History of the Great War

Based on Official Documents. By Direction of the Historical Section of the Committee of Imperial Defence.

Naval Operations.

Vol. I., To the Battle of the Falklands, December 1914
By Sir Julian S. Corbett, LL.M.
New Edition with new material and revised Maps.
8vo. With Maps.
Text Volume also issued separately.

Vol. II., From the Battle of the Falklands to the entry of Italy into the War in May 1915.
By Sir Julian S. Corbett, LL.M.
With 17 Maps and Plans. 8vo.

Vol. III., The Dardanelles campaign from May 1915 to the final evacuation, the opening of the Salonica operations, the Mesopotamian campaign to the Battle of Ctesiphon, operations in minor theatres, the German submarine campaign and events in Home Waters up to and including the Battle of Jutland.
By Sir Julian S. Corbett, LL.M.
With 7 Plans and Diagrams. 8vo.
46 Maps in a separate case. 8vo.

Vol. IV., June 1916 to April 1917.
By Sir Henry Newbolt, C.H.
With 11 Plans and Diagrams. 8vo.
14 Maps in separate case.

Vol. V., April 1917 to the End of the War.
By Sir Henry Newbolt, C.H.
With 11 Maps and Plans in the Text, and a Case of Maps. 8vo.
Text Volume also issued separately.

NAVAL OPERATIONS

NOTE BY THE LORDS COMMISSIONERS OF THE ADMIRALTY

The Lords Commissioners of the Admiralty have given the author access to official documents in the preparation of this work, but they are in no way responsible for its production or for the accuracy of its statements.

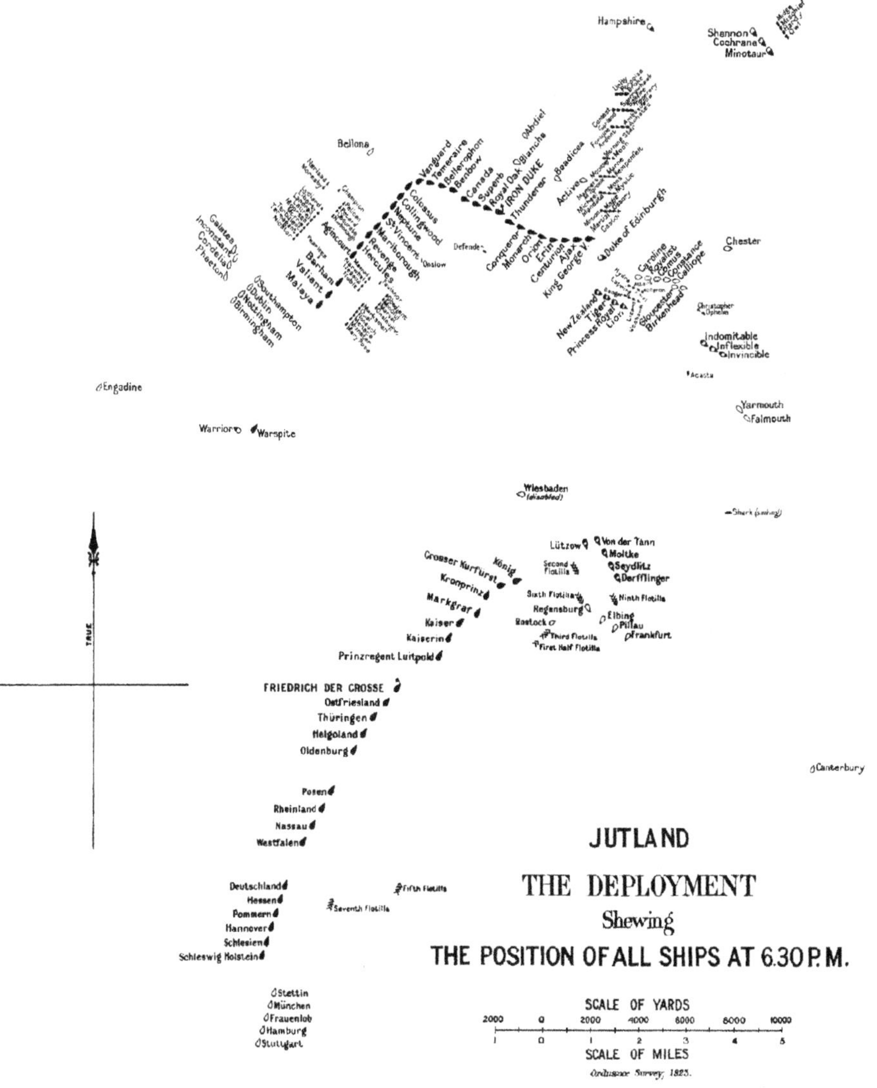

JUTLAND

THE DEPLOYMENT

Shewing

THE POSITION OF ALL SHIPS AT 6.30 P.M.

SCALE OF YARDS

2000 0 2000 4000 6000 8000 10000

1 0 1 2 3 4 5

SCALE OF MILES

Ordnance Survey, 1923.

Prepared in the Historical Section of the Committee of Imperial Defence.

NAVAL OPERATIONS

History of the Great War
Based on Official Documents

VOL. III

by

SIR JULIAN S. CORBETT

The Naval & Military Press Ltd

Published by
The Naval & Military Press Ltd
5 Riverside, Brambleside, Bellbrook
Industrial Estate, Uckfield, East Sussex,
TN22 1QQ England
Tel: +44 (0) 1825 749494
Fax: +44 (0) 1825 765701

PREFACE TO REVISED EDITION

The most important section of this volume is that which relates the story of the Battle of Jutland, and for its revision a great many authorities have been consulted, including the German Official History of the battle. The German account is based largely on Sir Julian Corbett's original narrative, and even many of the German charts have evidently been compiled from our own—sometimes at the expense of contradicting the text they are supposed to illustrate. Some hitherto unknown details, however, notably with regard to the initial activities of their submarines, and the opening movements of their forces are now available. These have been incorporated in the present edition, together with such additions and corrections as have come to light from this and many other authoritative sources, and the diagrams have been amended where necessary.

Among the more important additions are: the explanation of the absence of the seaplane-carrier *Campania* (Note A, p. 326a); the reason for the slow approach of the Grand Fleet to the battle area (Note B, p. 326b); and, in Appendix J (p. 442), a list of seven German signals received in the Admiralty but not passed to the Commander-in-Chief. It will be seen that the second signal in this list contained some words that were not included in the decipher. Had the officer responsible for the deciphering of this message realised the vital importance of the information it conveyed, it is hardly to be credited that it would have been withheld from Admiral Jellicoe.

In writing his narrative of the battle, Sir Julian Corbett had before him the official Admiralty study, but did not live to make due acknowledgment of its assistance. It is, therefore, here recorded.

For the revision of the first part of the volume a further large number of authorities has been consulted, including eight volumes of the German Official History, and recourse has again been made to the Naval Staff Monographs. From these and the other authorities many amendments have now been made.

Throughout the task of revision every endeavour has been made to preserve the work of the original author; indeed, no disturbance has been admitted except where it is essential for historical accuracy.

Assistance on points of detail, mostly technical, has been rendered by Captain A. C. Dewar, R.N. (Head of the Historical Section, Training and Staff Duties Division, Admiralty), and by his assistant, Lieutenant-Commander J. H. Lloyd-Owen, R.N., to whom my thanks are due.

I take this opportunity, too, of expressing my sense of gratitude, in particular, to Mr. C. V. Owen, Historical Section of the Committee of Imperial Defence, for his help and advice, which have been invaluable.

E. Y. DANIEL,
Lieut.-Colonel, R.M.
Secretary, Historical Section, Committee of Imperial Defence.

October, 1939.

PREFACE

THE present volume deals with the events in Home Waters from the spring of 1915 to the Battle of Jutland. It is also concerned with the Dardanelles Campaign up to the final evacuation and the opening of the Salonica Expedition; with the campaign in Mesopotamia as far as the Battle of Ctesiphon, and with operations in minor theatres.

It was only a few hours before his death that Sir Julian Corbett completed the last chapter. He had thus no opportunity of revising his proofs, nor of checking the accuracy of his narrative, as he had done in the preceding volumes, and this task devolved on me as having been closely associated with him in his work for many years and being fully acquainted with his methods. I had, therefore, to compare the text very closely with the materials upon which it was based, and, where any errors of fact were discovered, to correct it in such a way that the original form was preserved. Particular care has been taken to ensure that every passage in which the author has given expression to his own opinions or made deductions from established facts has remained unaltered.

In addition to the books referred to in the prefaces to his earlier volumes, the author drew largely from the following works for matters affecting German war policy and strategy :—

My Three Years in America, Count Bernstorff.

General Headquarters 1914–1916 and its Critical Decisions, General Erich von Falkenhayn.

My War Memories 1914–1918, General Ludendorff.

Die deutschen U-Boote in ihrer Kriegführung 1914–1918, Vols. II and III, Korvettenkapitän A. Gayer.

In describing the beginning of the Salonica Expedition he consulted :—

Mon commandement en Orient (1914–1918), Général Sarrail.

Joffre. La Première Crise du Commandement, Mermeix.

The German Official Naval History at present only covers a period of the war which has already been dealt with by the author.

The diagrams of the Battle of Jutland have been drawn from material prepared by Lieutenant-Commander J. F. H. Pollen, R.N. (retired), who was also responsible for the battle plans in the first and second volumes.

It was Sir Julian Corbett's intention to express his sense of gratitude to the members of the Staff of the Historical Section who prepared and digested the immense amount of material upon which the three volumes of his history are based. I, too, am indebted to them for the assistance they have given me in my task of revising the proofs and verifying the narrative.

E. Y. DANIEL.
Lieutenant-Colonel, R.M.
Secretary, Historical Section, Committee of Imperial Defence.

August, 1923.

CONTENTS

PLANS AND DIAGRAMS IN VOLUME

MAPS AND DIAGRAMS IN SEPARATE CASE

CHAPTER I

GENERAL SITUATION WHEN THE COALITION GOVERNMENT TOOK OFFICE—PROGRESS IN THE MINOR THEATRES—MESOPOTAMIA

By the end of May, 1915, the new Government was formed. Mr. Asquith, Sir Edward Grey and Lord Kitchener retained their former offices. The chief changes which directly concerned the conduct of the war were that Mr. Balfour became First Lord of the Admiralty and Mr. Lloyd George, from being Chancellor of the Exchequer, took up the Ministry of Munitions—a department now constituted for the first time as the best means of dealing with a need which, with ever-increasing insistence, had been clogging and weakening our operations both in France and the Dardanelles. At the Admiralty Admiral Sir Henry Jackson, whose masterly work in the direction of oversea operations designated him as Lord Fisher's natural successor, was apppointed First Sea Lord.

The general outlook which the new Government had to face was one of much anxiety—filled as it was with unsolved problems and unsolved situations all over the world. Our war plan had broken down, nor was there any hopeful prospect of regaining the initiative. On May 25, the day the new Ministry was formed, Sir John French had broken off the battle of Festubert for lack of ammunition, with no positive gain to set against his losses. Further south the French had gained ground, but the battle of Artois was still raging and showed little promise of giving a substantial improvement of the Allied position. As for the Eastern Front, neither the great French effort nor the imminent intervention of Italy had availed to relieve the pressure on the Russians in Galicia. In that theatre the Central Powers had made a sweeping advance, and were in the act of isolating the all-important fortress of Przemysl. The effect of their far-reaching success was to extinguish the hopes which had once been entertained of a decisive offensive movement from that quarter, and coupled with our own check at the Dardanelles, it also promised to be fatal to the Entente hopes of re-establishing a Balkan combination. Yet a united effort of the Balkan States was the only measure which could counter Germany's success in drawing Turkey into the war.

One of the first acts of the new Government was an effort to induce Bulgaria to enter the struggle against her hereditary enemy. But the minimum territorial consideration that was likely to prove an inducement to Bulgaria was far beyond what either Serbia or Greece was willing to consider. The attempt had no success, and only made it clearer than ever that if Germany were to be prevented from opening a road to Constantinople, and thus establishing an impassable gulf between Russia and the Western Powers, it was mainly upon our own strength we should have to rely. Had we strength enough? That was the crucial question, and it was one that was extremely difficult to determine. It really depended on whether our function in France was to be in the main defensive, or whether we were to participate directly with our French Allies in attempting to reach a decision there by offensive action. No clear, and certainly no unanimous answer to this question seems ever to have been given, nor, in view of the political frictions that are inseparable from acting with an Ally whose country has been invaded, was it easy for a clear answer to be made. Apart from such friction it seems almost beyond doubt that, so long at least as there was any hope of a decision coming from the Russian side, the correct course and the one most in accordance with our traditions was to assume an alert but general defensive in France and throw everything that was not required for that defensive into an alternative theatre where decisive success was attainable, and where consequently we could hope to influence definitely the course of the war. Such a theatre the Dardanelles provided when the enterprise was set on foot. Now the problem was not so clear. The collapse of Russia, while affording additional reason for striking with all possible strength in the Near East, also pushed opinion to the inevitability of the main Allied offensive being developed in France. The result was that it appears to have become a cardinal axiom of our war policy that, important as was the Dardanelles theatre, our enterprise there was no more than a secondary offensive, and that nothing must be devoted to it which would imperil the hope of a primary offensive in the main or central theatre at an early date. Our superfluous force, therefore, was all that could be used; but the measure of that force was no longer what was not required for a defensive attitude on the Western

Front, but how much of our disengaged strength the French could bear to see diverted to another theatre.

The superfluous force we had—that is, the force not already earmarked for the main theatre—was considerable, but it was far from free. Much of it was still engaged in the oversea attacks with which we had begun our vast effort to establish a permanent control of the seven seas. Everywhere, except in the Pacific and Togoland, the liabilities thus incurred were unliquidated. In two places—East Africa and Mesopotamia—the liabilities threatened to increase, and only at one point—German South-West Africa —was the situation really promising. There alone was there ample force for the work in hand, but the provision of that force was absorbing the whole strength of one of the three great self-governing dominions.

It was on February 6, as we have seen, that General Botha left Cape Town for Walfisch Bay to open his well-designed campaign.[1] The success he met with fully justified the completeness and strength of his preparations. From the first his progress was uninterrupted. After a month's work it was found that before the various Union forces that had been so skilfully co-ordinated the Germans were abandoning all the southern part of the colony and concentrating about the capital at Windhuk. Early in April, therefore, the plan was simplified, and the Central, Southern and Eastern forces were reorganised as a new Southern force, under the command of General Smuts. By April 20 he had occupied Keetmanshoop, the railhead of the Lüderitz Bay line, and then General Botha pushed forward to cut off the enemy, who were retiring northwards. So rapid was the movement that by May 5 his advance troops had cut the railway north of Windhuk, and a week later (12th) he seized Windhuk itself, with 3,000 Europeans all told, 12,000 natives, a large amount of rolling stock and the high-power wireless station still standing. The navy's influence on these operations had been exercised at the Falkland Islands and in the wide wastes of the Atlantic; its activities relieved General Botha from all anxiety with regard to probable interference from the sea, and thus he was able to operate on widely separated lines the masterly combination which completely baffled the Germans and gave to the Union forces their rapid and well-deserved success.

In the Cameroons the situation was much less satisfactory. Successful as had been the opening operations for the seizure of the coast, it had become clear, now that it was a question

[1] Vol. II., p. 235.

of reducing the vast expanses of the hinterland where naval co-operation was no longer possible, the troops on the spot were far too few for the task.[1] General Dobell had asked for 4,000 Indian troops, and when he was told that it was impossible to provide them, he was for standing fast on the line he then held, from Edea to the northern railhead, till reinforcements could be found. When, however, the French civil and military mission arrived at Duala to concert operations, they pressed for an advance on Yaunde at the great river junction where the Germans had established their headquarters. Their idea was that he should move on the place in two columns from Edea, with the British and French troops that were under his command, while General Aymerich advanced with two columns from the south and east by way of Lomie and Dumé. Such a scheme General Dobell could not approve. In his opinion the troops available were too few and the distances too great for it to constitute a co-ordinated converging plan of operations. Yaunde was 100 miles from Edea and 150 from Lomie and Dumé, which General Aymerich had yet to reach. Still, so eager were the French, that he gave way, and agreed to make the attempt in April.

Accordingly, on April 10 the movement began. It was made in two columns, the French troops working along the Midland railway for Eseka, and the British on their left along the direct road to Yaunde for the half-way post, Wum Biagas.[2] From the first the resistance was very strong and progress slow. To relieve the pressure and prevent the enemy concentrating it had been arranged with Captain Fuller that he should make diversions at various points on the coast with his marines and native levies, and to this work he devoted the squadron, so far as was consistent with stopping the flow of contraband from Fernando Po.

So difficult was this task, owing to the attitude of the Spanish local authorities, that it had been decided, on Captain Fuller's suggestion, to establish a blockade of the whole coast on the same lines as that for German East Africa. Measures for reinforcing the squadron for the purpose had been taken at home in the middle of March, and

[1] In March the French troops numbered about 6,000, the British 4,000 and the Belgians 600. The Germans were believed to have less than 3,000 formed troops with an unknown number of native irregulars. We and the French each had a cruiser and a gunboat, but we had also armed and manned eighteen sea-going and river craft.

[2] On April 3 the control of the operations had been taken over by the War Office.

on the 21st the *Sirius* and *Rinaldo* had been ordered to be prepared for foreign service.[1] Another ship was being taken up and armed locally, and the French, who had been asked to co-operate, were providing an armed trawler. The blockade, however, was declared without waiting for the arrival of the reinforcements, and put in force on April 24. It extended along the whole coast north of the Spanish enclave, a distance of about 200 miles. South of the enclave no blockade was necessary, for the coast was in the hands of the French. From the northern section the Cameroons River was excepted and Duala was declared an open port.

There the Senior Naval Officer's ship was stationed, but she was no longer the *Challenger*. Owing to the call for cruisers to watch the *Königsberg* on the east coast, the need of reinforcing the Cape station with a good ship had become so urgent that the long-contemplated exchange had to be carried out, and the *Astraea* had arrived. But, as General Dobell was as unwilling as ever to lose the services of Captain Fuller, the two captains exchanged ships before the *Challenger* left for Walfisch Bay (May 1).

During this time the advance of the troops had been held up. By the middle of April each of the Edea columns, after much hard fighting, had reached their first objectives, Ngwe on the road and the Kele river on the railway, which meant in each case an advance of about thirty miles. Then it was found the enemy was moving troops down from the north, threatening the British line of advance, and General Dobell had to detach a force to his left to hold Sakbajeme, on the Sanaga river, where it was crossed by the road from the north which joined the main road between Ngwe and Wum Biagas, his next objective.[2] At the same time General Aymerich sent word that he could not reach Lomie till the end of the month. The advance therefore was postponed. On May 1 it was resumed, and by the 4th the British were in Wum Biagas and the French in Sende again, on the 6th, after heavy fighting. On the 11th they had driven the Germans from Eseka and captured seven engines and two hundred wagons. The whole railway system was now in the Allies' hands, but General Aymerich had been unable to reach either Dumé or Lomie. To General Dobell it was clear that, as he expected, the ambitious concentric attack was no longer possible, and that the only chance of reaching Yaunde

[1] *Sirius*, light cruiser, 1889, 3,600 tons, 2–6"; 6–4·7"; 8–6 pdrs. *Rinaldo*, sloop, 1898–9, 980 tons, 4–4". Both had been hitherto devoted to coastal attack and defence in Home waters. See Vol. II., p. 234.

[2] See Vol. I., Map 16 (in case).

before the rains was a vigorous push along the shortest line with his whole force. His French column was therefore moved north to Wum Biagas, and the final effort began on May 25. But it was quickly found that the Germans had been able to bring about a concentration that made progress more difficult than ever. In ten days our men had only advanced a dozen miles, and in front of them the Germans held positions that swamps rendered almost impregnable. Dysentery was playing havoc with the troops, of General Aymerich there was no news, the rains were coming on, and by the middle of June General Dobell decided to abandon the attempt to reach Yaunde and fall back on the line of his first objectives. All there was to set against the failure was that in the north Garua had at last fallen (June 10), and on the coast the arrival of the naval reinforcements made it possible to render the blockade thoroughly effective.[1]

On the opposite side of the Continent affairs were in much the same position. There ashore the attitude of passive defence was maintained and military operations were confined to repelling German raids on the Uganda railway. The *Königsberg* still remained unapproachable, but at sea she led to much activity. The Germans evidently had no idea of leaving her to her fate, and early in April we began to get wind of attempts to relieve her and at the same time to run in arms and ammunition for the defence of the colony. The first attempt was planned for the spring tides in the second week of the month—a time which seemed to indicate that the *Königsberg* would try to break out and meet the relief ship off the Rufiji. The *Chatham* was ordered to return temporarily to the east coast as soon as her refit at Bombay was complete, instead of going at once to the Mediterranean, but her defects proved too serious, and Vice-Admiral H. G. King-Hall had to do his best with the ships he had.

To some extent the blockade had to be relaxed. Keeping the *Weymouth*, *Kinfauns Castle* and *Pioneer* off the Rufiji to prevent a break out, he himself in the *Hyacinth* made a cast for the relief ship. As was afterwards discovered, she was the British steamship *Rubens*, of 3,587 tons, with 1,600 tons of coal, 1,500 rifles and a quantity of ammunition and provisions.[2] As the time of spring tides drew near German wireless was heard by a British ship, and also by the French in Madagascar, at the north end of the Mozambique channel. The expected ship was evidently coming up that way, but the *Hyacinth* failed to find

[1] The *Sirius* and *Rinaldo* arrived on June 6.

[2] She was one of the vessels detained by the Germans at Hamburg on the outbreak of war, and was disguised as the Danish steamer *Kronberg*.

her on the anticipated course. Later on it was known that she was actually at Aldabra island, about 100 miles east by south of the Rufiji, from April 8 to 10. Then at the height of the springs she sailed and further wireless signals indicated she was moving northward. As the *Königsberg* had not stirred, it looked as though Tanga were her destination, and for that point Admiral King-Hall made, and at daybreak on the 14th sighted her in the Kilulu channel. At that moment, as ill luck would have it, the *Hyacinth's* starboard engine broke down. With only one engine it was impossible to overhaul the chase, and she was able to run into Mansa Bay and beach herself out of sight. But her steam blowing off betrayed her position, and the *Hyacinth* as she ran on shelled her over the land. When Admiral King-Hall got into the bay she was seen to be aground and burning forward. Boats were promptly sent in to try to salve her valuable cargo, but the heat was too great. Nothing of any value was recovered except her charts. From these it appeared she had left the Skaw on February 18, and making the Sumburgh head light after dark on the 21st, was able in the long hours of darkness to run the gauntlet of the Grand Fleet and pass out between the Shetlands and Orkneys and so by the west of Ireland southward.[1]

In the first week of March she was passing through the Canaries. Here, as in the North American area, we were still maintaining a considerable cruiser force to keep watch on the approaches to the Straits of Gibraltar, and on the German and Austrian vessels which, to the number of 120, had taken refuge in Spanish and Portuguese ports. It was now known as the squadron for the protection of trade from Cape Finisterre to Cape Verde islands, and although at this time it comprised eight British and three French ships, the *Rubens* passed through it undetected.[2] Thence she carried on south, following the ordinary track, till at the end of March she rounded the Cape and, keeping well out to sea, made

[1] The only cruiser squadron that happened to be out was the 10th, i. e., the Northern Patrol of armed merchant cruisers. During the week they had stopped 51 vessels.

[2] The squadron at this time was composed as follows:—

Finisterre—Canaries Division:—

Three cruisers—*Europa, Amphitrite, Argonaut,* and two armed merchant cruisers—*Calgarian, Carmania.*

French Morocco Division:—

Three light cruisers—*Cosmao, Friant, Cassard.*

Cape Verde Islands Division:—

One light cruiser—*Highflyer* and two armed merchant cruisers—*Marmora* and *Empress of Britain.* The first two divisions were based at Gibraltar and the last at Sierra Leone.

Aldabra island on April 8. It was at this time, as she passed up the Mozambique Channel, that her attempts to communicate with the *Königsberg* put our cruisers on the alert, with the result that her bold attempt ended as we have seen. As it was impossible to salve the cargo, the Admiral decided to destroy her by gun-fire at close range. She was soon on fire fore and aft, and after three explosions indicated that her ammunition had gone, the *Hyacinth* left her.[1]

But this was not the end of the German enterprise, and the strain on our cruisers increased rather than diminished. By the time the springs were over we had wind of another relief ship coming up. As she did not appear it was concluded she had received word to keep off till the next spring tides at the end of the month, when the *Königsberg* would have water again to break out. As the squadron was it could not count on stopping her. The *Hyacinth* could not steam much more than half speed and was sorely in need of an overhaul. The *Cornwall*, which had reached the Cape from home a week before, was therefore ordered up at high speed (she arrived on April 27), and the *Chatham* was also directed to the Rufiji, joining the squadron there on May 1. Meanwhile the islands north of the Mozambique Channel were searched, but no trace of the intruder could be found.

Under these conditions the need of making an end of the *Königsberg* was more urgent than ever. The two new seaplanes for which the Admiral had applied had proved unequal to the task. Though good enough for distant reconnaissance, they could not in that climate rise high enough for bombing in face of the enemy's anti-aircraft fire. On May 5 one of them crashed in the sea and was wrecked. Bombing having failed, the Admiral was for attempting a torpedo attack, but this the Admiralty would not sanction. Their solution of the problem was to send down two of the original monitors which then were at Malta, and he was directed to husband his seaplanes till they arrived. His work, therefore, was chiefly maintaining the watch on the Rufiji. It was kept up in full strength till the springs were again past, and then both the *Cornwall* and *Chatham* left for the Mediterranean (May 11 and 16). Till the monitors and more seaplanes arrived nothing further could be done.

Ashore the lack of force kept things equally quiet. From India little could be expected, the needs of Mesopotamia were too great, and on April 16 Major-General R. Wapshare sailed to take up a command there, leaving Major-General

[1] The destruction was not complete, and later on the Germans succeeded in salving part of the cargo of arms and ammunition.

M. J. Tighe as his successor in East Africa. The drain of Mesopotamia was indeed increasing ominously, and it was promising to be by no means the least of the liabilities which the new Government had to meet. Since the capture of Kurnah on December 9 no advance had been attempted. The Expeditionary Force had all it could do to secure itself. Till the end of the year it was engaged in entrenching a position on the Tigris about two miles above Kurnah, as well as at Muzaira'a, on the opposite bank, while in the river a ship always kept guard at night with its searchlights.

Since December 18, on which day Captain A. Hayes-Sadler sailed with the *Ocean* for Suez, the squadron attached to the expedition was in charge of Captain Wilfrid Nunn of the sloop *Espiègle*. He had besides her sister ship, the *Odin* (Commander C. R. Wason), the Indian Marine ship *Lawrence* and four armed launches. With this force he was able, so far as his guns would carry, to do a little to check the lawless tribes who inhabited the swamps and indulged themselves with perpetual sniping; but to control them entirely was impossible, for as they constantly moved their mat villages from place to place punitive raids were not easy to carry out. Most troublesome of these tribesmen were those living in the marshes of the Euphrates west of Kurnah. One of their Sheikhs, who lived at Kubaish, thirty miles up the river, secure in his swampy fastness, was found to be intriguing with the enemy, and Sir Percy Cox, the Chief Political Officer, consulted Captain Nunn as to the possibility of removing him.[1] The river was uncharted, but on January 6 they made the attempt together in the *Espiègle*, with three armed launches and two of Messrs. Lynch's river steamers, carrying troops. The navigation of the sluggish stream proved unexpectedly easy. The *Espiègle* got nearly up to the village, the launches penetrated into Hammar lake above it, and the offending Sheikh was brought down to Kurnah and deposed.

In their hostile attitude the Arabs were sustained by the southward movement of Turkish troops. After the capture of Kurnah a division of the Mosul Army Corps had concentrated at Bagdad, and by the end of the year an advanced force was established on the Tigris at Ruta, about eight miles above Kurnah. A combined reconnaissance, carried out on New Year's Day, found them entrenched on both banks of the river just above the Ruta creek, and below it they had blocked the river by sinking two iron lighters. Further reconnaissances, during one of which the *Espiègle*

[1] See Map 1.

sank a Turkish steamer above Ruta, showed the enemy's strength constantly increasing. Their outposts had been advanced to within six miles north of our entrenched camp at Muzaira'a. The General[1] therefore on January 20 moved out with a strong force, supported by the *Espiègle*, the launch *Miner* and the stern-wheeler *Mejidieh* in the reach above Abu Aran. The operation was entirely successful. The enemy were driven back in confusion, losing their original position and some two to three hundred killed. The infantry then advanced, but as the object was reconnaissance only, no attack was made. Having ascertained that the enemy numbered 5,000 men, mostly gendarmerie, the troops were withdrawn under cover of the ship's fire. Our losses were seven killed and fifty-one wounded.

But the situation was still full of anxiety. For some time past the Muntafik Arabs had been concentrating at Nasiriya, on the Euphrates, thirty miles above Hammar lake—a site once famous as "Ur of the Chaldees." It now became known that they had been joined by a number of Turks, and having crossed the river, were moving south of the marshes towards Basra.[2] Simultaneously another Turkish force moving from Amara on the Tigris had crossed the Persian frontier, and in conjunction with the local Arabs seemed to be making for Ahwaz, on the Karun river, and the pipe line which connected the oil-fields with the refinery At Abadan. On the night of January 29/30 a minor attack on our camp at Muzaira'a gave further evidence of the enemy's restlessness. There seemed to be little doubt that he meant to take the offensive and attack Basra, Kurnah and Ahwaz simultaneously; and no offensive movement on our part was possible. This was regrettable, for though our operations had been originally undertaken to confirm our command of the Indian Seas and secure our interests in the Persian Gulf, it was becoming evident that something of much greater moment was at stake. Thanks to the industry of the Germans, the whole Arab world was in ferment, and whether they or ourselves would profit by it depended mainly upon what we could do in Mesopotamia. It was making itself strongly felt in Central Arabia, where the Pan-Islamic movement had produced a deep impression. But here we scored the first point. The centre of the movement was at Hail, under the powerful Sheikh Ibn Rashid, and there on January 24 he was attacked by our partisan Ibn Saud, accompanied by Major W. H. I. Shakespear, our invaluable political agent at Kuwait. On

[1] Lieutenant-General Sir A. A. Barrett. [2] See Map 1.

both sides the losses were severe, including unhappily Major Shakespear himself. Neither side could claim the victory, but the action put it out of Ibn Rashid's power to move on Mesopotamia. Unfortunately the last chance of effective co-operation by Ibn Saud also passed away.

There the immediate danger was to the oil-fields and pipe line. The Admiralty were specially anxious about its safety, and two of the armed launches, *Shaitan* and *Comet*, were ordered up the river. They reached Ahwaz on February 1. Troops followed, and the Sheikh of Mohammerah mustered his men to assist, but for all they could do some of the oil stores were damaged and the pipe line was cut in several places during February. As for Kurnah, after the middle of the month it was made unassailable by the inundations that followed the rise of the river, and troops could be sent down to Basra in time to meet the attack which was developing from Nasiriya. The Turks and their Arab friends were slowly concentrating at Nukhaila, only thirty miles west of Basra, where supplies could reach them by water by way of the new channel of the Euphrates, which led out of the Hammar lake and joined the Tigris just above Basra. We were facing them at Shaiba, eight miles west of Basra, at the edge of the inundations caused by the new channel. From this point on March 8 an attempt was made with troops in *bellums*, or rude canoes of the district, propelled by punt-poles or paddles, to get at the enemy's line of communication. They were drawing their supplies from Nukhaila, on the Euphrates, and to this point, which was the objective of the operations, everything was brought down the river in *mahailas*.[1] The attempt failed, and a reconnaissance which had been pushed out to divert the enemy's attention was forced to retire before superior numbers. So formidable indeed was the concentration becoming that something clearly had to be done to arrest its further development.

The only way seemed to be to renew the attempt on the *mahailas* at Nukhaila with a regular combined operation, but whether or not it was possible for the flotilla to act was uncertain. At Kurmat Ali, seven miles above Basra, we had a post at the point where the new channel of the Euphrates joined the Tigris, but its navigation was quite unknown. So far as had been ascertained neither the sloops nor the *Miner* could operate in what was really a vast swamp with no more than three feet of water over the greater part of it. Consequently, as the *Shaitan* and *Comet* could not be spared

[1] The *mahaila* was a local kind of shallow-draft dhow usually of from 30 to 40 tons burden and occasionally a good deal larger.

from the Karun, a special flotilla had to be organised. The stern-wheeler *Shushan* was commissioned, with Lieutenant-Commander A. G. Seymour and six men from the *Espiègle*, and armed with two 3-pounders. Another, the *Muzaffri*, carried fifty men of the Norfolks, and a barge was armed with two 4-inch guns of the 104th (Heavy) Battery, and carried a crew of forty men under Major W. C. R. Farmar, R.G.A. A tug and a motor boat completed the little amphibious force, and on March 11 they started. By the second day they found their way through the shoals to within range of the enemy's camp at Nukhaila, and proceeded to shell it and the *mahailas* by which it was being supplied. The immediate effect was that the *mahailas* ceased coming down to Nukhaila and seemed to be stopping higher up. Next day, therefore, the flotilla moved on ten miles to Allawi, where there was a fort, with a depot near by at Ratawi. It was destroyed with more *mahailas*. So the work went on day after day in the wide waste of uncharted waters, with constant groundings as they tried to chase the elusive dhows which always made off and hid themselves in the jungle of high reeds that grew out of the floods. Above Ratawi the waters became more confined, and here it was found that a complete blockade could be established. Having ascertained this important fact they returned to Nukhaila and subjected it on March 20 to a full day's bombardment, setting the camp on fire, forcing numbers of Arabs out into the desert and destroying some of the *mahailas* that were there.

They were not many, for now it was found that the effect of the operations was that they came no further than a place called Ghabishiya, twenty miles above Ratawi, where they were unloaded and their cargoes transported by camels to Nukhaila. To Ghabishiya the flotilla therefore proceeded and found there a crowd of *mahailas* and camels. Here they stayed, doing what damage they could, and completely blocking the flow of supplies by water till they were forced to go down for more ammunition. Thus was set on foot what was known as the "Euphrates Blockade." Not only did it prove to afford invaluable protection to the west flank of the Basra position, but its moral effects were scarcely less important. The Arabs were peculiarly susceptible to ship fire, and the delay which the blockade caused in the attack so far disheartened them that, in spite of the Jehad, they began to fall away in large numbers.

On our right wing up the Karun river things were not so satisfactory. In attempting to anticipate the arrival of Turkish and Arab reinforcements our people had attacked the enemy west of Ahwaz on March 3, but we were too late, and met with a reverse from superior numbers, losing sixty-two killed and 127 wounded. The enemy lost over 200 killed and about 600 wounded. The Karun column had therefore to be increased to the strength of a brigade, but here, too, the Jehad was losing its force. The depressed Arabs began to desert, and by the end of the month, though the pipe line was still broken, the position at the oil-fields was better.

The whole situation, however, was still very serious, particularly in view of the failure of the naval attack on the Dardanelles. Ever since it had been realised how formidable was the effort the Turks were preparing to dislodge us from the Shatt-al-Arab, the question of reinforcements had been acute. Immediately the danger to the oil supply was known, the Admiralty, who were pressing for energetic military action to safeguard it, had ordered out the sloop *Clio*[1] (Commander C. MacKenzie) from Egypt, and they had also shipped two converted stern-wheelers armed with 4·7-inch guns. Troops were harder to find. The Government of India, owing to internal anxieties, could not see their way to providing more from their reduced garrison, but eventually General Melliss's Indian brigade was spared from Egypt, so that the Expeditionary Force was brought up to the strength of an army corps of two infantry divisions and a cavalry brigade, but without its full complement of artillery. On April 9 General Sir John Nixon arrived to command it. His instructions were to retain complete control of Lower Mesopotamia, including the vilayet of Basra and all outlets to the sea, and of all such portions of the neighbouring territories as affected his operations. So far as was feasible without prejudice to his main operations he was also to endeavour to secure the safety of the oil-fields, pipe lines and refineries, and further, in anticipation of possible eventualities, to study a plan for advancing on Bagdad.

So effectually had the Euphrates blockade checked the enemy that the long-expected offensive did not develop till after his arrival. It was heralded on April 11 by a bombardment of Kurnah from the Turkish position just above. Next day there was a demonstration against Ahwaz, and simultaneously the attack on our position at Shaiba developed in full force. We were holding the place with one cavalry and two infantry brigades, and after heavy fighting, which lasted till nightfall, the attack was repulsed with severe loss to the enemy. Next day Major-General C. J. Melliss, who was in command, counter-attacked and drove the enemy back on a

[1] Six 4-inch and four 3-pounder guns.

position they had prepared at Barjisiya, three or four miles to the south-west. This position he attacked on April 14, and by skilful tactics and indomitable persistence the valiant tenacity of the Turks was at last broken. A precipitate retirement began and quickly became a rout. The Turkish losses are estimated at one thousand. Four hundred prisoners and two guns fell into our hands. Pursuit was impossible for our exhausted troops, but the Euphrates flotilla was waiting its opportunity. It had been able to take no part in the battle, though the *Shushan* had had a little action of her own with two Thornycroft patrol boats, which she put to flight. In the evening, however, she was joined by a further force, so that the flotilla, which was now commanded by Lieutenant-Colonel R. P. Molesworth, R.G.A., could show two naval 4·7-inch guns, a 12-pounder and three 3-pounders, besides a military 5-inch and an 18-pounder. With this force he went up to Nukhaila. As they approached at dawn a number of *mahailas* could be seen making sail. As yet our people had no news of how the battle had gone; but what they saw could only mean that the enemy had been defeated the previous day and a vigorous pursuit was begun. Twelve of the largest dhows were destroyed or captured, but then came a gale which prevented anything being done for the whole of next day. When it abated they pushed on to Ghabishiya, but only to find it deserted. The enemy in scattered groups were flying in disorder. The truth was that our success had stifled the last breath of the Jehad. The Arab tribesmen had turned on the Turks, and were harassing and plundering them as they fled. It was a wholly broken and demoralised force that at last got back to Nasiriya. Their commander, Sulaiman Askari, had committed suicide before his assembled officers when the Arabs turned against him. Their total losses were about 6,000 men and a great quantity of arms and munitions which were found on the battlefield and at the river posts. Our casualties numbered 1,862 including 161 killed.

The work of the blockade flotilla was now done, and it could be withdrawn. The attempt to turn our Mesopotamian flank had failed, and failed so disastrously that its effects spread far and wide. Not only was General Nixon now free to operate in force up the Karun river in order to clear the enemy out of Persian Arabistan, but through all that district the Arabs began to renounce the Jehad. The result was that when Major-General G. F. Gorringe, towards the end of April, was sent up the river with his division the Turks fell back before him. The advance was one of the greatest difficulty. In a bold effort to cut off the enemy's retreat he left the river twenty miles short of Ahwaz and struck northward across the swampy desert to the hills. But their retreat had been too rapid for him; they had just passed ahead of his column, and all he could do was to press on their heels and drive them back the way they came. On May 14 he entered Bisaitin, and Persian Arabistan was again clear of the enemy, and the oil-fields and pipe line secured.

In this wholly successful operation the flotilla could take no part. Their turn was to come. For the present they were busy with work preparatory to further and larger operations by which General Nixon intended to follow up his victory at Shaiba. To consolidate the position in Lower Mesopotamia it seemed to him necessary to occupy Nasiriya and Amara, the two points from which the attacks on his flanks had originated. This forward movement had been sanctioned from home, and the minor units of the flotilla were investigating the channels about Hammar lake with a view to the advance up the Euphrates. About this phase, however, there was no immediate hurry. Far more important and more pressing was the capture of Amara. Since it was from that point the columns which attacked Ahwaz had started, it was probably there the baffled troops would retire, and if their retreat could be cut off it would mean a real and telling success.

The first operation would have to be the forcing of the Turkish position above Kurnah, where the enemy's advanced posts faced our own at a distance of 2,000 to 3,000 yards on both sides of the river. It was no easy matter.[1] The inundation was now at its highest; Kurnah itself was an island, and as far as the eye could see there was nothing but a reedy waste of water, broken by a few low detached sandhills on which the Turks were entrenched. The nearest, known to us as "Norfolk hill," was on the west or Kurnah bank. In rear of it was "One Tree hill," on the east bank, and "One Tower hill" on the west. Further back again was a stronger post, "Gun hill." Two miles in rear of this was the main position at Abu Aran village, and on the extreme horizon could just be seen the enemy's camps at Muzaibila and Ruta, below which was the obstruction they had formed by sinking iron barges.

To attack such a position involved work of an almost unprecedented character. Though the water was but two feet deep, it was intersected by so many deeper ditches and canals that wading was impossible. The only way to enable the infantry to move freely was to adopt the methods of the natives and embark them in the *bellums*. Three hundred

[1] See Map 2.

and seventy-two of these were collected, and ninety-six were lightly armoured to give protection against rifle and machine-gun fire.[1] As soon as the men had learned to use them brigade training had to proceed with every movement translated into terms of canoes. As for the cavalry, it could not be used at all. Its place had to be supplied by the flotilla, and on the flotilla, too, the force would have to rely for its artillery as soon as it had advanced beyond the range of the heavy batteries at Kurnah. Here the mobility of the water-borne guns gave us a valuable advantage, for though the main attack must be frontal up the course of the Tigris, it seemed possible at least to menace the flanks of the position. On either side of the river were two creeks which led northward, the one, Al Huwair creek, from the Euphrates, the other, Shwaiyib river, which joined the Shatt-al-Arab below Kurnah. These Captain Nunn was investigating while the elaborate details of the strange operation were worked out by the staff. He had now, besides the *Espiègle* and *Odin*, his third sloop, the *Clio*. She had been long on her way from Suez, for apart from its duties with the Expeditionary Force the squadron had to be continually showing the flag at any gulf port where there were signs of unrest or hostility. She had got as far as Muscat when it was found that German propaganda at Bushire, the headquarters of our political and naval activity in the gulf, had set up such a threatening state of affairs that she had to be diverted to that port, and there from March 12 to April 16 she had to remain till things were quieter. The Indian Marine ship *Dalhousie* was similarly engaged, but he had the *Lawrence*. The Al Huwair creek was found to have been mined, and some time had to be spent in clearing the neighbouring swamp villages and making all secure. It was not till the end of May that all the complex arrangements were complete, and the whole force concentrated at Kurnah under Major-General C. V. F. Townshend, who had arrived from India on April 22 to command the VIth Indian Division.[2]

[1] Each carried ten men and a reserve of ammunition and other supplies.

[2] The units of the division which took part in the operation were :—

16th Infantry Brigade.
(Brigadier-General W. S. Delamain.)
2nd Bn. Dorsetshire Regiment.
104th Wellesley's Rifles.
117th Mahrattas.

17th Infantry Brigade.
(Lieut-Colonel S. H. Climo.)
1st Bn. Oxfordshire and Buckinghamshire Light Infantry.
22nd Punjabis.
103rd Mahratta Light Infantry.
119th Infantry.

Divisional Troops—one battery, R.F.A., 1/5th Hants (Howitzer) Battery,

To him General Nixon committed the conduct and organisation of the fantastic adventure. Though the idea he had worked out was a combined frontal and flank attack, the frontal attack up the main channel was to be the decisive one, and was to be supported by the bulk of the artillery ashore and afloat. The *Espiègle*, preceded by two launches to sweep—for the river above Kurnah was known to be mined—was to accompany this attack with the General on board, and with her were to go the *Odin*, two naval horse-boats with 4·7-inch guns, and two gun barges with 5-inch and 4-inch guns. The *Clio*, *Lawrence* and *Miner* were at first to assist the fortress guns in covering the advance. The *Comet*, which had come down from Ahwaz, was to move in company with an armed transport up the Shwaiyib river abreast of the Turkish position to cover the turning attack which was to be made by the 22nd Punjabis against One Tree hill, the only post the enemy had on the eastern bank. Up the other creek the two stern-wheelers, *Shushan* and *Muzaffri*, were to make a demonstration against the opposite flank with the assistance of a swarm of Arabs under the friendly Sheikh of Medina in their own *bellums*.[1]

At 5.0 a.m. on May 31 the preparatory bombardment began. By that time the Punjabis in their *bellums* had already stolen up to a point within a mile east-south-east of their objective and had deployed in the water. As soon as the guns began they crept slowly on, and by 6.30 had rushed One Tree hill and captured its slender garrison. Easy as the surprise had been, it was of no small importance, for the Punjabis could now enfilade Norfolk hill on the opposite bank with their machine-guns. Against this point the rest of the 17th Brigade were now moving over the floods in their armoured *bellums*, making their way like rats through the jungle of reeds. No eye could see them nor could the enemy attend to anything but the squadron in the river. Preceded by the launches, *Shaitan* and *Sumana*, working a sweep, the *Espiègle* and *Odin* were pushing up stream, followed by the gun barges, with the *Clio* and *Lawrence* in support and the

---

R.F.A., two heavy batteries, R.G.A., one mountain battery, 2nd Bn. Norfolk Regiment, 48th Pioneers, two companies and Bridging Train, Sappers and Miners, one Divisional Signal Company.

Besides the three sloops, the *Lawrence*, the armed launches, stern-wheelers and gun-lighters, a very large flotilla of small craft had been organised. All supply and field ambulance was floating, and *bellums* had been provided for one whole brigade (about sixty to a battalion), besides those carrying rafts for the machine-guns.

[1] Medina is a village on the south bank of the Euphrates fifteen miles above Kurnah.

16th Brigade in steamers. Upon the leading ships the guns in the enemy's positions at One Tower hill and Gun hill were concentrated, but the sloops and the fortress guns and howitzers soon silenced them, and by 7.30 the Oxford and Bucks L.I. had Norfolk hill. In another two hours One Tower hill had surrendered. Only Gun hill remained. Upon this the naval guns concentrated, and at 11.40 it also surrendered to the 103rd Mahratta L.I. So by noon it was all over. Thanks to the admirable staff work, and the skill the troops had developed in managing the *bellums*, all had gone like the ticking of a clock, and the long-prepared position fell in a morning's work. Our own losses were negligible. The enemy's casualties in killed and wounded were over 100, and we had in our hands 250 prisoners and three guns.

This, however, was only a beginning. It was no more than an outpost line that had been taken. The enemy's main force, as we have seen, was higher up. Two miles above they had a position at Abu Aran, and two miles beyond that another on both banks at Muzaibila and Ruta, below which was the obstruction they had made on their first retreat from Kurnah. These were not to be attempted till next day. It was necessary to consolidate the ground that had been won and to rest the men after their exhausting spell of work in the intense heat that prevailed.

The coming day's work was to begin at dawn with a frontal attack on Abu Aran by the flotilla, while the 17th Brigade made a wide sweep to take in flank from the westward. The 16th Brigade would be landed at Abu Aran, and together they would deal with Muzaibila. But when the bombardment began there was no reply, and as soon as the aircraft got back from Basra, where alone there was enough dry ground for landing, they reported the enemy in full retreat. Instantly General Townshend decided to pursue and keep them on the run, and now the flotilla had to take up its cavalry function. The infantry were ordered to concentrate at Abu Aran, while the General pursued with the flotilla. The 16th Brigade was to hold Abu Aran, the 17th was to embark in their empty transports and follow him, and the Norfolks were also to come on. Then the General, with no more of his division than his staff and a guard of a dozen men, hurried on in the *Espiègle*, with the *Clio* and *Odin* in company and the *Shaitan* and *Sumana* sweeping ahead.

It was an exciting chase.[1] Several mines had been discovered, more were known to be ahead, but fortunately the engineer officer who laid them had been taken prisoner, and

[1] See Map 1.

being placed for custody in one of the sweeping launches, made no difficulty in pointing out where they lay. Still there were the sunken lighters below Ruta. As they approached the place they could see above it the gunboat *Marmariss*, with another steamer and other river craft flying up the river. A hasty reconnaissance seemed to show that the current had scooped a channel on one side of the obstruction. Captain Nunn decided to try, and in a short time all three sloops successfully scraped through the difficult passage. Then the chase began in earnest, and surely it was unique. Here was a General pursuing with his Staff far ahead of his army, knowing little of what was ahead except that the enemy was flying before him. It was all an improvisation. His idea as expressed in general orders was, if he got the Turks on the run, to hurry after the flotilla with the 16th Brigade. He had no intention to pursue in person, but still he permitted Captain Nunn to carry him onward mile after mile, bend after bend, and as they steamed against the surging current the river became ever narrower and more tortuous. So sharp were the turns and so swift the current that the sloops could barely get round them and never without bumping heavily against one bank or the other. For them, too, it was an adventure beyond sober imagination. Built for police work where the oceans spread widest, they were driving irresponsibly up an uncharted waterway in chase of flying infantry, where such ships had never sailed before, into the heart of an ancient continental empire a hundred and fifty miles from the open sea.

The *Shaitan* was leading alone, for the *Sumana* had been left behind to seize a quantity of arms which the enemy in the flight had abandoned near Muzaibila. The chase was long and arduous in the intense heat, but foot by foot the flying enemy was overhauled. Towards sunset they could be clearly seen—first the familiar white sails of the *mahailas* struggling against the current; then the steamer *Mosul*, full of troops and towing two barges equally crowded; and ahead of all the gunboat *Marmariss* similarly employed. Just as the sun dipped the *Shaitan* was able to open fire on the rearmost boats. The *Espiègle* followed quickly upon the *Mosul*, and then the reward began to be reaped. Both steamers hurriedly cast off their tows, and when before the brief twilight was done the blue dome of Ezra's tomb could be made out in its clump of palm trees, the *mahailas* could be seen lowering their sails and the small boats mooring under the banks. The *Odin*, as last in the line, was ordered to stop and take possession, while the rest went on in the dusk after the *Mosul* and *Marmariss*, firing till the targets could no longer be seen. At 8.0 navigation was no longer possible. They had to stop, and by aid of their searchlights they took possession of two large lighters and several more *mahailas* laden with troops, guns, mines and munitions, which the Turkish gunboats had abandoned. Here, too, they found the steamer *Bulbul*, which a shell from the *Shaitan* had sunk.

Two hours after midnight the moon rose and it was possible to move on. Leaving the *Odin* to guard the prisoners and booty, the *Espiègle* and *Clio* went on again with the *Miner* and *Comet*, who by this time had got up as well as the *Shaitan* and *Sumana*. As they proceeded the navigation became more and more intricate, until at 4.15, some six miles above Ezra's tomb, and just as the *Marmariss* was in sight again, the *Espiègle* had to stop with nothing but mud under her keel. Fire was opened at once on the Turkish gunboat. There was no reply, and an armed party sent to investigate found her cut to pieces, abandoned and on fire. The *Mosul* could also be seen round the next bend, and on her the *Clio* fired. The immediate response was a white flag, and the *Shaitan* went on and took possession.[1]

The evidence of the enemy's demoralisation was now complete. It was a sore temptation, with all the day before them, to carry on and see how things were up at Amara. But it was still fifty miles on, the sloops could go no farther and the army was fifty miles astern. But on the heels of a routed enemy much may be dared, and, after a short consultation the General and Captain Nunn decided to carry on in the *Comet* with the other launches. The *Miner* soon had to be left for lack of water, but the *Lewis Pelly* had come up, and she, with the *Shaitan* and *Sumana*, each towing a horse-boat with a 4·7-inch naval gun, continued the pursuit. No sign of opposition was encountered. At Qala Salih, half-way to Amara, which they reached in the early afternoon, some cavalry and an infantry company were dispersed with a few shells, and then the notables came off to make submission. Six miles further on they stopped for the night.

At daylight next morning, June 3, they moved again up the interminable succession of bends, less able than ever to tell what was round the next corner, but everywhere the villagers still greeted them with white flags and signs of obeisance. No troops were seen, but when they reached Abu Sidra, twelve miles short of their destination, it became

[1] The captures up to this time, besides the *Marmariss* and *Mosul*, were two steel lighters, seven *mahailas*, two field guns, large quantities of rifles and ammunition, 140 prisoners and treasure to the amount of over £1,000.

necessary to go more warily. The flotilla was concentrated, and Lieutenant M. Singleton in the *Shaitan*, the fastest launch, was sent three miles ahead with Captain B. G. Peel of the General's Staff and a small launch as despatch boat, to ascertain and report whether Amara was being held or evacuated. Then the *Comet*, leading the rest of the launches and the gun barges, followed.

By 2.0 the *Shaitan* was within three miles of the town without having found any sign of the enemy, but just as she turned into the Amara reach, troops in large numbers were seen leaving the place by a bridge of boats and getting into a barge on the other bank which was secured to a steamer. The bridge was immediately opened, but before the steamer could get through, a shot from the *Shaitan's* 12-pounder brought her to, and the troops took to the shore and made off up the river. The *Shaitan* followed through the bridge. As she passed it about half a battalion of infantry were just debouching on to the by-ways. At sight of her they hurried back up the narrow streets. Lieutenant Singleton went on. On rounding the westerly bend of the river above the town a number of troops were seen retreating on either hand, some 1,500 on the one bank and 1,000 on the other, both abreast and ahead of him, so that with those still in the town he was practically surrounded by the enemy. Still, though the river here was less than 200 yards broad, no shot was fired on either side, and he held on for 1,000 yards further, when 100 Turks came down to the bank and surrendered. After quietly taking their rifles on board and ordering them to march down stream parallel with the *Shaitan*, he turned back, and had not gone far when another 150 also surrendered. They were dealt with in the same way, and these also he continued to escort towards the *Comet*, which was just coming up the Amara reach.[1]

As she approached with the rest of the flotilla all was quiet under the burning afternoon sun; the steam craft and lighters at the quays were deserted, and abreast of them she anchored. Still no sign of movement or preparation for

[1] Of this incident Captain Peel in his report to the General wrote: "Thus *Shaitan* caused 2,000 Turks to evacuate Amara and captured some 250 with eleven officers by firing three shells and a display of cool audacity which even the Royal Navy would find hard to equal. . . . I am convinced had I been in command I should never have dared to proceed in the way she did, ignoring a strong force in my rear and with the knowledge that a few resolute Turks on either bank might easily have accounted for the crew at almost point blank." This was also Captain Nunn's opinion. Lieutenant Singleton was awarded the D.S.O., and the D.S.M. was given to his Coxswain A. J. Roberts and Gunlayer W. H. Rowe.

defence, but it was difficult to know what to do next. Amara was quite an important port and trading centre, it was the headquarters of a sanjak, and its population was estimated at 20,000, besides its garrison. Our own troops were a day and a half's steaming down the river, and in the whole flotilla, counting the General's Staff and guard, there were no more than 100 white men besides the Lascar stokers. Boldness had served them well, and with a culminating stroke of it they acted on the spot. A boat, manned by a couple of seamen and one marine, was sent off from the *Comet* with a corporal and twelve men of the West Kent and 1/5th Hants Territorial Battery, and the final scene of the fairy tale was played. The boat was met by an offer to surrender. In the barracks was found a whole battalion of the Constantinople fire brigade. *Corps d'élite* as they were, they gave themselves up to a few of the boat's crew—one officer, one seaman, one marine and an interpreter. The Turkish General, the Civil Governor, and a number of officers surrendered at the Custom House, where General Townshend, Captain Nunn and other officers landed on the arrival of the *Comet.* During the afternoon the British flag was hoisted over the Governor's house. up to a few of the boat's crew. The Turkish General, the Civil Governor, and between thirty and forty officers handed in their swords on board the *Comet*, and during the afternoon the British flag was hoisted over the Governor's house.

Still the position was highly delicate. With the *Shaitan's* captures there were now about 700 prisoners, and more, including the officers and crew of the *Marmariss*, were continually coming in for fear of the Arabs. As many as possible were put on board a lighter and moored in mid-stream, but it was little more than a tenth of the total, and it could not be long before such fine troops recovered their spirit and found out how slender was the force opposed to them. Messages were despatched down the river for the troops to press on. Hour after hour the southern horizon was eagerly scanned for a sign of them till darkness fell. What the morrow would bring none could tell, but towards morning the distant glow of a searchlight could be seen, and by dawn the smoke of the leading transport. So the position was saved. By 10·0 a.m. (June 4) the 2nd Norfolk came up in the *P.3.* But it was not a moment too soon. In the town the Arabs had discovered the real state of affairs, and had already started to fire and loot when they arrived. Then all was quiet, and Amara was securely ours with an abundant booty. In the four days' operations a gunboat and two steamers had been sunk, and the prizes were three steamers, a couple of motor boats, ten iron barges and other craft, on board one of which was £1,000 in gold coin. The prisoners numbered 139 officers and 1,634 men, and amongst the captured material were 17 guns, 2,700 rifles and over a million rounds of small-arm ammunition. Nor was this the whole tale of success. For they had been in time to cut off the retreat of the troops retiring from Ahwaz. Part of the advanced guard, ignorant of what had happened at Amara, was actually captured, the rest only escaped by dispersing with the loss of two guns, and these it seems were the fugitives whose retreat the *Shaitan* hurried on the east bank. The main body had to find its way northward to Kut, and there, too, the broken remnants of the Amara garrison eventually found refuge. The success was thus complete, and it was due not only to the audacity and alert resource in which the operation culminated, but in an equal degree to the skilful and patient staff work by which each Service from first to last had made good the inabilities of the other, and to the close co-operation between them which, as General Nixon wrote in his despatch, " stands out as a marked feature of the operations."

The British casualties in the four days, 31st May–3rd June, totalled only four killed and twenty-one wounded. The enemy lost 120 killed and wounded.[1]

[1] For a full account of the military operations outlined in this volume see : *Official History of the War, Military Operations, Togoland and the Cameroons, 1914–1916*, and *The Campaign in Mesopotamia, 1914–1918*, Vol. I.

CHAPTER II

THE DARDENELLES, MAY 5 TO JUNE 7—EXPLOITS OF *E 14* AND *E 11* IN THE MARMARA—LOSS OF THE *TRIUMPH* AND *MAJESTIC*—THE THIRD BATTLE OF KRITHIA[1]

THE success in Mesopotamia was the more welcome since in the main attack on the Ottoman Empire things had been going from bad to worse. The inability of the army had now extended to the squadron. It was not only that it was reduced in strength, but the long-expected hour had come when it could no longer claim a full working command of the Ægean. The *Queen Elizabeth* had gone (May 14), and under the Italian Convention Rear-Admiral C. F. Thursby had left with the *Queen* (flag), *Prince of Wales, Implacable* and *London* on the 18th. He joined the Italian fleet at Taranto on May 27. The four light cruisers which had been promised (*Dartmouth, Dublin, Amethyst* and *Sapphire*) were already at Brindisi; and Vice-Admiral J. M. de Robeck thus lost many of the ships which experience had made the most efficient at the work to be done. At the same time the *Exmouth* and *Venerable* joined from home, with the experience they had gained on the Belgian coast. The French had made up their contingent of six battleships by sending the *Suffren, Charlemagne* and *Patrie*, under Vice-Admiral E. E. Nicol, who was now in command of the French Dardanelles Squadron. The agreed number of cruisers was reached by the *Kléber* from Brest and the *Dupleix* and *Bruix* from patrol duty in the Mediterranean. All were comparatively old cruisers, which, though good enough for supporting troops ashore, could not make up for the light cruisers Admiral de Robeck had lost. They had to be replaced, and accordingly the *Chatham* and *Cornwall* were ordered to the Dardanelles from East Africa.

The squadron thus reconstituted might have served well enough but for the new danger that was menacing it. The supporting ships were now under Rear-Admiral Stuart Nicholson, Rear-Admiral R. E. Wemyss having resumed his duties as Senior Naval Officer at Mudros, and they were doing their best to assist the continual trench warfare that was going on and to keep down the fire of the new heavy batteries which had been established on the Asiatic shore, and which were beginning to hamper seriously the work of supply upon the southern beaches. The efforts of the ships in this direction

[1] See also *The Official History of the War, Military Operations: Gallipoli.*

were, however, soon to be checked. It had long been realised that the appearance of German submarines in the Ægean would naturally alter the situation for the worse. Sooner or later their arrival was inevitable, but so heavy was the strain in Home waters that little provision had been possible to meet the peril. No destroyers and few trawlers were to be had, and in default of them material had been sent out for closing the Straits with a barrier, but so strong was the current that it was found impossible to place it in position, and the idea had had to be given up. And now rumours were rife that German submarines had arrived, or were about to arrive. The Turks appear to have expected them on May 17, and the following day our Smyrna patrol reported that a large one had entered that port. The news was specially disquieting, for our intelligence agents were reporting that two new divisions had been brought to Gallipoli, and that submarine attack on the supporting ships at Gaba Tepe was to be expected. The inference was that the two new divisions were to be used against the Anzacs. General Liman von Sanders had made up his mind to combine the first effort of the submarines with a desperate attack to drive the Anzacs into the sea, and so remove the threat to his communications with Krithia and Achi Baba. The two new divisions were accordingly committed to Essad Pasha, and with the two old divisions already there he began the attempt before dawn on the 19th. At daylight the attack developed great intensity, but in spite of the danger to the supporting ships the Admiral had kept all four of them (*Canopus*, Captain Heathcoat S. Grant, Senior Naval Officer, *Triumph*, *Vengeance* and *Bacchante*) in position, as well as four destroyers, and they were able to play their part. As assault after assault was made they kept up a continuous fire as directed from the shore. Over much of the line of conflict the opposing trenches were so close that they could do little in actual support of the infantry. But the artillery fire they could keep down. No submarine appeared to disturb the bombardment. A ship in the Narrows tried to interfere, but was quickly driven off by the *Triumph*, and though the Turks had never fought with greater determination, by 11 a.m. the battle was over. Their losses amounted to 10,000 and more than 3,000 dead were counted that afternoon. A suspension of arms was arranged for them to bury their dead. The Australian losses were about six hundred. The result was very satisfactory. "After May 19," the Turkish War Office has stated, "it was realised that the British defences at Anzac were too strong to enable us to effect anything against them without heavy artillery and plenty of ammunition." The Turks also recognised the impregnable strength of their own position and withdrew two battalions. For nearly two months no major operation was attempted in this quarter.

But, though no submarine attack had been made on the supporting ships, the question of their exposure remained. For two days more there was no sign of the threatened danger, but on the morning of May 22 a submarine was reported by several ships between Gaba Tepe and Tekke Burnu. The transports were immediately ordered to raise steam and make for Mudros, and ships without nets to get under way. A thorough search failed to locate the enemy and no harm was done. It may even have been a false alarm—possibly due to dead mules, of which there were now many floating about—but that enemy submarines were in the vicinity could not be doubted, and steps had to be taken to minimise the risk. To the Admiral the problem was one of extreme difficulty. The presence of some covering ships he regarded as indispensable for the army. Its supply of artillery ammunition was so short that it was powerless to deal with the enemy's batteries without naval assistance. What he did, therefore, was to reduce the ships at Gaba Tepe from four to two, with one in reserve at Imbros, and those of the Southern Division from seven to four. That even six were to remain was solely due to what he felt was his minimum duty to the army, yet to the soldiers the change looked like a stampede. There can be little doubt, however, that Admiral de Robeck was taking the utmost legitimate risk that was consistent with safeguarding their communications.

Nor did it mean resting on a merely defensive attitude; for as it became clear that the enemy, having failed to dislodge us by direct means, was bent on breaking our hold by cutting up our sea communications, so we by the same means were doing our best to cut up his. How far we had succeeded was now known. Lieutenant-Commander E. C. Boyle had just returned from the Marmara (May 18) to tell the tale of *E 14*. Since his successful attack on his persecutors on May 1 the patrols had treated him with more discretion, but he had had little luck. Till May 5 no chance presented itself, but then he fell in with a large transport under convoy of one of the smartest of the enemy's German-built destroyers. The escort was being very well handled, and as it was a flat calm an attack was a very delicate matter. Yet by timing it when the destroyer was on the far side of the transport he was able unseen to fire his shot at 600 yards. It was a fair right-angled hit, but the torpedo failed to explode. Next day there was another good chance at a transport coming through the Marmara strait, but she saw the danger in time and turned back to Constantinople.[1] Day after day steamers were chased, but the few that were overhauled were full of refugees and were allowed to proceed. May 10 was a more exciting day. It began in the eastern part of the sea by a destroyer running over the submarine near Kalolimno island, but in the evening two large transports, escorted by another German-built destroyer, came along. The first torpedo fired at the leading transport did not run true, but then the bad luck ended. The second hit the other transport and exploded with such force that debris and men could be seen falling into the water. She was, in fact, crowded with troops proceeding from Constantinople to Gallipoli. Starting in life as the White Star liner *Germania,* she was now the Ottoman transport *Gul Djemal,* a ship of 5,000 tons, and on board of her were 6,000 men and a battery of artillery. What became of her could not be seen—night had fallen and she disappeared into the darkness. Later on an eye-witness on the island declared that she turned back on her course, but sank almost immediately with all hands.[2]

So at last Lieutenant-Commander Boyle could feel he had struck a blow of high material and moral consequence, but it had cost him his last torpedo, for the one he had left proved defective. Still, innocuous as he was, without a gun and with a single periscope left which he dared not expose to rifle fire, he held on. He could at least keep up the impression he had made, and so hope to hamper the flow of the enemy's reinforcements and supplies. One small steamer he did manage to force ashore, but that was all. Still he continued to cruise until May 17, when he was recalled in order to give his successor the benefit of his experience.

Meanwhile the enemy, pending the arrival of the German submarines, was developing his other means of disturbing our supply service. More and heavier guns were being brought into action against the beaches and inner anchorages, and the need of ship fire to keep them in check became every day more indispensable. Every day the duty battleships, in hourly expectation of submarine attack, were at their firing stations. For two days after the first alarm nothing happened, but then the crisis came. On May 25 Admiral

[1] See Map 3. [2] Prize Court Reports, *Lloyd's List,* Jan. 30, 1917. The German Official History, however, states that she was towed next day to the Golden Horn (*Der Krieg zur See: Die Mittelmeer Division,* pp. 160–1).

Nicholson in the *Swiftsure* was off Cape Helles, expecting the *Majestic* to relieve him.[1] The *Agamemnon* was anchored near by till the hour she was to go inside and assist the French in dealing with the Asiatic heavy batteries. Up at Anzac the *Triumph* was under way with her nets out off Gaba Tepe, ready to deal with any Turkish battleship that attempted to fire from the Narrows. On the Anzac north flank was Captain Heathcoat Grant in the *Canopus*. In the early morning he had been engaged in supporting another raid at Suvla Bay, where the observation post on Nibrunessi Point, destroyed a fortnight earlier, had been restored. About fifty troops in the destroyers *Chelmer* and *Colne* landed, and once more demolished it, and at 7.0 a.m. the *Chelmer* came down to protect the *Triumph*. The *Canopus* then moved off to meet the *Vengeance*, which was coming up from Mudros to relieve her. Special precautions were being taken, for it was clear at an early hour that a submarine was about.

It was a Grimsby trawler, the *Minoru*, that gave the first alarm—one of those maids-of-all-work of the fleet that were doing everything no one else could be found to do, and doing it well. Towards 7.30 a.m. off the entrance she began giving sharp blasts on her siren. It was all she could do. For the trawlers, having been sent out as minesweepers, were unarmed, and indeed when they started there were no guns to give them. Their only method of attack was to ram, and for this they had scarcely speed enough. They could, however, give the alarm to destroyers. The *Harpy*, which, with another destroyer was patrolling round the Cape Helles battleships, at once rushed to the spot and passed the warning signal. She quickly saw the submarine making apparently for the *St. Louis* off Sedd el Bahr, and pressed after it. Possibly for this reason the French battleship was not attacked, or it may be, as we had been informed, the submarine's orders were to deal with the ships at Anzac. At all events the enemy held on, and ten minutes later her periscope was seen passing between the *Swiftsure* and *Agamemnon* going north. The *Swiftsure* fired on her, but she disappeared, and nothing more was seen of her till shortly after 10.0. By that time the *Vengeance* was zigzagging up from Mudros, and when she was due east of Cape Kephalo the track of a torpedo was seen coming for her from shorewards. A smart turn to starboard swung her clear, and after a few rounds at her assailant's periscope she held on for Gaba Tepe, while the submarine made off up the coast. The *Talbot*, which was off Y Beach,

[1] See Map 4.

and all available destroyers and trawlers spread in search. Four times was her periscope seen and fired on, and once a destroyer ran right over her without touching. When the *Vengeance* reached Gaba Tepe Captain Heathcoat Grant transferred to her, and the *Canopus* started for Mudros, heading to take the safe course round the north of Imbros. As the hunt indicated that the submarine was coming northwards up the coast, Captain Heathcoat Grant ordered the *Manica* and all transports present to clear away for the protected Imbros anchorage at Kephalo Bay. Then the excitement quickened. A quarter of an hour later the *Canopus*, which was now half-way to Imbros, signalled a submarine 2,000 yards to the northward of her, steering south. The *Canopus* was working up to full speed, zigzagging hard, with the *Ribble* guarding her, and she was not attacked. On receiving the report Admiral Nicholson at noon signalled to Admiral de Robeck, who was at Kephalo in the *Lord Nelson*, for leave for all ships to retire there. All these attacks and alarms were the work of one submarine, the *U 21* under Lieutenant-Commander Hersing, who had left Wilhelmshaven on April 24, and so far the calm sea and good visibility had frustrated his efforts. But he had not long to wait.

Six miles away to the south-eastward was the *Triumph* at her firing station off Gaba Tepe, still under way, with her nets down, light guns manned and all watertight doors closed, and round her the *Chelmer* was patrolling at 15 knots. About 12.25, as the destroyer was rounding the battleship's bows, she saw a suspicious white wash 500 yards on the *Triumph's* starboard beam. Instantly she made a dash for it, but too late. The *Triumph* had started firing at the periscope, but in another minute a shock of extraordinary violence seemed to lift her, and then for a while she was smothered fore and aft in a shower of falling water and coal. The torpedo had got fairly home as though her nets had been a spider's web. When she could be seen again she had listed ten degrees. As she continued to heel over, the *Chelmer* rushed up under her stern walk, and by a fine display of seamanship was able to take off a number of men before, ten minutes after the battleship was struck, she capsized. For nearly half an hour she remained floating bottom upwards, and then, with a lurch that sent her stern high in the air, she slowly disappeared. As she went down the rescued men gave her a last cheer with cries of "Good-bye, old *Triumph*," for her requiem. Happily there were many to swell the sound of that farewell. The moment her list had become dangerous the "Retreat" had been sounded and the men had quietly dropped down from the nets and booms. Thus, thanks to the prompt action of the *Chelmer* and the other craft which hurried to the rescue, nearly all were saved. The *Chelmer* and her boats alone took up over 500 officers and men, and in the end only three officers and seventy men were lost.

Yet the loss was severe enough. For the Australians and New Zealanders it was like an old friend gone, so ready and skilful had she been to help at every turn of good or evil fortune. They were even loth to believe she was dead, and were for subscribing a month's pay all round towards salving her. Deep as was the moral impression of the brilliantly executed attack, it was small compared with the material effect on the whole plan of operations. Not only did it mean a serious new complication in the problems of supplying the various beaches, but the fact had to be faced that continuous battleship support for the army was no longer possible. Admiral Nicholson in the *Majestic* withdrew to Kephalo for the night, the rest of the ships were withdrawn to Mudros, and destroyers took their place. But the lesson was yet to be driven further home. On the following day (26th) nothing further happened, and all was quiet except for a submarine reported by the *Jauréguiberry* off the entrance. It was during the afternoon, and the French battleship was zigzagging between Kum Kale and Sedd el Bahr when a periscope suddenly appeared 100 yards from her. At the moment fortunately she was altering helm, so that instead of being torpedoed she ran over the submarine, and some on board believed they had cut her in two.[1] Another hunt was instituted, but nothing found, and Admiral Nicholson, who had returned to Helles in the morning, remained at his post taking every possible precaution against attack.

The objective of the submarine was clear enough. What had most hampered the enemy's operations was the fire of the battleships. This had first to be got rid of, and till that was done the transports could wait. Amongst the transports, therefore, a battleship could hope for a certain amount of security. Accordingly in the midst of those discharging stores at the southern beaches the *Majestic* was anchored with her nets out as close inshore as possible, and yet in a position where she could command the enemy's principal positions. Outside the transports destroyers were patrolling, and in the entrance of the straits was a cordon of unarmed trawlers. Even against the skill and boldness of the German submarine commander the berth seemed safe enough, but the sun was barely up on May 27 when it was

[1] Vedel: *Nos Marins à la Guerre*, p. 187.

shown how inadequate the precautions were. At 6.45 a periscope broke the water no more than 400 yards away on the *Majestic's* port beam. She opened fire immediately, but not before the track of a torpedo was seen coming through one of the few gaps in the surrounding screen of transports. It was a shot the best might envy. Striking the nets the torpedo went clean through them without a check and took its target fair amidships. Another followed instantly, and in seven minutes the famous old ship, the pride of the old Channel fleet, in whose design the whole thought and experience of the Victorian era had culminated, capsized. So good, however, was the discipline that all the officers and nearly all the men were saved. Of her whole complement, only about forty who were killed by the explosions or became entangled in the nets were missing. The ship did not sink, but being in only nine fathoms of water, lay resting on her foremast with the fore-end of her keel and bottom plating awash, looking like a stranded whale. Yet she was gone, and with her the last hope of clinging to what still was left of the system by which the army had been supplied and supported. Never before, perhaps, had a military operation been so deeply affected by means so small. For the brilliant way in which the enemy submarine had been handled, both services had nothing but admiration. It was indeed no more than was to be expected from the man in command. For later on he was known to be none other than Lieutenant-Commander Hersing, the determined officer who in April, as we have seen, in spite of every difficulty, had brought his boat *U 21* into the Mediterranean, and had thus demonstrated the possibility—till then not credited—of navigating a submarine to the Adriatic without a half-way base of supply.[1] Reaching Cattaro on May 13, with only half a ton of oil in his tanks, he had rested a week and then continued his voyage to the Dardanelles. The grave moral effects of the exploits in which his remarkable feat had resulted could not be disguised. Hundreds of Turkish troops, depressed by loss and failure and demoralised by the heavy shell from the sea, had seen the stampede of the ships they most dreaded; thousands of our own men had seen it and the loss of the ships as well, and they knew there was nothing now but the cruisers and destroyers to support them in their daily struggle in the trenches.

Fortunately there was something to set on the other side. The day the *Majestic* was lost a message was received from *E 11*, and the tale she had to tell was no less stirring than

[1] See Vol. II., p. 384 *n*.

that over which the enemy was exulting.[1] This was the boat which had succeeded *E 14*, and the same in which, after failing to get into the Baltic, Lieutenant-Commander Nasmith on Christmas day, 1914, had so brilliantly rescued four wrecked airmen in the Heligoland Bight while they were being attacked by a Zeppelin.[2] Lieutenant-Commander Boyle in *E 14* had safely run the gauntlet of the mines, nets and guns in the straits on May 18, and after learning all he could from him, Lieutenant-Commander Nasmith started the same night to find his way inward through the tangle of dangers himself. He was entirely successful. Though fired on by battleships and destroyers whenever his periscope showed, he reached the Marmara during the forenoon of May 19. All that day and the next nothing was seen in the western portion except torpedo-boats and armed trawlers. During the night, therefore, profiting by his predecessor's experience, he proceeded to the eastern end of the sea, where patrols were less active. There he seized a small sailing vessel, and trimming well down, lashed her alongside the conning-tower, and then cruised on a course which made him invisible from the eastward. But the ruse failed. His appearance going up the straits had evidently stopped all traffic. Nothing came along, and at nightfall he dismissed his prize and returned to the westward.

Here there was still nothing but the patrols, and early on the 23rd he was back at Oxia island, eight miles south of the entrance to the Bosporus. In this position, while capturing a small sailing vessel, he sighted an empty transport returning to Constantinople and followed her. Now came his first stroke of luck. At anchor off the city was a Turkish torpedo-gunboat giving a fine target, and he attacked at once. The torpedo hit her fair amidships and she began to sink. Before she went down, however, she gamely got off a few rounds with a 6-pounder, with the first of which she had the good luck to hit the submarine's foremost periscope, and Lieutenant-Commander Nasmith retired to Kalolimno island to repair it, but in this he was unsuccessful. Then, after going west again, he started next morning (the 24th) for a cruise north-east towards Rodosto, the chief Turkish port on the Thracian coast. On this course he soon met a small steamer coming west. She was summoned to stop, but took no notice, nor had the submarine a gun to enforce her signal. A rifle shot at the bridge, however, quickly brought her to, and when she was visited an American journalist on board explained she was taking marines to Chanak. They were already in the water, having capsized the boats in their hurry. As they

[1] See Map 3. [2] See Vol. I., pp. 237–8, and Vol. II., p. 52.

all had lifebelts they were left alone to right the boats and escape, but the steamer was found to carry a gun and a quantity of shell. She was therefore sunk with a demolition charge.[1]

But there was more to come. As she blew up smoke was seen coming up from the eastward. *E 11* dived to attack, but the chase, alarmed by the last explosion, altered course for Rodosto. When the submarine came to the surface the steamer was seen and chased till she was alongside the pier. With a gun she could easily have been finished, but the shallowness of the water made it very hazardous to dive within torpedo range. Still Lieutenant-Commander Nasmith was unwilling to leave her alone. Her deck was piled high with packing-cases which told she was a storeship heavily laden. So he took the risk and dived to attack. His periscope was greeted with rifle fire, but at one successful shot she burst into flames, and then the submarine, whose periscope could not be hidden owing to the shallowness of the water, made off out of the bay. Almost immediately a third steamer, laden with barbed wire, was seen. To a summons to stop she replied by an attempt to ram, and then made away and beached herself under the cliffs. A demolition party was got ready to finish her, but a body of horsemen on the cliff opened so hot a fire that Lieutenant-Commander Nasmith thought it best to beat a hasty retreat.

But appetite had grown with feeding. Nothing but small game was to be found in the open, and he now made his way eastward to see what could be found in the Bosporus. Shortly after midday (25th)—at the fatal hour when the *Triumph* was sinking—he was off the entrance, and there, to use his own words, he " dived into Constantinople." Rising close to the United States guardship, he saw a large vessel lying alongside the arsenal. By an ominous coincidence she was called the *Stambul*, and on her his blow fell. The first torpedo failed to run true, the second sank a lighter and also holed, but did not sink the *Stambul*. The result could not be seen from the submarine for she was suddenly swept aground by a cross-tide. But two explosions were heard, the stray torpedo which narrowly missed her exploding against the quay. As for the submarine, she behaved like a thing intoxicated by the wild adventure. Bouncing from shoal to shoal and spinning round with the current, she was quite out of control and in acute danger of destruction. Yet she survived, and when in twenty minutes she was calm enough to come to

[1] According to the German account, which wrongly allots this sinking to the *E 14*, this vessel, the *Nagara*, had on board a 5·9-inch gun from the *Goeben*. (*Der Krieg zur See : Die Mittelmeer Division*, p. 162.)

the surface, she found herself well clear of the entrance. "The next day," wrote Lieutenant-Commander Nasmith, "was spent resting in the centre of the Sea of Marmara."

Surely rest was never better earned. The material result of his unprecedented exploit was not great. The *Stambul* was an old ship, but the moral effect was all that could be wished. For over 500 years, since the Turkish flag first flew on the city walls, no foreign enemy had ever profaned the Golden Horn. All along the shores there was panic, shops were closed, troops disembarked from the transports, and sea communication between Constantinople and Gallipoli was practically stopped.

So much of what the adventurous submarine had done was known on the 27th, but it was not the end of her cruise. For another eleven days she remained in the Marmara as active as ever. Early on the 27th, as she was making her way back to the Bosporus, she encountered a large battleship, apparently the *Barbarousse Haireddine*, coming westward at high speed through the Marmara strait. She promptly trimmed low to attack, but just as she neared the firing position she saw in the moonlight a destroyer coming right on the top of her and was compelled to dive. Next morning she was consoled by catching a convoy of one large and four small supply ships, and in spite of the escorting destroyer, torpedoed the large one.[1] For the next two days there was no luck, but on the 31st she attacked a steamer making for Panderma. The torpedo failed to explode, although on its being recovered it was found to have hit; the vessel was towed ashore. Little else was moving, so on that day Lieutenant-Commander Nasmith decided to look into Panderma. There in the roads he found a large Rickmers liner and torpedoed her, but she also was towed ashore with a heavy list. All next day (June 1) he waited for transports which were reported to be coming with troops from Ismid, but nothing appeared. After reporting to the *Jed*, which was the linking ship in the Gulf of Xeros, he was proceeding on June 2 north-eastward up the northern coast when he met a vessel coming from the eastward. Diving to attack he got in a successful shot, and the explosion was so extraordinarily violent, seeming to heave her whole upper deck overboard, that there could be no doubt she was full of ammunition. She sank almost immediately, and in

[1] This vessel, the *Panderma*, carried some 500 Turkish soldiers, of whom about half were lost. This is claimed to be the only loss to the army caused by submarine. (*Der Krieg zur See: Die Mittelmeer Division*, p. 161.)

an hour or so another smaller storeship was attacked. The torpedo missed and could not be recovered owing to rifle fire from the shore, and for the same reason the storeship, which anchored and was abandoned close to shore, could not be demolished. Later on she attacked a despatch vessel escorted by two destroyers; again the torpedo missed, but this time it was recovered.

So the work went on, with hairbreadth escapes from the destroyers that were now hotly hunting her and no further success till June 7, when failing machinery warned her it was high time to return. She had still two torpedoes left, and these were reserved for the battleships she expected to find in the Straits on her way down. As far as Chanak she smelt for her prey, but nothing was seen except a large empty troopship lying off Moussa bank, eight miles above Nagara point. The torpedoes were reserved for better game, but when none was found Lieutenant-Commander Nasmith turned back, doubled the dangerous Nagara point once more, and torpedoed her. Then at last he started to go out, but only to meet an adventure that outdid all the rest.

He had passed the Narrows, diving deep to clear the mine-field beyond, when the boat began to grate as though on the bottom when no bottom was near. The only thing to do was to come up and investigate. As soon as the periscope was clear something ugly could be seen careering along twenty feet ahead of it. It could be nothing but a large mine with its moorings foul of one of the hydroplanes. There could be no worse company, but both shores bristled with guns and it was out of the question to come to the surface and clear it. There was no choice but to carry on with their evil shipmate in company. For an hour the nightmare continued till they were clear of the entrance. Then came the work of getting free. One false move must have proved fatal. What Lieutenant-Commander Nasmith did was to trim his vessel so that, while her bows were submerged, her stern was on the surface. In this position she went hard astern, till after a breathless interval the stern way, combined with the rush of water from the screws, caused the mine to slip free and drop off ahead like a necklace. The coolness and resource displayed was a fitting end to his brilliant cruise. In the course of it he had sunk a gunboat, two ammunition ships, two troopships, two storeships and beached and holed a third transport. He had also saved his vessel from an almost impossible situation.[1]

[1] For their exploits in the Marmara both he and Lieutenant-Commander Boyle received the V.C.

If, then, with equal skill and daring the enemy was disturbing our communications, it was not done without retaliation. To the enemy, whose lines of supply were almost entirely by sea for at least some part of their extent, the interference was serious. The number of ships available was very limited—those sunk could not be replaced, and the repair of those damaged was practically impossible. More and more they had to rely on land transport for troops and supplies, and it was quite inadequate. No railway ran to Gallipoli; the nearest station was on the Adrianople line at Uzun Kupru, fifty miles from Bulair.[1] The consequent delay and inconvenience were great, nor was there any relief except for the small quantities of stores that could be got through in small craft by night.

Our own case was not so bad, but for us the new development entailed a complete reorganisation of the system of supply. Transports could no longer anchor off the beaches and discharge into small craft. The only anchorage that as yet was safe for them was at Mudros. There a boom, which had been intended for the entrance of the Dardanelles, had just been completed across the channel leading into the inner harbour, and another was about to be laid at the entrance to the outer bay with material already on the spot. At Mudros, then, the transports would have to discharge, and this would mean for the already overworked fleet sweepers, trawlers and other small craft a trip each way of from fifty to sixty miles instead of a few thousand yards. It could only cause serious delay, and delay was specially untimely, for General Hamilton was preparing a last attempt to win Achi Baba and Krithia by a general assault. To add to the difficulty the strain on the flotilla and small craft had been increased by the necessity of keeping up a systematic search of the Ægean coasts and islands, whose multitudinous indentations offered endless facilities for submarine supply bases. In the course of this work the long-suspected port of Budrum was visited by the *Dupleix*. Finding the harbour full of shipping she signified her intention to examine them. The Vali asked for time, and on its termination boats were sent in under flag of truce. They were fired on, and suffered serious loss. The *Dupleix* then closed in, and having extricated them, bombarded the town. On hearing her report Admiral de Robeck sent away the *Bacchante* and *Kennet* with orders to destroy all the shipping. This they did on May 28, and having also laid the castle and barracks in ruins, came away.

[1] See Map 5.

So important was it now to restrict the enemy's sources of supply for his submarines that desultory operations of this character were not deemed sufficient. For the islands which were not in Turkish hands no more could be done, but with the mainland it was different, and at the Admiral's suggestion it had been decided to institute a blockade of the whole coast from the Dardanelles down to Samos. It was declared on June 2, and was thenceforth carried on from the land-locked harbour of Iero in Mityleni, where the officer in charge was stationed in a battleship or cruiser, and where with the sanction of the Greek Authorities an aerodrome was established.

Such, then, was the awkward situation which the new Board of Admiralty had to face, but in fact they found it had been discounted by their predecessors, for they had been making provision to meet it with all speed. Some of the monitors that were to replace the battleships were already in commission, and the work of providing four of the "Edgars" with protective bulges to render them immune from mine or torpedo was well advanced. But until they arrived on the scene of action there was need of a definite understanding as to how far the squadron could continue to give direct support to the army. The first telegram sent by the new Board to Admiral de Robeck dealt with the point. Their suggestion was that he should keep his battleships as much as possible at Mudros until netting patrols and other defensive arrangements that were in hand gave them reasonable security while bombarding, and that bombardments should be confined to occasions when important military operations were on foot. Even so their exposure should be reduced to the shortest possible time, and special precautions be taken to protect them with transports lashed alongside, and sea and air patrols. To enable him to act on these lines twenty more trawlers were ordered out, as well as thirty of the best drifters from Poole to work indicator nets.

In reply the Admiral explained how he had gradually reduced the number of battleships at sea as the submarine menace closed in upon him. He was now confining the support of the flanks to the "Beagle" class destroyers, with three battleships at short notice as supports, two at Mudros and the *Exmouth* at Kephalo, where her specially heavy nets would make her reasonably safe. Until he received similar nets for other ships it was all he could do pending the arrival of the monitors.

They could not, however, be in time for the next important military operations. During the week which had seen the coming of the submarines the Allied line had been advanced by local operations to within rushing distance of that of the enemy, and General Hamilton, rather than wait for his coming reinforcements, had determined to make one more attempt to carry the Achi Baba position before the enemy could strengthen it. Though submarines were still showing themselves the Admiral agreed to support the attack with two battleships. Accordingly on June 4, Admiral Nicholson took the *Exmouth* and *Swiftsure* with the light cruiser *Talbot* off Helles, while the little *Latouche-Tréville* went inside close off Kereves ravine to support the right of the French.[1] It was little enough the battleships could do. The aeroplanes were reporting submarines present, and though well covered by destroyers and indicator nets the ships had to keep circling, and indirect fire under way at unseen targets could be worth little beyond its moral effect. Still the attack opened brilliantly. It was a day of overpowering heat with a dust storm obscuring everything. At 8.0 a.m. the preparatory bombardment began afloat and ashore, and was kept up till past 11.20, when the men were ordered to fix bayonets and show them over the parapet. This was to bring the enemy into their advanced trenches to meet the attack. But the hour was not yet; the real bombardment had not begun. Not till the enemy's trenches were filled did it burst in full fury. For half an hour it was maintained in ever-increasing intensity. On the stroke of noon it lifted, and from end to end of the line the men sprang from the trenches. Bayonets were quickly crossing, but in spite of the fine resistance of the Turks the effect was all that could be wished. On the right the French, well assisted by the *Latouche-Tréville,* swept into the formidable work on the Kereves ravine, which had so long held them up; on their left the "Ansons" rushed a redoubt quite in old army style, and the "Howes" and "Hoods" captured the trenches in front of them. The "Collingwoods" which were sent forward in support suffered very heavily.[2] Even better was the work of the Manchester Brigade (with whom were the 1/5th and 1/6th Lancashire Fusiliers) on their left. In five minutes they had poured over the first line of trenches, which, the Turks state, had been rendered untenable by ship fire, and in half an hour they were masters of the second line 500 yards on. On their left again the XXIXth Division, including the Indian Brigade, were able

[1] The French Corps was now under the command of General Gouraud, who arrived on May 14 to relieve General d'Amade.

[2] The Royal Marine Brigade and the 1st Naval Brigade, less the "Drake" battalion, were in Corps Reserve.

to win the first line, but here the trenches had suffered less from the sea, and it was only gained after a fierce bayonet fight.[1] On the extreme left, which was dead ground for the ships, there was no progress at all. There the wire proved to be intact, and the most desperate work and devotion of Sikhs and Gurkhas could produce no result.

Still all promised well. The Manchesters were lying out on the slopes of Achi Baba with nothing between them and the coveted summit—waiting only for the word to go on. But that word never came. On the extreme right by the Kereves ravine, the work the French had so gallantly captured proved but a death-trap. They were simply blasted out of it by high explosive, and before an overwhelming counter-attack had to fall back to where they started. The Naval division, with its right exposed by the French retirement and cruelly enfiladed, was forced also to let go its hold, and the Manchesters were in the air. Yet for hours they held on while efforts were made to recover the lost ground. But the French had suffered too severely to renew the attack, nor was it possible for the XXIXth Division to get further forward while its seaward flank was pinned down. There was nothing for it but to get the Manchesters away. By sunset it was done—at the cost of further heavy loss; and the day, which had begun so well and brought us almost within grip of the forbidden height, ended with no more gain than the central sections of the enemy's first-line trenches—250 to 500 yards on a front of about a mile. It was little enough for what it had cost in death, wounds and heroic fighting.[2] Both armies were completely exhausted, and with this hard-fought battle in the dust storm the second act of the tragedy closed down like the first, in failure and disappointment. With both army and navy half paralysed, all on which hope had been built was gone—but on our part there was no thought of retreat. With the Turks it was different. So heavily had they felt the weight of our attacks that every man had to be pushed up into the trenches, and units became hopelessly mixed. The consequent demoralisation was so great that they saw it was impossible to hold against another assault, and the Chief of Staff urged a withdrawal from the position before Krithia to Achi Baba and Kilid Bahr.

[1] Late on this day Major-General H. de B. De Lisle took over the command of the XXIXth Division from Lieut.-General A. G. Hunter-Weston, who had been given the command of the newly-formed VIIIth Army Corps.

[2] The two Royal Naval brigades engaged had alone 1,170 casualties. Killed, 35 officers and 135 men; wounded, 24 and 608; missing, 5 and 368. Total casualties were: British, 4,500; French, 2,000; Turkish, 9,000.

CHAPTER III

THE WESTERN FRONT AND THE DARDANELLES—AFFAIRS IN HOME WATERS, WHITE SEA AND BALTIC, JUNE–JULY—THE END OF THE *KÖNIGSBERG*

WITH the failure of the original Expeditionary Force to seize the keys of the Dardanelles the whole outlook darkened. The bold plan for striking Turkey out of the German combination by a *coup de main* had finally broken down, and with it went all reasonable hope of bringing the war to a speedy termination. That hope depended on the power of the Allies to deliver a concentric attack upon the Central Powers in overwhelming force—and Turkey was the sole obstacle that stood in the way of its development. With Turkey gone the bulk of our troops in India and Egypt would be free, the vital communications with Russia would be open, and the attitude of the Balkan States would no longer be doubtful. Then, except for the little sustenance that could reach the enemy across the Baltic, the investment of the Central Powers would be complete, and the mass of force that could be launched against them would be as irresistible as the tide.

There are probably few now who do not see in that narrow area where General Hamilton's little army clung exhausted to their trenches before Krithia and Achi Baba the decisive point of the war. It was there, as at a new Thermopylæ, the struggle of the Anglo-Saxon and Latin civilisation with the German seemed to be finding the gate of destiny. Nowhere could anything like so much be achieved with so little force, nowhere could a small advance reach things so great, nowhere could the shedding of Christian blood promise so rich a prospect of an all-embracing peace.

It was this venture so rightly aimed—but aimed without the energy of true faith—that had been at first scouted as a blind dissipation of force, as a mere eccentric operation. Its significance was clearer now. With Russia, half paralysed for lack of material and equipment to reorganise her shattered armies; with Austria, relieved from pressure on the east and free for a new attack on Serbia; with Bulgaria under German temptation too obviously waiting till she could make up her mind which was the winning side, there could be little doubt where the key of the situation lay. Failure could not be admitted. When success had been so narrowly missed, when a little more would mean so much, it was impossible to drop the half-finished task.

A decision, however, to carry on energetically with the enterprise on which we had embarked presented the most thorny difficulties. The problem raised in acute form the fundamental differences between the traditional British method of conducting a great war and the Napoleonic method which with all continental nations had become the strictly orthodox creed. Our own idea had long been to attack the enemy at the weakest point which could give substantial results, and to assume the defensive where he was strongest. The continental method was to strike where the enemy's military concentration was highest and where a decisive victory would end the war by destroying his armed forces. By general agreement this method, being the quicker and more drastic of the two, was the better, provided there was sufficient preponderance of force to ensure a decision, and the reason why in past great wars we had never adopted it, when the initiative lay in our hands, was that we never had military force enough to enjoy that preponderance.

In the opinion of Lord Kitchener and the British Ministers concerned with the conduct of the war the Allies could not have any such preponderance in the main theatre for a long time to come. The obvious and logical policy, therefore, was to postpone offence in the main theatre and devote our combined energies to the work of gathering the needful excess of strength by every means in our power. From this point of view the Dardanelles offered an ideal objective. Havana, the Peninsula and Sevastopol were the leading cases which supported our doctrine, but not one of them was so perfectly adapted to our method as was now the Dardanelles. The instinct, then, to complete the arrested enterprise was very strong. That it was well within our grasp there was no doubt if only we could devote to it every man, gun and round of ammunition that was not required for holding the line in France and Flanders, as well as every ship that was not wanted in Home waters for dealing faithfully with the High Seas Fleet should it become active.

To those for whom the old tradition was still a living light all this was clear as day, but in the century which had elapsed since our last great war the light had become obscured by a misreading of the continental doctrine of concentration for a decisive blow at the strongest point. Insensibly that doctrine had been extended by a doubtful corollary. Given the truth of the main proposition, it was assumed that all available force should be concentrated in the main, or, as it was usually called, the decisive theatre, whether or not those forces were large enough to secure a decisive preponderance. It was, of course, a *non sequitur* which did not flow from the cardinal idea of the doctrine. Nevertheless, though it was widely held in military circles, civilian opinion, in this country at least, was not convinced—it was indeed thoroughly sceptical—but in the circumstances the military attitude was difficult to resist. The French were bent on a great offensive effort, which we had more reason than ever to regard with grave misgiving. The failure of our own spring efforts at Festubert and Ypres could no longer be disguised. The battles were just dying down and our Ministers were more deeply impressed than ever with the hopelessness of the idea of a "break through." On the other hand, it was to be argued that with Italy about to take the field and with the fall of Przemysl, emphasising the menace of the German thrust on her eastern front, it was the moment for a vigorous effort in the west, if only to relieve the pressure on Russia. To the other school, however, the new orientation of Germany was evidence that a defensive attitude in the west could safely be assumed while we concentrated our whole offensive strength on the point which was vital to a Russian recovery. On this view, however, it was impossible to insist. Premature and ill advised as our Government believed the French policy to be, they knew that no other could be accepted by a high-spirited people whose richest provinces were being exploited and trodden down by the hereditary enemy, and they knew that the only way of minimising the evil consequences was to give the attack what additional weight we could. For the present, then, there could be no thought of a strictly defensive attitude in France, and, if there had been, the minimum force required was very difficult to determine. The men on the spot were the men to judge, and they were also the men inevitably the most prejudiced for a high margin of safety.

Such was broadly the position when on June 7 the War Council met for the first time since the formation of the Coalition Government.[1] In the meanwhile much time had

[1] It was now assembled as a Committee of the Cabinet known officially as the "Dardanelles Committee," but the reactions of the Dardanelles operations in other theatres tended continually to extend the area of its delibera-

been lost. Of the two divisions which General Hamilton had asked for on May 10, only the LIInd Lowland Territorials had gone. Transports were ready for the other on May 30, but in the chaos of the Cabinet crisis they had been dispersed and it was still at home. He had thus only half of what he had asked for, and the two divisions for which he had stipulated were only a minimum, contingent on some neutral or allied power assisting him against Turkey. If he was to have no such help he would require two army corps. Moreover since he sent in his requirements his position had changed for the worse; for the assault of June 4 upon the Krithia position had failed with heavy loss, and the first duty of the Council was to decide how the depressing situation was to be dealt with.

The decision was to act on our time-honoured system as strongly as possible without an open conflict of opinion with France. The Dardanelles enterprise was to be carried on and General Hamilton was to have the first call on the new armies. Of the first army, which was ready, one division was already in France; the remaining three were to go out in time for a new assault on the Turkish position in the second week of July. The recall of the *Queen Elizabeth* stood, but in her place most of the monitors which Lord Fisher had prepared for carrying the war to the German coasts were to be taken, besides six submarines and two of the old 10th Cruiser Squadron, *Endymion* and *Theseus*, which had been fitted with bulges for coastal attack, and four of the new sloops.[1] This decision, being in effect a new departure in our war policy, was referred, in accordance with constitutional usage, to the Cabinet, and by them approved two days later.[2]

There only remained the question of reserves. It was to the omission to provide them that General Hamilton attributed his first failure, and now it was urged that two first line territorial divisions which were still in England

---

tions till in practice it was scarcely distinguishable from a general War Council. It was attended by the Ministers of the Departments concerned and their expert advisers as the questions under consideration required.

[1] Fifteen of these monitors were ready, or nearly so. In the first class were four, each carrying two 14″ guns mounted in single turrets. Six more had been armed with 9·2″ guns, and another five smaller ones with 6″ which had had to be removed from the five "Queen Elizabeths" owing to spray interference. A number of others were in hand, including two fitted with new 15″ turrets prepared for our "furthest off" new battleships and eight other large ones to carry a 12″ turret from four of the old "Majestics." For the sloops, see footnote, p. 50.

[2] *Dardanelles Commission Report*, II., pp. 23–26.

should be moved to Alexandria and Malta. With the ripening of the new armies the nervousness about invasion had begun to die away. The two divisions could well be spared from home defence, and eventually it was agreed that they should go out as soon as possible.

To detail the troops was one thing: to get them out another. Time was of the last importance. The new blow must be struck before the Turks could consolidate and reinforce the Gallipoli position and, above all, before further successes of the Central Powers on the eastern Front drew Bulgaria into their orbit and opened the road from Berlin to Constantinople. The transport problem was becoming very difficult. The war demands on the mercantile marine were already being severely felt. Tonnage was scarce, the voyage to the Dardanelles was long, and the transports were detained there; beyond all this there was the submarine danger, which meant that transports could only sail as and when escort could be provided from the overworked destroyers.

To devote them entirely to the transports was impossible, so constant was the call for commerce protection. Again and again the escort arrangements were interrupted by cries for help from merchant vessels against molesting submarines. The hope of being able to destroy an enemy submarine was naturally more in accordance with naval ideas than passive defence against their attacks, and a rush for the spot whence the call came was always made, often with the result that the sailing of transports was delayed. The frequency of such calls was evidence enough of the enemy's determination to do his utmost with the new weapon. In spite of the American protests about the *Lusitania*,[1] there was no sign that the German hand was faltering. Reports of enemy submarines were coming in from all round the coast at an average of seven a day, and so far as we could see the notes from Washington had produced no apparent effect; but in fact, unknown to us, the whole policy was in the melting-pot.

In Germany civilian ministers had from the first opposed the use of the submarine against commerce, believing it would inevitably bring America into the ranks of their enemies. The same conviction in this country had also a good deal to do with our backwardness in preparing to meet the new form of commerce warfare. Before the war we could not fathom that peculiar faculty of German mentality, their " imperturbable capacity for self-deception," as Admiral von Tirpitz calls it, which led them to believe they could wantonly destroy Atlantic liners and commerce and yet

[1] See *Official History of the War: Merchant Navy*, Vol. II, p. 1, et seq.

cajole or intimidate America into acquiescence. The original difference of opinion between the Chancellor and the General and Admiralty staffs was resuscitated by the American notes in all its intensity. Such differences must necessarily be acute where, as in Germany, soldiers and sailors had come to be regarded as the supreme experts in the conduct of war. They of course could be no more than experts in military and naval operations. Of the other two main factors in war—foreign affairs and economics—they had no special technical knowledge. In these matters the statesmen were the experts. Naturally, then, the Chancellor could not admit responsibility for what happened if the fighting services were allowed to persist in what he was convinced was so grave a mistake. He therefore pressed for a severe restriction in submarine operations. The navy resisted hotly, and the difference was referred to the Emperor. At the conference that ensued the military chiefs supported the Chancellor; the Emperor supported the Admiralty, and decided that unless the Chancellor was willing to be responsible for abandoning the submarine campaign altogether the existing orders must stand.[1] Apparently the Chancellor was not prepared to go so far, and the result was a re-issue of orders, previously given to submarine commanders, that they were to spare neutral vessels, but to sink all British without exception. With this compromise, however, the Chancellor could not rest—neutral non-combatants in British vessels were still in jeopardy, and the danger of raising up a new enemy was not removed. He therefore urged the Admiralty to give up all idea of another *Lusitania* incident. Again the Admiralty refused and there was another appeal to the Emperor; he gave way to the Chancellor, and on June 5, in face of continued naval protest, an order went out that all large passenger ships—even those of the enemy—were to be spared.[2]

Of these dissensions we, of course, knew nothing at the time. All that was apparent was that the submarines were more active than ever in all parts of Home waters. In the area of the Grand Fleet this activity was mainly shown in attacks on our North Sea fishing fleets. During May the trouble was already so bad that new measures were taken to deal with it. As a first step special trawler units were told off for their protection—one of them disguised to act as a decoy. In June the mischief was as bad as ever, but it was soon checked. On the 3rd off Peterhead the armed trawler *Hawk* saw a steamer blow up about ten miles away.

[1] The conference was held at Pless on May 31.
[2] Von Tirpitz, *My Memoirs*, Vol. II, p. 406.

She hurried to the spot rescued the crew and took them into port. Then she returned and with another armed trawler, *Oceanic II*, resumed the rôle of simple fishing vessels. The submarine appeared on the 5th, and opened fire on the latter, but the *Hawk* came up quickly to her assistance and after damaging the enemy by gunfire, rammed and sank her. Six officers and twenty-one men were saved, but the commanding officer refused to leave his ship. She proved to be *U 14*, which had destroyed two neutral steamers on her way out. This same day the armed trawler *Ina Williams* engaged the *U 35* off Mizen Head (South-West Ireland), and claimed a hit, but the submarine was able to continue her operations.

A fortnight later there was an attempt at bigger game. On June 19 the 3rd Cruiser Squadron, together with the *Nottingham* and *Birmingham*, were making one of the periodical sweeps across the North Sea from Rosyth. To screen them they had four destroyers—the most that could be provided—but all too few, and the *Birmingham* was attacked by *U 32*, but without success. Next day (the 20th) torpedo attacks were made on the *Roxburgh*, *Argyll* and *Nottingham* by *U 17*. They were all missed, but later the *Roxburgh* was hit by *U 38*, though not severely enough to prevent her getting back to Rosyth. The *Nottingham* was also unsuccessfully attacked by *U 6*.

At this time there were five submarines in the area, whose main object was to operate against the Grand Fleet. They were on a line running east from the Forth. The fifth was *U 40*, a large new boat which had begun her cruise on the 18th. Her identity was ascertained by means of a new and ingenious device which for a month past had been employed for the further protection of fishing fleets. The new scheme was to make use of the coast defence submarines, which hitherto had had little or nothing to do, in company with an armed trawler, which, while towing the submarine submerged, could act as a decoy ship to invite attack.[1] In pursuance of this idea the armed trawler *Taranaki* (Lieutenant-Commander H. D. Edwards) had been cruising for a month both with *C 26* and *C 27*, and on June 8 *C 27* by a piece of bad luck just missed getting the *U 19*. On the 23rd the *Taranaki* was out again, this time with *C 24* (Lieutenant F. H. Taylor). Leaving Aberdeen shortly after midnight, they found them-

[1] The idea was suggested in the Grand Fleet by Acting Paymaster F. T. Spickernell, Admiral Beatty's Secretary, and it was worked out and the crews trained by Captain V. H. S. Haggard of the *Vulcan*, depot ship of the 7th (Coastal) Submarine Flotilla at Rosyth.

selves at 9.30 in the morning in sight of *U 40*, the boat that had recently been identified. She was 2,500 yards away, trimmed low down for instant diving, and her gun ready. At sight of her Lieutenant-Commander Edwards signalled to his submerged consort to cast off for attack, but unluckily the slipping gear failed to act. Meanwhile *U 40* had called on the trawler to stop, but as it was essential to keep way on her till her submarine was clear, Lieutenant-Commander Edwards held on, but so coolly that the Germans' suspicions were not aroused. Finally after ten minutes, finding his submarine had not let go, he had to slip his own end of the towline and telephone wire to set his consort free. But *C 24* was still in trouble. With a hundred fathoms of 8½-inch wire and as many of telephone wire hanging to her bows she immediately dipped to thirty-eight feet. Only with the greatest skill and coolness could she be brought to trim. Still it was done, and in spite of having to tow the heavy line, and with the telephone wire beginning to foul her propeller, she managed to get into position for attack without breaking the surface. At the same time the trawler's crew were engaging the enemy's attention by scrambling into their boat as though panic-stricken, so that even the shy peeps of *C 24's* periscope were not observed. When right abeam at five hundred yards Lieutenant Taylor took his shot. The torpedo hit fair under the conning-tower, and the German immediately disappeared in a burst of flame, smoke and debris. Her two officers and a petty officer who were on deck were rescued—the rest all perished.

From the prisoners valuable information was obtained. We knew the Germans were getting disturbed at the unaccountable losses of their submarines, and now it was admitted they had already lost eighteen.[1] Naturally it was decided to extend the new system to other areas, and the crying need of such extension was simultaneously emphasised. For on this day and the next the *U 38* got into a fishing fleet fifty miles east of the Shetlands and sank no less than sixteen drifters.[2] Our losses in fishing craft were indeed at

[1] Admiral von Tirpitz states that on April 2, 1915, after the loss of several submarines in our traps, an order was issued that the safety of the boats was to come before all other considerations, and that it was no longer to be deemed necessary to come to the surface and give warning before an attack. *My Memoirs*, Vol. II., p. 414.

[2] According to Gayer, *U 19* and *U 25* were also at work about this time amongst the fishing fleets, and claimed between them to have sunk 27, when *U 25* was rammed while attacking submerged, and was forced to return for repairs (Vol. II., p. 32).

this time growing serious in spite of all the precautions that were being taken. On June 15 a special trawler patrol was allotted for fishing protection to the Dogger Bank area, but the havoc continued, and during the month no less than sixty boats were destroyed on the home fishing grounds—a heavy toll, seeing how great and never-ending was the call for trawlers and drifters for military purposes.

The new system, however, soon brought fresh fruit. Two more trawlers had been prepared for acting with submarines, and one of them, *Princess Marie José*, for these operations temporarily named *Princess Louise* (Lieutenant C. Cantlie), proceeded from Scapa on July 18 to cruise in company with *C 27* (Lieutenant-Commander C. C. Dobson), the same boat which had so narrowly missed the *U 19* with the *Taranaki* on June 8. When off the eastern entrance to the Fair Island passage on July 20 they fell in with *U 23*, which was four days out from Emden. The usual play was performed with perfect skill and coolness till *C 27* was in position to fire. Owing to the Germans seeing the track of her torpedo and going ahead it missed, but a second got home just abaft the conning-tower, and when the smother of spray and smoke had cleared the submarine was gone. Three officers and seven men were all that could be saved out of her crew of thirty-four.[1]

When *U 23* met her fate she was making for the west coast of Scotland, where the Germans were now keeping at least one submarine at work. To us it appeared that there must be more, for in June there were six engagements between submarines and the Stornoway Auxiliary Patrol. This disturbance meant a new burden on the Commander-in-Chief, for through these waters passed one of the main routes to Archangel, a line of communication which was rapidly growing in importance. Until the Dardanelles could be opened, Archangel was the only port through which we could supply the munitions and equipment which were vital to the Russian army. Already as early as February 5 the Tyne guardship *Jupiter* had had to be sent there to try to break a passage through. The regular ice-breaker had broken down, and the old battleship established one of the many records of the war as being, so far as was known, the first vessel that had ever reached Archangel in February. There she remained till the first week in May, when the ice-breaker returned; but the trouble only increased. Petrograd reported that the navigation would be open in about ten days; some

[1] Lieutenant Cantlie was awarded the D.S.C. and Lieutenant-Commander Dobson the D.S.O. The latter afterwards won the V.C. for his famous exploit in Kronstadt harbour on August 18, 1919.

thirty ships were waiting to get in, and the Russians feared that the enemy's mining activity would extend to the White Sea. Some form of examination service was essential if mining under neutral flags was to be prevented, and as usual they looked to us for help. Though they had plenty of suitable vessels[1] they expected the British navy to supply them with an examination service at Alexandrovsk, and a patrol to work between it and the North Cape.

Nothing was more probable than that the Germans would endeavour to disturb this now all-important trade route, and in spite of the daily increasing strain elsewhere we could not but take the new theatre in hand. Destroyers, of course, were not available, but a special White Sea group of six trawlers equipped with 12-pounders and sweeping gear were prepared at Lowestoft in June under Lieutenant-Commander L. A. Bernays. Before they could get away the need of them was proved. On June 10 a British steamer (*Arndale*) was lost on a mine in the White Sea and another (*Drumloist*) on the 24th, two days after the trawlers had sailed.[2] Still the Russians remained helpless. They could not exert energy to form an examination service, nor could they be induced even to buoy channels for the trawlers to sweep. As July advanced and submarines seemed to have become more active in the north their cries for help increased. One or two small auxiliary cruisers, or reserve ships, they said, would be welcome as an anti-submarine patrol, if we could not send regular ships of war. What they asked for would have been useless even if such ships had been available, and Lieutenant-Commander Bernays was instructed to see if an auxiliary patrol could not be organised from local craft. As, however, there was a strong suspicion, on Russian information, that the Germans might be forming a submarine base in the far north, the Commander-in-Chief on July 27 detached a light force to examine Spitzbergen and also Bear Island, between it and the North Cape, which, having been bought by a German before the war, was specially suspect. The force consisted of the armed merchant cruiser *Columbella* from the 10th Cruiser Squadron (Northern Patrol), with two armed trawlers and the *Acacia*, the name ship of the new class of sloops, four of which had just been allotted to Admiral Jellicoe. Nothing was found, and although the masters of

[1] *Bakan*, despatch vessel. *Vera*, armed yacht, three armed merchant cruisers, four armed and four unarmed small craft and trawlers.

[2] A minefield was laid by the German minelayer *Meteor* in the northern approaches to the White Sea on June 7/8. On the 17th the Russian vessel *Nikolai* was lost. The British *African Monarch* and the Norwegian *Lysaker* were lost on July 6.

the local coasting craft asserted that mines were still being laid under the Norwegian flag, no evidence was obtained that German submarines had yet appeared so far north.[1] No German submarine had in fact yet rounded the North Cape.

The middle part of the Archangel route was, of course, protected to some extent by the 10th Cruiser Squadron. It was still maintaining the Northern Patrol with undiminished vigilance and success. During four weeks in June, in spite of all interruptions, it intercepted no fewer than 290 vessels, and of these sixty-one were brought in for examination, and for the remaining three summer months its monthly average of visits and search were over 250. The blockade was thus well maintained, and the Germans seem to have made little effort to disturb it. Occasionally units were attacked as they proceeded to and fro to coal, but the danger was minimised by the establishment of their base under Rear-Admiral W. B. Fawckner at Swarbacks Minn, in the Shetlands.

There still remained, however, the danger area about the Shetlands through which the route passed and in which submarines were visibly active on their way north-about. The ordinary patrols could do little to check them, and yet another device was tried. It was again a form of decoy which afterwards became so famous as the "Q" ship. Since the beginning of the year a scheme had been in hand for taking up small merchant vessels on which the enemy would not be likely to waste a torpedo and arming them with concealed guns which could be suddenly unmasked when a submarine was tempted to molest them. The idea, of course, was not a new thing—time out of mind the trick of a wolf in sheep's clothing had been a commonplace of naval warfare. No one,

[1] The building of the "Acacia" sloops, which were just coming forward, was one of the remarkable feats of construction during the war. The class originated in the need which arose immediately after the outbreak of war for better and more numerous minesweepers, coupled with a continually increasing demand for general utility ships for carrying baggage and liberty men, and all the minor services of the fleet. It was to meet all these requirements that the new class of sloops was designed. They were single screw-ships of 16½ to 17 knots speed and 1,210 tons displacement, armed with two 12-pdrs. and two anti-aircraft 3-pdrs. and fitted with minesweeping and towing gear. Twelve were ordered on January 1, 1915, twelve in the following week and twelve more on May 4. Being designed on the mercantile system of construction, the orders could be placed with a large number of private firms not accustomed to naval work. The utmost rapidity of construction was thus secured, with the result that some were completed in nineteen weeks and the average was under six months. They proved so great a success that in July, 1915, thirty-six more were ordered of improved design giving a full 17 knots speed and allowing for 4·7″ or 4″ guns, instead of 12-pdrs. All were named after flowers, the first thirty-six being the "Acacia" class and the second the "Arabis" class.

therefore, could claim to be the inventor. The first ship of the class to get to work appears to have been the *Victoria*, which began operations in the Channel on November 29, 1914. In the next month the French fitted out another, a small collier called the *Marguerite*, but neither ship was a success nor had a long career.[1] Our next was the *Vienna*, renamed *Antwerp* (Lieutenant-Commander G. Herbert), which began cruising on January 27, but she proved a failure. Others followed in the spring, and amongst them the well-known *Baralong*. All of them worked in the Channel and its south-western approaches.

For northern waters Admiral The Hon. Sir Stanley C. J. Colville, who still held his Orkneys and Shetland command, prepared a small auxiliary fleet collier, the *Prince Charles*, at Scapa. Her concealed armament was two 6-pounders and two 3-pounders; the whole of her merchant crew volunteered for the cruise, and her guns' crews were volunteers from the guard and repair ships at the base. An officer on Admiral Colville's staff, Lieutenant W. P. Mark-Wardlaw, was placed in command, with orders to cruise on a specified route east and west of the Orkneys and Shetlands on the Archangel tracks. His instructions were to act strictly as a decoy; on sighting a submarine he was to make every effort to escape, but if she closed and fired he was to stop and all the crew except one engineer and the crews of the hidden guns were to set about abandoning ship. Simultaneously a slightly different application of this method was being prepared from Rosyth. Here no special ships were taken up, but Captain James Startin,[2] commanding the Forth Auxiliary Patrol base at Granton, had received permission to disguise an armed trawler and send her out to operate between Hoy Island and Aberdeen. Accordingly the armed trawler *Quickly* was disguised as a small Norwegian trader with a deck cargo, and in addition to her normal armament of one 6-pounder was given a 12-pounder with two gunlayers and two sight-setters from the *Zealandia*. At nightfall on July 19, with Captain Startin in command, she put to sea, and the following morning fell in with a submarine (*U 16*) on the surface. After about

[1] Vedel, *Quatre Années de la Guerre Sous-Marine*, p. 178. Commandant Vedel believed that the *Marguerite* was the first "Q" ship and that we borrowed the idea from her, but the *Victoria* was certainly prepared in November, and the idea had been suggested from many quarters in reply to a secret Admiralty letter inviting suggestions from the Service for thwarting submarines (December 4).

[2] Vice-Admiral (Retired), now serving as a Captain, R.N.R. See Vol. II., p. 47n.

half an hour's scrutiny the German opened fire, which, after striking neutral colours and hoisting the white ensign, the *Quickly* returned, and, assisted by the trawler *Gunner*, which soon joined her, she claimed to have destroyed the enemy. The claim was allowed, but the *U 16* had not been sunk. She returned to Heligoland for repairs arriving there on July 22.

On July 21 the *Prince Charles* sailed to try her luck. After proceeding through his assigned eastern positions Lieutenant Mark-Wardlaw rounded the Shetlands without seeing anything, but on the evening of the 24th, when near North Rona island (about 100 miles west of Scapa), he was aware of a three-masted steamer stopped, with a submarine standing by. Continuing his course to the westward, with guns' crews closed up behind the screens and the rest of the men standing by to get out the boats, he soon saw the submarine making for him at full speed on the surface. When about three miles off she fired. He then stopped and ordered the boats to be got out. As the submarine came on she fired again, and having closed to six hundred yards she altered course so as to bring her broadside on and continued to fire. Seeing there was no chance of the enemy coming nearer, Lieutenant Mark-Wardlaw unmasked his guns and opened fire. The German gun's crew were seen immediately to leave their gun for the conning-tower and the submarine began to dive. But it was too late; the *Prince Charles's* shooting was too good. The submarine had been hit abaft the conning-tower and had to come up again all out of trim, with her bows high above water. The *Prince Charles* promptly closed to three hundred yards and opened rapid fire; the submarine crew came scrambling out of the conning-tower, and with her bows reared thirty feet out of the water she suddenly plunged down stern foremost.[1]

The large ship with which she was seen was a Dane, and, after giving a satisfactory explanation that she had been stopped and compelled to jettison her contraband, she was allowed to proceed. The submarine proved to be *U 36*, a new boat which in June had been cruising between the Forth and Jutland. She was now about a week out, and after passing round the north of the Orkneys had taken up a cruising station west of the islands. In this area she had already sunk nine of our fishing trawlers as well as three steamers, Russian, French and Norwegian (*Rubonia*, *Danae*, and *Fimreite*), and had attacked unsuccessfully the *Columbella* of the 10th Cruiser Squadron. On the last morning of her cruise she had also captured an American sailing

[1] The *Prince Charles* saved four officers and eleven men from the submarine.

vessel with a cargo of cotton for Archangel. This ship had been stopped by the *Victorian* of the same squadron, and as her destination was suspicious she was being taken into Lerwick by a British armed guard. Contrary to the usual practice the German commander decided to make a prize of his valuable capture, and, ignorant that she was in British hands, for the guard kept themselves concealed, sent a petty officer on board to take her into Cuxhaven. Resistance was useless; the armed guard were told that the vessel was escorted by a submarine. This was not true, and the German petty officer took the prize into Cuxhaven entirely alone. There the armed guard gave themselves up as prisoners.[1]

The destruction of *U 36*, however, did not clear the area. Another boat, *U 41*, was working there, for on the same day (July 24) the British steamer *Grangewood* and on the 25th the American *Leelanaw*, both Archangel ships on the return voyage, were sunk. Five trawlers also met the same fate. The success of the *Prince Charles*, however, was sufficient to prove the value of the decoy ships if well handled, and in a short time four more were fitted out at Scapa.[2]

It may be said, therefore, that in the northern area the enemy submarines were far from having it all their own way, but they were a constant source of worry, and the strain they caused was increased by mining. In this work the Germans were becoming very active. A certain ship called the *Meteor* was a matter of special interest. She was known to have been out several times equipped as a minelayer, and special sweeps were made to catch her, but without success. Other ships were believed to be escaping from Germany along the Norwegian coast, and one patrol of the 10th Cruiser Squadron had to be devoted to watching this route. The work was very difficult. On June 22 the *Teutonic* intercepted a ship (*Konsul Schulte*), but on being chased she escaped into Norwegian waters. The danger from submarines was too great for an armed merchant cruiser to remain watching her, and Admiral Jellicoe asked for trawlers. He was told he could have no more and should use his four sloops. But these, he replied, were all he had to rely on for sweeping ahead of the fleet if he had to undertake any serious operation. The old fleet sweepers had proved too slow. Eventually, however, one armed trawler, the *Tenby Castle*, was sent. She succeeded in disabling one German vessel

[1] This ship, the *Pass of Balmaha*, was afterwards fitted out as a raider, the *Seeadler*, which operated in the Atlantic in 1917.

[2] *Vala*, *Duncombe*, *Penshurst* and *Glen Isla*.

and sinking another (*Pallas*, June 30, and *Friedrich Arp*, July 8), but as both incidents occurred between the Lofoten islands and the mainland, which Norway claimed as territorial waters, the result was a disturbance of our excellent relations with that country. Later in July, however, six more trawlers were sent up to Kirkwall for the Norway patrol.

A further effort to curtail German activity in this region took the form of a raid into the Skagerrak from July 28 to 31. The force employed was a large one—consisting of eight light cruisers and twenty destroyers supported by the 2nd Battle Cruiser Squadron and the 2nd Light Cruiser Squadron with a screen of six destroyers. It was carried out under Rear-Admiral W. C. Pakenham, commanding the battle cruisers in the *Australia*, but though it had been hoped, among other objects, to catch the German fishing fleet, no enemy was found except one trawler, the *Hanseat*, which was sunk. On the other hand, no effort was made by the enemy to interfere. In this it only repeated an experience which Commodore Tyrwhitt had had in the first week of the month. With three of his light cruisers, sixteen destroyers and five scouts he had proceeded off the Ems in support of another seaplane operation. Little or nothing was effected, but though he remained off Borkum for twelve hours the enemy made no move.

In the lower part of the North Sea, however, with the guard of which he was specially charged, they had been active enough in other ways. In this area, indeed, the strain had been perhaps the greatest of all; for here not only the sea but the air was alive with menace. In the first half of June, three airship raids took place on various points from Northumberland to London, and Commodore Tyrwhitt's light cruisers, each carrying a seaplane, were constantly out watching for Zeppelins, but attack from the sea either by gunfire or seaplane proved very difficult.[1] The only one that was caught (*LZ 37*) fell a victim near Ghent on June 7 to Flight Sub-lieutenant R. A. J. Warneford of the Royal Naval Air Service working from Dunkirk. For the cruisers it was risky work, since the Commodore never had enough destroyers to provide an adequate screen. Most of them were called away for escort duty in the south-west approaches

[1] Commodore Tyrwhitt had now received some more of the new light cruisers, and had as a separate squadron (5th Light Cruiser Squadron) *Arethusa*, *Penelope*, *Conquest* and *Cleopatra*, besides the *Undaunted* attached to the 3rd ("L" class) Flotilla and the *Aurora* to the 10th ("M" class) Flotilla. Each of them was to have a new type flotilla leader. Four more of the new light cruisers, *Calliope*, *Comus*, *Phæton* and *Royalist* were with the Grand Fleet forming the 4th Light Cruiser Squadron under Commodore Le Mesurier.

to the Channel, and what were left had multifarious duties of the same kind to perform, such as escorting the Portsmouth floating dock to the Tyne and the protection of "Paddler" minesweepers working south of the Dogger, and our own minelayers laying fields off the enemy's coast to check his submarines. Both in this area and off the Thames estuary and the approaches to the Dover Strait submarines were reported daily, and in searching for them we lost in the month of June two destroyers, *Mohawk* and *Lightning*, and two torpedo boats—the latter a specially disturbing experience, for torpedo boats were generally regarded as fairly immune from torpedoes owing to their shallow draft, yet both were sunk while hunting in company with five destroyers and four other torpedo boats.[1]

Fresh minefields, moreover, from now onward became a never-ending source of trouble, especially round the light-vessels, and it was at this time we began to perceive that the enemy were adopting the new and insidious plan of laying mines from submarines.

The Germans, in fact, were now developing a new form of the guerrilla warfare to which from the first they had decided they must confine themselves at sea. The weapon they were bringing into use was a new form of submarine, classed as "UC" boats and designed for minelaying. The earliest of them were fitted with four vertical tubes each charged with three mines, but the later ones had six tubes. Being small boats of limited range of action, their special plan of operations was to lay and maintain minefields round the light-vessels in the lower part of the North Sea, which, for the sake of the traffic, it had been found necessary to leave in place, and off the headlands and fairways which the trade passed between the Channel and the North Sea. The first intimation we had of this clever device was on June 2, and on the 18th minefields were discovered off Dover and near the Sunk light-vessel off Harwich. On June 30, off the mouth of the Thames, the *Lightning*, an old "A" class destroyer, foundered on a mine near the Kentish Knock light-vessel. Two days later a small tramp steamer, the *Cottingham*, bound from Calais to Leith, accidentally ran over and sank one of the new minelayers, *UC 2*, near Yarmouth Roads. As July advanced the "UC" boats grew bolder. On July 13, besides the field found off Dover, another beyond the net barrage was located off Calais,

[1] *Mohawk* of the Dover Patrol was mined on June 1, but was afterwards towed into harbour. On the 10th torpedo-boat *No. 10* was trying pluckily to take torpedo-boat *No. 12* in tow after she had been torpedoed and was herself torpedoed. Both the latter belonged to the Nore Defence Flotilla.

and others were continually being reported from the South Foreland as high as Lowestoft, and from this time forward the whole strength of the minesweeper flotillas had to be employed daily in keeping open a lane from Dungeness to Yarmouth, as well as the main channels into the Thames.[1]

The work put a strain on the Dover, Nore and Harwich areas which with the force then available was almost beyond bearing. All up the east coast the pressure of the enemy's activity was scarcely less, but crying as were the needs of the North Sea and the Dover Strait zone, they had at this period to be subordinated to those of the south-western approaches. Admiral Jellicoe was urging that special flotillas should be formed for hunting submarines and nothing else. The reply of the Admiralty was that his suggestion for a striking force of fast vessels was for the present impossible, owing to the paramount military necessity of protecting transports. Again, when Commodore Tyrwhitt had to represent that he sometimes had not a single destroyer to work with his cruisers, the Admiralty could only reply that the employment of his destroyers to the westward was unavoidable owing to the enemy's submarine activity in the entrance to the English Channel and the approaches to the Bristol and St. George's Channels, and the ever-increasing importance of the transport routes in those waters. Through them passed the tracks to the Mediterranean and the inward flow of food, remounts and munitions from America and troops from Canada. It was an obvious objective for the best of the German submarines, and it was clear they were trying to make the most of it. We have seen how in the later part of May the flow of reinforcements to the Mediterranean was held up owing to a political crisis, and how, of the two divisions which Sir Ian Hamilton had urgently asked for on May 10 only the LIInd Lowland Division (Territorial Force) had been sent.[2] At this critical period sinkings or attacks were reported daily along the south coast of Ireland, in the approaches to the Bristol Channel and on the transport route. The sudden calls raised difficulties enough for the harassed Transport Department; the insecurity of the route increased them threefold, and raised questions upon which naval and military requirements came into direct conflict. The Transport Department were at their wits' end to find the necessary tonnage. They complained that ships going to the Dardanelles were detained there apparently to meet unforeseen military emergencies. They did not return to time, and at

[1] From May 31 to July 31 UC boats laid mines in eleven positions.

[2] See *ante*, p. 43.

home it was impossible to provide shipping without dislocating the sparse trade that still existed, or unless the great liners, like the *Mauretania*, were used. She herself had been employed for the Lowland Division, and had made the passage to Mudros in nine days; two others followed and arrived within ten days, and each of them carried over 3,000 officers and men. At a push they could carry more. Doubts, however, now arose whether the risk of embarking so many men in one ship was justifiable. On May 27 a submarine, was definitely found to be operating between Scilly and Ushant directly on the transport track, and in the next three days six ships were sunk there, including an Admiralty collier. Moreover, since the submarines had appeared in the Ægean that terminal was equally dangerous, for the great ships could only enter the anchorages which had now been made secure against underwater attack. The risk was obvious, but it was not for the Admiralty to say if the end justified the risk. It was a question which only the Government could decide. It was referred to them, and after learning that the army was ready to face the danger they decided the large ships were to be used.

Still there remained the scarcely less thorny question of the port of embarkation. The army wanted Avonmouth, where the railway and wharfage facilities were excellent, but it meant a far greater strain on the destroyers than Devonport, which was the Admiralty choice. From there the destroyers had to cover no more than a hundred miles to see the transports clear of the danger area; from Avonmouth it meant a voyage of two hundred and fifty miles each way, and no anchorage where they could wait for the transports to come out. Seeing then that escort had become the real crux of the problem, the decision was given for the naval choice, and of the three divisions of the new army which were under orders for the Mediterranean only the XIIIth, for which preparations were complete, sailed from Avonmouth. All the rest embarked the troops at Devonport, except the big liners, which had to use Liverpool.

The strain that all this meant upon the naval, military and transport staffs, no less than on the unresting destroyers, is difficult to conceive. Had everything been normal at the ports the work would have been heavy enough. But conditions in the ports were far from normal. Owing to depletion of labour, due to intensive enlisting for the new armies, they were badly congested, and ships which usually took a week to prepare as transports now often took three weeks. But, bad as was the block, and sudden and great the call, the work was done, and done to time. By July 1 the move of the XIIIth Division was complete, by the 14th both the others (XIth and Xth) had sailed, and by the end of the month the two Territorial divisions (LIIIrd and LIVth), whose despatch had only been sanctioned on July 5, were well on their way. But, great as was the accomplishment, it by no means represents all that was being done for placing and maintaining our army where it was wanted. Both to the Mediterranean and to the northward for Scapa and the White Sea there was a steady flow of store and munition ships. Small craft to serve the needs of the increasing army at the Dardanelles had also to be prepared and sent forward; outgoing monitors and important store ships had to be provided with trawler escort, and during July the whole of the Second New Army was put across into France, besides more than the normal flow of drafts and the slowly increasing supply of ammunition. In the early days of the war the rapid transport of the old army into France had seemed an almost incredible feat of organisation. It was child's play to what was going on now.

Yet not a single troop transport was touched—only one was molested by gunfire—but it was not for want of German activity. During the first ten days of July two submarines, *U 20* and *U 39*, were at work in the critical south-western area, and between them they sank a round score of ships, British, allied and neutral, and at least a dozen more were attacked. Yet, in spite of every effort in the area, not a single submarine had been caught. Nor was it surprising. The immunity with which for months our Harwich submarines had maintained their watch inside the Heligoland Bight in face of the patrols and bombing aircraft with which it swarmed was proof enough of the difficulty of dealing with underwater craft in open waters. Still we could not admit failure. New methods must be tried. The remedy was sought in a better co-ordination of our auxiliary patrol. It took the form of a radical reorganisation of the western patrol areas, by which they were all to be under one command from the Hebrides to Ushant, with headquarters at Queenstown. To fill this all-important post, Vice-Admiral Sir Lewis Bayly, then serving as President of the Royal Naval College at Greenwich, was chosen on July 12. The selection was indisputable. It was he who in 1907 had been appointed the first Commodore of Flotillas and, having chosen Harwich for the centre of his labours, had earned his reputation in the Service as the father of destroyer tactics and organisation—a reputation he was destined to confirm and enlarge as his task increased in difficulty.

The number of units in his command was very large. At the time of his appointment to Queenstown (July 22), including those under the immediate command of Admirals Dare and Boyle at Milford and Larne, they numbered four hundred and fifty yachts, trawlers, drifters and motor boats. He had also at Queenstown a few torpedo boats, and by the end of July the first complete unit of four of the new sloops was added to his command. Many of the drifters were absorbed by the North Channel net barrage, and under Admiral Boyle the system had become so effective that it could be regarded as completely barring the passage of submarines. Whether or not any had attempted to get into the Irish Sea this way is uncertain, but in any case nothing was now passing. The problem which Admiral Bayly had to solve was to this extent simplified, and the system was now being applied to the St. George's Channel. Besides the Larne, Kingstown and Milford areas, the Scilly Islands sub-base was also transferred from the Falmouth command to Queenstown.[1] This was regarded as necessary for the main purpose of the new arrangement. The idea was that, if submarines in open waters had to be dealt with, numbers were essential, so as to ensure that whenever one was reported the locality could be surrounded by vessels numerous enough to cover a wide area, and so make it very dangerous for her to come to the surface.

It was not till August 1 that the new organisation came into force, and it was during the critical last half of July which followed Admiral Bayly's appointment that the Germans had probably one of the best chances in the war for dealing us a telling blow at sea. A determined attack on the Mediterranean route at this time could scarcely have failed to create a serious disturbance, but no exceptional effort was made.

During all this period our own oversea submarines were as active as ever. The Bight was never left alone, but in that quarter there was little to be done beyond the now established routine. Typical of the adventurous work are the activities of *S 1* (Lieutenant-Commander G. H. Kellett), a new class of submarine which it was desired to try for oversea work.[2] On her first cruise in the third week of June she began by winning her way through a combined Zeppelin,

[1] For the eastern half of the Irish Sea a new area (No. 22) was formed, with its base at Holyhead. The Bristol Channel also became a separate area, with its base at Swansea.

[2] She was one of those laid down in 1912 in a private yard to an Italian design, and was the first double-hull boat built for the British navy. The type was not continued.

seaplane, trawler and destroyer patrol, and reaching Horn Reefs, on the 21st. Then her engines broke down, and for two days she was busy repairing them under the constant annoyance of patrolling airships. As soon as one engine was repaired the other failed, but on the third day she could crawl well enough to capture a German trawler, the *Ost*, and employ it to tow her. Twice the trawler's engines failed, twice they were repaired by the submarine crew, until on the seventh day she met the *Firedrake*, who brought her in to Harwich with her useful prize.

Another typical cruise was that of Commander C. P. Talbot in *E 16*. On July 24 he left Yarmouth for the Ems. Reaching his station next morning, he was continually kept under by the air patrol, till near the Borkum Riff lightship he found himself foul of a submarine trap which dragged him down by the bows. In vain he struggled by every device that cool resource could suggest. Unable to get clear, he managed, with his bows still fast, to bring the conning-tower above water and open the lid. It was only to find a Zeppelin hovering a few hundred feet above him and evidently watching the trap. He had to dive again and continue his efforts—blowing, pumping and venting his tanks—going ahead and astern every few moments, and all to the accompaniment of exploding bombs which the watching airship dropped as his struggles disturbed the surface. Smaller charges also burst close to him. Still coolly as ever he and his crew struggled on, till after an hour of the nightmare the bows suddenly flew up and he was free. Then, after sending off a pigeon to warn the Commodore of the danger spot, he continued his patrol undisturbed. His reward came the following day (July 26). About noon, being then forty miles north of Terschelling on the outer edge of the German patrol lines, and having been kept down by a Zeppelin for three hours, he rose to find three large destroyers quartering the ground at high speed. In about an hour he got within six hundred yards of one of them, took his shot and blew off her stern. Yet he was not content. Though the other two enemy vessels at once made for him, he kept returning to the surface and interrupting their work of rescuing the crew of the sinking destroyer. Each time he appeared they broke off and made for him. Yet in spite of their persistent efforts to ram him he got in two more shots at them, which unfortunately they were easily able to avoid. That his conduct was highly commended and won him the D.S.O. will cause no surprise.[1]

[1] The destroyer sunk was *V 188*, a 32-knot boat of 650 tons with four 19·7 tubes and two 15-pounders.

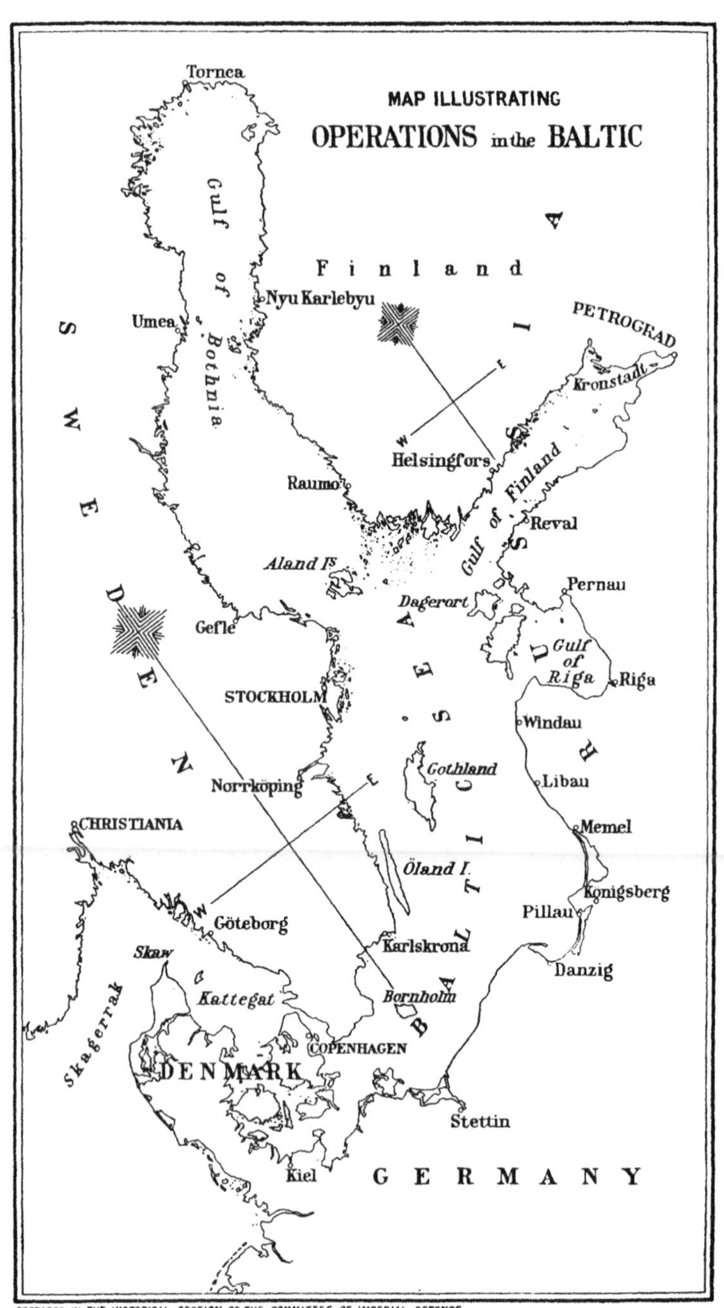

PREPARED IN THE HISTORICAL SECTION OF THE COMMITTEE OF IMPERIAL DEFENCE

[To face p. 61.

In the Baltic our submarines found possibilities of exerting a more direct influence on the course of the war. Towards the end of April the Germans, by way of creating a diversion for the thrust which in combination with the Austrians they were making in Galicia, had begun a menacing advance on Libau; a naval force was known to be concentrated in Danzig, and a cruiser squadron was located between the north end of Gothland and the mainland as though to cover the passage of transports eastwards. On May 4 both submarines were warned to prepare for a long cruise, and next day they were away, *E 1* for the Bornholm area and *E 9* to Dagerort, at the south side of the entrance to the Gulf of Finland, which was to be her base for operating against the enemy's covering force. Each of them found opportunity to attack light craft, but no hit was made before, on May 10, it was known that Libau had fallen and the enemy's covering force had withdrawn.[1] *E 9* was then ordered to work on the lines from Memel and Danzig to Libau, and here she at once fell in with three cruisers conducting three transports on the return voyage from Libau. Both the convoy and its escort had strong destroyer protection. Nevertheless Commander M. K. Horton proceeded to attack. Diving under the van of the port destroyer screen he fired his bow torpedoes at one of the cruisers, but unfortunately both missed. He then got into position for attacking the transports from right ahead as they came on. At two hundred yards he fired his port beam tube at the leading ship and again there was a miss by passing under. Then he tried his stern tube at her next astern. He was now under heavy fire, but the torpedo hit her just before the funnel, a second shot from a reloaded bow tube finished her, and notwithstanding the destroyers and an explosive sweep fired close to him he got safely away to Revel to replenish torpedoes. Both submarines continued their respective operations without success till June 1, when *E 1*, having fractured a main motor, was reported unfit for service. On reaching Revel they found that Admiral von Essen, the energetic and devoted officer under whose command they had been serving, had died (May 20) after a short illness.

Commander Horton in *E 9* had now to continue the work alone. Strong forces were reported west of the Gulf of Riga, and on June 4 news came in that the Russian minelayer *Yenisei* had been sunk by a submarine off Dagerort. He at once made for the spot, and there he found the offender and dived to attack, but the German submarine (*U 26*), also dived and was lost. Later on in the afternoon he came in sight of

[1] Libau was taken by the Germans on May 7.

four destroyers, two coaling from a transport, two patrolling, and a light cruiser of the "Gazelle" class standing by. Getting into position for attacking the cruiser and the coaling group simultaneously, he fired his port beam tube at the cruiser and missed. Both bow tubes, however, got home on the collier, and when, after avoiding being rammed by the patrolling destroyers, he came to the surface, the collier was gone, as well as one of the destroyers that had been alongside her, and a few survivors from each of them were rescued.

As June advanced the activity increased, for now the German demonstration was taking the form of an advance on Riga. The loss of Libau mattered little; it had in fact been discounted when it was evacuated early in the war. But Riga, besides being an important munition centre, was vital to the security of the capital. A new army had to be found for its protection, and in spite of Austro-German successes in Galicia it could only be formed by drawing on that front. Its right rested on the sea between Windau and Libau, and here on July 2 *E 9* was patrolling when the month-long sparring at sea culminated in a conflict. Early in the morning the Russian cruiser patrol, *Admiral Makarov, Bayan, Bogatuir* and *Oleg*, moving through a heavy fog off the east of Gothland, came upon an inferior squadron of Germans, consisting of the *Roon*, two light cruisers, *Augsberg* and *Lübeck*, with the mining vessel *Albatross*.[1]

Owing to the fog nothing decisive occurred, but the *Albatross* was cut off and forced to beach herself in a damaged condition on the neutral coast of Gothland, where she and her crew were interned.[2] The rest were lost in the fog, but as the Russian squadron made back for its own coast it was boldly attacked by the *Roon*, *Lübeck* and four destroyers. The *Augsberg*, which was severely damaged in the first conflict, did not appear. A desultory action seems to have ensued for half an hour, when the Russian cruiser *Ryurik* came upon the scene.[3] The *Roon* was then forced to retire, and though by her superior speed she was soon able to get clear, it was not before she had suffered a good deal from the *Ryurik's* heavy metal. But she was not left unsupported. In response apparently to her signals two of the older German

[1] *Bayan* and *Admiral Makarov* were cruisers of 7,700 tons armed with two 8″ and eight 6″, *Bogatuir* and *Oleg* were slightly smaller old cruisers, reconstructed with twelve 6″—all less than twenty knots sea speed. The *Roon* was 9,500 tons with four 8.2″ and ten 5.9″. The two light cruisers had nothing heavier than 4.1″.

[2] Casualties in the *Albatross* numbered 27 killed and 55 wounded.

[3] *Ryurik*, 15,000 tons, four 10″, eight 8″ and twenty 4.7″.

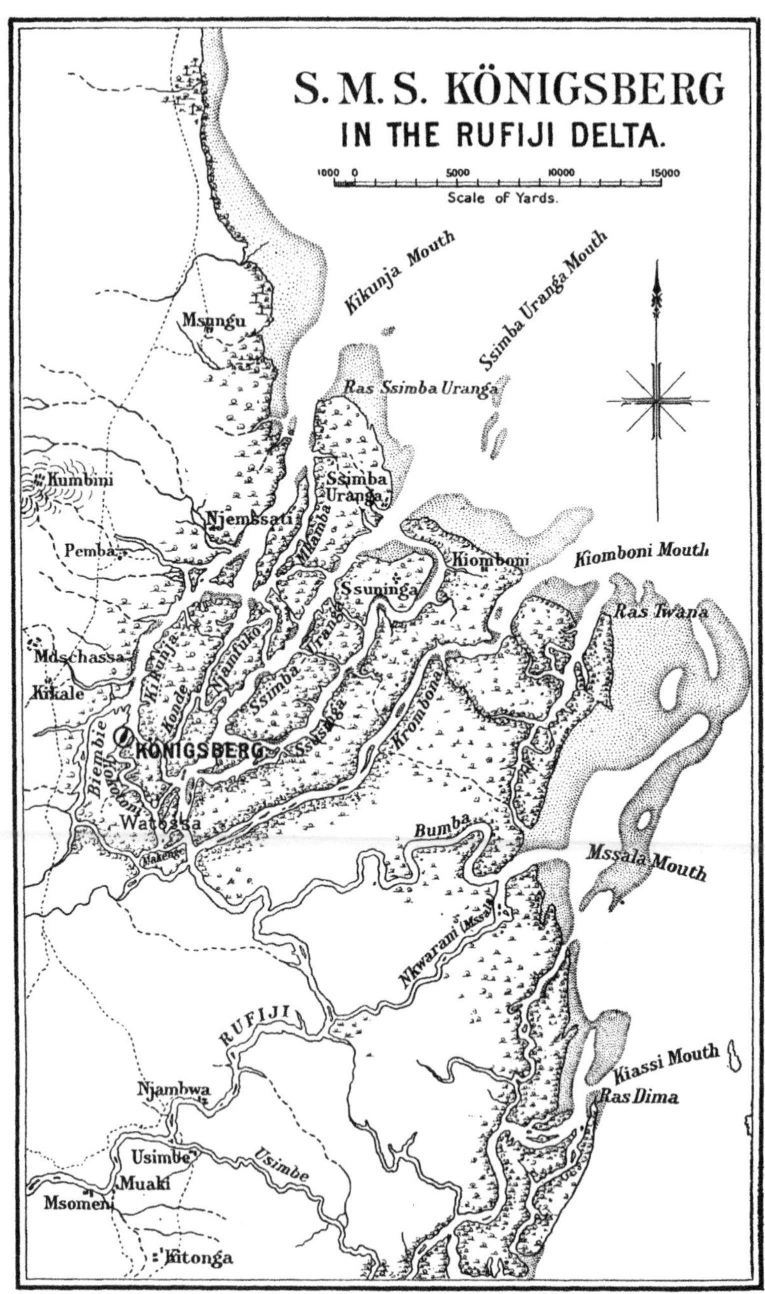
S. M. S. KÖNIGSBERG
IN THE RUFIJI DELTA.
1000 0 5000 10000 15000
Scale of Yards.
Kikunja Mouth
Ssimba Uranga Mouth
Ras Ssimba Uranga
Msungu
Kumbini
Ssimba Uranga
Njemssati
Mlamba
Pemba
Kiomboni
Kiomboni Mouth
Ssuninga
Ras Twana
Mdschassa
Kikale
Ki Kunja
Konde
Njamfuko
Ssimba Uranga
Krombona
Biembie
KÖNIGSBERG
Watossa
Bumba
Mssala Mouth
Nkwarami (Mssala)
RUFIJI
Kiassi Mouth
Ras Dima
Njambwa
Usimbe
Usimbe
Muaki
Msomeni
Kitonga

[*To face p.* 63.

battleships went to her rescue. To Commander Horton at least, who was lying right in their path, they seemed to have come out of Libau. As he saw them coming on he closed to attack, and at four hundred yards fired his bow torpedoes at the leading ship. Both hit, but with what result he could not tell, for only by a very smart dive did he avoid being rammed by an attending destroyer which for an hour would not leave him alone. It was certain that the ship attacked, the *Prinz Adalbert* was not sunk, but her consort had to escort her back to Kiel, for later on in the afternoon, when *E 9* sighted the *Roon* and her two light cruisers coming south, but too far off to attack, neither battleship was with them. The crippled ship reached Kiel on the 20th.

After this exploit *E 9* had to lie up at Revel for the rest of the month, but by this time *E 1* had made good her defects, and on July 30 signalled her reappearance by sinking the *Aachen*, one of three large auxiliaries which she encountered off Gothland escorted by a light cruiser. Yet in spite of all that had been done the strategical advantage of the campaign lay with the Germans. In the middle of the month their great change of front had begun to operate. From the Baltic to the Rumanian frontier the grand offensive against Russia was opening; the army of the Niemen, as it was called, operating from Libau, became the left of a great movement. To this army fell the first-fruits; within a week it had captured Windau, and with it one side of the entrance to the Gulf of Riga was in German hands.

While the whole Eastern front was thus astir with the new movements to crush Russia out of the Entente circle, far away on the coast of East Africa the last scene of the original German plan of commerce destruction on the high seas was being played out. There, in the Rufiji river, the *Königsberg* was still lying. At the end of April, when the new seaplanes arrived, they carefully reconnoitred her position, but as they proved unable to rise more than 800 feet over the land in that burning air, and a bombing attack was therefore impossible, she had been left alone till other means were provided for her destruction. So far as could be ascertained she was still capable of breaking out, and Admiral King-Hall of the Cape Station had been keeping up the blockade of her and the adjacent coasts with his available forces.

Such a position on the flank of our far eastern route could not be tolerated indefinitely, and it was now, (April 19), that the Admiralty detached two of the 6-inch monitors, which had been sent to the Mediterranean, to see what they could do. On May 9 and 10 they recalled the *Chatham* and *Cornwall* to the Dardanelles, leaving the Admiral only one light cruiser, the *Weymouth*, capable of chasing and engaging the *Königsberg* if she broke out. In accordance with the new plan Captain E. J. A. Fullerton left Malta on April 28 in the *Severn* in company with the *Mersey* (Commander R. A. Wilson), the fleet messenger *Trent*, four tugs and a collier. The voyage before him was as arduous as any in the war. The ships of his squadron were wholly unfit for the intense heat of the Red Sea, but thanks to the devotion and spirit of all concerned, especially in the engine-rooms, Aden was reached on May 15. In two days he was away again, and as the motley squadron struggled down the African coast against head seas and abnormal currents, the difficulties they encountered increased beyond measure. But they were encountered only to be overcome. There were times when scarcely any progress could be made without the *Trent* and the collier assisting the tugs, but in the end they were rewarded, and on June 3, after five weeks' struggle, the squadron anchored at Mafia island.[1]

Here at Tirene Bay, where, since the occupation of the island, the blockading force had its base, an aerodrome had been established under a Major of marines, Squadron Commander R. Gordon, with two good aeroplanes, and here the monitors had to remain to prepare for the operation. Its interest lies in its novelty. To destroy by a combination of aircraft and heavily armed shallow draft vessels a ship of war lying concealed ten miles up a tropical river with unknown defences at its mouth was a new experience. Consequently, besides making good defects developed during the arduous voyage, the monitors had to be fitted with deck and side plates and sandbag protection, and spotting with the aircraft needed careful rehearsal. It was not until July 5 that all was ready, and on this day, in order to prevent reinforcements being sent to the Rufiji, the *Laurentic*, with three transports carrying a few Indian troops from Zanzibar, made a demonstration of landing at Dar-es-Salaam and returned after dark.[2]

At 5.20 next morning the two monitors entered the Kikunja, a northern mouth of the river, accompanied by an aeroplane to cover them by bombing the *Königsberg* while

[1] In recognition of the successful conduct of this arduous voyage Captain Fullerton and the commanders of all his auxiliaries received letters of appreciation from the Admiralty.

[2] Admiral King-Hall now had with him four light cruisers (*Hyacinth* (flag), *Weymouth*, *Pioneer* and *Pyramus*), two armed merchant cruisers (*Laconia* and *Laurentic*), and two monitors (*Severn* and *Mersey*). The *Challenger* joined his flag on July 8, after the first attack on the *Königsberg* had been made.

they were taking up their firing position. On entering the river they came under fire from 3-pounders, pom-poms and machine guns concealed in the density of the trees and the rank undergrowth, but it was easily dealt with and did no harm. As they felt their way up the river the Admiral followed in support in the *Weymouth* (Captain Denis B. Crampton), attended by the *Pyramus* (Commander Viscount Kelburn) and the whalers *Echo*, *Fly* and *Childers* sweeping and sounding ahead. By 6.30, when he was scraping over the bar, the two monitors had anchored head and stern at a point judged to be 11,000 yards from their objective and were opening fire, with Flight Commander J. T. Cull spotting for them in the other aeroplane, while the Admiral, as soon as he was anchored, did what he could at long range to keep down the fire which greeted him and to search the Kumbini hills on the north side of the river, where it was believed there was an observation station. As a further diversion the *Pioneer* (Commander T. W. Biddlecombe) engaged and silenced the defences of the Ssimba Uranga mouth by which the *Könisberg* had entered.

The firing position selected for the monitors was just below an island some four miles up, and no sooner were they anchored than it was apparent that the enemy expected them there and had their range to a nicety. The *Königsberg* was firing salvoes of four and sometimes five which straddled them at once. The enemy evidently had a well-placed spotting station, but where the spotting station was it was impossible to discover. All that could be done was to fire into the jungle at any suspicious sign of movement, while the enemy's shells continued to fall within ten or fifteen yards. Yet, by a miracle, for nearly an hour neither ship suffered a direct hit, till, at 7.40, a shell struck the foremost 6-inch gun shield of the *Mersey*, put the gun out of action, and inflicted eight casualties including six killed. Within a few minutes she was again struck and holed near the waterline; she, therefore, shifted her berth 1,000 yards back, but only just in time to escape a salvo which pitched exactly on the berth she had left. The *Severn* then carried on alone, the enemy's salvoes still straddling her, for half an hour and was scoring hits when the aeroplane had to go home. She then also shifted to open the range, and as she did so was able to wipe out what seemed to be an observation party in a tree on the bank. The action now slackened, till at 1.30 another aeroplane arrived. Both ships then moved up again to a spot near the first position and came into action. But the results were disappointing; the *Königsberg* was still firing, but with less accuracy and fewer guns, and at 3.30 the monitors proceeded down the river with the crews worn out and dispirited at the failure to complete their task.

They retired to Tirene, but not to rest. All was unchecked activity to prepare for a renewal of the attempt. The frail ships had been badly shaken by so much firing at extreme elevation and needed tightening up, there was the *Mersey's* gun to repair, and well as observation had worked in rehearsal, it had been far short of success in action. Out of 635 shells fired only for 78 had spotting correction been received, and no more than six hits had been registered. It was therefore decided that only one ship should fire at a time, and on this plan, after four days' work on strained frames and bulkheads, they went in again on July 11. At the entrance they had the same reception as before, but though the ships were hit, no harm was done. As soon as the *Mersey* reached the first day's firing position she anchored to draw the enemy's fire, while the *Severn* steamed on. One salvo was fired at the *Mersey*, but after that the *Königsberg* concentrated on the *Severn*. For a mile she steamed on under a rain of salvoes, untouched till about 12.30 she was securely anchored and could open fire. By this time Flight Commander Cull was again ready to spot for her. Seven salvoes were fired before he got her on, but the eighth was a hit. After that "H.T." (hit) came in almost continuously. In ten minutes the *Königsberg* was firing only three guns—but then came a signal from the aeroplane, "We are hit, send a boat for us." In fact, hits had been numerous, but though the engine was pierced and failing, the intrepid pilot would not come down so long as he saw it was possible to plane down into the river. Even as he did so his observer, Flight Sub-Lieutenant C. V. Arnold, continued to signal, with the result that in a couple of minutes more the *Königsberg* was firing only two guns, and as the wounded machine came down into the water between the two monitors one only was in action. The last spotting signal was "H.T. All forward." The *Severn's* guns were at once trained further aft to get the target amidships, and at 12.52 a large explosion was seen, followed by thick clouds of smoke. Amidst the cheers that greeted the success the *Mersey's* boat was rescuing the gallant pilot and his observer. The doomed ship was now clearly near her end, but before closing, the *Severn* continued to fire where she was for nearly an hour. By 1.46 seven more explosions occurred though no gun was firing at her; it is probable that these were the result of an attempt to destroy the ship which could no longer be defended. Captain Fullerton then signalled to the *Mersey* to move up to the second position well above the island. From this point, as the other aeroplane appeared, she fired twenty-eight salvoes—the third was a hit, and by 2.20 the target was a wreck blazing from stem to stern. The monitors were recalled by the Admiral at 2.30, and so ended the last of the German cruisers on the high seas.[1]

For eight months she had defied all the efforts we were able to spare for her destruction, and had fought gamely to the last. Inglorious as had been her career as a commerce destroyer, her end redeemed her honour, and the survivors of her crew with some of her guns went to swell the local defence force. So they continued the struggle, but the menace to our communications which she had so long maintained was now finally removed, and Admiral King-Hall was free to devote himself to the general blockade of the coast and to such assistance as the military authorities should require for operations against the enemy's garrison.

[1] The only British casualties on this day were two men of the *Mersey* slightly wounded.

CHAPTER IV

THE DARDANELLES JUNE 20–JULY 31—THE NEW PLAN—SUBMARINE ACTIVITY IN THE SEA OF MARMARA—ARRIVAL OF REINFORCEMENTS

WHILE the question of reinforcing General Sir Ian Hamilton was under consideration, doubt had been expressed as to whether it was physically possible to develop a powerful offensive from the position he held. On the assumption that he merely had in mind a more powerful attack on the Achi Baba position, it was objected that the ground he occupied was obviously too limited to give room for another army corps to deploy. But to seek success by mere weight of numbers was foreign to his idea of generalship. Fully alive to the freedom of manœuvre which the sea afforded, he was bent on making further use of it for strategical surprise by breaking in upon the enemy at a fresh point.

The idea had originated at Anzac. The costliness and even the futility of pressing the attack on the Achi Baba position, which was now only too apparent, drew attention more strongly than ever to the possibility of turning it. For some time past General Birdwood had had his eye on the Sari Bair ridge, the dominating feature of the neck of the peninsula. Rising from the sea directly in front of his left, it stretched away about north-east to the Boghali valley, so that once established on the summit he would be able to command all the communications both by sea and land by which the Turkish forces holding Kilid Bahr and the Achi Baba position were nourished. Nor was its value only military, for in the opinion of the naval staff it would mean securing a spotting station for effective bombardment of the Narrows. So promising was the plan, even as first conceived, that as soon as General Hamilton knew that another army corps was coming, he saw the possibility of developing General Birdwood's plan into the main line of operation.

With the new reinforcements, all the troops necessary for giving effect to his project could now be allotted to him. More than this, the surplus forces could be used to give an important expansion to the scheme and so overcome its technical difficulties. Its defect had been that from the cramped and insecure Anzac beaches it was impossible to nourish the increased force which was necessary to promise success against Sari Bair. But hard by, Suvla Bay offered an ideal anchorage for the purpose. Its conformation was such that it could be quickly closed by anti-submarine nets. True it was open to south-westerly gales, but six miles further up the coast, at Ejelmer Bay, was an alternative anchorage completely sheltered from them, and over and above the six brigades destined for Anzac there would remain sufficient force to seize both bays. Thus the primary object of the Suvla landing was to secure an adequate base for the new development, but incidentally the force employed could, by a comparatively small advance inland to the eastward, effectively protect General Birdwood's exposed left flank and generally operate in support of the main attack.

With every precaution for secrecy the new ground was reconnoitred from the sea, and was found to be practically unentrenched and occupied by little more than the usual look-out posts. Surprise, which the sea put in General Hamilton's power, seemed certain, could secrecy be preserved long enough. The confidence of the British Staff was confirmed by an appreciation received from General Gouraud on June 14. He was proving himself an ideal colleague, and between him and General Hamilton the closest harmony existed. The French still had their eyes on the forbidden Asiatic side, but realising that the expected reinforcements would be insufficient to enable the allied force to operate astride the Straits, he was seeking an alternative method of breaking the deadlock. One was a descent at Bulair, the other a development of the Anzac zone. The Bulair idea, as he frankly admitted, depended on the assumption that the naval authorities did not regard the difficulties as insuperable, and on this they were more strongly convinced than ever. Admiral de Robeck had, in fact, just been called upon to go once more into the whole question of a landing at the head of the Gulf of Xeros. After full consideration he could only report that since the advent of the submarines the original risks and difficulties of a disembarkation so far from the base at Mudros had so materially increased that nothing could justify the attempt but the prospect of a quick and decisive military success, and this he understood was not to be expected. His view was endorsed by the Admiralty, and Bulair was thus definitely ruled out. The only alternative that remained was General

Gouraud's third one, and this was to use the new divisions for developing the Anzac line of operation with much the same general idea of seizing the Maidos neck as was in General Hamilton's mind.[1]

So high was the impression for capacity and knowledge of his profession which General Gouraud had created, that his independent and spontaneous approval of the general idea was all the encouragement that was required to confirm the wisdom of the plan. So vital, however, was the preservation of secrecy that his staff were not informed, for the part assigned to the two French divisions was to be no more than a share in a holding attack on the Krithia positions by the Helles force. Of our own staff only the few officers needed to work out the plan were let into the secret. Even the authorities at home were told no more than enough to satisfy them that the General knew how to use the three new divisions. But Lord Kitchener did independently suggest the very plan that was in course of preparation.

So the famous Suvla movement was set on foot, but it must be many weeks before it could be carried out, and General Gouraud at least was not content to wait inactive so long. Already, just before news of the coming reinforcement arrived, he was arranging with General Hamilton for a carefully prepared attack on the formidable Turkish trenches in front of his left and centre, and after the news came the elaborate preparations continued. Owing to the submarine menace the ships could give but little assistance. All depended on the massing of artillery fire and the accumulation of unlimited supplies of ammunition. By June 20 all was ready, and on that day the *Lord Nelson*, with a kite-balloon spotting for her, bombarded the docks and shipping at Gallipoli over the land, inflicting considerable damage. For several days the front of attack had been kept under a hot fire by the French artillery which opened the attack on the 21st with a greatly intensified bombardment. The *St. Louis*, screened by trawlers with nets, and protected by British destroyers and trawlers, did her best to keep down the fire

[1] General Gouraud's plan differed in detail. He proposed a landing south of Gaba Tepe, and thence, in concert with the Anzac force, to capture the heights which dominated the Maidos plain. The establishment of a new base at Suvla did not enter into his plan. The technical naval considerations on which the need of such a base rested had probably not been brought to his notice. He was probably also unaware of the reasons we had for thinking the Turks were prepared to meet an attack south of Gaba Tepe. They had actually a division deployed on this part of the coast and another in reserve. General Gouraud's letter, which is dated June 13, is given by General Hamilton in his *Gallipoli Diary*, Vol. I., p. 296.

of the Asiatic guns: otherwise the fleet took no part. After a long day's desperate fighting, in which, under General Gouraud's inspiration, the French infantry displayed all their best qualities, the fierce resistance of the Turks was overcome. By nightfall the obnoxious "Haricot" redoubt in the Kereves ravine, which hitherto had baffled all his efforts to gain ground on this side, had been won.

Nor did the effort end here. While the question of another army corps was under debate at home General Hamilton had reported that he had enough ammunition left for one more day's assault. He was now preparing to deliver it with the idea of doing against the Turkish right what the French had done on their left. The first of his original reinforcement, the LIInd (Lowland) Division, arrived on June 19, and with the XXIXth Division and the Indian brigade he meant to make the attempt supported by a holding attack at Anzac. No battleship was to be risked in its support. Naval assistance was to be confined to a light cruiser and four destroyers. On the 28th, the day fixed for the operation, the *Talbot*, which was now the ship of the Senior Naval Officer at Gaba Tepe, took station off the left of our Helles line, with Admiral Nicholson on board to direct operations. From 10.0 a.m. onwards, with the *Manica* spotting, and four destroyers (*Racoon, Beagle, Bulldog* and *Basilisk*) screening, she shelled the enemy's trenches and silenced several batteries, while the other destroyers *Renard, Scorpion* and *Wolverine*, starting at 9.0 a.m., were at work where the enemy's trenches came nearly down to the sea. Again the bulk of the battery work came from our artillery ashore, assisted by French 75's, and it exceeded all that it had been able to do before. But there seems little doubt that the ship fire was a material assistance. According to the Turks it entirely destroyed the front-line trenches of the division that was on the sea flank, with the result that when at 11.0 our infantry got the word to advance they were able to occupy them at once with little loss. And not only that, but before the second line could be properly organised they had rushed that as well, and by noon all the assigned positions were in their hands. The advance made was about 1,000 yards, and it gave us five lines of trenches and the notorious "Boomerang" redoubt, which for so long had been holding up our left. During the night the Turks counter-attacked heavily. The chief effort was on the coast, but here a strong attempt to turn our sea flank along the beach was detected by the searchlights of the *Scorpion* and *Wolverine*, and was swept away by their guns. Nor were the attempts upon the rest of the front any more successful or less costly. All were repulsed with heavy loss and the whole of the new ground was retained.

Materially the gain to the general position was substantial. The Allied line was not only advanced, but straightened, and in every way improved. The moral effect was even greater. Since the first advance no such success had been won, and it had been won in spite of the reinforcement the enemy had received and of the time he had had to consolidate the position. There was a feeling of elation in the air—the light of victory was in all eyes, and could the blow have been followed quickly, all agreed that the victory could have been made complete. In this view we were certainly not over-sanguine. General Weber, who was now in command of the southern zone, was deeply enough impressed by our success to advise a retirement to the line of Soghanli Dere and Kilid Bahr. It was the last ditch for saving the Narrows forts, and General von Sanders would not consent. He was for recovering at all costs what we had gained on our coast flank, and for this purpose he brought over a division from the Asiatic side and moved another down from Anzac. This was an important result of our success. After General Birdwood had delivered his holding attack he was strongly counter-attacked, but the Turks were repulsed with heavy loss.

By July 4 the two Turkish divisions were in position, and from then onward the enforced delay till our new reinforcements arrived gave our troops in the southern area little rest. At short intervals the Turks delivered counter-attacks with a desperation and persistence that seemed regardless of cost and were testimony enough to the value of our newly-won ground. All was in vain; they gained nothing by their courageous efforts but incurred a loss of 6,000 men. We were even able to react, for on July 12–13 the Turks, with their attention fixed on our left, found themselves attacked by the French and the LIInd Division on the British right. About 400 yards more ground was gained and the position further improved. So far spent was the British artillery ammunition that the preparation and counter-battery work was all done by the French, with the assistance of the *Prince George*, *Chatham*, *Suffren* and half a dozen destroyers which were in action against Krithia, Achi Baba and the Kereves ravine.

It was little, however, that the fleet could do to give direct assistance to the land operations during the period of waiting, and the opportunity was taken to send the ships away to Malta to refit. Above all it was necessary to husband ammunition for the next great effort. But whenever an objective of sufficient importance presented itself a battleship would come out. These special targets were points where depots of ammunition were reported to exist, and in this way, amongst other places, Gallipoli, Chanak, Eren Keui and Examil, the centre of the Tenedos front, were all bombarded in turn. For this work the Admiral now had the assistance of another kite-balloon ship, the *Hector*. The monitors and the " Edgars," with their bulge protection, were also coming in and were available to take over the bombardments. The first to appear was the *Humber*, one of the original three monitors bought from Brazil. She had arrived on June 4, and shortly afterwards was sent to Gaba Tepe to deal with a large number of guns concealed in the Olive Groves along the Axmah ravine south of Gaba Tepe, which were enfilading the main Anzac beach and making it almost impossible for craft to approach it in daylight. Assisted by the Kephalo destroyers she was apparently successful, for after July 17 the guns were silent for the rest of the month. She was followed (on July 15) by the *Roberts*, one of the new 14-inch monitors. She was told off for the Asiatic batteries. Proceeding to Rabbit Island, north of Tenedos, she was securely anchored, netted in and connected up with the shore by telephone. Here she was joined by *M 19*, the first of the new 9·2-inch monitors to arrive. She was established in the same way, and the two, with the *Ben-My-Chree* to spot for them, settled down together to the sorely needed counter-battery work. By the end of the month the other three 14-inch monitors, *Abercrombie*, *Raglan* and *Havelock*, had arrived, as well as the 6-inch monitors, *M 29*, *32* and *33*, and the rest of the bulge ships of the old 10th Cruiser Squadron, *Theseus*, *Endymion*, *Grafton* and *Edgar*.[1]

The new arrivals, which henceforth became the main naval support for the army, were under Admiral Stuart Nicholson, who flew his flag in the *Exmouth*, in the now well-protected anchorage at Kephalo in Imbros.[2] At Imbros, too, owing to its position midway between Anzac and the

[1] A " bulge ship " was a ship fitted with an outside hollow belt as a protection against torpedo attack. The belt was termed a " bulge " or " blister," and these vessels were known later as " blister ships." From the autumn of 1914 onwards bulges were included in the designs of all large ships.

[2] It had now submerged defences in the form of a net boom, placed in position by the special net-layers *Queen Victoria* and *Prince Edward*, which had been sent out after proving their capacities on the Belgian coast. See Vol. II, p. 387.

southern beaches, General Hamilton had established his headquarters ever since the advent of the submarines. What was most to be feared during the period of arrested activity was that the efforts of the Turks on our flanks would develop into a violent attack all along the line. The month of Ramadan had begun, when Moslem religious enthusiasm was at its highest, and we expected that on the 23rd its driving power would be used to the utmost extent. So real was the expectation that it was deemed advisable to reinforce the Allied line with some of the new army that had just arrived. Accordingly the three brigades of the XIIIth Division and one of the XIth were landed at Helles to give the old XXIXth a sorely needed rest. By the 21st they were in position, and on the same day Admiral Nicholson, in consultation with the General Staff at Anzac, assigned to all the supporting ships (*Talbot*, *Humber*, *Colne* and *Pincher*) definite stations and areas of fire should an attack take place. The expected did not happen. Nothing but another attack on our left was made—it was the tenth they had launched—and was easily beaten off, like the rest.

For the monitors, however, there was other work. In the crowded end of the peninsula, particularly at Helles and at Sedd el Bahr, where General Gouraud had his headquarters, the Asiatic guns had become more and more galling, and it was mainly to check the disturbance that the recent bombardments had been ordered. Even so the beaches were never safe. All work in the daytime had to be done under fire, from time to time ammunition dumps were exploded, one of the beaches used by the French had to be abandoned and, worst of all, on June 30 General Gouraud himself was so severely wounded by a heavy shell from Asia that he had to relinquish the command to his second, General Bailloud, and go home. It was a catastrophe destined to have far-reaching consequences arising out of the appointment of his successor, and even at the moment, coming, as his loss did, immediately after the successful push, the blow was severely felt. " Gouraud's loss," wrote General Hamilton, " almost wipes out our gains." General Bailloud, on whom the command temporarily devolved, seeing no other way of ending the trouble, was setting his heart on landing part at least of the new army on the Asiatic side, but General Hamilton would not hear of it—nothing must be done to compromise the new plan. Meanwhile another means of relieving the annoyance at Sedd el Bahr and Helles was in hand, and the navy did its best with its own means. Two 4·7-inch naval guns, landed from the *Alnwick Castle*, and two French 5·5-inch naval guns were already in position, and were to be supplemented in a short time by another 4·7 and a 6-inch naval gun. In this way, by getting the monitors off the coast about Yeni Shehr, it was hoped to bring an effective cross-fire upon the obnoxious batteries. In this service they were principally employed during the rest of the period of waiting, with occasional bombardments, in combination with aircraft, of depots such as Chanak and Maidos, in the hope of crippling the enemy's supply of ammunition.

But the real work of breaking the flow of Turkish supplies was done by the submarines. All through June and July their activity never ceased, and during much of the period there were two operating in the Marmara.[1] On June 10 Lieutenant-Commander Boyle went up again in *E 14* and remained there over three weeks, keeping the whole sea in a state of disturbance. On his first day he met a brigantine and forced her to stop. As it was too rough to go alongside, Lieutenant R. W. Lawrence, R.N.R., swam off to her, and finding she was laden with heavy stores, he set her on fire with her own matches and paraffin, while the crew looked on from their boat. Next day at Panderma, the principal port on the Asiatic side, he torpedoed a steamer in the harbour and sank four dhows alongside her. But large steamers had disappeared from the sea; nothing was left but small ones of the ferry-boat type and sailing craft, and beyond a gunboat and destroyers that hunted him and a few grain dhows which he sank he saw nothing till, on the 20th, he had to go back to meet *E 12*, which was coming up under Lieutenant-Commander Bruce.

The career of the newcomer was beset with trouble. She arrived at the rendezvous in the evening of the 21st, and the following two days were spent in repairing her main motors, which were causing trouble. She then proceeded to cruise in the eastern part of the sea while Lieutenant-Commander Boyle remained in the western in order to report her condition by wireless to the connecting destroyer the other side of Bulair. This was on June 24, and the following day the crippled *E 12* began her adventures. Entering the Gulf of Mudania, in the south-eastern extremity of the sea, she came upon two small steamers which seemed to be passenger packets. But as they were towing between them five sailing vessels Lieutenant-Commander K. M. Bruce chased the first one and stopped her. Seeing all her crew on deck with life-belts and no trace of a gun, he ran his bow up alongside, with his 6-pounder and rifles ready, and ordered his first

[1] See Map 3.

lieutenant to board. Then suddenly it was evident the lesson of our decoys had reached the Turks. As the boarding party stepped over the side a bomb was thrown which hit the submarine forward. Luckily it did not explode, but it was followed by fire from rifles and a small masked gun. The fire was promptly returned, and an action began at ten yards during which the two sailing vessels which the steamer was towing also opened fire with rifles and tried to foul the submarine's propellers. They were soon silenced by her small-arm men, and she slowly got clear. By this time *E 12's* gun, which, after dealing with the steamer's masked gun, had been holing her from forward aft, must have found the ammunition she was carrying, for she suddenly blew up and sank in fifteen minutes. Having also sunk her two tows, Lieutenant-Commander Bruce gave chase to the other steamer, which had three sailing craft in tow. They promptly slipped and made off, while he engaged the steamer till he was within range of a gun on shore. Then he could do no more; his starboard main motor was again showing defects, and as the chase was in flames he left her to beach herself. Still he carried on with his cruise round to the Gulf of Ismid, the easternmost arm of the sea, and there he forced another steamer ashore. A second had disappeared towards Mudania, and in hunting back for her he met *E 14*, who passed to him an order to return to make good his defects. Crippled as he was, his struggle with the cross-currents going down the Straits was very severe, but, by a fine display of seamanship, all difficulties were overcome, and in the evening of June 28, in the midst of the elation at our success ashore, *E 12* crawled safely into Kephalo harbour. She had sunk three steamers and three sailing vessels. Five days later Commander Boyle[1] followed him down. On this cruise *E 14* sank one large steamer and 13 sailing vessels.

Lieutenant-Commander A. D. Cochrane, who commanded *E 7*, had difficulties no less great than *E 12*, but of a different character. To begin with he and his crew were suffering from the depressing form of dysentery with which both services were affected, and to add to the trouble during his first exploit, which was to destroy a steamer and some dhows at Rodosto, on the north coast, his first lieutenant and an able seaman were so badly burnt by an explosion that both were unfit for service for the rest of the cruise. In spite of everything, however, during the next ten days he destroyed four brigantines, two small steamers and sixteen dhows, ending on July 10 by torpedoing a 3,000 ton steamer at

[1] Promoted to rank of Commander on June 30.

Mudania pier. Still not content, he made for the Bosporus, and in the afternoon of the 15th, while aground on the Leander Shoal, fired a torpedo with a T.N.T. head into the arsenal. There was a resounding explosion, but the effect could not be seen, and proceeding out of the Bosporus he, at midnight, bombarded the Zeitunlik Powder Mills, in the western suburbs of the city.

His next exploit against the enemy's rear communications was quite a new departure. Near Kava Burnu, the cape at the entrance to the Gulf of Ismid, the railway from Constantinople passes through a cutting close to the sea. This point, early on the 17th, he bombarded till the track was blocked. He then proceeded up the Gulf for some twenty miles, where at Derinji there was a shipyard. It was found to be closed and nothing was there, but while it was being observed a heavy troop train was seen going towards Constantinople. Hoping the line ahead of it was blocked he gave chase at full speed, and sure enough about twenty minutes later the train was seen coming back. It stopped in a belt of trees, so that spotting was difficult, but, nevertheless, after twenty rounds three ammunition trucks blew up, and later on he caught and damaged a second train near the same spot. After these exploits there was a few days' cruise in Mudania Gulf and along the north shore, during which more steamers and sailing vessels were destroyed and some munition sheds blown up. Then he returned to the railway, and on July 22 caught another train in motion, but did little harm. A railway viaduct was then attacked, without better result, but the vulnerability of the line at this point had been demonstrated. In the evening he met Commander Boyle, who was at the rendezvous on his third trip and had a new difficulty to report. On approaching Nagara Point, where the navigation of the Narrows was most dangerous, he found the Turks busy on a net obstruction from shore to shore. A line of lighters marked its position, but seeing a gap which he believed to be the gate he dived to eighty feet and passed clear.[1]

Three days later Lieutenant-Commander Cochrane had to face the obstruction on his way down. Fortunately when

[1] The obstruction was probably incomplete at this time. The Turks state it was laid in July and that the gate was off Nagara Point, where there was only a depth of four fathoms over the shoal. It was afterwards ascertained that the net was seventy metres long, made with meshes four metres square of three to five inch steel wire rope and that the depth corresponded with the depth of water. The fairway through it was closed by torpedo netting. It was watched by five armed motor gunboats with searchlights and carrying bombs, and was commanded by ten guns in three batteries.

he reached the boom he found it had apparently dragged, so as to leave plenty of room to pass between it and the Point, but lower down he twice fouled moorings. From these, however, he cleverly managed to get clear, and reached the base safely with his sickly crew to be highly complimented on the skill, judgment and fine spirit which he and his men had shown.

Even with nothing to contrast it with, the appreciation must have been high, but, unhappily, the luck and skill of these two boats was emphasised by a reverse. A comparatively new French submarine, the *Mariotte*, slightly smaller and less powerful than our "E" class, went up on the 25th to join Commander Boyle next day. All went well till 5.30 in the morning, by which time she calculated she was clear of the Narrows minefield, when she suddenly found herself foul of something. Everything possible was done to free her, but she could move neither ahead nor astern, and in her struggle she suddenly rose till her conning tower was exposed. It could then be seen she was some 250 yards away from one of the Chanak batteries, which immediately opened fire. To complete her plight there was a mine foul of her forward. An attempt was made to dive, but before she was under she had received so much damage to her conning tower and after ventilation hatch (*manche d'aeration arrière*) that diving was no longer possible, and nothing was left but surrender. Accordingly, after wrecking all her engines and gear and making sure she would sink, the conning tower was opened and the ship abandoned. Officers and crew were all taken prisoner, to the keen regret of their British colleagues.[1]

Her unhappy loss was but one more testimony to the desperate nature of the service on which they had been engaged, and cannot but increase our wonder at the almost incredible endurance and resource which made it thoroughly effective. For two months or more they had held the Sea of Marmara in a panic. The sudden appearances which their restless activity enabled them to make, now here, now there, in quick succession from end to end of the Sea, multiplied their numbers in the Turkish imagination till the supply of Gallipoli by water was thoroughly crippled and the passage of troops entirely ceased. Nothing like a transport was seen, except hospital ships, and so numerous were these that grave suspicion was aroused. But all that were examined proved to be in order, and the explanation of their number was

[1] Report of the officer in command, communicated by the *Service Historique de l'Etat-Major General de la Marine.*

doubtless the heavy losses the Turks were suffering in their determined and incessant attempts to recover the ground they had lost at the end of June.[1] The disturbance which our submarines were thus producing was supplemented by the work of the Black Sea Fleet. We had urged the Russians to continue their raids on the Turkish coal supply, and they claim that up to the end of July they had set one coal depôt on fire, destroyed three shipyards and sunk over a hundred sailing vessels engaged on the supply of fuel and munitions. To cover these operations they had got a submarine mine-layer to work in the entrance of the Bosporus, and on July 18 the *Breslau* struck one of the mines and had to go into dock.

In the Ægean outside the Straits the main work of the navy, beyond the operations of the bombarding ships, was maintaining a blockade of the Turkish coast.[2] To some extent, in that it stopped the inflow of supplies, it was supplementary to what the submarines were doing. Reports of the scarcity of food in Constantinople were growing in coherence, and something at least was to be hoped from efforts to increase the distress. But the chief object was naval. The menace of German submarines was the most serious feature of the situation from all points of view, and now that the anchorages had been made proof against their attacks, the main concern of the fleet was to stop supplies for them and to prevent them establishing bases in the Ægean. On June 2, as we have seen, a formal blockade of the whole coast had been declared.[3] Smyrna, of course, was the best port for the enemy's purpose, and this area was allotted to the British and watched by the Smyrna patrol, from the Gulf of Adramyti to Khios. It was based at Port Iero in the south-east of Mityleni, where the Greek population was found to be sympathetic. The patrol normally consisted of two ships of force, two destroyers and a boarding steamer, with two trawlers to work indicator nets and the fleet sweeper *Gazelle* fitted for mine-laying. Here, too, was stationed the seaplane-carrier *Ben-My-Chree*. South of the patrol area all the lower Ægean, down to a line from the southern point of Greece to Marmarice on the Asiatic

[1] The Turks admitted using transports as hospital ships in breach of the Hague Conventions. It was therefore lawful to sink them, but neither the General nor the Admiral was willing to embitter the conflict by exacting the extreme penalty. The instructions, therefore, which our submarines received were, if possible, to hold up any transport coming from Constantinople, and if troops or munitions were found on board to destroy her.

[2] See Map 5. [3] See p. 37.

coast, was watched by a French patrol, which was also based at Port Iero and maintained the blockade down to Samos.[1] The system was completed by two more British patrols. Two light cruisers with armed boarding steamers formed the " Southern patrol " to watch the area between Mudros and the Smyrna patrol and to search for submarine depots, which were being continually reported from all quarters amongst the islands off the Greek coast. The " Northern patrol," which consisted of armed boarding steamers only, was charged with watching the north Ægean, and especially Salonica and Dedeagatch, to prevent contraband going into Turkey through Greek or Bulgarian ports. Finally in the Gulf of Xeros was the destroyer which was always stationed to keep up wireless communication with the submarines in the Marmara, to watch enemy movements about Bulair and to keep an eye on the island of Samothraki.

On these dispositions, so far as the limits of Admiral de Robeck's command were concerned, we had to rely for the safe arrival of the reinforcements, both naval and military, that were now going through the Mediterranean.[2] For the safety of the rest of the transport route, except the vicinity of Gibraltar and Malta and the Egyptian and Syrian coast, the French Commander-in-Chief was responsible. We had urged him to provide destroyer escort, but this he was unable to do. His available destroyers, he said, were all absorbed in patrolling between Sicily and Malta, south of Malta, the Ionian Islands, and between Crete and Cape Matapan. Consequently the transports had to proceed unescorted, except when outgoing armed boarding steamers could be used to convoy the slower ships. For the rest all the French Commander-in-Chief could do was to see that no submarines passed in or out of the Adriatic from Pola, where it was reported German boats were arriving by rail in sections and being assembled, and from time to time to give routes for the transports as the conditions of the hour suggested.

The whole question was further complicated by the requirements of the Army Staff. For military reasons they insisted that all transports should proceed in the first instance to Alexandria. As this meant exposure to submarine danger

[1] The French patrol consisted usually of two cruisers, five destroyers, eight armed sweepers and ten armed trawlers with drift nets.

[2] By an arrangement made with France and Italy in June 1915 the British Dardanelles zone was bounded by Eubœa and the chain of islands that stretch south-east of it to Mykonos. Thence the line ran across to Nikaria and on through Samos to the Turkish mainland. All the rest of the Mediterranean, except British and Italian territorial waters, was under the French.

for another seven hundred miles, Admiral de Robeck pressed for at least a modification of the order. But on technical grounds General Hamilton felt unable to give way. As a general rule he was not prepared to take the risk, but the two largest transports, *Aquitania* and *Mauretania*, were permitted to proceed to Mudros direct.[1]

From Egypt the transports came on into the British Ægean zone through the protected channels to Mudros, where they could find shelter behind the now double boom, and here, except for small store ships, the voyage ended. Large ships discharged into destroyers, fleet sweepers, trawlers and other small craft, and these proceeded to the various beaches by night unescorted, but for this critical part of the voyage no more than five hundred troops were permitted to be carried in one vessel. The need for these precautions had been unhappily demonstrated on July 4. About the 1st a fine French transport, the Compaigne Transatlantique liner *Carthage* of 5,600 tons, had arrived with munitions and stores. No ship had been attacked in the Helles area since June 17, when two torpedoes were fired at a supply ship, which both missed. So badly was the ammunition needed at the time to resist the Turk attempts to recover their lost ground, that it was decided to risk breaking the rule, and the *Carthage* was sent on straight to Helles. There she had been discharging for four days, and had landed with other stores 5,000 shells for the 75's, when she was torpedoed and sank in five minutes with what was left of her cargo. Besides the ship little was lost, but the lesson was severe enough, and the new system was thenceforward adhered to strictly.

Owing to the deficiencies of Mudros—where as yet the Engineers had been able to do little to construct piers—the system was necessarily slow, and this was the main cause of the Home Transport Department's complaint that transports were detained so long at their destination. It further entailed very heavy work on the beach parties, for owing to the landing places being exposed to fire, the troops and all

[1] These two ships made the voyage out in a week, against a fortnight taken by other transports via Alexandria. Their value for effecting a rapid concentration of troops at a distance is best testified by their performances. The *Mauretania*, which was originally destined to go via Alexandria, but was subsequently diverted, left Liverpool with 3,470 officers and men of the Xth Division on July 9, and reached Mudros on the 16th. The *Aquitania* with 5,800 men of the XIth Division, sailed on July 3, and arrived on the 10th. Returning immediately she sailed again on the 30th with 5,860 of the LIVth Division, and was back at Mudros by August 6. Thus, in a little over a month she carried nearly 12,000 officers and men over a distance of 3,000 miles.

personnel had to be put ashore in the dark, and as yet no deep-water piers had been constructed.

As the reinforcements arrived and Mudros became more crowded the difficulties of making military requirements square with naval limitations increased. Admiral Wemyss was still in command as Senior Naval Officer, and he was also acting as governor, though a Greek governor was also on the island. Since the resignation of M. Venizelos on March 6, on King Constantine's refusal to co-operate against the Dardanelles, relations with the governor had not been smooth. Difficulties of all kinds arose, particularly in regard to the native population and undesirable strangers, until the general election, which in the following August (22nd) returned M. Venizelos to power and ended the friction. Admiral Wemyss had now also a ship, the *Europa*, for his flag, in which there was room for a proper office. His staff, too, had been established on a more adequate scale. He had a Principal Transport Officer, Captain R. C. K. Lambert, whom he established afloat in the same ship with the military Inspector-General of Communications, and in this way difficulties that arose through the exigencies of the two services were more easily smoothed. Kephalo and Port Iero, of course, did something to relieve the pressure at Mudros, and just west of the bay was Port Kondia, where the auxiliary patrol was established, consisting of the *Osiris* and nearly a hundred trawlers and drifters. The air base was at Tenedos, where Commander C. R. Samson had formed an aerodrome for his squadron. Here Captain E. K. Loring, R.N., was governor, with a garrison of Marines, and it was from this point the air bombardments of the Turkish depots were carried out.

To all the other anxieties under which the navy laboured during the period of preparation was added the question of small craft. From the first it had been difficult to maintain a sufficient supply, and now the great increase of the army, a new line of operation and the impossibility of taking the transports further than Mudros, had rendered the problem two-fold more exacting. In view of the possible interruption of communication owing to bad weather and other causes, it was considered necessary to keep a ration supply of at least twenty-four days on all beaches, and this it was desired to increase to thirty. Water had always been scarce. The distillery plant at Mudros barely sufficed for the navy, and for the army water had to be brought from Egypt and other places and then distributed in barges. The call for small craft was indeed endless, and from all parts our officers were buying anything they could lay hands on. The problem, however, was to some extent simplified by better provision having been made for the actual landing of the troops. Thirteen specially designed motor lighters, each capable of carrying five hundred men or forty horses under a bullet-proof deck, had come out from home. The idea was that they could run up to the beach by their own power—thus doing away with the need of tows—and each was fitted with a brow or gangway forward so that at the last moment the men could emerge from their shelter and march straight on to the beach over the bows. They were taken up to Kephalo, for from Imbros were to start the troops forming the covering force for Suvla. It was to consist of the XIth Division and the infantry of the Xth Division, less one brigade. On the last night of the month the brigade belonging to the XIth Division, which had been landed at Helles, was silently transferred to Imbros, where the rest of the division was being exercised with the motor lighters. The concentration point of the Anzac reinforcement, whose main strength was the XIIIth Division, under Major-General F. C. Shaw, was Lemnos, and there three brigades which General Bailloud had agreed to replace were brought in the same way. To the Anzac force was also attached the 29th Indian brigade and one brigade of the Xth Division; of its two remaining brigades which were to be landed at Suvla, three battalions were at Lemnos and six at Mityleni. With these movements the long and difficult concentration was completed without mishap in spite of the hazards, and with every hope of success the great effort to break the deadlock was ready to be launched.

CHAPTER V

SUVLA [1]

In the long history of British warfare there is a special feature which distinguishes it from that of any other country. The precession of years is marked by a series of great combined expeditions which, over and above those which were planned as diversions or for seizing subsidiary strategical points, were aimed as definite thrusts at the decisive points of a world-wide war. Quebec, Havana, Walcheren and the Crimea, to name only the more conspicuous, occupy a position in our annals which, at least in modern times, is not to be matched elsewhere till we come to the decisive use of the device by another Island Power in the Russo-Japanese War.

Our record in the late war was true to type. It has given rich proof that the British genius for that most difficult and least appreciated form of operation, and the instinct for seeking in it the solution of baffling strategical problems, has in no way diminished in vigour and resource. Admittedly the first landing at Gallipoli outshone all precedent. So forlorn a hope did it seem at the time that even its partial success for a while struck dismay into the counsels of our enemy, and its moral effect bade fair to give a wholly new colour to the war. Apart from the high place which the actual fight for a footing won for it as a feat of arms, as a piece of subtle planning and finished organisation it was quite on a par with Quebec or Walcheren. Had it stood alone it would have served well enough to mark the vitality of the old spirit, but in these respects the Suvla operation even surpassed it. Nothing quite equal to it, either in conception, difficulty or magnitude, had ever been attempted before, and when we try to visualise the operation as it presented itself to its originators in the nakedness of its birth, we can only bow before the men who could see it clothed and nourished into a full-grown possibility.

After over three months' campaigning in a strictly limited area a strategical surprise was to be attempted—not at a

[1] See Map 6, and Vol. II., Map 4.

distance, but at a point within the area, half a day's march from the enemy's reserves. The surprise was to be not only strategical, it must be tactical too. In the dark the troops must start and in the dark they must be put ashore, and this must be done in great part on a beach that it had been impossible to survey or reconnoitre adequately, and by a force exceeding in number anything that had been attempted before. In the original descent at Helles the navy had been unable to guarantee the landing of a much smaller force before daylight, and therefore it had been agreed that the advantage of preparation by the guns of the fleet was greater than that of surprise. Now the conditions were different. The might of the fleet could no longer be brought up in support, and at the new landing-points the currents which the navy feared at the southern beaches did not interfere. On this occasion, therefore, surprise naturally took precedence.

To secure it to the full no elaboration of plan was omitted. A period of moonless nights was the first essential, and this would occur in the first week in August. The new moon was on the 10th and the attack was fixed for the night of the 6th-7th. As a preliminary step it was necessary to get from 7,000 to 8,000 Anzac drafts ashore. This was done during the nights following July 31, and by August 3 they were all ashore, together with forty guns and extra transport, without being detected. The next step was to land the new force of five brigades which were to reinforce the Anzac Corps from Mudros, and not only to land them secretly, but to keep them hidden till the last moment. For this purpose General Birdwood had constructed an elaborate series of dug-outs.

To cover these delicate operations dispositions were made to attract the enemy's attention to the Asiatic coast. At Mityleni the six battalions of the Xth Division, which had been sent to wait in their transports till they were wanted, were landed every day for route marches and inspected by General Hamilton, while in concert with some French ships every effort was made to create an impression of an attack from Adramyti Gulf on the railway from Smyrna to Panderma, a line of supply which the operations of our submarines in the Marmara had doubled in importance. Lower down the coast a more elaborate menace was staged by Admiral Nicol, the French naval commander, who was now flying his flag in the *Patrie*. During the afternoon of August 3 a French squadron, escorting transports and our seaplane carrier *Ben-My-Chree*, appeared before Sighajik, a small port some twenty miles from Smyrna, lying on the south of the neck of the peninsula which divides the Smyrna Gulf from the Gulf of

Scala Nuova. After a line of trawlers with their nets out had been stationed across the entrance to the bay, guarded by tugs patrolling inside, the squadron proceeded to bombard the coast till 4.0 p.m.; at dusk the transports came in, the small craft gathered to meet them, boats were lowered and formed into tows, and as night fell a regularly formed flotilla headed for the shore.

During the next three nights (August 3–5) the reinforcements for Anzac were moved to their positions in the ordinary way by destroyers and troop carriers, undetected by the enemy. Towards the first morning, it is true, the Olive Groves batteries woke up again after their long slumber and rained shells upon the beach. A steamer and two horse-boats were sunk, but that was all. After that they went to sleep again as though it had been all a bad dream, but to make sure the next night the bulge ship *Grafton* was there to drop shells into the trees and remind the enemy of the unwisdom of revealing their position by gunflashes.

The work of reinforcement being successfully completed, all was in order for the Suvla operation to proceed. The risk attending it, as it was finally settled, was considerably greater than that of the Anzac landing. The original intention, as agreed between the Admiral and the General, was to land the whole of the force on the Nibrunesi beach, which lies outside and just south of the bay. It was admirably adapted for the purpose. Not only did it afford ample elbow room, but during the naval raid that had been made upon Nibrunesi observation post on Lala Baba Hill it had been found to be so " steep-to " that destroyers could run in with their bows almost touching the beach. Both from a naval and a military point of view nothing better could be desired, and so it stood in the operation orders which the Commander-in-Chief issued to Lieutenant-General The Hon. Sir F. W. Stopford on July 29. He it was who, as commander of the new army corps (IXth), was to have charge of the Suvla part of the operation. These orders laid down as the primary object " to secure Suvla Bay as a base for all the forces operating in the northern zone." If he found this could be done without using the whole of his force, he was to assist General Birdwood's attack by an advance on the village of Biyuk Anafarta, with the object of moving up the eastern spurs of Sari Bair. On discussing these orders with the General commanding the XIth Division, which was to lead off, he came to the conclusion that the bay could not be secured without seizing the whole of the high ground between Ejelmer Bay and Sari Bair known as Anafarta Ridge, and for this it would be necessary to land two brigades inside Suvla Bay on its eastern shore.[1] But Admiral de Robeck and his staff saw serious objections. Having already reconnoitred the place, as thoroughly as could be done, from the sea and the left of the Anzac position, they reported that a landing by night inside the bay was inadvisable. Though a proper survey was impossible for secrecy's sake, they could see enough to tell them the old chart they had was not to be relied on. The eastern shore had apparently silted up and the north shore was clearly foul with reefs. Under these conditions of uncertainty they could not undertake to land two brigades at once. One it might be possible to get ashore, but they could not promise to get up a second till four hours after the first had landed, the reason being that the motor lighters would probably take the ground and would not be able to return for the second brigade. For these reasons they were still for landing the whole force at Nibrunesi.

The soldiers, however, still had to insist. From the northern point of the bay there ran north-eastward and parallel to the coast a ridge known as Karakol, and this at least it was necessary to seize at once as part of the covering position; otherwise, they urged, the bay would be untenable and could not be used as a base. Between the southern end of this ridge and the Nibrunesi beach was a salt lagoon which left only a narrow spit of sand between it and the southern half of the east shore of the bay, and it was along this spit that a force landed at Nibrunesi beach would have to make its way north. Whether the lagoon was dry or not could not be seen, but if it proved to be impassable or defended there was little likelihood of the ridge being seized at the first onset by troops advancing from Nibrunesi. The General, therefore, was anxious to land half his force within the bay north of a cut which was believed to connect the lagoon with the sea.

The two Commanders-in-Chief thus found themselves face to face with one of those delicate questions which cannot fail to arise in the conduct of combined operations. Continental Powers had never seen but one way to deal with them, and that was to make the General supreme and the Admiral subordinate. Our own long experience had taught us at an early stage that in practice this plausible solution tended to raise more difficulties than it removed. The British method was to have two co-equal Commanders-in-Chief, the

[1] Properly speaking, the Anafarta Ridge is a low spur taking off from this high ground; but in the narrative the expression has been used to describe the group of heights now known as Kavak Tepe Sirt.

Admiral being paramount at sea and the General on land. By tradition the Admiral was to land the troops and re-embark them as and where the General desired, so far as was, in his opinion, technically possible and consistent with the safety of the fleet. If the General's plan involved, from a naval point of view, risk to the army, it was for him to say, after the sea risk had been explained, whether he would accept it or not. Naturally such an arrangement could only work by mutual goodwill and understanding between the two officers concerned, but we had found it the only practicable method, and this case affords an excellent example of its merits.

The difference to be settled was one of unusual complexity, for the naval and military exigencies were tightly interwoven. To the navy the command of Suvla Bay was indispensable. Not only was it essential to their ability to give continued support to the army, but it could so easily be closed by nets that large ships would be able to lie there, and thus the difficulty of supply for the whole northern zone would be materially reduced. The nets, of course, would only prevent the entrance of submarines; they were no bar to torpedoes, and in the initial stages of the operation, when the bay was crowded, ships would have to lie so close to the net that they could easily be hit by torpedoes fired from outside. This was a risk which to the utmost extent the Admiral was ready to run, for by no other means could the army he was there to assist carry out its last hope of breaking through the deadlock ashore; but with guns on the heights commanding the bay and always forcing the transports close up to the net, the risk would become so great as to bar entirely the working of the base. On these grounds he could but agree to what the divisional General considered absolutely necessary for securing the ridge; and finally on August 2 the operation orders were so far modified that one brigade was to be landed north of the cut and the other, with the rest of the division, on Nibrunesi beach, whence, as soon as Lala Baba was rushed, they could march northward along the shore of the bay. Having reluctantly decided to take the risk of landing a whole brigade simultaneously in the dark on an unsurveyed beach, the Admiral at once set about minimising it. In case things went wrong with the destroyers and motor lighters orders were issued for an alternative landing flotilla, consisting of ketches (trawlers and drifters) with tows of the transports' lifeboats, to be anchored off the mouth of the bay, —a typical example of the spirit by which from first to last all concerned testified to the vitality and virtue of our traditional method of command in the hands of men of goodwill and understanding.

The question of naval support, now that the monitors and bulge ships had nearly all arrived, was comparatively simple. It was these specially prepared craft, which, with the cruisers and destroyers, had of late been doing most of the battery work on the flanks, that were to be used. All the battleships had been kept back in reserve for action that would be needed if the new plan proved successful in throwing open the Straits. The supporting ships were organised in three squadrons. The 1st under Admiral Nicholson, with his flag in the *Exmouth* at Kephalo, was to be devoted to the southern or Helles zone, for an integral part of the coming operation was an attack in force on the Krithia and Achi Baba position.[1] For the left flank in this area were detailed the *Edgar*, two monitors, (*Raglan, Abercrombie*), three destroyers (*Scorpion, Wolverine, Renard*), and the kite balloon ship *Hector*. Support of the right flank, except for two French and two British destroyers (*Harpy, Savage*) at Helles, was confined to counter-battery against the Asiatic guns by the *Roberts* and two small monitors from Rabbit Island, with a French battleship in reserve at Kephalo in case more weight was required. The 2nd Squadron, under Captain The Hon. A. D. E. H. Boyle in the *Bacchante*, was for Anzac, with four monitors (*Havelock, Humber, M 33, M 20*) on the right flank and the *Endymion* (bulge ship), a small monitor (*M 15*) and two destroyers (*Chelmer, Colne*) on the left. The 3rd Squadron, under Captain Fawcet Wray in his light cruiser the *Talbot*, was for Suvla, with two bulge ships (*Grafton* and *Theseus*) and three small monitors (*M 29, M 30, M 31*) and to this division were attached one destroyer and the balloon ship *Manica* for spotting. The general conduct of the Suvla landing was assigned to Rear-Admiral A. H. Christian, who had recently come out in place of Rear-Admiral R. S. Phipps Hornby, and for the time flew his flag in the sloop *Jonquil*.[2]

In addition to the usual artillery support the navy had also undertaken to arrange for two small diversions designed to hold certain enemy troops away from the northern beaches. The Turks, who were fully aware that large reinforcements had arrived—they believed them to amount to 100,000 men—had collected large forces in the peninsula. In what zone the expected attack would fall they could not tell, and could do no more than dispose their troops in relation to the most

[1] During the operation he flew his flag in the *Scorpion* on the left flank.

[2] Admiral Phipps Hornby had arrived in the *Glory* from the North American Station in June, but was invalided in July.

likely points of attack. Besides three divisions watching the Asiatic coast about Bashika Bay, five divisions facing our southern force and three in the Anzac zone, they had three more guarding the Bulair beaches and another south of Anzac, where the Chanak Plain runs out to the sea at the Olive Groves. Here a demonstration of landing was to be made by a flotilla of trawlers, while at the head of the Gulf of Xeros the *Minerva* and *Jed* were to land a force of three hundred and fifty irregulars under two French officers for a raid on the north shore.

The operation began with the movement in the southern zone. It was now temporarily under Major-General W. Douglas of the XLIInd Division, for unhappily Lieutenant-General Hunter-Weston's health had broken down under the long strain.[1] Although it was intended primarily as a holding attack, it was hoped that certain tactical progress would be made which might soon lead to the capture of Krithia. The attack, which was to be confined to our own right and centre, while the French stood fast in the trenches they had taken over, was timed for 3.50 in the afternoon on August 6, and had been prepared during the previous days by the supporting ships occasionally bombarding Achi Baba and other gun positions. In support of the actual attack the whole of the 1st Squadron was to join in the final artillery preparation, each ship with her appointed group of batteries, with special instructions to fire a proportion of shots on the weather side of both Krithia and Achi Baba so as to raise a dust screen across the enemy's observation posts, while the destroyers fired as required by the military direction officers ashore. At the prescribed moment the infantry rushed forward, and all appeared to be going well, but only for the first few seconds. Our centre and right found themselves up against heavy masses of Turks, and in spite of long and persistent fighting, involving many casualties, no impression could be made. The Turks, unable to divine where we meant to strike, had concentrated five divisions in their southern zone, so that of their own accord they had done what General Hamilton intended to force them to do by his diversionary attack. The result, however, was that only on our extreme left was a precarious hold won and maintained on a corner of the Turkish position. Everywhere else their lines were intact.

Simultaneously a similar attack was made against the Turkish left at Anzac, where a system of formidable trenches,

[1] On August 8 Lieutenant-General Sir F. J. Davies took over the command of the VIIIth Corps, and Major-General Douglas reverted to the command of the XLIInd Division.

known as Lone Pine Hill, constituted the strongest section of the enemy's line. Though here again the main idea was diversionary, its capture was keenly desired. It commanded an important source of the enemy's water supply, and had further marked tactical importance which would render its seizure a clear step on the road to the ultimate object of getting astride the neck of the peninsula. To reinforce the Australian artillery the 2nd Squadron was brought up. The preparatory bombardment was assigned to the *Bacchante* [1] with the monitors protecting her from disturbance by the enemy's artillery: the *Havelock* with her 14-inch guns kept an eye on any ships that might fire from the Narrows, while the *Humber* and the *M 33* dealt with the guns between Gaba Tepe and the Olive Groves. At 4.30 the bombardment began, and an hour later the Australians went over and rushed the wire, but not until they had torn up the massive timber covering of the trenches could they penetrate, and then the impossible was done. As a feat of arms it could hardly be surpassed, but the occupation of the redoubt was far from the end. Hour after hour as the *Bacchante* lifted to the ravines that formed the approaches to the captured trenches an heroic struggle raged for their retention. Mass upon mass the Turks hurled forward with splendid pertinacity, and upon these the *Bacchante* and *Grafton* took their toll as they made their way to the front. Yet neither side would give way. All night long and for the next forty-eight hours the fight went on as fiercely as it began; since the first landing there had been nothing like it, but for all the Turks could do, the stubborn Australians were still in possession, with large numbers of prisoners.

By that time General Birdwood's real attack was in full swing. Its objective, it will be recalled, was the Sari Bair Ridge, which dominated both the Anzac and the Turkish positions. Where the ridge begins to fall to the sea, at a point known as "Battleship Hill," the main line of Turkish entrenchments ended. It was, however, prolonged towards the sea at Ocean beach by a system of entrenched positions. Beyond the main line and to the right of it was a minor feature, Chunuk Bair, which was still unentrenched, and once in our hands would give us the whole Sari Bair Ridge. The enemy's flank could then be turned and his rear threatened. The plan meant that the attack must start from the Anzac extreme left in a north and north-easterly direction, and then turn up the main ravines which led to the ridge easterly. To carry out so complicated an operation over a maze of broken ground

[1] *Bacchante* 2–9·2″; 12–6″; 12–12-pounders.

through thick scrub and in the dark required the nicest adjustment. The operating force was organised into two assaulting columns and two covering columns. The function of the covering columns was to clear and occupy the ground to the north, so that the assaulting columns could be free to march straight to the entrance of the ravines up which the main attack was to be thrust.

In the preliminary or covering stage the Turkish advanced positions must be won before the ground was made good, and here the navy could give direct assistance. The first of them was our "No. 3 Old Post," 800 yards from the beach. At the end of May it had been snatched from us by the Turks, and ever since they had been engaged in turning it into a well-nigh impregnable redoubt. But what is difficult by force may be easy by guile. Its capture was assigned to the right covering force, composed of New Zealanders, under Brigadier-General A. R. Russell, who, with Commander C. Seymour of the *Colne*, the left flank destroyer, arranged a pretty little stratagem. To ease their task, the *Colne* for several nights before the assault turned her searchlight on the post and then bombarded it for ten minutes. After a short interval she did it again, always at the same time, 9.20 to 9.30, till the Turks seem to have acquired the habit of retiring into cover as the hour approached. Needless to say, it was also the hour the assault was to be made. At the appointed moment, with the guns of the *Colne* still covering the sound of their steps, the New Zealanders moved forward in the dark shadow that fringed the beam of the searchlight. Half of them crept up the bush-covered spur on which the post stood, and then the moment the guns stopped and the searchlight was switched off they sprang up out of the scrub, to find the redoubt empty. So the first point was scored without a blow, and a good half-hour before midnight the whole system of trenches was in their hands. Meanwhile the rest of General Russell's column passed to attack Bauchops Hill, the next post to the northward, and the valley between it and "Old Post." By 1.0 a.m. all this zone was won, the way for the right assaulting column was open, and General Russell could proceed against his final objective, Table Top, to which the *Colne* had shifted her fire and searchlight. It was a scarped hill sloping at an angle which, according to our regulations, was impracticable for infantry, but, nevertheless, when the *Colne* threw her beam up and ceased fire its precipitous sides were scaled, and soon after midnight, in face of a fine resistance put up by the Turks, that post too was in our hands, at the point of the bayonet and almost without a shot. As an example of perfect

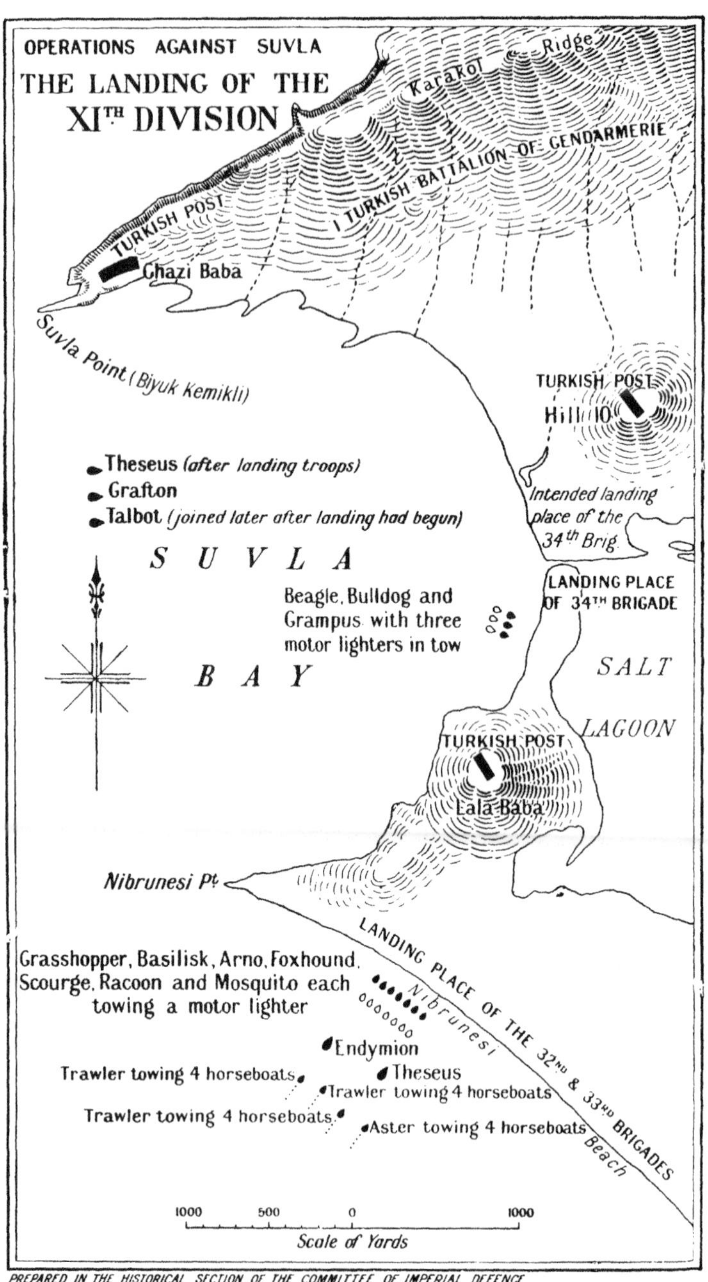
OPERATIONS AGAINST SUVLA
THE LANDING OF THE
XITH DIVISION
Karakol Ridge
1 TURKISH BATTALION OF GENDARMERIE
TURKISH POST
Ghazi Baba
Suvla Point (Biyuk Kemikli)
TURKISH POST
Hill 10
Theseus (after landing troops)
Grafton
Talbot (joined later after landing had begun)
Intended landing place of the 34th Brig.
S U V L A
LANDING PLACE OF 34TH BRIGADE
Beagle, Bulldog and Grampus with three motor lighters in tow
B A Y
SALT
LAGOON
TURKISH POST
Lala Baba
Nibrunesi Pt.
LANDING PLACE OF THE 32ND & 33RD BRIGADES
Grasshopper, Basilisk, Arno, Foxhound, Scourge, Racoon and Mosquito each towing a motor lighter
Nibrunesi Beach
Endymion
Trawler towing 4 horseboats
Theseus
Trawler towing 4 horseboats
Trawler towing 4 horseboats
Aster towing 4 horseboats
1000
500
0
1000
Scale of Yards

PREPARED IN THE HISTORICAL SECTION OF THE COMMITTEE OF IMPERIAL DEFENCE

[To face p. 93.

combination between land and sea, and a dashing push home of surprise, the movement could scarcely be surpassed.

Meanwhile the left covering column, consisting of two battalions of the XIIIth Division, under Brigadier-General J. H. du B. Travers, had passed on, before Bauchops Hill was entirely ours, and in spite of enfilading fire from the trenches still in the enemy's hands the New Army troops, unshaken, rushed the trenches in the next ravine northward and then stormed Damakjelik Bair, the hill beyond it. It was the last height towards Suvla, and so the New Army not only proved its metal, but cleared the way for the left assaulting column, and completed the security of the left rear of the main attack, which the *Colne* was now doing her best to cover.

Away to the left the landing at Nibrunesi beach of two brigades (32nd and 33rd) of the XIth Division had been going equally well. As at the first landing, the weather was perfect, with the sea like glass, and at Kephalo the leading troops were embarked without a hitch, five hundred in each motor lighter and five hundred in the destroyer that was to tow it. Seven destroyers and seven lighters carried the covering troops for this beach. The remainder, three thousand men, followed them, crowded into the supporting ships, *Endymion* and *Theseus*, the sloop *Aster* and six trawlers, the *Aster* towing a motor lighter and each of the trawlers four horse-boats with guns and horses. With a destroyer anchored close in to the beach as a guide, the leading troops arrived accurately and to time about 10.0 p.m. and the lighters cast off and went in. An hour later they had discharged their men, and two battalions were moving for the spit between the lagoon and the sea to seize Lala Baba Hill. Returning at once to the destroyers, the lighters went in again, and by midnight all the covering troops were ashore and the lighters could come back to meet the cruisers, which had already arrived with the rest of the troops. The surprise was complete. Beyond a few rifle shots from amongst the sandhills there had been no opposition, and there was not a single casualty.[1] With equal success the cruisers were cleared, so that by 1.30 a.m. the whole of the two brigades were ashore with the guns and horses, and the two cruisers were able to take up their supporting stations for the coming day's work, while the rest of the troops advanced against their first objectives. These were Chocolate Hill, which lay about a mile and a half north-east from the beach east of the lagoon and the guns on Ismail Oglu Tepe or " W " Hill a mile further to the eastward. Both these positions commanded Suvla Bay, where the most doubtful

[1] One naval rating was killed by a shot from the shore.

part of the operation, the disembarkation of the remaining brigade (34th) of the XIth Division, was proceeding. Only three destroyers (*Bulldog*, in which was Brigadier-General W. H. Sitwell, commanding the brigade, *Beagle* and *Grampus*) with three motor lighters were required for this landing, but here also by dawn were to come two brigades of the Xth Division from Mityleni and Mudros, and the brigade that was now being landed was, in fact, its covering force. Here, too, General Stopford took his post of command with Admiral Christian in the sloop *Jonquil*, while Admiral de Robeck came over from Kephalo in the *Chatham*. The landing was planned to take place five hundred to a thousand yards north of the cut, directly opposite a knoll known as Hill 10, but in the blackness of the night, with no mark to guide them, the destroyers deviated slightly to starboard, and at 10.20 p.m. anchored six hundred yards from the shore a little to the south of the cut. Ignorant of the error, the lighters cast off and pushed straight inshore, and almost immediately the trouble which the Naval Staff had anticipated began. One after the other they went hard aground a hundred yards short of the beach, and from the sand dunes snipers opened fire. So far, however, little harm was done. There were only three feet of water, and though it deepened shorewards all the fifteen hundred men by the aid of ropes run out from the lighters got ashore without serious loss. But how to support them was the difficulty. They were soon under fire from the Turkish outposts on Ghazi Baba, on the north arm of the bay, as well as from Hill 10 and from Lala Baba, which had not yet been taken; two small-calibre guns were searching the bay with shrapnel, and the lighters were so hard aground they could not move to go back to the destroyers. As soon as their plight was known picket boats were sent off to fetch reserve tows, but it must be long before they arrived. Meanwhile every effort was being made to get the lighters off, and by 11.30 the *Grampus* had hers alongside again. An hour later her men were ashore, and by 2.30 the *Bulldog's* contingent had also been landed. It was not till nearly five o'clock that the *Beagle* had sent her men ashore in the reserve tows, and the delay was already serious. General Sitwell, when he landed, seized a sand dune in front of him, and believing it to be Hill 10, seems to have waited for the 32nd Brigade from Nibrunesi to join up. The Turks thus had time to be fully on the alert, and when the advance to Hill 10 was made it was held. Eventually, however, the position was turned. By 6.0 a.m. it was in our possession, and only then could the deployment begin which had been timed for 1.30.

Unhappily the delay did not end here. At break of day, as Hill 10 was being occupied, Brigadier-General F. F. Hill arrived from Mityleni with five battalions of the Xth (Irish) Division, and the question at once arose where they should land. Commander E. Unwin had just come on board the *Jonquil* to report that he had hastily surveyed the beach and found that the whole eastern side of the bay was so shoal and beset with rocks that it was impracticable. Admiral Christian was for sending the troops round to Nibrunesi at once, but it was not till General Stopford had consulted General Hill that he assented and the troop carriers were ordered there.

Before, however, they were all away Commodore R. Keyes, Chief of Staff to Admiral de Robeck, came on board to report that two practicable beaches had been discovered on the north side of the bay where from a distance the rocks had seemed to bar all approach to the shore. After reconnoitring the Karakol Ridge to the northward, Admiral de Robeck had returned at 8.0 a.m., and could at once see that the reefs really ran out to seaward, so as to form two convenient coves, afterwards known as "A East" and "A West." It was obviously by far the best point for the left-wing troops to land, and knowing by this time of the troubles at the original beach, he sent away Commodore Keyes to urge the newly-found coves as an alternative. As they lay right under the Turkish look-out post on Ghazi Baba, and troops could be dimly seen on the Karakol Ridge beyond, he ordered up a monitor and two destroyers to cover the landing. Meanwhile Commodore Keyes had ascertained that the troops were our own; in fact the 11th Manchesters, who were on the left of the XIth Division, were already established there. Commodore Keyes could, therefore, with increased confidence urge the Admiral's view of what should be done to recover lost time. Lieutenant-General Sir B. T. Mahon, with the remaining three battalions of the Xth Division, had also arrived; his idea was that the division should be landed immediately on the north shore. As orders had already been given to General Hill's five battalions to go round to Nibrunesi, General Stopford was unwilling to recall them, but General Mahon was directed to land his force where the Admiral advised, as well as one of General Hill's battalions which had arrived late and had been deflected to the northern arm of the bay.[1]

The new landing-place, besides saving the men a long

[1] This composite force of four battalions, landed in the northern part of the bay, together with the 11th Manchesters, came under the command of Brigadier-General L. L. Nicol.

march along the beach from Nibrunesi, had another advantage. At dawn the Turks had begun shelling the other beaches, this one they could not reach. Moreover, owing to the first landed troops not having reached their initial objective, all the inner part of the bay was unsafe. At 8.30 the Commodore had returned to the *Jonquil* with Admiral de Robeck, and while they were conferring with General Stopford about the new scheme of landing, the destroyer *Scourge*, which had been trying to get off some lighters that were still aground was hit by a shell in the engine-room and had to retire for repairs. Shortly afterwards a definite signal was made that the new beaches were to be the main landing-place.

Unhappily they had not proved all they seemed, for when the men began to land at " A East " land mines, placed there apparently to defend the Ghazi Baba post, exploded, with disaster to the leading files, but the landing proceeded without interruption. The other cove was found to be clear, and though the disembarkation was slow, owing to there being room for no more than three lighters abreast, progress was soon made. With the destroyer *Foxhound* operating on the left and another monitor searching the ground in front from Ejelmer Bay, General Mahon was able to push along the ridge till the new beach was practically safe. By this time, moreover, half the anti-submarine nets were in place and the two paddle net-layers had gone back for the remaining sections.

In the centre and on the right the position was less satisfactory. Here the covering troops were little more than clear of the beach. The line actually ran from the right of the Nibrunesi beach through the lagoon, which was found to be dry, and Hill 10 to a point on the Karakol Ridge which General Mahon had reached nearly two miles in advance of his landing-place. The main cause of the halt was said to be want of water. Ample provision had been made in the fleet for bringing it up as soon as the troops were landed, but owing to the need of shifting the point of disembarkation in Suvla Bay the first water lighters could not begin to get in till after noon; even so it was only at the narrow beach on which the troops were crowded. Later on one got in under shelter of Lala Baba, and the *Foxhound* was doing all she could to supply General Mahon's men by way of the Karakol cliffs. Unhappily the arrival of the lighters did not end the trouble, for it was found that the troops were entirely unprovided with gear for the reception or distribution of the water. Baths, canvas tanks, buckets and tins were hastily requisitioned from all the craft within reach, but the supply was all too small for the demand on that burning August day, and the troops were declared incapable of further effort till their thirst had been quenched.

With the main attack at Anzac things had gone better. By a display of leadership, hard fighting and endurance that nothing in the war surpassed, the two assaulting columns had never ceased to grope their way forward up the scrub-filled ravines and over the tortuous ridges. No wire was too thick, no trenches too well held, no scarps too precipitous to stop them. Higher and higher they fought their way, and the stubborn Turkish resistance melted before them like shadows of the night, till when the Sari Bair Ridge was taking shape in the first light of the dawn the right column was on the Rhododendron spur, which led straight up to their goal at Chunuk Bair, and the left was just below Hill Q and Koja Temen Tepe, the two culminating points of the ridge where Victory was holding out her hand. In the growing light they still pressed on, exhausted as they were, but only to find the enemy's resistance was hardening. His reserves had hitherto been held back on Battleship Hill by a desperate attack which the Anzac centre was making on the trenches at its foot. Now part of them were being hurried forward. By this means about 7.0 a.m. the great attack was held up, and a call went out to the guns. The supporting ships heard it and joined in. For two hours the *Endymion* with her 6-inch guns was smothering Battleship Hill with lyddite. The *Bacchante* had her 9·2's on Chunuk Bair, where she claimed to have silenced two guns, while with her 6-inch she was doing her best, like the *Endymion*, to stop the advance of the enemy's reserves. Then at 9.30 the guns ceased fire and the weary troops were called on for another effort. The response was all that human endurance could give, but it was not enough, and in the end they could do no more than dig themselves in on the ground they had so gallantly won just short of the summit.

Up to this time it does not appear that the failure of the main attack to gain the ridge was materially affected by the delay of the Suvla force, but on that side progress was slow. Owing to the exhaustion of the men, want of water and the displacement of units due to the changed landing arrangements, no further advance was made till late in the afternoon. It was not till about 5.30 that an attack on Chocolate Hill was launched under cover of the guns of the *Talbot, Thesus* and *Grafton*, but soon after 7.0 the whole position was occupied, while on the left General Mahon had fought his way along the coast ridge to its highest point at Kiretch Tepe Sirt. From this point the line ran roughly southwards and well east of the lagoon as far as Chocolate Hill. The interval from this point to Damakjelik Bair, where the left of the Anzacs rested, was unoccupied. This meant it was but half-way to the line it had been hoped to seize on the first night.[1]

In front of them still lay the ridge that ran down from Ejelmer Bay to " W " Hill, and not only was the occupation of these heights deemed essential for the command of the bay, but about the two Anafartas was the pastoral country on which the army counted for its water. It had been the hope that both places would be in our hands by the first morning. Yet all the second day (the 8th) passed without any further advance being made. General Stopford urged the divisional Generals to push on; they could only reply that owing to the disorganisation of the line and the lack of water and exhaustion they could not move. There was also another reason for delay which weighed with the General. Hitherto, owing to the need of getting mules ashore for the distribution of water, only two batteries of mountain guns and one of field artillery had been landed, the latter without horses; and without proper artillery preparation he did not think the troops should be allowed to make frontal attacks on entrenched positions. The naval guns had done excellent work the previous day against Chocolate Hill, and this he acknowledged. But now he pointed out it was no simple question of a definite target, but of searching broken ground where it was impossible for ships to do all that was required.

His objection was one that goes to the root of disembarkation tactics, as evolved from long tradition in the British Service. It was on this tradition Sir Ian Hamilton had made his plan. " Normally," he wrote, in his despatch, " it may be correct to say that in modern warfare infantry cannot be expected to advance without artillery preparation. But in a landing on a hostile shore the order has to be inverted. The infantry must advance and seize a suitable position to cover the landing and to provide artillery positions for the main thrust. The very existence of the force, its water supply, its facilities for munitions and supplies, its power to reinforce, must absolutely depend on the infantry being able instantly to make good sufficient ground without the aid of artillery other than can be supplied for the purpose by floating batteries. This is not a condition that should take the commander of a covering force by surprise. It is one already foreseen." Whether or not the latest experience goes to show that under modern conditions this principle will no

[1] British casualties on the 7th amounted to 1,700, rather more than the total of the opposing force.

longer hold good, may be regarded as an open question until it is proved that the control and nature of floating fire cannot be developed so as to meet the new conditions. But that at the time the plan was made it was the traditional principle, admits of no doubt whatever.

At General Headquarters the state of affairs at Suvla was unsuspected up to the morning of August 8. But as the forenoon wore on with no news of any further advance, General Hamilton began to feel that all was not well and he must get to the spot himself. Hitherto, as the main attack was from Anzac, and those at Helles and Suvla were subordinate, he had remained at Imbros, as the best post of command for keeping his hand on the whole of his extensive combination. The destroyer *Arno* had been placed at his disposal by Admiral de Robeck, so that he could move at once to any point where he was required, but when about 11.30 a.m. he asked for her, he was informed she was drawing fires owing to boiler trouble and was not available. He begged the order should be revoked and that she should go to the military water ship to fill her boilers. This was not done, and as there was nothing else ready at Kephalo except the Commander-in-Chief's yacht *Triad*, the General had to stay where he was. Fortunately an hour later Admiral de Robeck, no less uneasy than the General, telegraphed for the *Triad* and informed him she would sail for Suvla at 4.0 p.m. Still, owing to further difficulties it was not till 4.30 that he got away. So anxious indeed was the Admiral that he seems to have drafted a signal to General Hamilton saying it was important that they should meet either at Suvla or Imbros, but presumably when it was known that the General was coming in the *Triad* the message was not sent.[1]

He arrived, at 6.0 p.m., to find that throughout the whole precious day no further progress had been possible. The failure to get on was the more to be regretted, for at Anzac an attack which had been launched at dawn on Chunuk Bair and Hill Q had not succeeded. In spite of another day's exemplary fighting all they had done was to get a lodgment on the saddle between those two heights. There the Anzacs had been able to entrench, but everywhere else the troops had been met by overwhelming numbers and had had to fall back on the position of the day before.

[1] The only direct communication between the two Commanders-in-Chief was by wireless through *Chatham* and *Exmouth*. The message does not appear in the signal log of either ship nor in that of the *Triad*. By 1.15 a.m. on August 7 a cable had been run out from Imbros, but it was brought ashore at Nibrunesi Point.

It was therefore of the last importance to give the main effort, which was to be resumed next day, all possible support. General Stopford had ordered an attack for dawn, but General Hamilton, feeling there was not a moment to lose if the enemy's reinforcements for the coveted positions were to be anticipated, was for attacking immediately. He therefore went ashore, and overruling all objections made by the corps and divisional commanders, himself ordered the only brigade (32nd) which seemed to be concentrated to advance at once on Tekke Tepe and the heights north of Anafarta Sagir. At the same time one battalion of the 33rd Brigade was directed to fill the gap between Chocolate Hill and Damakjelik Bair. The LIIIrd Division, under Major-General The Hon. J. E. Lindley, which had been retained at Mudros with the LIVth in general reserve, arrived at Suvla and landed during the night.

From the other quarters of the field the news was little better. At Lone Pine the fighting had been incessant, but it was still held. In the Helles zone also fighting had been continuous. Again and again the Turks had counter-attacked in great force, only to be driven back with heavy loss. To this extent the operation was succeeding as a holding attack, but no real progress towards Krithia and Achi Baba had been possible. Yet from the naval effort to assist the general plan there was one cheering success to record. It came from the Marmara submarines. After a further adventurous cruise during the last week in July Commander Boyle in *E 14* had come down to meet his successor, Commander Nasmith in *E 11*, who came up on August 5, ten days after the *Mariotte* was lost. Without incident Commander Nasmith reached Nagara Point, but on rounding it was caught in the new net. In a few minutes, however, he broke through, and immediately afterwards (7.0 a.m.) torpedoed a three-masted transport in Ak Bashi harbour, which was being used for troops and supplies coming from Asia. The following afternoon the two submarines met, and *E 11* was able to give Commander Boyle his orders for combining with the great attack. It was now well ascertained that all troops coming from Constantinople had to march by the Gallipoli road, and at two places it was exposed to the sea—at the Bulair lines and at the Dohan Aslan Bank, five miles to the eastward. Here they were to lie and watch the road. They were about to proceed to their station when a gunboat, the *Berc-i-Satvet* came in sight. Both boats gave chase, and eventually at 4.30 *E 11* torpedoed her off Silivri, an ancient port midway on the northern coast, where she managed to beach herself.

As soon as it was dark they made back to the Straits, and at daybreak were submerged watching the road, *E 14* at Bulair and *E 11* to the eastward. For some time nothing appeared out of the dust that arose on the road except bullocks, but by 11.30 *E 11* could see troops, and rising to the surface she quickly scattered them. Half an hour later another column appeared, and this she compelled to open out and take cover. Apparently the men crept forward unseen, for presently *E 14* got them, and *E 11*, who had followed them down, soon joined her, and for the best part of an hour they had them under shell fire. Still the troops were not stopped. In spite of the punishment they hurried on, "marching at high speed," and suffered heavily, especially from *E 11*, who had mounted a 12-pounder in place of her 6-pounder. Only when a field gun opened an accurate fire were they forced to dive. But yet they had not done. Rising again they found the Turks resting and again they took toll till the field gun once more interfered.[1]

Still this was by no means the end. Bigger game was at hand. Before the submarines appeared in the Marmara it will be recalled that the Turks were in the habit of sending down battleships to disturb our ships bombarding over the land and to harass the anchorage at Anzac. Since May 21 none had appeared, but now that everything was at hazard they had decided to send down the *Barbarousse Haireddine* with sorely needed munitions to support the defence of the peninsula.[2] At dawn on the 8th *E 11* could see her steaming westward past the Bulair lines. She had a destroyer screening her, but Commander Nasmith attacked and at 5.0 a.m. torpedoed her amidships. The battleship at once took a heavy list, altered course for the shore and opened a rapid fire at his periscope. A second shot was impossible, but in twenty minutes a large flash as of an explosion was seen and she slowly rolled over and sank. With her were lost 253 Turkish seamen. Against the troops little more could be done, for the exposed roads were now too well protected by artillery, but though foiled in this work *E 14* was able to torpedo a 5,000-ton supply ship as she approached Dohan Aslan. She was able to beach herself, and there was shelled by both boats till she was in flames. But this was not her end. A day or two later she was to suffer another attack of an entirely novel character.

For some time past the *Ben-My-Chree* had been practising dropping torpedoes from her seaplanes, and the difficulties

[1] On the 6th *E 11* was bombed by an aeroplane without effect.

[2] *Barbarousse Haireddine*, 9,000 tons, 6–11″. For her orders, see Liman von Sanders' *Fünf Jähre Turkei*, p. 117.

had now been so far overcome that the first attempt was to be made. The scouting planes had reported a large transport lying close inshore near the Bulair lines. Proceeding up to the head of the Gulf of Xeros the *Ben-My-Chree*, on the 12th, successfully got off one of her planes, piloted by Flight-Commander C. H. K. Edmonds. Passing over the Bulair isthmus at a height of 1,500 feet he saw his quarry lying just west of Injeh Burnu. To ensure a successful attack it had been found that the shot must not be taken at a greater height than fifteen feet. Passing the ship at this elevation and at a distance of three hundred yards he released his torpedo. As he rose again rapidly under fire the track could be seen running true till it took the enemy amidships with a big explosion. She was too close in to sink, but she settled down, and Flight-Commander Edmonds on his return from his brilliant and unprecedented exploit could be congratulated on having rendered useless one of the last of the enemy's large transports and in adding a new terror to naval warfare. Nevertheless, although this detracted little from the merit of his exploit, he had really killed the slain, for as the ship was reported to be of 5,000 tons and to be lying between the Dohan Aslan bank and Injeh Burnu, she was without doubt the one that Commander Boyle in *E 14* had disabled at this spot, on the 8th.[1]

As the seaplane was finishing his victim he himself, having completed his cruise, was again coming down the Straits. This time he was caught in the Nagara net, but he quickly broke through it, and so, after being missed by a torpedo as he passed the Narrows and fouling an electric contact mine whose wires his propellers carried away, he got safely back, with his crew exhausted by sickness, having completed his sixty-eighth day in the Marmara.[2]

How much exactly the submarines had done to retard the ever-increasing strength of the enemy in the peninsula cannot be told, but as units in the great amphibious combination they had certainly pulled their weight. All that we can affirm is that neither their activity nor any other of the subsidiary operations availed to prevent the enemy bringing up their reserves to the critical zone. So well had they been disposed by the German Staff that the time which had been lost after the first surprise had proved ample for bringing them into action at Anzac and Suvla. On August 9 another desperate attack was made on Chunuk Bair and Hill Q, the next height on the ridge. At daylight the *Bacchante*, supported

[1] Two more vessels were torpedoed on the 17th by another seaplane.

[2] On this cruise of 22 days he had sunk two steamers and 22 sailing vessels.

by the *Endymion*, a monitor and three destroyers, and every gun ashore that would bear were concentrating on it, till in three-quarters of an hour the whole ridge was a mass of flames and smoke. Then in three columns the attack was launched. The saddle between the two hills was rushed, and the troops that gained it were able to look down the other side upon the Dardanelles. In spite of every effort to turn them out they held on; elsewhere the attack failed, and by night the troops were back practically in the morning's positions.

Next day (the 10th) the attack was renewed, but only to meet ever-increasing forces and to collapse without result. Up on Sari Bair the accumulation of the enemy was so great that by sheer weight of numbers our men were swept off the dearly won saddle, but there the Turkish success ended. Flushed with victory and confident in their numbers, they advanced to drive our exhausted men down the way they had come, but as soon as the first line topped the ridge it was caught by the artillery and the ships and simply swept away. Undismayed, they came on again, line after line and mass after mass, in splendid style, giving a target such as our gunners seldom saw, and every time their gallant men disappeared in the storm of shell and were seen no more. On this day also the Turks made two determined attacks on the foothills where the Suvla and Anzac forces had joined hands. Both were repulsed, and so in glorious failure the great attempt came to an end.

From Suvla there had been little support, in spite of all General Hamilton could do to provide it. The night attack of the 32nd Brigade had failed. Both General Hamilton and Admiral de Robeck, who had been watching the attack from the bridge of the *Triad*, were eager to secure the Anafarta Ridge from Ejelmer Bay to the village of Anafarta Sagir, in order to make Suvla Bay safe from the enemy's guns. With this object in view the General again went ashore early on the 9th and began urging that General Mahon should be pushed on from the point on the sea ridge where, in spite of the assistance of ship fire on his flank, he was being held up by a small force of gendarmerie. General Stopford, however, saw difficulties, and General Hamilton, finding the corps too dispirited for an immediate attack on the Anafarta Ridge, went off to Anzac to confer with General Birdwood. There still remained one division in reserve, Major-General F. S. Inglefield's as yet untried Essex Territorials (LIVth), and as General Birdwood said he could not use it against Sari Bair, owing to the difficulty of getting water forward, and agreed that Anafarta Ridge was for the moment more important, it was decided to land it at Suvla. Whilst they were being disembarked on the following day (10th), an unsuccessful attack on Chocolate Hill was made by the LIIIrd Division, and the 11th was spent in reorganising the line. With the fresh troops now under his command General Stopford was urged to make a dash for Kavak Tepe and Tekke Tepe, the two culminating heights on the Anafarta Ridge. Still the inertia of the IXth Corps could not be overcome. General Stopford had no faith in his troops, he was nervous about advancing before he had cleared the rough ground on his right up to the Anafarta village, and nothing came of it but a few half-hearted attempts which still further dispirited the whole corps. General Hamilton could not believe the fault lay with the men; he knew them, and knew that precisely similar new formations had just been doing all that soldiers could do under vigorous leadership at Anzac, and could not believe that a real effort to secure the peace of the bay would not succeed. At all costs the attempt must be renewed, for it had now become too evident that the capture of the dominating heights was vital to the whole plan. On the 12th, while the navy was working its hardest at completing landing-places and getting ashore the gear and supplies most urgently needed, and at the same time was evacuating the crowds of wounded, shrapnel began to rain on the supporting ships, and before they could get away they had suffered fifty casualties. It was now General Hamilton decided on a change in the Suvla command, and on the 15th he called up Major-General De Lisle from Helles to supersede General Stopford in command of the IXth Corps pending the arrival from France of Lieutenant-General The Hon. J. H. G. Byng. Other changes were made at the same time and Major-General W. E. Peyton was, moreover, expected on the 18th with his 5,000 dismounted Yeomanry from Egypt.

General De Lisle's instructions were to land at Suvla and reorganise his corps for the new attack which General Hamilton had in mind.[1] It was designed on a different plan from the last. The main force of the attack was to be thrown against the Anafarta Spur, with its two dominant heights Scimitar Hill and "W" Hill, the possession of which he now considered would best secure the safety of Suvla Bay and open the way for a further advance through Anafarta Sagir to envelop the force that was defying the Anzacs

[1] The IXth Corps would be composed as follows:—Xth Division (less one brigade, the 29th, at Anzac, but with the 5,000 Yeomanry attached); the XIth, LIIIrd and LIVth Divisions. Owing to casualties the corps could only concentrate 10,000 rifles for the projected attack.

on the coveted Sari Bair Ridge.[1] The Anzacs would be able to do no more than swing forward their left, which had remained bent back south-west along the Damakjelik Bair Spur, and endeavour to seize the important wells at Kabak Kuyu and Hill 60. This height with " W " Hill formed, as it were, the gallery of the Anafarta Valley and commanded its whole extent, so that their possession would decide whether the valley was a road for our further advance or a highway for the enemy's reinforcements. The rest of the force, that is, the XIth Division, was merely to hold the line from Scimitar Hill northwards to the sea.

For the present, of course, a renewal of the attempt to gain the main objective at Sari Bair was out of the question. The new troops had lost too heavily and were too much disorganised for such an operation without a large increase of force, and General Hamilton was asking for 45,000 drafts to fill his depleted ranks and 50,000 new reinforcements.

For the preliminary work immediately in hand General De Lisle could only report that it would take several days to get the corps fit for the attack. But time was of the utmost importance, for with every day that passed the Turks were increasing their strength. Their efforts in this direction fortunately gave a solution of the dilemma. Word came up from Helles that in spite of all we could do there to hold down the Turks troops were being withdrawn to the northward. On this General Hamilton decided to move up the old XXIXth Division and call on them for one more effort. They began to arrive on the 18th, and the effect of their presence amongst the new troops became rapidly apparent, so that the operation could be fixed for the 21st.

Much was hoped for from the preparatory bombardment, for, though the artillery, which it had been as yet possible to land, was not up to strength, a special new scheme of fire was worked out for the supporting ships, and the *Venerable* came into Suvla Bay to reinforce them. In order, moreover, to take all possible chances from the advantage of the light, the attack was timed for the afternoon, when the low sun always sharply defined the lines of the enemy's trenches and was full in the eyes of the defending force.

As things turned out, all that had been arranged to give the infantry the utmost support proved unavailing. By one of the many ill turns the weather did us, the atmospheric conditions which had prevailed so long suddenly changed. The morning of the 21st revealed the whole Suvla region enveloped in a low mist. Spotting both for the shore and

[1] "Instructions to General De Lisle," *Gallipoli Diary*, Vol. II., p. 335.

ship guns was practically impossible, and the infantry had to do the work with no effective help. Yet they did wonders. In spite of forest fires that held them up in places, in spite of some confusion caused by certain units losing their direction, the XXIXth Division with splendid dash reached the top of Scimitar Hill, the Yeomanry, coming on in support over the open like veteran troops, forced their way up "W" Hill, but neither point could be held—they were simply swept away by shell fire, which the ships in the low visibility could not check, and they had to fall back to the old front line, whence the fine attack had started.

On the other side of the valley General Cox, who now had the Anzac left, had better fortune.[1] That evening the invaluable wells at Susak Kuyu were won and a lodgment effected on Hill 60, and, in spite of desperate efforts by the Turks, were held. Next morning (22nd) the counter-attack continued, but in spite of it most of the ground was made good and connection established both with the rest of the Anzac line and with General Peyton's Yeomanry. The situation was thus much improved. Though the whole of Hill 60 had not been gained, the line had been straightened, much elbow room had been won, which opened a freer communication between Anzac and Suvla, and the burning question of water supply was materially eased.

Both at Suvla and Anzac the following three days passed quietly, but on the afternoon of the 27th another effort was made to capture Hill 60 by a force of 1,000 fit men. These had to be drawn from no fewer than nine battalions owing to sickness and battle casualties having greatly reduced every unit in the area. After very severe fighting against determined opposition a firm hold was gained on the southern slopes of the hill and on the spur to its immediate right. The upper half of the enclosed work still defied capture, however, and reinforcements pushed into the attack that night could make little progress. On the 28th the captured position was retained and improved, and, with an additional reinforcement, the attack was renewed an hour after midnight. Fighting continued till after daybreak and this time persistence seemed at long last to be rewarded with success, but the morning revealed that the captured trenches did not encircle the hill. The actual summit was still in the hands of the

[1] Besides his own 29th Brigade of Indian infantry he had the 4th Australian Brigade, two battalions of the New Zealand Mounted Rifles, two of the 29th Brigade from the Xth (Irish) Division, and the 4th South Wales Borderers.

enemy. One more thrust might have finished the work, but the truth seems to have been that the whole corps was now completely spent.

In the great August offensive (6th to 29th) the British casualties totalled nearly 38,000. Still the well-planned strategical surprise had failed. What that failure meant for the Central Powers is well put by General Liman von Sanders. " Had the campaign," he says, " been brought to the tactical decision which the landing at Anafarta had in view, the batteries in the coastal forts, which were not well supplied with ammunition, would have been destroyed. The mines would have been swept in the Narrows, and the victorious army and fleet would have had no difficulty in combining against Constantinople. A Russian landing would certainly have followed. Our intelligence reports from Athens and Bucharest were quite explicit about the transports being assembled at Odessa. The Western Powers would then have established secure communications with Russia and have torn Turkey away from the Central Powers. Under such conditions it is most improbable that Bulgaria would ever have abandoned her neutrality and plunged into so unpromising a military situation."[1] Such were the results which the brilliant management of General Hamilton's design had seemed at first to promise. By a hair's breadth it had failed, and now nothing more was to be hoped from the Dardanelles without reinforcements so large as materially to affect the position in other theatres and demand a reconstruction of the whole Allied war plan.

[1] *Fünf Jähre Turkei*, p. 116.

CHAPTER VI

GENERAL SITUATION AFTER SUVLA—THE COLLAPSE OF THE RUSSIAN FRONT—CHANGE IN THE FRENCH ATTITUDE —PERIL OF SERBIA—BRITISH SUBMARINES IN THE MARMARA

THE news of the failure to turn the Turkish position at Gallipoli, or even to establish a secure footing at Suvla from which there was hope of turning it in the near future, reached the Cabinet at a moment when the cup of their difficulties was already brimming over. They were face to face with one of those striking developments of the war which must always be a landmark in its course. " On account of the general situation," so Lord Kitchener had telegraphed to General Hamilton on the eve of the battle of Scimitar Hill, " it is very desirable at the present juncture that a success should be obtained either in France or the Dardanelles." So desirable indeed was it felt to be, that at the same time Admiral de Robeck was informed that if any of his old battleships could make any really decisive or important contribution to the success of the land operations, he might use them in any way he thought desirable.

At the moment there was nothing to be done, nor after the failure at Suvla was there any present hope of such an occasion arising for at least several months. General Hamilton had further been told that a serious offensive in co-operation with the French was being organised on the Western Front, and that he was not to count on any large divisional units being diverted from France. He must rely on such drafts and reinforcements as were on the way to him and on such further troops as could be spared from Egypt. These, as he pointed out in his reply, would be barely sufficient to enable him to hold on to the new ground he had seized; and the whole situation at the Dardanelles sank into a deadlock of trench warfare, with no prospect of obtaining there the success which was so sorely needed to break the gloom of the general outlook.

The cloud that had settled down on the prospects of the Entente was due to the successful German campaign in the

East. The vast offensive which they had begun in the middle of July in concert with the Austrians had given startling results. On August 5, after a third tremendous battle before Warsaw, the city had been occupied by the Germans. Simultaneously an Austro-German army entered Ivangorod, the great railway centre to the southward, sixty miles up the Vistula. Another Austrian army, advancing northward from Galicia against the Russian left, was already in possession of the next junction at Lublin, and to the northward the Germans were pressing on through the Baltic Provinces against the enemy's right. It was clear the whole Russian Front was broken; on August 17 Kovno fell to the Germans, who thus directly threatened Riga; on the 25th/26th Brest-Litovsk, the key of the Russian centre, was in their hands, and they had definitely pushed the enemy back to a line that ran roughly southward from the Gulf of Riga.

At present, therefore, all hope of carrying through the original plan of the Dardanelles enterprise was gone. Even if we succeeded in breaking through to the Bosporus, Russia would not be able to join hands with us for crushing Turkey out of the hostile alliance. With the overpowering moral impression of the Austro-German advance, Bulgaria must be looked upon rather as a probable enemy than a possible ally. From Italy no help could come, as at one time we had hoped. Her first great effort against Austria was exhausted. By August 10 the fighting on the Isonzo, which had begun at the end of June, had come to an end, and although our Allies had established themselves on the river in enemy territory, the defensive front which the Austrians had taken up remained unbroken.[1] To make matters worse, the relaxation of the Italian pressure was marked by an Austro-German concentration on the Serbian frontier. We had therefore to face the prospect that at any time a third invasion of that unhappy country might begin, with Rumania in a position which made it difficult for her to move, and Bulgaria lurking in keen anticipation for the moment when she could safely play jackal to the Central Powers.

In France—in political circles at least—the deepening danger of seeing the German dream of expansion in the East come true was being realised with scarcely less apprehension than it was by our own Government; but we had no conception that it was likely to affect their war plans until, on September 1, they applied to know if we could

[1] What the Italians call the first battle of the Isonzo began on June 29 and ended on July 7. The second battle was from July 18 to August 10. The third did not begin till October 18.

supply transport for four divisions from Marseilles to the Ægean. At first sight the request seemed to promise a new light of hope for the Dardanelles, but, on the other hand, so sudden a change of our Ally's attitude to the ill-starred enterprise was difficult to understand. Were they converted to our Easterners' view that the best way to weld the efforts of the Entente into unity was a decisive blow at Turkey, or did the new departure spring from some obscure political origin? We could not tell, and so further uncertainty was added to the tangled situation.

Possibly the French proposal was a hybrid that had the stamp of both parents. On July 22 General Joffre, without consulting the Minister for War, had deprived General Sarrail of the command of the Third Army. His action came with something of a shock to the Government. General Sarrail was the man who had held Verdun against the first rush of the Germans and saved it for France. An officer of already high professional reputation, he thus became a national hero, especially with the politicians of the "Left." There was consequently a strong desire to soften his fall. The recent news that General Gouraud would be incapacitated by his wounds for a long time offered the required opportunity, and as soon as General Sarrail reached Paris he was offered the command at the Dardanelles. He refused on the ground that he could not accept a command inferior to that of which he had been deprived. His conditions for taking up the proffered post were that a separate "Army of the East" should be formed, that he was not to be under the British Commander-in-Chief, and that he was not to leave France till he could sail with the reinforcing divisions.

The first condition was the only one on which any assurance could be given. It happened to be entirely in accord with the views of certain members of the Government, and in particular M. Briand, a former premier and now Keeper of the Seals. Ever since December 1914, when the Serbians had so triumphantly flung the Austrians out of their country, he, like some of our own Ministers, had seen the key of the war in a vigorous intervention in the Balkans, his idea being that an army should be specially formed for the purpose. To this project he now recurred, and on August 3 General Sarrail was gazetted to the command of "L'Armée d'Orient." It was, of course, as yet a mere phantom army which was far from satisfying General Sarrail's conditions, but as a first step he was called on to furnish a plan of campaign.[1] The

[1] Général Sarrail. *Mon commandement en Orient*, pp. vii–ix; Mermeix, *Joffre. La Première Crise du Commandement*, pp. 82–3.

memorandum he presented was very comprehensive, embracing a number of alternative plans, but as a condition of all of them he insisted on the Gallipoli theatre being left to the British, while his own army, including the two French divisions then under General Hamilton, was to be employed elsewhere. Various lines of operation on the Asiatic side were considered. They included a direct attack to clear that side of the Straits, a more ambitious advance from the Gulf of Adramyti, the capture of Smyrna, and lastly the old idea of a descent at Alexandretta. But preferably to all these plans he finally recommended as the best means of securing a definite effect in the East an intervention in Serbia from Salonika.[1] The memorandum was referred to General Joffre, who was as firmly as ever opposed to any withdrawal of troops from France, and General Sarrail was told he had cast his net too wide. Operations at Anzac, Bulair, or on the Asiatic shore of the Straits were all that could be contemplated, and he was called on for a second memorandum on this restricted basis.

At this point a further complication set in. At the moment when General Hamilton's request for large drafts and reinforcements came to hand he had been told that no answer could be given till Lord Kitchener returned from France, where he had gone to confer with our Ally about a radical change of plan which the gloomy outlook on the Eastern Front seemed to demand. At an earlier conference held at Calais in July it had been settled that no serious offensive should be attempted in France till our joint strength had been developed to a point at which our preponderance of force would give definite hope of a telling success. But now, in view of the alarming collapse of the Russian Front, it was felt that this decision could not be adhered to. Unless something was done to relieve the pressure on our Eastern Ally, there was a possibility of her making a separate peace, as she had done under similar conditions with Napoleon in 1807. This was the fear that was echoed in the telegrams which Lord Kitchener sent to General Hamilton as soon as he returned, telling him how the general situation called for a success in France or the Dardanelles. Nothing appears to have been settled definitely, but although objection was raised that we could not hope to acquire an adequate preponderance this year, it was taken as settled that no increase of the Dardanelles force could be drawn from France

[1] See Sarrail, *Mon commandement en Orient*, p. 297, where the memorandum is given in full.

till after the offensive had been attempted—probably in September. The utmost that could be done was to supply General Hamilton with drafts to replace his casualties, and for the conveyance of these troops the whole of our available transport was earmarked for two months to come.

In these circumstances the French request for transport for four divisions came with all the greater surprise. While on our side we had decided to postpone a decision as to increasing the strength of our effort in the Dardanelles till a full report had been received from General Hamilton, in France the movement for providing General Sarrail with his Armée d'Orient had never ceased. Besides four divisions from France, it was to comprise, as General Sarrail had stipulated, the two already at Gallipoli, and these Lord Kitchener had hinted he would have to replace with two from Sir John French's army. In addition to this stumbling-block the difficulty of providing transport from the French marine was proving so great that in Paris the Opposition were using it as an insuperable objection to the whole plan. Hence the application for our assistance. The Admiralty were already up to their eyes in transport difficulties, but they had never yet refused to provide what military exigencies demanded. With increased effort, they said, it might be done, but the French should be called on to provide destroyer escort. Owing to the growing menace of submarines in the Mediterranean, the protection of transports was an increasing anxiety. Nevertheless, so anxious were we to fall in with our Ally's proposal that, in spite of the fresh burden the French request would entail, a telegram was sent saying that arrangements were being made to transport the required troops and stores to Mityleni by the end of September, and no demand was made for assistance in protecting them.

Yet there was reason enough for such a demand. Hitherto the anti-submarine organisation in the Ægean had seemed to be all that was required, but on August 13 the *Royal Edward*, a transport of 11,000 tons, carrying drafts from Egypt for the XXIXth Division and other details to the number of nearly 1,400 officers and men, was torpedoed just as she was approaching Kandeliusa island, off the Gulf of Kos.[1] It was a landfall on the direct route into the Ægean from Alexandria which the transports for Mudros were still taking, and was in the patrol area assigned to the

[1] Besides drafts for the XXIXth Division, she carried 300 R.A.M.C., 200 Labour Corps—in all 31 officers and 1,335 men.

French. It would appear that the German submarine *UB 14*, one of the new small class that had been brought overland to the Adriatic in sections, had put into the Gulf of Kos on her way from Cattaro to the Bosporus in order to operate against the transport line. Her lurking-place was in a lonely little cove called Orak bay, ten miles east of Budrum, in the vicinity of which we had long suspected that a submarine base had been established, but whether or not it existed it had never been discovered. As soon as the loss was known two French destroyers were ordered to the spot; the hospital ship *Soudan* was also there and a trawler or two, but between them they saved less than 500 souls.

After this catastrophe the route was changed. Transports were ordered to give the Asiatic coast a wider berth, and passing through the channel east of Crete, to proceed inside the Greek islands, and not debouch till they reached the Doro Channel south of Eubœa. For a fortnight the plan was successful, but on September 2, a few hours after the reply to the French request for transport went out, news arrived that another transport from Egypt to Mudros had been torpedoed south of Strati island, within thirty miles of her destination. This was the *Southland*, a ship of 12,000 tons, with over 1,400 men on board, nearly all for the IInd Australian Division. It was the same submarine which was apparently now making for the Bosporus that dealt the blow, but this time it was not fatal. The ship did not sink at once, so that all but about forty men were able to take to the boats, and as another of this group of transports, the *Neuralia*, boldly insisted on standing by, in spite of the risk she ran, they were quickly picked up. When two hours later the nearest patrol destroyer, *Racoon*, arrived on the scene, the *Southland* was still afloat, and, thanks to the devotion of her engineers and both naval and military volunteers, the destroyer's captain, Lieutenant-Commander H. N. M. Hardy, was able to get her into Mudros that evening without further loss.

The same day that the news of this second attack was received in London the appreciation which General Hamilton had been called upon to furnish came to hand. It was to the effect that no fresh line of attack was possible. The only chance of success was to carry on from Suvla and Anzac in order to get possession of the neck between Maidos and Gaba Tepe. The difficulty was that until his exhausted troops had recovered their tone a further effort would mean mere waste of life. There must be a period of rest, during which the Turks would be able to strengthen their position so formidably that there was no hope of mastering it until the large reinforcements he had already asked for reached him. Meanwhile he intended to do what he could to worry the enemy, but for the present, unless new strength came from fresh allied troops or from a change in the political situation in the Balkans, offensive action must be confined to the navy. Here he saw some light to relieve the darkness of his outlook. It shone from the submarines in the Marmara.[1] So striking had been the success of the few which had been operating there, that he believed an increase of the number would avail to stop entirely the sea communications of the enemy. They would then have no line of supply except the Bulair road, and once confined to that precarious route they would be unable to maintain so large a force as had now been accumulated in the peninsula.

In the latest exploits of the submarines he certainly had ground enough for his confidence in their abilities. Day by day their activities had been growing more daring and successful. After sinking the battleship *Barbarousse Haired-dine* near Gallipoli, on the following day (August 9) Commander Nasmith in *E 11* communicated with *E 14* at a secret rendezvous and replenished with torpedoes. He then went on to San Stefano. As this was the first headland west of the Bosporus on the European side, it was the most vulnerable point on the coastwise route to Gallipoli. It was defended by guns and a small destroyer, which he engaged, but without hitting her before he was forced to dive. Then after burning half a dozen sailing craft he proceeded across to Mudania. This port, it must be remembered, was the sea outlet of the Brusa area, with which it was connected by rail, and as such it was never left long in peace. Having bombarded the railway station and secured three hits before he was put under by the shore guns, he disappeared, to turn up again at San Stefano. He now found it watched by an aeroplane, which bombed him off, and as his ammunition was nearly spent he returned to the westward to communicate with the *Aster* sloop, which at this time was the linking ship on the other side of Bulair.

After a short bombardment of Artaki on the Asiatic side, on the next day (August 14) he met *E 2* at the rendezvous. Lieutenant-Commander D. de B. Stocks had just brought her up successfully, in spite of having been caught in the Nagara net with a half turn of 3½-inch wire round his 12-

[1] See Map 3.

pounder. Smaller wires were foul of the conning tower and wireless mast, and depth charges were exploding all round him. For a while things looked ugly, but by boldly giving his boat negative buoyancy and alternately backing and speeding up he broke through in eight minutes. The weight of the boat as she got free carried her down to 140 feet before he could regain control, but he then was able to carry on, and before joining *E 11* at the rendezvous he had sunk an armed steamer off the entrance of the Gulf of Artaki.

He had brought up a fresh supply of ammunition for his consort, and after taking it on board, Commander Nasmith went back to the Bosporus, where with admirable skill and patience he next day (August 15) torpedoed a steamer which was lying alongside the Haidar Pasha railway pier. In the evening he was back at the rendezvous with *E 2*, and after doing some gunnery together they proceeded in company to San Stefano. Here they engaged a patrol steamer, and hit her three times before being forced to dive. She then retired into the Bosporus. *E 11* then went over to Ismid Gulf and bombarded the railway viaduct. After securing several hits she disappeared, and by the 18th was once more scattering troops on the Bulair neck. *E 2*, after repairing her gun mounting, which had carried away in the action with the patrol steamer, was equally active in all quarters, and the ubiquity of the two boats, and the havoc they played almost every day with the coastwise traffic, multiplied their number in Turkish eyes to a paralysing degree.

Still unsatisfied, Commander Nasmith was planning a more serious attack on the railway, which the bombardment had hitherto failed to damage effectively. When all preparations were ready for the highly adventurous plan he had in mind, on the night of August 20–21 he stole into the Gulf of Ismid and worked the submarine in till her bows just touched the ground at a little cove half a mile east of Eski Hissar village. His second in command, Lieutenant G. D'Oyly-Hughes, then slipped into the water, pushing before him a little raft which had been previously prepared to carry his clothes and accoutrements and 16 lbs. of gun-cotton. Finding the cliffs were unscalable at the point where he landed, he had to relaunch the raft and swim further along the coast till he reached a less precipitous place. Armed with a revolver and a bayonet, and carrying an electric torch and a whistle for signalling purposes, he laboriously dragged his heavy charge up the cliffs, and in half an hour reached the railway. Finding it unwatched, he followed alongside the track towards the viaduct, but he had only gone about a quarter of a mile when he heard voices ahead, and soon was aware of three men sitting beside the line in loud conversation. It was impossible to proceed further undetected, and after watching them for some time, in hopes of seeing them move away, he decided to leave his heavy charge of gun-cotton where he was and make a detour inland to examine possibilities at the viaduct. Beyond stumbling into a farmyard and waking the noisy poultry, he managed to get in sight of the viaduct without adventure, but only to find he was again beaten. A number of men with a stationary engine at work were moving actively about, apparently repairing the damage which the bombardments had caused. Clearly there was nothing to be done there, and the only course was to retrace his steps and to look for a vulnerable place up the line where he could explode his charge effectively. A suitable spot where the track was carried across a small hollow was soon found—too soon, in fact, for it was no more than 150 yards from where the three men were still talking. But the place was too good to leave alone, and deciding to take the risk, he laid his charge, and then, muffling the fuse pistol as well as he could, he fired it, and made off. For all his care the men heard the crack, started to their feet and gave chase. To return by the way he came was now impossible. His only chance was to run down the line as fast as he could. From time to time pistol shots were exchanged. They had no effect on either side, and after about a mile's chase he had outdistanced his pursuers and was close to the shore. Plunging into the sea, he swam out, and as he did so the blast of the explosion was heard, and débris began to fall all about him, to tell of the damage he had done.

Yet his adventure was far from over. The cove where the submarine was lying hidden was three-quarters of a mile to the eastward, and, when about 500 yards out he ventured to signal with a blast on his whistle, not a sound reached him. By this time day was breaking and his peril was great. Exhausted with his long swim in his clothes, he had to get back to shore for a rest. After hiding a while amongst the rocks he started swimming again towards the cove, till at last an answer came to his whistle. Even so the end was not yet. At the same moment rifle shots rang out from the cliffs. They were directed on the submarine, which was now going astern out of the cove. In the morning mist the weary swimmer did not recognise her. Seeing only her bow, gun, and conning tower she appeared like three small boats, and he hastily made for the beach to hide again amongst the rocks. Once ashore, however, he discovered his mistake, and hailing his deliverer, he once more took to the water. So after a short swim he was picked up in the last stage of exhaustion, and his daring adventure came to a happy end.[1]

As for *E 11* her remarkable cruise was still far from finished. On her way out of the gulf she met *E 2*, who had been operating at the other end of the sea, and the previous day in Artaki Bay had torpedoed a steamer of about 1,500 tons, armed with three or four guns, and cut her completely in two. After exchanging experiences they separated again, *E 2* making for Mudania and *E 11* for the Bosporus. Here at nightfall she fell in with a convoy of three armed tugs with eight sailing vessels in tow with a destroyer as escort. Preceding them in the moonlight through the night, Commander Nasmith attacked at dawn. Three times he nearly got into position for torpedoing the destroyer, but thrice her clever handling foiled him. By this time, however, the convoy was broken up, the tugs had slipped their tows, and eventually, after engaging them with gun fire all the morning, he sank one of the tugs and a dhow, and severely injured several others. The sunken dhow proved to have an important passenger on board, for amongst the prisoners he picked up was the manager of a German bank taking a quantity of money to the bank at Chanak—an eloquent testimony of the straits the enemy was put to for keeping up communication with the Gallipoli peninsula.

His time was now nearly up, but he had still to crown his cruise with a telling blow. The following day (August 23), being then well to the westward, he heard from the *Aster* that a number of transports were in the Dardanelles. On getting the news he proceeded to the rendezvous to find *E 2*. She, however, was not there. The previous day she had sunk a large steamer off Mudania pier, and was still busy in that quarter. Commander Nasmith therefore carried on alone, going right down the Straits to Ak Bashi Liman.[2] Here, just short of the Nagara net, the main Turkish sea base had been established when the more convenient Kilia Liman opposite Nagara Point was made untenable by our ship fire over the neck of the peninsula. The harbour was full of shipping, with a gunboat on guard, and at this vessel he fired a shot. The torpedo passed beneath her keel, but

[1] For his service Lieutenant D'Oyly-Hughes was awarded the D.S.O.

[2] See Vol. II., Map 4.

exploded amongst the shipping behind her. What damage was done could not be seen, for the gunboat and a destroyer at once came for him. After diving to avoid them, he three hours later returned to the attack, and firing both tubes, succeeded in sinking two large transports. Then, moving up a little, he got another. After this exploit he carried on up the Straits to Chardak Liman, the port at which grain from the Asiatic provinces was collected and ground for the supply of the Gallipoli army, and here he completed the day's work by sinking a fourth large transport with his last torpedo. As he entered the Marmara again he fell in with his consort and arranged that she should go down to Ak Bashi Liman next day to finish what he had left undone, while he took a well-earned rest to clean up. To *E 2* fell the same bad luck. She, too, missed the gunboat, and saw her torpedo explode amongst the shipping still afloat around the wrecks of her consort's victims. After vainly trying to get in another shot, she fired at a transport near Bergaz Iskalessi on the Asiatic side. The torpedo exploded well abreast the funnel, but it was doubtful whether it had not hit a small craft alongside her.

On August 28 they were both together again, once more bombarding Mudania railway station. Then after another attack on the Ismid viaduct and destroying a number more of the coasting craft (between them they had up to this time accounted for some forty of these vessels) *E 11* prepared to go down, while *E 2* went up to Constantinople, where she found nothing to attack. On September 3, Commander Nasmith, having dismantled his gun and fitted extra jumping wires, started at 2.0 a.m., and after easily breaking through the Nagara net arrived safely at Helles after a seven hours' run. Thus ended his record cruise, during which in twenty-nine days he had sunk or destroyed a battleship, a gunboat, six transports, and an armed steamer, as well as twenty-three sailing vessels, from whose cargoes of fresh victuals and fruit he had been able to keep his men in good health.

So far success had been uninterrupted, but there was now to be a reverse to the picture. On September 5 *E 2* went to the rendezvous to meet *E 7*, which was coming up to be her consort in relief of *E 11*, but she was not there. Under Lieutenant-Commander Cochrane she had reached the Nagara net in safety at 7.30 the previous morning, and at 100 feet had actually got her bows through when one of her propellers got foul of it. In vain she tried to push on with the other, but the only effect was to bring her broadside on to the net hopelessly entangled. Hour after hour, in spite of mines bursting round him, her gallant commander with every device that coolness and resource could suggest strove to get free. For nearly twelve hours the struggle went on dauntlessly, till a depth charge was dropped close to the hull and exploded so violently that the electric light fittings and other gear were broken. Realising then that there was no more to be done, he decided to surrender. Having first burnt his confidential papers and made all arrangements to sink and blow up his ship, so that if possible the explosion would destroy the net, he came to the surface, and he and all his crew were taken as prisoners to Constantinople, where both officers and men were kept till the end of the war.[1]

Lieutenant-Commander Stocks had now to carry on alone with *E 2*, and what he had in mind was to repeat the exploit of *E 11* against the enemy's railway communication. The point he chose was Kuchuk Chekmejeh, where, three miles west of San Stefano, the Adrianople line runs close to the sea. Here, after destroying several more sailing craft, Lieutenant H. V. Lyon was landed in the early hours of the 8th with the same apparatus that Lieutenant D'Oyly-Hughes had employed. He was seen to disappear in the darkness towards a bridge which had been marked for destruction, but nothing was ever heard of him again. For two days *E 2* cruised about the place in vain hope, and finally, after destroying some dhows, she went down through the Straits on September 14 without further trouble, having torpedoed a ship off Bergaz Iskalessi on her way. Her cruise had lasted thirty-three days, during which she had covered over 2,000 miles and destroyed six steamers and thirty-six sailing craft.

By dint of thus keeping two submarines always in the Marmara what General Hamilton hoped from them had already come near to attainment. The movement of troops, except those ferried across the Dardanelles, was entirely confined to the Bulair road, and supply by sea, if not actually stopped, was so restricted and precarious that the maintenance of the Turkish army in Gallipoli was a matter of grave concern. Satisfactory as this was from our point of view, it could not be regarded as a solution of the anxious situation which General Hamilton's report had revealed. Clearly unless a great offensive effort could be made in the near future there would be nothing left but evacuation.

[1] Lieutenant-Commander Cochrane succeeded in making his escape shortly before the close of the war.

But evacuation with all its horrors, the loss of life and prestige which it was assumed it must involve, was a measure of despair that no one could face while there was a ray of hope. Hope there still was from the new proposal of the French, and on September 10 Lord Kitchener went over to Calais to ascertain definitely, in conference with the French Government and High Command, what we might expect.

CHAPTER VII

HOME WATERS AND THE BALTIC, AUGUST AND SEPTEMBER, 1915—THE *ARABIC* AND THE *BARALONG*, AND AMERICAN PROTEST AGAINST THE SUBMARINE CAMPAIGN

By this time the outlook in Home waters, which during that dark summer had been scarcely less gloomy than on the Continent, began to show signs of brightening. Ever since the spring the guerrilla warfare of the Germans had been increasing in activity, and the means of meeting it had proved of so little effect as to shake the national faith in our old power of commanding the sea. It appeared, indeed, we were faced with a new problem in naval warfare for which our old experience would not serve. As the enemy seemed more and more obstinately committed to a policy of minor offensive—in such striking contrast to what he had been doing so successfully on land—the hope of a decisive fleet action was growing dimmer than ever, but never for a moment were arrangements for meeting a sortie of the High Seas Fleet relaxed. Subject to this paramount preoccupation the energies of the Admiralty and the Commander-in-Chief were absorbed in developing all kinds of expedients for dealing with the unprecedented form of warfare on which the enemy had pinned his faith. Minelaying by submarines in the southern area of the North Sea was increasing every week, and the discovery of a minefield in the Moray Firth,[1] forced further precautions in the zone of the Grand Fleet. Submarine attack on our trade and transport routes kept pace with the mining, and in the latter half of August it reached its highest point of intensity since the war began. Moreover the guerilla warfare had now definitely spread to the air. Continual Zeppelin raids were disturbing our eastern shores and much of Commodore Tyrwhitt's attention was taken up with trying to intercept the airships at sea with his cruisers.[2]

[1] Laid on August 7/8 by the German minelayer *Meteor*.

[2] No Zeppelin raids took place between June 15 and August 9, but during the next five weeks to the middle of September there were no fewer than eight directed against the Eastern counties and London.

For Admiral Jellicoe the immediate concern was the surface minelaying, and in particular the *Meteor*, which, as we have seen, was known to be active in northern waters, but had hitherto eluded all his attempts to catch her. The last one had been made at the end of June, when she laid a minefield in the White Sea, and a submarine was sent over to the coast of Norway to lie in wait for her.[1] No trace of her presence was found, but early in August there was reason to believe that she was out again, and it was imperative to put an end to her career. Extensive mining in the Grand Fleet zone, such as she was capable of, might well prove a bar of the utmost consequence to its power of operating against the High Seas Fleet on the fatal day.

Accordingly on August 6 Admiral Jellicoe ordered Commodore C. E. Le Mesurier to take out the 4th Light Cruiser Squadron (*Calliope*, *Carysfort*, and *Phaeton*) to form an intercepting patrol off the coast of Norway in about the latitude of Bergen.[2] After maintaining this patrol till the afternoon of the 8th he started to return to the base. No sign of the *Meteor* had been seen, and he was back within eighty miles of Scapa when, shortly after midnight, Admiral Jellicoe directed him to steam at twenty knots for the Horn Reefs light-vessel.[3] Another signal told him that at 6.0 p.m. on the 8th the *Meteor* had been located in a position off Cromarty Firth about seventy miles E.N.E. of Kinnaird Head (Lat. 58° 20′ N., Long. 0° 5′ W.), and that she was probably making for the Horn Reefs light-vessel. "Go," it continued, "as fast as fuel admits. Two Rosyth squadrons and another of Commodore T. are co-operating. Keep wireless silence."

The time given as 6.0 p.m. appears from what follows to have been an error in transmission for 6.0 a.m. What had happened was that at daybreak that morning the *Meteor*, flying the Russian flag, had met in the vicinity named, but nearer to Cromarty, with the *Ramsey*, an armed boarding steamer attached to the Grand Fleet. This ship, after signalling the stranger to stop, closed her to about eighty yards and was about to lower a boat to examine her when the *Meteor*, hauling down her false colours and hoisting the German ensign, suddenly attacked her with masked guns and torpedo tube. In three minutes the *Ramsey* went down and her commander and the survivors of the crew were taken on board the *Meteor*.

The news of the whereabouts of the *Meteor* put a new

[1] See *ante*, pp. 49, 53. [2] See Map 7.

[3] Owing to having insufficient fuel the *Phaeton* could not take part in this sweep.

and graver aspect on the situation. It could only be inferred that the field of her mining operations was not the White Sea but the Grand Fleet zone of concentration, and this was the reason why the Admiralty at once set on foot the elaborate hunt for her of which Commodore Le Mesurier had been informed. Seeing how grave was the danger of her activities, she had to be caught at all costs, and nothing is more eloquent of the change that had come over naval warfare than that so large a force had to be devoted to the search for a single fleet auxiliary.

Commodore Tyrwhitt was the first to get the word. At 8.40 p.m. the Admiralty informed him of the loss of the *Ramsey* north of Kinnaird Head, and told him also that at 6.0 p.m. (*sic*) the *Meteor* had been located approximately in Lat. 58° 20′ N., Long. 0° 5′ W. "She will probably," the message continued, "return to Heligoland going east of Lat. 56° N., Long. 5° E., and will probably make for Horn Reefs. Take all available light cruisers and steer for Horn Reefs to intercept her. . . . Do not make wireless, or German directional stations will get you." Commodore Tyrwhitt had come in only forty-eight hours before from a sweep into the Bight with his cruisers, but as usual he was ready, and at 10.30 p.m. he was away with the *Arethusa*, *Conquest*, *Cleopatra*, *Aurora* and *Undaunted*. Two hours later (12.40 a.m. 9th) Commodore W. E. Goodenough with the 1st and 2nd Light Cruiser Squadrons was coming out of Rosyth with orders designed to cut off the *Meteor* if the Harwich Force should head her back. As soon as they were clear of May Island, they diverged slightly, the 1st Squadron, under Commodore E. S. Alexander-Sinclair, making at full speed for a point twenty miles to the westward of Horn Reefs, and Commodore Goodenough with the 2nd for a position midway between the Forth and the Skagerrak.[1]

All through the night the *Meteor*, unconscious of the net that was being spread for her, was making her way homewards. So confident indeed was she of having run out of danger that the previous evening she had stopped midway over to burn a Danish bark laden with pit-props for Leith. It was not long, however, before she was undeceived, for now another feature of the new naval warfare was introduced into the operations. About 8.0 a.m. on the 9th, as Commodore Tyrwhitt sped northward, a seaplane passed over the squadron from seaward. His anti-aircraft guns failed to bring it down,

[1] The 1st Light Cruiser Squadron—*Galatea*, *Caroline*, *Cordelia*, *Inconstant*. The 2nd Light Cruiser Squadron—*Southampton*, *Birmingham*, *Nottingham* (*Lowestoft* detached).

and it passed away towards Borkum. About the same time a Zeppelin picked up the *Meteor*, and warning her that British cruisers were between her and the Jade, for which she was making, led her northward for the Skagerrak on a course which was nearly the same as that upon which Commodore Tyrwhitt was coming up forty miles astern. He was going perhaps twice the *Meteor's* speed and rapidly gaining. The danger in which she stood cannot have long been unknown to her, for about 9.30 a Zeppelin, *L 7*, possibly the same that had given the original warning, approached the Harwich squadron from the westward and proceeded to keep it company at a distance of ten miles.

Thus the chase stood when a message was received from the Admiralty to say they had located the *Meteor* as having been at 4.0 a.m. about ninety miles to the westward of Horn Reefs (Lat. 55° 50′ N., Long. 5° 03′ E.). The Commodore did not know what to make of it. He could not reconcile it with the "6.0 p.m." position of the previous evening; directional wireless at that time was not too reliable, and after getting the message repeated he decided to ignore it and hold on on his way for his Horn Reefs rendezvous. Commodore Alexander-Sinclair received the position shortly before 11.0, and then altered course for a point a little to the southward of Commodore Tyrwhitt's rendezvous, and a little later Commodore Goodenough, having reached his midsea position at 11.15, also turned for Horn Reefs.

The *Meteor's* chance of escape in any direction was thus very small. At the German headquarters they were doing all they could to save her. In addition to *L 7* another airship, *P.L. 25*, was now dogging Commodore Tyrwhitt. One submarine which had gone out with the *Meteor* had apparently parted company, but another, *U 32*, put to sea from the Ems and a third, *U 28*, which was just returning from a successful cruise, was informed of her plight.[1] The moral effect of the Heligoland action was apparently still paralysing the ardour of the German cruisers, and without ships in support such measures could avail little. By noon Commodore Tyrwhitt had reached his position off Horn Reefs and then, turning to the westward, he spread his five ships at ten miles intervals. On the opposite course the two Rosyth squadrons were coming on for points north and south of the Reefs, and the obnoxious minelayer was fairly caught between the three. At 12.30 Commodore Tyrwhitt had sight of her, apparently in trouble; she was turning in a small circle, and as he closed her it was seen she was sinking by the stern.

[1] Gayer, Vol. II., p. 48.

He did not know, however, till 3.30 when the *Ramsey's* crew were taken on board his ships that this vessel was the *Meteor*.[1] Thanks to the completeness of the enveloping plan, all that the aircraft had been able to do in their first effort to intervene in a regular naval operation was no more than to spare us the trouble of sending to the bottom the ship they had come out to save. The weakness of operating with minor naval types unsupported by surface ships of force could scarcely require more cogent illustration. At the moment a sortie would have involved little risk. Since the Germans had practically blocked Cromarty,[2] the Grand Fleet could not concentrate except at great hazard and without freedom of manœuvre, and had they seized the occasion to push even their battle cruisers out to sea with judgment, one or more of our light cruiser squadrons would have been at their mercy.

It was just before Commodore Tyrwhitt caught sight of the *Meteor* that her commander, Captain von Knorr, knew that escape was hopeless and decided to scuttle his ship. He with his crew and the British prisoners boarded a Swedish lugger, which was seen as our cruisers came on, but it was impossible to stop and pick her up. A submarine had just been reported by the *Undaunted* four miles from the wreck, the two airships were still hovering round, and for all Commodore Tyrwhitt knew the *Meteor* might have sown the vicinity with mines. For this reason he signalled to a number of Danish trawlers that were present to clear away to the south-west for safety, while he made off north-west, and the other squadrons turned back on a signal which the Commander-in-Chief had sent to recall them as soon as he knew the *Meteor's* end. In an hour Commodore Tyrwhitt found his manœuvre had shaken off the airships and he turned back with two ships to pick up the survivors. The prisoners from the *Ramsey* he soon found in a trawler, and they were alone with a curious tale to tell. With the appearance of an overwhelming British force a nice point of naval law had arisen, and on board the Swedish lugger a hot dispute ensued as to whether Germans or British were prisoners. Lieutenant P. S. Atkins, R.N.R., the commander of the *Ramsey*, insisted on Captain von Knorr obeying the Commodore's signal to steer south-west. He had seized the helm, but the Germans were armed and his men were not. Still the Germans, who all along had been treating our men with courtesy, politely refrained from taking command of the vessel, and when

[1] The armed boarding steamer *Ramsey* was sunk by the *Meteor* on August 8.

[2] At Cromarty were the *Iron Duke*, the 4th Battle Squadron, the 1st Cruiser Squadron and half the 2nd Destroyer Flotilla.

Lieutenant Atkins by way of compromise proposed that he and his men should change into a Norwegian lugger near by, the arrangement was accepted. So in mutual goodwill they parted—Lieutenant Atkins with £7 in English notes which the German captain insisted on lending him, and which was subsequently returned with compliments to the friendly lender through the American Embassy.

So with all the courtesies of war the career of the *Meteor* ended. One source of trouble was removed, but the trouble itself remained. The mines she had laid were found to have been scattered over a wide area and the draft on the sweeping flotillas was very heavy. On August 9 the destroyer *Lynx* struck a mine and sank in Moray Firth with a loss of all but twenty-four of her crew. So important was it to clear away what might prove an obstacle to rapid concentration of the various sections of the Grand Fleet, that the new sloops which had been assigned to Admiral Jellicoe as fleet-sweepers had to be used, and one of them, the *Lilac*, while working in Cromarty Firth, struck a mine (August 18). The accident proved the excellence of their construction. Their forepart had been specially designed in view of mine danger, and though her bows were practically blown off, she was safely brought in to dock. Later on another, the *Dahlia*, also struck a mine while sweeping the same field, and she, too, was saved (September 2). Even with their help the local minesweepers were unequal to clearing the area quickly enough, and as the southern sweepers were more than occupied with the submarine minelayers in their own area, the Clyde sweepers had to be brought round. But prevention had to be thought of as well as cure. Since the loss of the *Hawke* in October 1914 the old cruiser patrol areas which Admiral Jellicoe established had ceased to be regularly occupied, but now that so many more of the new light cruisers were available the Admiralty decided that a more active watch might be resumed. In place of the original discredited system of patrol areas a series of light cruiser sweeps was substituted. It was a tactical advance directly due to war experience, but it meant, of course, an increased strain on the light cruisers and the destroyers that had to screen them.

Against the enemy's guerilla tactics little more than this could be done offensively. We had to face the fact that if the High Seas Fleet came out—and at this time it was frequently at sea doing tactical exercises—we might find at the enemy's selected moment the movements of the Grand Fleet seriously hampered. The only way seemed to be to discount the advantage which the enemy was apparently seeking to obtain by counter-mining. We had hitherto shrunk from this device, as likely to impede our own freedom of manœuvre, but in view of the German attitude opinion for some time past had been crystallising in favour of closing in the Bight by a semi-circle of minefields, as complete as was consistent with channels being left clear for the operations of our "oversea" submarines. The idea had been revived by Admiral Jellicoe early in June, and after full consideration it was now decided to carry it out in a modified form.

The first operation was fixed for August 14. The mines were to be placed off the Ems, but this plan was rendered needless by the discovery that the Germans themselves had just laid a new minefield in the same position. It was therefore changed to one on more modest lines. One minelayer only, the *Princess Margaret*, under escort of two divisions of the 10th Destroyer Flotilla, and supported by the Harwich Light Cruiser Squadron, with four destroyers of the 4th Flotilla[1] was to proceed to the coast north of the Bight and lay a minefield off Amrum Bank, twenty-five miles north of Heligoland. At nightfall on August 17 the force made the Horn Reefs light, having passed through a number of trawlers who, though ostensibly fishing, were using wireless. One was boarded and, being German, was sunk. The force then turned southward to its assigned position and very soon ran into a division of the German 2nd Torpedo Boat Flotilla. They at once attacked with torpedo, and the *Mentor*, in leading the escort to engage, was hit. The *Princess Margaret* had turned back to avoid them, and as standing orders were against wide chasing on these expeditions, the enemy was soon lost in the darkness. In an hour's time the *Princess Margaret* decided to carry on, but now she learnt of the *Mentor's* mishap, and in the confusion the rest of the escort had lost touch. They were still not to be found when a signal came from the Admiralty recalling the whole force, as directional wireless indicated that larger enemy forces were moving in the vicinity. By a fine display of seamanship the *Mentor*, with her bows fairly blown off, came in under her own steam, but the expedition had failed.

The failure had obviously been due mainly to lack of support. It was decided to repeat the attempt, this time on a much larger scale. Three minelayers were to be

[1] 10th Destroyer Flotilla: *Mentor, Minos, Moorsom, Miranda, Manly, Matchless, Medusa.* Harwich Light Cruiser Squadron: *Arethusa, Penelope, Cleopatra, Conquest,* with the *Undaunted* and *Aurora.* 4th Flotilla destroyers: *Laurel, Lysander, Lookout, Llewellyn.*

used.[1] They started from the Humber early on September 10 with the *Meteor* and five other " M " class destroyers for escort. To the north was a supporting force from Rosyth, consisting of the 1st and 3rd Battle Cruiser Squadrons and the 1st and 2nd Light Cruiser Squadrons, with the *Fearless* and *Botha* (flotilla leader) and four divisions of the 1st Flotilla: to the south was another, composed of Commodore Tyrwhitt's Light Cruiser Squadron, the *Nimrod* and five destroyers.[2]

This time the success was complete. After dark, as the night was very clear with bright starlight, the escorting destroyers were withdrawn to Commodore Tyrwhitt's force, to give the minelayers every chance of doing their work unobserved. The device proved entirely successful. During the night they laid their mines rapidly without mishap or hindrance to the number of 1450—the biggest night's mining work until the last year of the war. They were laid in three fields west and north-west of Amrum Bank between Latitude 54° 30′ and 55°, exactly as arranged, and the whole enterprise was cordially commended both by the Admiralty and the Commander-in-Chief.

For the present no more was done. The fields were probably discovered by the enemy, just as their own off Cromarty had been by us, but they must have remained a source of danger which necessarily restricted the free movement of the High Seas Fleet.

Four days later (15th) our own measures to check the enemy's activity off the Norwegian coast met with another success. At this time the Commander-in-Chief was using the submarines now attached to him to keep up a regular patrol in that area. On this duty Commander C. P. Talbot in *E 16* left Aberdeen on September 12. An enemy submarine, *U 6*, was also on the station cruising against trade, and during the week she was out sank three British sailing vessels and captured a Dane. This boat Commander Talbot fell in with on the 15th near Stavanger, and cleverly torpedoed her. Rapidly as she sank five of her crew were rescued; the rest, with their commander, perished, and for a long time no more was heard of " U " boats in this quarter.

[1] *Princess Margaret*, 6,000 tons (Canadian Pacific Railway Co.), *Orvieto* 12,130 tons (Orient Steam Navigation Co.), and *Angora*, 4,298 tons (British India Steam Navigation Co.).

[2] The destroyers *Loyal*, *Legion*, *Lysander*, *Lucifer*, *Linnet*; the *Nimrod* was the first of the new " Kempenfelt " class of " flotilla leaders " of the War Programme. They were of about 1,600 tons displacement; designed speed 34 knots; armament four 4-inch guns, two pompoms and four torpedo tubes (21″). Six more ships of the class were in course of construction and six of a similar " Grenville " class had been ordered.

In other areas where the German submarine activity had been increasing, our offensive counter-measures had continued to be developed by means of the latest devices. The "C" class submarines were still acting in company with trawlers. In the first week of August one of them, *C 33*, which had been operating off the Norfolk coast with the armed trawler *Malta*, was lost with all hands as she was returning to the base on relief—probably on a mine near Smith's Knoll. On August 29 another, *C 29*, working in company with the armed trawler *Ariadne*, was lost in the same way near the Outer Dowsing light-vessel off the Humber. The disaster was thought to be due to their having got out of their reckoning, and thenceforth these combinations of "C" boats and trawlers were forbidden within fifteen miles of any mined area. The difficulty of keeping true reckoning was only one of the troubles attending this form of operation; the fouling of the tow and telephone line, as we have seen, was another. It occurred again on August 11, when thirty miles off the Forth the trawler *Ratapiko* and *C 23* fell in with a submarine, the *U 17*. The consequence was that *C 23* was unable to get in a shot, and though the *Ratapiko* got to close range and opened fire, the enemy escaped.

For the protection of our sailing smacks special measures were introduced at this time. These vessels worked mainly in the Lowestoft area (Patrol Area X), in which they were specially exposed to attack from the small "UB" boats operating from Zeebrugge, and had suffered severely. Four of them, the *G. and E.*, *Pet*, *Glory* and *Inverlyon*, were now taken up and armed with 3-pounders. The device met with considerable encouragement. By the end of the month all of them except the *Glory* had been in action with a "UB" boat and claimed to have destroyed her by gunfire. The three claims were allowed, but only one, the destruction of *UB 4* by the *Inverlyon*, was ever verified. Several other successes were reported by other means, but the only certain one among them was the *UC 2* which on July 2 had been accidentally run over by the s.s. *Cottingham*.[1] This boat was raised shortly afterwards, and from it was obtained our knowledge of the structure of the minelaying class. However, notwithstanding every effort, the trouble continued. During August thirty Lowestoft smacks were destroyed, and anxiety began to be felt for our supply of fish, but the intrepid fishermen continued to ply their trade in spite of all the enemy could do.

It was not only in these waters that the growing intensity

[1] See *ante*, p. 55.

of the submarine attack was causing anxiety. Far more important was the zone of the south-west approaches, where the enemy was making his most energetic and dangerous effort, and through which his larger submarines were passing to the Mediterranean. On August 19 the trouble in this area may be said to have culminated. Three submarines *U38*, *U27* and *U24*, had left Germany on August 3–5, to operate between Ushant and St. George's Channel. The *U24*, Lieutenant-Commander Schneider, was the same boat which on New Year's morning had sunk the *Formidable.* Her orders were to begin by going up the Irish Sea to attack the naphtha and benzol works of the Harrington Coke Oven Co., on the Cumberland coast of the Solway Firth. The plant had been installed by two German firms, whose agents had been careful to carry away complete plans of the works, including photographs taken from the sea. The submarine therefore knew exactly what to do, and on August 16 carried out a deliberate bombardment. There were no coast defences and she was quite uninterrupted, yet in spite of this and the complete information she had, little harm was done. The explosion of a drum of benzol at the outset caused so dense a smoke as to screen the works, and after firing some fifty rounds she moved away to join her consorts to the southward, believing the destruction to be complete, whereas in truth only £800 worth of damage was done, and in four days the works were going again.

During the next few days the three boats did a good deal of damage. Two of them in the Irish Channel sank ten vessels on the 17th, and though the auxiliary patrols had been in frequent contact with the marauders they had been able to do no more than impede their operations. On the morning of August 19 *U 27* (Lieutenant-Commander Wegener) was at work in the Scilly Area ; Lieutenant-Commander Schneider in *U 24* had come down to a position south of Kinsale, and *U 38* was between them, off the Bristol Channel. The tale of destruction on this eventful day, when again ten vessels were sunk, began at daybreak with the loss of a Spanish steamer off Newquay. By 9.0 a.m. two British steamers had been sunk by *U 38* to the northward of Scilly—the *Restormal,* of 2,100 tons, and the *Baron Erskine,* of 5,500 tons, with 900 mules. Further north another ship, the *Gladiator,* of 3,300 tons, had fallen to *U 27*, and to the westward of her, about fifty miles south of Old Kinsale Head, *U 24* had stopped the *Dunsley*, of 5,000 tons. The submarine was standing by, endeavouring to sink her by gun-fire as the crew got away in the boats when a much larger steamer was seen coming up from the eastward. Lieutenant-Commander Schneider now began to feel uneasy, and not without reason. Coming down the Irish Sea he had had anxious moments. Twice he had narrowly escaped destruction while molesting ships ; on each occasion he was nearly rammed—first by the armed yacht *Valiant II* and then by the fishing trawler *Majestic* of Fleetwood, who, unarmed as she was, made a dash for him as he was about to sink an Admiralty collier, and so rescued her with the help of the patrol vessel *Bacchante II*. Moreover, when entering St. George's Channel he had attacked the Ellerman liner *City of Exeter*, who at first ran for it, but on meeting the armed yacht *Sabrina II*, turned on him and tried some rounds at long range with her defensive armament. The experience made him wary of big ships. The one he now saw coming on was zigzagging, and according to his own account he took an alteration of her course for an attempt to attack, which entitled him to ignore the instructions not to sink passenger ships without warning. As soon therefore as she was in position he fired a torpedo at close range with violent effect. In about ten minutes the great ship went down, and he made off without knowing, so it was asserted, what she was or how far-reaching were to be the consequences of his hasty action.

The ship he had sunk without notice was none other than the White Star liner *Arabic* of 15,800 tons from Liverpool for New York. Crew and passengers numbered 429, and of these, thanks to the skill and readiness of her commander, Captain W. Finch, and the splendid discipline of his company, 389 were saved.

As the news spread far and wide that another *Lusitania* outrage had occurred the activity of the patrol all over the area increased. Off Kinsale for a time all was quiet, but at noon the *Ben Vrackie*, of 4,000 tons, was sunk by *U 27* fifty-five miles to the northward of the Scilly islands, and about two hours later another large steamer, the *Samara*, was sunk by *U 38* to the westward of that group. Half-way between this point and that where the *Arabic* had gone down in the morning a " Q " ship was cruising in hope of falling in with the boat that had done the mischief. This was the *Baralong*, Lieutenant-Commander Godfrey Herbert. She was an ordinary tramp steamer, 4,200 tons, armed with three concealed 12-pounders, being one of the first of the type to be regularly commissioned for this special service. Ever since the beginning of April he had been cruising independently without any luck—at first in the Channel ; but when in June the south-west approaches became so deeply affected he had been moved into that area.

At about 3.0 p.m. on August 19, when his search had brought him on an easterly course about eighty miles west-north-west of Scilly, he was aware of a large steamer south-west of him making a wide alteration of course. Almost immediately he took in a signal that she was the *Nicosian*, a "Leyland" ship of 6,300 tons, and that a submarine was in chase of her. Three minutes later came another signal, "Captured by enemy submarine." Hoping, however, she might still be free to act, he signalled her to steer north-east towards him, while he, flying neutral colours, headed to meet her. But she could only repeat that she was captured—this time by two enemy submarines—and that most of the crew had already left her. We can easily imagine the tense excitement that was throbbing through the decoy ship. The shock of the *Arabic's* loss that morning was still fresh, and with tingling hope that the hour of her destroyer was at hand they hurried towards the cry for help. On this course a couple of miles were covered and then a submarine was sighted about seven miles away on the port bow. They could see she was steering for her victim at slow speed while the crew got clear in the boats, till she was within 1,000 yards, and then for the first time they witnessed German gunners firing into an unarmed British ship.

With deepening indignation the *Baralong* steamed on, while the Germans continued to fire till she was about two and a half miles from them. Then the submarine's gun's crew were called in while the boat trimmed down a little and turned to meet the interrupter at high speed. Lieutenant-Commander Herbert promptly altered course for the *Nicosian's* boats, which were on her starboard bow, as though to save life, and the submarine responded by manning her gun again and returning to her previous course, with the evident intention of cutting him off from the boats. He then stopped his engines so that the submarine would pass him on the other side of the *Nicosian*, and as soon as the enemy was out of sight behind her he struck his neutral colours, hoisted the white ensign, unmasked his two 12-pounder guns and trained them just forward of the *Nicosian's* bows. The moment the submarine was clear of them Sub-Lieutenant G. C. Steele, R.N.R., who was in charge of the guns, opened fire at 600 yards, and simultaneously the ten marines she carried started in with their rifles.[1] The effect of the surprise was crushing. The submarine was almost helpless to reply, and after the *Baralong* had got off thirty-four rapid rounds she heeled over twenty degrees. The crew jumped overboard, and in another minute she disappeared in a boil of escaping air that told she would never rise again.[2]

But the end was not yet. Lieutenant-Commander Herbert now called the *Nicosian's* boats alongside, and was busy clearing them when about a dozen of the submarine's crew were seen to have swum to the abandoned vessel and to be swarming up the rope ends and pilot ladder, which had been left hanging down her sides. What was he to do? The *Nicosian*, like the *Baron Erskine*, was full of mules and fodder from New Orleans—it would be possible for the desperate survivors of the submarine to scuttle or set her on fire and, moreover, only one of the two submarines reported had been accounted for. If the valuable cargo was to be saved it was necessary to act at once; there was no time to think, and he ordered the guns and marines to shoot.

Even so a number of Germans got on board. The danger of losing the ship therefore continued, and as soon as possible Lieutenant-Commander Herbert placed his ship alongside the *Nicosian* and ordered a party of marines to board her and recover possession. It was not an easy piece of service. The Germans were nowhere to be seen, and it was not known how many of them had succeeded in climbing on board. They had made no sign of surrender, and in the chart-house rifles and ammunition had been left readily accessible. He therefore warned the men to be on their guard against surprise and to be careful to get in the first shot. Over what happened next he had no control. It would seem that after a short search the Germans were found in the engine-room, and were shot down. The total number of the enemy thus summarily dealt with was four. The crew of the *Nicosian* then returned to her, and in spite of the holes which she had received in her hull from the submarine's gun she was brought safely into Bristol.

Such are the facts of this much-discussed incident so far as the truth could be obtained after a searching investigation. Many other stories were circulated, some mutually contradictory, others obviously invention. All were traced to Americans of the rolling stone type who had signed on for

[1] Besides her ordinary crew, which was mainly R.N.R., the *Baralong* bore one corporal of Marines, three lance-corporals and six privates.

[2] The submarine was afterwards identified as the *U 27*.

the *Nicosian* as muleteers or crew. These men when they returned, disgusted with the food and accommodation they had found on board, were easy tools for the German propagandist organisation in America, and the neutral and German press was assiduously flooded with accusations that an inhuman breach of the laws of civilised warfare had been committed. Though these stories were contradicted by others of the *Nicosian's* crew who enlisted in the British army, they were believed in Germany, especially as we took no steps at the time to contradict them.

The upshot was that, relying on the depositions obtained in America from these more than questionable witnesses, the German Government, with charges of barbarity, demanded the trial of the Captain and crew of the *Buralong* for murder, and threatened reprisals in default of obtaining their demand. Our reply, while calling attention to their own long list of excesses both by land and sea, expressed satisfaction at their consideration for the laws of war. We expressed ourselves quite ready to have the whole question of irregularities investigated by an impartial tribunal, and as it would take too long to go into the whole of the counter-charges of the Allies, we were ready to confine the inquiry to events at sea which had occurred during the forty-eight hours in which the *Baralong* incident had taken place. Of these there were three. The first was, of course, the affair of the *Arabic*, a large passenger ship sunk without warning; the second was the case of the *Ruel*, a collier transport on her way from Gibraltar in ballast to Barry. In the afternoon of August 21—her fourth day out—she fell in with a submarine, *U 38*, three miles distant, which began firing at her. She then turned to the westward to keep her assailant astern according to standing instructions, and tried to get away. But the submarine was too fast for her, and after an hour and a half's chase was able to put two shells into her which forced her to stop and get out the boats. The submarine then came close up to the ship and fired six shots into her, and then as she was sinking began to fire with shrapnel and rifles at the crowded boats; the result was that the Captain and six men were severely wounded and one man was killed.

This was bad enough, but the third case was even worse. The incident was not remarkable merely as further evidence of the lengths to which Germany was prepared to go in defying the old comities of naval warfare, but also because it had a definite place in the great strategy of the war. On the Russian front, where the strongest cards were being played, the campaign, in spite of all the Germans had won, was not giving the decisive results for which they had hoped. The Russians, as though pursuing their traditional tactics, were falling back upon their illimitable hinterland, slipping out of every trap that was laboriously set for them. The only prospect the Germans could see of dealing their enemy a crushing blow was to drive them from the great roads and railways which led eastward from Brest-Litovsk. The fortress fell on August 25/26, but the Russian armies had retired in time and the blow failed. It had synchronised with a determined effort against the northern end of the line, where the Germans had endeavoured to turn the extreme right flank of the Russians on the Gulf of Riga. Success depended on their ability to carry out a combined movement of their land and sea forces, and so important was the object, that they had decided to attempt a naval operation to force an entry into the gulf and to cover the attack with their battle cruisers.

As soon as Petrograd suspected what was in the wind a request came to us to know whether we could not increase our force of submarines in the Baltic, or what else we could do to relieve the pressure upon Riga. It was represented by our own people on the spot that as the Russians had only one submarine fit for service, the two we had there did not make up a force adequate for effective interference with the new German plan. On this representation the Admiralty were already preparing to act, and on August 14, the day before the Russian cry for help reached us, Lieutenant-Commander F. H. H. Goodhart with *E 8* and Lieutenant-Commander G. Layton with *E 13* were ordered to proceed from Harwich through the Sound and make for Dagerort, the advanced base at the entrance of the Gulf of Finland from which our *E 1* and *E 9* were now working.

They were off immediately, and all went well till the night of August 18. During the afternoon of that day Lieutenant-Commander Layton had successfully dived through the Sound and was about to debouch into open water when, shortly after 11.0 p.m., his magnetic compass failed, and before he could rectify the error of his course he ran hard on the south-east edge of Saltholm flat between Malmö and Copenhagen. While his consort was passing safely through without seeing what had happened, every effort was made to get the boat afloat again, but she would not move an inch. At 5.0 a.m. the night-long struggle was still proceeding when a Danish torpedo boat arrived to inform them they would be allowed the usual twenty-four hours to get off if they could, but no assistance could be given and that an armed guard would be anchored close by. The torpedo boat then left with one of the officers of the submarine to visit the Danish guardship. Meanwhile a German destroyer had appeared on the scene and remained near till two Danish torpedo boats came up, when she withdrew. About 9.0 a.m., when the promised guard had been completed by another Danish torpedo boat, two German destroyers were seen approaching from the southward. The leading one, *G 132*, when within half a mile hoisted a commercial flag signal, but before there was time to read it she fired a torpedo. It hit the bottom close to *E 13* and did no harm, but simultaneously she opened fire with all her guns at 300 yards. The submarine was in flames in a moment, and the men were warned to take to the water and swim for the shore or the Danish boats. As they did so the Germans opened fire on them with shrapnel and machine guns, and kept it up remorselessly till one of the Danish boats steamed in between the Germans and the swimmers. Both the destroyers then made off, while the Danes did all they could to rescue; but in spite of their efforts fifteen petty officers and men were lost by shrapnel or drowning. The outrage was perpetrated in cold blood, by men well under control of their officers, upon a helpless wreck on a neutral shore. For a cumulation of illegality it would surely be hard to match in the annals of modern naval warfare. It is therefore scarcely surprising that the Germans, with some irritation, refused to entertain our proposed enquiry and fell back on their threat of reprisals.

The real explanation of their treatment of *E 13* is their extreme annoyance at the activity of our submarines in the Baltic at that particular juncture. The powerful force of battleships and cruisers with which they had decided to co-operate in the attempt to turn the Russian right was already at sea; four days earlier, on August 15, they had begun testing the strength of the defences of the Riga Gulf, and were taking every possible means to prevent more of our submarines passing in through the Sound. The actual attack to force an entrance into the Gulf of Riga had begun on the 18th; the defences were partly penetrated, and the two British submarines already on the spot were very active in trying to get a chance at the enemy's battle cruisers which were covering the operations. The weather was foggy, and the ships were so well handled and so strongly screened with destroyers that every effort to get into a position for attack was foiled by the Germans' bewildering tactics. On the morning of the 19th, however, almost in the same hour that saw the destruction of the *Arabic* and the *E 13*, Commander N. F. Lawrence in *E 1* found himself within attacking distance of four battle cruisers in line abreast. In ten minutes he was in position to fire at the wing ship, and the torpedo hit forward. He saw no more, for only by a very prompt dive could he escape by a few feet one of the screening destroyers that dashed at him. Owing to the fog and the large number of destroyers that were hunting him he could not get off another shot, but the ship he had hit was the *Moltke*, eight men being killed. She was seriously damaged, but was able to go back to Hamburg for repairs and was out of action for about a month.

Whether or not this blow was the final cause, it marked the end of the attack on Riga. It was the first operation of the kind which the Germans had attempted, and it had proved a failure. After partly forcing the entrance, the Germans persevered for some days without meeting any great success. Losses were sustained on both sides.[1] But the day after the *Moltke* was disabled the attempt to turn the Riga flank was abandoned. It is not, therefore, impossible that the presence of our submarines in the Baltic was as disconcerting to the Germans as the arrival of theirs at the Dardanelles had been to us. Be that as it may, by the morning of August 21 the German squadrons had disappeared. All that remained on the coast were light forces to see what could be done with the British submarine base. On the 25th Dagerort was bombarded by two cruisers and a division of destroyers, but without result, and the outcome of the whole affair was that the Russian right remained secure on the line of the Dvina.

Simultaneously with the withdrawal of the Germans from the coasts of Livonia and Courland, in our south-west approaches their submarines also disappeared. In the four days that followed the *Arabic* and *Baralong* incidents nine British ships were lost and a number of attacks frustrated by the auxiliary patrol, but after August 23 all was quiet. Yet August had been a very bad month. In this area alone thirty-eight British ships had been sunk, besides two fishing craft and four neutrals, and nine British ships had escaped

[1] The German naval losses in the whole undertaking were : two destroyers and three minesweepers sunk by mine ; three other vessels struck mines but were brought into port ; *Moltke* damaged by torpedo ; four ships each hit once by shore batteries. Casualties numbered sixty-five. The Russians lost two vessels and one seaplane ; five other vessels were damaged and eleven merchant ships lost. *Der Krieg zur See : Ostsee*, Vol. II, p. 283.

after being attacked. The new organisation of the Queenstown area had so far been undeniably disappointing. No one was more dissatisfied with the result than Admiral Bayly himself, and on August 24 he submitted a memorandum pointing out why no better results could be hoped for with the resources at his disposal. Besides the regular patrols of trawlers and drifters allotted to the areas within his command, the actual offensive force based at Queenstown was eight sloops, three yachts and twenty-four trawlers. To the sloops were assigned cruising areas between Latitudes 50° and 51°, extending to about 350 miles westward from Land's End, while the yachts cruised on certain selected routes, but neither sloops nor yachts had succeeded in encountering a submarine. As for the trawlers, not only were they too slow to deal with the larger submarines the enemy was now using, but they were constantly engaged in escort duty. The Admiralty reply on this point sheds a vivid light on those little-noticed, but never-ceasing, preoccupations which were more and more hampering the possibilities of offensive operations. The pressure on their resources, they explained, was due to the increasing number of troops abroad, of munition ships coming from America, of others going to Archangel for the Russians, and of large ships detached for refitting and other purposes from the Grand Fleet. All required escort, as well as ships not under the Geneva Cross conveying wounded, and ships proceeding across the Atlantic with bullion, a traffic that was indispensable for keeping up the flow of munitions from America. With so many pressing calls they could do no more than protect the interests which were most important.

While submitting that there was no effective cure for the evil except by blocking and destroying the submarine bases, Admiral Bayly had asked for more sloops and disguised ships. No more sloops were yet available, but he was told at once that the *Baralong* would now be placed definitely under his orders, as well as two other "Q" ships to be taken up, and that his force of sloops would be brought up to eighteen during the next two months.

His faith in the "Q" ships was soon justified by another success. After ten days of quiet there was another short outbreak of submarine trouble, but now it was further out to sea, as though the Germans were finding the actual Queenstown area too full of danger. During September 4 and 5 five British steamers and two Norwegian sailing vessels were sunk between the Fastnet and the Bishop rock, and the patrol vessels which Admiral Bayly hurried to the spot at the first alarm failed to find anything. The fact was there was no renewal of the attack on Admiral Bayly's area. The mischief had been done by boats on passage to the Mediterranean.[1] One of them, *U 39*, after unsuccessfully attacking a single ship, carried on through the Straits, where she did some damage before going on to Cattaro. Another, *U 33*, was responsible for two British steamers and a neutral sailing vessel out of a total of seven vessels sunk on the 4th and 5th. On the following day she destroyed a British steamer off Finisterre. After passing the Straits she was attacked by torpedo boat *No. 95* of the Gibraltar patrol, but escaped, and she also got safely to Cattaro. A third boat, *U 20*, present in Irish waters at this time, seemed to have had a special mission to harass the flow of supplies into La Rochelle. Between Scilly and Ushant on her way down she contributed to our losses on September 4 and 5. In the Bay on the 6th she caught a French ship, and next morning she appeared off the Gironde. This day she sank another British vessel and a French steamer close off the port. Then she left as suddenly as she had appeared, being presumably at the limit of her sea endurance. As she retraced her course across the Bay she got yet another British steamer, and then no more was heard of her.

After this there was another lull of about a fortnight, during the last half of which the cruiser *Terrible* and the battleships *Mars*, *Magnificent* and *Hannibal*, which had been deprived of their turrets to arm the new monitors, sailed as troopships for the Mediterranean. The last of them, however, was hardly away, together with the *Olympic* carrying 5,500 officers and men, when there were signs that the quiet which had fallen on the south-western approaches was only a respite. On September 23 three ships averaging over 4,000 tons were sunk by gunfire to the westward of Scilly in the area of the *Baralong's* recent exploit. This ship, now altered in appearance, with a new Captain (Lieutenant-Commander A. Wilmot-Smith), was in Falmouth at the time, and in the evening, directly news of the first loss reached Admiral Bayly at Queenstown, he ordered her to put to sea on a course which would intercept the submarine if she were making for Ushant or the Bay. This course Lieutenant-Commander Wilmot-Smith had already taken on his own initiative, and he therefore held on as he was during the night. The movement could not have been better judged. At 9.45 next morning he was aware of a ship stopped and blowing off steam some eight miles right ahead. She proved to be the Wilson liner *Urbino*, of 6,600 tons, homeward bound, which

[1] See *post*, p. 169.

had just been stopped by *U 41* sixty-seven miles south-west of the Scillies, and was now being sunk by gunfire.

Keeping on as he was, and making all ready for action, Lieutenant-Commander Wilmot-Smith in the fine clear weather that prevailed could soon make out the submarine on the far side of the *Urbino*, and he held his course directly for her, till when about five miles distant the submarine dived. He responded by altering six points to the southward, to a course which would take him outside her maximum submerged danger angle, and so force her to come to the surface if she meant attacking. The manœuvre had the effect intended. She quickly reappeared and proceeded at full speed on the surface to head him off, and on his hoisting neutral colours signalled him to stop. Though he obeyed immediately he was careful to keep his engines working in such a way as to maintain a position on the bearing most favourable for attack. Without any trace of misgiving the submarine continued to approach, and when about two miles and a half away signalled for his papers to be sent on board. This order he used to close her gradually while clearing away a boat, and so they both kept on upon converging courses till they were only 700 yards apart, when Lieutenant-Commander Wilmot-Smith swung to port as though to give the boat a lee for lowering into the water. By this means he cleverly brought his starboard quarter and stern guns to bear, and with the range down to 500 yards he gave the order to unmask them. The screen and poop rails fell and with them the neutral colours on the jack staff, the white ensign was hoisted on the main back-stay, and fire was opened both with guns and rifles. The second shot hit the submarine at the base of the conning tower and she was doomed. As shells and bullets rained upon her she tried to dive, then she partly reappeared, but only to plunge convulsively down again, and that was her end. Of her crew of five officers and thirty-two men only a lieutenant and a petty officer remained afloat to be rescued, the rest all perished with their boat.

This was the last encounter in the south-west area for many a day. With the second exploit of the *Baralong* the first submarine campaign against our commerce came to an end, and to many it seemed that the defence had mastered the attack. But in fact this was not the reason for the respite. It was due to two entirely different considerations. One was, as will be seen directly, that the enemy was once more changing the direction of his primary offensive; his attention was turning to the Balkans, and for the moment the most important theatre for his submarines was in the Mediterranean.

The other lay not in the great strategy of the war, but in diplomatic considerations which forced the High Command to give way to the statesmen.

The disturbing influence arose from the destruction of the *Arabic*. The reception of the news in America filled the German Ambassador with alarm. For months he had been deliberately spinning out the negotiations over the *Lusitania*, and American patience was showing signs of exhaustion. A note, sharper in tone than any of the numerous communications that had preceded it, had been sent to Berlin. It demanded an apology and indemnification for the American lives that had been lost and an undertaking that no passenger ships should in future be sunk without warning.[1] For nearly a month Berlin had been silent and the only reply was the sinking of another great liner without warning or provocation and with the loss of more American lives. The United States Government immediately asked for an explanation : Count Bernstorff sent an urgent warning that American opinion was now dangerously exasperated, and counsels in Berlin began driving confusedly in a storm of controversy between the Chancellor and Admiral von Tirpitz. The Chancellor, on Count Bernstorff's alarming representations, was for offering arbitration and definitely forbidding attacks on all passenger ships if America in return would press the British Government to stand by the Declaration of London. Admiral von Tirpitz and his men protested that such a reply would admit the illegality of the campaign and that the submarines, their only hope, must not be sacrificed to America. The Emperor was inclined to agree, and Admiral von Tirpitz suggested that if something must be done to quiet American resentment the submarines could be temporarily withdrawn from British waters and sent to the Mediterranean. But the Ambassador's account of public feeling was too disturbing for so easy a makeshift to restore confidence in Berlin. The Emperor wavered, then changed his mind to the Chancellor's view, and Admiral von Tirpitz tendered his resignation, (August 27). It was refused and the orders which had been secretly issued after the *Lusitania* incident, that no liner was to be sunk without warning, were extended. Admiral von Pohl at Kiel was now told that all passenger ships were to be spared. As Commander-in-Chief he protested in reply that this restriction, which involved the examination of vessels before attack, would involve so much risk to the submarines that further effort was useless, and he too tendered his resignation, (September 1) with the same result.[1]

[1] Bernstorff, *My Three Years in America*, p. 138. [2] Von Tirpitz, *My Memoirs*, pp. 411–12. Von Pohl, *Letters*, Sept. 3 and 4, 1915.

Seeing how far we had developed the system of defensively armed merchantmen and decoy ships, the Admiral's attitude was fully justified by the experiences of the year. At the beginning of 1915 the Germans had no more than twenty-four "U" boats fit for commerce destruction, and in the succeeding months new construction had barely covered the losses. If therefore the losses were likely to reach a higher rate, there was little hope that they could have a decisive effect upon the war.[1] At the same time his objections bring out clearly the inherent limitations of the submarine as a commerce destroyer. Owing to its essential vulnerability it could not operate in a true offensive spirit. Immunity from attack was the first consideration, and it therefore had to act by stealth and evasion. Consequently its only chance of avoiding destruction was too often to sink at sight with the inevitable risk of inflicting on powerful neutrals an unpardonable affront. The Germans thus found their new method of disputing the command of the sea was involving them in an insoluble dilemma. The more vigorous, extended and ruthless their submarine campaign against commerce became, the more likely it was to increase the strength opposed to them by sooner or later forcing neutrals into the ranks of their enemies.

Faced with this dilemma the German Government agreed on September 7 to send a Note expressing regret for the loss of American citizens but without admitting responsibility to pay an indemnity, and proposing, if agreement on this point could not be reached, reference to a Hague Tribunal. At the same time they forwarded an account of the affair, which was taken in America as an attempt to justify the action of the submarine commander on the ground of self-defence, and although the Ambassador on his own authority had already made public the secret orders about the treatment of liners, in hopes of quieting the storm, popular opinion only became more inflamed at the grudging admission of the Germans. Eventually on October 5, seeing no help for it, Berlin disavowed the officer and agreed to negotiate an indemnity. This proposal America at once accepted, and the storm which had brought the two countries to the brink of war rapidly died down.

So far as we were concerned the most important outcome of the diplomatic storm was that Admiral von Tirpitz's suggestion was also adopted. On September 18 an order went out for withdrawing all submarines from our west coast and the Channel, where American traffic was most abundant. In

[1] Scheer, *Germany's High Sea Fleet in the World War*, p. 258.

the North Sea ten of them were still kept at work, and the mining activities of the Flanders Flotilla remained unrestricted. But for a field where submarine operations against the commerce and communications of the Allies could be carried on effectively and with little risk of another gale from Washington, the German Admiralty had to look to the Mediterranean. In this way, moreover, the political and military exigencies of the moment were reconciled. For it was upon the operations in the Eastern Mediterranean that the issue of the war seemed at this time likely to turn.

CHAPTER VIII

THE GERMAN CHANGE OF FRONT—ATTITUDE OF BULGARIA—NAVAL OPERATIONS IN SUPPORT OF THE AUTUMN OFFENSIVE IN FRANCE

In the orientation which the war was now taking there was reason enough why Germany should shrink from setting a hard face towards so powerful a neutral as America. While the nervous negotiations about the *Arabic* were proceeding they were in the act of giving another direction to the main current of the war. The new development which the Allies were already expecting was what gave special urgency to the question which Lord Kitchener on September 10 had gone over to Calais to settle with the French.[1] To an influential section of British opinion it seemed that the best way of turning the tide which was flowing so strongly in favour of the Central Powers was to concentrate the whole of the Allied offensive power on bringing our well-conceived, but ill-provided Dardanelles enterprise to a successful issue. This appeared at least the most effective means of restoring the shattered power of Russia and of eventually confining the main theatre of war to Europe. In Paris this view was not without support, but the bulk of opinion regarded the Dardanelles enterprise as an eccentric movement, and was pinning its faith on direct offensive action in France. It was only natural. Not only was the invader on French soil, but the whole French outlook was traditionally continental. It was not to be expected that they could see the struggle against Germany as the world war it was to us. Between the two Western Powers there was a difference of outlook so deeply rooted in the distinctive history and conditions of each country that it was naturally hard to reconcile, as appeared only too clearly when the discussion took place.

The conference met on September 11. It was attended by Lord Kitchener, Sir John French, Lieutenant-General Sir

[1] See *ante*, p. 120.

Henry Wilson and the Secretary, Committee of Imperial Defence, and by M. Millerand, Generals Joffre and Sarrail and two French staff officers. Nothing really definite was decided. M. Millerand had to suggest that General Sarrail should have the supreme command, but on the ground that the British troops in the theatre greatly outnumbered the French the proposal was firmly declined. It was agreed, however, that if it was eventually decided that the British forces should operate on one side of the Dardanelles and the French on the other, the European and Asiatic commands might be independent. It was also agreed that if the French sent out four divisions we would send two to relieve the two French divisions which had hitherto been operating in Gallipoli. Transport sufficient for the six divisions was to be prepared, but no definite decision was taken till the result of the coming offensive in France was known. Throughout the discussions General Joffre, feeling that at any moment the Germans might choose to change their front again and sweep back to the west, made no secret of his dislike of the whole affair, and neither he nor Sir John French would commit himself to a date when it would be possible to extricate the six divisions from the Allied line.

The prospect of prompt action was therefore still remote, and prompt action was what was most important if the only other spark of hope was to be blown into flame. That spark was a glimpse of anti-German feeling in the ranks of the opposition parties in Bulgaria, of which, in a last forlorn effort, the Allies were now trying to take advantage. Early in August a note had been presented to Serbia advising her to make certain territorial concessions to Bulgaria if her old enemy would declare for the Allies. On September 1 she had replied accepting the proposals but with certain reservations, which led to further discussions between the Allies. They ended in a resolution that the Serbian reservations must be overruled, and on the 14th a note went to Sofia offering the whole of the concessions if Bulgaria would conclude with the Allies at a short date a convention binding her to take military action against Turkey. As soon as the proposal reached the ears of the Bulgarian opposition they took it up warmly. In a deputation to King Ferdinand they solemnly warned him of the danger of the policy he was pursuing, and demanded the formation of a coalition government and the convocation of Parliament. But the King was far too deeply committed to the Central Powers to give way, and the immediate result of the Allied overture was rumours that he was preparing to mobilise.

The fact was that the Germans, as we now know, were taking the same view of the crisis as the British Government. The Imperial aspirations which had been so actively fostered by Prussia up to the eve of the war, and which in some measure at least accounted for her precipitating it, had so far mastered her continental traditions that she too saw that the key of the future now lay in Constantinople, and to secure it the Great General Staff had decided to abandon for the present any further action to crush the Russian military power. For a while, it is true, the German Commander-in-Chief in the East continued his attempt to turn the Russian right in spite of the failure at Riga, and this he hoped to do by an enveloping movement pushed against Vilna between Riga and Brest-Litovsk. The movement was already beginning when the attempt on Riga failed, but within a week Brest-Litovsk had fallen (August 25–26). For the Great General Staff that was enough. Even if after the failure at Riga and with their coastwise communication in the Baltic insecure the turning movement could have been successfully continued, they regarded the complete destruction of the Russian military power as not immediately necessary. She was already crippled enough to prevent her interfering with their wider ambitions for a long time to come. They had reached the shortest attainable defensive line, and they were not so fanatically wedded to their dominant war maxim as not to see that the moment had come to relax it and seize the opportunity of using the advantage of interior lines to divert their main offensive to a more urgent direction.

The Dardanelles, and not the Russian army, was now their preoccupation. There lay the channel through which alone stricken Russia could be healed of her wounds—there, too, lay the key to the most telling offensive against the British Empire, and the road to it ran through Serbia. Whether or not that road could be taken depended on the attitude of Bulgaria and Rumania. How far King Ferdinand was committed to the German cause at this time is difficult to say, but it is certain that the German Great General Staff considered that the negotiations were going too slowly and that they required speeding up with a military gesture to encourage King Ferdinand and overawe Rumania. Accordingly, as soon as Brest-Litovsk fell, Austria was informed that in pursuance of previous arrangements certain German troops were to be withdrawn from the Galician Front for the Danube. To this Austria objected. For her the final crushing of Russia was the paramount object, and she wished the troops to reinforce the Kovno Army Group, which was about to commence its thrust for Vilna. Germany was inexorable. The troops began at once to move and the Chief of the Great General Staff explained that they were indispensable for assisting the Bulgarian negotiations by appearing on the Rumanian flank and within easy reach of Bulgaria. " A reinforcement of the Kovno Army Group," he wrote, " is certainly desirable, but it is incomparably more important to secure the Dardanelles and to strike the iron in Bulgaria while it is hot. Consequently the forces which we are able to withdraw from the zone of Brest-Litovsk must go to the Danube." [1]

To the Danube the troops therefore went, and the Vilna envelopment had to proceed without them. The attempt very nearly succeeded, but at the last moment it proved too weak and the Russians were able to settle down on the line of their choice, from which there was no moving them. To this extent our power of influencing a European military situation by naval and combined operations in the Baltic and Mediterranean reasserted itself as of old, and to this extent the Dardanelles enterprise, inert as it seemed to have become, did avail to relieve the pressure on Russia and give her breathing time, had she been capable of using it.

The effect of the change in the German front of attack was soon felt. It was within three weeks of the withdrawal of the German troops from the Eastern Front that the rumours of a Bulgarian mobilisation began to be heard. At the same time Serbia reported that Bulgarian troops and munitions were being dispatched to Vidin and that two Austro-German forces were concentrating on her northern frontier.[2] For her the evil day was obviously at hand. Invasion from the north the Serbs had twice heroically repelled, but a third invasion with a third enemy pressing in from the east rendered resistance almost hopeless. Greece by treaty was bound to come to her assistance if necessary, but Greece without support was too weak to save the situation, and Serbia threatened from the north could not provide the 150,000 men against Bulgaria which, as Greece contended, was a condition of the defensive alliance becoming operative. Rumania might turn the scale, but it was more than doubtful if she dared move, and, failing her, M. Venizelos and the

[1] Von Falkenhayn, *General Headquarters, 1914-1916*, p. 133.

[2] The German troops had gone to Orsova, which is on the Danube at the " Iron Gate," where the frontiers of Austro-Hungary, Rumania, Serbia and Bulgaria practically meet. Vidin is in the north-west corner of Bulgaria, just below the " Iron Gate."

Serbian Prime Minister appealed to the Allies for the immediate assistance of 150,000 troops to provide the required force for dealing with the Bulgarians.

In London the proposal was taken into consideration on September 23, but no definite reply could be given. It was impossible to say whether or not the troops could be spared from France till the result of the coming offensive was known. The first preparatory moves were already being made not only on land but also at sea, where the navy had its definite part to play in the Franco-British combination. The general idea was to cut off the salient of the enemy's line in Artois by the French driving northward against its southern face in Champagne, with a subsidiary British push eastwards against its western face in the region of Arras. The part of the navy was to be a demonstration on the Flemish coast to menace the German sea flank, and so prevent the salient being reinforced from that quarter. As early as September 7 Rear-Admiral R. H. S. Bacon had been secretly informed that at any moment he might be called on to support the sea flank of the Allied army by gunfire from his ships, and to this end he was to keep in close touch through General Bridges, our liaison officer at Dunkirk, with General Foch, commanding the coast sector.

As in the crisis of the first race for the sea the previous year, it was to the Dover Patrol that the duty fell. It was now far better composed for the work and far better trained. Admiral Bacon had had attached to his command three of the new monitors which had been armed with the turrets and the 12-inch guns of the discarded "Majestics," as well as the old *Revenge*, now furnished with bulges and renamed *Redoubtable*, and for some time past he had been training them and experimenting with fire observation on a specially prepared range in the Thames Estuary, where the natural features, conditions and leading marks of the vital part of the Belgian coast were sufficiently well reproduced.[1] He was then absorbed with the idea, which he shared with Admiral Bayly and many others, that the only way of dealing with the enemy's submarines was to destroy the bases in his area from which they were acting, and with this object he had been rehearsing on the Thames range an attack upon Zeebrugge and Ostend and the adjacent coast batteries. To overcome the key difficulty of all coastal bombardments

[1] These 12-inch monitors were *Lord Clive* (Commander N. H. Carter), *Prince Rupert* (Commander H. O. Reinold), *Sir John Moore* (Commander S. R. Miller), *Prince Eugene* (Captain E. Wigram), and *General Craufurd* (Commander E. Altham).

he had devised a novel form of observation station, consisting of tall iron tripods which could be carried in specially fitted vessels and planted in shallow waters at convenient points. On the top were platforms to carry an observation party and their instruments, but so small that when the structure was immersed it was hoped they would not attract attention.

After three months' work the first attempt was to be made on August 21–22 against Zeebrugge.[1] Owing to the proximity of the enemy's submarines and aircraft, no less than the strength and number of the coast batteries and the danger of fixed and floating mines and the intricate navigation, the difficulty of the operation was very great, and only to be overcome by a very numerous and complex force. Nearly a hundred vessels of all types took part. Besides the *Lord Clive*, carrying Admiral Bacon's flag, and two other monitors, *Sir John Moore* and *Prince Rupert,* there were two minesweeping gunboats (*Seagull* and *Spanker*), ten shallow draft paddle minesweepers, ten destroyers, and forty to fifty drifters of the Dover Patrol, four observation ships to carry the tripods, a seaplane carrier and other minor auxiliary units. It was, in fact, like the naval force operating at the Dardanelles, a fragment of the organisation on which Lord Fisher had pinned his faith for seizing the initiative from Germany, and which he had been so actively preparing up to the time of his retirement. In effect it was what a recent French authority has aptly termed a "Siege Fleet," whose operation against the enemy's naval strongholds was to be covered by the Grand Fleet. Its organisation was closely analogous to that of a siege army whose operations are covered by a field force. Such a device we had been compelled to employ again and again in former wars, but had never prepared in time of peace.

After being delayed a day by unsuitable weather, the fleet sailed in the evening of August 22, while the French destroyers *Oriflamme* and *Branlebas* were sinking a German torpedo-boat off Ostend. Thanks to their careful training under Captain F. G. Bird the drifters accurately formed there a zareba of explosive mine nets forming three sides of a rectangle open to the coast to enclose the firing position of the monitors ; the two observation tripods were successfully placed, unnoticed by the enemy, and at 5.36 a.m. on the 23rd fire was opened. So far, in spite of every difficulty, all had gone well, but now the defects of the old gun fittings of the monitors, which had been a perpetual source of trouble

[1] See Map 8.

during the rehearsals, again declared themselves. The *Prince Rupert's* director broke down at once and she could only fire very slowly. The *Sir John Moore* had to cease fire after the eighth round, but the *Lord Clive* was able to carry on for the allotted time, and in spite of the poor visibility, which made it difficult to identify the landmarks with their imitations on the practice range, good execution was done upon the Solvaye submarine factory and the docks and basins. In order not to risk a concentration of submarines on the return home, to punish the daring attempt it had been decided that the bombardment should last no more than two hours. Accordingly at 7.30 the " cease fire " was signalled and Admiral Bacon withdrew his motley force in the same orderly manner in which it had arrived upon the scene. No submarine or other interference, except some gunfire on the observation ships as they went in with their sweepers, was attempted, and he was able to report himself well satisfied with the first performance.[1]

The day's work had in any case been encouraging enough for the same treatment to be applied to Ostend at the earliest opportunity. Owing to unfavourable weather it could not be arranged till a fortnight later. The force employed was much the same as before, except that the squadron was reinforced by the *General Craufurd* (12-inch) and *M 25* (9·2-inch), which had just joined Admiral Bacon's flag. The 6th Flotilla light cruiser *Attentive* was also there, while the *Redoubtable* and the two gun-vessels *Excellent* and *Bustard* were detailed to keep under the fire of the guns at Westende. After two efforts frustrated by bad weather the main force was in position off Ostend by 6.0 a.m. on September 7th, but though the morning was beautifully fine Ostend and its vicinity were concealed by haze, so that fire could not be opened for fear of damaging the town, and while waiting for the haze to clear, the force was so heavily bombed by aircraft, which hit the *Attentive*, killing two men and wounding seven, that Admiral Bacon had to order the ships to separate. Another serious disappointment was that two tripods which had been placed in position were discovered by the enemy and destroyed.

In the afternoon, however, the weather cleared, and he again took up firing positions, this time further out, at 18,000

[1] The report of the result received from Holland by our Intelligence Division was—Two submarines and two dredgers sunk, the Solvaye Factory and the first lock destroyed. This report, however, was much exaggerated, for an air reconnaissance two days later reported the lock gates intact, and the submarine factory was not destroyed.

to 19,000 yards. As the range of the batteries was uncertain, the power of the German shore guns had to be tested, and the test brought an ugly surprise. No sooner was fire opened than heavy shell from the enemy began to fall so close that it was necessary to turn the monitors 16 points to open out the range by 1,000 yards. The enemy's shell followed as the range increased, and when the monitors turned again to engage their targets they were still under heavy fire. The shooting of the new battery was extraordinarily good; but though the flagship was hit four times little damage was done. Still, as it was clear the battery was good for at least 22,000 yards, and could not be located, it was obviously only common prudence to retire and wait till these formidable guns could be located and the 15-inch monitors be brought up to deal with them.[1] After about half an hour's action Admiral Bacon therefore withdrew. It was disappointing, but some success had been obtained, and a reconnaissance next day reported the Ostend lighthouse wrecked, a shed in the naval arsenal (*Atelier de la Marine*) and the eastern pier carried away, while at Westende there were considerable signs of damage done by the *Redoubtable* and her two consorts.

It was with this fresh revelation of the difficulties of his task that Admiral Bacon received the warning to be ready to assist the army when called upon. His instructions were to keep a proportion of the monitors and other vessels required for the service in a state of immediate readiness and to arrange with the French authorities to have them berthed at Dunkirk. This was done, and on September 16 as a preparatory measure he made an attempt to destroy the military works at Ostend and the newly discovered Tirpitz battery, which had now been located in the south-western suburbs. This time, in hopes of avoiding the arc of fire of these formidable guns, the attempt was to be made from West Deep.[2] For two days the weather stopped the operations, and on the 18th, while waiting for it to improve, Admiral Bacon was invited to St. Omer to confer with Sir John French and arrange the best manner of co-operating with the army in the coming offensive. There he learnt it was to take place on the 25th, and hurrying back on the 19th he found the weather suitable for his delayed operation.

With the *Marshal Ney* (Captain H. J. Tweedie), the first

[1] The new work was known as the Tirpitz battery. Its range was actually 35,000 yards.

[2] The West Deep is the channel inside the Outer Dunkirk banks which leads to Nieuport and Ostend. It is reached from Dunkirk Roads by a narrow channel through the inner banks known as Zuidcoote Pass.

of the 15-inch monitors, and the *Lord Clive* he proceeded to engage and test the coast batteries between Ostend and Nieuport, particularly the Tirpitz, and another heavy battery a little to the westward at Raversyde, as well as the guns at Middelkerke, halfway between Nieuport and Ostend.

While the two monitors from eastward of La Panne—that is, about four miles west of Nieuport—engaged the three targets, the French batteries and naval guns about Nieuport joined in to keep those at Westende quiet. The results were not encouraging. It was found that both Tirpitz and Raversyde batteries could range the ships with accuracy, and after firing intermittently for two hours they retired through the Zuidcoote Pass with three of the Tirpitz guns following them up to an extreme range of 29,000 yards. In the afternoon they tried again, this time moving up inside the inner bank to La Panne to test the enemy's arc of fire. Here one of the Tirpitz guns could still find them, and after half an hour they withdrew to Dunkirk. No damage had been done, but the *Marshal Ney* had had so much trouble with her engines that she had to be towed in by a destroyer, and the day's work convinced Admiral Bacon he must return to Dover to recast his whole plan for the diversion.

There were only four days in which to do it, but in that time the new arrangements were completed. His guiding idea was that the diversion would be more effective if the operations were extended over several days, than if all the limited supply of ammunition was fired away at once; and further, that to get the utmost effect from the demonstration it should be made at both ends of the German sea front. In order to give the impression of an intended landing, a number of the new troop motor lighters had been brought to Dover, the troops of the garrison were exercised with them in embarkation and landing, and it was hoped the double demonstration would leave the enemy in doubt whether the descent was intended at Knocke, near the Dutch frontier, or to combine with an advance from Nieuport. Thus the new plan involved operation orders for several days and the reorganisation of the fleet into two separate squadrons.

By the night of September 24 all was ready, and punctually next morning, while our army's first intensive bombardment began between La Bassée and Lens, the *Prince Eugene* and *General Craufurd* were opening on the coast from Knocke to Blankenberghe, and the *Lord Clive* (flag), *Marshal Ney* and *Sir John Moore*, assisted by the Nieuport batteries, were attacking Westende and Middelkerke. That day the Eastern Squadron fired seventy-eight rounds of the precious ammunition and the Western Squadron a hundred and sixteen. The damage done appeared to be considerable, and none of the monitors was hit. The casualties were confined to the drifter *Great Heart*, which was blown up with the loss of her commanding officer and seven men, and the auxiliary patrol yacht *Sanda*, which was acting with the Eastern drifters and was sunk by gunfire from Blankenberghe with the loss of her commander and twelve officers and men.[1] In the evening the Eastern Squadron rejoined the Admiral at Dunkirk, to receive the news of the capture of Loos and the promise of our first successes in other parts of the front of attack.

In good heart the naval demonstration was renewed next day, but only on Middelkerke and Raversyde. Ostend was considered out of the question, owing to the Tirpitz battery. Its range was so great that to attack it effectively the monitors would have to crawl in under its accurate fire for at least 8,000 yards, and with their low speed this would mean almost certain destruction before they could get even into extreme range. The only chance was to deal with it at night, and this was being arranged when the weather changed and nothing beyond some desultory firing at extreme range could be done for a week. It was not till October 2 that the weather mended. On that night the Admiral with four monitors steamed up the coast past Ostend under clouds of star shells from the enemy, which seemed to tell the anxiety ashore, and in the morning fifty rounds were spent on Zeebrugge to keep up the alarm. There the operation ended. Though the battle of Loos had not yet come to an end, the Admiral, feeling that he had exhausted the possibilities of a pretence of landing, reported that he could do no more to assist the army till an advance from Nieuport was intended, and that he proposed to devote his force to preparing for this eventuality, and to trying to destroy the heavy coast batteries. So the whole fleet was withdrawn to Dover, without the enemy having made any attempt to interfere with it by torpedo attack.

As a measure of what such coastal work under modern conditions was worth, the operations were inconclusive. The defective gun mountings in the first four monitors, the failure of the *Marshal Ney's* engines, the breakdown of the observation arrangements and the shortage of ammunition

[1] The loss of the commander was specially deplored. He was Lieutenant-Commander H. T. Gartside-Tipping, the oldest officer serving afloat, being one of the veterans who early in the war had volunteered to serve in any capacity desired.

deprived the test of most of its value. Such drawbacks were in themselves enough to deprive the attempt of any chance of a real success, and the result could not be regarded as satisfactory.

In so far as the operations were intended to destroy the German submarine bases and coast batteries, they had failed, and what effect they had had in holding German troops to the coast could not be determined. All we know was that the Allies' long-planned and premature military offensive had failed in its immediate object, as our own higher authorities only too rightly anticipated. True we had gained some ground, but they could only reflect with regret that, had that ground been gained on the Gallipoli front, it would have availed to settle in our favour what the German Great General Staff was regarding as "the incomparably important point" of securing the Dardanelles. Had a tithe of the men and the ammunition lavished on the abortive offensive been spent upon the exhausted and disappointed Turks, there can be little doubt that the Germans would have found their effort in the Near East too late. As it was they were well in time, and there being no present hope of direct action, we had, in order to parry the new German stroke, to agree to a counter-move that involved us in complexities beyond anything we had yet experienced.

CHAPTER IX

SALONICA

WHILE the ill-fated offensive was proceeding on the Western Front the French idea of stretching out a hand to Serbia from Salonica had taken more definite shape. When, on September 23, the joint request of Serbia and Greece for 150,000 men had been considered, and it had been found impossible to give a categorical answer till the result of the coming battles in Artois and Champagne was known, the British Government had gone so far as to say that a small contingent might be quickly landed at Salonica as evidence of their intention to support Serbia. From this small concession began our entanglement in the French design, which was destined to strain the resources of the navy and mercantile marine beyond what they were fully able to bear.

At the moment there was reason to believe that no further committal would follow. Russia had no doubt that a contingent of even 5,000 men would suffice to bring Bulgaria to reason, and was for accompanying it with her favourite diplomatic card of an ultimatum. France, however, was insisting that a military demonstration must be made in sufficient force to prevent the resignation of M. Venizelos, on whose ascendancy rested the only hope of saving the situation in the Balkans, and she was urging that he should be informed that if Greece would mobilise in defence of Serbia a Franco-British force would be sent to support her in resisting a Bulgarian invasion. There was no time to deliberate on the possible consequences of our reluctant consent, for Bulgaria had ordered a general mobilisation for September 25. Nor were we without hope that what we then contemplated would suffice. We had just learned that the King of Greece had consented, (23rd), to a general mobilisation, though "only as a measure of precaution, not committing the country to participation in the general war." In these circumstances it was decided on the 24th to fall in with the French plan, and to assure M. Venizelos that we were ready to make the necessary arrangements for the first large contingent of troops " on hearing definitely that their dispatch to Salonica would be welcomed by the Greek Government."

Late the same evening the reply came from Athens. Its effect was that M. Venizelos understood the whole force of 150,000 men would be sent and that he " would be pleased at the arrival at Salonica of any force of Allied troops, however small." At the same time it was explained that the King's attitude was doubtful, for when it was just too late he had tried to stop M. Venizelos from asking for the 150,000 men. This was far from satisfactory, and next day our Minister at Athens was instructed to ascertain definitely whether the Greek Government accepted officially our offer to send troops to Salonica and would welcome them on arrival.

Steps were already being taken to find the men. In view of the offensive in France the only apparent means was to draw upon the Dardanelles, which could be done if Suvla Bay were abandoned. Such a shortening of our line, it was calculated, would set free two divisions of General Hamilton's army, and by adding some 8,000 Yeomanry who were on their way to Egypt, about 37,400 men would be available. Telegrams had already been sent out during the afternoon of the 23rd both to General Hamilton and Admiral de Robeck asking for their opinion whether, if Suvla were given up, Anzac could be supplied from its own beaches, and assuring them that there was no idea of abandoning the Dardanelles. To the men on the spot such a suggestion was highly disconcerting, and they replied strongly deprecating any idea of abandoning Suvla unless the whole situation in the Balkans had changed. They hoped, by establishing a new harbour at Ari Burnu beach, to be able to supply the new Anzac position, but if the Suvla position were abandoned the enemy's guns could make this beach untenable, and in that case they would have to abandon everything that the Anzacs had won in the recent attack.

General Hamilton's apprehensions for the fate of the Dardanelles enterprise were increased by the receipt of an urgent telegram from General Bailloud (September 25) saying that he had received an order from Paris to arrange for sending away one of his divisions. There was no explanation of the object or destination, but General Hamilton was soon to be enlightened. Late that night he received a message from Lord Kitchener explaining the new situation that had arisen out of the Bulgarian mobilisation and the Greek invitation, as it was then understood, and telling him that two of his divisions were required for Salonica and that the French wanted a brigade or a division of their expeditionary force for the same destination. No sooner, however, had the telegram been dispatched than the reply to our request to Athens for an official assurance of welcome came in, and it only reflected the shifting no-man's-land that lay between the policy of the King and that of his Ministers. True it stated that they were now in agreement, but it was only too obvious from the rest of the message that they were not. "The King," it went on to say, "hoped that the Allied troops would not be sent to Salonica for the present, but M. Venizelos trusts that preparations to send them will be rapidly pushed on, and that they will be sent to Mudros or some other convenient base so as to be available when wanted, which he thinks the course of events will soon prove to be the case." In a later telegram Sir Francis Elliot, our Minister at Athens, explained that M. Venizelos had suggested Mityleni as an alternative half-way house for the troops, but that there would be no objection to stores and horses proceeding direct to Salonica and being taken up country by men in plain clothes under the pretence of being destined for Serbia.

To men burdened with the tremendous anxieties of the offensive in France which was then beginning, such a shifty reply was in the last degree exasperating. It added greatly to their difficulties, especially in regard to their advice to Serbia. From the first she had been eager to seize the advantage of her own complete mobilisation to take the offensive before Bulgaria was ready to move. The Allies had held her back, hoping still to induce her and Greece to make the territorial concessions on which they relied for drawing Bulgaria out of the influence of Germany. That hope, although Russia had not ceased to press Serbia to consent, was now very faint, but still she must be held back. If she struck the first blow the Greek King would seize the excuse for contending that no *casus fœderis* had arisen under his defensive alliance with her, and the ground would be cut from under the feet of M. Venizelos. The Bulgarian mobilisation had begun, news of a great concentration of Austro-German forces on the Serbian frontier was coming in, but nothing more could be done while the Greek factor was shifting from hour to hour in nervous irresolution between the devil and the deep sea.

At the Dardanelles there was no less anxiety. General Hamilton was sending a long and reasoned message pointing out the serious consequences of abandoning Suvla, and the naval objections were insisted on no less forcibly by Admiral de Robeck next morning. But as soon as the General's message reached Whitehall he was informed that owing to the hesitating attitude of Greece no definite action could be taken, and that Paris had been intimated that the definite order to General Bailloud to withdraw his division was premature. To determine the Greek attitude was the first essential, and next day (September 27) a message went to Athens pointing out the impossibility of the situation as it stood. The idea of smuggling troops and stores through Salonica was summarily rejected, with a clear intimation that the work of collecting transports to comply with the original invitation must be suspended till we had a definite understanding about the landing of the troops, and that it was of the last importance that it should come without further delay.

The remonstrance had scarcely gone when we were faced with another of those bewildering shifts of front which rendered the whole Salonica question little less than a nightmare to our baffled Ministers. Their message was crossed by one from Athens, announcing that M. Venizelos had obtained the consent of the King to the dispatch of British and French troops, and requesting that they should come at once if possible, before the Greek troops, who we knew were to begin concentrating in Macedonia on the 30th, required the use of the Salonica railway. So far the message was satisfactory enough, but it was added that the King was to know nothing officially until the troops were on the point of arriving, and then a formal protest was to be made.

Clearly this would never do, and our reply was that we were already making arrangements to send the troops, but the difficulty of landing them in face of even a formal protest was obvious. Such a protest was therefore inadmissible, and M. Venizelos was once more urged to make it perfectly clear that the troops would be welcome. The message concluded with a suggestion that the Greek navy should co-operate in the laying of anti-submarine defences for the port. The Greek answer, which was received in the course of the day (September 28), was staggering. While thanking the British Government cordially for the offer of troops, they "thought there was no present need to avail themselves of it in view of the declaration of both the Bulgarian and the Serbian Governments." These declarations referred apparently to an assurance received from Serbia that she did not mean to take the offensive and one from Bulgaria that her attitude, like that of Greece, was one of armed neutrality. To all appearance the telegrams indicated a complete *volte face;* but next day (September 29), before we could adjust ourselves to the kaleidoscopic situation, word came in from Athens that no notice was to be taken of the last telegram; the real message was that of the 27th, desiring the Allies to take action.

At the Dardanelles the pirouettes which Athens was forced by her difficult position to dance produced a bewilderment of cross purposes, as orders and countermands followed each other in quick succession. On September 26 General Hamilton, in pressing the objections to abandoning Suvla, had stated that he thought he could arrange to hold the position if he sent away the Xth and LIIIrd Divisions and no more than a brigade of the French; and the following day, after we had been told that the King had consented to the landing at Salonica, he was instructed to prepare to withdraw the two divisions he had specified and that the French had been told he could spare one of their brigades. But before the telegram arrived General Bailloud informed him that he had an order from Paris to proceed to Mudros with a division from Helles. General Hamilton, as Allied Commander-in-Chief, could only reply that having received no intimation of such a decision, and as his own orders were specific, he could not permit him to move without further instructions.[1] The instructions when they came were to concentrate the Xth Division at Mudros and to stand fast with the LIIIrd till it was clear whether the French meant to move a brigade or a division. The preparations which had been ordered for a landing at Salonica now began, and a party of British and French officers left in the destroyer *Scourge* to make preliminary arrangements for the reception of the troops, with the *Latouche-Tréville* to keep up wireless connection.

All seemed now fairly well, but it was far from well. The staff officers found, instead of the welcome they believed to be assured, a reception cold to the verge of hostility. It was obvious that something was wrong at Athens. What it was they could not tell, but it would seem that, for reasons which it is difficult to fathom, M. Venizelos had become suspicious of the Allies' intentions. Russia had never ceased to urge that Greece and Serbia should be pressed even at this late hour to make the suggested territorial concessions to Bulgaria. The sacrifice required from Greece was Kavala and its hinterland.[2] It was scarcely a secret that this

[1] *Gallipoli Diary*, II., p. 218.

[2] By the unratified Treaty of London, which closed the first Balkan war, the new boundaries of the Balkan States were to be settled by an international conference (Art. VI). No decision was given; but it was generally understood that Salonica would be ceded to Greece, Kavala to Bulgaria, and that the frontier between the two would be the River Struma, as this was roughly the territory which their armies had occupied. During the second Balkan

solution of the Balkan difficulty was also favoured in other Allied quarters, and a series of unforeseen chances now changed the vigilant Minister's attitude to one of alarm that the real intention of the Salonica design was to seize the zone and hold it as a means of purchasing Bulgaria's adhesion to the Allied cause. It would seem that it was with the object of countering the suspected scheme that the Greek army was about to concentrate in the Salonica area. To make matters worse, at the moment the Allied officers arrived the atmosphere of grave suspicion was thickened by a mangled report of a speech of Sir Edward Grey's in Parliament which seemed to leave no doubt that Greece was to be betrayed. To confirm M. Venizelos' worst fears it was discovered that the chief of the British staff officers who had arrived at Salonica was General Hamilton. It was in fact Brigadier-General A. B. Hamilton, but it was at once assumed that the Commander-in-Chief had come in person, and it looked as though the main British effort in the Near East was to be transferred to Salonica without Greek consent. The truth was quite otherwise. General Bailloud had just announced that he had definite orders from Paris to withdraw a whole division composed entirely of European troops, and that he was taking steps to execute the order, and Sir Ian Hamilton had to send home word that, in accordance with a discretion which he had by this time been allowed, he must retain the LIIIrd Division and dispatch only the Xth. It was already being quietly withdrawn by night from Suvla without molestation by the Turks, and by the evening of October 1 it had been concentrated at Mudros, ready to embark for Salonica as soon as Admiral de Robeck got the word.

During the afternoon Vice-Admiral Dartige du Fournet, who had just relieved Admiral Nicol in command of the French Dardanelles Squadron,[1] and was now at Mudros, informed the British Admiral that he had had a telegram from the *Latouche-Tréville* saying that there was a complete

---

war, the Greeks pressed up the coast as far as Kavala, and forced the Bulgarians to cede it by the Treaty of Bucharest. There was thus a port—Kavala—and a strip of territory between the Struma and the Mesta over which the Bulgarians felt that they had a right, and their claim was strengthened by the fact that the inhabitants were admittedly Bulgarians. The cession required of Serbia was that part of Macedonia which lies to the south of a line running north-eastwards from Lake Ochrida to the Bulgarian frontier near Kustendil. In the treaties of alliance preceding the first Balkan war, it was intended that this territory should be given to Bulgaria: it was called in consequence the "uncontested zone."

[1] Admiral Dartige du Fournet was succeeded by Vice-Admiral Gauchet in the command of the Syrian Coast Squadron.

entente at Salonica. He was therefore sending off the first French contingent, and wished our anti-submarine net-layers to get away at once. They were ordered to sail accordingly, and on receipt of instructions from home our first contingent was embarked on board the battleship *Albion*.

Once more all seemed plain sailing. The alarm into which M. Venizelos had fallen had not yet been felt, but during the night a signal came in from the *Doris* which put everything back to the beginning. She had been sent to Salonica to assist the *Latouche-Tréville*, whose wireless was not satisfactory, and what she had to say was that M. Venizelos had refused to permit a man to be landed or a net laid. Captain F. Larken had therefore, with great promptitude, intercepted the French troops and our own net-layers as they were on the point of arriving and turned them back. Admiral de Robeck also stopped our own contingent from putting to sea, and another impasse had to be faced.

Nor was it only about Salonica that M. Venizelos had turned obdurate. He was protesting with equal vehemence about what was going on at Milo in the French patrol zone.[1] Since the French Admiral had established a patrol base there, Admiral de Robeck, at his request, had been taking steps to secure it with anti-submarine nets, and access to it was forbidden by night. The island was an integral part of Greece, and the infringement of Greek sovereign rights was undeniable. Wherever the Allies went, so the Greek Premier protested, "we acted as though the place belonged to us." We could scarcely resent the complaint in view of what had been done elsewhere in the Ægean, but without Milo our line of supply through the French zone could not be made safe. At present it was far from safe. Even with Milo the Kithera channel, between Crete and the Greek mainland, which the transports were now using, would be insecure. Storeships and colliers were being lost almost every day in its approaches, and both Admiral de Robeck and Admiral Limpus at Malta were urging that another patrol base should be formed at Kithera or Antikithera—that is, Cerigo or Cerigotto.

In view of the check at Athens nothing could be done at the moment. It indeed had come at a most untimely juncture. Russia, seeing herself likely to lose her place as the dominating power in the Balkans, had suddenly overridden our efforts to find a formula on which all could agree for opening the eyes of Bulgaria to the risks she was running, and had sent (October 4) an ultimatum to Sofia. It bluntly

[1] See Map 5.

announced that the Russian Minister had instructions to leave, if within twenty-four hours the Bulgarian Government did not openly break with the enemies of the Slav cause and of Russia. Confronted with this *demarche* the Western Powers could do nothing but fall into line, and we were to find ourselves committed to war with Bulgaria with scarcely a possibility of help from Russia and with our only line of operations barred by Greece.

Everything now depended on disabusing M. Venizelos of the sinister impressions under which he had so unexpectedly fallen. Between Paris, London and Athens the wires were promptly alive with explanations. We were able to assure him that all offers to Bulgaria had now lapsed, and at his request to give him a categorical assurance that in passing troops through Salonica the Allies had no intention of encroaching on the sovereign rights of Greece or of interfering in the administration of the country. With this formula he was content and assented once more to the landing of the troops at Salonica with no more than a formal protest, on the understanding that they would at once proceed up country. To this last proviso we could not agree. To dispatch the troops in driblets into the interior was an inadmissible military operation. It was essential first to concentrate in the vicinity of Salonica and prepare a base there. To this condition no exception was taken, and during the night of October 2-3 the *Doris* was able to signal to Mudros that she had received written permission for the troops to land. The French received orders direct from Paris to proceed, but Admiral de Robeck was told not to move till the permission was confirmed from Athens. The confirmation came next day. The net-ships with the leading French transports started immediately, the *Albion* with 1,500 British troops followed in the evening with the second French contingent; next day (the 5th) the French artillery ships sailed and 2,000 more British troops, and at last our effort to face the new Austro-German front was well under way. All was ready for the rest of the troops to follow in due course, and arrangements were being made to transport a French cavalry regiment from Egypt, as well as our Yeomanry brigade which would shortly be concentrated there.

We could not, of course, disguise from ourselves, in view of intelligence of the enemy's activity on the Serbian frontier, that the movement was late. Still there was hope. Hitherto, owing to the political instability at Athens and the lack of machinery for rapid co-ordination of the counsels of the Allies, it had been beyond the wit of man to frame a coherent policy. Now that the outlook was clearer Lord Kitchener on the 5th went to Calais again for another conference, to ascertain definitely what force the French were likely to send and to concert a plan of operations. At the same time steps were taken to arrange for the Greek navy, which was relatively strong in destroyers, to co-operate with ours on the new lines of communication. On the same day M. Venizelos, after explaining his foreign policy to the Chamber, carried a vote of confidence. On the whole, indeed, the prospects of the enterprise upon which we had reluctantly entered at the instance of France looked brighter, when before the day was out the delicate web that had been spun with so many set-backs was suddenly torn to pieces. A telegram came in to say that M. Venizelos was no longer in power. On proceeding to the Palace to report the result of the debate, the King had informed him that in his speech to Parliament he had gone beyond his authority, and that in spite of the vote of confidence he could not endorse the policy of his Ministers. Under a constitution based at least ostensibly on Ministerial responsibility there was but one course for M. Venizelos to adopt, and he had handed in his resignation.

To complete the confusion into which the whole situation was thrown by the collapse at Athens, the conference at Calais had decided the same day to proceed on the basis of the previous state of affairs. To provide the promised 150,000 men France, besides the division and the cavalry regiment already detailed, would at once add a Marine brigade. These troops were to be followed as soon as possible by a second brigade, two cavalry divisions and another division of infantry—in all 64,000 men. As for the British contingent, besides the division and a Yeomanry regiment already under orders, three divisions were to be taken from Sir John French's force. This would give a total 20,000 short of the number promised, but it was agreed that the deficiency could not be made up by drawing more troops from Gallipoli, since the operations there were inseparable from those at Salonica. In addition, the French stipulated that we were to provide transports for their two cavalry divisions as well as our own three divisions. In spite of the breaking strain it meant upon our shipping resources we agreed, but the question of command was not so easily settled. In this connection a preliminary agreement on the plan of operations was essential, and here the views of the two Governments were fundamentally opposed. The French, on the promise they had given merely to pass through Greek territory into Serbia, had ordered General Bailloud to proceed at once to Nish. To reach it from Salonica fifty miles of difficult mountainous country had to be traversed, and we on our part refused to commit ourselves to so hazardous a movement. Our intention from the first, as we were obliged to remind our Allies, was not to move from the port till we knew definitely that the Greeks were to take part with us in rescuing Serbia, and the resignation of M. Venizelos could leave us in no doubt that we must adhere to our resolution.

The actual situation at Salonica was that most of the French division had landed, the last units were leaving Mudros, the *Albion* with 1,500 of our Xth Division had arrived, and our anti-submarine nets were in place across the mouth of Salonica bay. General Sarrail, in spite, as he tells us, of being urged by influential politicians in the ranks both of the Government and the Opposition to refuse to proceed now that M. Venizelos had fallen, left Paris on October 6 and embarked next day, but without any troops. At the same time General Bailloud's orders to advance were cancelled. He was to remain at Salonica till General Sarrail arrived, and General Sarrail was not to move from the port till another brigade came from France.[1]

There was now nothing to do, so far as our Government could see, but to stand fast till the situation was cleared, and yet it was the moment when definite action was most urgent. The day before M. Venizelos fell Russia presented her ultimatum to Bulgaria; it was rejected; on October 6 we knew that Petrograd had broken off relations with Sofia; it would be impossible for us not to conform, and in spite of all our efforts we found ourselves being forced into a hostile attitude to Bulgaria, without having secured the co-operation of Greece. Paris was accordingly informed that we could not send another man to Salonica till we knew where we stood, and our Minister at Athens was instructed to press for a frank declaration of what the policy of Greece was now to be. He was further to insist that the presence of the French and British forces at Salonica involved no breach of neutrality as the German propaganda was actively representing it: the troops had come on a definite understanding that Greece desired their presence in order to enable her to fulfil her engagements for the defence of Serbia. The answer was that the question of supporting Serbia was not yet decided.

On ground so uncertain it was impossible to treat further, and it began to look as though the effort to check the German advance towards Constantinople must be too late. The

[1] Sarrail, *Mon Commandement en Orient*, pp. xv and 308.

invasion of Serbia had begun, Russia was doing nothing to back her ultimatum with force, and it became necessary to consider alternative lines of action. The choice seemed to lie between another desperate effort to force the Dardanelles and the evacuation of Gallipoli. In the latter alternative we could use the troops to strike at Alexandretta or some other vital point in Asia, or else concentrate everything on assisting Serbia by striking in from Dedeagatch or the Gulf of Xeros, while the French pushed on, as they still wished to do, from Salonica. A joint appreciation from the Admiralty and the General Staff was accordingly called for.

By October 11, when the appreciation was ready, we were in possession of General Joffre's considered opinion. It proved to be more in conformity with our own than previous French utterances. General Sarrail had in fact been ordered not to advance into Serbia without further instructions. General Joffre's view was that the operations should be confined to securing Salonica as a base, to holding the railway thence to Uskub, the old Serbian capital, and to preventing the enemy from penetrating into the heart of the country by covering the Serbian right. For this he considered the force available would suffice, particularly if Italy could be persuaded to send a contingent to Salonica and open a second entry from the Adriatic at Durazzo. Regarding the question from a purely strategical point of view, our joint Staff conference had no doubt that without the assurance of Greek co-operation and strong Russian support the risk involved in sending 150,000 men to Serbia was too great to run on a slender hope of stopping munitions reaching Turkey, and to attempt it from any point on the Bulgarian coast would be more hazardous than from Salonica. In whatever way we acted the operations were only too likely to develop upon a scale which would put an unendurable strain upon both our land and sea forces. They therefore concluded that the best way of cutting the tangled knot was to renew the offensive in Gallipoli, provided sufficient force could be spared without prejudice to the fundamental war plan—that is, seeking a decision in France with all possible forces—and for a period of three months they believed the necessary troops could be spared from the main theatre.

So far the strategical problem was fairly simple, but its political deflections could not be ignored. Politically the most desirable way was to persevere at Salonica, but naval and military considerations all condemned it. It was further felt that, heavy as were the moral and political objections to abandoning Serbia to her fate, the objections to abandoning

Gallipoli were heavier still. All, therefore, the conference could suggest in the prevailing uncertainty about the attitude of Rumania and Greece was that the troops which were then being assembled for action in the Balkans should be used for a renewed offensive at the Dardanelles. The objections to increasing our military commitments in Greece and Serbia were represented as being so serious that, when the War Council (Dardanelles Committee) met on October 11, they decided against proceeding further with the despatch of troops to Salonica and directed that the available forces should concentrate in Egypt ready for prompt action when the sky was clearer. It was further decided that a specially selected general officer should proceed to the Mediterranean to study the situation on the spot as it developed, so that he could advise on what line the troops could be employed with the greatest effect as conditions stood when the proposed concentration was ripe. It was hoped that General Haig or Lord Kitchener himself might undertake this all-important mission. On the following day we undertook to provide an army of 200,000 men for operations in the Balkans by January 1, if Greece and Rumania would declare war at once on the Central Powers.[1]

By this time Greece had finally declared her intention to remain neutral. Her neutrality, however, would be so far friendly that we could continue to use Salonica as a base and she would keep her army ready to oppose the Bulgarians at the first sign of an intention to invade her territory. All attempts to move her from this attitude proved unavailing. The King declared frankly he was thoroughly afraid of the German army and no less afraid of the Allied fleet, and no inducement would tempt him to side openly with either. Every effort to revive the Balkan League was equally fruitless. Without strong support from Russia Rumania dared not move, even to threaten a diversion against Bulgaria, and Russia, exhausted and already threatened with signs of internal unrest, could do nothing effective.

In this tangle of difficulties there was clearly only one way of acting that could be regarded as really effective, and that was a quick decision at Gallipoli. A successful effort there would untie all knots and solve all problems. But at Gallipoli affairs were in such a state as to give little hope. True, since the last battle the Turks seemed to have lost all spirit, and sporadic trench warfare had been going on the whole time, generally in our favour, but the enemy—whose hopes we had reason to believe now rested on the arrival of

[1] *Dardanelles Commission Report*, II., p. 53.

Germans to their rescue—made no move, except in the air. There the exchange of compliments with our own bombing planes was frequent, but little or no harm was done. The work of our airmen was supplemented by the constant activity of the monitors and bulge ships. Every few days they were bombarding the Turkish bases and depots or other points selected by the army, and fire observation had by this time so much improved that their practice seems to have been very good.

In the Marmara, moreover, our submarines were as busy as ever. When in the middle of September *E 2* concluded her fruitful cruise, she had been succeeded by Lieutenant-Commander Bruce in *E 12*.[1] She was the first submarine to carry into the Sea of Marmara a gun heavier than a 12-pounder, and the result of the experiment was all that could be desired. On September 16 on her way up the Straits she torpedoed and sank a large steamer in the shallows of Burgaz Bay. Then, finding nothing at Rodosto, on the north shore, she made across for Mudania. On her way, near Kalolimno Island, she chased and fought a torpedo-boat. With her fourth shot she secured a hit, and the enemy, who was quite outranged, made off at high speed for the Golden Horn in a disabled condition. Mudania was dealt with next day, and here she made eight hits on the magazine, silenced the battery and damaged the railway. Two days later she was back at Marmara Island, where she sank a steamer of 3,000 tons laden with cattle and provisions. A spell of foul weather succeeded. When it was over she was to the eastward again, with intent to bombard the San Stefano powder factory outside the city, but she found the place too well patrolled by destroyers and aircraft for her to keep on the surface. On October 4 she was back at the rendezvous to meet *H 1*, which Lieutenant W. B. Pirie had just brought up successfully. The " H " class boats were little more than half the tonnage of the " E's," and nothing so small had yet been tried in the Marmara, but she had already proved her endurance, for, though she had run aground in nearing Nagara and had fouled the net, she came safely through without damage.[2]

[1] See Map 3.

[2] *H 1* was the first of a new class, lighter than the " E's," which formed part of Lord Fisher's programme. Until he returned to the Admiralty on October 30, 1914, no fresh order for submarines had been given, but a large programme of new ones was then quickly inaugurated. Thirty-eight more " E's " were allotted to various private firms, and twenty others (the " H " class) to the Bethlehem Steel Works in America. The first ten were to be built as quickly as possible in Messrs. Vickers' Works in Montreal from American

After the meeting Lieutenant-Commander Bruce ordered his newly arrived consort to the eastward, while he had another look at Rodosto. This time the road was full of shipping, and with gunfire he sank a small steamer and seventeen sailing craft. They met again on October 7 and *H 1* reported she had sunk a steamship at Mudania the previous day. They then in company made another attempt to get at the San Stefano Powder Works, but were again driven off by the patrol. Before, however, they got back to Gallipoli to report their proceedings, *E 12* had torpedoed a steamer in Lampsaki Bay.

So far our submarines were continuing to do all that was expected from them, but on the enemy's side there was also a tale to tell ominous of what the new burden that a further development of the Salonica policy would mean for the navy.

When, after our landing at Suvla, Germany was forced to turn her main offensive front to the Balkans, the movement of troops to the Danube was supplemented by a special naval effort to hamper our operations in the Ægean. Lieutenant-Commander Hersing in *U 21* had already demonstrated the possibility of the larger submarines reaching the Adriatic without the need of an intermediate supply base.[1] In spite of his remarkable success in sinking the *Triumph* and *Majestic* at the end of May, the experiment had not been repeated. Already, however, the attitude of Washington was bringing the Germans to the conclusion that it would be prudent to confine their submarine attack on commerce to waters where few American ships were found. When therefore they became seriously alarmed for the fate of Constantinople, the Mediterranean was obviously the field in which their submarines could most effectively meet both the military and political needs of the situation, and during August four large new submarines were despatched in Hersing's track. The first two, *U 35* and *U 34*, got through our Gibraltar patrol unseen. It was at this time under Vice-Admiral F. E. E. Brock, and comprised the old light cruiser *Pelorus*, ten torpedo-boats and a couple of armed boarding steamers

---

material. To facilitate rapidity of construction they were to be on the lines of those supplied by the Electric Boat Company for the United States navy. The contract was signed on November 10, the first one reached British waters in June, and the whole ten were delivered within seven months. The home firms did no less well with the much larger "E's," for whereas before the war they took from twenty to thirty months to complete, several were now turned out in from eight to ten months.

[1] See *ante*, p. 31.

with some aircraft. As an anti-submarine patrol it left much to be desired, but as it was impossible to provide the destroyers and trawlers he asked for, he was doing his best with what he had. With one patrol line outside the Straits and another inside from coast to coast just west of Alboran Island, he might hope to catch them before or after their submerged run through the Gut. On August 30 the Admiral was warned from home that two more "U" boats were on their way. These were *U 33* and *U 39*. Both were sighted by the Eastern Patrol line, and though *U 33* was engaged by torpedo-boat *No. 95*, both got away and proceeded to do considerable damage along the Algerian coast on their way to Cattaro. Besides these five large boats, all under officers of experience, several smaller "UB" and "UC" boats, a mining class, had been sent overland in sections to Pola. Of them by the middle of September there were five "UB's" and four "UC's," or fourteen in all.

During the first three weeks of September five vessels were sunk off the coast of Crete by *U 34* and *U 35*, but it was not till the end of the month that the first organised raid was made on the Entente communications in the Eastern Mediterranean.[1] No part of it, except the British Ægean zone, was reasonably safe.[2] During the fortnight from September 28 to October 11 nineteen ships were sunk.[3] Of these, nine went down in the approaches to the Kithera and Anti-Kithera Channels, one of which was the *Arabian*, a large vessel full of sorely-needed ammunition, and the same day (October 2) the *Olympic*, eight days out from England with 5,500 Yeomanry, was chased by a submarine west of Cape Matapan. On the route she had traversed between Malta and Cape Matapan four ships that had not her high speed were lost, including one that was bringing the much-wanted motor lighters. Two more were sunk on the direct route from Malta to Alexandria, and three between Alexandria and Crete, where also a fleet sweeper was unsuccessfully attacked. Seeing that to the ordinary war traffic would soon be added numbers of troop transports from Marseilles,

[1] See Map 5.

[2] The only recorded attack in the British zone was made on the *Swiftsure*, proceeding from Mudros to Suvla (September 18), but, as the incident is not mentioned in the German Official History, it is not possible to name her assailant. It may have been *U 21*, which left the area on the 16th and reached Cattaro on the 21st, or one of the "*UB*" or "*UC*" boats, five of which were now working from Constantinople. On September 15 the British Steamship *Patagonia* (6,000 tons) was sunk by *UB 7* in the Black Sea, ten miles from Odessa.

[3] Seven by *U 39* and twelve by *U 33*.

the situation was serious, and steps were quickly taken to meet it. The French Commander-in-Chief, with many expressions of regret at what had happened in his area, withdrew a destroyer flotilla he had with the Italian fleet to guard the route from Malta to Matapan. At the same time Admiral de Robeck detached the sloop *Jonquil* with six trawlers and six drifters down to Milo to assist the French patrol, and also sent his last-arrived submarine, *H 2*, to act with a decoy ship, the *Clacton*, in the way that had proved so successful in the North Sea. By the middle of October the worst of the raid was over, and for some time no further losses were reported, but as it was certain to be repeated shortly orders were given for transports moving through the area to be armed with 12-pounder guns.

Thus the navy met the new call upon it as it had met all others, and it had done all the work of transporting our own and the French troops without touching the arrangements for supplying Gallipoli. But nothing could disguise the strain which the new line of operation would mean both to the navy and our diminished shipping resources. It was still another reason for doubting whether the operations from Salonica could possibly be in time to prevent the Germans from pouring new life into the Turkish defence of Gallipoli. In the opinion of the Admiralty this danger looked more remote than it did to the General Staff; for even if the Germans forced a way through to Constantinople the process of getting supplies into the peninsula must be slow and precarious, owing to the action of our submarines in the Marmara and to the fact that the accurate long-range fire of our ships prevented the use of any convenient port in the Straits. Their view appears to have carried little weight with the Government. When, on October 11, it was decided to send to Egypt all troops that could be spared from France, and that an independent general officer should go out and advise how best to use them, the possibility of evacuating Gallipoli was already a factor in the problem, and as a preliminary step Lord Kitchener the same day telegraphed to Sir Ian Hamilton that although no decision had been taken to evacuate, he wished to have his estimate of what loss evacuation would be likely to cost.

General Hamilton's reply next day (October 12) did not conceal his immediate determination that if so lamentable a decision was taken he must decline to have a hand in carrying it out.[1] What he answered was that the loss must to some extent depend on the circumstances of the moment,

[1] *Gallipoli Diary*, II., p. 249.

but it could scarcely be less than half the men and all the guns and stores, and that possibly with so many still raw troops at Suvla and the Senegalese at Helles it might mean a veritable disaster. This estimate so far exceeded the worst that had been calculated at home that it seems to have fixed a growing feeling that a fresh mind must be brought to bear upon the situation, and consequently that a change in the Dardanelles command was inevitable. Without such a change it was clear the crucial decision could not be taken with an open mind. The resolution to recall General Hamilton was reached with the greatest reluctance. Seeing how much he had done with wholly insufficient means the blame of the failure could scarcely lie heavily upon him. Yet there was no doubt the thankless step had to be taken, and on October 15 the telegram went out. "The War Council," it ran, "held last night decided that though the Government fully appreciate your work and the gallant manner in which you personally have endeavoured to make the operations a success in spite of the great difficulties you have had to contend with, they consider it advisable to make a change in the command." Until his successor could arrive, General Birdwood was to be left in charge. The officer chosen to succeed General Hamilton was General Sir Charles Monro, then commanding the Third Army in France: a military leader of wide experience and with a high reputation for dispassionate judgment. He was also the officer selected to advise the Government on the general situation in the Near East.

At the same time the Expeditionary Force was to lose the services of another man who had borne the heat and burden of the day. This was Vice-Admiral Guépratte, now 2nd in Command of the Dardanelles Squadron, who on promotion had been appointed Préfet Maritime at Brest. From the first his co-operation with his British colleagues, no less than the gallant manner in which on all occasions he had fought his squadron, had won him the affection and esteem of everyone who had to work with him. Longer acquaintance had only deepened the impression of his loyalty, spirit and ability, and he left with the sincere regret of his British comrades. This was not the only change of command which now took place in the Mediterranean. The Commander-in-Chief, Admiral Boué de Lapéyrère, had asked on October 10 to retire for ill-health, and Admiral Dartige du Fournet, who had been commanding the French Dardanelles Squadron, took his place. He was succeeded by Vice-Admiral D. M. Gauchet, and Vice-Admiral F. P. Moreau was appointed to the command of the 3rd Squadron on the Syrian Coast.

In France itself the situation was further confused by a cabinet crisis. The shock which the complete failure of the recent offensive had caused could scarcely leave things as they were. On October 13 M. Delcassé, the Minister for Foreign Affairs, resigned, on the ground, it was believed, that he disapproved of the Salonica venture. For the time the crisis stopped there, and M. Viviani, the Premier, taking the vacant portfolio as acting Minister, endeavoured to weather the storm.

We were still holding back from the desperate Balkan adventure, but the French now authorised General Sarrail to advance into Serbia as soon as his base was secure. It was a lead we could not follow, but, on the other hand, we were urging that the break of relations with Bulgaria which Russia had brought about should be followed at once with a declaration of war. For some time past Admiral de Robeck, in spite of all his other preoccupations, had been ready to declare a blockade and bombard Dedeagatch. A proposal had been made that in view of the doubtful attitude of the Greek army, which was continuing to move to Salonica, we should strike at Bulgaria from the port of Enos, but this had been vetoed by the Admiralty, on the ground that there was no shelter there from prevailing winds and no landing facilities, and that it would entail a further dispersion of force to which their overstrained resources were unequal.

In view of the crisis in France the negotiations for a joint declaration of war proceeded slowly. We, however, broke off relations on October 13. Bulgaria declared war on Serbia next day, and Admiral de Robeck was immediately instructed to declare a blockade of the Bulgarian coast with two days' grace, and to ascertain by air reconnaissance whether there were any objectives of military value that could be reached by bombardment. This step we accompanied (October 15) by a declaration of war, and France issued hers the next day.[1]

So far we were in agreement, but no further. We were pressing upon Paris that our position in the Near East and India called for the release of eight divisions from France (including two for India). We were ready to send our contingent of the promised 150,000 men to Salonica, but it was only from France that the troops could come, and then only if General Joffre took over the line south of Arras. At the same time we made it an express condition that we did not bind ourselves to advance beyond Salonica unless Greece

[1] Russia and Italy declared war on Bulgaria on October 19.

joined the Entente, and as an inducement for her to do so we were offering her Cyprus. None of our conditions was acceptable to the French Government, and M. Millerand, the Minister for War, came over to London to try to arrange matters. The day after he left Paris (October 17) the situation had grown distinctly worse. News arrived that the Bulgarians had cut the railway south of Uskub and that General Sarrail was advancing in order to restore communications with the Serbians. To us the movement seemed rash in the extreme. Rumania had just definitely refused to move unless the Allies sent half a million men; Italy was protesting she could give no help till her coming offensive against Austria on the Isonzo was delivered, and Greece could not be tempted from her attitude by any territorial concession. We therefore had no hesitation in informing General Mahon that he must not follow General Sarrail's lead without further instructions.[1]

The only prospect of immediate help came from Russia, and it was little enough. She had told us that she was ready to bombard the Bulgarian Black Sea port of Varna on the 21st, and Admiral de Robeck was now given definite orders to attack Dedeagatch on the same day. From this operation there was some hope of producing a diversionary effect. Our scouting trawlers had been reporting a nervous activity along the Ægean coast. At various points entrenching and wiring was incessant, pointing to serious apprehension of a descent in force. We had also ascertained that there were points of high military value that could be reached by ship fire. At Dedeagatch the railway from Salonica ran down to the coast and thence it continued to Constantinople. For about ten miles the latter section was exposed to attack from the sea, but five miles inland from the port, at a place called Bodoma, a by-pass had been constructed behind the hills so that traffic east and west could pass in comparative security without going into Dedeagatch. The junction itself, however, could easily be reached by the heavy guns of the monitors, and it was this vital point which Admiral de Robeck chose for his main objective. The bombarding force was organised in two squadrons. The main squadron, under Captain F. Larken, in the *Doris*, comprised the bulge cruiser *Theseus*, two 9·2 and one 6-inch monitor with the *Ben-My-Chree* for observation and four destroyers and ten ketches. With this force he was to operate against Dedeagatch and the coastline as far as the Bulgarian frontier

[1] General Mahon had been appointed to the command of the British troops at Salonica.

and the Maritza river (that is, ten miles south-east), with orders that the destruction of Bodoma junction and the subsequent destruction of the rolling stock and stores was to be its principal object. The second squadron (*Kléber*, *Askold*, with four British destroyers and four trawlers), under Captain S. Ivanov of the *Askold*, was to operate along the coast thirty miles westward as far as Porto Lagos (Kara Agatch), where, as well as at Dedeagatch and the estuary of the Maritza, oil stores for submarines were suspected. The instructions were to watch the coast road and endeavour to locate batteries which had been reported at various points. Damage to neutral shipping was to be avoided and civil residences respected as far as possible.

The operations, which were watched by the Admiral in the *Triad*, began on the morning of the 21st by the destroyers rapidly sweeping before the town. No mines were found, but before the ships could take up their positions the airmen reported the visibility too low for observing fire on Bodoma. Attention was, therefore, devoted to Dedeagatch. The monitors, delayed by a head wind, had not yet arrived, and at 1.0 the *Doris* and *Theseus* began on the barracks, closing in from 4,800 yards. At this range every shot told. Hundreds of troops were seen flying to the hills, and the whole range of buildings was soon a heap of blazing ruins. Other military works were then taken on, and finally the railway station and the long lines of trucks on the sea front. In this work two of the destroyers shared, going close in and firing deliberately on the rolling stock with great effect and setting on fire many trucks which seemed to be full of oil. As soon as the first monitor, *M 16*, arrived she was given a railway bridge east of the town for a target and quickly destroyed it. The other two, *M 19* and *M 29*, on arrival joined in the general holocaust of rolling stock, railway and harbour work, warehouses and shipping, while the destroyers set fire to a coal-heap and an oil store. By 4.0 the work was done and the squadron ceased fire. By this time the other squadron had dealt with the storehouses at Porto Lagos and the signal stations along the coast. Nowhere had there been any opposition, and when, during the night, a feint of landing was made on each side of the port there was still no sign of resistance.

The attack had apparently come upon the Bulgarians as a complete surprise. They were at the moment concentrating their efforts on Uskub, and the day after the bombardment it fell into their hands. For the British Government it was an additional reason for not following General

Sarrail's lead. It was no longer possible for the Serbians to prevent the Bulgarians and Germans joining hands; they were threatened with an overwhelming disaster, and if this occurred it was likely that Greece would be unable any longer to resist the pressure which Germany was bringing upon her. This view was urged upon the French with an intimation that General Sarrail could not maintain the forward position he had occupied. Their reply was that for them the new situation called for the immediate despatch of more troops and a naval demonstration to counteract the influence of the German army. It was a view we could not share. Every telegram from the Near East added a deeper shadow to the alarming situation of Serbia. She was even protesting that unless 150,000 men came to her rescue in ten days she was lost. This was quite impossible. A large proportion of our available transports were carrying the French divisions. Even could transport be found the troops could not be landed quickly at Salonica, for the port would soon be thoroughly congested by the Greeks, who were on the point of increasing their force there by sending round the First Army Corps by sea from Piræus. Yet the French continued to urge us on.

The only ray of light in the situation was that our bombardment and feint seemed to have alarmed Bulgaria. The Greek Minister at Sofia reported that the attack had been taken very seriously. As a port and a railway centre Dedeagatch was ruined, wild rumours spread that thousands of troops had been killed in the bombardment, and three regiments of territorials were hurried off to the threatened spot. At best it was far too little to restore the situation. We were more firmly convinced than ever that it was now impossible to save Serbia, but it was equally evident that perseverance in the venture had become a political necessity in France. General Joffre, who on military grounds had opposed the precarious scheme from the first, was now urging that, having once begun, it was impossible to turn back. British military opinion was practically unanimous in opposition, and the Admiralty objection to being saddled with the protection of another important line of communication had just been deepened by a very regrettable occurrence.

On October 19 the transport *Marquette* (7,000 tons) had left Egypt for Salonica with the Ammunition Column of the XXIXth Division and the New Zealand Stationary Hospital. On board were thirty-six nurses, twenty-two officers and 588 other ranks, besides 541 animals. Unmolested, she entered the Gulf of Salonica on October 23, and there, only some thirty miles short of the anti-submarine net, she was torpedoed by *U 35*. British and French patrol boats were quickly on the spot, and before she sank were able to rescue the greater part of those on board, but the first reports that had come in put the missing at little less than half the whole number.[1] Intelligence from a Greek source gave reason to believe that the submarine which had done the mischief was operating from the Euripo Channel behind Eubœa, and representations were made to Athens. At the moment probably nothing could have been more unwelcome to the Greek Government than that such use should be made of their territorial waters when they were straining every nerve to preserve a precarious balance between the Entente and the Central Powers, and two destroyers were at once despatched to search the suspected channel. Her anxiety not to give cause of offence to the sea Powers was probably genuine. In France, Italy and England the Press were in clamorous chorus supporting the French idea and calling for coercion of the Greeks. The ships of the Allies were within striking distance and the Austro-German army still far away.

In taking this attitude Greece was certainly well advised. So long as she maintained formal neutrality we were not to be persuaded into coercing her to take sides with the Entente. On the purely strategical question we were more firmly convinced than ever that the action on which France had set her heart was wrong. But unfortunately it was now obvious that the question could not be settled on naval and military grounds alone, and we had to recognise that for other reasons, if we blankly refused to go further than we had originally undertaken to do, the solidarity of the Entente would be in jeopardy. The only course seemed to be to suggest a Franco-British Staff conference for a frank interchange of views. As the issue to be decided turned so much on the naval factor, to which it appeared the French were not attaching sufficient weight—particularly in the matter of transport and its defence—it was agreed that naval as well as military representatives should attend. Meanwhile the concentration of troops in Egypt was to proceed; eleven transports were ordered home from the Ægean for the purpose, and Admiral de Robeck was called on to report on how many men could be maintained in Serbia with our existing naval resources.

How vital a point the extent of our capacity for main-

[1] By October 28 there were still unaccounted for 128 troops, ten nurses and twenty-nine of the crew, all of whom were eventually reported as killed.

taining the sea communications was, had just been brought home to all concerned. Russia had promised to send a contingent of troops from Archangel to join the Franco-British force, but the project had had to be abandoned for lack of transport. On the other hand, there was a new though faint ray of hope that she might still come to the rescue. A project was now being considered of a large Russian force being brought to bear by way of Rumania, if only rifles could be provided for her, and these would probably be available from Italy and our own resources. In the Black Sea also she was taking action on the Bulgarian coast in concert with our own fleet in the Ægean. On October 26 the spell of bad weather had mended, and on that day Admiral de Robeck tried once more to get at Bodoma. The ships employed were the *Theseus* and the monitors *M 28* and *M 15*, but the attempt was not very successful. At an early stage the 9·2-inch gun of *M 28* had a premature burst and had to cease firing, but the airmen reported ten hits on the railway station, and some rolling stock destroyed. It was probably enough to keep up the alarm, especially as the Black Sea Fleet next day appeared off Varna and dropped into it 178 rounds of 12-inch and 8-inch and a score of bombs from an aeroplane.

In the Marmara we were still holding our own.[1] In the third week of October there were four submarines up the Straits. *E 12* and *H 1* were still operating. For several days the weather had been very bad and they had no luck, but on the 20th *H 1* succeeded in torpedoing two steamers of about 3,000 and 1,500 tons near Injeh Burnu, and both were seen to sink. On the 22nd they were joined by the French boat *Turquoise* and next day by *E 20* (Lieutenant-Commander C. H. Warren), who on her way up had torpedoed two steamers in Bergaz Iskalessi above the net. It was now time for *E 12* to return. Lieutenant-Commander Kenneth Bruce had surpassed all previous records by prolonging his cruise to forty days, during which time he had accounted for five steamers and thirty-two sailing craft, besides damage done to patrol vessels and to magazines and railways ashore. On October 25 he started to go down, but only to meet adventure surpassing in peril all he had yet encountered. In passing the net he seems to have carried away a part of it. The effect was to force the boat down by the bows and jam the foremost hydroplane so that she began rapidly to dive, and in spite of every effort to get the bows up she continued to sink till she reached a depth of 245 feet. The pressure of the water then

[1] See Map 3.

burst in the conning-tower glasses, the conning-tower filled, and a number of leaks developed forward so dangerously that the fore compartment had to be closed. At last by getting three men on the hydroplane handgear a little movement was obtained and the boat began to rise. As she approached the surface whatever it was she was towing revealed her position and she was attacked by six patrol vessels. Then, being quite unmanageable, she plunged down again, and so continued to struggle on with continual sudden and uncontrollable inclinations till when 150 yards off Kilid Bahr she was brought up by what sounded like a chain mooring. Speeding up to full power she found that in four minutes the obstruction was scraping aft and, what is more, that it apparently had cleared away the incubus which had been distracting her since she passed the net. For suddenly the boat took a steep angle upwards and rose so rapidly that she was into new peril. It was impossible to trim quickly enough to prevent her bows and conning-tower breaking the surface, and the moment they appeared shore batteries and patrol vessels opened a hot fire at close range. Two torpedoes were also seen coming from Kilid Bahr; one missed the conning-tower by ten yards, the other passed astern, and though she was hit several times by small shell no serious damage was done before she was able to dive again. Then all was plain sailing, and without further adventure she reached Helles in safety. Seldom can officers and men have had nerves and resources more severely tried. "The passage down the straits," wrote Admiral de Robeck in his report, "when the control of the boat is entirely vested in the commanding officer, was an experience the like of which few officers have had to undergo, and the successful accomplishment of the journey speaks volumes for Lieutenant-Commander Bruce's determination."[1]

Lieutenant Pirie in *H1* had not yet done. Two days after *E 12* went down he sighted a gunboat escorting a steamer of about 7,000 tons which sought refuge in Panderma. He attacked the gunboat, but the torpedo missed, and before he could get into position for the steamer she ran into safety behind the harbour mole. Still he had not yet done with her. On the 28th he communicated with *E 20*, whose programme was arranged, and on the following day *H1*, by boldly hugging the western shore and turning at the last moment, got an end-on shot and hit the steamer on the starboard bow.

Her engines were now causing trouble. Small as she was she had done over 2,000 miles, and on the 31st she

[1] For this cruise he was awarded the D.S.O.

safely negotiated the dangers of the passage down. In her cruise of twenty-nine days *H 1* sank four steamers and eight sailing vessels. Of the *Turquoise* nothing had been heard since the 26th. Her endurance was not great, and she was expected back before the end of the month. The next news of her was from an intercepted German telegram received in the *Patrie* announcing that she had been sunk by gunfire on the 30th and that her two officers and twenty-four men were saved. This unhappily was not the whole truth. While preparing to go down she had stranded and stuck fast on the surface under the Turkish guns. Being quite helpless her commander had surrendered. The boat was thus captured almost intact and taken to Constantinople, where it was found that her confidential papers had not been destroyed. The result was that all the rendezvous she had arranged with *E 20* were disclosed. These facts were, of course, carefully concealed, and the serious consequences of the strange neglect did not appear till later.[1]

At the time the check which our hitherto successful attack on the Turkish communications received was quite overshadowed by what had been taking place at the higher end of the war scale. The Franco-British Staff conference which was to examine the technical aspects of the attempt to save Serbia by operating from Salonica had met at Chantilly, and, mainly owing to an initial difference of opinion on the capacity of the port and its communications with the interior, had proved abortive. To our military representatives the French seemed to be exaggerating the carrying power of the railways, while from actual experience our naval representatives knew that the port could not possibly accommodate traffic on anything like the scale upon which the French staff were relying. To add to the seriousness of the situation, it could not be concealed that the French officers were not entirely free to base their opinion on purely technical considerations. A wave of enthusiasm for Serbia was being spread by the Press all over France, filling the bulk of the nation with what seemed to be a passionate desire to save her heroic army, until at Paris it was felt as a controlling factor in the situation. At Chantilly General Joffre, up to this time the most determined opponent of the Salonica adventure, was already bending under the pressure. The next day (October 29) M. Viviani, the Premier, and his War Minister, M. Millerand, resigned, and a new Government was formed under M. Briand, who more than any other French statesman was identified with the idea of the new line of

[1] See *post*, p. 206.

operation in the Balkans.[1] His political position now depended on that policy being carried through; General Joffre's future was no less critically involved, and on the day M. Viviani resigned he came to London to persuade the British Government to modify its attitude of opposition in deference to the disturbing political situation in France.

The proposal he had to make, though far from satisfying the desires of the French Government, led quickly to a healing compromise. What he asked was that we should undertake to safeguard the position from Salonica as far as Krivolak on the Serbian frontier, so as to secure the communications of the French army operating to maintain touch with the Serbians. These operations it was understood were not to extend beyond Uskub; and with a proviso that we did not hold ourselves responsible for our Ally's view of the capacity of the port and the railway we agreed to active co-operation as the French desired.

In this way the tension which was straining the solidarity of the Entente was relieved, but only at the cost of our Government having to raise the precautionary demonstration, which was all that was intended when ground had first been broken in the Balkans, to the status of a new line of major operations. The seriousness of the departure was fully realised, but in loyalty to our embarrassed Ally, who had been bearing so large a share of the struggle, it was unavoidable. Alone, the commitment could only be regarded with the gravest concern, but it was not alone. In another quarter beyond the horizon of the French outlook we were simultaneously involved in another commitment, where the critical situation in the Near East was also forcing a sound defensive into an offensive, of which no man could foresee the limit or count the cost.

[1] Mermeix, *Joffre. La Première Crise du Commandement*, p. 86.

CHAPTER X

THE MESOPOTAMIA CAMPAIGN—JULY TO OCTOBER

THE brilliant capture of Amara by General Townshend and Captain Nunn in the first week of June,[1] though undertaken solely as a measure indispensable for the security of Basra and the oil supply, had led almost inevitably to a wide extension of the Mesopotamian operations beyond what the Home Government originally considered necessary or even possible. It indeed offered temptation to enterprising military and political officers that was difficult to resist, particularly when they had been led to believe that the intentions of the Government were as ambitious as their own. When on March 18, General Nixon had been appointed to command the Expeditionary Force, which then consisted of an army corps of two divisions, his instructions from the Commander-in-Chief in India were, after mastering the situation on the spot, to prepare a plan for the effective occupation of the vilayet of Basra, and, secondly, a plan for a subsequent advance on Bagdad. The last instruction was given in ordinary course merely as a precautionary step. As yet neither at Simla nor at Whitehall was there any intention of reaching out so far. At present the object was purely defensive—to secure the head of the Persian Gulf for naval and political purposes: that is, to ensure the safety of the invaluable oil supply, and to prevent the Arabs and Persians from joining the Jehad, which, if it spread eastward, could scarcely fail to have undesirable reactions in Afghanistan. With the seizure of Amara General Nixon not only saw his way clear to carrying out the first and legitimate clause of his instructions, but beyond the limits of the vilayet —and as it seemed, in the light of recent high achievement, only a little beyond it—glittered the domes and minarets of Bagdad.

Ninety miles to the north-west of Amara, but twice as far by the writhing river, was Kut, the point to which the remnants of the armies broken by Generals Townshend and

[1] See page 22.

Gorringe were retreating. It lay just beyond the boundary of the Basra vilayet, at the apex of a triangle formed by the Tigris and a channel known as the Shatt al Hai, which was shown on the maps as flowing into the Euphrates at the important town of Nasiriya, and the capture of this strategical point seemed necessary before an advance on Kut could be undertaken.[1] The truth was, that the Shatt al Hai lost itself in marshes far short of the town, and was only navigable at the season of highest floods. Still Nasiriya had an importance of its own, for it was not only the administrative centre of the western sanjak of the Basra vilayet and the natural focus of influence over the powerful tribes of the Arabian borderland, but it was also the base from which the previous attack on Basra had been developed. Hitherto, as we have seen, in times of emergency it had been masked by the Euphrates naval blockade, but this would no longer suffice, and immediately after the capture of Amara General Nixon applied for permission to reduce it into British possession. Apart from all ulterior objects its value for securing the western sanjak, as General Gorringe's Karun expedition had secured the eastern, was so great that the Government of India, assuming that the home authorities agreed, sanctioned the advance on June 22 as being expedient to complete the security of our hold on Basra and the pipe line.

It was no easy task. With the hottest and most unhealthy season of the year coming on, and the navigation of the falling rivers growing ever more precarious, it was naturally a time to rest the hard-worked troops, but the high advantage of allowing the enemy no time to recover from the blow under which he was reeling overweighed all other considerations. As the approach to Nasiriya by the desert route at that season would be very hazardous it was decided that the advance should be made by water. To reach it eighty miles had to be covered by way of the old channel from the Euphrates, which joins the Tigris at Kurnah. As a waterway it presented at this time every kind of difficulty. Some forty miles to the west of Kurnah the river pours through the Hammar lake, a shallow expanse of water over ten miles broad, by a tortuous and narrow channel, which was no longer navigable for ships, and only with difficulty for the shallowest river craft. Everything therefore depended on the resources the navy could develop, and on June 8 Captain Nunn had come down with his ships from Amara to make his preparations and to confer with General Gorringe, to whom the military command of the expedition was entrusted.

[1] See Map 1.

The work of assisting in the Nasiriya expedition was not, however, the only call upon the navy. Though the capture of Amara and General Gorringe's recent operations on the Karun had so far settled the country up to the Persian frontier that the pipe line was never again disturbed, the situation beyond the frontier was calling for active precautionary measures. About this time it was ascertained that a German agent, Wassmuss, who had been German Consul at Bushire and Bagdad, was in Persia with a mission to raise the gendarmerie and Tangistanis against us in the maritime province of Fars, where, at Bushire, we had our long-established and all-important diplomatic outpost. As we had nothing there but a small agency guard, prompt measures had to be taken for its security. A battalion was withdrawn from General Nixon's force to garrison the place, and Captain Nunn was ordered to send away the *Lawrence* (Commander R. N. Suter) to reinforce the squadron which was to operate in the Gulf. It was to be under Captain D. St. A. Wake in the *Juno* as Senior Naval Officer, and with him were to be the *Pyramus* (Commander Viscount Kelburn), the *Dalhousie* (Commander E. M. Palmer), and some small craft for inshore work. Captain Nunn's force was further reduced by the *Clio* being away at Bombay for repairs, and by the necessity of sending such other ships as were not immediately required to Ceylon in turns in order to recruit the health of the crews at the naval hill station during the worst of the hot weather.

By June 26, when the General had his three Indian brigades concentrated at Kurnah, Captain Nunn had the remainder of his force assembled just short of the Hammar lake. Further than this point the three ships that were still with him—the *Espiègle*, *Odin* and *Miner*—could not go, and from them he proceeded to man and arm his flotilla, such as it was. Three small stern-wheelers, the *Shushan*, *Messoudieh* and *Muzaffri*, all crazy with age, formed the strength of it. Besides these were two horse-boats armed with naval 4·7-inch guns, an armed launch, the *Sumana*, a convoy of *mahailas* with two tugs to tow them and a number of *bellums*, some of them in pairs, carrying the mountain guns as before. Here he was joined by General Melliss with the 30th Indian Brigade [1] in three river steamers, each mounting two 18-pounder field guns in the bows, and at 4.0 next morning (the 27th) Captain Nunn led off into the Hammar lake in his stern-wheeler, the *Shushan*. By 1.30

[1] 1/4th Hampshire Regiment, 24th and 76th Punjabis and 2/7th Gurkha Rifles.

he had groped his way across the waste of reed and water to the end of the tortuous channel, where a creek known as the Akaika channel led into the new channel of the Euphrates, which runs down through a waste of marshes to Basra. Here he had first contact with the enemy. Two Thornycroft launches in the main river opened a smart fire with pom-poms, but they were soon driven off, and at 4.0 p.m. the whole force was anchored in the creek before a dam which, about six miles short of the river, barred further progress.

It was found to be very strongly constructed—a solid bund of mud piled on a foundation of sunken *mahailas*—very different from the clumsy obstacles that had been encountered on the Tigris. Only by blasting could a passage be cleared. All next day the work proceeded in the almost unbearable heat, aggravated by swarms of mosquitoes and the pom-poms of the Turkish launches. It was not till midday on the 29th that a channel 150 feet wide was open, and then so strong was the rush of water that none of the crazy flotilla could get through under her own steam. Despite the exhausting conditions, every one of them had to be hauled up by man power, but by 5.0 in the evening the *Shushan* was through. Another stern-wheeler, the *Messoudieh*, followed the same night, and next morning, when Captain Nunn had been joined by the two horse-boats with their 4·7-inch guns, he proceeded to reconnoitre the enemy's first position.

It was established on the west or right bank of the river, immediately opposite the point where the Akaika creek flowed out of it, and here were two guns with a clear field of fire for 2,000 yards down the channel, which it was impossible for the frail gunboats to face.[1] It was therefore only by getting the troops across the river to carry the entrenchments that protected the guns that the Turks could be turned out, and nothing could be done till they were all above the obstruction. This took four days more, and it was not till dawn on July 5 that the attack could be launched, nor could the flotilla advance further till the banks had been cleared by the troops sufficiently to enable the channel to be swept for mines which were known to exist.

On the north or left bank of the creek were landed the 24th and 76th Punjabis, the former with their *bellums*, with which they were to make their way through the inundations, cross the river above the enemy's position and cut the garrison off from Nasiriya. Supported by all the guns of the flotilla, they pushed steadily on in the face of considerable opposition,

[1] See Map 9.

till they reached a spit of dry land along the river bank over which they had to carry their *bellums* before they could launch them again. Meanwhile the other bank of the creek was being cleared by the Hampshire Regiment and the 7th Gurkhas, and the flotilla, drawing slowly on, was keeping up so hot a fire over the high reeds that by 9.0 a.m. the enemy's guns were silent and the garrison began to stream out of the entrenchments towards Nasiriya. But it was only to find the 24th Punjabis on their path, and then they put up the white flag. While most of the Arabs stole away we captured the guns and 91 prisoners, including seven Turkish officers, at a cost of twenty-five of our own men killed and eighty-four wounded.

By nightfall the creek had been cleared of mines under direction of a Turkish officer who had been brought in by the fickle Arabs, and Captain Nunn was able to pass out into the open river and anchor there for the night. The *Sumana* had been put out of action during the day by a shell which cut her main steam pipe, but next morning, with the *Shushan*, *Messoudieh* and the two horse-boats, he went down to deal with Suq ash Shuyukh, the chief trading centre of the district, which lay about three miles below the captured position. He arrived to find white flags flying, and after solemnly hoisting the British flag in the presence of Sir Percy Cox, the Chief Political Officer on the General's staff, he returned up the river to reconnoitre the next position above.

The enemy were found strongly entrenched on both sides of the Euphrates near Majinina creek, about six miles below Nasiriya.[1] In the river itself, 3,000 yards below the position, was another obstacle formed by two steamboats which had been sunk to block the channel, but so hastily that they were easily passable and a reconnaissance could be carried out. The enemy had evidently been reinforced; their outer flanks rested on the marshes with a Thorneycroft launch at the bend of the river and their artillery was numerous and well emplaced. On such a position the flotilla could make no impression. The decks of the old stern-wheelers were already giving way under the recoil of the guns, and the 4·7-inch guns in the horse-boats were too low down for direct firing, so that in spite of the higher calibre of our guns, we had no real superiority over the enemy. To make an attack still more hazardous the only approach to the position was along the river banks, which were no more than spits of dry land between the river and the marshes, and even they were cut at frequent intervals by dykes. General Gorringe,

[1] See Map 10.

therefore, decided to send back for the 12th Brigade [1] and two 5-inch howitzers. The water was falling fast; only with the greatest difficulty could they be brought up through the Hammar lake, and it was not till the night of July 13–14 that the attack could be delivered.

Its success depended on an outflanking movement over the marshes on the right or western bank. The objective was a group of sandhills on which the right of the Majinina position rested. It could be reached by water, and as soon as the rest of the 30th Brigade had rushed the advanced enemy trenches at Shukhair, the 24th Punjabis began to move over the marsh in their *bellums* with the mountain guns. By dint of wading and paddling they managed to reach the sandhills, but found them too strongly held to be rushed, and before anything could be done swarms of Arabs could be seen coming down upon their left and rear out of the marshes, which made a retirement imperative. Though it was skilfully conducted it cost many casualties, nor could anything more be done. So long as the Majinina position was held in force it was impossible for the flotilla to advance in support of an attack on the trenches on the other side of the river, and General Gorringe decided to break off the operations.

The situation was now critical. Owing to the intense heat sickness was rife and the effective strength of the force growing less every day. Moreover, the water was falling fast, so that communication with the base was getting very difficult. Nevertheless, there was nothing for it but to send for the third brigade,[2] as well as more guns and howitzers and two aeroplanes, doubtful as it was whether they could get through. Still it was done. By superhuman labour in the fiery air they were forced through the slime of the lake bottom, and at dawn on July 24 a new attack was begun.

The opposing forces were now about equal, each side having about 5,000 men, but the preponderance of heavy artillery was with the British, and we also had a flotilla, an advantage difficult to overestimate against an enemy astride a river. Our aircraft,[3] moreover, were able to give the General an accurate picture of what lay before him and his plan was quickly formed. The Majinina position was to be attacked, this time on its left, where the lines bent back against the river. But here the unfordable mouth of

[1] 2nd Bn. Queen's Own Royal West Kent Regiment, 67th and 90th Punjabis and 44th Merwara Infantry.

[2] This was the 18th Indian Brigade: 2nd Bn. Norfolk Regiment; 110th Mahratta Light Infantry and 120th Rajputana Infantry.

[3] Four aeroplanes were now available.

the creek had to be passed, an operation of no small difficulty, but means were at hand in the Sappers and Miners' bridging barge. It was accordingly protected as well as possible, and the *Sumana*, just returned from repairing her steam pipe, was told off to the hazardous work of towing it into position. At dawn a concentrated fire of the naval and artillery guns was opened on the point of attack, and while it proceeded the 12th Brigade on the other bank advanced against the Maiyadiya creek. Brilliantly led by the West Kents, the attack in an hour's time (6.40), after heavy fighting, gave us the southern salient of the position, and the whole bend of the river opposite Majinina was soon in our hands.

As the attack was seen to be progressing the 30th Brigade was ordered to advance from its trenches between Shukhair and the river, with the Hampshire along the bank and the Gurkhas next. Simultaneously Lieutenant W. V. H. Harris in the *Sumana* made his way up-stream towing the bridging gear, and in spite of the storm of fire that met him he laid the barge accurately across the mouth of the creek. It was a brilliant performance and well worth the casualties it cost. The thirty-five Hampshire men that formed the guard and the fifty-five Sappers of the bridging train each lost twenty of their number. Still, by 9.45 the bridge was completed, but it proved too difficult to use. So well, however, had the barge been placed on the mud that it stopped the flow of water from the river, so that when the troops came up on the left they found the creek fordable, and by 10.0 the whole position was in our hands. At the same time the 12th Brigade, which had been stopped by gun-fire owing to the palm trees preventing its own artillery from seeing how to support them, made another desperate rush and got across the Maiyadiya creek.

Now was the time to pursue the retiring enemy, before they could establish themselves in the second position they had entrenched at the Sadanawiya creek, about a mile and a half higher up at a bend, where the Nasiriya reach is entered. But pursuit was difficult. The heat, the water-courses and a galling fire made it very arduous for the troops, and here was where the flotilla made itself decisively felt. By about one o'clock both brigades had advanced some 2,000 yards beyond the positions they had taken up, and the *Shushan* and *Sumana* were nearly level with them. Below, the transport steamers were bringing on the artillery and beginning to land the Norfolks for an attack on Sadanawiya. This was still going on when it was reported that the enemy were leaving the trenches. The Norfolks were immediately re-embarked and the flotilla advanced. Whether the Turks had actually decided to abandon the position is uncertain, but the doubt was quickly settled by Captain Nunn laying the old *Shushan* close alongside the trenches and blazing into them at point-blank range with everything she carried. The *Medjidieh* with her two 18-pounders also came into action at 1,000 yards, and even before the Norfolks could land the enemy were in full retreat.

In similar circumstances on the Tigris Captain Nunn had immediately pushed on to take all advantage of the enemy's demoralisation. He did so again. Labouring up the Nasiriya reach at the best speed the *Shushan* could paddle with the small craft in company, he was fired on by the remaining Thornycroft launch. She was quickly reduced to a burning wreck on the bank, and as white flags were flying over the town Captain Nunn held on to find the Commandant, but as he proceeded he was met by a heavy fire from the roof of the Turkish barracks, which wounded Lieutenant-Commander A. G. Seymour. As it was now too near dark to do anything, he could only fall back. Next morning (25th) a deputation of Arab inhabitants came down to report the Turks had all left and to invite us to occupy the place. Turkish casualties are estimated at 2,000 killed and wounded and 950 prisoners, against British losses of 104 killed and 429 wounded. Naval casualties numbered only 5 wounded.

With the consolidation of our hold on Nasiriya General Nixon found it possible to proceed to perfect our occupation of the Basra vilayet by an advance on Kut. Here, 120 miles up the Tigris above Amara, Nur-ud-Din Bey was known to be concentrating a considerable force, and before long his activity became so menacing that by July 20 it was thought advisable to withdraw all our advanced posts north of Amara, but the "River Column," that is the *Comet* and *Shaitan*, with two steamers carrying infantry and sappers continued to keep observation by patrolling up the river.

So far the prospect of a further advance up the Tigris was not too promising, but the fall of Nasiriya immediately reversed the situation. For some time past the Government of India had been considering an advance on Kut, and they now applied for the movement to be sanctioned. Still in India at least it was not regarded as the last step on the way to Bagdad. The application was pressed on the ground that the capture of the place would complete and secure the occupation of the Basra vilayet, and at the same time, since it was the irrigation centre of the surrounding districts, it would mean so strong a control over the powerful Beni Lam tribe which had gone over to Nur-ud-Din that they would not be able to disturb the oilfields or pipe line. The plan, in short, was presented as a necessary defensive operation within the limits the Home Government had laid down. Yet the assent of Whitehall was not immediately forthcoming. General Nixon had said that in order to make sure he would require drafts to fill up his British battalions. His force was much reduced by sickness, besides the loss of the battalion sent to Bushire. The Government of India, in recommending the advance, was hoping for a brigade which had been sent from Egypt for the defence of Aden and was no longer required there. But seeing how urgent was the need of troops in the Near East, Lord Kitchener had to order it back to Egypt, and General Townshend[1] could only be reinforced from Nasiriya and Ahwaz; or, in other words, by endangering the oil supply, about which the Admiralty were at the moment concerned more deeply than ever. Eventually, however, it was agreed that the oilfields and pipe line could be left to the protection of the subsidised Bakhtiari, and on August 20 the Home Government sanctioned General Nixon's plan.

He had already begun his preparations. On July 28, the Turks were found to be falling back on Kut, and Ali Gharbi was again occupied (31st) to cover the concentration for the operation which he proposed.[2] He knew the concentration must be a long process. The only line of advance was by the shallow bends of the Tigris, and the brigades from the Euphrates that were to join General Townshend had to be hauled back to Amara through the mud of Hammar lake before they could begin to move northwards.

While the weary movement was proceeding the expected trouble in the gulf had broken out. On July 12 the activity of the German agent had made itself felt by an attack of Tangistani tribesmen on our lines at Bushire; satisfaction was demanded from Persia: none was forthcoming, and on August 8 a proclamation was issued announcing our intention of occupying the whole Bushire island, including the native town and port, until reparation was forthcoming. Action was also taken to meet the menace of the Tangistani. Their headquarters were at a fortified village called Dilwar, twenty miles down the coast from Bushire, and during August 13–14 it was destroyed by a small combined force under Captain Wake, of the *Juno*, and Major C. E. H. Wintle (96th Berar Infantry). It was followed by the ships actively searching for Tangistani dhows along the coast and destroying all that

[1] A few days after capturing Amara General Townshend went to India on sick leave and was back in Basra on August 21. [2] See Map 1.

were found. On this service the *Pyramus* and *Dalhousie* were ordered down to Bahrein with the Political Resident on board, and in the course of their search they visited the port of Al Bida, where on August 20 they forced the Turkish garrison of Doha fort to evacuate it and hand over its armament and munitions to the local Sheikh of Katar.[1]

At Bushire the Tangistanis were again threatening trouble. The 96th Berar Infantry which formed its garrison had to be reinforced from Basra by a squadron of the 16th Cavalry and the 11th Rajputs, and now that a serious attack was clearly in the wind, counter-measures to meet it were carefully concerted between Captain Wake and Brigadier-General H. T. Brooking, commanding the garrison. Joint staff rides were instituted and from time to time a naval brigade was landed to train and manœuvre with the garrison. On September 9 the threatened attack took place on the British lines south of Bushire. The *Dalhousie* was still away in the Bahrein area, but the *Juno*, *Pyramus* and *Lawrence* were on the spot, and a naval detachment of fifty men and the marines, under Captain G. Carpenter of the Royal Marine Light Infantry, was ashore. For some hours the point of the lines which they occupied was hard pressed, but they held on till the infantry came up and scattered the enemy with a bayonet charge. A cavalry charge completed the rout, and Bushire settled down again to its accustomed repose.

Small as the operation was, the intense heat had made it very trying to the endurance of the force. In Mesopotamia it was even worse. With a thermometer varying from 110° to 120° in the shade, the laborious concentration of General Townshend's force was at last nearing completion. To make matters worse, the navigational difficulties of the shrinking river increased daily, but by September 11 the whole division was assembled at Ali Gharbi. To this point the troops had been brought in the river craft, but now most of them had to march painfully along the dusty banks, while the flotilla and transport craft struggled up beside them.

The naval section of the force was very weak, and no longer under Captain Nunn. After Nasiriya he had been invalided to Ceylon. His successor, Captain C. Mackenzie, was also in hospital, and Lieutenant-Commander E. C. Cookson in the *Comet* was Senior Naval Officer. One other gunboat, the *Shaitan* (Lieutenant Singleton), was with him and the launch *Sumana* (Sub-Lieutenant L. C. P. Tudway), as well as four naval 4·7's in horse-boats. But this slender

[1] Katar lies about 100 miles from Bahrein harbour down the west coast of the gulf. It includes the villages of Doha and Al Bida.

force was supplemented by two heavy batteries of Royal Garrison Artillery with 4-inch and 5-inch guns mounted in barges.[1]

As the column moved forward the enemy's advanced troops fell back before it, and by September 16 the village of Sannaiyat, some fifteen miles below Kut and seven miles from the Turkish position which covered it, had been reached. Here a halt of ten days had been made to allow of adequate air reconnaissance and give time for reinforcements to join. Most important of these were aircraft. One of the military machines had come down in the enemy's lines and two others were badly damaged. Fortunately on September 5 four seaplanes, which had done so much for the success of the final operations against the *Königsberg* in the Rufiji river, reached Basra, under Squadron-Commander Gordon, and by dint of great exertions they were got off up the river in a week, and were able to give some assistance to the military airmen in providing General Townshend with the information he required.

The Turkish position, which was found to be elaborately organised on the latest principles, lay astride the river.[2] On the right or southern bank it extended five miles into the desert along a line of mounds admirably adapted for defence and commanding a perfect field of fire. The river itself was completely blocked by a formidable boom constructed of barges and wire cables and commanded at close range from either bank by guns and fire trenches. On the left or north bank the lines ran northward for about seven miles, but their continuity was broken for over two miles by the Suwada swamp. The section between the swamp and the river was again broken for 1,000 yards by another swamp known as the "Horseshoe," so that the actual defensive front of this section was only 3,000 yards. Some three miles north of the Suwada marsh the position terminated in a well-designed system of redoubts, about 2,000 yards short of a third swamp, known as Ataba marsh. Here General Townshend saw the weak point of the position which the enemy seems to have regarded as practically impregnable to anything he could bring against it. South of the Ataba marsh it could be turned, and if a frontal attack on the Horseshoe or central section could hold the enemy down and the boom could be

[1] 86th Battery: four 5-inch in barges; 104th Battery: two 4-inch in barges. The two horse-boats had been under Lieutenant-Commander Cookson, and Lieutenant M. A. B. Johnston, R.G.A., had been lent to command them when Lieutenant-Commander Cookson became Senior Naval Officer.

[2] See Map 11.

forced so as to permit of pursuit by the flotilla, there was a good prospect of annihilating Nur-ud-Din's army and settling the fate of Mesopotamia at a blow.

On each bank the enemy had a division with a bridge of boats five miles above the position and a reserve of four battalions close to it. On our side a similar bridge was to be thrown across the river, for the plan the General had formed involved a rapid and secret transference of one of the two columns in which he had organised his force from the south bank to the north.[1]

Nur-ud-Din had, besides his reserve at the bridge, two divisions, each consisting of three two-battalion regiments, two regiments of cavalry, two squadrons of Anatolians and 400 Camel Corps, with three heavy guns, two howitzers, eight quick-firing field guns and sixteen 15-pounders, besides others more or less obsolete. He thus had twelve battalions against our fourteen, and was also slightly inferior in artillery.

On September 26 an advance was made to Nukhailat, between three and four miles below the Turkish position, the main column, under Brigadier-General Delamain, marching by the south bank, and the other, under Major-General C. I. Fry, going by river. On reaching Nukhailat they disembarked on the north bank and the bridging train rapidly threw their boat bridge across the river. At dawn on the 27th a preparatory attack on the Horseshoe position began under cover of the flotilla guns and artillery, while General Delamain demonstrated against the trenches on the south bank. By 2.30 the flotilla and artillery had so effectively silenced the enemy's guns that General Fry had been able to establish himself with little loss 2,000 yards from the enemy's trenches. At the same time the demonstration on the other bank was renewed and the troops began ostentatiously to entrench. Then, as soon as it was dark, the whole column, with the exception of a bridge guard, silently crossed to the north bank, and by midnight was assembled at the south-east corner of the Suwada marsh. From this point, at 2.0 a.m. on the 28th, the enveloping attack began. Though unfortunately delayed by the brigade on the extreme right marching round the Ataba marsh instead of between it and the enemy's redoubt, the attack succeeded in forcing

[1] General Townshend had only one division, the 6th Indian and half the 30th Brigade. In Column "A" were three and a half squadrons of cavalry, two batteries Royal Field Artillery, one howitzer battery and two brigades of infantry. In Column "B" was one infantry brigade. With the divisional troops the fighting strength was: British, 264 officers and 2,797 men; Indian, 206 officers and 7,603 men—total 10,870, with twenty-eight guns and forty machine guns.

the extreme left about 10.30, but General Fry's column, which had been steadily working forward, had to be stopped till the flank attack developed further.

While they were thus waiting, at eleven o'clock it was seen that the enemy on the south bank were moving a detachment to the Chahela mounds abreast General Fry's force to enfilade this line. It was a dangerous movement, but the Turks had not counted with the flotilla. It at once moved up to close range, and quickly drove the enemy back to their entrenchments. General Fry's column was thus left free from flank disturbance, but they still had long to wait. The day was exceptionally hot, and since 9.0 a.m. a strong wind had been raising clouds of dust that stopped all possibility of visual signalling. For the troops fighting on in the long turning movement the conditions were in the last degree trying; progress was slow, yet, in spite of the enemy's stubborn resistance, the whole of the position north of the Suwada marsh was in our hands by 1.45 p.m.

While the exhausted troops rested and reassembled at the west end of the swamp, before sweeping down on the rear of the Horseshoe position, the flotilla concentrated upon it to prepare for the culmination of General Fry's frontal attack. In the frequent mirage and dust-laden air observation was scarcely possible. Yet so effective was the fire, combined with that of the artillery ashore, that the enemy's guns were silenced, and by 4.30 his right was within nine hundred yards of the trenches between the Horseshoe and the Suwada marsh. It lacked only the appearance of General Delamain's column for the final rush to be made, but as yet there was no sign of it. It had begun to move in time, but meeting with opposition had to fall back to replenish ammunition and seek for water. They failed to find any, and it was not till nearly 5.0 that, worn out with thirst and marching, they began finally to move southwards. At 5.30 General Delamain was able to send a message that he was about to turn east, when he was aware of a force advancing against him from the south. It seems to have been Turkish troops from the other side of the river whom the delay had given time to come up across the bridge, and there was nothing to do but turn against them. Springing with new life at the prospect of a bayonet fight his men dashed forward, and in one magnificent rush completely routed the new-comers and captured four guns. It was only the rapid approach of night that permitted the remnants of the force to escape back to the river. There was now no more to be done. Utterly exhausted and parched with thirst the men bivouacked on the ground they had won, and General Fry had to entrench five hundred yards short of his objective.

But the Turkish position was obviously no longer tenable. The morning must see the enemy driven out of it, and now was the time for the flotilla to make the success decisive. The boom alone seemed to stand in the way, and General Townshend requested Lieutenant-Commander Cookson to go up and see what could be done with it. As soon as it was dark he started in the *Comet* with the other two gunboats, but though he proceeded without lights, he was met with a very heavy rifle and machine-gun fire from both banks. Steaming through it, he made to ram a dhow which lay in the centre of the boom between two iron barges. The dhow withstood the shock. Not to be baffled, he tried gun-fire, and then, as that would not sink her, he laid the *Comet* alongside and himself sprang upon the dhow, axe in hand, to try to cut the wire hawsers that secured her. It was a desperate attempt. The enemy were less than a hundred yards from him, and he fell almost at once, riddled with bullets. On board the *Comet* hardly a man was untouched, and the helpless gunboats, holding their ground long enough to sink the dhow by gunfire, retired downstream, and anchored for the night.[1]

Early next morning (29th) the Horseshoe was found to have been abandoned; the airmen a little later reported the whole force in full retreat, and the pursuit could begin. While the cavalry went after them by land, General Fry's column embarked in the transport steamers, and led by the flotilla, under Lieutenant Singleton of the *Shaitan*, started upstream. The obstruction, being now undefended, was quickly cleared; about 10·0 the gunboats were off Kut, and proceeded to chase two Turkish steamers that could be seen making away. All seemed fair for turning the victory into a crushing decision by cutting off Nur-ud-Din's retreat, but here unexpected troubles began. As far as Kut, in spite of the low state of the river, there had always been water enough to make navigation comparatively easy, but once above the town they found themselves so beset by shoals that in the first twenty-four hours the ships had covered little more than two miles. At daylight on the 30th the two steamers could still be seen, but the *Shaitan* had stuck fast close to Kut, the *Sumana* had broken both her rudders by grounding, and the *Comet* had to continue the chase alone. She could do no more, however, than force one of the retreating

[1] For his devoted action Lieutenant-Commander Cookson was awarded a posthumous V.C.

steamers to drop two ammunition barges she was towing and hurry on out of range. The barges were captured by the cavalry, who came up with the enemy on October 1. The Turks were then found to be making an orderly retreat with an organised rearguard, which the cavalry could not touch, and they were forced to wait for the river column to come up.

It now consisted of the *Shaitan* and *Comet* with four steamers, in which were the General and a brigade. After four days' grounding and steaming they reached Aziziya (5th), sixty-one miles by land and 102 by river above Kut. The enemy, however, were already securely established in a long-prepared position at Ctesiphon, twenty miles below Bagdad, and all hope of destroying Nur-ud-Din's army was for the time at an end.[1] True we had captured 1,700 prisoners and fourteen guns and inflicted heavy losses in men and material, and had the prestige of having broken a position deemed impregnable. At least it could be said that the vilayet of Basra had been finally cleared of the enemy, and the defensive objects of the expedition had been completely attained.[2]

With this General Nixon could not rest content. He at once announced that although the pursuit had failed, he felt strong enough to open a road to Bagdad, and that he proposed to concentrate for the purpose at Aziziya. The place was no more than fifty miles by a good road from Bagdad, but as it was also about five hundred above the base at Basra, the proposal was received by the home authorities, both civil and military, with the gravest doubt. Assuming he could break through and occupy Bagdad, there seemed no possibility of his holding it against forces which in a month or two could be brought to bear upon him from the adjacent theatres. On the other hand, the political importance of capturing the ancient Arab capital, if only as a means of isolating Persia from the dangerous activities of the German agents, was so great that the idea could not be lightly dismissed. The Government, therefore, immediately appointed an Inter-departmental Committee from the Admiralty, the General Staff and the Foreign and India Offices to consider the question, and meanwhile General Nixon was ordered to stand fast.

But before the order reached him, new considerations of the profoundest import had arisen. The day the Committee was set up, October 5, was the day that General Nixon's

[1] See Map 1.

[2] British casualties totalled 1,233 (94 killed). Turkish losses were about 4,000.

advanced troops reached Aziziya, but it had hardly got to work on the multitudinous and complicated factors of the problem, when new ones still more intricate were introduced. For it so happened that October 5 was also the day on which the sudden resignation of M. Venizelos had broken to pieces the frail barrier we had been so laboriously constructing to stem the German push for Constantinople. With the hope of stopping the enemy short of his goal thus reduced to the slenderest proportions, Bagdad began to assume an importance second only to that of Constantinople itself.

The reasons for sanctioning General Nixon's plan had thus increased in strength. He was reporting that he had overcome the navigational difficulties above Kut by lightening the ships, using them to tow barges, and leaving the troops to march with the land transport. Firmly convinced that he could quickly push through to Bagdad, he knew he could not hold it without another fresh division. India declared she could not spare one; Egypt, being the reserve for the Near East, was in like case; and it was only from France a reinforcement could come. Before any decision was taken the question was again referred to General Nixon. The high military and political importance which the Home Government now attached to the capture of Bagdad and its continued occupation was put before him, and he was asked what force was necessary to carry out the policy. The reply was still that he had enough to beat Nur-ud-Din and take Bagdad, and that one more division with another cavalry regiment would enable him to hold it. The Government of India, watching with deepening anxiety the German propaganda which, centred at Bagdad, was growing active in Afghanistan, endorsed the opinion of the General on the ground that the man on the spot was the best judge, and only added that the reinforcements must arrive not more than a month after the city was occupied.

In view of the extent to which General Nixon's successes had depended on the support of the flotilla and the river transport, it is noteworthy that attention seems to have been almost entirely confined to the number of troops required. In the Viceroy's despatch no special emphasis was laid on the difficulty of the flotilla giving support in the shallow and extraordinarily tortuous stretch of the river between Aziziya and Bagdad, or the vastly increased strain on the river transport that the occupation of the city would entail. It is true that General Nixon had applied for a considerable increase of river steamers. The Commander-in-Chief in India had endorsed his demand, but as they could not be obtained locally, an urgent request was sent that they should be built in England. It was some time before the Admiralty knew of this; and, when they did, their assistance was necessarily limited to hastening the construction and delivery of the steamers, as the dockyards, already occupied to their utmost capacity, could not meet the requirements. Of all this, the Inter-departmental Committee appears to have been unaware, and in their report, which was completed on October 16, they took it for granted that the General had the necessary transport. Agreeing as to the political advantage of the venture, they concurred in the local view that it could be done with the force for which General Nixon stipulated, but advised that another Indian division should be held in readiness for eventualities. This conclusion, however, was expressly stated to rest on the understanding that the existing numbers of vessels on the Tigris was sufficient to enable the advance to be made and to ensure the supply of the advanced troops. Their caveat was natural enough, since they had nothing to reassure them on the point except General Nixon's original allegation that he had overcome the navigational difficulties and knowledge that the new small "China" or "Fly" class gunboats were in course of erection at Abadan, and would before long begin to be available for protecting the river line of communication.[1] This service, besides the safe transport of troops from Marseilles or Egypt to Basra, was all the Admiralty could contribute. Since the expedition had penetrated so far inland, they regarded it as in effect a military, and not a combined campaign. The puny flotilla could no longer provide tactical assistance of any real value and the transport steamers were under military direction.

With these considerations before them the Government on October 14th endeavoured to come to a definite conclusion, but so many difficult technical points were raised on which authorities differed, both in regard to the Bagdad advance

[1] In November 1914, when Lord Fisher returned to the Admiralty, he gave Messrs. Yarrow carte blanche to design and get built twenty-four gunboats—twelve small ones known as the "Fly" class for policing the Tigris, and twelve larger ones (named after insects) for the Danube. During construction they were given the *camouflage* designation of "China" gunboats. As the smaller ones were completed they were shipped out in sections to the Persian Gulf, and were now being rapidly put together by Messrs. Yarrow's men at the Anglo-Persian Oil Company's works at Abadan. Each carried a 4-inch gun, one 12-pounder, one 6-pounder, a 2-pounder pom-pom and four Maxims, but being designed originally for police work against the Arabs, they had nothing but bullet-proof protection. For stern wheels, however, was substituted a less vulnerable propeller working in a tunnel in the hull, an original device by which was solved the problem of combining a big diameter screw with shallow draught They were fitted with good wireless installations.

and subsidiary operations from Alexandretta in support of it, that a decision was postponed to give time for the General Staff, in conjunction with the Naval War Staff, to furnish a full appreciation on the existing and prospective situation in Syria and Mesopotamia, the Syrian outlook being also vital to the security of Egypt. The result of the report was to rule out Alexandretta on naval grounds. With the resources at their disposal the Admiralty declared that another line of operations in the Near East was out of the question so long as the Dardanelles operations continued. Descents at various points on the coast further south were more within their capacity, but only if the operations were limited to raids to hamper a Turkish advance on Egypt.

Over and above their confession of inability to maintain yet another line of communication, they specially deprecated a repetition of the difficulties they were suffering at the Dardanelles, where the supply beaches were under shell fire and open to submarine attack. In their opinion no combined expedition should be sanctioned unless it was practically certain that enough ground could be seized by the military covering force to ensure the landing-places immunity from artillery fire. On the other hand, the occupation of Bagdad was declared by the General Staff to be feasible on the assumption that two Indian divisions could be added to General Nixon's force by the end of the year, but it should not be occupied if it was likely that for political reasons the place could not be abandoned at any moment. In any event, if no Allied army was to be landed at Alexandretta, they recommended that the military authorities should be empowered to withdraw—whatever the political advantages of holding the place—if on military grounds its occupation was considered to involve unwarrantable risk. Otherwise the operations should be limited to a raid with the object of rendering it useless as a base. The contribution of the Admiralty to the problem was necessarily small. They could guarantee the safe transport of the two divisions to Basra, but the date by which they could move them would depend upon what other calls were made upon the limited supply of transports. They could also guarantee the effective patrol of the Tigris with the new gunboats as they came forward, and assist to a limited degree with seaplanes, but that was all.

After a full discussion in the light of this appreciation and the report of the Inter-departmental Committee, on October 21 the whole question as it was now displayed was referred to India. Special emphasis was laid on the probability that the Germans could not now be prevented from breaking through to Constantinople and that our prospects in Gallipoli were most uncertain. The Arabs, too, were wavering and inclining to join the Turks, and a striking success in the East was urgently needed. The reply of the Viceroy was that the situation in the Near East as now explained to him proved conclusively the need for action in the Middle East. For the Government of India the prospect of a German break-through into Asia had a special significance. The activity of German agents in Persia was for them an increasing pre-occupation. Should the enemy succeed in bringing it under their domination the neutral attitude of Afghanistan might become untenable, and the inevitable reaction on Indian unrest was a picture that no one cared to contemplate. From the Viceroy's point of view, therefore, the political outlook was now so disturbing that it swept away all hesitation he had felt in accepting the military view that the operation was not beyond their power. Given a reinforcement of two divisions, the balance of risk obviously dictated the occupation of Bagdad with the least possible delay. The Government reply, which went out on October 23, was to tell General Nixon that if he was satisfied the force he had immediately available was strong enough, he might march on the coveted city.[1] With this telegram the Government finally abandoned the defensive idea to which the Mesopotamian operations had hitherto been restricted, and, with their hands forced by the German thrust into the Balkans, committed themselves to a counter offensive from which there could be no turning back till the issue of the war in Asia was decided.

[1] See *Official History of the War : The Campaign in Mesopotamia 1914–1918* Vol. II, p. 28.

CHAPTER XI

THE DOOM OF GALLIPOLI AND THE BATTLE OF CTESIPHON

In view of the adventurous decision to attempt the occupation of Bagdad it was obviously desirable to keep the Turks occupied as fully as possible with the defence of their capital, and here it was that our Mesopotamian policy and that of the French in the Balkans came most gravely into conflict. Ever since the failure at Suvla a general conviction had been growing that only two courses were open to us in the Near East: we must either push on in increased force or abandon the attempt to open the Dardanelles. Now, committed as we were by the importunity of our ally to more than we had ever contemplated in the Balkans, the necessary increase of force for Gallipoli was not to be found, and for all but the determined men on the spot and those at home who had seen in the ancient seat of Empire the decisive theatre of the war, evacuation was becoming defined as the only possible alternative. Not for the first time had a mysterious destiny seemed at the last moment to intervene to save the Turk from what not once nor twice in the past century had threatened to end his history as a great power, and once more the grip of destiny was holding fast.

The time had come when a final decision could no longer be deferred. On that decision would turn the future drift of the war not only for ourselves, but for the whole alliance, and on the course taken might well depend the issue—victory or defeat. The question itself was beset with every kind of difficulty which can complicate the direction of a war conducted by allies against allies, and for some time past it had been growing evident that the machinery of our higher direction was not sufficiently well designed to deal with the ever-increasing intensification and complexities of the struggle. This conviction had just come to a head.

On November 2 the Prime Minister announced that henceforward the war would be directed by a new War Council to consist of from three to five members of the Cabinet. To this body, sitting from day to day and assisted by such experts as they should call in to advise them, was to be entrusted the control of all our war activities. They would have authority to deal with the "daily exigencies of the State" without reference to the Cabinet as a whole, but when any substantial change of policy or a new departure was in question Cabinet confirmation of their decision would be necessary. This arrangement had been the constitutional practice during the great wars of the past, when the comparatively small Cabinets of those days had been found too large for the rapid discharge of current war business. To some extent it had been used in the present war in the shape of various committees of the Cabinet, the most important of which had been the Dardanelles Committee, but it was not till this time that the old practice was fully revived and placed on a permanent footing.

The original members of the Council, which was known officially as the "War Committee," were the Prime Minister (Mr. Asquith), in the chair; Mr. Balfour (First Lord of the Admiralty); Lord Kitchener (Secretary of State for War); Sir Edward Grey (Foreign Secretary); and Mr. Lloyd George (Minister of Munitions), with Colonel Hankey as Secretary. Their first meeting was on November 3. It was attended by the Prime Minister, Lord Kitchener and Mr. Balfour, to consider the question of evacuating Gallipoli in the light of the latest information. It was on this question that General Monro was now concentrating his attention, as all our military policy in the Near East hinged upon it. On October 31, after conferring with the Corps Commanders and making a short visit to each sector, he had telegraphed a very unfavourable account of the situation. In his view the troops were too much exhausted and had lost too many officers to make a further effort with any prospect of success, and he had no hesitation in advising evacuation. Next day, however, came a message from General Maxwell, who, as being responsible for the defence of Egypt, strongly urged that we should hold on if possible. General Monro was then (November 1) asked to report whether the three Corps Commanders were of the same opinion as himself. The reply had just come to hand. General Birdwood, while admitting the gravity of the situation, shrank from the loss of prestige and loss of life that evacuation would probably entail. He was, therefore, opposed to evacuation unless we could strike elsewhere immediately, and he did not see where a blow was possible. General Byng at Suvla thought that as things stood a voluntary withdrawal from his section was possible without much loss, but later on, if German reinforcements arrived, a retirement would be compulsory and very costly. General Davies at Helles expressed agreement with General Monro, who reiterated his original conclusion.

The divergence of military opinion was embarrassing enough, but Ministers were also confronted with an equally wide divergence from the naval side, and this was the more embarrassing, since it was most pronounced amongst the highest authorities on the spot. The War Committee had before it a carefully considered appreciation which the Eastern Mediterranean Naval Staff had been working at for months, and it contained a detailed plan by which they were confident another attempt to force the Straits would succeed. From the experience they had gained, and counting on all the increased resources that were now at their disposal, especially in ammunition, monitors and aircraft, as well as their greatly improved mine-sweeping service, they felt no doubt that with a few more obsolete battleships and some minor reinforcements the difficulties which led to the original failure could be overcome. In this view Admiral Wemyss fully concurred, but Admiral de Robeck was less sanguine. In his eyes the plan, good as it was, was certainly attended with high risk, while he was unable to see any definite advantage to which it could lead even if it attained the highest degree of success that could be expected. In short, the certain risk seemed to him out of all proportion greater than any salutary effect the venture could have on the course of the war. The principle on which he reasoned was sound, and with reluctance he felt he must make it quite clear that he could not recommend the adoption of the Staff plan.

Yet with this expression of opinion he could not rest content. The moving spirit of the proposed scheme was his Chief of Staff, Commodore Roger Keyes, and it was endorsed by Admiral Wemyss. For both men he had the highest regard and with both he had always worked in the closest harmony. Simply to overrule their considered and confident opinion was more than his position seemed to warrant. In any case he felt it only right that in a matter of such capital importance, the Admiralty, in making its final decision, should be placed in full possession of the weighty opinions which were opposed to his own, and that this should be done in the fullest and most forcible manner, he took a step to which few men in his position would have risen. It was to send home his Chief of Staff, that he might lay his plan before the Admiralty and freely explain the situation as he and Admiral Wemyss saw it.

This was decided on October 19 just before the bombardment of the Bulgarian coast. Waiting only to see the operations through, Commodore Keyes started for London, and arrived there late on the 28th. No time was then lost in laying his scheme before the Naval War Staff. The general idea on which it rested was to rush the Straits by surprise at dawn with two squadrons under support of a third. The first squadron, consisting of ten of the best battleships, with eight sloops and ten destroyers for sweeping, would engage the forts inside below the Kephez minefield. The second squadron would be composed of five or six old battleships, two cruisers of the "Theseus" class and eight destroyers, and would go straight for the minefield. If possible the squadron would also contain some of the special service ships—that is, the old merchant steamers disguised to look like battleships which Lord Fisher had ordered for his North Sea project. The ships that survived the minefield would then rush the Narrows, accompanied by sloops and destroyers to set up a smoke screen, and proceed to sink the Nagara net barrage and destroy any minelayers that might be encountered. Meanwhile the third squadron, comprising all the monitors, the *Swiftsure* and the heavy cruisers off the western shore of the peninsula, would be firing over the land, with all the heavy guns registered on the Narrows forts. With this assistance it was hoped that at least half of the second squadron would be able to reach security at Pasha Liman harbour, above Nagara, from which they would proceed to engage the Narrows forts in reverse, while the first squadron attacked from below. If at the same time the army could develop an attack, or at least make a demonstration in force, to which the first and third squadrons would give full support with their secondary armament, success, he felt, would be assured. The plan concluded with detailed arrangements for maintaining the successful ships in the Marmara and a scheme of operations by which all communication with Gallipoli both by sea and land could be effectually cut.

Daring as was the conception, it seemed at least the only way in which success could be snatched from the failure. To every one at home, except the strictest adherents of continental war doctrine, it was clear that even partial success would profoundly affect the course of the war, and the War Staff, without committing themselves to the details of the plan, thought that something of the kind might have to be done, but as combined action of the army was, in their opinion, essential, nothing could be decided till General

Monro's report came to hand. By the time it arrived the effect of Commodore Keyes's advocacy had gone far to convince the immediately responsible Ministers that he had found a way out of the impossible situation. The result was that when on November 3 the War Committee met, they found it impossible to accept General Monro's opinion out of hand. The effect of the Commodore's presentation of his own project on Lord Kitchener was to stiffen to apparent rigidity his determination not to sign an order for evacuation. If the Admiralty were ready to sanction the new plan, he was ready to back them with the army and to give General Birdwood the command. Still the fundamental technical factors were too uncertain to warrant Ministers coming to an irrevocable decision. The problem, moreover, now presented itself as a balance of risk which could only be measured in the light of the political situation, and was far too complex to be decided on an appreciation made on military grounds alone. A much wider view was required, and to obtain it they decided to request Lord Kitchener to go out in person and report on the whole situation, including Egypt.[1] Taking Paris on the way, where he found the French High Command as strongly opposed to evacuation as he was himself, he reached Marseilles on November 7. Here the *Dartmouth* was waiting to take him to Alexandria, but at the last moment a request reached him to proceed direct to Mudros.

It was not till this day that Commodore Keyes started to return, for at Lord Kitchener's request he had waited till the despatch of naval reinforcements was definitely assured. Having been authorised to impart the scheme to the French, in passing through Paris he saw Admiral Lacaze, the Minister of Marine, who embraced the idea with enthusiasm, and promised to support the operation with six old battleships. With the assurance of French support he continued his way, feeling sure that the idea of evacuation was now dead.

Meanwhile, Admiral de Robeck, who had been ordered to detail a flag officer to command the naval forces at Salonica, was reporting that the port and its communications were quite unfit to receive or supply so large a force as was intended. All his efforts to improve matters were being obstructed by the Greeks, and until we took the place out of their hands it could not be regarded as a safe base. The possible necessity of coercing Greece by naval pressure was a burning question of the moment, and on November 4, the day after the War Committee considered Commodore Keyes'

[1] *Dardanelles Commission Report*, II., p. 55.

plan, Admiral de Robeck was informed that four battleships were coming out under Rear-Admiral S. R. Fremantle, to be used as a detached squadron as desired. He was also told that his light forces were to be strengthened by four destroyers and two submarines.

The following day (5th) Admiral de Robeck, whose health for some time had been giving way under the strain of his long and arduous command, was granted leave to come home for a long-needed rest, but he was requested to wait at Mudros till Lord Kitchener arrived. At the same time the fluid condition of opinion at home on the burning question was indicated by instructions that, before sailing, he should arrange for the officer left in charge to be ready for an urgent appeal from the army to co-operate with them, and that this might entail an attempt to force the Straits. To this extent the plan which Commodore Keyes had brought home had made its impression, but at the same time Admiral de Robeck was warned that nothing was yet decided and the secret preparations for evacuation were not to be taken in hand. It was a case, in fact, of arranging for every eventuality, and he was to be careful to keep sufficient light craft at Mudros so that any sudden and large call for tugs and lighters could be met. In reply he said that a joint naval and military committee was at work on plans for evacuation, and added his final opinion on the questions at issue. So far as he was aware the position of the army was not at present critical, but he and his staff agreed that unless it was established that a definite object was to be gained by a portion of the fleet forcing its way through to the Marmara, the sacrifice entailed would be a grave error, since it was likely to leave him too weak for safeguarding the army at Gallipoli and Salonica.

This was a very serious consideration. In the Mediterranean the security of the transport routes was becoming as haunting a preoccupation as it had lately been in Home waters. The enemy's submarines were again very active, particularly along the African coast from Algiers to Alexandria, and the need of small craft to deal with them was increasing. To make matters worse it was known on November 7 that the French submarine *Turquoise* had been captured in the Marmara intact and had been taken into the Turkish service. On the same day the Germans announced that our own *E 20* had been sunk. At the time there seemed no connection between the two losses. As we have seen, Lieutenant-Commander Warren had taken the *E 20* up on October 17, three days before the

Turquoise had started. He was known to have begun well, but nothing had been heard of him since the 30th. Two or three days later he had met his fate. How it happened was still a mystery, but a month later it leaked out that when the two boats met they arranged a rendezvous near Rodosto and then separated.[1] The *Turquoise* very soon afterwards ran aground under a Turkish battery and was forced to surrender. Practically intact she was taken up to Constantinople, and in her captain's cabin was found a book, which he had forgotten to destroy, giving the rendezvous with *E 20*.[2] In the Bosporus was the German submarine *UB 14* undergoing repair. In twenty-four hours she was made ready for sea and proceeded to the fatal spot. There she found *E 20* lying unsuspecting on the surface. Without difficulty the German was able to stalk her and get in a torpedo at 550 yards. She sank at once, and of her crew only nine men, including her commanding officer, could be saved.[3] These losses left us with only one submarine in the Marmara —*E 11*—which Commander Nasmith had brought up on November 6 for another cruise, and for over a month he kept up the disturbance single-handed.

The extent to which we could continue to control the Turkish communications with Gallipoli by sea was a question which closely affected that of our ability to maintain a hold on the peninsula. On this main point Lord Kitchener quickly convinced himself. After his first inspection he came to the conclusion that as things stood—that is, so long as the enemy was not reinforced by German troops and guns—our men had nothing to fear, but, on the other hand, what he had seen convinced him that the fleet could never break through to the Marmara. As it was on its ability to do so that depended the power of preventing the Turks being reinforced from Germany, his determination never to sign an order for evacuation seems to have been shaken. His objection to confessing failure was at least so far overcome that he was now willing to assent to a withdrawal provided the evacuation was accompanied by a telling blow against the Turks elsewhere. Such an enterprise, it will be remembered, had always been his preference, and now, as ever, in common with other high authorities, the dominating consideration that he had in mind was the loss of prestige which a simple confession of failure would involve all over the East and the consequent perilous situation which would

[1] See Map 3. [2] See *ante*, p. 179.

[3] *U-boote gegen U-boote* (Die Woche, 10th March, 1917), by Lieutenant zur See von Heimburg. The *E 20* was sunk on the 5th.

arise in Egypt. From the first he had seen in Alexandretta the best objective for our Expeditionary Force, where at the nodal point of the Turkish railway system our position both in Egypt and Mesopotamia could be most effectively supported. French opposition to the project had turned the scale against its adoption, but now he thought that he had found a way out. On the opposite shore of the Gulf of Alexandretta lay the small but well-sheltered port of Ayas. Being beyond the extreme confines of Syria, it was well out of the French sphere of interest, and close by, at Adana, was a point where the main Turkish line of communication was equally vulnerable. With two divisions and 3,000 cavalry that were available from Egypt he believed the port could be seized, and as soon as it was in our hands the evacuation of Gallipoli could safely begin. Admiral de Robeck reported that at their first conference the Generals were unanimously in favour of this solution of the difficulty, and that he believed the extra burden it would lay on the navy was not an insuperable difficulty.

At the Admiralty the design was received with grave misgiving. There, where the needs of every theatre met in never-ceasing importunity, it was felt that the new idea would strain their anti-submarine resources to breaking point. A new base like Mudros would have to be established, a new line of communication would be entailed, and by no means could they see their way to providing the small craft for their protection for two or three months, if then.

In the War Committee there was no less doubt. At the moment the chief anxiety was the attitude of Greece. It had recently grown so suspicious and even menacing that it was a serious question whether the Salonica troops would be extricated from the precarious position in which General Sarrail's adventurous advance had placed them without adopting the French proposals for drastic coercive action with the fleet forthwith. Such high-handed action against a neutral our own Government could not regard as justified by the undefined situation. They could go no further than to inform the French Government that, unless Greece declared she would demobilise or agree not to molest the Allied troops in their withdrawal from Serbia and Salonica, we were ready to apply coercion and to settle the method of applying it in immediate conference between the French Naval Staff and our own.

The existing state of affairs at Salonica naturally added weight to the objections which were generally held at home to the Ayas project. By the General Staff it was argued that while Ayas and Alexandretta were nodal points of the Turkish railway system, and, as such, important objectives, they were, for the same reason, the points where it was easiest for the Turks to concentrate against a descent. Consequently, although the first landing might be easy, subsequent developments would be sure to involve a greater proportion of our land and sea forces than we could spare. It would be far better, then, if we withdrew the Dardanelles force to Egypt and defended the line of the canal at the extreme end of the enemy's difficult lines of communication, with no new line of our own to protect. Moreover, when the winter was over and the desert impassable, Egypt would be safe for eight months and the troops could be used wherever they were wanted. Finally was formulated the real objection to Lord Kitchener's plan. It was that we must retain the power of concentrating our utmost strength in the main theatre at a favourable moment. But as decisive action in France could only be hoped for if the Russian armies were making a simultaneous effort along their own front, it was not clear how a favourable moment could arise so long as Turkey was barring the only practicable line by which the Western Powers could restore the fighting force of Russia. Still, the doctrine of the main theatre had too strong a hold not to dominate the situation. It was decided, therefore, to telegraph these views to Lord Kitchener, and beyond ordering a division which was about to proceed to Salonica to stand fast in Egypt, no decision was to be taken till his reply was received.

It came promptly, and in unequivocal terms. Seizing at once upon the most obvious fault in the General Staff appreciation, he pointed out that to treat the canal as the defence of Egypt was bad politics as well as bad strategy. On the technical objections to his alternative plan he urged that the staff at home were obviously misinformed, both as to the number of troops the Turks could concentrate at Ayas and also as to the nature of the terrain, which would demand a much smaller force for holding it than they assumed. Moreover the political considerations were in this case far more important than the military. To retire from Gallipoli and do nothing would be to leave the Germans free to develop their plans in the East and to throw the Arabs into their arms, with fatal results, not only to our own position in Asia and Egypt, but also to the French and Italian possessions in North Africa.

Admiral de Robeck had also been asked for his opinion. Seeing that his mistrust of the new scheme for forcing the

Straits and his unwillingness to admit complete impotence were as strong as ever, he as promptly replied that he was fully prepared to do all that was possible to co-operate in Lord Kitchener's plan. The proposed base in the Gulf of Alexandretta he regarded as far easier to protect than Mudros, and far handier for giving tactical support to the army than Gallipoli. The only doubt he felt arose from the attitude of the Greeks at Salonica. There, in his opinion, lay the most serious danger, but if that were settled the rest would be comparatively easy.

On the day (November 14) that his telegram reached the Admiralty another went out to him to say that steps were being taken by the French and British Governments to frame a note to Greece and to back it with a naval demonstration by an Allied squadron in Salonica Bay. As it was in the French sphere a French Admiral would command, and he was immediately to organise a squadron to join him. Till all was ready the note would not be presented, nor would anything be done till the time limit of the ultimatum expired. Then, if the reply was unfavourable, the Greek fleet was to be destroyed.

Here, then, was a further complication standing in the way of the quick decision for which Lord Kitchener was pressing. One step, however, the War Committee now took towards clearing the board. On November 15 they came provisionally to the conclusion that the Ayas project should be dropped. In view of the danger of a new military commitment in the Near East while the situation at Salonica was so uncertain, and of the naval difficulties of a new line of communication, and finally of the objection of the military authorities and the French Government, his bold project seemed inadmissible. He was at once informed that our whole policy in the Near East was to be discussed at a conference with the French which was to meet in Paris on November 17.

It had been called at the instance of General Joffre with the main object of considering the whole tangled situation, and generally to co-ordinate the efforts of the two allies. Its conclusions were that no new line of operation in the Near East was possible and that our two divisions which had been ear-marked for strengthening the Mediterranean Expeditionary Force, and on which Lord Kitchener was counting for his *coup de main* at Ayas, should go direct to Salonica. Meanwhile the evacuation of Gallipoli was to await the final appreciation of Lord Kitchener and Colonel Girodon, whom the French had sent out for the purpose. As for the note to Greece, it was not to be presented till Salonica was rendered safe from surprise by the Greek army and the eventual retreat of the Anglo-French forces secured, nor until the necessary naval measures for enforcing the note had been taken. It was further decided to set up an Inter-Allied Council of War with a permanent staff in close touch with the naval and military staffs of the two countries to secure better co-ordination between the Entente Powers. It was to be composed, in the first instance, of the British and French Prime Ministers and such expert members as they deemed necessary. Its office was to advise the two Governments, but Italy and Russia were to be invited to participate in the arrangement.

This was the end of the Ayas project, but, so far, nothing had been settled about Gallipoli, nor did Lord Kitchener see his way to giving a final opinion till the question of Greece was cleared up. The naval preparations for enforcing the intended ultimatum were well advanced, but as a last chance of weaning the harassed King from the influence of his Germanophile staff our Minister at Athens was suggesting that Lord Kitchener, who was coming to Salonica, should go on to Athens and see if he could not open the King's eyes to the mistake he was making in assuming a German victory as a foregone conclusion. It looked like a forlorn hope, but the mission was one for which Lord Kitchener's peculiar diplomatic power was well adapted, and the suggestion was adopted. This was on November 18, and next day, in reply to his request for instructions as to the line he should take, the Prime Minister told him he was to make it clear we were not attempting to force Greece to join the Allies against Germany, but that any attempt to intern or disarm our retiring troops would be taken as an act of war. Further, he should try to convince the King that Germany was going to lose the war, that Russia and ourselves were only beginning, and that our determination to win was unchanged by recent reverses. Our vast resources as yet had hardly been touched, and this view he was to press as strongly as possible. As this was Lord Kitchener's own unshakable opinion, no man could do it better, and he was completely successful.[1] The impression he made was deep and lasting; every undertaking we required was given, the unmolested retirement of General Sarrail's force was promised, as well as all we required for making Salonica safe as a base, and the embarrassing need for violent naval action passed away.

With the Near Eastern problem so far simplified it was

[1] *Official History of the War : Gallipoli*, Vol. II, pp. 419–20.

possible to come to a conclusion about the Dardanelles. Just as Lord Kitchener was leaving Mudros for Athens he had received word that the conference had vetoed his Ayas project, and had been asked if he could not now give a considered opinion on the burning question of Gallipoli. It was on November 22, after he had returned to Mudros and had held a further combined conference with Admiral de Robeck and the Generals, that he at last gave a reluctant opinion for evacuation.[1] In his view the Salonica venture, into which we had been drawn against our better judgment, left no other course open. But for that he believed we could have stopped the German designs in Egypt, either by turning the Turkish right from Suvla or by breaking in from the Gulf of Alexandretta. Entangled as we were in the Balkans, neither operation seemed possible, and we now had to face the necessity of defending Egypt in Egypt, a task so formidable in the eyes of all who knew the political situation, that it must inevitably compromise the possibility of a serious offensive on the Western Front in the Spring. So it was he saw the future. His recommendation was that the troops withdrawn from Gallipoli should in the first instance remain at Imbros, Tenedos and Mytileni, where they would still menace the Turkish communications and hold back considerable forces in Asia Minor. He was therefore of opinion that Suvla and Anzac should be evacuated at once, but that, on naval grounds, Helles should be retained at least for the present.

On this telegram a prolonged discussion took place next day (November 23) in the War Committee. They had also before them a carefully considered appreciation by the General Staff and another from the Admiralty. That of the General Staff, while frankly admitting the extreme complexity of the problem, concluded regretfully with the opinion that the military reasons for the evacuation outweighed all others, but that, on naval considerations, Helles might be retained for the present provided it was tactically suitable to be the last point evacuated. Admiral de Robeck was for its retention, mainly on the ground that if it were abandoned it would be practically impossible to prevent the enemy using the Dardanelles as a submarine base. With all the relevant considerations fully before them the War Committee in the end decided to advise the Cabinet that on military grounds the Gallipoli peninsula should be evacuated and that the naval advantages of a permanent

[1] The Admiral took no part in the discussion. He left the conference as soon as it appeared that the questions at issue were purely military.

occupation of Helles were outweighed by the military disadvantages it involved.[1]

For the navy it was a severe blow. The idea of holding on to Helles was one which Admiral de Robeck had been urging ever since he had been instructed to prepare for a possible evacuation. For him Helles was on quite a different footing from Suvla and Anzac. Were it abandoned the Turks could quickly mount heavy guns at the mouth of the Straits and permanently deny entrance to the fleet. Not only would it be impossible to keep up the menace of seizing the Dardanelles, but a submarine base could be established at a point where it would be most disturbing to our Near Eastern operations. Now he did not conceal his regret that even Suvla and Anzac were to be given up. This was not, he said, favoured by the navy, but was entirely a military necessity, in which the navy must co-operate if wanted. When asked if he concurred in the military decision, he replied on November 25 that he could not understand it. This was his last word before he started home for the short leave which was now indispensable for the restitution of his health.

Admiral Wemyss, who for some time past had been engaged in working out evacuation plans, was left in command to carry them to completion. But, as we have seen, he fully shared Commodore Keyes' belief in another attempt to break through, and was even more firmly opposed than his chief to letting go anything that had been so hardly won, and he clutched resolutely to the last threads of hope. The word had not yet been given, and his first act was to beg that it should be held up till he had been able to consult further with the Generals and prepare a naval appreciation. The point upon which he now insisted was the dangers of a winter evacuation, which he said he could only regard with the gravest misgiving. For this view he had good grounds. At the end of October the weather had broken, with a south-westerly gale, which in the early hours of November 1, besides doing much other damage, had driven the destroyer *Louis* ashore in Suvla Bay. For several days it prevented all attempts to salve her, and she became a total loss. For the next three weeks strong south-west winds were almost incessant, culminating on November 22 in a heavy gale, which blew for thirteen hours and played havoc with the piers and small craft, and even broke the back of one of the blockships that formed the makeshift harbour at Kephalo. As this was the advanced

[1] *Dardanelles Commission Report*, II., p. 57.

base for the evacuation, Admiral de Robeck had reported the damage before leaving, with a request for old battleships or cruisers to be sunk for the better protection of the piers and beaches, and Admiral Wemyss was requested to send in an appreciation explaining his views without delay.

It came to hand on November 28. While fully realising the military reasons for the decision, he considered the evacuation of the army was almost entirely a naval operation, the difficulties of which he proceeded to point out. In the first place, a lengthy spell of fine weather was essential at a season when every north-easterly wind was quickly followed by strong south-westerly weather, to which all the beaches were open. Then the shelving nature of the shore involved the lengthy process of embarking men in lighters, the number of piers was inadequate, most of them had just been swept away, and owing to the submarine danger, transports, except at Suvla, could not come nearer the beaches than Kephalo. Moreover, the beaches were all under fire, and the Turkish guns so accurately registered on them that they could work effectively at night. He agreed with General Monro that thirty per cent. of the force must be lost, and before accepting such a disaster he begged that one more joint naval and military effort should be made to retrieve the situation. He had ready a plan for the naval part, and was sure General Monro would be willing to co-operate. In reply he was directed to submit his plan at once.

It came promptly next day, and proved to be the same which Commodore Keyes had taken home. Its main lines, as before, were the rushing of the Straits by a squadron of old ships in the night, so as to seize Pasha Liman harbour at dawn, establish control of the upper reaches, and then take the Narrows forts in reverse, while the first squadron attacked from below and the third squadron over the land from the neighbourhood of Anzac. The only modification was that the army would not necessarily be expected to attack simultaneously, but a vigorous diversion would materially assist the fleet by holding the enemy to his ground so as to prevent him reinforcing the light gun defences of the minefield. The demoralising effect of such a surprise attack from the sea he hoped would give him control of the Straits, and then the question of immediate action against Constantinople could be settled from home.

The impression this message made was strong enough for it to be referred to the Cabinet, together with the resolutions of the War Committee, and for some time longer the question of evacuation remained open. Indeed, it was practically impossible to come to a final decision until we had reached a definite understanding with France as to what was to be done with the Salonica force. The way was now clearer for the withdrawal of General Sarrail's army to the base, but, while we were determined to stand by the limit we had fixed when we were first induced to join in the enterprise, we could not ascertain what the French intended to do.

When, on December 1, Lord Kitchener was back in London, he expressed an unqualified opinion against proceeding with the Balkans enterprise, and, having seen the French Minister of War in Paris, believed General Sarrail would be ordered to fall back on Salonica. We, in any case, felt the time had come to remind our allies that with the failure to join hands with the Serbian army the limit of our commitment had been reached and we were at liberty to withdraw. Next day Admiral de Robeck arrived. On the problem of Gallipoli his opinion was unshaken, that another attempt to force the Straits involved risks that were unjustifiable, since he was still unable to see any clear advantage to which it would lead. He was also hopeful about evacuating Suvla and Anzac successfully, but was firm as ever in pressing for the retention of Helles, in which opinion he had Lord Kitchener's support.

The latest news from the Dardanelles added further doubt. Another north-easterly gale had been blowing for three days (November 26-28) with heavy rain. Ashore, particularly at Suvla, which was fully exposed to the storm, the effects were lamentable. Trenches were flooded out, the nullahs were raging torrents and the flats a swamp. Most of the roads became impassable and many trenches were wrecked. To make matters worse, there came with the gale a bitter spell of cold. The high ground was white with snow, ten degrees of frost were registered, and the drenched troops in their summer clothing suffered terribly. Over two hundred died from exposure and more than 5,000 became casualties from sickness and frost-bite. At sea things were as bad; piers were destroyed; and at Kephalo, the most essential point for the coming operation, the damaged blockship broke up. It was the middle one of the three forming the breakwater, and the raging sea drove in through the gap, spreading havoc in the harbour. Here, as well as elsewhere, numbers of small craft, including a torpedo boat, were wrecked, and until the damage was made good it was impossible to attempt evacuation. The news, in fact, told as strongly for the need of a speedy withdrawal as for the difficulty of carrying it out. Finally it was agreed that no decision could be reached without another conference with the French, and a meeting of the new Allied Council was called for December 4 at Calais.[1]

It was one of the crises in the Entente when its harmony was likely to be severely tried. The main question was whether or not the Salonica enterprise was to be abandoned, and in this the views of the two Governments were diametrically opposed. Our General Staff was actually at work on arranging transport for removing our troops at Salonica and taking them to Gallipoli. In short, the question of evacuation was again in the melting-pot, as the Cabinet, with whom the final decision rested, was not persuaded. To Lord Kitchener the idea of abandoning the enterprise was as obnoxious as ever, and having found on his return home that the Admiralty were ready to make another attack on the lines of Commodore Keyes's plan, provided the army gave it its full support, the distasteful conclusion he had come to at Mudros was shaken. Two days before the conference was to meet he sent General Monro an urgent query as to whether four divisions from Salonica could be landed at Suvla before the stormy season set in, and, if so, whether sufficient depth could be gained to make its retention possible. The navy, he added, were ready to co-operate with a big offensive operation. But General Monro replied next day that the terrain at Suvla did not lend itself to support from ship fire, that the transfer of the Salonica divisions could not be made in time to avoid bad weather, and that in any case the utmost we could hope for was an advance of a few hundred yards. He was, moreover, apprehensive about the difficulty of maintaining so large a force after the bad weather had made the flow of supplies irregular; nor did he think it possible to interrupt the enemy's line of communication along the Bulair road for any length of time. The General on the spot was, therefore, persuaded that the Dardanelles expedition ought to be liquidated. Those with whom the final decision rested were still in doubt, and the idea of transporting our Salonica force to Suvla remained a possibility.

In this highly charged atmosphere the critical conference met. The discussion that took place was very frank, we,

[1] It was attended by Mr. Asquith, Mr. Balfour and Lord Kitchener; and on the part of France by M. Briand (Premier and Foreign Minister), General Gallieni (Minister of War) and Admiral Lacaze (Minister of Marine). The experts assisting were General Murray, Chief of our General Staff, and for France General Joffre and the Chiefs of the General and Naval Staffs. Neither Russia nor Italy was represented.

on our part, insisting that the original object of the expedition was no longer attainable, and that we did not feel that 150,000 men should any longer be risked in so precarious a position; the French, on the other hand, pleaded that the Serbian army had not been destroyed, and was capable of resuscitation. They urged the lamentable moral and strategical effects of retirement empty-handed, the possibilities of future action in the Balkans, and the objection to evacuating without first consulting Italy and Russia, both of whom we had been urging to co-operate and who had promised assistance in Albania and on the Rumanian frontier. We could only reply that we required the troops for the security of our eastern possessions, and if they wished us to provide a sufficient force for operations in the Balkans, the men could come only from France. Still, the French pleaded to retaining at least a *pied à terre* at Salonica. Their troops were already falling back upon the town, and in any case it must be held and placed beyond the possibility of attack before evacuation was possible.

On these lines a kind of compromise was reached. In the end we formally announced that with all sympathy with the views of our Allies, and without prejudice to further possible operations in the Balkans, our General Staff were of opinion that to keep 150,000 men at Salonica was at present a dangerous measure, which might well end in disaster. We could not, therefore, consent to retain the place, and wished steps to be taken forthwith to evacuate it. To this end, Greece should be informed that we intended to occupy all positions necessary for the security of the troops, with an assurance that there was no intention to trench on her sovereign rights. As we had expressly reserved the right to retire on the conditions which had arisen, M. Briand could only bow reluctantly to our decision. All he asked was that General Sarrail should be placed in supreme command of the operations for retirement, and that all Senegalese and Creoles at Helles, who were rapidly wasting away from disease, should be immediately withdrawn. To both these requests we readily agreed.

An important point was thus left undecided. The naval objection to the evacuation of Salonica appears to have been overlooked. Nothing had been said about taking precautions to prevent the port being ultimately used as a submarine base against us. Attention was quickly called to the omission, with a suggestion that Greece should be required to hold the port neutral, on pain of failure being regarded as a *casus belli.*

An Allied Military Conference, moreover, which met at the French Headquarters on December 6 to define a concerted policy for all theatres of the war, declared that opinion was unanimous on the extreme urgency of organising the defence of Salonica, and with equal unanimity they required the immediate and complete evacuation of Gallipoli. This decision was the final blow to the greatest combined campaign that history records. From this moment the idea of reinforcing Suvla was dropped and the conclusions of the conference were in the main accepted by the Cabinet and sent out to the Dardanelles on December 8.

There, as was only to be expected, the verdict could not be meekly accepted. For the devoted men who had so gallantly borne the burden and reverse of the long struggle in the Ægean it was a judgment to which they could not bow without passionate resistance. On December 7 Admiral Wemyss was informed that in face of unanimous military opinion it had been decided "to shorten the front" by evacuating Anzac and Suvla. To him and his staff, who had not ceased to press for leave to make one more attempt to force the Straits, the decision was specially disappointing. The latest intelligence had further increased their confidence. Their agents were reporting that the demoralisation of the Turks which their abortive and costly attacks had caused was greatly deepened by the effect of the late storms and by the growing accuracy of the ship-fire on their billets, reserves and magazines. There was, moreover, excellent news of Commander Nasmith in *E 11.*[1] After failing to get in touch with his lost consort, *E 20*, on November 15, he found two large steamers in Bergaz Bay. One he torpedoed, but his shot at the second did no more than sink two schooners that were protecting her.[2] Eleven days later he found two more at anchor in Artaki Bay, and though both were protected by a cover of dhows he managed with his gun to sink one and damage the other. The first week in December was specially full of adventure. On the 2nd he was lying in wait for a passing train on the railway in the Gulf of Ismid. The first one that came he hit and set on fire, and next day as he was leaving the gulf he cleverly torpedoed the Turkish destroyer *Yar Hissar*, which was coming from the westward to look for him. Out of her total complement of seventy Turks and fifteen Germans he was able to rescue the captain, another officer and forty

[1] See Map 3.

[2] This ship proved to be one that had been beached after he had torpedoed her on August 23 on his last cruise.

men, five of whom were Germans. It was clear, as well as encouraging, to find that our chief enemy was feeling acutely the effect of our submarine work and using every effort to stop it, and in addition to what Commander Nasmith now learnt, he ascertained from a prize a few days later that the Germans had established and were manning no less than eleven anti-submarine batteries at various points of vantage or refuge.[1] Again, next day (December 4), while he was attacking off Panderma a 5,000-ton steamer with his gun, a torpedo boat came hurrying up, opened fire and started circling round his quarry. But for all she could do he continued to attack, and finally, while the torpedo boat was on one side of the ship, he, on the other, got in a shot on the steamer's water line at twenty yards and finished her. His next encounter was near Gallipoli with a despatch vessel coming out of the port, with which he was in action for two days, finally leaving her on fire fore and aft on the north shore of Marmara Island. On December 10 he met *E 2*, which had just come up, and leaving her to the westward went up himself to the entrance of the Bosporus, where he sank another large steamer proceeding across from the Golden Horn to Haidar Pasha. So he continued, in spite of every effort to catch him, till December 23, when, after narrowly escaping an attempt to torpedo him at the rendezvous, he went down in safety.[2]

The work of stopping the enemy's sea communications was now practically complete. From one of his prizes he had learnt that only three large steamers then remained, and two of these he had destroyed. From the same prize he also learnt that the success of his and his comrades' work was so effective that the Germans had built a railway from Uzun Kupru, the nearest point on the Adrianople—Constantinople line, to Kavak, at the head of the Gulf of Xeros, and that all munitions and troops were going that way and thence by road across the Bulair lines into the Gallipoli peninsula. But this line of supply had also been taken in hand. After several unsuccessful efforts by various craft, the *Agamemnon* with the *Endymion* and the monitor *M 33*

[1] They were Gallipoli, Karabuga, Rodosto, Erekli, Silivri, San Stefano, entrance to Ismid ,Mudania, Panderma, Artaki and Kalolimno.

[2] Commander Nasmith's cruise had lasted forty-seven days, making his total time in the Marmara only three days short of a hundred. In this last cruise he had destroyed or rendered useless five large and six small steamers, as well as one destroyer, five large and thirty small sailing vessels. For the remarkable tenacity and skill he had displayed he was promoted to captain after only a year's service as Commander, and the admirable behaviour of the ship's company received proportionate recognition.

had succeeded on December 2 in destroying the three central spans of the Kavak road bridge and so cutting up the road as to make it impossible for anything to pass that way. Everything, in fact, gave the Admiral and his staff increased faith in their ability to afford the troops support enough to enable them to hold their ground, and brighter hope of a successful naval surprise. So confident, indeed, were they that they could now completely isolate the Turks in the peninsula, that the decision to evacuate on military grounds came as a complete surprise. The despatch of naval reinforcements, for which they had asked, and the prefatory steps that had been ordered for the transfer of the Salonica troops to Gallipoli, had led every one to believe the naval staff views had prevailed with the Government. General Monro himself, having no doubt he was overruled, had declared his determination to do all in his power to make the new offensive a success. To the Admiral and his staff the decision to evacuate was in the circumstances incomprehensible. They could not even believe that it had really turned on the strategical possibilities of the theatre. It would seem to them as though a conviction was growing in military circles that the sole way to win the war was by "killing Germans," a method which could only be effective in the main theatre. To men whose outlook had been so long fixed on the promise of a great strategical stroke in the Near East, such a view of the war meant mere bankruptcy of leadership. It meant, moreover, entirely ignoring the fleet and its oft-proved capacity for substantially increasing the power of the army. It was impossible not to protest, and in a long reasoned telegram Admiral Wemyss endeavoured to show how unsound was the idea on which he believed the decision rested.

It involved, so he urged, the conclusion that our only way of defeating Germany was to fight her with one arm. The navy was practically being left out of the account. Nor was he without ground for his complaint. For he knew, and had had to point out, that in calculating the military force necessary for the defence of Egypt the General Staff had omitted to take any account of the naval guns; and this although, since the Turkish attempt to invade in February, practical experience at the Dardanelles and improved methods of gunnery had immensely increased their power of finding military targets ashore. Further, he urged that since the war was now admittedly one of exhaustion, nothing could increase our staying power so much as the opening of the Black Sea and the settlement of our preoccupations in Asia and Egypt by cutting Turkey out of the Central Powers combination; and, could any doubt remain as to this not being our right policy, he pointed to the now obvious indications that Germany's paramount war aims were the markets and industrial resources of the East.

His protests and arguments were in vain. The Admiralty could only reply that to them his proposed operations looked so precarious that they did not feel justified in risking a defeat which might well prove disastrous enough to shake our naval prestige and make our position in the East still more difficult. A new attempt to force the Straits by the fleet alone could not, therefore, be sanctioned. Nor could they, in face of the overwhelming military opinion and the strain of Salonica, press any further objections to the evacuation of Suvla and Anzac. The only consolation they could offer was that the retention of Helles would enable the kind of attempt he desired to be made later on. This final decision Admiral Wemyss acknowledged on December 12 " with the greatest regret and misgiving," and announced that he hoped to carry out the evacuation of Suvla and Anzac on the nights of December 19–20 and 20–21, and at once set about arranging for the concentration of his detached units so as to provide the number of officers, men and small craft that the operation would require.

As the preparations proceeded his misgiving increased. The compromise under which Helles was to be held only deepened his anxiety, till, on December 13, he felt compelled to lay before the Admiralty the very serious situation that would arise at Helles when Suvla and Anzac were evacuated. As it was, the daily casualty list ashore with no regular fighting going on amounted to hundreds, and the abandonment of the northern area to the enemy would mean that the artillery fire to which the whole area was always exposed from the Asiatic shore and the north of Achi Baba would be doubled in intensity. Unless therefore Achi Baba was captured before the Turks could move their guns down from the evacuated area, or German howitzers and ammunition arrived, Helles would be untenable. He was quite ready to support an attack upon the long-coveted position, but unless it was held, there was no naval advantage great enough to justify the sacrifice of the army, which the retention of Helles would entail. Judging from the admitted effect of ship fire he did not doubt the success of a determined combined attack.

The fact was that in both services confidence in the power

of the fleet to give tactical support to an army ashore had been growing rapidly during the past two months, and with no one more than General Davies, who, as commanding at Helles, was in the best position to know. His supporting squadron was under Captain D. L. Dent of the *Edgar*, an accomplished gunnery officer, to whom the recent improvement was greatly due. On November 15 the General had put his faith to the test by arranging with Captain Dent for tactical co-operation in an attack he had planned for driving in an awkward salient in the enemy lines at the junction of the two Krithia ravines. The operation proved a rapid and complete success. After springing three mines our men rushed forward, and so completely did the fire of Captain Dent's squadron demoralise the Turkish gunners, that we were able to seize and consolidate the captured section with trifling loss.[1] In this case there could be no doubt about the navy's contribution, and the Headquarters report for the day contained much more than the usual acknowledgment of the ships' assistance. The result, it said, "was mainly due to the effective fire from the *Edgar*." General Davies' full staff report went further, and was no less appreciative of the monitors. "All who saw it," the report says, "agree as to the accuracy and value of the monitors' fire, but the chief point is that it has been established that co-operation in an attack has now become a practical reality, and that a system has been established which with further development will prove a powerful factor both in attack and defence." It was not too much to say, for the weather had been too bad for aircraft to go up, and the remarkable results had been obtained without their assistance in spotting.

General Davies, though he agreed with General Monro on the question of evacuation and was equally opposed to a further attempt on Achi Baba, was much impressed as to the tactical value of fire from the sea. After November 15 he had thought it all out, and on December 4 he presented a long memorandum detailing the classes of ships that were required and what each class could do. What he wanted was a permanent squadron of "Edgars" and heavy monitors, with the addition of battleships for large operations requiring a great volume of fire. For his left flank he desired destroyers, and if possible the same he had hitherto had, since they knew the local conditions and their work had been as valuable as it was important.[2] His reason for asking for heavy monitors

[1] Captain Dent's squadron comprised the *Edgar*, two 14-inch monitors, *Abercrombie* and *Havelock*, *M 21* and two destroyers.

[2] The destroyers he referred to were *Scorpion*, *Renard* and *Wolverine*.

was that he had found they afforded a steady enough platform to enable them to fire on works close in front of his line, but if the weather happened to be too bad for them to be at sea he would be content with two or three "Edgars."

Admiral Wemyss had, therefore, ample grounds on the experience gained for urging a combined attack on Achi Baba and for insisting that the possibility of capturing it was not a purely military question. With the support of the ships he felt sure it could be done if it were attempted at once. Soon it would be too late, and he therefore begged for an immediate decision. Finally he pointed out that it was the real key of the situation. If it were captured we should then be in the position we had hoped to attain at the first landing. Not only could Helles be held, but with the essential observing station in our hands the main difficulties which had foiled the first attempt on the Narrows would disappear and the forcing of the Straits would become a task well within the power of the reinforced fleet. If, on the other hand, no attempt to take the dominating heights was to be allowed, then Helles should be evacuated while evacuation was still possible.

Whether right or wrong, his proposal for securing the position at Helles had now little chance of being accepted. A corrupting blight too familiar in some of our older combined expeditions was making itself felt; for the naval and military leaders held views about the future conduct of the campaign which were utterly opposed. General Monro, though in command of both sections of the Mediterranean Expeditionary Force, had been at Mudros for less than a week, and after one short visit to each sector had left for Salonica. Though personally his relations with Admiral Wemyss were excellent, his absence necessarily prevented that close and continuous interchange of ideas that is the essence of successful combined work. On December 14, on his return from Salonica, the Admiral's telegram containing the proposal to attack Achi Baba, a copy of which the Naval Staff had already given him, was sent to him from home. His immediate reply was as follows: "In this telegram Admiral Wemyss deals with the military situation at Helles and urges an attack on Achi Baba without delay. I wish to dissociate myself from the views expressed by the Admiral."

His final opinion was that, while the capture of Achi Baba would improve our position, the resources at his command were unequal to the operation. Emphatic as was this opinion, it did not silence the controversy. The difference between the naval and the military views was as marked as ever and, as so frequently happens, Ministers were left to decide a vital question of war policy while their most trusted and competent expert advisers were in open conflict upon its essential technical factors.

Even this difficulty was but one strand in the tangle of uncertainties that perplexed their deliberations. They had also to face the fact that the question of retaining Salonica, which they considered had been closed at Calais, was still open. In spite of the Conference having come to a clear decision on the matter, the French were showing strong disinclination to abide by it. At the Allied Military Conference at Chantilly which, as we have seen, followed the Ministerial Conference at Calais the Russian, Italian and Serbian representatives strongly urged the retention of the place, and the Russian Emperor, in a personal telegram to King George, backed the appeal, and the French were already presenting a formal request that the decision to withdraw should be reconsidered. It was difficult to tell what to do. All we knew was that there was a growing feeling in Paris which once more threatened to overthrow the Ministry, to wreck the Entente and to render all co-ordination of effort impossible. So acute was the crisis that it was decided that Sir Edward Grey and Lord Kitchener should go over to Paris to explain our views and should remain there until a definite understanding was established. They arrived there on December 9.

They found the atmosphere as bad as could be, but when they pointed out that in spite of our written agreement, which entitled us to retire at once, we had no thought of doing so, but were actually sending another division to secure the place for the retreat of General Sarrail, the air quickly cleared. M. Briand was able to explain to the Chamber that, so far from desertion. we were actually going beyond the commitment to which we had explicitly bound ourselves. So the crisis passed, but only at the cost of our being still tied for an indefinite time to an adventure of which we heartily disapproved and which made the defence of Egypt a task of increased difficulty.

It is possible the anxiety in the last direction was more than the conditions warranted, but the phantom of the February invasion had never ceased to haunt the Egyptian authorities, and a new spectre was walking on the western frontier. The Lybian desert was dominated by the Senussi, an independent Arab organisation on the strictest Mussulman lines. Of late years it had become powerful enough to be a factor with which both the Egyptian authorities and the Italians in Cyrenaica had to calculate as a dangerous field for German and Pan-Islamic propaganda. For some time past signs of unrest, religious in character, but with unmistakable indications of outside inspiration, had been causing increased anxiety, and now apprehension was suddenly confirmed by the appearance of an enemy submarine at Sollum. Here was our slender frontier garrison, two hundred miles from the railhead west of Alexandria, and connected with it by no more than a chain of weak coastguard stations. For practical purposes the line of communication was by sea, but owing to the pressure of the anti-submarine work in the Eastern Mediterranean there was nothing to spare for its adequate protection beyond four armed boarding steamers of the Egyptian Coast Patrol. It was organised in two sections, the Eastern working from Alexandria and the Western from Sollum. At this time the Western section was commanded by Captain R. S. Gwatkin-Williams in the *Tara*, which had just come out from serving in the Irish Sea with the North Channel Patrol. His instructions were to co-operate with the Italian Coast Patrol. Italy was at war with the Senussi and had established a patrol of the Gulf of Sollum, to which the Senussi had access, in order to prevent contraband from reaching them. We were the more concerned in the matter seeing that, though still nominally at peace with us, the Senussi were threatening Sollum with a large force and continually sniping the place. Captain Gwatkin-Williams, therefore, had orders that one of his vessels was to visit it once a day so as to evacuate the garrison if the port was rushed.[1] In the morning of November 5, in pursuance of these orders, the *Tara* was coming in with no thought of danger when she was suddenly torpedoed by a submarine. She sank immediately, but seventy of her crew of a hundred got away in the boats and were towed by the submarine into Bardia, which though nominally an Italian port, was claimed by the Senussi and was actually in their possession, and there they were handed over as prisoners to the Turkish commandant. Thence the submarine went back to Sollum and sank an Egyptian coastguard gunboat at her moorings and damaged another.

It was *U 35* that effected the surprise, the same boat which three weeks before had sunk the transport *Marquette* in the Gulf of Salonica, and it was soon discovered that what damage she had done was only incidental to her real mission.

[1] The garrison was only about one hundred men of the Egyptian Army, under Colonel Snow. The *Tara* was a London and North-Western Railway Company's steamer of 1,800 tons, armed with three Hotchkiss 6-pounders. She was still under her old captain, Lieutenant Tanner, R.N.R.

From the Gulf of Salonica she had gone to a rendezvous in the Gulf of Xeros, known as "Hersing Stand," and had there received orders to proceed to Budrum and take a Turkish mission and war material to Bardia. After embarking ten Turkish and German officers and some stores she left Budrum on November 1, and taking in tow two sailing vessels similarly laden, reached her destination three days later, having sunk a British tramp steamer on her way, besides unsuccessfully attacking a transport, the *Japanese Prince*, with troops from Alexandria to Salonica. The *Jonquil* and her roving patrol of eleven trawlers were quickly ordered to the area to hunt for the offending submarine, but with no success. The result of this energetic move of the Germans was that on November 15 Sollum was attacked. The garrison held its ground, but the fact that the Senussi were now in open war with us, and the fear that their move was not an isolated operation, gave deeper colour to the rumour of an impending invasion from Palestine. Steps were therefore promptly taken to deal with the minor menace before the greater one could materialise. The idea was to concentrate a sufficient force at Marsa Matruh, the post half-way between Alexandria and Sollum, and to that point the Sollum garrison was withdrawn by the coastguard gunboat on November 23, the day on which the main force began to be transported there by sea. Since there was nothing but trawlers available as transport, the work was very slow, nor could Vice-Admiral Sir Richard Peirse provide proper protection. But on his urgent entreaties Admiral de Robeck detached his other roving patrol, the *Clematis*, and six trawlers, to his assistance.

It was only with the greatest difficulty that the ships could be spared, for the second organised raid of the German submarines on our Mediterranean communication was in full swing. On November 3 another boat, *U 38*, had passed the Straits unseen, and between Gibraltar and Alboran had caught the British transport *Mercian*, with a regiment of yeomanry on board. The submarine attacked with shell-fire which immediately took effect, and some of the crew got out of hand. The *Mercian's* Commander, Captain Walker, had to take the helm himself, and, unknown to him, boats were lowered by order of a ship's officer, two of which capsised. For an hour the attack continued, yet by zigzagging Captain Walker was able to dodge most of the shells. Meanwhile the troops had been ordered on deck and behaved admirably. A soldier relieved the captain at the wheel and several more assisted in the stokehold. The regiment's machine-guns were got going, and with a parting salvo the submarine gave up. By that time the casualties were seventy-eight, including twenty-three men killed, besides an officer, twenty-two men and eight of the crew missing from the capsized boats.[1] Continuing her way, *U 38* sank eleven vessels by the 11th, and for two days held up the sailing of transports. So severe were the losses that the French could not help complaining of the inadequacy of the Gibraltar patrol, and it had to be reinforced by two sloops.[2]

In the vital Mediterranean area the destruction was no less. There, besides the *U 35*, two others, *U 34* and *U 33*, were at work again, and between them all during November fifty-two ships were attacked, of which forty were sunk. Of these three were armed, and of the twelve that escaped five were armed.[3] At this time, indeed, defensive armament seemed to be the best answer to the submarine campaign. Escort had been found impossible for lack of sufficient destroyers, and neither the roving squadrons, the patrols, nor the disguised ships had had any apparent success.

Fortunately, by the end of November, when all possible small craft had to be called in for the evacuation of Suvla, the activity of the submarines died down again, and by moving only at night 4,500 troops were safely disembarked at Marsa Matruh by December 7, and in position to begin the operations.

The new disturbance on the Western Frontier of Egypt was not the only cause for the anxiety that existed. As one looks back now it seems to have been excessive, but it must be remembered that at this time our whole position in the East was felt to be quivering under a blow from which no man could see a quick recovery. The rash attempt on Bagdad had failed. On October 5, it will be recalled, General Townshend had stopped his pursuit of the Turks retiring from Kut at Aziziya, and there he was ordered to concentrate for a possible further advance.[4] On October 23 General Nixon had received a guarded permission to make the

[1] The officer, thirteen men and five of the crew were picked up later. Captain Walker was awarded the D.S.C. for his conduct.

[2] See Note on p. 229.

[3] From November 15 to December 6 *U 33* sank sixteen merchantmen, including one neutral. Her British victims included the *Clan Macleod*, sunk by gunfire on her way home from India. Her Master (Captain H. S. Southward), who describes in his report the treatment he received from the U-boat commander, made a gallant effort to escape, but after a two hours' chase found the submarine had the advantage of speed and was obliged to surrender. See *Official History of the War : The Merchant Navy*, Vol. II, pp. 192–4.

[4] See Map 1.

attempt on which he was bent, but so difficult was the work of transport from the far-away base at Basra, with the river at its lowest, that it was not till a month later that General Townshend was ready to strike. Meanwhile the Turks had been preparing a strong position athwart the river at Ctesiphon, about eighteen miles below Bagdad. It consisted of three lines of entrenchments extending on either bank of the river and well connected by a bridge of boats. By November 21 General Townshend had his whole force of four brigades and one cavalry brigade concentrated about five miles from the Turkish position by the main Bagdad road, but twice as far by the bend of the river of which the road formed the cord. The flotilla consisted of the new Yarrow gunboat *Firefly* (Lieutenant C. J. F. Eddis), the old *Comet* (Lieutenant G. E. Harden), the two armed launches, *Shaitan* (Lieutenant A. C. Thursfield), and *Sumana* (Sub-Lieutenant Tudway), with four 4·7-inch naval guns in horse-boats towed by the armed stern-wheelers *Shushan* and *Messoudieh*.[1] Of these vessels Captain Nunn, having just rejoined, took command on November 22, as General Townshend's attack was developing. It was on identical lines with that which had been so successful at Kut—that is, a turning attack on the enemy's left or landward flank, and with a minor holding attack along the river supported by the flotilla. But it was little the flotilla could do, for in the reach below the Turkish position the banks were too high for direct fire, and when at the first rush the army captured the advanced line of trenches and were advancing on the next line, Captain Nunn found it impossible to move forward into the reach above. He was held up by a battery on the right bank; on that side we had no troops to trouble it, and it was able to develop a fire which the frail gunboats could not face. Thus, when the Turks counter-attacked to recover the part of the line which the troops had penetrated, the flotilla could give no adequate assistance, and after a prolonged struggle General Townshend was compelled to withdraw to the first position, with the loss of nearly a third of his force.

After maintaining himself there till November 25 to evacuate his wounded and prisoners, General Townshend, thinking the enemy was receiving large reinforcements, decided that the force must retire, and for the next week the flotilla, with incessant toil and self-sacrifice, devoted itself to expediting and covering the retreat of the river transport.

[1] The *Firefly* was the first of twelve "small" river gunboats designed by Messrs. Yarrow on Lord Fisher's instructions. See *ante*, p. 197.

The whole movement was one of extraordinary difficulty. In the advance up the shallow river, with its swift current and innumerable loops, the navigation had been difficult enough, but going down it was much worse. The transport craft were continually grounding, and when one grounded all above it were held up. From morning till night the gunboats were incessantly employed in getting them off under sniping fire from the local Arabs, who, as usual, were turning against the beaten side. Slowly as the exhausted army was able to retire along the direct road, it was only with the greatest exertions that the river craft were able to keep up with them. On November 28 the old camp at Aziziya was reached, but a little above it the *Comet* and *Shaitan* had taken the ground. The *Comet* was soon afloat again, but the *Shaitan* was immovable. All day the *Comet*, *Firefly* and *Shushan* strove to get her off under a sniping fire, until, when the Turks' advance guard began to join the Arabs, General Townshend, at the request of Captain Nunn, sent out the cavalry brigade to clear the snipers away. Even so, all attempts to move the *Shaitan* were in vain, and she had to be abandoned. On the 30th, after a rest of two days to reorganise troops, the retreat was continued as far as Umm-at-Tubal, only eight miles further on, and here the flotilla and all the transport anchored abreast of the bivouac. During the night it was shelled, and though the enemy soon desisted it was clear that the pursuit was overtaking the retreat. But for the sight which greeted the gunboats at dawn no one was prepared.

Barely more than a mile from our northern front was a large Turkish camp. It was owing to the absence of their cavalry that they had stumbled into so perilous a position, and full advantage of the mistake was immediately seized. Our artillery opened at once on the enemy's massed formations, the gunboats joined in with high explosive and the camp was quickly a confused scene of men and tents falling in clouds of dust and bursting shell. Under cover of the devastating fire and an infantry demonstration the troops and transports were quickly withdrawn, and the Turks had suffered far too heavily to pursue with any vigour. For the time the army was safe, but the flotilla was no more. As the gunboats were pouring destruction into the masses of the enemy, guns opened fire from a position on the bank where they could enfilade the reach in which the river craft had anchored. The *Firefly* soon received a shell in her boiler and was entirely disabled. Captain Nunn steamed up to save her and got her in tow, but the *Comet's* engines were unequal to the task and both vessels went hard aground under the left bank, upon which the Turks were advancing. The little *Sumana* then pushed up to the rescue, but only succeeded in getting the last men away from her doomed consorts when the Turks were already swarming upon their abandoned decks. But their main duty was done, and without further molestation the troops reached Kut on December 3. Here they met two more of the new gunboats, *Butterfly* and *Cranefly*, but these, with all the river craft and the cavalry, were sent down the river, and on December 7 Kut was invested.

In the three days of the battle of Ctesiphon, the engagement of Umm-at-Tubal and the retirement of December 1 and 2, the British losses, exclusive of "followers," numbered 711 killed, 3,890 wounded and 369 missing, a total of 4,970. The Turkish casualties at Ctesiphon including many desertions, are given in the Turkish account as over 9,500. Another Turkish official estimates their actual fighting losses at 6,188. At Umm-at-Tubal their losses amounted to 748.

So it was that, instead of achieving a success which could be looked to for countervailing the moral effect of our withdrawal from Gallipoli, we had met with a rebuff which, unless General Townshend could speedily be relieved, was likely to end in resounding disaster. That was for the moment the paramount consideration, and to the French importunity for more and still more transports for Salonica we could only reply (December 15) that the first call on the ships available must be to get the remaining Indian division out from France to the Persian Gulf.

Note.—On November 3 the *U 38* also attacked the armed steamer *Woodfield*: Before she was sunk by torpedo a search party discovered the Admiralty secret instructions to armed steamers and naval guns' crews. This document heavily weighted the arguments of the German Naval Staff in favour of regarding armed merchant ships as men-of-war, and on February 8, 1916, the German Government issued a memorandum, together with what purported to be a photographic reproduction of our secret instructions, and warned neutrals against using "the armed merchant vessels of the Powers with whom the German Empire is at war." An Imperial Order, to come into force on February 29 (issued on the 11th) instructed all naval commanders to destroy "enemy merchant ships armed with guns by every means." This order was modified on the 24th to the effect that "enemy passenger steamers are to be spared until further orders, even when armed," a restriction due mainly to the attitude of America with whom the correspondence about the *Lusitania* had not yet reached a conclusion.[1]

[1] *Der Kreig zur See: Der Handelskrieg mit U-Booten*, Vol. III, pp. 26, 85–89.

CHAPTER XII

EVACUATION OF GALLIPOLI

THE controversy over the retention of Helles was still proceeding with unabated animation when the withdrawal from Suvla and Anzac was well under way. It was an operation which, as we have seen, no one concerned could contemplate without the gravest misgiving. Nothing of the kind on a scale so great or under conditions so formidable had ever been attempted before. From beaches under artillery fire, without any safe natural harbour, some 92,000 men with two hundred guns had to be re-embarked in the face of an undefeated enemy whose trenches were nowhere more than three hundred yards from our own, and in some places only five, and it had to be done at a season of treacherous weather in confined waters open to submarine attack, while to ensure secrecy the whole work must be carried out at night. It is difficult to conceive of any operation in which so many possible mishaps menaced success or so much depended on the steadiness and discipline of all ranks, strict punctuality, absolute secrecy and accurate, exhaustive and harmonious staff work between land and sea. As a piece of combined work—which a large proportion of those engaged and directing believed to be a needless sacrifice of dearly won advantage—it must surely stand as a feat of arms unparalleled in the annals of war.

So vital was secrecy that the labour of working out the scheme had to be confined to the few naval and military officers to whom it was necessary to disclose what was in the wind. From the first day that warning had been given that withdrawal might be necessary a joint staff conference had been at work, and had quickly decided the operation must be conducted in three stages. The first was purely preparatory, in which were to be evacuated all troops, animals and material not required for a defensive winter campaign, should it be decided to hold on till the spring. This stage was completed by December 10, when Admiral Wemyss received definite orders to proceed with the evacuation, and when about

9,000 sick, mainly victims of a sudden spell of cold winter weather, had been re-embarked.[1] The next was an intermediate stage, in which would be withdrawn all men, guns and animals not required for the tactical defence of the positions during the final stage, which it was hoped would take only two days more, though if the weather proved unfavourable it might last a week. For the final stage, then, nothing but fighting men and medical personnel were to be left, and all told they must not exceed what the navy could undertake to embark in two nights with the resources at their disposal. It was mainly a question of small craft. Even the limited number available could not all be used, for Admiral Wemyss felt it essential to hold about one-third of them in reserve to replace casualties in case of bad weather and enemy action. Twenty thousand men at each place was the utmost found possible, for with them must be withdrawn the last of the guns. It was few enough—seeing that we believed they had 80,000 to 100,000 enemy opposed to them, and that the Turkish front trenches were fully manned. During this stage, moreover, the troops would have to rely almost entirely on the ships for artillery support.

To arrange that such support should be adequate was no easy matter. Any unusual movement at sea would be sure to attract the enemy's attention, and everything depended on lulling him to sleep. So important was this precaution that the idea of making a feint elsewhere—the usual device for securing surprise—was rejected. Nothing of the kind was to be permitted except such offensive action as might be possible at Helles. Having received instructions to that effect for the last day, General Davies decided on an operation like that which had been so successful on November 15, and applied for the assistance of Captain Dent with an increase of his squadron. Elsewhere, so far as possible, the usual routine was kept up. All through the intermediate stage a show was made of landing animals and stores, while ashore care was taken that wagons should be heard as usual making their way to the front. The only observable change that was allowed was that all firing after midnight was to be avoided as far as possible, so as to accustom the enemy to a routine of nocturnal inactivity. Similarly it was decided to allow nothing but the normal supporting ships to be seen off the beaches, and not till the last day of the intermediate stage were the ships detailed for reinforcing them to be brought up. Even so they were to remain out of sight at Aliki and Kephalo in Imbros, while the Naval Air Service

[1] The cases of frostbite alone numbered 3,700.

maintained a permanent patrol to prevent their presence being detected by the enemy's scouting aircraft.[1]

In this way it was hoped that ship fire would be able with some efficiency to supply the place of artillery. The area of fire for every ship had been settled with the military, and to ensure the utmost attainable precision in working the scheme the corps and divisional artillery staffs were to be distributed amongst the two squadrons to assist in fire direction. But the problem of support from the sea was not the same at both beaches. At Anzac, where the enemy trenches were comparatively close to the beach, and to which the weaker squadron was allotted, it was the simpler of the two. For here the hills sloped steeply to the shore, and any attempt to follow our retirement before dawn would be fully revealed to the searchlights of the ships, which would at once blind the enemy and expose him to heavy punishment. At Suvla, on the other hand, where the retirement had to be made across a plain from two to three miles wide, searchlights would dazzle our own men, and if the enemy followed close, ship fire would be too dangerous. To some extent, however, these drawbacks were modified by the protruding conformation of the coast, which afforded good flanking berths for the ships and better possibilities for enfilading fire.

This advantage was emphasised by the fact that at Suvla there was room for a succession of retiring positions. The main embarkation places were at the extremes of the two horns of the bay, and to facilitate the evacuation General Byng had divided his force into two approximately equal sections separated by the Salt Lake. For the northern section he had a position extending from the lake over Hill 10 to the sea, and a similar one over Chocolate Hill for the southern section. In their rear were two second positions extended across the base of each horn of the bay, with a final position immediately covering the beaches allotted to each section. General Fanshawe, who commanded the northern or left half, was assigned Suvla Cove, just outside

[1] The normal guard for Anzac at this time was one bulge cruiser (*Grafton*) and two destroyers. The reinforcement concentrated at Aliki was another cruiser (*Talbot*), three monitors (*Humber*, *M 15* and *M 16*) with three more destroyers and the balloon ship *Hector*, all under Captain Boyle, who was to be in charge of the Anzac evacuation in the sloop *Honeysuckle*, his own ship, *Bacchante*, being in reserve at Kephalo. Inside the nets in Suvla Bay were two battleships (*Cornwallis* and *Prince George*), one monitor (*M 29*) and two destroyers, while in reserve at Kephalo there were to be the bulge cruiser *Theseus*, the heavy monitor *Earl of Peterborough*, and the small one *M 31*, and to this squadron was attached another balloon ship (*Canning*).

Suvla Point, and a well-organised harbour inside at Ghazi Baba, known as "West Beach," which had been the main base of supply for the Suvla force. For the south or right section Major-General F. S. Maude, who had succeeded General Shaw in command of the XIIIth Division on August 23, had for his main point of embarkation the beach inside Nibrunesi Point, and for certain troops on his extreme right a small beach, outside the bay. At Anzac General Godley had no such facilities. Practically the whole of his force had to use Anzac Cove and the adjacent beach just north of Ari Burnu. Both being opposite his right centre, a good deal of flank marching was involved, over steep and broken ground, with no good defensive position to cover the embarkation should the Turks attack. All that was possible was a "keep" close down to the beach to cover the last movements of the withdrawal. Here, therefore, the efficiency of the ship fire was of the last importance.

The hope was, however, that no retiring positions would be required. The plan for the final stage was to keep our front trenches occupied till the last possible moment, gradually thinning the numbers holding them, and to march the troops as they were stealthily withdrawn in successive groups straight down to the beaches. What that meant for the military staff in elaboration of detail and sagacious organisation to provide against all possibilities of confusion in the night, what steadiness and intelligent discipline from all ranks, what subtlety of device to lull suspicion in the enemy, needs no telling, and for the navy the strain was no less.

Ten days had originally been allotted to the intermediate stage—the final one being fixed for the nights of December 19-20 and 20-21. Owing to the necessity for repairing the breach in the Kephalo breakwater before the last stage could be begun, an earlier date was thought to be impossible. So important was it, however, to expedite matters while the fine weather lasted, that instead of waiting for a blockship which had been asked for, it was decided to sink a laden collier at the gap. This was successfully accomplished by December 13, and it was possible to anticipate the final stage by a day.[1] It was only just in time. Two days later it came on to blow hard from the north-east, and had the breakwater been open the intermediate stage must have been held up for a day. As it was, by dint of great exertion it was completed by the night of the 17th. Otherwise the weather had been perfect, with a glassy sea and a waxing moon giving light enough to

[1] The sinking was so cleverly done that after the evacuation she was refloated and left for Mudros with her valuable cargo under her own steam.

facilitate the work at sea, but not enough to reveal anything to the enemy. In driblets, with little more than the ordinary service of ferry steamers and small craft, there had been withdrawn to the islands in eight nights, without a hitch, no less than 44,000 men, about a hundred and thirty guns and 3,000 animals, besides quantities of stores and ammunition.[1] Before each dawn all sight of unusual movement had ceased, beaches and roads had assumed their normal appearance and the enemy had made no move. Still there remained ashore 40,000 men with fifty guns, a few animals and carts and stores sufficient for four days in case of bad weather prolonging the final stage to that extent.

These 40,000 men, as we have seen, were the utmost number the navy considered they could deal with in two nights with the flotilla resources at their command. The number of vessels of all kinds, large and small, found to be necessary, exclusive of pulling boats, was little short of a hundred. To provide the number of boats and, above all, the number of officers required for the complex operation was quite beyond the capacity of ships immediately at hand, and to supply his needs Admiral Wemyss had to call in Admiral Fremantle's squadron at Milo, which was watching the Piræus in case drastic pressure on Greece became necessary for securing General Sarrail's retreat.[2] First in the throng of vessels that were assembled came the dismantled battleships *Mars* and *Magnificent*, with the large transport *Huntsgreen*, capable between them of accommodating 6,000 men. These were brought up to Imbros from Mudros at the last moment, together with fourteen ferry-boats and armed boarding steamers, each with a carrying capacity of from 1,000 to 1,500 men. Some of them had been engaged on the two previous stages, the rest were brought up to Imbros as required. The main work of embarking the troops and taking them to the transports was to be done by the new motor lighters, which had proved so useful during the Suvla landing. Admiral Wemyss had now thirty of them, but half had been kept back at Mudros pending the repair of the gap in the Kephalo breakwater, and these had now to be brought up.[3] Of the whole thirty, ten were allotted to Suvla, and ten to Anzac. The remaining ten, with a number of other small craft, formed the reserve at

[1] The work had been done by six ferry steamers, thirteen motor lighters, ten gun, horse and store ships and a few steam-boats.

[2] The Milo squadron consisted of three battleships, one cruiser, two monitors, two sloops, four destroyers, and two net-layers.

[3] They were designated officially as "K" boats, but from their turtle-back construction, and the derricks for handling their forward gang-board, which suggested antennae, they were known to the army as "Beetles."

Kephalo. The motor lighters were all to work from the piers at the main points of embarkation, but as it was found necessary at Anzac to embark the flanking parties north and south of the main beaches, twenty-eight pulling boats (launches, pinnaces and cutters) were provided. For towing them and other duties twenty-five steamboats were told off, of which twenty had to be brought up from Mudros on the last day of the intermediate stage. In addition, there were fifteen trawlers, five of which, with three tugs, were held back at Kephalo in the reserve, and the rest divided between Anzac and Suvla with the main duty of guiding the motor lighters and pulling boats to their proper transports and troop carriers, and generally assisting in case of accident.

The marshalling of such a heterogeneous mass of ships and small craft was no light task. The elaboration of detail to prevent confusion and secure minute precision in time-keeping and for working in accurate harmony with the system of the movements ashore, obviously demanded from the navy no less just imagination and mastery of technique than was called for from the staff of the sister service, and no less steadiness, intelligence and discipline from all afloat. But no matter how highly these qualities were displayed, they could scarcely avail without a perfect system of communication both ashore and afloat, as well as between land and sea; and, further, it must be a system which could control not only the actual work of evacuation, but also the fire of the two supporting squadrons in case of need. The problem was solved on the basis of devoting all wireless communication between ships and shore to fire control. The rest had to be done by a system of cables, though this again increased the complexity of the work afloat, for the greatest care was needed to guard against ships fouling the cables when they anchored. The shore ends were connected up with the military signal station in each sector, and the other ends buoyed so that they could be picked up by the two sloops in which the two corps commanders intended to establish their posts of command so that they might move rapidly to either flank as necessary. For Anzac General Godley had the *Heliotrope*, and General Byng the *Peony* for Suvla, while Admiral Wemyss and General Birdwood were together in the *Arno*. At Anzac Captain A. D. Boyle of the *Bacchante* was in sole command afloat in the *Honeysuckle*, while at Suvla Captain C. Corbett directed the embarkation in the *Anemone*, and Captain A. Davidson of the *Cornwallis* commanded the supporting squadron.

By the morning of December 18 everything was in place ready to move, with no sign that the enemy had any suspicion of what was going on. The weather was still perfect, but it had now lasted ten days and might change at any moment. Yet the day wore on serenely with no indication of disturbance, and as soon as night fell the still waters between Imbros and the peninsula were alive with dim shapes as everything required for the first night's work moved silently and in perfect order to its allotted station in the kindly moonlight.

Punctually at 6.45 p.m. the motor lighters were at the piers, while the transports and troop carriers steamed up to their berths and anchored. At Anzac particularly it was an anxious moment. Though light clouds dimmed the full light of the moon, it seemed impossible that a great ship like the *Mars* could come in and anchor within 2,000 yards of the beach without arousing attention. Anzac Cove was still open to enfilading fire from the Olive Groves guns to the southward, which we had never been able to master, and on the Gaba Tepe bluff the Turks evidently had an observation post to direct their fire. All precautions had been taken for the prompt arrival of supporting ships should the guns become troublesome, and off Gaba Tepe Captain Boyle had stationed the destroyer *Rattlesnake*, with orders to keep her searchlight thrown across the enemy's line of vision and do her best to blind the enemy's observation post there. The device appears to have proved entirely successful. The first batch of troops was ready at the piers as the "beetles" arrived, and by 8.25 the *Mars* was steaming off again with her 2,000 men, and all was quiet ashore except for a fairly hot fire on the *Rattlesnake*. Still she held her ground, merely shutting off her light when the guns found her and switching it on again after shifting her berth. So, under cover of her beam, the work went on. Trip after trip the "beetles" made, always to find their batches of troops silently waiting and punctual to the minute. Beyond an occasional rattle of maxims ashore nothing broke the death-like quiet. General Godley came off to the *Heliotrope* in the middle of the night from his headquarters ashore, but owing to trouble with the cable and fear of using flashing signals, nearly all communication had to be made by boat. In spite of this difficulty all went like clockwork: one by one the troop carriers filled and steamed off, and by 5.25 a.m. on the 19th the last of them was away.

Up at Suvla General Byng had remained ashore in cable communication with his headquarters in the *Peony*, and under his immediate supervision all had gone equally well. Here,

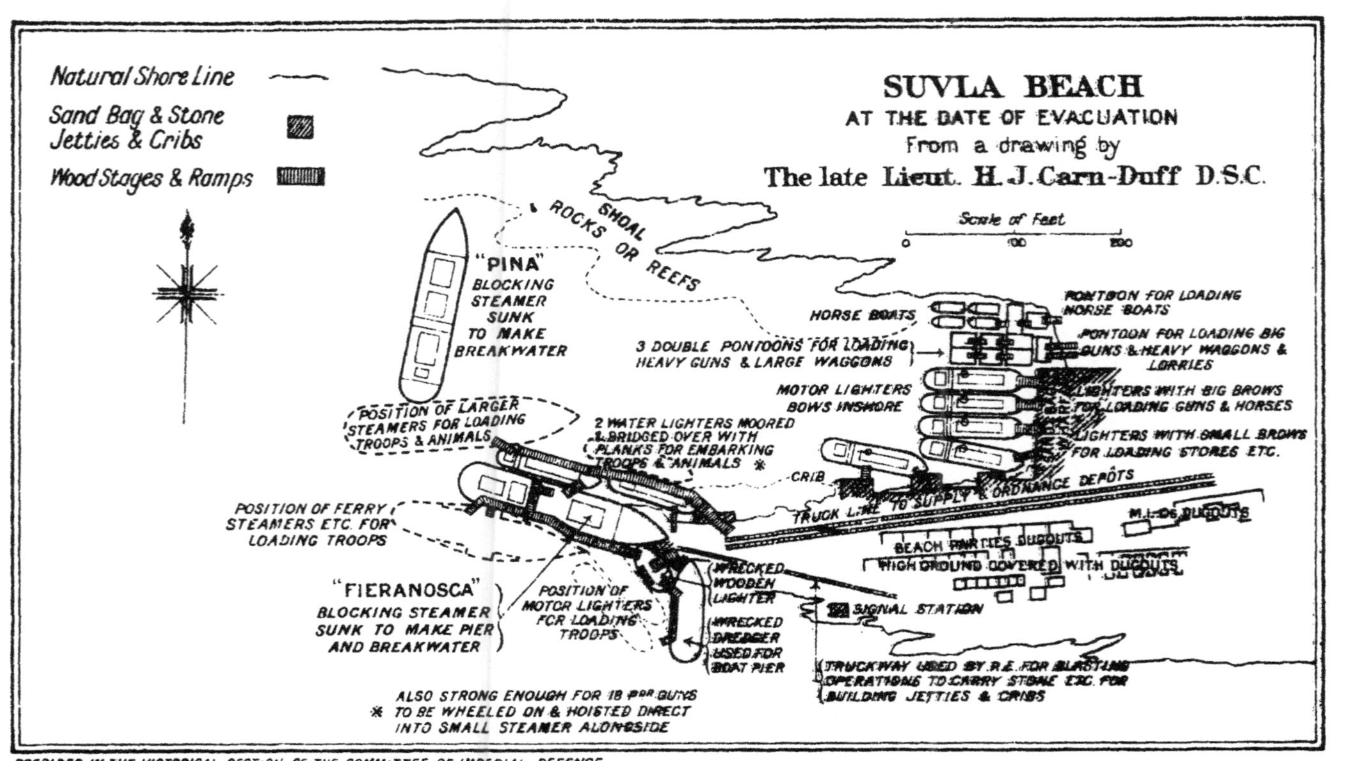
SUVLA BEACH
AT THE DATE OF EVACUATION
From a drawing by
The late Lieut. H. J. Carn-Duff D.S.C.
Natural Shore Line
Sand Bag & Stone Jetties & Cribs
Wood Stages & Ramps
Scale of Feet
0
100
200
SHOAL
ROCKS OR REEFS
"PINA" BLOCKING STEAMER SUNK TO MAKE BREAKWATER
POSITION OF LARGER STEAMERS FOR LOADING TROOPS & ANIMALS
HORSE BOATS
PONTOON FOR LOADING HORSE BOATS
3 DOUBLE PONTOONS FOR LOADING HEAVY GUNS & LARGE WAGGONS
PONTOON FOR LOADING BIG GUNS & HEAVY WAGGONS & LORRIES
MOTOR LIGHTERS BOWS INSHORE
LIGHTERS WITH BIG BROWS FOR LOADING GUNS & HORSES
LIGHTERS WITH SMALL BROWS FOR LOADING STORES ETC.
2 WATER LIGHTERS MOORED & BRIDGED OVER WITH PLANKS FOR EMBARKING TROOPS & ANIMALS *
CRIB
TRUCK LINE TO SUPPLY & ORDNANCE DEPÔTS
M.L.O's DUGOUTS
BEACH PARTIES DUGOUTS
HIGH GROUND COVERED WITH DUGOUTS
POSITION OF FERRY STEAMERS ETC. FOR LOADING TROOPS
"FIERANOSCA" BLOCKING STEAMER SUNK TO MAKE PIER AND BREAKWATER
POSITION OF MOTOR LIGHTERS FOR LOADING TROOPS
WRECKED WOODEN LIGHTER
WRECKED DREDGER USED FOR BOAT PIER
SIGNAL STATION
TRUCKWAY USED BY R.E. FOR BLASTING OPERATIONS TO CARRY STONE ETC. FOR BUILDING JETTIES & CRIBS
ALSO STRONG ENOUGH FOR 18 PDR GUNS
* TO BE WHEELED ON & HOISTED DIRECT INTO SMALL STEAMER ALONGSIDE

PREPARED IN THE HISTORICAL SECTION OF THE COMMITTEE OF IMPERIAL DEFENCE

Ordnance Survey, 1922.

where the enemy was accustomed to large ships entering the netted bay, the risk of detection was less and the work of embarkation easier. Here, too, there was plenty of room, so that the troops could be brought down to two safe "forming-up" places behind the last covering position, and there they were told off in parties of 400 for the "beetles." Thus the beaches could be left clear—an important consideration, seeing that, besides the 20,000 troops, the main embarkation of the remaining guns and transport had been done in this sector. All the heavy guns except one 60-pounder had been removed already, as well as all but two anti-aircraft guns, but there still were left thirty field guns and four howitzers, half in each sector, besides some motor and horse lorries and ambulance transport, 250 horses and mules and about a hundred mule carts. During the preparatory period the quays and piers had been continually improved, and in calm weather even the larger troop carriers could be brought alongside the sunken blockships.

With these conveniences the embarkation proceeded under Captain Corbett, with Captain Unwin, of *River Clyde* fame, as beach-master, without a hitch. As at Anzac, it had begun at 6.45 p.m. From the "forming-up" places the troops arrived punctually at the beaches, whence they could rapidly be taken off to the *Magnificent* and her accompanying transport and troop carriers lying off in the bay. There, too, was Captain Davidson in the *Cornwallis*, with the *Prince George* and the rest of his supporting squadron, all with guns trained on their assigned fire areas, the guns' crews standing ready at a moment's notice to act as the artillery staff officers might direct. But no call was needed. Batch after batch of troops moved silently to their transporting vessels, and by 3.30 a.m. 11,000 men and nearly half the guns were well on their way to Kephalo or Mudros. By dawn there was no sign of them to be seen from the shore; nowhere was a trace of what had happened, and so the first night passed without hitch or accident of any kind.

Such a bloodless success was more than any one had dared to hope. Still less could another such night's work be expected. Eagerly the weather-wise watched the face of the sky, and not without misgiving as they noted indications of a change. With no less eagerness the enemy's lines were scanned for any trace of activity—but nothing unusual could be detected beyond the increase of artillery fire in which the Turks were wont to indulge on Sundays. During the afternoon one of the southern Suvla piers was hit, but the Australian bridging section quickly repaired it. Most of the fire was on our front trenches. Indeed, the indications were that if the enemy had noticed anything he had concluded that reinforcements were being landed for a new attack. The Turks could be heard digging and were busy all day fixing new wire, while in the early afternoon reinforcements were reported marching down from the central plateau towards Anzac. Then suddenly loud explosions were heard away at Helles, followed by a roar of naval fire, and the oncoming troops seemed to disappear whence they came.

It was General Davies's holding attack that had begun against the enemy's extreme right. The explosions meant that at 2.15 he sprung a series of mines which he had prepared between Fusilier Bluff and the head of Gully Ravine, and under cover of the artillery and rapid fire from the supporting squadron the troops rushed forward to seize the shattered trenches. At General Davies's request Captain Dent had been given for the operation, besides the *Edgar* and his regular destroyers, three monitors, *Abercrombie, Sir Thomas Picton* and *Raglan*, and such was the increased weight they gave to the artillery that the attack was little less successful than the one which had been delivered on November 15. In vain the Turks launched counter-attacks; except at Fusilier Bluff, where the mine had failed to make a crater, all the seized trenches were maintained.

At dusk the firing died away, and in the northern area nerves were already being braced for the desperate adventure beside which the previous night's work seemed an easy thing. There were increasing indications, of which no one cared to speak, that a break in the weather was at hand. As yet the sea was like a mill-pond. Again the nearly full moon was dimmed by fleecy clouds, while ashore a damp mist was rising to obscure the stealthy movements of the troops. It was an ideal night for the work if it would only last. But would it last?—that was the absorbing question as once more that motley throng of vessels stole like dreams across the sleeping sea. The naval arrangements were the same as on the previous night—nothing had been found to need alteration, and as every vessel slipped into her place Admiral Wemyss and General Birdwood came up in the *Chatham* to keep a finger on the pulse of the panting crisis. As before, the arrival of the ships caused no stir in the enemy's lines. Punctually at 6.45 p.m. the "beetles" were at the piers, and as punctually their quotas of men were there to meet them. Eight of the remaining ten guns in the southern section of Suvla, after firing their parting rounds, were being run down for the West Beach, and there at midnight they and all that were left in the northern section were embarked. At 8.0 General Maude's last two guns had been withdrawn to a special pier at Nibrunesi Point, and on the crews closed round the guns in the barely visible ships the thinning remnants of General Byng's corps now depended for support in those last intense hours. At Anzac alone a few guns remained. Here, where no covering position was possible, it had been reluctantly decided to leave four 18-pounders, two 5-inch howitzers, an old naval 4·7-inch and three smaller guns, all worn out, to deceive the Turks by firing till the last and to be destroyed before they were abandoned.

So far all was going well. By the time the guns ashore were no longer available the first embarkation was complete; at 8.0 p.m. the battleship transports were away, and as the men told off for the second embarkation with all the trench mortars were assembling, every one knew the operation had reached its crisis. It was past believing that now the enemy would not awake to the chance that lay in their hands, but minute by minute went by without any sign that the precautions that had been taken were failing. On a slender remnant of devoted men success depended, and on them the most anxious thought was centred. The word had gone forth that at all costs the front trenches must be held till the last moment, however thinly, and the ranks that held them were now very thin. At Suvla by midnight General Fanshawe had no more than 677 men in his front line and General Maude only 200, with 350 in his rear position. As the minutes crept on towards the hazardous hour when the last trench would be empty, even at the beaches, far out of enemy hearing, the men were speaking in whispers. Still wave after wave of men stole down through the covering positions and passed on to the beaches; the faint shadow of the "beetles" glided incessantly between ships and shore, and the troop carriers as they filled crept silently away, and still the enemy slumbered. Ashore all looked the same. The hospital tents were standing as usual; and few as were the men in front, they were busy keeping the usual bivouac fires burning and giving the last touches to the devices by which the final retirement was to be masked and a possible advance of the enemy checked. Nothing that ingenuity or experience in France could suggest was omitted. On the parapets rifles were left with their triggers attached to tins into which water dripped until they were heavy enough for the pull. Quantities of explosives were arranged to fire by means of candles of different lengths so as to keep up the delusion that snipers were still alert. Other detonations were provided with slow matches. In the communication trenches frames of barbed wire were ready to block them, mines were made active and deadly traps of all kinds awaited an oncoming enemy.

Half-past one was the hour fixed for the last desperate act—the withdrawal of the rear parties from the front trenches—to commence. Then the danger of the movement being detected had reached its acutest point, and as the devoted parties stole away, with boots muffled in sackcloth, men down at the beaches and afloat, strung to the highest pitch of subdued excitement, hardly dared to hope. Yet the rhythm of that immortal symphony went on unbroken, save when from time to time the sounds that were to deceive the enemy broke the silence on the hills.

At Suvla the second embarkation, which had begun at 9.45 p.m., was complete, and the third was just starting. As the numbers ashore thinned, the risk of great disaster lessened, but there still remained the dread of what would happen if the Turks discovered the front trenches were empty and began shelling the beaches on which they had so accurately registered. For Anzac the anxiety was deepest, for here our front trenches were so close to those of the enemy that their evacuation could not be long undetected, and here too the Olive Groves guns enfiladed the beach. Punctually at 1.30 a.m. the last parties in the front trenches crept away; in the course of the next two hours the last posts which covered Anzac Cove were emptied. Still nothing was heard but the popping of the rifles that had been left behind, till suddenly the air was rent with the roar of a huge explosion.

At the head of Monash Gully, under the Turkish trenches on Russell's Top, General Birdwood's engineers had prepared a series of mines, and at the last moment (3.24) they fired them. It was now only that the Turks took alarm, and as the devoted men who had just abandoned the last held posts poured down upon the beach, a tremendous fire of artillery, machine-guns and rifles opened all along the enemy's line, but it was upon the empty trenches that it rained. The waste of ammunition only served to mask the last embarkation at the Cove and the work of the pulling boats as they took off the two flanking parties north and south, and at 4.15 the beach officers could signal to the Admiral "All clear at Anzac." A quarter of an hour later the Suvla beaches had also done their work. Only 100 men who had held the last position remained ashore. By 5.30 a.m. on the 20th these were embarked at Suvla Point, and then, and not till then, General Byng and Captain Unwin, with the naval beach parties, went off to the destroyers awaiting them. So the impossible was done without the loss of a single life, and ashore nothing was left of the two army corps and all their material except a few shattered guns, a few dead mules, some broken transport carts and the blazing dumps of the stores which there had been no time to remove. At Suvla it was very little—no more than the reserve stores which had been kept in case the evacuation was delayed—and General Byng was able to report that he had not left behind him a single gun, wagon or animal. At Anzac, where there were no such facilities as the West Beach in Suvla Bay provided, there was a greater sacrifice of material. Besides the guns that were destroyed, large dumps of rations and forage to a considerable value, which could not be removed, had to be abandoned and set on fire.

Some of the covering squadrons had orders to remain behind to complete the destruction of the stores, piers and stranded lighters, and at dawn there was nothing else to be seen.[1] Except for these vessels and a few patrol boats, the sea was deserted. Transports, lighters and boats had all disappeared, nothing but the blazing dumps marked what had happened, and it was only this unaccountable sight that seems at last to have roused the Turks and their German staff from their lethargy. Even then they hardly understood, for, believing apparently that the conflagrations were accidental, they opened a hot fire on them, as though to hinder their being extinguished, and thus at Anzac the few onlookers enjoyed the strange sight of the *Theseus* and the enemy guns pouring shell into the same targets. But as the light grew the amazing truth was discovered, and at Anzac men could be seen cautiously advancing in the open. As they gathered in ever denser formation the *Grafton* and *Theseus* held their fire, and then suddenly opened on them with high explosive.

The terrible slaughter that ensued was the last word in this unexampled feat of arms. Since the night of December 10 there had been withdrawn in the face of the hypnotised enemy 83,048 troops, 186 guns, 1,697 horse-drawn vehicles, 21 motor vehicles and 4,695 horses and mules, and the casualties were only two wounded men. When we consider that in the Mediterranean hospitals provision had been

[1] At Anzac were the *Grafton, Talbot, Humber, M 15, M 16* and *Beagle;* the last named, however, did not fire. At Suvla were the *Cornwallis, Theseus, Laforey* and *Prince George;* the last named did not fire. In addition to these, the *Chatham* (flying the flag of Admiral Wemyss), escorted by *Basilisk,* also fired upon the abandoned camps at Suvla.

made for 30,000 wounded, it is possible to get some idea of the high moral effect of the success. It was all as far beyond hope as it was beyond precedent, but it was only just in time. During the afternoon, as vessels of all kinds were making their way back to Mudros, the wind got up from the south, and by nightfall it was blowing a gale. But for the happy decision to put the operation forward a day there is no knowing what would have happened. It was luck, but luck that comes from the maxim of "never losing a wind" is own brother to judgment, for which Admiral and General may take full credit.

With experience enriched by this astonishing success and by the narrow escape from the treacherous weather, the still unsettled question of Helles had to be faced. All through the intermediate stage of the evacuation Admiral Wemyss had not ceased to urge his views in opposition to those of General Monro, who persisted in his opinion that the capture of Achi Baba would in no way reduce the dangers of the military position at Helles, and that in any case it could not be taken with the force at his disposal. Admiral Wemyss could not agree that the question of retention was purely military, as it involved the question of supply, which was a purely naval factor. Nor could he understand why the General had so low an opinion of the value of Achi Baba, seeing that all the higher military commanders had long agreed that it was the key of the southern position. On the naval side, moreover, its possession would render us independent of precarious air observation in winter, and our supporting ships would be able to lie close in to Gully Beach, whereas if the Turks still held it when the German heavy guns arrived, our ships would be forced out of effective supporting range. He repeated that if the General's view was accepted, Helles, in his opinion, should be evacuated at once.

The question of Helles was not the only problem with which General Monro was faced. Salonica and the defence of Egypt still called for a decision, but these were matters upon which he did not feel able to offer a final opinion until he understood what the policy of the Government was. In reply to his request for further information on this point he was informed that the intention was to hold on at Salonica for the present, but that the Russian plan of developing from it a large offensive movement was regarded as impossible, and it was hoped to withdraw our troops later on, if the French consented. Further, it was desired to make the defence of Egypt more active. For this eight divisions, eight cavalry brigades and two independent infantry brigades with fifteen garrison battalions for internal defence were considered as necessary, and as the Gallipoli troops would not be fit for some time, the force was to be made up from home as soon as transports were available.

This telegram was sent on December 18, but three days later General Monro was ordered to return to France and left the peninsula on January 1. While the evacuation was being carried out a far-reaching reorganisation of army commands was put in force. Sir John French was recalled from France and Sir Douglas Haig took his place (19th). General Monro was to take over the command of the First Army and Sir Archibald Murray was to succeed him in the Near East, but his headquarters were to be in Egypt, where his main duty would be the defence of the canal, while General Maxwell confined himself to military affairs in the interior. General Birdwood was to command at the Dardanelles, but both he and the Salonica force were to be under General Murray's supervision. Egypt, it will be seen, was resuming for British strategists its natural place as the central point of our Near Eastern activities. On the same day Admiral Wemyss was offered, and accepted, the East Indies command, which included Egyptian waters. The appointment was to take effect on January 11, and meanwhile he was to detail a squadron of two battleships, a cruiser and four monitors for the Suez Canal, to arrive by January 4.[1]

What did these orders portend? In Egypt it was calculated that by the end of January the enemy could bring against the Canal 200,000 men who might be increased to 300,000 a month later, and on this basis the defence had been reorganised. There were now three lines of defence eastward of the Canal extending eight miles into the desert, with light railway and water-pipe connections, and from there it was intended, in concert with ships and aircraft, to strike continually at the approaching enemy before he could complete his concentration. In a similar way the Egyptian western force had just struck the Senussi a severe blow from Marsa Matruh, though without further reinforcement and naval co-operation they were not yet in a position to recapture the frontier post at Sollum. But there were not lacking indications that the last resolution of the Home Government for a more active defence of Egypt contemplated some more ambitious plan. The idea was to undertake a large

[1] The ships detailed were *Cornwallis*, *Glory*, the monitors *Roberts*, *M 15* and *M 31* and the *Euryalus*, but the monitors did not sail owing to the evacuation of Helles. Admiral Peirse's term of command, three years, was about to expire.

offensivé operation through Palestine and Syria, which, if French objections could only be overcome, had long been at the back of Lord Kitchener's mind, and which in its final shape was destined to have so decisive an effect on the war.

So things stood when on December 23 the War Committee met to decide the question of Helles. For Ministers the position was extremely difficult. Military opinion at home was unanimous for evacuation, but in the course of the discussion it became apparent that naval opinion was scarcely less unanimous for retention. Admiral de Robeck had gone out to resume his command with a firm conviction that the retention of Helles was of the highest naval importance. On the other hand, the grounds of Admiral Wemyss's opinion, that if Achi Baba was not taken evacuation should be carried out at once, was misunderstood, and it was assumed that he had changed his mind. A telegram had gone to Admiral de Robeck asking him to explain the apparent inconsistency, but no reply had yet come to hand, and it was under the false impression that Admiral Wemyss now agreed with General Monro that the Committee, in spite of all that Admiral de Robeck had urged, were in favour of evacuation. So large a change of policy was beyond their province to decide. Their conclusion was to refer it to the Cabinet, and pending its decision to send out orders for a plan of withdrawal to be prepared, with the proviso that nothing was to be done which would prejudice the possibility of holding on.[1]

The conclusion of the War Committee had already been passed to the Cabinet when Admiral de Robeck's explanation of the puzzle arrived. It revealed at once what was the matter. The essential principle that in combined operations the naval and the military commanders must be in the closest personal communication—consecrated though it was by our unique experience—had been violated, and the usual crop of misunderstandings had sprung up in the shadow of the sin. General Monro had explained, so the Admiral telegraphed, that he had understood Admiral Wemyss did not regard the retention of Helles as being of sufficient naval importance to warrant the military risks of holding on. Clearly that was not an adequate presentation of Admiral Wemyss's view; but about Admiral de Robeck's there was no doubt, for he included in his reply a reiteration of his opinion that if the army could hold the end of the peninsula, its retention should be insisted on, adding that he was leaving at once for Kephalo to get General Birdwood's opinion. As General Birdwood would become the responsible

[1] *Dardanelles Commission Report*, II., p. 60.

military officer at the Dardanelles in two or three days' time, this seemed the best thing he could do. Accordingly the following morning, which was Christmas Day, he reported that both General Birdwood and General Davies thought that Helles could be held, and that a meeting had been arranged between them and Admiral Fremantle, who was now in command of the supporting squadron, with his headquarters at Kephalo, to consider the defence. He further reported that the Turks were actively shelling the southern beaches, as though expecting a repetition of the Suvla and Anzac surprise, and that therefore in any case the evacuation ought not to be attempted till they had quieted down. His own conviction still was that it should not be attempted at all. "Personally," he concluded, "I maintain that the holding of Helles is of great naval importance."

This last desperate effort to bring about a real co-ordination between naval and military opinion did not affect the issue. On December 27 Admiral de Robeck received a telegram from the First Lord telling him "with great regret," and in confidence, that the Cabinet had decided for evacuation. Next day came the official order, with leave to keep the squadron detailed for Egypt till the operation was complete.

It is impossible to follow step by step what has been called this agony of indecision with a clear conviction that the Gallipoli question was finally decided on its intrinsic merits. Overshadowing its tactical possibilities were two powerful considerations. One was the disbelief of General Monro and the General Staff that the decisive power of our army could be increased by using a substantial part of it with the fleet, and their consequent determination to see it concentrated to the utmost possible extent in France. The other was probably that Lord Kitchener, with his Eastern outlook, saw salvation in active operations from Egypt. Though the two views were in opposition, both were fatal to Gallipoli. Nor did their reactions end there. Both looked to a speedy withdrawal from Salonica and the abandonment of the Bagdad venture. Indeed it was at this time (December 29) that orders went out to India that as soon as Kut was relieved there was to be a retirement to defensive positions about Kurnah and in the Shaiba area.

When the momentous order that was to end the tragedy of the Dardanelles went forth, to the deep regret of the navy, the plans for the evacuation were well forward. To the last they had hoped that it would never materialise. With the broader outlook their world-wide activities gave them, they were in a better position to know all that the order meant than men whose view of war had for long been almost entirely confined to the continental aspect of the great wars of the past, and who had been nurtured on doctrine bred in France and Germany. As naval thought read our long and rich experience, it was by close co-ordination of naval and military force that we had always held the balance and had built up the Empire. Now there was to be a complete divorce, and each service was to play a lone hand. Whether inevitable or not, at the moment it was a thousand pities; for not only did it mean that, so far as could be seen, all hope of free strategical design which sea power gives was abandoned, but never did the true method and spirit of combined action attain a higher manifestation than was exhibited in the last act of the great adventure.

As originally drawn up, the plan of operations closely followed that for Suvla and Anzac. There were to be the same three stages. The preliminary one was already complete when the order arrived. It left on the peninsula 37,500 men, 142 guns, nearly 4,200 animals, over 1,900 vehicles and vast quantities of ammunition and stores which had been accumulated for a winter campaign.[1] Difficult as had been the evacuation of the northern area, and encouraging as was its success, it could not be disguised that the work now in hand was a much more delicate affair. The enemy was obviously expecting another surprise, as the activity of their artillery and aircraft testified. Their heavy guns on the peninsula were obviously increasing in number, and, what was still worse, the main beaches were exposed to the accurate fire of the Asiatic batteries. The weather, too, was thoroughly unsettled and the stormy period was close at hand. For this reason the intermediate stage was started on December 29, the day after the orders were received, so that it could be completed in time to leave two nights for the final withdrawal before January 10—the last day on which experience could hold out hope of favourable weather conditions. During this stage the remaining French troops were withdrawn, so as to leave complete unity of command. General Brulard, however, who, with Admiral le Bon, was giving every possible assistance, readily agreed to leave at our disposal six old heavy guns, which he suggested should be destroyed. For the final stage some 22,000 troops and sixty guns would be left. About 7,000 of them would be withdrawn on the first day, leaving about 15,000, which was calculated to be the utmost the navy could deal with in one night.

[1] The figures given in this chapter do not include the statistics of the French evacuation.

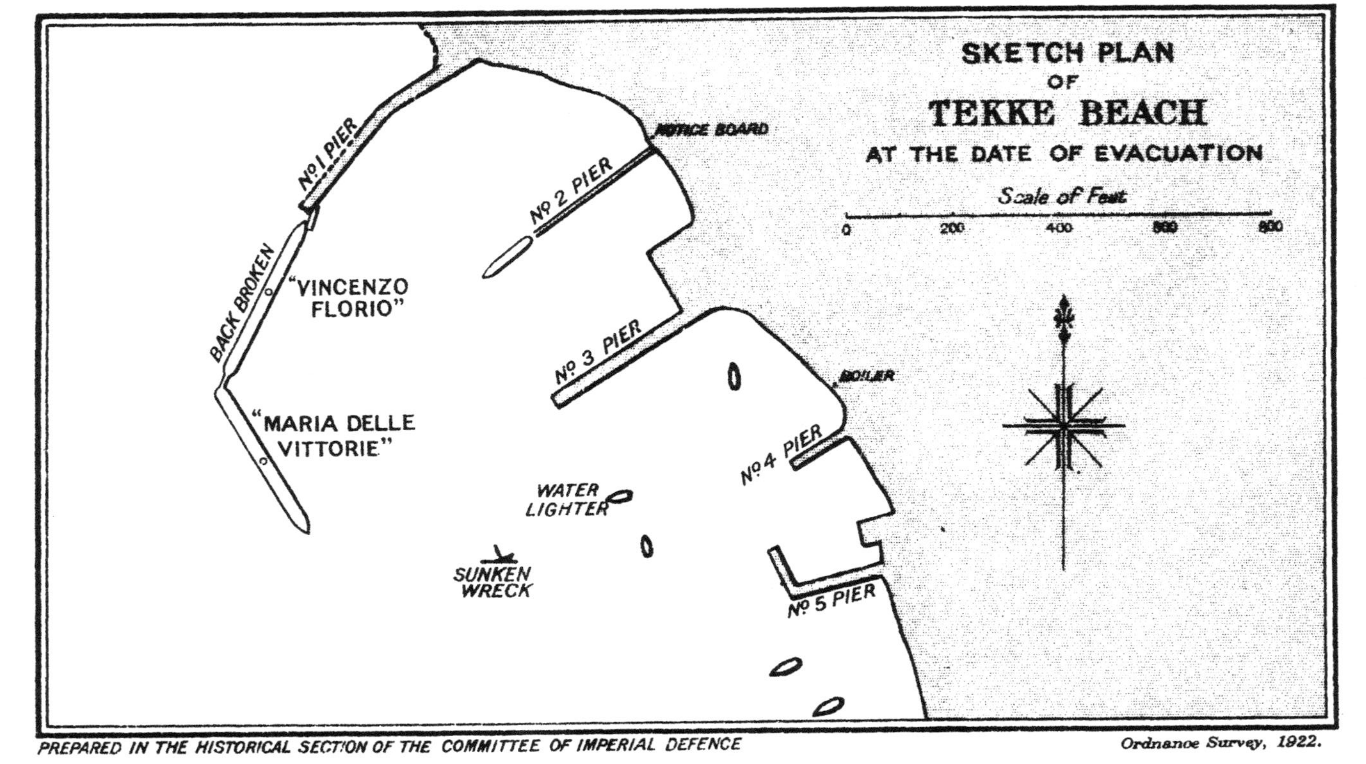

PREPARED IN THE HISTORICAL SECTION OF THE COMMITTEE OF IMPERIAL DEFENCE

Ordnance Survey, 1922.

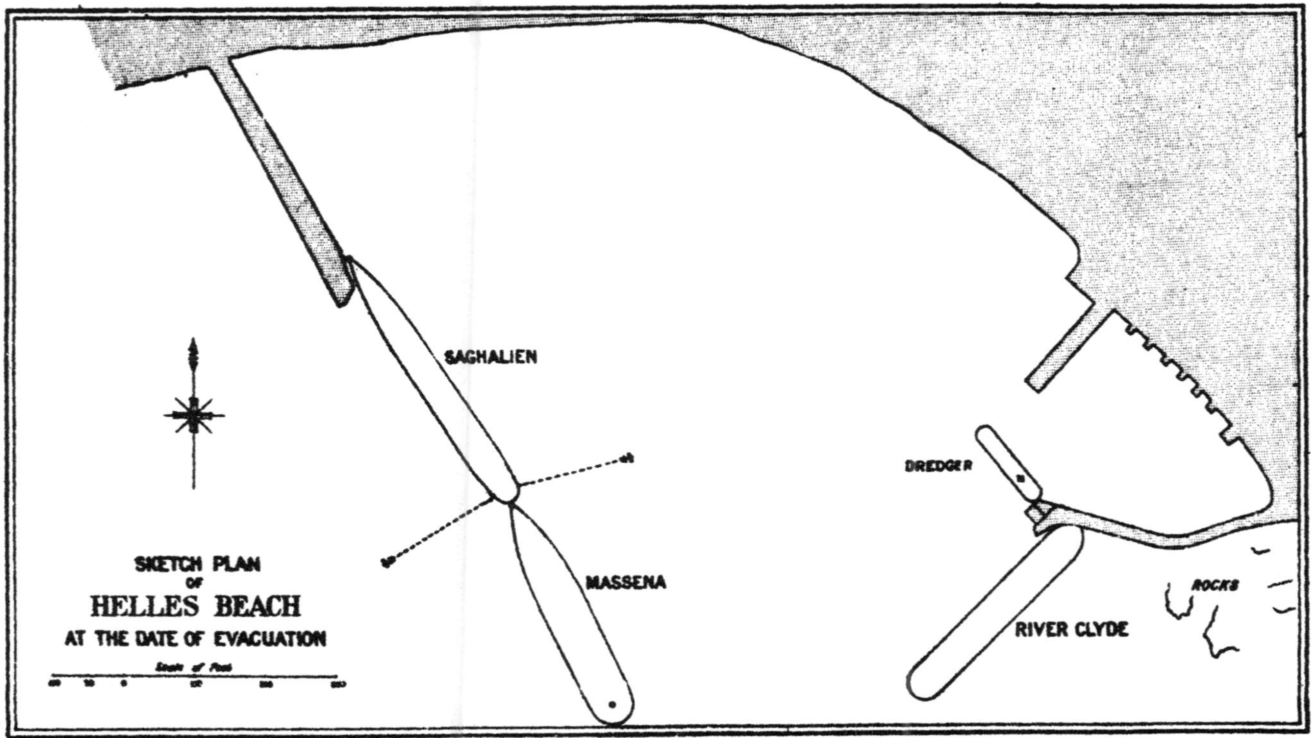

SKETCH PLAN
OF
HELLES BEACH
AT THE DATE OF EVACUATION

Scale of Feet

SAGHALIEN

MASSENA

DREDGER

RIVER CLYDE

ROCKS

PREPARED IN THE HISTORICAL SECTION OF THE COMMITTEE OF IMPERIAL DEFENCE

Ordnance Survey, 1922.

The measure of their ability was the capacity of the beaches, and particularly the two main ones—that is, the old "W" (Tekke) beach or "Lancashire Landing," under Tekke Burnu, at the extreme south-western end of the peninsula, and "V," or Helles beach, between Cape Helles and Sedd el Bahr. At both places regular harbours had been formed by sinking blockships to form breakwaters, but both were open to southerly weather, and during the late gale all their piers had been broken up. At Sedd el Bahr the famous *River Clyde* was still where she had run ashore at the first landing, and was now connected with the land by a mole which formed an inner harbour. At the other end of the beach the French, to whose use it had been allotted, had prolonged the breakwater by sinking a large transport and beyond it the old battleship *Massena*.[1] The other beach had a similar but less well-protected harbour, with five good piers, off the westernmost of which two Italian ships had been sunk, giving shelter to the next two from northerly and westerly winds. Outside on the western coast of the peninsula were three other beaches all open. Nearest to our left front was Gully Beach, at the end of Zighin Dere or Gully Ravine; then came the old "X," or "Implacable," Beach, and between it and Cape Tekke "Bakery" Beach, but none of them was practicable in even moderate weather from south, west or north.[2]

Ever since the last gale work had been proceeding incessantly to restore the piers, and when the intermediate stage was begun all could be employed. The greatest care, however, had to be taken to preserve secrecy. It was no easy matter, for so great was the accumulation of stores and animals that to save time it was found necessary to load the lighters during the day, and the process was constantly interrupted by the curiosity of the enemy's aircraft. Whenever one appeared the work had to stop, but means were found for reaping advantage from the annoyance. Whenever a "Taube" appeared the rule was to reverse the process. Everything on the march to the beaches turned back, and a show was made of discharging stores and mules already in the lighters, so that the Turkish observers could only take back intelligence that we were still strengthening our position

[1] She was a ship of 12,000 tons displacement launched in 1895. As ordinary merchant vessels were found to open out after being beached, she was specially fitted out as a hulk for running ashore, and was towed from Toulon. When she was in place the breakwater was nearly four hundred yards long.

[2] See Vol. II., Map 4.

as if for a winter campaign. The weather, too, was a constant source of trouble. Up till New Year's Day it was fairly good, and each night between 2,000 and 3,000 men were embarked, including all the French, except the guns which General Brulard had agreed to leave behind for our use. In their place the hard-worked XXIXth Division had been landed after the withdrawal from Suvla, to enable the Royal Naval Divisions to take over the French trenches, while two brigades of General Maude's division, (XIIIth) rich in recent experience, relieved the exhausted XLIInd Division, which had borne the brunt of the recent fighting on the extreme left.[1] On January 2 it came on to blow, and the bad weather continued all next day and night, but as it came from the north-east it mattered little to the two main beaches and, by the morning of the 4th, 6,300 more men and forty-two guns had been got away.

To these difficulties was added the continued activity of the enemy's guns, but this the navy could do a good deal to reduce by means of a special organisation of supporting ships under the general charge of Admiral Fremantle. It comprised the regular "covering" squadron, under Captain Dent, which it was not thought prudent to increase during the intermediate stage. In the Ægean for the support of our left we had the *Edgar*, *Theseus*, the heavy monitor *Abercrombie* and two destroyers (*Scorpion* and *Wolverine*). For keeping under the Asiatic fire we had five other monitors, known as the "Rabbit Island Squadron," and so called from its station being behind those islands off Yeni Shehr.[2] Under his own hand Admiral Fremantle kept at Imbros a reinforcing squadron consisting of two battleships, *Hibernia* (flag) and *Russell*, the bulge cruiser *Grafton* and two heavy monitors, *Raglan* and *Havelock*. During the intermediate stage the battleships of this reserve were not required. In spite of the reduction of our guns ashore, it was found that the covering squadron was sufficient, with the remaining artillery, to keep the enemy's fire under control, so that it was an irritation rather than an interference, and the casualties it caused were negligible. But other causes for anxiety now arose.

All day on the 4th it was calm, but in the evening the

[1] During these three nights there were withdrawn 7,700 men (including the Greek labour corps), thirty-four guns with some 7,000 rounds of ammunition, 250 animals, over 600 tons of stores and nearly 9,000,000 rounds of small arms ammunition. The removal of animals was seriously delayed by the *Suffren* colliding with one of the largest horse transports on December 31 and sinking her, so that none could be embarked that night.

[2] *Sir Thomas Picton*, *Earl of Peterborough*, *Roberts*, *M 18* and *M 31*.

weather broke again, and all night it blew a gale from the north-east, and it became evident that the plan as it stood involved too great a risk, and that something more drastic than had sufficed for Suvla and Anzac must be devised. With the weather as it was it would be little short of madness to expect two calm nights in succession, which the final stage required. With the 15,000 men and forty guns that were to be left, General Davies was fairly sure that after the first night he could hold on for twenty-four hours, but it was only too likely he might find himself weather-bound at the last moment, possibly for several days. With eight miles of front to maintain he felt he could not do with less than 17,000 men and fifty-four guns. If only the navy could compress their last two nights' work into one, it could be done; and with this idea he consulted Captain C. M. Staveley, with whom, as Naval Transport Officer and Principal Beach Master in charge of the evacuation, he had been arranging the details. To increase the difficulty Captain Staveley had already come to the conclusion that, seeing what the weather was, it was impossible to count on any of the exposed western beaches being used. This would mean that everything must be embarked from the southern harbours, but still he thought that all might be crowded into one night if the necessary troop carriers could be found for the increased numbers and room made for more lighters at the already crowded piers, provided always that no more guns were embarked.

Next day (the 6th) he proceeded to "V" and "W" beaches to see what could be done, and there, in consultation with Colonel A. B. Carey, R.E., who had been doing wonders for improving the piers, a solution was found. By blowing large holes in the hulks as entry ports and connecting them up with No. 1 pier, it would be possible to march the troops straight into them and embark them without need of clogging the piers with more lighters. About the French harbour there was no difficulty, but at "W" Beach there was a gap between the end of No. 1 pier and the hulks which could only be filled by a floating bridge. Hitherto this had not been possible, but now he found it could be done. During the previous day the weather had mended, and the calm night that followed had been seized to complete the breakwater. By a clever piece of seamanship a steamer had been sunk exactly off the gap, so as to give shelter to the necessary bridge from the action of the sea. As soon as he returned he reported his plan to a staff conference which was being held at General Davies's headquarters. Commodore Keyes then suggested an improvement. By employing destroyers the difficulty of finding more troop carriers would be overcome, and their commanders could be relied on to bring them alongside the hulks, so that no more lighters would be required. General Birdwood sanctioned the plan and Admiral de Robeck authorised the employment of the six destroyers needed. To recast the elaborate arrangements for so delicate an operation at the last moment meant both afloat and ashore a vast deal of labour, but it was done with remarkable speed, and by the morning of the 7th the new naval schedules were issued.

Thanks to the improvement in the weather the intermediate stage was well up to time. During this night nearly 3,000 men had been embarked with six more guns, over 1,200 animals and large quantities of ammunition; another such night would complete the stage, and the final act was definitely fixed, weather permitting, for the night of the 8th–9th.

There was still no sign that the thinning lines and diminishing dumps had roused the enemy's suspicions. Every possible precaution had been taken to deceive him and to preserve all normal appearances. As the guns were removed the same rate of fire was kept up by those that were left and, as in the northern area, the Turks were carefully drilled for the last critical hours. For some time past the order had been to let fire die away about an hour before midnight: the enemy had soon followed suit, and as though by agreement used the respite for sleep. But could the deception hold for another forty-eight hours? By the morning of the 7th General Davies had but 19,000 men and sixty-three guns left. Should the enemy now awake and make a resolute attack anything might happen. That they were growing uneasy was evidenced by the vigorous shelling of the beaches during the last few days and the activity of their airmen, and now their patrols were busier and artillery fire on our trenches had increased.

So in deepening anxiety the morning hours went by and the immediate danger seemed to be passing when suddenly about midday a terrific artillery attack opened on both our flanks. Upon the Royal Naval Division holding the old French trenches a storm of shell burst from the Asiatic side, and still worse was that rained on General Maude's XIIIth Division on the left. Nor did the XXIXth Division and the LIInd in the centre escape. Nothing like it had been seen on the peninsula before. Those who knew said it was like the worst in France, and the long-talked-of coming of the German guns and ammunition seemed now a reality. For over three hours the bombardment continued, till by 3.0 it developed into drum fire which the supporting ships were unable to control. For three-quarters of an hour the intensive period continued, and our trenches were fast being wrecked when the Turks sprang two mines on Gully Spur. Then it could be seen the enemy's trenches were bristling with bayonets. At 4.0 the artillery fire slackened and our people could watch the Turkish officers trying to force their men over the parapet all along the line. But in vain. Nowhere did the attack begin to develop except opposite the North Staffords near Fusilier Bluff, and there their steady fire dropped every man who showed himself. At the same time Captain Dent was amply compensating for General Davies's diminished strength in artillery. With his cruisers, monitors and destroyers he was enfilading the enemy's position and taking a terrible toll from the helpless Turkish infantry crowded in the reserve and communication trenches.[1] It was more than flesh and blood could stand, and at 5.0 all was over, with our line intact. Our casualties were no more than 164 killed, but what the massed enemy must have suffered cannot be told. It was enough to leave them no heart for more when the hour came for the last reduction of General Davies's force.

That night, in continued fine weather, 2,300 men and nine more guns were withdrawn, as well as nearly 1,000 animals. Over 500 were still on the peninsula, as well as 1,590 vehicles and a vast quantity of stores, little of which could be removed without risking another day's delay.[2] On the morning of the 8th General Davies was left with just under 17,000 men and fifty-four guns, but, small as the force was for holding eight miles of trenches, his confidence had been stiffened by the complete defeat of the Turkish attack. Though evidently intended as a supreme effort, and in spite of the lavish expenditure of ammunition, it had failed even to shake the British line. In every way it was encouraging. Clearly General Liman von Sanders cannot have been aware that so many guns had been withdrawn, or his main effort would not have been made at the very point where the navy could best make good the need of artillery support, and seeing how

[1] On January 7th and 8th Captain Dent's squadron was composed of the bulge ships *Edgar*, *Grafton* and *Theseus*; the monitors *Abercrombie*, *Havelock*, *Raglan*, *Earl of Peterborough* and *M 17*, and the destroyers *Scorpion* and *Wolverine*. The *Russell* also took part on the 7th, when the *Edgar* herself fired 1,000 6-inch shells.

[2] The total embarkations during the intermediate stage were: troops, 20,714; guns, 102; animals, 3,649; ammunition, 32,000 rounds for artillery and 12,718,000 for small arms; vehicles, 303, and stores, 1,500 tons.

effective that support had been, General Davies's anxiety about his special weakness was happily diminished.[1]

As the last crucial day advanced the good effects of the success became further manifest in a distinct diminution in the amount of fire on the beaches, due probably as much to a depression of spirit as to exhaustion of ammunition. The weather promised no less well, though for a little time a southerly breeze caused some anxiety. Should it increase a postponement might be necessary, but towards the afternoon it died away and at 5.0 p.m. the Admiral made the signal to " carry on." Captain Dent's ships were already in position, having been engaged all day replying to the fitful fire from the enemy, and Admiral Fremantle now began to move his reinforcing squadron from Kephalo. The *Grafton* and his two reserve monitors, *Raglan* and *Havelock*, were to anchor in selected berths where they could best answer any call from the army, while he himself, with the battleships *Hibernia* and *Russell*, cruised off Gaba Tepe in readiness to enfilade the enemy's trenches at dawn should a hitch occur.

Ashore all was in order. Two covering positions, one for each beach, had been prepared along the heights which had been so hardly won at the first landing, and during the afternoon they had been quietly occupied by the troops to whom the post of honour was due—six hundred men of the XXIXth Division for " W " Beach and four hundred of the Royal Naval Division for the other. The embarkation was to be in three flights in diminishing numbers, so as to allow for accidents to the boats. For the first time the troops were to be at the forming-up places behind the covering positions between 7.0 and 7.30. As soon as they arrived, General Davies, leaving General Lawrence, who commanded the LIInd Division, in charge, embarked in the *Triad*, which had been placed at his disposal by Admiral de Robeck and was connected up by cable with the shore. Punctually at 8.0 Captain H. F. G. Talbot, who had the direction of the operation afloat, had all his troop carriers and small craft in their assigned berths, and the embarkation began with smooth precision and proceeded rapidly. At " V " Beach four trawlers and a horse-boat were alongside the old *River Clyde*,

[1] This view is confirmed by an officer on the German staff who wrote a highly coloured account of the evacuation. It is of little value for facts —being mere propaganda—but may be quoted for impressions. Of the attack on the 7th he says : " But for the ever-active hostile fleet not an enemy would have been left alive on the peninsula "—little more, of course, than a boast to save the face of the staff, but none the less evidence of the effectiveness of the ship fire.

and alongside the other two hulks, six motor lighters, which, as they filled, went off with 2,000 of the Royal Naval Division and 1,200 of the LIInd to two troop carriers. All went like a clock, and the work began no less well at "W" Beach, where 4,000 troops of the XXIXth and XIIIth Divisions were embarked. The troop-carrier *Ermine* was at the outer hulk on the inner side and the destroyer *Lawford* at the other, while the *Lydiard* waited to take the *Ermine's* berth as soon as she was filled. Here, however, the breeze was causing a lop in the harbour and the floating bridge had already had to be hurriedly secured with anchors taken from the lighters. So for an hour the troops passed over it securely, but by 9.0 the wind was freshening and a rising sea soon began to cause difficulties. It was 10.15 before the *Ermine* cleared away. The *Lydiard,* in spite of the sea, was skilfully berthed in her place, but before she was filled the bridge had become impassable, and the rest of her complement had to be brought out to her in lighters as they became available.

Meanwhile, though only two iron-decked gun-lighters remained, seven 18-pounders and a 5-inch howitzer had been embarked at the same beach with their teams, as well as an anti-aircraft gun with its motor lorry, while at "V" Beach by 10.30 fourteen British guns and all the French 75's were afloat. At 11.0 the ships for the second flight had anchored, the *Mars* for "W" Beach and the *Prince George* for the other, each accompanied by a troop-carrier. The two battleships took between them 3,400 troops, and 2,600 were embarked in the troop carriers. As the *Prince George* steamed away, there came an alarming signal that she had been struck by a torpedo. Two destroyers at once rushed to the spot but there were no further alarms. Actually, as no submarine was present that night, the *Prince George* must have struck a piece of wreckage, but the report was disturbing enough to compel Admiral Fremantle to take his two supporting battleships back to Kephalo.

The last flight was to begin at 1.30, but by this time things were growing alarming. A nasty sea that was running into "W" Beach threatened to bring everything to a standstill, and it began to look doubtful whether a second embarkation of guns would be effected. By dint of great exertion, however, eight more 18-pounders, four 5-inch howitzers and three limbers were got away in two more trips, but unhappily it was found impossible to save their valuable gun teams, and they had to be destroyed. About 3,700 troops with the beach parties now remained. At "V" Beach were

1,600, and for these the destroyers *Grasshopper* and *Bulldog*, in spite of the wind and sea, were brought alongside the hulks by a fine display of seamanship which deeply impressed all who saw it. By 3.20 they were both clear, but at "W" Beach the difficulties were much greater. Here, with higher risk and no less skill, the *Staunch* and *Fury* were brought in to the outer hulk, but the bridge had long been impassable, and the troops had to be ferried to them in the "beetles," which in the sea that was running were almost unmanageable, and the work went very slowly.

The strain of anxiety was now at its highest tension. Since 9.0 p.m. only snipers and bomb-throwers about one to ten yards had been left in the front trenches, and soon after 11.30, when the regular silent period for which the enemy had been so carefully drilled began, they were all stealing away with muffled boots. As they passed through the covering positions the troops holding them were withdrawn, but as each successive line of the maze of trenches had been firmly closed with wire and the mines made active by the last of the retiring troops, there was little danger now of an attack. Yet at any moment the Turks might awake to the fact that the front trenches were empty and begin a deadly shelling of the beaches.

Graver even than the position at "W" Beach was that of General Maude and his last party isolated at Gully Beach. There were over 680 of them, and at midnight the *Talbot* had arrived towing two "beetles" and two steamboats from Kephalo to take them off. The orders were that, for fear of alarming the enemy, the "beetles" were not to use their engines till they were leaving. In spite of the increasing swell on the beach the first one attempted it only to be driven ashore. The second had better fortune. The R.N.R. sub-lieutenant in charge started his motor and very skilfully brought his boat up to the pier. With the greatest difficulty 525 men were got into her and she cleared away. It was the utmost she could safely carry in such a sea, and as the other was now a wreck the beachmaster had to inform General Maude that, as he had been previously warned might happen, the remaining 160 must make their way to "W" Beach. The General with his Medical Officer and a dozen men attached to his headquarters stayed with the naval beach party to be taken off by two of the *Talbot's* steamboats, but this, after several attempts, proved impossible, and all of the little headquarters party had to follow the men in an adventurous march against time. It was now getting on for 3.0 a.m., they had two miles to go, and at the covering positions they had to cut their way through the controls which they found closed, but thanks to the difficulties at " W " Beach they arrived in time.

The sea was now rapidly rising and by 3.30 it seemed that only a few minutes remained before further embarkations would be quite impossible. But only little now remained to be done. General Maude and those with him were hurried into the boats, the fuzes to the main magazine were lighted, and the abandoned stores set on fire. At 3.45 a.m. the last picket boat left the shore and the evacuation was complete. The only life lost was that of a seaman who was unfortunately hit when a shower of debris fell from the magazine which exploded prematurely. With the sound of the explosion the Turks seemed at last to awake. All along their lines the glare of red lights illumined the distance, but still nothing happened. The surprise, it would seem, had been too complete. A second time they had been tricked past all belief; and unmolested, as the enemy's signal of alarm spread, the rest of the lighters, under the admirable handling of their Royal Naval Reserve officers, were slowly moved out in the light of the blazing dumps without accident. By dawn the last of them was clear and Captain Staveley was able to join Captain Talbot in the *Colne*.

So once more the impossible had been performed. " In spite of all our vigilance," wrote General Liman von Sanders, " the withdrawal was successfully carried out." With the exception of the single accidental casualty General Davies's whole force and all the beach parties had been got away intact; and afloat only one lighter and a picket boat had been lost—a marvellous testimony to the seamanship and resource of all concerned, and to none less than the Royal Naval Reserve officers in charge of the troop carriers and lighters, on whom chiefly fell the perilous inshore work. Ashore there was a much greater sacrifice than before. Over 500 animals had to be slaughtered and 1,600 vehicles and vast quantities of stores abandoned, as well as fifteen guns, only one of which was fit for service, but all of them were blown to pieces so that they might not be paraded as trophies.[1] As for the sunken hulks that formed the breakwaters, their demolition was undertaken a day or two later by picket boats with torpedoes, while the ships of the supporting squadron dealt with all other serviceable craft that had been driven ashore.

Those shots were the last salute over the grave of an

[1] This is exclusive of the six French heavy guns, which were also destroyed.

operation that, as both friend and foe admitted, had no parallel in history. Looking back on the final acts of the whole campaign, the uppermost feeling can only be one of deep regret. In that marvellous evacuation we see the national genius for amphibious warfare raised to its highest manifestation. In hard experience and successive disappointments the weapon had been brought to a perfect temper, and when the hour of fruition came to show of what great things it was capable it was used only to effect a retreat. It may be that retreat was inevitable. The wisdom of the decision will long be a matter of debate. As to Suvla, without which Anzac was useless, General Byng's opinion can hardly be gainsaid. The grounds on which he based his advice for evacuation were quite independent of "western" doctrine, nor is there any sign that his judgment was warped by his service in France. It was the tactical conditions that left him no room for doubt. On taking over the command he had quickly made up his mind that we must get on or get out. Later he was sure he could gain ground on his left if sufficient reinforcements and ammunition were given him, but after the gales which changed the terrain so much for the worse, he declared that he could neither deploy the needed reinforcements nor shelter them when they arrived. Unless, therefore, the fleet could break through, the evacuation of Suvla seems to have been imperative, and with it must go Anzac.

The question of Helles was not so simple. The men on the spot believed it could be held through the winter if Achi Baba were taken, and those immediately concerned, having proved how far combined tactics had advanced during the campaign, were convinced they could do it. The weight of high military authority was against them. Undoubtedly military opinion was within its province in contending that, given all possible naval support, the capture of the position was still on military grounds impossible, but it is no less certain that they measured the value of naval support by what the fleet had been able to do when, half starved for ammunition, it was first faced by a problem of which it had no experience, rather than by what its capacities were with an ample ammunition supply after a year's training under actual war conditions. In both services the men on the spot, deeply imbued as they now were with the amphibious spirit, had complete trust in the weapon they had forged, and by their conduct of the evacuation they proved it could do things beyond all military experience.

To compensate for the lack of solidity in the foundations

of the tactical argument the strategical considerations, if not convincing, were at least not without weight. The retention of Helles, it was urged, even if practicable, could serve no purpose. In view of its naval value, as insisted on by Admiral de Robeck, this was going too far. The naval reasons for retention may have been inadequate, but if right judgment be desired they must not be simply ignored. The military advantages of keeping our hold were that by maintaining our menace of the Turkish capital we were in a better position to develop a decisive offensive from Egypt, with the assistance of the troops which we were still hoping to withdraw at an early date from Salonica. There was no lack of authority that this was the line on which our efforts could be used most effectively for the common cause if France would agree, and only later experience showed how hopeless it was to get French consent. The dominant idea of the French high command was to mass every possible man and gun against the front upon which the enemy was strongest, regardless of whether within measureable time such a concentration would give sufficient preponderance to secure a decision. If the abandonment of the Dardanelles could have given the necessary preponderance, then undoubtedly it was right; if it only meant a slightly increased power of "killing Germans" in France, while at the same time shutting out our navy from the continental struggle, then, however desirable on political grounds, it is far from clear that its strategical advantages balanced its drawbacks.

We have seen how in August, after the landing at Suvla, the increasing gravity of the menace to Constantinople had forced the German Great General Staff to arrest their offensive against Russia. Just when a crushing decision seemed within their reach the necessary troops had to be diverted to the Danube. It is incomparably more important, General Falkenhayn had then written, to secure the Dardanelles. With the abandonment of Helles the menace was entirely removed. There was no further need to press their offensive in the Balkans. Now that the Serbian army was for the time off the board, it sufficed for the Central Powers to set up a defensive front with the Bulgarian army against Salonica, and they were free to resume the great lines of their war plan. With the cessation of the disturbance at the Dardanelles that at Salonica became negligible.

Untimely and regrettable as was the evacuation, the apparently wasted sacrifice and effort were not without tangible result. The strain of the defence—sickness and privation, losses in battle—told heavily upon the Turkish army, and deserters, who continued to come in freely up till the final days of the withdrawal, indicated a serious demoralisation. The resistance had been stubborn, but it succeeded only at the cost of enormous loss. General Liman von Sanders gave the total casualties as 218,000, including 66,000 dead, and of the wounded only 42,000 returned as likely to be fit for further service.[1] The Turkish official account, however, gives a total of 251,000, while other Turkish authorities place the total as high as 350,000. Our own losses were 115,000 killed, wounded, and missing, and 90,000 evacuated sick. Many of the latter, owing to the lack of hospital accommodation, were only suffering from minor sickness or light wounds. The French casualties numbered 47,000. For the Ottoman power their heavy losses meant a degree of exhaustion from which it was never able to recover. To provide sufficient force to meet our advance up the Tigris was all it could do, and the immediate result was seen in Armenia. From the time of our first landing the pressure on General Yudenitch's army had been sensibly relieved, and within a week of our retirement from Helles he was advancing on Erzerum. With nearly all the Turkish shipping destroyed by our submarines, a rapid reinforcement of the Armenian army was impossible. On February 16 Erzerum fell, and two months later the Turkish sea base at Trebizond was in Russian hands (April 17). So it happened that just as we withdrew, Russian co-operation, on which we calculated when we first undertook military operations at the Dardanelles, was beginning to develop with brilliant promise. Turkey, indeed, was at this time in so precarious a position that the political consequences of the evacuation which had most been feared were not realised. Loss of prestige in the East had all along been the strongest objection to admitting failure, but happily the effect seems to have been to raise the reputation of British arms, and nowhere was it more evident than in the frank admiration of the way the withdrawal was managed which was expressed in Germany.

[1] Liman von Sanders, p. 135.

CHAPTER XIII

HOME WATERS SEPTEMBER 1915 TO MARCH 1916 AND THE CRUISE OF THE GERMAN RAIDER *MOEWE*

THE reactions of the Dardanelles enterprise, which Lord Fisher foresaw when he resigned rather than remain responsible for the policy he condemned, went even further than his immediate apprehension. It was because he was convinced that the new departure in the Near East must put it out of the power of the fleet to influence the general course of the war by high offensive action in Home waters that he threw up his office. There is room for doubt whether his plan or that which took its place was the better calculated to bring about a quick decision. It may be that the Government's plan, had it been possible to carry it out as a true combined operation, was the more wisely chosen of the two. But it had failed, and the consequences were asserting themselves more gravely than its strongest opponents had foretold. It was no longer a question of whether the navy could exert its most powerful influence by pressing home its offensive efforts into the enemy's waters, but rather whether the strain was not sapping the power of the Grand Fleet to perform its cardinal function of defeating the enemy decisively in the open sea.

The danger was felt in many ways, but what finally drew from Admiral Jellicoe a deliberate protest was the reinforcement of the Mediterranean by the withdrawal from Home waters of Admiral Fremantle's division of the 3rd Battle Squadron. New ships of the most powerful class were coming forward for service. In themselves they, of course, amply made up for what the Dardanelles was absorbing, but all required crews, and the skilled ratings that are the life-blood of a ship could only be drawn from the Grand Fleet. Foremost among the new ships were the five "Queen Elizabeths." The *Barham* and *Warspite* had already joined their nameship at Scapa, though the *Warspite*, having grounded in the Forth, had had to be docked in the Tyne, and did not rejoin till November 23. Following them another Dreadnought, the *Canada*, and the light cruisers, *Birkenhead* and *Liverpool*, had arrived.[1] In February the other two "Queen Elizabeths," the *Malaya*, which the Federated Malay States had given, and the *Valiant*, were due, to be followed in March by another Dreadnought, the new *Revenge*. It was in the first days of November that the *Hibernia*, flying Admiral Fremantle's flag, *Zealandia*, and *Albemarle* were withdrawn from the 3rd Battle Squadron, and the *Russell*, which was in dock at Belfast, was to join them *en route*. They left Rosyth on November 6, but only to meet in Pentland Firth a gale of quite unprecedented fury—the herald of that terrible winter—which drove them back into Scapa. The *Albemarle's* bridge was swept clean away by the terrific seas, and she had to go into dock.[2]

The withdrawal of these ships seemed to promise no end to what the Dardanelles was already devouring, and towards the end of November Admiral Jellicoe felt compelled to make a serious representation of what it entailed. So long as so large a force of old battleships was retained in service for the Mediterranean the demand for necessary ratings for the new ships meant constant changes in the personnel of the Grand Fleet ships, to the inevitable detriment of their fighting efficiency. To stop the mischief he urged that the crews for the new ships should be formed by bringing home some of the older battleships, and declared that the method now being adopted could "no longer be pursued with safety." The letter necessarily made its impression. The reply was an assurance that the exchange of ratings of which the Commander-in-Chief complained would be suspended till April. The difficult question of the Mediterranean force, he was told, was being considered, as indeed we know it was, in all its baffling perplexity, and that it was hoped to effect a reduction in the spring.

To that extent the special anxiety for the fighting efficiency of the fundamental element of our war strength was allayed, but there were others scarcely less serious. Since the end of September it had become apparent that, except for minelaying in the southern area, the German submarine activity had ceased. The knowledge did much to relax the strain on our overworked destroyers, a welcome relief as the stormy winter season approached, but it was not

[1] At the end of November the new "C" type light cruiser *Castor* joined and the *Liverpool* was withdrawn for service in the Mediterranean.

[2] She rejoined the 3rd Battle Squadron at Scapa in December, and was subsequently employed in the White Sea.

to be believed that the disappearance of the submarines meant the cessation of the known German policy of seeking to cripple our battle strength. The successful operation of the *Meteor* in August and the continued activity of the submarine minelayers in the southern area suggested that the enemy's effort was likely to be directed to fouling the approaches to the Grand Fleet bases by means of surface minelayers. In the long winter nights it would be a promising policy, difficult to meet, and from now onwards Admiral Jellicoe's main efforts were directed to thwarting it.

Obviously the best way to intercept the minelayers was to seek them at their starting point, and a series of light cruiser sweeps to the Skagerrak was instituted. Usually they were supported by the Battle Cruiser Fleet, either at sea or in immediate readiness to sail; sometimes the Battle Fleet went out with the same object and also to exercise battle tactics, not always without causing new trouble. On one such occasion, (December 3), a week after the *Warspite* had rejoined from the Tyne, that unlucky ship collided with the *Barham*, and both were condemned to a long absence in dock. These temporary losses were the more severely felt since two others were suffered in the last quarter of the year. On October 28 the cruiser *Argyll*, while making for Rosyth after a refit at Devonport, in thick weather ran on the Bell Rock, near Dundee. The heavy sea that was running soon reduced her to a total wreck, but in spite of it all her officers and men were successfully taken off by destroyers from Rosyth. More tragic was the fate of the *Natal*. On December 30, while lying in Cromarty harbour, she was observed to be on fire, and before any assistance could be given, her after magazines blew up and she went to the bottom. At first it was thought her destruction must be the work of a submarine, but inquiry proved that it was due to defects in some of her ammunition. The loss of life was great, and amongst those who perished with her was her commanding officer, Captain E. P. C. Back.

These two disasters sensibly increased the strain on the Grand Fleet cruisers. For, over and above the insistent need of watching for minelayers, there were constant calls for gold escort, for conveying missions to and from Archangel, for protecting ships carrying munitions from France to the White Sea and for other similar services. The strain, indeed, could scarcely have been met but for the vigorous co-operation of Commodore Tyrwhitt. The Harwich Force now consisted of the 5th Light Cruiser Squadron and the 9th and 10th Flotillas, to which were attached the *Undaunted* and *Aurora*, and the two Flotilla leaders *Lightfoot* and *Nimrod*.[1] Though, owing to the never-ending calls for troop escort across the Channel, his destroyers were sometimes reduced to a single flotilla, his activity during the last quarter of the year was incessant in all weathers. On September 30 in a sweep to the Bight he captured thirteen German trawlers and sank one. These vessels were believed to be acting as scouts to give warning when our cruisers were operating. The following week he made another raid to the Skagerrak and came back with fifteen more. Seeing how insistent was the demand for this class of craft for the Mediterranean, it was a useful haul. They were taken into our service, six being sent to the Dardanelles and six to the Suez Canal. Nor were these captures without effect in increasing the pressure of our blockade. The restriction it meant on the enemy's food supply was at this time causing the German Government ever-increasing anxiety. All the boats were found to be fishing on Government account, and from this time onward no more were seen. Yet Commodore Tyrwhitt's hold on the enemy's waters was never relaxed. Every week he was in force off the German or Danish coast, and all he met with was the Swedish *Osterland* carrying ore on German account from Narvik to Rotterdam, and her he brought in. Twice he was driven in by heavy gales, till at last, at the end of December, the Admiralty had to restrain him by a caution not to expose his force during the stormy season unless some exceptionally favourable opportunity presented itself. There was, indeed, little need at this time for special exertion, for the enemy was feeling the restraint of the weather even more keenly. Their main oversea activity had been confined to airships. Up to the middle of October their bombing raids on our coast had been a constant source of annoyance. Commodore Tyrwhitt had been no less occupied with seeking to intercept them than with his search for surface minelayers, but the violence of the weather that had set in was more than they could face, and they had ceased altogether.

Beyond the reach of our surface vessels, and to keep up a more permanent watch on the enemy, our submarines were from time to time stationed in the Bight and the Skagerrak. Their objective was the enemy's trade and minelayers, and sometimes submarines and destroyers whose presence had been reported in the entrance to the Baltic. Yet nothing

[1] In August the old 7th and 9th Flotillas had been amalgamated as the 7th, under Rear-Admiral G. A. Ballard, Admiral of Patrols. Commodore Tyrwhitt's 3rd Flotilla was then renamed the 9th, so that the more modern flotillas might be numbered 9th, 10th, etc.

was met with until, on December 22, *E 16* sank a German naval auxiliary vessel, but against this success four days later *E 6* on her way to the Bight, was lost with all hands on a mine laid by *UC 5* near the Sunk light-vessel.

So far as could be judged, the strenuous scouring of the seas for minelayers was successful. Since the *Meteor* had laid her field off Cromarty nothing had appeared till December 30, when one was sighted near the Outer Gabbard, apparently at work in the fairway between the British and the German mine-fields. Our own mining activity, however, continued undiminished. Early in October, Admiral Jellicoe, having heard that as an outcome of the submarine controversy changes in the German flag commands had taken place, thought it probable the High Seas Fleet would engage in tactical exercises in the North Sea for the benefit of the new admirals, and suggested the laying of fresh minefields to stop them.[1] Accordingly on October 13 the minelayers *Biarritz* and *Paris* had been sent out, under escort of a detachment of the Harwich Force, and they laid a new field off the Ems without being detected. The Germans discovered the mines a week later, but mistook them for part of an earlier field. No mention of them appears in their official history. On November 8 a similar expedition was made, escorted in the same way, and supported by Commodore Tyrwhitt with the *Cleopatra* and six destroyers. On this occasion the *Princess Margaret* and the *Angora* spread 850 mines in the northern exit from the Bight off Amrum Bank. Its object was to replace the field laid in the same vicinity in September, which the Germans had easily detected owing to the defective mooring of the mines, and again the operation was completed without a single vessel appearing to interfere.

During all this time, when our fleets were completely dominating the North Sea, the part which the 10th Cruiser Squadron silently played in the shadow of the Grand Fleet must not be forgotten. It was still under the command of Rear-Admiral D. R. S. de Chair, and had reached its full complement of twenty-four armed merchant cruisers under Royal Navy captains. Undeterred by the incessant gales, in all but continuous darkness as the season advanced, and blinded with snow and fog, they held their ground. Uncomplaining and vigilant, the merchant seamen and officers who manned the ships kept their grip on the enemy's throat with no less spirit and resource than their comrades in the fleet. "The

[1] On September 3 Admiral von Holtzendorff succeeded Admiral Bachmann as Chief of the Staff, and the Deputy Chief of the Naval Staff, Admiral Behncke, was replaced by Admiral Reinhard Koch.

work of these officers and men," wrote the Commander-in-Chief, "merits the very highest commendation. They deserve all their country can do for them." [1] But ostensibly at least it was no longer a purely British force. On November 5 the American Government had delivered a protest against our blockade in stronger terms than they had hitherto used. As a counter-move it was thought desirable to demonstrate that the doctrine of legitimate restriction of neutral trade upon which we were acting was not confined to ourselves. France was ready to endorse it openly by showing her flag in the blockading forces, and as she had no ship available for the purpose, it was arranged that one of the squadron should be transferred to her flag. The *Digby* was accordingly sent down to Brest, and after receiving a French crew and commission, rejoined the squadron as the *Artois.* Then, on the French request for another ship, the *Oropesa* was handed over in the same way. She was rechristened the *Champagne,* and though she did not join Admiral de Chair's flag, she was associated with his White Sea work as a monthly packet between France and Archangel. The calls upon him for this, the only line of communication with Russia, were frequent. It was one of his ships, the *Arlanza,* who took out General Wolfe-Murray and the Allied Mission to Russia. She was to bring back a similar Russian Mission, but on starting to return she struck a mine, and there being no possibility of repairing her damage where she was, another ship, the *Orotava,* had to be detached to take her place. The White Sea, indeed, continued to be a source of perpetual irritation owing to the apathy and incapacity of the local authorities. They seemed quite unable to help themselves. Not only was the sea a permanent drain on our mine-sweeping trawlers, but the Russian Admiralty never ceased to call for further naval protection. In order to keep the channel to Archangel clear of ice as long as possible we sent out the *Albemarle* to join the old cruiser *Iphigenia* as a guardship and ice-breaker.

Though the advent of winter naturally increased the difficulties of the squadron, it brought certain compensations. The cessation of the submarine campaign reduced the danger of search and eased the difficulty of persuading neutrals to proceed for examination to ports within the declared danger zone. The Clyde and the Mersey, moreover, could again be

[1] *Alsatian* (flag), *Alcantara, Almanzora, Andes, Arlanza, Cedric, Changuinola, Columbella, Digby, Ebro, Hilary, Hildebrand, Mantua, Motagua, Orcoma, Oropesa, Orotava, Otway, Patia, Patuca, Teutonic, Victorian, Virginian.* The *Bayano* and *India* had been sunk by submarines, and the *Clan Macnaughton* and *Viknor* had foundered in heavy weather with all hands lost.

used as bases, though here labour troubles sometimes caused delay and increased the strain on ships overdue to be relieved. No less important were the measures designed by the various Government Committees which, besides the Trade Division of the Admiralty, under Captain Richard Webb, and the Foreign Office Contraband Department, under Sir Eyre Crowe, had been set up for controlling neutral trade by agreement. The most effective of these expedients was the Order which began to operate in October restricting the supply of bunker coal. Notorious offenders were placed on a "black list" and their owners could not get bunker coal at British ports; others could only obtain it on certain conditions, such as undertaking not to carry goods of enemy origin and to reserve a proportion of space for Allied cargo. The immediate effect upon the work of Admiral de Chair's squadron was that Dutch and Scandinavian owners began to agree to their ships calling voluntarily at specified ports for examination.[1] Still recalcitrants made the work anxious enough, particularly a certain firm who took to running the blockade at night without lights and at high speed. As these ships were fine liners, carrying numerous passengers, the risk of a regrettable catastrophe was very great. They might well be taken for escaping raiders and sunk at sight, and the Commander-in-Chief had to endorse Admiral de Chair's emphatic representations that the practice must be stopped. But the Government was already taking action, and shortly afterwards the matter was settled by agreement, the offenders undertaking to confine their ships to a certain well-defined route.

Still with all mitigation the work was heavy. What vigilance and endurance it meant may be judged by what was done. During the year 1915, in all weathers, and in spite of submarines, an area of 220,000 square miles had been regularly patrolled. No less than 2,281 vessels, in and out, had been visited, besides 817 fishing craft, and of the total of over three thousand 743 had been sent in for examination. So effective indeed was the control that during the last five months Norway and Denmark had received no more than seventy-seven cargoes which we did not know to be innocent, and only eight vessels that were believed to carry important contraband evaded the patrol, while Germany's outward bound trade, except in the Baltic, was absolutely stopped.

No less successful to all appearance had been Admiral de Chair's share in preventing commerce raiders and minelayers

[1] For a full account of these measures see Fayle, *Seaborne Trade*, Vol. II., chap. ix.

from breaking out into the high seas. To such vessels, if handled with skill and daring, no blockade had ever been absolutely impervious, and with the New Year came a sudden warning that the old rule held good. On January 6 the pre-Dreadnought *King Edward VII*, on her way from Scapa to Belfast for a refit, fouled a mine off Cape Wrath, the north-west extremity of Scotland. At first it was believed to have been the work of a submarine, and the *Kempenfelt* and twelve destroyers were hurried to her assistance. No minefield was known to exist in the vicinity, and the *Africa*, proceeding to Scapa, had passed the spot safely a few hours before. Efforts were made to tow the doomed battleship, but by 4.0 p.m., after nine hours struggle, it was clear that in the heavy weather that prevailed she was doomed. Captain C. Maclachlan therefore decided he must abandon his ship. In spite of the sea that was running the destroyers *Musketeer*, *Marne*, *Fortune* and *Nessus* were skilfully brought alongside, and every soul was saved, and four hours later the stricken ship turned over and sank. It was long before the mystery of the new minefield was solved, partly because of the terrible weather that prevailed throughout the month, and partly because of the ceaseless call for sloops and trawlers everywhere. Eventually it was found that the number of mines laid was so great that the work could only have been done by a surface vessel.

Though it was weeks before the inference was verified, it was true. With the cessation of the submarine campaign in our Home waters it would seem that the German public became increasingly restive at our being left in undisturbed control of the North Sea and the Atlantic, and towards the end of the year it was decided to revert to the policy of surface commerce raiders as a demonstration that British control was not undisputed. So at least Commander Count zu Dohna-Schlodien believed when he was ordered to proceed to sea in a ship called the *Moewe* to lay mines in various places along the enemy's coasts and then to carry on cruiser warfare. She was a converted merchantman of 4,500 tons which had been fitted as a minelayer, and armed fore and aft with two groups of guns and two torpedo tubes. Her appearance as a trader was carefully preserved, and she had the Swedish colours painted on her sides. Thus equipped she put to sea on December 29, 1915, and taking advantage of the long hours of darkness and the dirty weather to elude our patrols, she proceeded round the Faroe Islands and reached Sule Skerry on January 1 just before dark. There in a gale of wind and snow she proceeded to lay her first field of 252 mines across the western entrance of the Pentland Firth where the *King Edward VII* was caught. At this time, owing to the heavy demands for sloops and trawlers in the Mediterranean, the local patrols were specially weak, and she entirely escaped detection.[1] She made away out into the Atlantic, and it was not till January 9 that she next made herself felt by a second field of 238 mines off Rochelle.[2] Two days later her presence in that quarter was marked by the capture of the s.s. *Farringford*, with a cargo of copper ore, 160 miles west of Finisterre.[3] It was the first stroke of her commerce raiding, and on that fertile route it was quickly followed by others. Moving southwards, by the 13th she had made four more captures in the vicinity of Madeira.[4] The first, the *Corbridge*, being full of coal, was kept, and in accordance with the practice of his predecessors Count zu Dohna despatched her to a secret rendezvous at Maraca island, on the north coast of Brazil. The other three vessels he sank. Two days later, being then about 120 miles north of the Canaries, he captured the *Ariadne* (3,035 tons), with maize for Nantes, which he also sank, and then the *Appam* (7,781 tons), for the west coast, in which was a large sum of bullion and a number of passengers, including the Governors of Sierra Leone and Nigeria. This vessel Count zu Dohna was obliged to spare for the accommodation of his now numerous prisoners, and after taking the bullion out of her, directed her to proceed to Norfolk, Virginia.

By this means he did all that was possible to conceal his presence, and as yet nothing had been heard of him either by the Admiralty or on the stations affected. The whole of the great southern highway, which for nearly a year had been undisturbed, was being held by cruiser squadrons as before, mainly as a precaution against German ships which had sought refuge in neutral ports. In the Madeira–Canaries area Rear-Admiral Sir Archibald Moore had the *King Alfred* and *Essex*, with two armed merchant cruisers, *Carmania* and

[1] Cape Wrath marked the dividing line between the Stornoway Patrol Area (No. 1) and Area III, which guarded the Scapa zone.

[2] See Map 12.

[3] Count zu Dohna in his published narrative does not mention laying the Rochelle minefield, but says he remained twelve days in British waters—a statement difficult to reconcile with the known locality of his first five captures, but a venial exaggeration in view of his conviction that the object of his cruise was mainly political.

[4] *Corbridge*, 3,687 tons, January 11, Barry to Rosario with coal; *Dromonby*, 3,627 tons, Cardiff to St. Vincent with coal; *Author*, 3,496 tons, London to Port Natal with general cargo; *Trader*, 3,608 tons, St. Vincent to Falmouth with sugar—all three on the 13th.

Ophir. Further south was Captain H. T. Buller, with the *Highflyer* and the armed merchant cruiser *Marmora*, to watch the Cape Verde islands, while on the south-east coast of South America Captain J. Luce was still on his old station with the *Glasgow* and *Vindictive* and the two armed merchant cruisers *Macedonia* and *Orama*, the *Glasgow* being at the moment recommissioning at St. Vincent, Cape Verde. As in the previous period of commerce raiding, there was nothing to spare for the area of St. Paul Rocks and Fernando Noronha, where in the approaches to Pernambuco the *Karlsruhe* had found her best-stocked hunting ground.

For this area Count zu Dohna was now making, but not without danger. On January 16, half-way between Madeira and the Canaries, he fell in with the *Clan Mactavish*, a defensively-armed ship of over 7,000 tons from Australia to London. Though the commanding officer, Captain Oliver, opened fire and made a gallant attempt to escape, he was soon overhauled and forced to surrender, but not before his wireless operator had sent out a call for assistance. The message was received in the wireless room of the *Essex*, but by a reprehensible neglect of duty was not communicated to her captain. But for this the whole of Admiral Moore's squadron might have been on the *Moewe's* track next day and the alarm would have spread to all quarters. As it was the Admiralty remained as unconscious of her cruise as Admiral Moore. It was not till the 30th that the captain of the *Essex* found out that the call for help had been received. Whether or not it meant that a submarine was on the route was doubtful, but next day the *Appam* reached Norfolk, Virginia, with the *Moewe's* prisoners and the truth was known. Dispositions, to which the French contributed four cruisers, were then rapidly made to put a stop to the intruder's career.

Meanwhile Count zu Dohna had struck out into the Atlantic, away from Admiral Moore's station, and after sinking the barque *Edinburgh* on January 22 far off the trade route made for Maraca island, where, having re-coaled from the *Corbridge*, he scuttled her in deep water (February 1). Then with full bunkers he proceeded to the Fernando Noronha area, but instead of the crowded seas he expected, nothing was seen for some time, thanks, as he realised, to the admirable way in which the British system of warning and reporting was worked. Not till February 4 did he capture a solitary Belgian steamer, the *Luxembourg*, outward bound from Newport with coal to La Plata. He was then eighty miles to the eastward of Fernando Noronha and in acute danger. Straight for him down the highway was coming Captain Luce in the *Glasgow* to rejoin her squadron, but they did not meet. Sometime late on February 5 they must have passed each other just out of sight, and next day Count zu Dohna was able to capture the *Flamenco*, another outward bound coal ship. From her he learnt that his presence was known, and altering the appearance of his ship he turned northward for St. Paul Rocks. But it was only to increase his danger, for Captain Buller in the *Highflyer* had left St. Vincent on the 4th, and it was for the same point that he was making. By the evening of the 8th he was rapidly nearing the area when Count zu Dohna captured the *Westburn*,[1] 120 miles west-south-west of the Rocks, and early next morning sank the *Horace*, ninety miles west-north-west of them. He had now nearly 200 prisoners, and these he humanely sent away in the *Westburn* in charge of a prize crew. While thus engaged his danger was acute; to all appearance nothing but luck could prevent his bold career from coming to an end before the day was out. The *Westburn* had managed to get off a call for help. It was taken in by a Spanish vessel bound from Cadiz to Tenerife, and Captain Buller was then only ninety miles away, steering almost directly for the *Moewe*. By noon he was only thirty miles from the scene of the *Horace's* destruction. Had he held on another half-hour he could scarcely have failed to see the *Moewe's* smoke. But, as luck would have it, he had not taken in the *Westburn's* call. So, instead of holding on for the position given, he made a cast for the west-north-westward, and did not turn back for the Rocks till 6.30. For three days more he actively patrolled the vicinity, but the *Moewe* was gone. How she avoided him we cannot tell. But she did, and while Captain Buller was still patrolling the area of her hairbreadth escape she had turned homewards.

Apparently Count zu Dohna, considering that the moral purpose of his cruise had been fulfilled, decided to run no further risk on the trade routes. For twelve days he made no more captures. The only ship he met with, being then 200 miles west-south-west of Madeira, was the passenger steamer *Demarara*, which showed him a clean pair of heels aud spread the alarm. But Count zu Dohna had not yet done. On February 24, far out in the Atlantic, he captured and sank the French ship *Maroni* (3,000 tons), and on the next day, the same fate befell the British steamer *Saxon Prince* (3,500 tons). After that nothing more was heard of him till, on March 5, it was publicly announced in Germany that he was home again. The official wireless message by

[1] Sunk off Tenerife on February 23.

which the news was spread gave a list of his prizes, and made clear at last that it was in the minefield he laid that the *King Edward VII* had perished.

An enterprise so successful, so brilliantly conducted and so inspiriting, could not but encourage further efforts of the same kind, and a revival of the hopeful days of the *Emden* and *Karlsruhe* seemed possible. It was only what Admiral Jellicoe had been expecting all through the winter. With unrelaxed attention he was still taking all possible precautions that the resources in his power permitted, and with good reason. The *Moewe* was not yet safely in a German port before the stirring effect of her success began to be felt.

About noon on February 28 the Admiralty had warned Admiral Jellicoe that a decoy ship, possibly with a submarine in company, was coming out of the Skagerrak. Two light cruisers and four destroyers were ordered away from Rosyth to intercept her if she came westward, and three other light cruisers from Scapa (*Calliope, Comus* and *Blanche*), each with a destroyer attached, were directed to search an area off the coast of Norway in case she came north. Shortly after midnight this route was indicated by our directional wireless finding a German ship close off Ekersund, on the south-west coast of Norway, and the Scapa light cruisers were ordered to search on an arc from that centre, while the *Columbella* and *Patia*, of the 10th Cruiser Squadron, were to take up a patrol line north-east from the north of the Shetlands. Two other ships of the squadron were in the same area, the *Andes* (Captain G. B. W. Young) having just arrived to relieve the *Alcantara* (Captain T. E. Wardle), which was on the point of going to Liverpool to re-coal, but before leaving the station Captain Wardle had arranged to meet his relief ship in mid-sea, sixty miles east of the north of the Shetlands. He was nearing the rendezvous when he was told not to quit the area till further orders, as a disguised enemy merchant auxiliary from the southward might pass the patrol line during the day. This was shortly after 8 a.m., and by 8.45, while steaming about north-north-east up the patrol line, he was aware of smoke on his port beam. Then came from the *Andes* the words "Enemy in sight north-east 15 knots," and at full speed he turned north-west. Almost immediately he sighted her. She was flying Norwegian colours and had one funnel, whereas a second message from his consort, as he took it in, described the enemy as having two. There was some doubt therefore whether she was what he was after, and in two or three minutes the doubt was increased by a sight of the *Andes* on his starboard bow steaming apparently fast north-east, as though in chase of something else. Before going to her assistance Captain Wardle felt he must examine his own chase. Two rounds of blank brought her to a standstill, but as the number she made could not be identified the *Alcantara* went to action stations and held on for the stranger with guns trained on her. By this time (9.20) Captain Wardle had heard from the *Andes* that her chase had altered south-east, and that she herself was following on the same course. This only increased the doubt. From the situation as he saw it the stranger he had in sight could not be the ship the *Andes* seemed to be chasing. Moreover he could now read *Rena* on her stern and her appearance corresponded to that ship. As he had full information about her particulars and voyage he determined to send an armed guard aboard of her, and informed Captain Young of his intention. Then as the boat was being lowered about 1,000 yards astern of the stranger came the startling reply, "This is the suspicious ship," and even as it was being read the *Rena's* ensign staff dropped over the stern, her poop steering box opened out to unmask a gun, falling flaps on her sides revealed others, and in a moment the *Alcantara* was under a hot fire. Before she could reply the boat was wrecked and her own telemotor steering gear disabled. But she was soon hard at work and doing great execution as she continued to close the now moving enemy. For a quarter of an hour the duel raged, with some assistance from the *Andes* as she came up, till the enemy was almost lost in a cloud of smoke. She had ceased fire, and out of the smother crowded boats could be seen leaving her. But the *Alcantara* was in no better case. She too had to cease fire with a heavy list to port. She had apparently been hit by a torpedo, and as she was obviously sinking Captain Wardle gave the order to abandon ship. The two auxiliaries had, in fact, fought each other to a finish in a spirit fully worthy of their betters. At about 11.0 a.m. the *Alcantara* was on her beam ends and quietly sank; 69 of her crew were missing. Captain A. G. Hotham in the *Comus*, the northernmost of the Scapa cruisers, had taken in the *Andes'* signals, and coming on at twenty-seven knots with his destroyer, the *Munster*, he was already in sight when the action ceased, and by the time the *Alcantara* sank the *Munster* was on the spot to save her crew. It was fortunate, for the look-out of the *Andes* had reported a submarine between her and the boats, and she could not approach. As for the chase, she was still afloat. Owing to further alarms of submarines the *Comus* and *Andes* forebore to close her, but finally sank her with deliberate fire with her German ensign still flying.

From the prisoners it was ascertained that she was a new ship built for the German Australian line, originally called the *Guben*, which had just been taken over by the Government and been secretly armed with four 5·9-inch guns and two torpedo tubes. Re-named the *Greif*, she had been commissioned with a crew of about 360, of whom 220 were saved by our vessels. Setting aside her torpedoes, of which she fired two, her gun-power was considerably superior to that of the *Alcantara*, and seeing that the British ship is believed to have succumbed to a torpedo, it is little wonder that Captain Wardle and his crew were adjudged to have "fought their ship in a creditable manner." The *Greif* had left Germany on February 27 under orders to proceed round the north of Iceland into the Atlantic to raid commerce, and if unable to get back she was to make for German East Africa, the only colony which was not yet in the Allies' hands.

The dispositions which so promptly cut short her career, it will have been observed, were made by Admiral Jellicoe. Admiral de Chair had nothing to do with them, for he was no longer in command. The political and administrative measures for crippling the enemy's resources culminated in the creation of a Ministry of Blockade under Lord Robert Cecil on February 23. A competent naval adviser was essential to its effective working, and Admiral de Chair's record made him the natural choice for the office. Thus when the action took place he was on his way in the *Alsatian* to Liverpool where he hauled down his flag on March 6. His successor was found in Vice-Admiral R. G. O. Tupper, who since the beginning of 1915 had been senior naval officer, Stornoway. In this position he had been practically a limb of the 10th Cruiser Squadron. His work had been in a great measure the same, and the able manner in which he performed the arduous and responsible duties of that tempestuous station, no less than the experience he had gained, naturally pointed him out as the man for the work.

His period of command began with long months of the usual exhausting routine unbroken by special incident. The sudden end to the *Greif's* activities marked for the time the cessation of the revival of the enemy's policy of cruiser-raiding on the ocean highways. Materially its success against commerce, though probably as good as the Germans expected, had been negligible, and the moral reasons which prompted it no longer existed, for once more the partisans of submarine warfare against Allied trade had gained the upper hand in the shifting counsels of the German State.

The long inaction to which, for political reasons, the German navy had been forced to submit was for our authorities difficult to interpret. The quiescence of the High Seas Fleet was the darkest part of the mystery. While to Admiral Jellicoe it seemed that it was only preparing to deal a desperate blow at some selected moment in the near future, the Admiralty took the opposite view, that it had no present intention of risking a battle. What they expected to be in preparation was a vigorous use of mines and submarines accompanied by a widespread attack on our commerce all over the world, of which the *Moewe's* raid was taken to be the prelude. The effective counter was a close blockade of the Bight, and the only way in which it could be done was to seize as a base for submarines and aircraft one of the islands off the Schleswig coast. This it was believed was a cardinal feature in Lord Fisher's rejected plan, and the outlook was now grave enough for the idea to be revived. But conditions had changed. The range and number of heavy artillery had so much increased that all the islands were open to a bombardment from the mainland that would render any one of them untenable as a naval base. Apart from this, the execution of the plan raised very great difficulties. The operating force of old battleships, monitors and cruisers would require for their protection a large number of destroyers, which could only be taken from the Grand Fleet, as the Dardanelles operations left us no residue of light craft from which to draw. As a result the Grand Fleet would be driven to cover the operation without its usual complement of flotillas; an objection which, to the Admiralty, seemed without remedy. After full consideration by the Government, the project was, therefore, set aside, and beyond continual cruiser and destroyer sweeps against the enemy's coastwise trade, and to intercept minelayers, which had no success, our offensive was confined to the air.

Since December a plan had been in preparation by which Commodore Tyrwhitt, with the bulk of the Harwich Force and some submarines, was to take the seaplane carrier *Vindex* close up to the estuary of the Ems and endeavour to bomb the airship bases at Hage, north of Emden and Hoyer, on the Schleswig coast. On January 18 the attempt on Hage was made, but before the final position was reached a dense fog came down which rendered further operations useless, and the force could only withdraw. There had been no sign of interference, and the retirement was made leisurely and without loss, except for one of the submarines, *H 6*, which grounded off the Ameland Gat. Ten days later the attempt was renewed. This time the weather was favourable. By 5.0 a.m. on January 29 Commodore Tyrwhitt had reached the assigned position, and the *Vindex* was hoisting out her seaplanes when a torpedo grazed the stern of the *Arethusa*, which was still carrying his broad pendant. Another quickly followed, which also narrowly missed. No sign of a submarine was seen, but clearly the enemy were on the alert, and seeing it was useless to carry on, the Commodore again withdrew, and as he did so the force was enveloped in a fog which in any case would have rendered the operation abortive.

With this failure the deadlock seemed more immovable than ever. But, in fact, unknown to us, it was beginning to break. Early in January Admiral von Pohl, stricken with a mortal sickness, had to resign the command of the High Seas Fleet, and on the 18th, the day Commodore Tyrwhitt was starting his first raid on the Emden aerodromes, Admiral Scheer was formally appointed Commander-in-Chief. He it was who had been in command of the new Third Squadron, recently completed to seven Dreadnoughts of the latest type, and for Chief of his Staff he chose Captain von Trotha, who had been commanding the *Kaiser* under him. No two men had chafed more restlessly under the defensive policy of the Government, and once in chief command Admiral Scheer began to press urgently for the change which his predecessor had been already advocating. While recognising that the fleet had hitherto played as good a part as its weakness permitted—relieving the army from coast defence and keeping doubtful States neutral (by which he apparently meant Holland and Scandinavia)—he realised that this would no longer serve. The " hunger blockade " was being too severely felt, and Germany could not endure the strain nearly so long as her arch enemy. Moreover the British military power was growing rapidly, and this in Admiral Scheer's opinion was a sure sign that the determination for war was increasing in order to make up for the mistakes which had been made, the chief of which he, like all German strategists, held to be the surrender of Antwerp and the abandonment of the Dardanelles. By some means or other the British sea-power must be broken. In battle there lay no hope, for it was only under exceptionally advantageous conditions in their own prepared waters that it was possible to meet the Grand Fleet with success, and that was a chance it was vain to expect. The British people, he was sure, knew too well the security Admiral Jellicoe was giving them as he sat immovably on the ocean communications ever to throw it away by clamouring for a hazardous advance into German waters. But short of that he believed that with his increased forces much might be done to make them weary of the war, and he lost no time in bracing the fleet for the schemes that were teeming in his mind.[1]

It was not long before Whitehall began to feel the stir of his vigorous personality. On February 9 the Admiralty warned the Commander-in-Chief, as well as Admiral Beatty at Rosyth, that the German fleet was showing signs of activity. They were, therefore, ordered to move south and concentrate, while Commodore Tyrwhitt was to watch off Texel. In a few hours, however, they were told to stand fast, but the indications that something was in the wind continued, until on February 10 it was discovered that a considerable force of light cruisers and destroyers was proceeding west from the Jade. A raid on our coast being suspected, Admiral Beatty was ordered south to cut them off as they returned, and Commodore Tyrwhitt to put to sea. But scarcely had they started when the blow, such as it was, had fallen. To the eastward of the Dogger Bank the newly formed 10th Sloop Flotilla (*Buttercup*, *Arabis*, *Alyssum* and *Poppy*) had during the week been sweeping one of the war channels which were constantly kept clear for the concentration of the fleet. On the previous day they had run into Bridlington bay for a few hours and had put to sea again before the Admiralty got the alarm. As a rigid wireless silence had been ordered for fear of alarming the High Seas Fleet, which was then believed to be coming out, they could not be reached. All day on the 10th they continued sweeping, and at nightfall marked their progress with a lighted dan buoy. The *Arabis* (Lieutenant-Commander R. R. Hallowell-Carew) was ordered to stand by it while the other three steamed on and off. In so doing towards midnight they were aware of the tracks of torpedoes passing through the line, and they turned away. At the same time the *Arabis* was engaged with three destroyers. There was a sharp fight, but her steam-pipe was soon cut and her wireless disabled, so that she could neither manœuvre nor call up her consorts. Still so spirited was her reply that the enemy hauled off, apparently for reinforcements, for presently she was attacked by six destroyers, which soon brought her to a standstill and sank her with torpedoes. Lieutenant-Commander

[1] Scheer, p. 96. The whole passage is specially noteworthy in view of the criticism of Admiral Jellicoe's attitude, which was widely circulated in some of the British Press at the time.

Hallowell-Carew[1] and one other officer, one warrant officer and eleven ratings were rescued by the Germans, and treated with all the honour and courtesy his conduct had won them. His consorts all escaped, and the enemy retired without further action. The mountain had been in labour, but nothing had been brought forth beyond a strong destroyer patrol. It had been sent out apparently for no particular purpose as part of the method by which Admiral Scheer was tuning up his fleet for the part he was determined to see it play —and to this all the alarms were due.

The loss of the *Arabis* was in itself no serious matter, but unhappily it did not stand alone. As soon as the insignificance of the German operation was known, Commodore Tyrwhitt was recalled, and was leading his Light Cruiser Squadron into Harwich through the Sledway channel, which was believed to be clear, when the *Arethusa* struck a mine which had been laid by the *UC 7* on the previous night, (9th), close to the North Cutler buoy. The explosion killed six men. Her engines stopped at once and she began to settle, yet, in spite of the heavy sea that was running against the tide, the flotilla leader, *Lightfoot* (Commander C. K. MacLean), got her in tow, but the hawser parted. Lieutenant-Commander F. Burges Watson then tried with the *Loyal*, but only with the same result, and the *Arethusa* drove upon the Cutler shoal and broke in two. Not till then did Commodore Tyrwhitt order her to be abandoned, transferring his broad pendant to the *Lightfoot*. Till August the ship whose name he had rendered worthy of her famous predecessor lay where she was, when all hope of salving her was abandoned and she was left to break up.

In the approaches to the Thames and the Straits of Dover these enemy submarines were specially active. During January and February a number of vessels fell victims to them, about half of which were neutrals from Holland and Norway. More and more boldly were their operations pushed home, till on February 27 the P. & O. liner *Maloja*, (12,431 tons), was struck within half a mile of the entrance to Dover harbour with a loss of 122 lives, and the Canadian *Empress of Fort William* was mined in going to her assistance. The next day two trawlers were lost in locating the new field, and a Dutch steamer with passengers foundered in the same way at the Galloper. No device had yet been hit upon for checking the trouble, and the only submarine encountered at this time was the *UC 6* which on January 11 the armed

[1] Awarded the D.S.O. in 1919 for his service on this occasion.

yacht *James Fletcher* met near the Goodwins and rammed. The submarine, however, was able to return to Zeebrugge for repairs. Since the stoppage of all other submarine operations against trade in the declared war zone, mining, and the almost negligible bombing from the air, were all the Germans could do in reply to our blockade.[1] It was with countering these efforts that Admiral Bacon at Dover, and Admiral Sir George Callaghan at the Nore, were mainly occupied. At Dover Admiral Bacon still had the monitors ready for any calls that General Foch might make for assistance on the Belgian coast. One such call was made towards the end of January. It was for a bombardment of the Villa Scolaire batteries in conjunction with the French army. On the 26th it was carried out by five heavy monitors protected by the Dunkirk drifter flotilla, Admiral Bacon flying his flag in the *General Wolfe*, with Rear-Admiral de Marliave representing the French as his second-in-command in the *Lord Clive*. There was no reply from the enemy, but what, if any, damage was done could not be ascertained. Then, so multifarious were the duties of this hardworked force, that an order came to mass the monitors, light and heavy, in the mouth of the Thames, to protect London against Zeppelin raids during the coming favourable phase of the moon.[2] There were nine monitors in all, and for a week they kept their watch. On January 31 the expected raid took place; but the attacking airships were too far north for our forces in the Thames to be of any use; nor could the Harwich Force move out to intercept them owing to fog. The raid was very severe. Nine Zeppelins passed over the coasts of Norfolk and Lincoln between 5.0 and 7.30 in the evening and went further inland than they had ever done before; Burton, Derby and six other towns were all bombed during the night.[3] Apart from this, the Germans did not risk their airships during the winter, and their bombing raids were confined to aeroplanes and seaplanes. On January 23 and 24 the Downs and our aerodrome at Capel were bombed, and several attempts were made on shipping in the Thames estuary. On February 1 the Admiralty collier *Franz Fischer*

[1] Other minelaying submarines of the Flanders Flotilla active at this time were the *UC 1, 3, 5* and *10*.

[2] On September 3, 1914, the Government had decided to give the navy charge of the air defences of the country, and a year later (September 12, 1915) Admiral Sir Percy Scott became responsible for the special defence of London. On February 10, 1916, the army took over the whole organisation ashore, the navy being left to deal with aircraft on their way oversea to attack.

[3] One of the raiders, *L 19*, sank in the North Sea on her way home on February 2. She was sighted in a sinking condition by the trawler *King Stephen*. For full details of this raid see *The War in the Air*, Vol. III, pp. 135–44.

was sunk when at anchor near the Kentish Knock, and this loss has been recorded as the first caused by a bomb dropped from a Zeppelin. There is, however, no doubt that the real agent of her destruction was a torpedo from the German submarine *UB 17*.[1] On the 20th seaplanes attacked the Kentish coast and Lowestoft with little damage; and on March 1 a number of bombs were dropped on the Margate area, which did considerable damage at Cliftonville. On the 19th a heavy daylight raid on Dover and Ramsgate resulted in the loss of thirteen lives and injury to twenty-six people.[2] A hundred houses at Dover were damaged but otherwise in a military sense the raids were ineffective.

[1] *Der Krieg zur See: Der Handelskrieg mit U-Booten*, Vol. III, p. 82.
[2] *The War in the Air*, Vol. II, p. 430.

CHAPTER XIV

CALL OF THE GERMAN ARMY FOR NAVAL ASSISTANCE AND THE CATASTROPHE OF THE *SUSSEX*

ALL that the enemy had been able to do against us in Home waters during the winter amounted to little more than pin-pricks, but they were an irritation which acted like a spur to the keenness to bring the High Seas Fleet to action. The hopes which the signs of its restlessness had aroused were dying away. Yet, unknown to us, there was developing in Germany itself a situation which, as though the hand of destiny was upon men whom the gods had doomed to perish, was pushing her to her fate.

Between the Chancellor and the naval and military headquarters the struggle over the use of submarines had never ceased to smoulder since, in September, after the destruction of the *Arabic*, the order had gone forth " to cease all forms of submarine warfare on the west coast of Great Britain or in the Channel." Under such a prohibition the navy could not sit quiet, and Admiral von Pohl, some time before his death (February 23), had represented that it would compel him to reconsider the passive attitude of his command. The Note in which the United States on November 5, 1915, had emphasised their protest against the blockade had encouraged the German Government slightly to relax the restrictions with which they had fettered the navy, and on the 15th " U " boats were authorised to sink at sight all enemy ships entering or leaving French ports between Le Havre and Dunkirk, but neutrals as well as passenger and hospital ships were to be spared. Seeing how many merchant vessels were now defensively armed, and how great was the danger of approaching them to ascertain their character, it was but a small concession, but still a step towards the unrestricted warfare for which the navy was striving, and now the army was coming into line. The sanguine illusions with which the Great General Staff plunged into the war had faded away. Their cherished doctrine was failing them. The cardinal article of their creed was to crush the armed forces of the enemy by a swift and unrelenting offensive. But the preponderance of strength and energy that is essential to the method was no longer theirs, and they had to face the disquieting fact that they were practically reduced to the defensive. To some extent our failures in Mesopotamia and the Dardanelles relieved the gloom of their outlook, but although they told as points of brightness, they were casting ominous shadows. Ill-planned as these adventures were, they had been too well chosen as strategical objectives to be unproductive. As diversions their effect had been far-reaching. They had compelled the Central Powers to spend their existing balance of offensive strength in the Balkans, and had forced the Turks to concentrate on the defence of their capital. As a direct consequence Russia was able to seize Erzerum (February 16), and she was beginning to push southwards towards Mesopotamia and to the northward menaced the vital Black Sea port of Trebizond. She was even attempting a new offensive in Galicia, with the obvious intention of depriving Germany of her last source of food supply in Rumania, but from this there was little to fear, seeing how unmistakable were the signs of internal unrest in Russia. It was in the western theatre that Germany's outlook was gravest, and it must be frankly appreciated if we are to judge with any fairness the desperate expedient to which she was about to be driven.

We can see it all with the eyes of the German High Command in an appreciation which at the end of the year General von Falkenhayn, Chief of the Great General Staff, prepared for his new year's report to the Emperor.[1] For him Great Britain, with her strangle-hold upon the sea, was the arch enemy, and the key of the whole war problem was how to break her domination over the other Entente Powers, and tire the British people of the struggle. The method he proposed was to give the German defensive the most active possible energy. Italy could be left to Austria now that the menace of Serbia was removed. It was against France, "England's most trenchant sword," as he called her, that the prospects seemed most promising. He saw her on the brink of exhaustion, and, devotedly as she was enduring her sacrifices, he believed that any severe moral shock would bring the tension to breaking strain, and close in rear of the French lines, before Belfort and Verdun, were the required objectives for the limited offensive still open to him. Verdun was his choice, for here the dangerous salient which the Germans had failed to drive in with their first rush still formed a sally port from which their whole line of defence could be brought to ruin.

[1] See von Falkenhayn, *General Headquarters*, 1914–1916, p. 209 *et. seq.*

But the highest success he could hope for at this point would not suffice. Even if France were lost to Great Britain —nay, even if all her allies failed her—it was only too probable she would continue the struggle alone, as she had done in the last great war, a century before. Without simultaneous blows delivered directly at her national existence, the policy he formulated would be useless. For this purpose, contrary to the belief that prevailed in high quarters on our own side, he held the army to be powerless. The memorandum indeed passed the point as beyond controversy, and no feature of it is of so permanent an interest, since our failure to appreciate it was the source of so much of the embarrassment which crippled our offensive action up to the end. "The island itself," he pronounced, "cannot be reached by our troops. Of that the navy is profoundly convinced." Since, therefore, as he had demonstrated, there was no chance of dealing England a decisive blow on the continent or in the east, nothing remained but the unrestricted use of submarines on her sea communications. In that way alone could the navy give the necessary assistance to the army, and only with a free hand could they do it.

But here the spectre of America stood in the path. As he frankly admitted, unrestricted action would mean her hostility; but if the definite promise of the navy were justified, she would not be able to interfere before the arch enemy was terrorised into peace by famine. True, it was possible the promise might not be fulfilled—past experience was none too encouraging—but the dockyards were ringing with new submarine construction, and with the already increased numbers at their disposal there was good ground for confidence and none for not using ruthlessly their most effective weapon. No doubt he felt that his ruthless proposals might raise qualms of conscience, but Britain's unconscionable behaviour at sea justified it. America, of course, would not admit the plea, and was not likely to intervene actively on the continent of Europe.

So with all the dangers of his proposal faced and half brushed aside, he turned to the navy for assistance. Hitherto the assistance it had given to the army had been confined to the defensive. Its value as an adjunct to the army had been used only to relieve the land forces of the distraction of coast defence. Now something more, on British lines, was to be required of it. The navy was only too ready to respond, and the High Command (Jan. 7) gave the assurance that if once the submarines were given full freedom of action they could bring Great Britain to her knees in six months. But the Chancellor was unconvinced. The arguments used to substantiate the assurance were questionable, and the Foreign Office still had hanging over their heads the shadow of the *Arabic*, now deepened by the strong Notes which the Austro-Hungarian Government had just received from the United States over the *Ancona* incident, in addition to which the demands of America in regard to the *Lusitania* were not yet settled.[1]

But now suddenly the naval and military combination found further assistance, and it came from the most unexpected quarter. On January 18, with the best intention in the world, Washington presented a new Note on the submarine question, and this time it was addressed to all the Entente Powers. Hitherto the Americans had grounded their objections on the danger to American citizens. Now they took a higher stand as the guardians of humanity. The destruction of merchant ships without securing the safety of their crews was denounced as incompatible with the principles which should control the conduct of naval operations, but at the same time they admitted that submarines must be recognised as a legitimate instrument for the interruption of enemy commerce. On this basis the Note formulated proposals for bringing submarine warfare "within the rules of International Law and the principles of humanity." Before attack ships should be summoned to stop, and none must be destroyed till all on board had been removed to a place of safety, nor should any ship be attacked unless she attempted to escape or resist. So far the proposals were but a plain reassertion of the tradition by which every Entente Power was ready to abide. But, unhappily, the Note went further. As a corollary it declared that merchantmen should cease to be armed. Admittedly the demand was not within the tradition, but it was urged that the submarine was a new development of warfare and its fragility on the surface justified the departure. Without such a concession the recognition of the submarine as a commerce destroyer under the restrictions proposed would be nugatory, and the suggestion was backed by a plain hint that in the event of the proposal being rejected they intended to treat all armed merchantmen as auxiliary cruisers liable to internment.[2]

[1] The *Ancona*, a large Italian passenger steamer with American citizens on board, had been torpedoed by the *U38* flying the Austrian flag in the Western Mediterranean on November 7. The Austro-Hungarian Government conducted the consequent diplomatic correspondence.

[2] American opinion was sharply divided as to the propriety of this attitude, and afterwards, when the Note was made public, the right to arm merchantmen for defence was so warmly maintained as an established usage by Senators Lodge and Sterling that the objections to it were dropped.

The solution of the difficulty was plausible enough, but it had the one fatal flaw that the ancient right of arming merchant vessels was one we felt unable to forgo. Possibly, in view of later experience, it would have been better if we had done so, provided always that Germany had been loyal to the proposed restrictions, but at that time the mistrust which her treachery to Belgium had engendered had killed all possibility of crediting her good faith, and the Note could not be accepted.

No one doubted the high motives of the American Government, but unfortunately the consequences of this move were not what they hoped. German sailors knew that for submarines to act in accordance with the old rules of commerce warfare so long as any merchant vessels were armed and retained the right to resist, was impossible. It was on this very ground they were pressing the Government to allow them greater liberty of action, and the Note played directly into their hands. The veiled menace with which it ended was especially unfortunate. The almost incredible capacity which the Germans displayed for misunderstanding the psychology of their opponents during the war was one of its surprises, and they at once rushed blindly to a false deduction. In the tone of the Note's conclusion they read a determination of the United States to retaliate against the British blockade. In vain their Ambassador warned them that the feeling which dominated American public opinion was resentment at the sinking of the *Lusitania*. His words fell on deaf ears. It was on fear of American hostility that Ministers were basing their opposition to the fighting services, and the ground was so far undermined by the Note that the Chancellor could no longer stand firm. The most he could do was to plead for delaying unrestricted warfare at least till April, that he might improve the diplomatic opening that had been given for coming to an agreement with America. In this attitude he was supported by Admiral von Holtzendorff, the new Chief of the Naval Staff, on the ground that by that time new submarine construction would amply compensate for the delay, and so far he succeeded in restraining his sanguine opponents. In February, orders for a revival of the submarine campaign were issued, but under restrictions which gave them at least a colourable appearance of meeting American views. Submarines were again to act against commerce "according to the rules of prize law for the time being." Armed merchantmen and transports were to be sunk at sight, but on no account were passenger ships to be attacked. The immediate result of the well-meaning Note was that in the latter part of February submarines reappeared on the old hunting grounds off our west coasts. During the following month the usual succession of two boats in consort was maintained, and in the space of four weeks they accounted for the total destruction in these waters of 35,000 tons, besides a number of ships damaged.

In America the new orders, combined with the promptitude with which they were executed, made a very bad impression. It is difficult to believe that the Germans really imagined that, ingeniously as the orders seemed to them to be worded, they could avert the storm that was brewing across the Atlantic. Yet so it was, and they continued to plunge blindly forward nearer and nearer to the abyss they most wished to avoid. For the unequivocal advocates of unrestricted submarine warfare the half loaf they had been given only strengthened their determination to get the whole. From a purely military point of view the attitude they took up was exceptionally strong. Except on political grounds there was, in fact, no disputing their declaration that if the "U" boat campaign was to bring the relief which the High Command regarded as essential for avoiding a disastrous end to the war, it must be carried on ruthlessly. But there was just the point on which the Chancellor's opposition turned. If ruthlessness was essential to the "U" boats' success, their success could not save the country, for the moral and political reactions would bring new forces into the war against which Germany could not hope to stand. Yet, where else was ultimate victory to be looked for—nay, more, how else could they avoid defeat?

In the eyes of the High Command the need of taking the final step was growing daily more insistent. The attack on the Verdun salient began on February 21. For a fortnight the battle raged, and no real success had been won against the heroic French resistance. The goal was still far away, and when it was reached the end would be no nearer. Even if Verdun fell, it meant, as the Chief of the Staff knew, little more than improvement of the German line of defence. A war of endurance would still have to be faced. But it was the Chancellor's turn to play. He was on the point of opening the negotiations for which he had stipulated. At Washington the German Ambassador was preparing the ground, and his way of doing it was to try to persuade the American Government to prevent their citizens from travelling in armed merchantmen. The move was typical of the maladroitness which did so much to injure the German cause. With a complete lack of sympathetic understanding it ignored the all-important fact that President Wilson's idealism had now taken its stand on the interests of humanity at large. It demanded, moreover, an interference with the cherished liberty of American citizens in the interest of a foreign Power, and the result was a further exasperation of American resentment.

If the Great General Staff and the Naval High Command had no faith in such diplomacy, it is no matter for wonder. Their expostulation continued, and it resulted in a joint conference at Pless. It was held on March 6, and no summons to attend it was sent to Admiral von Tirpitz. Now that the number of submarines warranted unrestricted warfare he was the most powerful advocate of ruthlessness, and the slight brought about his long-threatened resignation. Yet, although the Chancellor procured as his successor at the Admiralty Admiral von Capelle, a man of his own way of thinking, General von Falkenhayn's support of the navy's demands was so strong that again he had to give way a step. Unrestricted warfare was still to be postponed, but he had to consent to the submarine orders being "sharpened." Officers were now (March 13) directed to sink without warning all British vessels found within the war area, with the exception of passenger ships. Seeing what the Ambassador was trying to do in Washington, nothing could well have been more exasperating to the resentment which he was hoping to placate. Still the ruthless party had gained an advance, little thinking it was to lead in precisely the opposite direction to that they expected.

The startling result came quickly. About 3.0 in the afternoon of March 24 Lieutenant Pustkuchen, in *UB* 29, of the Flanders flotilla, encountered a steamer between Dungeness and Boulogne, and torpedoed her without warning.[1] His first explanation seems to have been that from her crowded decks he took her to be a transport, but as she proved to be the *Sussex*, which was the regular packet plying between Folkestone and Dieppe, the excuse would hardly serve, and it was afterwards maintained that he mistook her for "one of the new minelayers of the 'Arabis' class." [2] She had, in fact, 380 passengers on board, many of whom were killed or injured by the explosion which blew up her bows. With better luck, however, than the *Lusitania*, she remained afloat, but in imminent danger of sinking before any assistance arrived.

Her S.O.S. signal, as taken in an hour later, placed her

[1] Gayer, Vol. III., p. 48

[2] *Sussex*, 1350 tons, owned by the French State Railways, and managed by the London Brighton and South Coast Railway.

well within the French patrol sphere. Admiral de Vigneau sent out all available help; Admiral Bacon despatched the *Amazon*, and at 9.0, when he heard the French had failed to find her, he ordered all ready destroyers to join the search. At 11.10 the *Afridi* found her still afloat about fourteen miles west of Boulogne, with a French trawler alongside taking off the women and children.[1] Eventually 250 survivors were landed at Boulogne and 120 at Dover. Nine of the crew had made off to the Colbart light-vessel. The destroyer *Greyhound* was dispatched to bring them back, and while so engaged in the early hours of the next morning a torpedo passed six feet ahead of her. As further evidence that a submarine was at work in the area, another ship, the *Salybia*, homeward bound from the West Indies, was torpedoed as she was approaching Dungeness about two hours after the *Sussex* was struck. Both ships were towed into port, but that slight alleviation of the disaster could make no difference to the consequences.

Seeing that amongst the passengers in the *Sussex* were several American citizens, and that the German Ambassador had just opened his tactless negotiations for an agreement in Washington, the incident could only be taken both as a glaring evidence of bad faith and an intolerable defiance. To add to the gravity of the incident two Spanish subjects had been killed by the explosion, so that Spain, to whose benevolent neutrality Germany attached great importance, joined her protests to those of America. At his wits' end how to weather the storm the German Foreign Minister lost his head, and in his reply to America endeavoured to attribute the disaster to a mine. But the evidence of submarine work was too clear, and his idle excuse only fanned the flames. The German Ambassador, Count Bernstorff, has characterised the communication as the most unfortunate document that ever passed from Berlin to Washington. Having taken full time to probe the facts to the bottom, the United States Government presented a Note whose plain speaking left nothing to be desired. After exposing the German position with merciless frankness, it closed with this unequivocal declaration, " Unless the Imperial Government should now immediately declare and effect an abandonment of its present methods of submarine warfare against passenger and freight-carrying vessels, the Government of the United States can have no choice but to sever diplomatic relations with the German Empire altogether." (April 18.)

[1] The difficulty in finding her was due to the fact that her position as given in the S.O.S. signal was fifteen miles in error.

It was not till April 20, nearly a month after the offence, that the Note reached the German Foreign Office. The deliberation with which it had been presented only added to its weight, and the Chancellor, who was at Army Headquarters, hurried to Berlin. All Easter Sunday and Monday an Imperial Council sat in distracted session. The Chancellor and his satellite Herr Helfferich, the Secretary of State, were for temporising with a reply that would use the President's desire for " Freedom of the Seas " to entangle the two questions. The Chief of the Naval Staff, on the other hand, while ready to conduct submarine operations under the recognised rules of visit and search applicable to cruisers, was firm for no further concession to America. A middle course was sought, but the Spanish Ambassador, being in intimate touch with his American colleague, was able to inform them that Washington would be satisfied with nothing less than unconditional acceptance. At Headquarters General von Falkenhayn was pressing the Emperor to cede nothing.[1] At Verdun he was making little progress. Its reduction would obviously take a long time, and he had told the Emperor plainly that success was impossible unless the enemy's supplies from overseas were interrupted. Only by unrestricted action by the submarines could this be done. The Chief of the Naval Staff was as firm as ever that this was the only way in which the navy could co-operate with the army, since, owing to the superiority of the British, any attempt to use the High Seas Fleet, except in specially favourable tactical conditions, would only jeopardise defence of the coast, the command of the Baltic, and consequently the vital flow of Swedish ore to German ports.

His protests were useless, for while the decision swayed in the balance news came in which so far brightened the outlook at sea as to cut from under his feet the main part of the ground on which he had taken his stand.

[1] Helfferich, *Der Weltkrieg*, II., pp. 341–3.

CHAPTER XV

THE AIR-RAID ON THE SCHLESWIG AIR BASE AND THE BOMBARDMENT OF LOWESTOFT

WHETHER or not the Spanish Ambassador's solemn warning would have turned the scale without added weight we cannot tell, but by a bold stroke Admiral Scheer had created the impression that it was not by unrestricted submarine warfare alone that the navy could influence the situation. He too agreed that nothing could be done against the Grand Fleet except in specially favourable tactical conditions. But he was not content to wait for them to appear. Ever since his accession to the command he had never ceased to work for an opening and to fit the fleet for taking advantage of the moment when it occurred, while, as an essential preliminary to the offensive scheme he had in mind, he was doing everything possible to make his home waters in the Bight impervious to attack.

Having been accorded a fairly free hand with his battle cruisers and light forces, his general idea was to use them in such a way as to entice similar enemy units acting against them within reach of his battle fleet, and so produce the stipulated situation of exceptional tactical advantage. He began cautiously in the first week in March with an attempt to entrap our southern forces. Sections of them were so continually operating in what the Germans called the Hoofden, that he hoped, by a move against them with a strong cruiser force, to draw out a similar force to the rescue, and by judicious dispositions entice it between his cruisers and the battle fleet.[1] The movement began on March 5, the day after the *Moewe* returned. The general idea was for the cruiser force to be off Terschelling at daybreak, and then to advance to the limit of the British minefield, while, at an interval of thirty miles, the two Dreadnought squadrons would follow them until 10.0 a.m. Each section of the force was attended by two flotillas of destroyers, and, as security against surprise, one airship accompanied the fleet and three others recon-

[1] The Hoofden or Flanders bight corresponds to our southern area—that is, the portion of the North Sea which narrows down south of the Wash-Terschelling line between the coasts of East Anglia and Holland.

noitred well to the northward with instructions, if conditions were favourable, to bomb Rosyth. The movement was further supported by twelve submarines of the Flanders Flotilla, who took station on our south-east coast. But no enemy was seen, and nothing came of it except the air-raid. Struggling through storms of snow and hail and an increasing north-westerly wind, which drove them off their course, two of the airships (*L 11* and *L 14*) found themselves towards midnight crossing the coastline south of Flamborough Head, and made for Hull. As the clouds cleared and revealed a starlit sky, the snow-clad landscape and the course of the Humber could be read like a map, and though the town was well darkened it was easily located. Its streets, quay and harbour basins were seen below as though drawn on a sheet of white paper, and a number of bombs were dropped, but without any military effect.[1] Thence Immingham was found and treated in the same way, but here searchlights and anti-aircraft guns interfered, and little damage was done. Both ships returned in safety and were only just in time to escape the full fury of the weather, which had developed into a heavy easterly gale, and put a stop to all further activities.

How far the German fleet advanced was unknown. So far as we could ascertain it never went beyond Terschelling. Early on March 6 we discovered it was in that vicinity, and the Grand Fleet was ordered to make a sweep to the southward, while Commodore Tyrwhitt with the Harwich Force and a group of submarines to act with him was sent to the North Hinder to reconnoitre, with orders, if pressed, to retire on the Dover Straits. By midday, however, it was clear the enemy were still in the Terschelling area, moving north, and that they intended to return to harbour at dark. Commodore Tyrwhitt was recalled during the evening, and the Commander-in-Chief, who continued to push southwards until he learned there was no chance of contact with the retiring enemy, turned back about 10.0 p.m., and the episode came to an end without result.[2]

[1] The actual damage done was less than the Germans believed. Four terraces of houses were destroyed, and the casualties were seventeen killed and fifty-two injured.

[2] It was not only by his handling of the fleet that Admiral Scheer sought to remove from the navy the reproach of inactivity. He afterwards continued the work with his pen. Commenting on this affair he wrote: "On the occasion of the advance of March 5–6, as we learnt afterwards by intercepted wireless messages, the enemy preferred withdrawing all his forces into port as soon as he had news of the advance" (*High Seas Fleet*, p. 123). The facts, of course, were the exact reverse. The alleged intercepted messages can only have been the usual recall of the auxiliary patrol and minesweepers.

Why the German attempt was not repeated at once is not clear. It was not that our light forces did not offer plenty of opportunity. Within the next fortnight cruiser sweeps were made to the Norwegian coast in search of German merchant vessels, with the object of enticing the enemy to sea. Again, on March 20, an extensive mining operation was started to close the mid-sea approaches to the Thames and to the straits of Dover between the North Hinder and Galloper. The work was entrusted to four minelayers from Sheerness, *Paris*, *Biarritz*, *Princess Margaret* and *Orvieto*, escorted by two divisions of destroyers from Harwich. Simultaneously an air-raid in force was to be made on the Houtlave aerodrome, near Zeebrugge, from which originated the incessant raids on the Kentish coast and Dunkirk. About fifty bombing aeroplanes, British, French and Belgian, with fifteen fighting machines, were assigned to it, and the *Riviera* and *Vindex* were to co-operate with their seaplanes by attacking the seaplane base on the Zeebrugge Mole. For escort they were given a division of the 9th Flotilla, *Lance* (Commander W. de M. Egerton), *Lookout*, *Lucifer* and *Linnet*, which incidentally also covered the minelayers. Owing to the *Orvieto* running aground they were delayed some hours. The minelaying had not yet begun when at 8.0 a.m. Commander Egerton's division patrolling near the North Hinder light-vessel was attacked by three large German destroyers, but after a sharp little action, in which the *Lance* suffered somewhat severely, they were driven off, and the minelaying proceeded without interruption. Two lines were laid that day, and a third line on the 23rd. It was reported that considerable damage had been done at Zeebrugge by the aeroplanes, all of which returned in safety.

Two days later another air-raid was attempted from the sea, and as it was supported in force it gave Admiral Scheer, as he says, an opportunity of testing his preparations. The Hull airship raid, no less than the previous one on January 31, had shown us that little reliance could be placed on cruisers for intercepting such attacks at sea. With the coming of spring, therefore, the more drastic method of destroying the airship bases by counter-attack had been revived, and it was decided to carry out a plan which Commodore Tyrwhitt had been elaborating.[1] The objective was the Zeppelin station which was believed to exist at Hoyer, on the coast of Schleswig, behind the island of Sylt.[2] The attacking force was to be seven seaplanes (afterwards reduced

[1] The plan was first suggested by Commodore Murray F. Sueter.
[2] See Map 13.

to five), carried in the *Vindex*, which was to take them well inside the Vyl light-vessel, south of Horn Reefs, under escort of the whole available Harwich Force, with Admiral Beatty and the Battle Cruiser Fleet from Rosyth in support.[1]

Starting at daybreak on March 24, Commodore Tyrwhitt made his way south of the German mid-sea mined area.[2] It was bitterly cold throughout the day and night, with constant snow squalls, but by 4.30 next morning he was well inside the Vyl light-vessel, and the *Vindex* was ordered to proceed further in towards the Graa Deep light-vessel. Scarcely was she away with her escorting destroyers when a torpedo narrowly missed the *Cleopatra*, (Commodore's broad pendant), and gave warning of submarines being about, but the usual precautions were taken, and nothing further happened.[3] By 5.30 the *Vindex* got her seaplanes away, and stood by, waiting for their return, with her destroyers circling round her and two patrolling to the south-eastward, while the Commodore patrolled east of the Vyl light-vessel.

The weather was getting worse, and while he awaited the return of the seaplanes the snowstorms grew heavier and more frequent, till about 7.0 the first two machines appeared. They had to report there was nothing at Hoyer, but that a base had been formed further inland at Tondern. Only one of them, however, had located it, but her dropping gear had jammed, and she brought all her bombs back. Of the others there was no sign, and at 7.45 the Commodore ordered his two flotilla leaders, *Lightfoot* and *Nimrod*, with the remaining eight destroyers, to sweep south-east for them while he himself searched the Graa Deep.[4] So far no enemy had been seen, but towards 9.0 the destroyer sweep, having pushed as far as Röm island, had just turned to seaward, when they sighted two armed trawlers. The Germans, in continual expectation of a powerful stroke against the Bight, had elaborated as part of its defence a system of trawler outposts, and these two belonged to the group which watched

[1] Commodore Tyrwhitt's force consisted of the 5th Light Cruiser Squadron, *Cleopatra* (broad pendant), *Penelope* and *Conquest*; two flotilla cruisers, *Aurora* and *Undaunted*; two flotilla leaders, *Nimrod* and *Lightfoot*; two divisions of the 10th Flotilla, *Meteor*, *Mastiff*, *Minos*, *Manly*, *Medusa*, *Murray*, *Mansfield* and *Morris*; and two of the 9th, *Laforey*, *Liberty*, *Llewellyn*, *Laurel*, *Laertes*, *Lassoo*, *Laverock* and *Linnet*.

[2] This area, known to us as "Area I," lay about half-way between the Danish and Northumbrian coasts. It was of rhomboidal shape, thirty miles from south to north, and fifty from south-west to north-east.

[3] There is no record of German submarines being present, but one of our own, *H 7*, had left Yarmouth for these waters on March 19.

[4] The pilots of these three machines were taken prisoner.

the Lister Deep between the islands of Röm and Sylt. After a few minutes' chase both were sunk. While our people were picking up survivors aeroplanes appeared and began to bomb them. No destroyer was hit, though the Germans believed a bomb fell on one of them. But in fact the supposed success was the result of an accident. As Commander R. G. Rowley-Conwy of the *Nimrod* was re-forming his flotilla to carry on the search, the *Medusa* was rammed by the *Laverock*, and so severe was the damage that she could not steam more than six knots. The situation thus suddenly became full of anxiety. The disaster occurred right in the northern exit from the Bight, and it was to be presumed that the trawlers had given warning before they sank, and in any case the enemy's aircraft had located them.

The Commodore, having given up hope of finding the missing seaplanes, had just ordered the *Vindex* and her destroyer escort to return to the base, but on hearing of the *Medusa's* plight and the German air attack he recalled the *Lightfoot's* flotilla and went off at full speed towards the Lister Deep to meet it. But the *Lightfoot* had taken the *Medusa* in tow, and keeping the *Laertes* and *Lassoo* with him as escort, Commander C. K. MacLean ordered away the *Nimrod* and the rest of the destroyers to rejoin the Commodore. It was not till about 11.0, when they were in contact, that he was aware of the seriousness of the situation. Seeing how long his presence must have been known to the enemy, it was high time to withdraw. To do so with the *Medusa* in tow was full of risk, yet he could not bring himself to abandon her. There was no sign yet of the High Seas Fleet being out, our battle cruisers could not be far away, and ordering the *Aurora* and the destroyers that he still had in company to form a screen for the *Lightfoot* and *Medusa*, he began a slow retirement westward.

Admiral Beatty had in fact pushed his advance so far that by noon he was only twenty miles west of the Horn Reefs light-vessel, and no more than fifty miles west-north-west of the *Cleopatra*, but in another half-hour Commodore Tyrwhitt received a message from the Admiralty ordering him to withdraw without delay, and then came another, warning him to expect destroyer attacks during the night. As he was already withdrawing he felt justified in clinging to his hope of saving the *Medusa*. All he did was to call four of the destroyers that were with the *Vindex* to rejoin him, and in a rising sea, which made the work of towing the damaged destroyer more and more difficult, he held on as he was.

The meaning of the recall was that the Admiralty had

discovered that the High Seas Fleet was moving. So much was true, but for the present Admiral Scheer was at a loss to divine what our air attack, with its powerful support, portended. It might be a prelude to another raid on the Hage aerodrome, near the mouth of the Ems, or it might mean a trap to catch any force he sent to the north. He therefore held the main fleet back, and, he says, contented himself till our intentions became clearer with sending his "cruisers and several flotillas to pursue the retiring enemy." But, he adds, owing to the weather becoming worse, they were unable to come up with them, and had to report on their return empty-handed that one destroyer had been lost on a mine.

Every hour, indeed, the gale had been growing in violence. The German aircraft which in the early afternoon had been endeavouring to harass Commodore Tyrwhitt's retreat had to go back. But the situation only increased in anxiety. The *Vindex* destroyers had joined him about 5.30, and he had just ordered them to reinforce the *Medusa's* screen when he took in a message from the Admiralty warning him that strong enemy forces were sweeping west and north-west. This meant they were making straight for him, and the tension became acute. But relief was at hand. At 12.30 Admiral Beatty had intercepted the Admiralty order to Commodore Tyrwhitt that he was to withdraw without delay; but, concerned for the safety of the Harwich Force, he continued to hold his ground. Nor was he content with this. The situation that was developing closely resembled that which he had had to face in the first month of the war during the Heligoland action. At its crisis he had felt it his duty to stretch his instructions by boldly advancing into the Bight, and the result had fully justified the risk he took. So now, as the anxiety grew, he could no longer endure to keep his patrol station off the Horn Reefs, and at 2.0 he decided to run down to the southward to his colleague's assistance. So slow, however, was Commodore Tyrwhitt's retirement that about 4.0 the battle cruisers had passed across his course several miles ahead. Thick as was the weather, they were near enough for each to make out the other, and Admiral Beatty held on, till by 5.30 he was as far down as the latitude of Hoyer and well to the south of the Harwich Force. Here he took in the Admiralty's last warning. In view of the previous caution to beware of destroyer attacks in the night, he could no longer retain his covering position so far south, and he turned back to the northward, with the result that just before dusk the two forces were close together again.

About the same time it became evident that with the increasing violence of the weather the *Medusa* could not be saved. The towing hawser had parted, and the Commodore gave orders for her to be abandoned and sunk. No sooner was the order given than a message from the Admiralty told Admiral Beatty to remain at sea to cover the retreat in the morning, and he kept on to the northward to resume his patrol station north of Horn Reefs. The difficulty of clearing the *Medusa* in the sea that was running was very great, but by 9.0 it was very brilliantly done by the *Lassoo.* Through some misunderstanding, however, she was left afloat with an idea of picking her up next day.[1]

Rid of this incubus the Commodore was free to withdraw as he liked, and he now had from the Admiralty more precise information of the enemy's movements, showing there were two danger areas, one along the Frisian coast and the other inside a line running north-westward from Sylt. Although Admiral Beatty was within the latter zone, he himself was just outside it. The accuracy of the information was soon apparent. Having left the *Medusa*, the *Aurora*, *Lightfoot* and *Lassoo* were carrying on astern of the 5th Light Cruiser Squadron, and ahead of them was the *Nimrod*, with the bulk of the destroyers. All lights were doused, and the three groups were not in visual touch. In this order the force was steering north by west when in the intense darkness Captain F. P. Loder-Symonds, who commanded the *Cleopatra*, was aware of the flaming funnels of two enemy destroyers steaming across his bows. Putting over his helm, he made for the second one (*G 194*) and cut her clean in two. The other got away, but the consequences of his unexpected movement in the dark were disastrous. It brought the *Cleopatra* across the bows of the *Undaunted*, and as the squadron was in close order and steaming without lights, a collision could not be avoided and the *Undaunted* crashed into the flagship.

The result of the collision was that the Commodore's movements were more dangerously hampered than before he gave up the *Medusa*. The *Cleopatra* was but slightly damaged, but the *Undaunted's* bows were stove in, and it was quickly found that her collision bulkhead could not bear the strain of a speed exceeding six knots. In the confusion, moreover, the squadron and the flotillas had become scattered, and were entirely ignorant of each other's movements, while our battle cruisers were by this time fifty miles away and

[1] On April 3 she was found by a Dutch trawler whose skipper towed her 150 miles to Terschelling. She, however, ran on to a sandbank at the entrance and eventually became a total loss.

still steaming northward. Had Admiral Scheer ventured to pursue there can be little doubt he would have found the chance for which he was working, and the trial of strength between the British and the German battle cruisers might have come sooner than it did. But, as it happened, in view of the obscure situation and the heavy weather, he had recalled everything for the night, and by 11.0 we knew it. The information was sent out by the Admiralty with a warning that although the German destroyers were returning, their cruiser force would come out in the morning. Seeing how widely the Harwich Force was scattered, it was still in grave danger, and Commodore Tyrwhitt, who was steering northwest to get round the German minefield, signalled for everyone to make for the base. Up to this time the Admiralty knew little or nothing of his plight. Admiral Beatty scarcely knew more, and shortly before receiving the Admiralty message that the enemy were expected out in the morning, he asked leave to join the Commodore for a combined sweep south of the mined area, but permission was refused, and he continued patrolling to the northward. It was not until past 1.0 that the Admiralty intercepted a signal from the Commodore to Admiral Beatty telling him of the *Undaunted's* plight, and they immediately ordered Admiral Jellicoe to put to sea and concentrate all sections of the Grand Fleet east of the Long Forties. As the stormy night wore on the intentions of the enemy became clearer. The indications were that the battle cruisers and light forces would assemble off the Lister Deep in the morning, and then, supported probably by the two Dreadnought squadrons, make a sweep to the westward. It could hardly be doubted therefore that they had located the Harwich Force, and at 4.30 Admiral Beatty turned south-eastwards straight for the Amrum Channel, south of Horn Reefs, by which the Germans would debouch, and so if possible interpose himself between the enemy and his colleague. In another half-hour, by which time the Admiralty seem to have been certain that the German fleet was out, Commodore Tyrwhitt received orders to retire on Admiral Beatty. Having ascertained his exact position, he issued the necessary orders, and by 6.0 a.m. all the light cruisers were heading back to the eastward to join the battle cruisers.

An action now seemed inevitable, and it must begin long before our battle fleet could appear. It was only just clear of its ports, and the south-westerly gale was still raging with undiminished violence. For over three hours more the battle cruisers and light cruisers laboured through the mountainous seas towards their meeting-place, eager for the expected fight.

Hardened by their continual activity in the past terrible winter, no weather could deter them. By 9.30 Admiral Beatty was only sixty miles from the Horn Reefs light-vessel, the *Cleopatra* was almost as near, and in another hour or more either an action must be imminent or the enemy's retreat cut off. But it was not to be, for there came in word from Whitehall that the enemy were returning to port.

Whether an action could have taken place is doubtful, but it could only have begun in conditions advantageous for the enemy, such as Admiral Scheer was hoping for. His battle cruisers, with a squadron of light cruisers, had orders to steam out as far as Lat. 55′ 10″ N., Long. 5′ E., and two battle squadrons were out in support of them. But at 6.30 the cruisers reported the sea was so rough that an engagement was impossible, and he gave up his attempt as hopeless.[1]

So he missed his chance, and the great fleet movements which had developed out of a weak raid of five seaplanes came to an end. But our fleet kept the sea for a while longer. Towards noon all the light cruisers except the *Undaunted* had joined Admiral Beatty, and not till then did he and Commodore Tyrwhitt turn back. At 4.0 the Grand Fleet had reached its concentration point, but by that time the sea was impossible for destroyers, and knowing the danger was passed, Admiral Jellicoe ordered all squadrons back to their bases, except Admiral Evan-Thomas's " Queen Elizabeths," which he detached to cover the retreat of the *Undaunted*.[2]

While the difficulties of the *Sussex* affair dominated the counsels of Berlin, Admiral Scheer was quietly maturing his plans for the High Seas Fleet, and German offensive action was confined to air-raids. Attacks were launched on six successive nights, and five of them reached our coasts. The first, on March 31, was directed against the southern counties, and five Zeppelins—*L 13*, *L 14*, *L 15*, *L 16* and *L 22*—took part in it. Bombs were dropped at Cleethorpes and Bury St. Edmunds, and 29 soldiers killed and 53 injured ; but one of the raiders—*L 15*—was so damaged by our anti-aircraft guns that she was forced to come down near the Kentish Knock in the early hours of April 1. All her officers and crew, with the exception of one man, were rescued by the drifters *Olivine*, *Kitty George* and *F. & G.G.*, but though the *Electra*, which was patrolling the vicinity with a division of destroyers, appeared and took the wreck in tow, our attempts

[1] Scheer, *High Seas Fleet*, p. 119. During the night another German destroyer, *S.22*, struck a mine and sank.

[2] The *Undaunted* reached Seaham Harbour on the 28th.

to get her to land were fruitless, and she sank. This was the first loss which our defences had inflicted on the enemy's airship fleet, and the German commanders noticed what advances our organisation had made.[1] After this, their attacks followed rapidly. On April 1 two airships, *L 11* and *L 17*, started to attack in the south, but the wind veering against them for the return they tried further north. *L 17* apparently attempted Hull, but dropped about seventeen bombs into the sea off Tunstall (twelve miles north of the Humber), and none fell inland at all. *L 11* reported that she made the Tyne, but, finding that the strong north-north-westerly wind prevented her from manœuvring into a good position for dropping her bombs on the docks, she tried for Sunderland, where she did extensive damage, and believed she had blown up a blast furnace. Thence she made for Middlesbrough, where she reported having bombed two more blast furnaces, but in fact no damage of military value was done anywhere. On the following night four Zeppelins came across: two of them bombed Leith and Edinburgh; another attacked the coast of Northumberland, whilst the remaining two made for Norfolk and Essex. On April 3 *L 11* started again with *L 17*. They reached the Norfolk coast, but were unable to do anything. On the next night four or five airships started but failed to get across the North Sea. On April 5, however, *L 11*, *L 13* and *L 16* attacked the northern counties, and again the raid was a failure. *L 11* reported having been driven off Hull by anti-aircraft fire, but to have destroyed blast furnaces and iron works at Whitby, though that place was not attacked at all. They seem indeed to have lost their bearings, but a large number of bombs were dropped at various places between Durham and the Humber.

With this attempt the raids ceased for the time, while we on our part never abated our efforts to goad the enemy to sea. During April two more sweeps were made to the Norwegian coast against German trade, but nothing was found, nor did they induce any movement of the German fleet. From April 13 to the 19th Admiral Scheer was being held back in constant expectation of a British attack, which the German Government were led to believe was imminent.[2] The impression may well have arisen from the extensive preparations which we now had in hand for another attempt on the Schleswig airship base, and also for a large mining operation off the Belgian coast, while at the same time certain

[1] The German official account (*Der Krieg zur See: Nordsee*, Vol. V, pp. 105–6) claims that three airships in this raid bombed London, but *The War in the Air*, Vol. III, pp. 189–95, makes it clear that the German account is inaccurate.

[2] Scheer, *High Seas Fleet*, p. 123.

communications were passing between the Naval Staffs in London and Petrograd. Now that the Baltic ice had broken up it became necessary for the Russians to re-lay their mine-fields, and an arrangement was being made for a demonstration by the Grand Fleet to hold the enemy to the North Sea and prevent them from interfering with the operations. Possibly they got wind of this, but if so their information was curiously inaccurate. On April 20, when the Germans considered the danger was past, a cruiser force left for a raid into the Kattegat to operate against German trade and engage any enemy vessels which the move might draw out of the North Sea ports, while three submarines were to be stationed in the exits from the Baltic to deal with anything that might appear that way. Next day, however (April 21), the orders were altered. The Admiralty had become aware that the High Seas Fleet was getting ready to put to sea in the evening. They knew it had been held in readiness to meet an attack all the past week, but what the new development meant they could not tell. The whole Grand Fleet was therefore ordered to put to sea for a sweep to the Bight. As usual, the bulk of it was to concentrate the following morning east of the Long Forties—that is, 100 miles east of Aberdeen—with the battle cruiser fleet forty miles ahead, while the 3rd Battle Squadron and 3rd Cruiser Squadron from Rosyth took up a station from which they could join later if required. During the forenoon of the 22nd Admiral Jellicoe had word from the Admiralty that the enemy were returning to port. Their battle cruisers, so they informed him, had gone beyond Horn Reefs, and the rest of the High Seas Fleet as high as Lister Deep. They therefore suggested he should carry out the light cruiser sweep as far as the Skaw and keep the fleet at sea in support. The 4th Light Cruiser Squadron with destroyers was, accordingly, detached to the Skagerrak, while Admiral Beatty was ordered to push on ahead of the battle fleet, and by 6.0 p.m. he was seventy-five miles north-west of Horn Reefs. Here he was to cruise during the night, and then steer for the reefs, where the battle fleet would be closing him. But it was not to be. By the time Admiral Beatty reached his night station a dense fog came down, and he had to report that the *Australia* and *New Zealand* had been in collision and must return to the base. Slowly the fog spread northward, and by 10.0 Admiral Jellicoe, who, after steering eastward till dark, was heading for the reefs, was enveloped in it. For a while he held on, but as the weather grew thicker and thicker he felt he could not venture nearer to the Danish coast, and at 4.30 a.m. on the 23rd, when west of the Little Fisher Bank off Jutland, he decided to turn north. Three destroyers had been in collision about midnight, and one of them, the *Ardent*, had to be taken in tow stern first, and the battleship *Neptune* was subsequently damaged by a neutral merchantman running into her. During the morning—it was Easter Sunday—the weather cleared a little, but it was unsuitable for a sweep, and the Commander-in-Chief, having heard from the Admiralty that all was quiet in the Bight, returned to Scapa to refuel.

The Russian operations in the Baltic had not been completed, and there was further reason for being on the alert. In the southern area the mining operations off the Belgian coast were about to start. For some time past Admiral Bacon at Dover had been preparing a scheme for a mine and net barrage against the minelaying submarines of the Flanders Flotilla. Several times, for various reasons, its execution had been postponed, but it was now in operation under Admiral Bacon's direction. The idea was to close the passage between the Thornton Ridge shoal and the Belgian coast by a double line of deep mines extending across the entrance to Zeebrugge, supplemented by mine nets on the same line, as well as at the North Hinder.[1] The force detailed was considerable—six divisions of net drifters, four large minelayers and six minelaying trawlers, the monitors *Prince Eugene* and *General Wolfe*, a division of "M" class destroyers from Harwich, and the Flanders coast patrol working from Dunkirk. At 4.0 a.m. on April 24 all were in place. By 7.30 a double line of mines fifteen miles long had been completed, as well as a barrage of over thirteen miles of mined nets, and the minelayers were returning to port with their escort.[2] The drifters with the supporting ships remained to watch the nets. Here they were attacked by seaplanes, but no harm was done, and a seaplane was brought down by one of our machines and blew up as she struck the water. Then three enemy destroyers appeared off Zeebrugge, steering north-east. Our "M" class boats, *Medea*, *Murray*, *Melpomene* and *Milne*, broke away after them and opened fire. In the eagerness of the running action that ensued our people pressed the chase so hotly that they came under fire from the shore batteries. All of them were hit, and the *Melpomene* was brought to a standstill with a shell in her engine-room.

[1] "Mine nets" were a modification of the earlier nets. Mines were hung in them in such a way that when a submarine fouled them, the drag exploded the attached mine.

[2] The minelayers proceeded and returned under escort of two divisions of "L" class destroyers from Harwich.

The *Milne* and *Medea* took her in tow, and the German destroyers, seeing their opportunity, came out again from under the shelter of the batteries. The *Medea* promptly slipped her tow, and with the *Murray* engaged them again, but by this time the two monitors had come into action and the enemy went back to cover. For the rest of the day there was no further interference, and the watching vessels were left in peace to reap the outcome of the operation. Two submarines had already been caught in the nets and destroyed, and explosions in the line of the mines were believed to have accounted for two or possibly three others.

It was at least a promising beginning, but the day was destined to live in evil memory. The Grand Fleet was hard at work refuelling when at 4.0 in the afternoon Admiral Jellicoe received from Whitehall news of the gravest import. A rebellion had broken out in Ireland, Sinn Fein was in possession of Dublin, the High Seas Fleet appeared to be moving, and there was reason to believe that the Germans intended to support the insurgents with a demonstration against our east coast. About a week earlier Admiral Bayly at Queenstown had been warned that Sinn Fein intended to start a rebellion about Easter, and that arms were being shipped from Germany for the coast around Limerick, the point from which the movement was expected to begin. He accordingly stationed armed trawlers to watch the Kenmare river, Dingle bay and the waters between the Shannon and the Aran islands, and on April 20 he was reinforced by the *Gloucester* and four destroyers from the Grand Fleet. Meanwhile the German auxiliary *Libau*, disguised as a Norwegian tramp steamer the *Aud*, had arrived on the coast with arms.[1] The intention was that she should be met by the German submarine *U 19*, with the notorious rénegade Sir Roger Casement on board. He was to put her into communication with the rebels, who would assist the gun-running. He reached his destination on the 20th, but failed to recognise the *Libau*, who had put into Tralee the same day. He was, therefore, landed from *U 19* during the night, while the *Libau*, after hanging about the place for twenty-four hours, moved southward, and next day (April 21) ran into our patrols. Ordered to proceed to Queenstown under escort of the sloop *Bluebell*, she held on during the night, but next morning scuttled herself near the Daunt rock light-vessel. Three officers and nineteen men of the German navy were

[1] There was a real *Aud*, and the patrol trawlers accepted the disguise as authentic. She was originally the Wilson liner *Castro* (1,062 tons) detained in a German port at the outbreak of war.

taken prisoners. Casement had already been captured by the police near Tralee, and Admiral Bayly could devote his attention to the safeguarding of the troops that were being hurried over from Liverpool to Dublin, and was assisting the military from various points on the coast.[1]

There was thus good reason to expect some sympathetic action from the High Seas Fleet, and we proceeded to take the necessary steps on the well-considered lines. Commodore Tyrwhitt, who had been authorised to put to sea for a practice cruise, was recalled to refuel, and at 3.50 p.m. on April 24 the whole Grand Fleet was directed to be at two hours' notice as soon as it was complete with coal. Admiral Beatty, who had returned to Rosyth at 8.30 the previous evening, reported at 5.0 p.m. (24th) that he was ready. The Commander-in-Chief, however, could not complete for sea till 7.0 p.m. Moreover he had reported that a strong southerly gale was blowing which his destroyers would be unable to face, and against which his light cruisers could only steam at low speed. By 6.0 p.m., however, he had news that three hours earlier the German battle cruiser force was forty miles west of Heligoland, and apparently steering north-west, while the battle fleet seemed to be moving out in support. By 7.50 it was found that this appreciation was incorrect, and informing Admiral Jellicoe that the weather was better in the south, the Admiralty ordered him to put to sea and concentrate for intercepting the enemy. But he had already taken action. On receipt of word that the High Seas Fleet was moving he had begun to raise steam for full speed, and had ordered Admiral Beatty to proceed at once down the swept war channel west of the German minefield in Area I, and informed him that as he was now short of two of his battle cruisers, Admiral Evan-Thomas with the fast 5th Battle Squadron ("Queen Elizabeths") would start to join him as soon as possible, but he was to be careful not to get engaged with a superior force till the main fleet was within supporting distance. The reserve force at Rosyth, that is the 3rd Battle Squadron and the 3rd Cruiser Squadron, were to take up a position off Farn island to cover the Tyne.[2]

It was all he could do till the situation was clearer. Meanwhile, along the coast every precaution was being taken to meet any emergency. All auxiliary patrols and minesweepers were recalled, the local defence flotillas had orders to be in readiness to act, the submarines were to be outside in signal touch. Aircraft were to scout at daybreak and

[1] The rebellion came to an end on May 10. Casement was found guilty of high treason and executed on August 3.

[2] See Map 14.

every available machine was to attack the enemy as soon as they were sighted. While the east coast was all quietly astir with these orders, fresh light was obtained. At 8.10 the Commander-in-Chief had word that the *Seydlitz*, flagship of the battle cruisers, had struck a mine, but that the rest of the 1st Scouting Group were operating from a position fifty miles north-west of Borkum. The 3rd Battle Squadron, which comprised the latest German Dreadnoughts, was steaming along the Frisian coast for a position thirty-five miles north of Terschelling, whence they would steer south-westward, and the other two battle squadrons seemed to be in company. Besides the expected demonstration on our east coast, it was therefore evident that the enemy were contemplating something more serious to the southward. The situation was extremely grave. We had long thought it possible for an enterprising enemy to operate in the Flanders bight and the Straits of Dover. We knew that under cover of a sortie of the High Seas Fleet a force might be detached to raid our bases at Yarmouth or Lowestoft, or even the Thames Estuary. In spite of the hindrance of the Dover minefield it was also possible for a strong force to push through the Straits and attack our cross channel communications. Another attainable objective was the mass of shipping which accumulated every night in the Downs; for a squadron of battleships which had penetrated into the Straits for a few hours would have been presented with a target of a hundred defenceless merchantmen. The havoc that a well-supported raid in the Dover Straits would have brought about in our supply of food and materials was therefore beyond calculation. Nor was this all; blocking operations might also be attempted against the vital French ports through which the army was drawing its supplies, and finally we had to be on our guard against an endeavour to turn the Allied sea flank by landing a force at La Panne, between Nieuport and Dunkirk. In view of the large numbers of lighters and barges which had been collected at the German bases in Flanders, military authorities regarded such an enterprise as a danger that could not be ignored, and the Admiralty had undertaken that if attempted it should fail. Measures for meeting any of these eventualities had long been worked out, and the Admiralty proceeded to make their dispositions accordingly.

An essential feature of them had always been to place our flotillas and submarines in such a way as to give them a fair chance of laming one or more of the enemy's capital ships, and so to delay the movements of the High Seas Fleet sufficiently to allow our own fleet to come up with it or to intercept its retreat. Captain Waistell, who, as " Captain S," had charge of the Yarmouth submarines, was accordingly ordered to send six of them with a destroyer to a mid-sea position between Southwold and The Hook of Holland (52° 10′ N., 3° 5′ E.) and look out for large German ships steering south-west. To ensure as far as possible the success of the plan, Commodore Tyrwhitt was to proceed with his light cruisers to a position twenty miles north-north-east of the submarines on the presumed track of the battleships, and endeavour to lead them into the trap. All his destroyers, both from the Nore and Harwich, were to rendezvous at daylight near the submarines and await his instructions. What the German battle cruisers actually were doing the Admiralty did not yet know, and at 10.40, as no further news of them had been obtained, Captain Waistell was ordered to place six submarines at gun range off Yarmouth.

It was not till an hour later that the Admiralty were able to fix the movements of the German battle cruisers. At 11.40 p.m. it was ascertained that in two hours they would be on the far side of the Southwold danger area, steering to the westward on a course that led across it direct for Yarmouth, while the battle fleet was following them at a distance of about fifty miles. Admiral Bacon was immediately ordered to stop all operations on the Belgian coast and to keep the Dover force concentrated for local defence, and the *Vindex* seaplanes were to fly up the coast and attack the enemy when they appeared. A rapid attempt was also made to adapt the original disposition to the situation as it was now seen. To this end the destroyer *Melampus*, which had just started with the mid-sea group of submarines, was directed to take them thirty-three miles north-east of the original position. With the bulk of the Grand Fleet only just clearing its ports and the advance squadron still far to the north no more could be done to stop the expected raid, and so, as the Grand Fleet sped southwards, the night wore on, while on the east coast prowling Zeppelins under a starlit sky heralded the coming attack.

Why it was Admiral Scheer chose this moment for repeating his attempt of the previous month, is now clear. In his own account, no mention is made of the Irish rebellion, but the Naval Staff had agreed to support the Easter Sunday rising with a demonstration of the German fleet towards the Flanders bight, " but it was to be extended further so as to force the enemy out of port." " I expected," he says, " to achieve this by bombarding coastal towns and carrying out air-raids on England the night the fleet was out." Constant reports of our activity on the Norwegian coast and in the southern area convinced him that our fleet was divided, and that he had a chance of engaging one section or the other. We know, of course, that the German naval intelligence left much to be desired, but it is scarcely credible that it was so bad that they did not know our home fleets were permanently organised into a northern and a southern force. Read with similar explanations later on, it suggests that what was really in his mind was to deliver a sudden blow on our coasts and retire before either section could touch him. The bombardment was not to last more than half an hour, and the whole course of the operations points to evasion being his governing idea. The plan was to take the objective towns by surprise " in order to prevent counter-measures by the enemy, such as calling up submarines from Yarmouth." Every available ship of the High Seas Fleet was to be used, but the striking force detailed was under Admiral Boedicker, and consisted of four battle cruisers of the 1st Scouting Group and four light cruisers of the 2nd, with two fast destroyer flotillas and their cruiser leaders. The rest would be the support. They were to keep in the open waters west and north of Terschelling. " That," he explains, " was the only position where, in case it came to fighting, liberty of action could be ensured." It was also the best position to secure a prompt retreat. As a further precaution his disposable submarines were sent to the Forth and one of them, (*U 71*), mined its southern exit. From the Flanders Flotilla six submarines were sent out, of which two proceeded off Lowestoft, and the rest were held in readiness to assist as required ; whilst, in addition, six Zeppelins were to accompany the fleet as a scouting force.[1]

At noon on April 24 the whole force[2] started along the Frisian coast to pass through the southern opening of the German barrage off Nordeney, intending then to turn north round our minefield laid out of sight of the Dutch coast in the previous November. It was in this area that the battle cruiser flagship was disabled by a mine. Owing to an alarm of submarines Admiral Boedicker could not transfer his flag to the *Lutzow* until 7.0. Apart from the loss of time and strength which the mishap entailed, its effect was to prejudice the chance of surprise. For fear of further mishap

[1] Two (*L 16* and *L 13*) dropped bombs during the night on Newmarket and Honingham, but very little damage was done, and there were only two casualties.

[2] The German force numbered 22 capital ships, 5 older battleships, 12 light cruisers and 48 destroyers.

Admiral Scheer had now to alter his line of advance and continue along the coast. So clear was the weather that the movement could not fail to be seen from the Dutch islands, and might be reported to London. Towards sunset, however, he was relieved by two messages from headquarters : one was to say that on the previous morning large British squadrons had been seen off the northern entrance of the Skagerrak—these were probably our 4th Light Cruiser Squadron—and the other that since daylight numerous enemy forces were assembled off the Scheldt. Their intentions were unknown, but it was probably connected with a bombardment of the Belgian coast. For Admiral Scheer, so he says, it confirmed the presumption that our fleet was divided. It must also have assured him that both sections were fully occupied and well out of the way, but the news was soon tempered by more that was less agreeable. At 8.30 he heard that a British message had been intercepted recalling all patrols. It indicated that his advance had been detected, and he attributed the misfortune to his battle cruisers meeting with our submarines when the *Seydlitz* was mined. Although, as we have seen, the Admiralty half an hour earlier were sending out their first detailed account of his intended movements, it was not from submarines that they obtained the information, nor did Admiral Scheer suspect how much of his mind was being read. He was now well past the Ems on a north-westerly course, and by midnight had reached his rendezvous, some thirty miles north of Terschelling.

About the same time Commodore Tyrwhitt was hurrying out to sea with the *Conquest*, *Cleopatra* and *Penelope* of the 5th Light Cruiser Squadron and the *Lightfoot* leading seven destroyers that were ready. The *Nimrod* followed with eight others. The two divisions of "L" class destroyers which had been operating with Admiral Bacon, and had just returned to the Nore, were unable to get away till two hours later. By 1.30 a.m. on April 25 the Commodore was well to sea beyond the Sunk light-vessel, but instead of carrying on to his assigned decoying position beyond the mined area, he turned north to run up inside it.[1] Just before he started the Admiralty message at 11.40 came showing that the enemy battle cruisers were about to cross the danger zone towards Yarmouth. It was obvious therefore that his old orders would no longer serve. The *Melampus* and her submarines were on their way to take up their more northerly station, and though they were making for it directly across the danger

[1] See Map 15.

area, they could now only arrive in time to intercept the enemy on their return. He was thus in the difficult position of knowing that the orders under which he was acting had been based on a false appreciation, and with the fearless independence of judgment characteristic of his high qualities for command, he decided to act on his own responsibility. The decision he took was no less worthy of his fine record. It was to make straight for the point of the German attack. With only three light cruisers the odds against him were overwhelming, nor could he count on his destroyers to redress the balance. By 2.0 a.m. the moon was up in a clear sky, and with dawn at hand it would be too light for a torpedo attack to be attempted. Yet it was not to be endured that our arch enemy should boast of having insulted our coasts without interference on the sea, and he might at least entice them to chase him and draw their fire upon himself.

So with his two flotillas on either hand he held on north-north-east, hoping to get contact with the enemy before they sighted the shore. Nor was he disappointed. About 3.50, with the moon well up and the first glimmer of dawn beginning to brighten the sky to seaward, he was aware of some strange vessels about ten miles away to eastward, steering a north-westerly course. He at once turned parallel to them and as the dawn brightened, he sighted six light cruisers with a number of destroyers, and ahead of them were the shapes of four battle cruisers. Here was the chance he was seeking, and after standing to the westward towards Lowestoft for a few minutes to give the enemy a good sight of him, he suddenly turned south as though to escape. For a while it looked as though the enticement would succeed. The light cruisers started to chase, but soon turned away. Whether or not the main purpose of the German operation was to overwhelm a section of our forces, Admiral Boedicker was not so easily turned from his determination to strike the blow which was now almost within his reach, and he held on for the land.

So near was he now that at 4.10, as the Commodore continued his enticing retreat, the battle cruisers were seen to open fire. The first salvoes fell in the water. In a minute or two he could see them bursting over the town, but the enemy were no longer in sight. Only the flashes of the guns told where they were, and seeing he was not followed he stopped his retirement. Turning to starboard he now moved inshore for a few minutes to tempt them again, while the lessening thunder of the bombardment told him they were moving away from him. At 4.20 it ceased altogether. Clearly the enemy must be heading for Yarmouth, and determining to make an effort to save it, the Commodore turned north again to regain contact.

There was now better hope of doing something. The Germans were moving into the waters where the Yarmouth submarines were apparently expected to be, but in fact one only was in position at gun range off the town. This was *H 5*, near the Cross Sands light-vessel; two others, *H 10* and *V 1*, were on a line extending east-north-east to Smith's Knoll, as though the Admiralty's order had been taken to mean that they were to guard the approach to Yarmouth north of the danger area.[1] *H 5* was consequently the only one that saw the enemy when they appeared off Lowestoft. She dived to attack, but being too far to the northward the enemy was steaming back to the eastward before she could get within effective range. The other two made a similar attempt as the enemy retired, but with no better result. Not only had they further to go, but their approach was hampered by our own aircraft, which knew nothing of the Yarmouth submarines and attacked them with bombs. It was not the airmen's fault. They were doing their best to carry out their orders, and with such pertinacity did they endeavour to bomb the enemy that though some of them went sixty miles to sea, their gallant efforts had no success.

The appearance of our submarines, combined with the Commodore's turn northward, saved Yarmouth from the fate of her sister town. The German light cruisers had turned to the south-east at 4.23, and seven minutes later Commodore Tyrwhitt had sight of them to the north-eastward. He opened fire at 14,000 yards, but all the shots fell short. Owing probably to his having the land behind him the enemy seem to have been unable to make him out. At all events, they made no reply, but began manœuvring as though to lead our ships to the battle cruisers. Possibly they had been detached for this purpose. If so the device was successful. On hearing the firing the German battle cruisers, abandoning any further attempt to attack Yarmouth, turned south at full speed to the support of their light cruisers, and in five minutes (4.45) the Commodore could see them ten miles to the northward, steaming directly for him. He immediately turned back sixteen points together, but at once came under a

[1] Of the other three, *H 7* was stationed in the Haisborough Gat. *E 53* and *E 37* were coming up from Harwich.

heavy and accurate fire. In five minutes the *Conquest*, which was now the rear ship, was hit on the superstructure by a 12-inch salvo. The casualties were heavy—twenty-five officers and men killed and thirteen wounded—and her aerials were shot away, but she could still steam twenty knots. Ordering the destroyers to scatter and set up a smoke screen, he held on, but in another five minutes the enemy's fire ceased and they disappeared to the eastward. For thirteen minutes the Commodore had been under fire, but no further damage had been done except for a hit on the *Laertes* which wounded five men and put a boiler out of action.

Seeing that the time allowed for the bombardment was half an hour, and that it had lasted barely half as long, there can be little doubt that Commodore Tyrwhitt's spirited movement had to some extent achieved its object. Lowestoft had suffered severely, but without his intervention the destruction might have been far worse. As it was, though some two hundred houses had been wrecked, there was little loss of life, while Yarmouth had hardly been touched. And now, with their work half done, the bombarding force was retiring rapidly eastward upon Admiral Scheer. But the Commodore was not yet satisfied. After the battle cruisers ceased fire he had turned east-south-east in company with Captain Waistell, who, with another destroyer, had joined him in the *Lurcher*. The course led to the entrance of what was known as the " K " channel, a passage running north-eastwards which had been kept swept through the danger area. The channel was the direct route for the Bight; off Terschelling there was still a chance of regaining touch with the enemy and seizing any opportunity that occurred; and at 5.40, having done emergency repairs, he turned up the channel at his utmost speed.

Meanwhile Lieutenant-Commander G. O. Hewett in the *Melampus* when he was approaching his last assigned position with his five submarines, and was beginning to place them, received an order (5.47) from Captain Waistell to extend them as high as 53° 15′ north across the probable line of the enemy's retreat and to return south himself. But, having just heard German ships were about twenty-five miles to the westward and coming on at high speed, he remained to hurry the disposition, and was now steaming northward when at 6.0 he sighted an enemy force far ahead. He was just too late, and still hoping his foremost submarine might get a chance, he obeyed the order to retire. The leading boat, *E 55*, did actually sight the enemy about ten minutes later, but they steamed past her four miles ahead and so got clear away.

That seems to have been their only thought. There was no waiting to engage forces their raid might have brought out, yet had they really sought them they were not far away. Admiral Beatty, it is true, was still six hours' steaming from the German battle fleet's position off Terschelling, where, as Admiral Scheer says, if we wished to cut off his retreat the waters were favourable for offering battle. But an engagement can scarcely have been what he intended even in waters of his own choosing. There seems to have been no attempt even to get another blow at our light forces—this was left entirely to the Flanders submarines which were now covering the retirement. Commodore Tyrwhitt as he swept north-eastwards with his cruisers disposed abreast passed the *UB 18* at 6.35, but still he pressed on, till at 8.30, after his three hours' chase, he saw the enemy's smoke ahead. With increased eagerness he continued the pursuit, but in ten minutes came a recall from the Admiralty. He obeyed it at once, and a little before ten o'clock on the run back the *Penelope* was torpedoed. Though the torpedo blew away her rudder and wrecked her steering gear, she was still able to steam twenty knots, and by 3.0 p.m. the Commodore, in spite of all he had so brilliantly risked, was back in Harwich.[1] Admiral Beatty's battle cruisers turned back at 12.30. The 5th Battle Squadron and the Battle Fleet came down to meet them, and by 2.30 p.m. the whole force was on its way home.

We were not slow in retaliating. Ever since our attack upon the Schleswig coast in March, which had so nearly ended in a fleet action, plans for repeating the operation had been under discussion, and by the end of April a new project had been worked out in every detail. On the night of May 3, two minefields were to be laid at the outer ends of the German swept channels: the first to the north-west of Borkum by the *Princess Margaret*, and the second to the south of the Vyl light-vessel by the *Abdiel.* Each was to be reinforced by a group of watching submarines, three working off the Terschelling bank, and six in the Horn Reefs area. Early in the morning of May 4, the 1st Light Cruiser Squadron was to appear off Sylt with the seaplane carriers *Vindex* and *Engadine* and sixteen destroyers of the First Flotilla. A raid of seaplanes was then to be sent out against the Zeppelin sheds at Tondern, and, as soon as the raiders returned, Commodore Alexander-Sinclair was to withdraw to the northward with his light cruisers.

[1] At 11.45 a.m. *E 22* was attacked and sunk by *UB 18* (Lieutenant Steinbrinck) near the patrol line laid out by the *Melampus* between 5.0 and 6.0. This loss and the damage to the *Conquest*, *Laertes*, and *Penelope*, were the only British casualties, while in addition to the battle cruiser *Seydlitz* striking a mine, the Germans lost incidentally two submarines, *UB 13* and *UC 5*.

The difference between this raid and its predecessor in March was that, in the present case, the bombing of the Zeppelin sheds was an incident in a larger plan, whereas, before, it had been the primary object. On the experience gained, we could assume that even a temporary threat to the security of the German coasts would bring out the whole High Seas Fleet, and our project was laid accordingly. The minefields and submarines were to be placed across the enemy's most probable lines of advance, and, to complete the trap, Admiral Jellicoe was to take the battle fleet to a position in the southern approaches to the Skagerrak, whilst Admiral Beatty with his battle cruisers took up an advanced station to the south of him.

Overnight and early in the morning of the 3rd our squadrons got under way ; but a singular chance made the situation very complicated. During the night a squadron of eight Zeppelins (*L 11, L 13, L 14, L 16, L 17, L 20, L 21, L 23*; *L 20* was destroyed in Norway) had raided the East Riding of Yorkshire and Scotland and were thus returning across the North Sea during the very hours that our fleet was steaming to its position off the Bight.[1] We could be fairly certain that large sections of the High Seas Fleet would come out to support them ; and this movement might very seriously affect the operation to which we were committed.

The added uncertainty was not in itself enough to alter the orders given; nor indeed could new orders have been devised for a situation in which so many factors were now beyond calculation or even forecast; and during May 3 our squadrons moved across the North Sea to their allotted stations.

Late in the afternoon the Admiralty relieved Admiral Jellicoe's uncertainty by telling him that a light cruiser squadron and Admiral Hipper's battle cruisers had come out during the day, but that both groups were then going back to harbour. The position was, therefore, quite promising, for, as Admiral Scheer and his battle squadrons had not put to sea, nothing would prevent him from moving out to meet us on the first alarm.

The first part of the plan now went forward without a hitch. By half-past one on the morning of the 4th Commander Lockhart Leith in the *Princess Margaret* and Commander B. Curtis in the *Abdiel* had laid their minefields, and by dawn the Grand Fleet was inside the area it was to occupy during the day. Off Sylt matters did not go so well. Shortly after 3.0 a.m. Commodore Alexander-Sinclair's light cruisers arrived at the position from which the raid was to start, but when the eleven

[1] It had been preceded by two raids on the nights April 25–26 and 26–27, carried out by military airships *LZ 87, LZ 93, LZ 88, LZ 97* ; no casualties occurred. No more airship raids were attempted until the last week in July.

seaplanes were put into the water all except two failed to rise, and had to be hoisted in again with damaged propellers. Of the two which rose from the water only one got away, for the destroyer screen was manœuvred so close to the other that she fouled the *Goshawk's* aerial, and came down a mass of wreckage: the unfortunate pilot, Flight Commander O. N. Walmesley, sank with his machine and was never seen again. By half-past five the one seaplane which had dropped her bombs returned, and two hours later Commodore Alexander-Sinclair had taken up his station in the screen of the battle cruiser fleet.

Unsuccessful as our raid had been, the mere presence of our forces off the German coasts would probably suffice to bring out the German fleet, and it now remained to be seen how soon they would move.

For two hours nothing happened; but at half-past nine the *Galatea* and *Phaeton*, at the western end of the light cruiser screen, sighted Zeppelin *L 7* to the southward of them. For half an hour they strove to close the range, and then, after exchanging a few shots, both ships turned back to resume their station. Almost as they did so, the airship was seen to turn sharply into an almost vertical position and then come down. As the light cruisers were well inside the area in which hostile submarines were reported to be operating, it was not safe for them to complete the Zeppelin's destruction, but in fact she needed no further attention. She had only been hit once, but the shot had got home in the petrol tanks and started fires which rapidly got the upper hand. In a few minutes the flaming gas and petrol had wrecked her, and when our submarine *E 31* came up alongside, she had nothing to do but to save as many survivors as she could.[1]

Our forces had now been off the Bight for well over six hours, and still the High Seas Fleet showed no signs of moving. Admiral Jellicoe, therefore, held his position until 2.0, when he decided that it was useless to wait any longer, and turned for home.

Admiral Scheer had meanwhile returned to bring a ray of light into the gloomy Berlin Council Chamber. The elation his exploit against Yarmouth and Lowestoft had produced in Germany was out of all proportion to its intrinsic value. It was taken as inspiriting evidence that the arch enemy could no longer command her own seas. How far the reaction it produced affected the submarine question we cannot tell. It at least raised the prestige of the High Seas Fleet and can scarcely have been without effect. All we know is that the Chancellor won his case. Without a word to the Chief of the General

[1] *E 31* picked up seven survivors in all.

Staff it was decided to postpone the unrestricted campaign, and on May 4 a note accepting all the American conditions was placed in the Ambassador's hands.[1] The Chancellor, it is true, made some attempt to soften the humiliation by introducing the question of "Freedom of the Seas" in order to loosen the stringency of our blockade. But his effort only earned another rebuff. "Respect," he was told, "by German naval authorities for the rights of citizens of the United States upon the high seas should not in any way or in the slightest degree be made contingent upon the conduct of any other Government." So the capitulation was ostensibly complete.

[1] An order to Admiral Scheer on April 24 that "U-boats are to carry out war only in accordance with prize regulations" was a precaution to prevent further complications with America before a decision was reached. (Scheer, pp. 129–30.)

CHAPTER XVI

THE EVE OF JUTLAND

THE impunity with which the enemy had insulted our East Coast after his long inactivity came with something of a shock to public opinion. There was nothing approaching to panic—the faith in the navy was scarcely shaken—but the Admiralty thought it desirable to issue a reassuring pronouncement. It took the form of a letter from Mr. Balfour to the Mayors of Lowestoft and Yarmouth, in which he stated that our home forces were about to be redistributed in a way which would make a repetition of a raid against our East Coast highly dangerous to the enemy. In the early stages of the war, it was explained, it was necessary to keep our main fleet in northern waters, where it could be concentrated against any prolonged operation of the enemy such as attempted invasion, but could not be sure of intercepting raids. Now, however, that new construction had materially increased our strength, we not only had better means of coast defence, but it was possible to bring important forces south from the Grand Fleet without imperilling our preponderance elsewhere.

A redistribution of the character he indicated had in fact been under consideration since the beginning of the year. The old difficulty of inadequate bases in the North Sea had held it up, and it had been found necessary to postpone it till the work of providing what was required was further advanced. On February 17, at a meeting of the War Committee which Admiral Jellicoe came down to attend, the whole strategical aspect of the naval situation had been fully investigated. In the first place the Committee had explored the possibility of a naval offensive on the lines of Lord Fisher's still-born plan. Its precise nature had never been divulged, but it was understood to aim at seizing any opportunity of the moment which would serve to upset the German war plans by forcing them to dissipate forces for the defence of their northern front. There were various possible objectives. One of the German coastal islands might be seized as an aircraft and submarine base, or for operations for blocking their harbours. A landing on the Schleswig coast was another possibility, or, better still, in Denmark, if the neutrality of Denmark, like that of Belgium, should be violated by the enemy. Finally, as an ultimate objective, there was the coast of Pomerania, within a hundred miles of Berlin, where, with the then incalculable Russian force at hand, a threatened invasion could not be ignored. The whole scheme presupposed military co-operation and the preservation of the Grand Fleet intact to deal with the High Seas Fleet if it came out. The Grand Fleet was not to be used; the whole of the combined work was to be entrusted to the special fleet which Lord Fisher had under construction. That fleet, we know, had been eaten away by the Dardanelles operations, but whatever chances of success the scheme may have had at its inception, it was agreed that they had now disappeared. Owing to the increased range and power of heavy artillery, a coastal island was no longer tenable as a base, and no troops were available for a landing. Moreover, with the enhanced effectiveness of mines and submarines, the difficulties of supplying a fleet in the Baltic were greater than ever, and on these and other minor grounds it was decided that no naval offensive such as Lord Fisher had planned was possible. There remained nothing but minor aggression, such as closing the enemy's ports with blockships and mines, but here again the objections seemed insuperable. To begin with, a very large number of ships would be required if the blocking was to be effective, and we had none to spare. Owing to the diversion of skilled hands from the shipyards into the army, our mercantile construction was not keeping pace with the destruction by mines and submarines. Efforts were being made to recover the wasted men, and mercantile shipbuilding had been declared "war work," but already grave anxiety was being felt for the maintenance of our oversea supplies. As for attempting to close the ports with mines, they were too easily removed on the coast, unless continually watched, and until the enemy main fleet was defeated this could not be done. The conclusion, therefore, was that the only possible course was to preserve the old expectant attitude, while persevering by every means in our power to goad the High Seas Fleet to expose itself in the open sea.

But even for this the distribution of the fleet left much to be desired, and early in April the question was thoroughly re-examined. Admiral Sir Henry Jackson, First Sea Lord, pointed out that while the existing disposition provided no real protection for the southern area, the main fleet was based too far north to be able to seize such opportunities as had hitherto occurred and the only ones which were likely to occur again. So long as we kept our greatly superior fleet concentrated, the enemy would never come within its reach to commit suicide. If we did not divide it we could never get victory. All we could expect was raids by airships and small craft which, under the new German Commander-in-Chief, the High Seas Fleet might come out to support, and to meet it the Grand Fleet must be based further south by dividing it between Rosyth and the Humber. Steps were already being taken to render both places capable of receiving the required number of ships, but until the southern bases were ready redistribution must stand over.

There was, however, an expedient which if adopted would improve the situation, and that was to detach the 5th Battle Squadron, the fastest in the fleet, to act with the battle cruiser fleet. There were, moreover, special reasons why this change was regarded in some quarters as admitting of no delay. It was known that two new and powerful ships, the *Lützow* and *Hindenburg*, were about to join the German battle cruisers. Some corresponding reinforcement was consequently required for the Rosyth force, and the proposal was that the "Queen Elizabeths" should join Admiral Beatty to take the place of the 3rd Battle Squadron. This solution was warmly recommended by Admiral Beatty, but the Commander-in-Chief saw serious objections. High as was the speed of the 5th Battle Squadron, it was believed not to be sufficient for them to be sure of bringing the *Lützow* and *Hindenburg* to action. An even graver consideration was that in Admiral Jellicoe's battle plans the "Queen Elizabeths" were given the function of a free wing squadron, which, not forming part of the main line of battle, could be used at any opportune moment in an action for bringing a concentration to bear on part of the enemy fleet, or otherwise by independent attack to modify the rigidity of the old single line ahead formation on which the battle orders were based. It was decided therefore to leave things as they were, at least till we knew for certain that the German battle cruiser force was superior to our own, and that the larger distribution should not be attempted until the new battleships that were coming forward had brought the main fleet up to a strength of twenty-four Dreadnoughts.

Meanwhile the East Coast had to lie open to a raid. So weak was its defence that to the Admiralty it was inexplicable why the Germans did not attempt a blow. The risk to us was obvious, but it was one that must be run for the greater end. Indeed, the acceptance of the risk was the only means in sight by which the greater end could be attained. Convinced that so long as we kept our fleet concentrated where it was, a decisive action was out of the question, the Admiralty saw in the temptation to raid the only effective means of getting the enemy to expose himself. All, however, that could be done at present was to take steps to ensure that a raid would involve the exposure we desired, and by the middle of April something was possible. The main fleet had reached the stipulated strength, and on the 15th the Commander-in-Chief was informed that the proposed redistribution was to begin as soon as the work of defending the outer anchorage of the Forth was completed. Meanwhile, as the Humber was ready to receive a contingent, the 3rd Battle Squadron and 3rd Cruiser Squadron were to move there. The effect would be that the Germans, if they attempted a raid with light craft, would be compelled to bring out a battle force to support it. A chance might then occur, but to obtain full advantage of it Dreadnoughts must be ready to support the Humber Squadron. The Commander-in-Chief was therefore directed to consider whether as the new Forth defences progressed he would not be able to base some of his ships there. He was also informed that in order to expedite matters it had been decided to utilise the material that had been prepared for the Dover Strait boom and send it up to the Forth.

Then, on the eve of the first step being taken, came the Lowestoft raid. The expected blow had fallen; nothing had been near enough to prevent it or to retaliate; the chance of an action had been missed. It was now imperative that something must be done at once, and the Admiralty hastened to ask the Commander-in-Chief what he would propose. "The enemy," they said, "have practically tested our weakness in southern waters and will probably act on the offensive in those waters shortly." Commodore Tyrwhitt, they pointed out, had now only one light cruiser available, and until the damaged ships were repaired they must call on the Commander-in-Chief to safeguard the threatened area. What he advised was that the 3rd Battle Squadron and the 3rd Cruiser Squadron should proceed south at once from Rosyth, and be based not in the Humber but in the Swin—that is the northern passage of the Thames estuary—or at Sheerness or Dover, and that the Rosyth submarines should move down to Yarmouth. If minefields were laid off the East Coast they should provide, with the increased force of submarines, an ample defence against bombarding raids, while the 3rd Battle Squadron, with the *Dreadnought* added, as soon as she was refitted, would constitute a covering force quite able to deal with the German battle cruisers at their present strength. This was so far approved that the submarines, except two which were to remain in the Forth, went south, and the 3rd Battle Squadron and the 3rd Cruiser Squadron were ordered to proceed to Sheerness at the first opportunity and to regard the Swin as their war anchorage. By May 2 they arrived, and were next day formally detached from the Grand Fleet and placed under the orders of Vice-Admiral Sir Edward Bradford, commanding the battle squadron.

But this was no more than a temporary expedient. It was now obvious that if the main redistribution was to be made at all, it should be done with the least possible delay. In giving his advice Admiral Jellicoe had stated that until the outer anchorage below the Forth bridge was made proof against torpedo attack he could not move any part of his battle fleet to Rosyth, and he urged that the defensive work both there and in the Humber should be pushed on with the utmost energy. As soon as ever the work was sufficiently forward he intended to base one Dreadnought squadron and the 1st Cruiser Squadron on the Humber and the rest on the Forth.

A conference was accordingly assembled (May 12) at Rosyth, at which the First Sea Lord presided, to come to a final decision as to whether the proposed redistribution was strategically sound and to concert with the military authorities what defences were immediately necessary for both bases, and how they could be most speedily carried out. The conclusions were that, whether or not the centre of gravity was to be permanently shifted to the southward, the constitution of the Forth as a primary base was urgent. Of this the Commander-in-Chief was now convinced, but in deference to his views and experience it was agreed that Scapa was too valuable to be disestablished. It was to remain as an alternative base for the exercise of squadrons and individual ships, as well as a base for the 10th Cruiser Squadron and its supporting force as necessary. As for the Humber, it was also to be an alternative secondary base, and by a reorganisation of the battle fleet all the 12-inch-gun Dreadnoughts (except the *Dreadnought* herself) were to be formed into a new 4th Battle Squadron which would be detachable there or elsewhere as required. The Forth, it was agreed, could be made capable of holding the 1st and 2nd Battle Squadrons and the 2nd Cruiser Squadron, as well as the battle cruiser fleet and the necessary light craft, and it was hoped that all would be ready before the winter.[1] No conclusion, however, was reached as to whether the shift south was strategically advisable, and pending a final decision the propriety of at once attaching the "Queen Elizabeths" to the battle cruiser fleet was again raised, but to this the Commander-in-Chief was still opposed. It was, however, agreed that it would be well to move them or the new 4th Battle Squadron to Rosyth occasionally, and as the 3rd Battle Cruiser Squadron (*Invincible, Inflexible* and *Indomitable*) was about to proceed to Scapa for exercises, Admiral Jellicoe announced his intention of replacing them temporarily with the "Queen Elizabeths." So it came about that when the long-expected day was at hand, the distribution was not that on which his considered battle orders were based; in one important particular the organisation they contemplated was dislocated. The free fast battle squadron was no longer under his hand.

At Scapa he had two battle squadrons with their attached light cruisers: the First, under Vice-Admiral Sir Cecil Burney in the *Marlborough*, with Rear-Admiral E. F. A. Gaunt as Second Flag, and the Fourth, under Vice-Admiral Sir Doveton Sturdee in the *Benbow*, with Rear-Admiral A. L. Duff as his Second. Besides Rear-Admiral The Hon. H. L. A. Hood's 3rd Battle Cruiser Squadron with the attached light cruisers, he had with him the 2nd Cruiser Squadron and the 4th Light Cruiser Squadron, with the 4th, 12th and part of the 11th Destroyer Flotillas, numbering in all one light cruiser, four flotilla leaders and thirty-five destroyers ready for action. At Cromarty was the 2nd Battle Squadron, with one attached light cruiser, under Vice-Admiral Sir Thomas Jerram in the *King George V*, with Rear-Admiral A. C. Leveson as his Second. Here, too, was Rear-Admiral Sir Robert Arbuthnot's 1st Cruiser Squadron, with the rest of the 11th Flotilla, whose available strength was the flotilla leader *Kempenfelt* and ten destroyers. Recently, in order the better to secure combined action, the whole of the battle fleet flotillas, whether at Scapa or Cromarty, had been constituted a single command, under a Commodore "F," a post to which Captain J. R. P. Hawksley had been appointed only a month before, with his broad pendant in the light cruiser *Castor*. But this was only one feature of the flotilla reorganisation which was in course of procedure. In August 1915, as the new destroyer programme began to materialise, it had been decided that the Grand Fleet should have six flotillas, one for each of the five

[1] Admiral Sir Robert Lowry, Commanding the Coast of Scotland, had been made Commander-in-Chief, Rosyth, on March 1 owing to the increasing importance of the Scottish naval command.

battle squadrons and one for the battle cruiser fleet, that is, 100 destroyers in all. At that time, however, they numbered only sixty-five, and would remain at that total till all the old boats of the 1st, 2nd and 4th Flotillas were relieved by the first new ones coming forward. The process of relief was proceeding when early in 1916 the pressing need everywhere for more light cruisers suggested a further reorganisation. At a conference in the Admiralty on January 17, 1916, a plan was formulated for setting free the flotilla cruisers by organising the destroyers into four flotillas instead of six—three for the battle fleet of twenty-four boats each and one for Rosyth of twenty-eight. Each half flotilla would have a flotilla leader, in one of which was to be the flotilla Captain (Captain "D"), and in the other the senior Commander, a system which approximated to that of the Germans. The only light cruiser required would be one for the Commodore who was to command the whole, while retaining the post of Captain "D" in his own flotilla. On March 18, however, the Commander-in-Chief expressed his opinion that sixteen to eighteen destroyers were the utmost a Captain "D" could handle efficiently from a flotilla leader, and one such vessel was required for every eight or ten boats. He proposed, therefore, a reversion to five flotillas, four for the battle fleet of eighteen boats each, which, allowing for two spares, would give an effective strength of sixteen. Each flotilla was to have a light cruiser and flotilla leader or two flotilla leaders. The fifth, for Rosyth, was to consist of twenty-eight boats with a light cruiser and two flotilla leaders, the light cruisers to be relieved by flotilla leaders as they came forward. Thus on the eve of the battle the Grand Fleet flotillas were in a state of transition, and with new boats continually joining. Commodore Hawksley had had as yet no time to exercise his command.

Under Admiral Beatty, whose fleet flagship was the *Lion*, was Rear-Admiral H. Evan-Thomas, with his flag in the *Barham*, and three other ships of the 5th Battle Squadron, the *Queen Elizabeth* being in dock at Rosyth. The battle cruiser fleet now consisted of the 1st Squadron, under Rear-Admiral O. de B. Brock in the *Princess Royal*, and the 2nd, under Rear-Admiral W. C. Pakenham in the *New Zealand*, his flagship, the *Australia*, being also in dock. Together, with the *Lion*, they numbered six ships. The three light cruiser squadrons which formed the remainder of the force were the 1st, under Commodore E. S. Alexander-Sinclair in the *Galatea*, the 2nd, under Commodore W. E. Goodenough in the *Southampton*, and the 3rd under Rear-Admiral T. D. W.

Napier in the *Falmouth*. The available strength of the attached flotillas was twenty-seven—nine boats of the 1st Flotilla led by the light cruiser *Fearless*, ten of the 13th led by the light cruiser *Champion*, and two divisions (eight boats) of the 9th and 10th Flotillas, which had joined from Harwich.[1] At the moment, therefore, the Grand Fleet consisted of twenty-four " Dreadnoughts," four " Queen Elizabeths," nine battle cruisers, eight cruisers, nineteen light cruisers, besides four attached to the battle squadrons. The flotillas numbered seventy-two boats, with three light cruisers and five flotilla leaders. At Scapa was also a balloon ship and the seaplane carrier *Campania*, while another, the *Engadine*, was at Rosyth ; she alone sailed with the fleet. Measures were also on foot for enabling submarines to take part in an action, and a new flotilla was being formed at Blyth, whence it was hoped it would be able to join the final concentration.[2]

Over and above this great fleet, the most formidable that had ever sailed the sea, there was the Harwich Force, whose available strength was now five light cruisers, two flotilla leaders and about seventeen destroyers. Under the war plan it had always been contemplated that it would be available at least for the concluding phases of a battle in the North Sea. But it was far away, and it was more than doubtful whether it could reach the scene of action in time.

So the distribution remained until such time as the southern bases were ready. But pending the change Admiral Jellicoe did not wait with his arms folded. Satisfied that much might be done with the fleet as it was, he continued his efforts to entice the enemy to sea. Hitherto all his devices had failed to bring them far enough north, but by the end of the month he had prepared a plan that went beyond anything he had yet hazarded. Two squadrons of light cruisers were to proceed to the Skaw, which they were to reach by dawn on June 2. Thence they would sweep right down the Kattegat as far as the Great Belt and the Sound, while a battle squadron would push into the Skagerrak in support. Such a bait, it was hoped, could scarcely fail to draw a strong enemy force from the Bight. Possibly, as had happened before, they would not come far enough north to ensure an action, but at least they might be lured into a trap. To this end three of the Harwich submarines were to be in position from June 1 to 3 westward from the Vyl light-vessel, which is just southwards of Horn

[1] These Harwich destroyers were asked for, as there were not enough otherwise to provide an efficient screen for the heavy ships.

[2] For distribution of the fleet see Appendix A.

Reefs. South of them the *Abdiel* would extend to the westward the minefield she had laid on May 3–4 due south of the Vyl, while the seaplane carrier *Engadine*, escorted by a light cruiser squadron and destroyers, would be off the Reefs on the look-out for Zeppelins, and east of the Dogger Bank would be two of the Blyth submarines. Finally, somewhere north of the mined area the battle fleet and battle cruiser fleet would be cruising, ready to move south and attack directly they heard any strong forces of the enemy were out.

The plan, however, was destined never to be put to the test. By pure coincidence Admiral Scheer had already elaborated a strikingly similar combination with a practically identical object, and while the British operation was being worked out he was only waiting for favourable weather to carry out his own, all unaware that it was precisely what his adversary was bent on forcing him to do.

For Germany the situation which had developed out of the destruction of the *Lusitania* and *Sussex* was one which called loudly for action on the lines of his desire, and at the same time seemed to have increased the chances of success. With the indefinite postponement of unrestricted submarine warfare, the bulk of the "U" boats could be used against the armed forces of the enemy, while offensive action of some kind against us at sea was imperative if the German navy was to justify its existence in the eyes of the people. A disillusioned nation which had borne the heavy burden of creating it was groaning under the increasing severity of the blockade, and calling ominously for retaliation. On land hope was waning. The appalling sacrifices which had been made in the desperate effort to win the Verdun salient had so far been made in vain. For the first time the spirit of the people was sick, and in the fleet alone was their present hope of a restorative. Only too pleased with a situation so favourable to the free hand he wished, Admiral Scheer proceeded to develop still more ambitious plans for crippling his overpowering adversary. His hopes were also brightened by Mr. Balfour's announcement that part of the Grand Fleet was being moved into the southern area. For Admiral Scheer this could only mean a loosening of our concentration, and he had now little doubt that another well-designed raid would bring about the kind of conflict he desired.

The plan he conceived was of greater boldness than anything he had yet ventured. It was based on a bombardment of Sunderland, the nearest vulnerable port to Rosyth, where lay Admiral Beatty with the southernmost section of the Grand Fleet. Owing to the need of repairing the serious damage which the *Seydlitz* had suffered during the raid on the East Coast, and to the fact that several of his battleships were crippled with machinery defects, it must be some weeks before Admiral Scheer could be ready. He had therefore ample time to work out elaborate precautions to reduce the risk he meant to run. To this end he intended to use the whole of his submarines. Sixteen of them were to be stationed off the Grand Fleet bases, the bulk of them being naturally allotted to Rosyth. Others were employed defensively as part of the extensive dispositions he made for securing the safety of his bases in the Bight. The actual bombardment was to be carried out by Admiral Hipper's battle cruisers and the light cruisers of the 2nd Scouting Group, and when the Rosyth force came out to engage him he was to endeavour to lead all that escaped the submarines to within reach of the battle fleet.

The weak point in the scheme was that, owing to Admiral Jellicoe's habit of making sweeps down the North Sea at odd times, the danger of being caught at a disadvantage could not be ignored, and Admiral Scheer, with whom boldness was never allowed to pass the limits of sane prudence, regarded adequate reconnaissance by airships as essential in order to make sure the field was clear. But experience had shown that this novel weapon fell far short of what had been hoped from it as a fleet auxiliary. For distant reconnaissance airships could not be relied on except in the most favourable weather, and it was therefore necessary to provide an alternative plan which in case of need would dispense with their assistance. Should, therefore, the weather render the Sunderland design too risky, he intended to proceed up the Danish coasts as though to strike at our cruisers and merchantmen which were reported so frequently in the Skagerrak. By this means he could safely dispense with airships, for his one exposed flank could be guarded from surprise by his cruisers and flotillas.[1]

In the latter half of May, however, it was reasonable to count on a sufficiently long spell of fair weather for the more ambitious plan to be feasible, and to this Admiral Scheer adhered. Accordingly, on May 17 it was inaugurated by the submarines of the High Seas Fleet putting to sea for their allotted stations.[2] They were to form lines of observation between Norway and the Forth, and from the 23rd onwards, when it was expected that the fleet would be ready for action, they would take up their intercepting positions.

[1] Scheer, *High Seas Fleet*, p. 136, and his report in *Battle of Jutland Official Despatches* (Cmd. 1068), p. 587.

[2] *U52, U24, U70, U32, U66, U47, U43, U44, U63, U51*

In addition to these, the *U46* was detailed to patrol off Sunderland during the night of May 21/22, and subsequently until June 2, to take up a position off Peterhead. As she was not ready in time, however, the *U47*, one of the ten submarines assigned to the North Sea, took her place. The submarine minelayers, *U72*, *U74* and *U75*,[1] put to sea on May 13, 23 and 24 respectively to lay lines of twenty-two mines each in the Firth of Forth, the Moray Firth and westward of the Orkneys, while on the 20th *UB 27* sailed to force her way into the Firth of Forth beyond May Island with the object of attacking warships entering or leaving. On the 21st *UB 21* and *UB 22* went out to keep watch on the Humber, and on the 22nd *U67* and *U46* were sent to guard the fleet from flank attacks westward of Terschelling.

Though these initial movements were immediately detected by the Admiralty, the High Seas Fleet had been too long quiescent for any inference to be made that a big operation was in the wind. During our raid on Tondern in the first week in May we knew the fleet had been ordered out, but we quickly detected that the 3rd Battle Squadron had been sent to the Baltic for exercises, and our diving patrol reported all quiet in the Bight beyond the routine minesweeping and outpost duty of the flotillas. Consequently, although by the 22nd we knew that at least eight and probably more submarines were in the north part of the North Sea, nothing but a fresh attack on commerce was expected.

Meanwhile Admiral Scheer, with everything in readiness, was eagerly watching the weather for the moment when he could safely give the word to carry on ; but day after day passed and nothing came from the airship commander but monotonous reports that it was impossible for any of his craft to go up. This went on till the time was near when the submarines would have to return. May 30 was the last possible day to which Admiral Scheer's operations could be postponed, and at midnight on the 28th/29th he made a general signal for all units to be prepared to sail next morning when the *Seydlitz* would be ready. Still the weather remained unchanged, and finally he had to confess his favourite scheme was impracticable. On May 30, therefore, he directed Admiral Hipper to proceed early on the 31st with the scouting divisions to the Skagerrak, with orders to show himself off the

[1] *U75* laid the mines on which the *Hampshire*, with Lord Kitchener on board, foundered a week later. *U74* in action with armed trawlers, was sunk with all hands on the 27th.

Norwegian coast so as to ensure his presence being reported to the British Admiralty, while he himself would follow secretly with the battle fleet.

In Admiral Hipper's orders to show himself there is a pleasant old-world flavour of the days before directional wireless. The precaution was needless. During the morning of the 30th there were indications that the High Seas Fleet was assembling in the Jade roads outside Wilhelmshaven, and this, connected with the mystery of the submarines, pointed to some movement of unusual importance. Accordingly at midday on the 30th it was decided to warn Admiral Jellicoe that the German fleet might go to sea early next morning and that there were as many as sixteen submarines out, most of which were believed to be in the North Sea. No definite orders were given. Beyond further indications that a large operation was at hand, all was still obscure. Its object could not yet be divined, and as a precaution the Harwich destroyers and the East Coast minesweeping sloops were recalled and all submarines ordered to be in readiness for sea. It seemed possible that an operation which we thought had been planned some time before was about to commence, but further than this Admiral Scheer's intentions could not be fathomed. Shortly after 5.0 p.m., however, it became known that all sections of the High Seas Fleet had received an important operation signal. This could not be wholly deciphered, but there was no time to lose, and at 5.40 a telegram was sent to the Commander-in-Chief and Admiral Beatty conveying to them the latest information and ordering them to concentrate as usual eastward of the " Long Forties " —which stretched about a hundred miles east of the Aberdeen coast—and be ready for eventualities. They were further informed that both the Harwich and the Nore forces would be held back till the situation became clearer, but that, as Admiral Jellicoe's plan provided, three submarines were being sent to the Vyl light-vessel.[1]

It was, of course, possible that the German move northwards might only be a blind to cover some design in the southern area. Admiral Bradford at Sheerness had already been ordered to have the 3rd Battle Squadron ready to sail at daylight and to send his cruisers out to the Swin, and all the East Coast Auxiliary Patrols were now recalled. Com-

[1] Two submarines from the Blyth Flotilla, which, as we have seen, was being formed with the idea of co-operating with the Grand Fleet in battle, were sent east of the Dogger, and four others sailed at noon on the 31st with the destroyer *Talisman*.

modore Tyrwhitt was also warned for action at daylight with all available light cruisers and destroyers. We were thus well prepared to deal with any serious operation in the southern area.

To the northward all was equally ready, and by 10.30 p.m. all available units of the Grand Fleet except the *Campania*[1] were at sea making for the rendezvous which Admiral Jellicoe had chosen east of the Long Forties. For himself, with the main portion of the fleet,[2] he fixed a position off the Skagerrak (57° 45′ N. 4° 15′ E.), on a line between Buchan Ness and the south of Norway some ninety miles to the westward of the Naze, and there at 2.0 p.m. next day Admiral Jerram would meet him from Cromarty with the 2nd Battle Squadron, the 1st Cruiser Squadron and nine destroyers of the 11th Flotilla with its flotilla leader. At the same time Admiral Beatty with the battle cruiser fleet and the 5th Battle Squadron was to be at a rendezvous sixty-nine miles to S.S.E. of the Commander-in-Chief—that is, in the direction of the Bight.[3] For a true advanced squadron whose function was to bring the enemy within reach of the main fleet the interval was undoubtedly too great, since in the North Sea visual connection could not be counted on over such a distance. But, as we have seen, this was not at the time the primary function of Admiral Beatty's force. As the prospect of a fleet action grew ever more remote, its tactical character as an advanced squadron became secondary to the ever-present need of intercepting raids on our coast. To this end a disposition was needed which, while the battle fleet could be kept far enough back to prevent the enemy evading it to crush the 10th Cruiser Squadron and raise the blockade, at the same time allowed the advanced force to be far enough to the southward to deal with a direct attack across the breadth of the North Sea. A distance of fifty miles between the two parts of the Grand Fleet was the least that could satisfy these conditions, and the disposition which Admiral Jellicoe now adopted had, after long consideration, become the approved normal whenever there were indications that the Germans

[1] See Note A, p. 326a.

[2] 1st and 4th Battle Squadrons, 3rd Battle Cruiser Squadron, 2nd Cruiser Squadron, and 4th Light Cruiser Squadron, with the 4th and 12th Flotillas and a division of the 11th, comprising one light cruiser, four flotilla leaders and thirty-five destroyers.

[3] 1st and 2nd Battle Cruiser Squadrons, 5th Battle Squadron (less the *Queen Elizabeth*), 1st, 2nd, and 3rd Light Cruiser Squadrons, and twenty-seven destroyers of the 9th, 10th and 13th Flotillas.

were contemplating some large operation with an unknown objective. It was only when we ourselves were operating offensively that the interval was reduced to a mean of about forty miles. On this occasion, in the absence of any indications that the Germans had changed their policy, neither the Admiralty nor Admiral Jellicoe had any reason for altering the established practice.

So through the short summer night the three sections of the fleet steamed for their rendezvous with nothing to encourage them to believe that what had set them in motion was anything more than one of the many alarms which had so often ended in disappointment. A few hours before Admiral Beatty sailed, a submarine *U 63* off the Forth had attacked the *Trident*, one of the destroyers attached to the Blyth Submarine Flotilla. Earlier in the afternoon the sloop *Gentian* had been attacked by *U 43*, also unsuccessfully, off the Pentland Skerries, while another submarine had been reported off Aberdeen, but this was all that had been seen of them that day. Later on, at break of day (3.50), when Admiral Beatty was about seventy miles out, the *Galatea*, port wing ship of his advanced screen, had a torpedo fired at her, and shortly after 8.0 a.m., eighty miles or so further on, the *Yarmouth* reported another. As she was "linking" ship right ahead of the *Lion*, Admiral Beatty turned eight points to port for twenty minutes to avoid the danger. Before he resumed his course, the destroyer *Turbulent*, which formed part of the battle cruisers' screen, reported another steering south, but by this time they had passed the "U" boat line and the trap had failed. Nor as scouts did Admiral Scheer's submarines prove more successful. The glimpses they had of the various squadrons and the scraps of intercepted signals they were able to pass on gave him no picture of concerted action. The conclusion he formed was that, whatever their purpose, the movements had no connection with his own enterprise. The reports indeed rather indicated a dispersal of our fleet on distinct missions, and being even less able to visualise the pregnant situation than our own authorities, he was more hopeful than ever of success.[1]

Our own appreciation was still far from clear. On the eve of sailing, Admiral Scheer, in accordance with the usual practice, had transferred the call sign of his flagship to the naval centre at Wilhelmshaven, so that, although it was thought he had sailed that morning, our directional wireless

[1] Scheer, *High Seas Fleet*, p. 141.

up till noon could only indicate that the battle fleet was still in the Jade. Thus, Admiral Jellicoe, who was informed of this by the Admiralty,[1] had no special reason to expect the chance of an action. The natural deduction from the information he had was that another of the now familiar cruiser raids was on foot, and that, as before, the battle fleet was preparing to cover the retirement. This being so, there was nothing to call for a modification of his dispositions.

Note A

On May 30 the *Campania* had left Scapa on one of her routine co-operation exercises, and throughout the day successful spotting flights had been made by her aircraft for ships carrying out firing practice. Her balloon had also been sent up and four officers had been given the opportunity to observe the firing. These exercises were finished by 3.30 p.m. and the carrier returned to Scapa where she anchored at 5.15 p.m. at a spot six miles to the north-eastward of the fleet anchorage.

At 5.35 p.m. she received the preparatory signal for the fleet to leave Scapa, and at 7.0 p.m. she received a further signal ordering her to raise steam for full speed ; by 9.30 p.m. she was ready to proceed. Her stationing signal was sent at 10.54 p.m., but this she did not receive. At 11.45 p.m. she was asked by the Rear-Admiral, Scapa, if she was leaving that night, and then only did her Commanding Officer (Captain Oliver Schwann) realise that the fleet had sailed, for neither the ships nor their lights could be seen from his anchorage. The *Campania* at once weighed anchor and proceeded out of harbour some two-and-a-quarter hours after the *Iron Duke*.

It was some time before the Commander-in-Chief was aware that the carrier had not sailed. She had been ordered to take station astern of the light cruiser *Blanche*, and that vessel advised accordingly. At 11.20 the *Blanche*, having no sight of the *Campania*, enquired of Commodore F if he could see her, and received the reply " No ; I am asking last destroyer." As the *Mons* replied to the question in the negative the *Blanche* reported to the C.-in-C. at 11.58 p.m. that the destroyers could see no sign of the *Campania*, and one minute later the C.-in-C. signalled direct to the carrier giving the speed and course. It was not until two hours later (2.0 a.m. May 31) that Admiral Jellicoe learned that the *Campania* had left harbour.

[1]See Note B, p. 326b.

Enemy submarines had been reported in the North Sea during that morning and at 3.55 a.m. the *Galatea* signalled that she had been attacked by one. As the *Campania* had no destroyer escort and was so far astern of the fleet that, in the C.-in-C.'s opinion, there was very little chance of her overtaking it in time to be of any assistance, he ordered her at 4.37 a.m. to return to her base, where she again dropped anchor at 9.15 a.m.

Her engine room staff had made a splendid effort to regain the lost time, and in fact she was overhauling the Grand Fleet at the rate of at least three miles an hour when she was ordered to return. If therefore, no accident had occurred, she could have joined up by about 1.30 p.m.—some hours before the action began. As she carried ten seaplanes it is possible that she might have rendered valuable reconnaissance service and thus have amply justified the risk of submarine attack.

Note B

Directional wireless indicated that the German flagship was still in the Jade at 11.10, and a telegram from the Admiralty passed the news on to Admiral Jellicoe in the following terms at 12.30 p.m.:

" No definite news of enemy. They made all preparations for sailing this morning. It was thought Fleet had sailed but *directional wireless places flagship in Jade at 11.10 G.M.T.* Apparently they have been unable to carry out air reconnaissance which has delayed them."

This message remained for many hours the only news Admiral Jellicoe had, and he therefore held on his course at economical speed.

On the evening of the previous day (May 30), however, at 5.41 Admiral Scheer had sent out the following signal:

" C.-in-C. to High Seas Fleet: The head of the 3rd Battle Squadron will pass Jade war lightship A at 4.30 a.m. (M.E.T.) 2nd Squadron will take part in the operation from the beginning and will join up astern of 1st Squadron. Wilhelmshaven 3rd Entrance will control W/T in German Bight." (*Der Kreig zur See*: *Nordsee*, Vol. 5, p. 519).

This was intercepted by the Admiralty but could not be deciphered. Had it been possible for Admiral Jellicoe to receive this information he could have arrived much earlier in the battle area, and the daylight thus gained would have been an immense advantage. As it was, it was not till the evening of May 31 was well advanced, as we shall see, that contact with the enemy battle fleet was made.

CHAPTER XVII

JUTLAND[1]—THE FIRST PHASE[2]

Battle Cruiser Action

ADMIRAL BEATTY, who was leading the 1st Battle Cruiser Squadron (*Lion*, *Princess Royal*, *Queen Mary*, *Tiger*), had been zigzagging at nineteen knots on a mean course a little south of east towards the Jutland bank, and at noon made his position about forty miles short of the rendezvous, but this was an error, and in fact he was over five miles further away to the north-westward.[3] On either side of him was his destroyer screen, and eight miles ahead his light cruisers were spread in pairs on a front of thirty miles facing south-east, with the *Yarmouth* as linking ship and his seaplane carrier *Engadine* about the middle of the cruiser line. The 2nd Battle Cruiser Squadron (*New Zealand* and *Indefatigable*) was three miles on his port bow, while Admiral Evan-Thomas with the " Queen Elizabeths " (*Barham*, *Valiant*, *Warspite* and *Malaya*) and the 1st Flotilla[4] was five miles astern. In this disposition he

[1] The following symbols are used in the diagrams of the Battle of Jutland:

Battle squadrons.	Battle cruiser squadrons.
Battleships.	Battle cruisers.
Armoured cruiser squadrons.	Light cruiser squadrons.
Armoured cruisers.	Light cruisers.

›››› Destroyer flotilla.

›› Half flotilla.

• Individual destroyers.

Note.—Flagships are denoted by the symbol attached to individual ships or squadrons.

For detailed information as to damage sustained by German vessels see the German Official History, *Der Krieg zur See* : *Nordsee*, Vol. 5.

[2] In this account of the Battle of Jutland courses and bearings are magnetic : compass variation 13° 15′ W. Times are G.M.T.

[3] *Lion's* noon position is recorded in her signal log as 56° 44′ N., 3° 45′ E., but comparison with the mean of the observed positions of the rest of the ships shows that she must have been in 56° 46′ N., 3° 36½′ E. See Diagram 16.

continued till 1.30, when, in preparation for the designed turn to the northward on reaching the rendezvous, he changed the line of bearing of his screen to E.N.E. and W.S.W., with the centre to bear S.S.E. from the *Lion*, so that when he came to make the turn it would be between him and an enemy advancing from the Bight. Similarly he advanced the 2nd Battle Cruiser Squadron and the 5th Battle Squadron two points, to bring the battle cruisers three miles E.N.E. of him and the battleships five miles N.N.W., so that on turning north they would be on either bow of the *Lion*. At 2.0, when he believed he was only ten miles short of his assigned position, though in fact the distance must have been over fifteen miles, having no news of the enemy, he made a general signal, in pursuance of Admiral Jellicoe's instructions, for the fleet to turn northward at 2.15. The only information he had was the Admiralty telegram, (12.30 p.m.), stating that, although it was thought the High Seas Fleet had put to sea in the early morning, by directional wireless the German flagship seemed to be still in the Jade at 11.10.

The truth was that Admiral Hipper, with the German scouting force, consisting of five battle cruisers, five light cruisers and thirty destroyers, had left the Jade about 1.0 a.m. and was as high up the Danish coast as the Jutland bank, approximately in the same latitude as Admiral Beatty's rendezvous and about fifty miles to the eastward of the *Lion*.[1] His light cruisers were spread on the quadrant of a circle from seven to ten miles ahead of him, but between his port wing ship and our nearest cruisers there was still a distance of twenty-two miles. Following him, over fifty miles astern, was Admiral Scheer with his two Dreadnought squadrons and six ships of the second squadron of "Deutschlands," which corresponded to our "King Edward VIIs" of Admiral Bradford's squadron at the Nore. As yet the German admiral had no suspicion of the presence of our fleet, but since the morning broke in all the beauty of a clear summer day he might well count on his dispositions for securing him from surprise. Yet, seeing what the actual situation was, this was by no means certain. It looked indeed as though Admiral Jellicoe's dispositions were exactly what was needed, and that if nothing incalculable happened Admiral Scheer would have little chance of avoiding the battle for which we

[1] First Scouting Group: Battle cruisers, *Lützow* (flag), *Derfflinger*, *Seydlitz*, *Moltke* and *Von der Tann*. Second Scouting Group (Light cruisers): *Frankfurt* (flag), *Wiesbaden*, *Pillau*, *Elbing*. The fifth light cruiser was the *Regensburg* leading the 2nd, 6th and 9th Flotillas. Scheer (*High Seas Fleet*, p. 140) states that Admiral Hipper was ordered to leave the Jade at 2.0 a.m.

had so long been striving, and would be brought against the whole Grand Fleet with his line of retreat in jeopardy.[1]

But the incalculable did happen, just as it did in March 1805 when Villeneuve's chance meeting with a neutral revealed the trap Nelson had laid and enabled him to escape out of the Mediterranean. So now it happened that about the time Admiral Beatty made the signal for turning northward, the *Elbing*, Admiral Hipper's left wing light cruiser, sighted a steamer (the Danish S.S. *N. J. Fjord*) to the westward and detached one of her attendant destroyers to ascertain the stranger's character.[2] At the same time Commodore Alexander-Sinclair, who, with his broad pendant in the *Galatea*, and with the *Phaeton* in company, was on the eastern wing of our cruiser screen, and was just about to turn north with the Admiral, also saw the vessel about fourteen miles E.S.E., and decided to hold on to the eastward a little to examine her. So luck would have it that the German destroyer as she came west sighted the *Galatea's* smoke and reported it. The *Elbing* at once altered course towards it, followed by the *Frankfurt*, *Pillau* and *Wiesbaden*. The result was premature contact. Admiral Beatty had only just settled down on his northward course to join the Battle Fleet when, at 2.20, the *Galatea* hoisted the welcome signal "Enemy in sight" and reported he could see "two cruisers, probably hostile, bearing E.S.E., course unknown."

For Admiral Beatty this was enough. Hitherto the *Galatea's* reports had not been definite enough to warrant his departing from his instructions to close the Commander-in-Chief. Now he saw them overridden by a chance of cutting off the enemy in sight, and at 2.25 he ordered his destroyers to take up positions for forming a submarine screen upon a S.S.E. course. Meanwhile the *Galatea*, increasing speed, was coming within range of the enemy, and at 2.28 she opened fire, whereupon Admiral Beatty, seeing his cruiser screen engaged, made a general signal (2.32) to alter course in succession to S.S.E. and to raise steam for full speed to intercept the enemy's retreat.[3] By this time the *Galatea* had discovered the ships she first saw were only destroyers, but at the same moment a hostile cruiser appeared, and with this ship, which was the *Elbing*, she and the *Phaeton* became engaged while the rest of the light cruisers were hurrying

[1] At 11.30 a.m. five Zeppelins were sent up, one towards the Skagerrak, the others to patrol between the second and fourth meridians. Owing to the hazy weather, however, they were able to see nothing and shortly after 4.0 p.m. were recalled. For organisation of the German fleet see Appendices C and D.

[2] See Diagram 17. [3] See Diagram 18.

eastwards to support their engaged consorts. Four minutes earlier Admiral Hipper knew that the *Elbing* had got contact, and still without knowledge of the import of her news he had turned towards her.

"It was thanks to that steamer," writes Admiral Scheer, "that the action took place. Had the destroyer not proceeded to the steamer and thus sighted the smoke of the enemy to the west, our course might have carried us past the English cruisers."[1] This could scarcely have happened. The conjecture rests on the German admiral's belief that our battle cruisers turned to north after contact was obtained, but in fact they had done so before, according to plan, and had it not been for the neutral steamer, would have continued north. Assuming, therefore, that no similar chance befell for two or three hours, Admirals Beatty and Hipper would have held on upon converging courses about abreast of each other. What would have happened then? Owing to the unfortunate Admiralty signal, which had not been corrected, Admiral Jellicoe assumed his opponent had not left the Jade by noon, and he had, therefore, been making for his rendezvous at 15 knots. The speed was governed by the fuel endurance of the destroyers, the aim being to ensure that they should reach the rendezvous with fuel enough to fight an action even if, as was likely, the fleet had to remain out more than two days. Continuous steaming at this speed would bring him to the rendezvous at the appointed hour, but, as it happened, suspicious vessels were met with which the destroyers had to examine, and he had to ease down for them to rejoin. He was consequently behind time. At 2.0 p.m. he was short of the rendezvous by eighteen miles, but according to his intention he would soon be heading for Horn Reefs to meet Admiral Beatty coming north, so that, unless something supervened, Admiral Hipper, who was proceeding to show himself on the coast of Norway, would know nothing of his danger till he ran into Admiral Jellicoe's cruisers. It is, however, very doubtful whether he could have got so far without being aware that there was something near him to the westward. The course he was then steering apparently would take him to the westward of the Naze, and if he had not soon altered more to the eastward, as he possibly might have done, his own course and that of Admiral Beatty's right wing cruisers would have been inclining so much that within half an hour at most they would scarcely have failed to sight each other's smoke. In any case there would have arisen a situation differing materially from that which actually

[1] Scheer, *High Seas Fleet*, p. 141.

occurred, and one much less favourable for the Germans. Admiral Hipper would have been committed further to the north and further ahead of his supporting battle fleet, while the two sections of the Grand Fleet would have been closer together. It is even possible that Admiral Hipper might have found retirement on Admiral Scheer impracticable, and that his only line of escape would be through the Skagerrak, where pursuit could have been safely pressed to the last. But the vision of what might have been remains a shadow land where fancy may wander and no approach to certainty is attainable. All we can assert is that Admiral Scheer thought it good fortune that he chanced to gain contact when and where he did.

Sixty-five miles away to the northward Admiral Jellicoe had taken in the *Galatea's* signals, and though there was nothing to lead him to expect anything more than an affair of cruisers, he ordered steam to be ready for full speed.[1] A few minutes later he heard the *Galatea* reporting a large amount of smoke as though from a fleet bearing E.N.E. of her, and he then (2.43) ceased zigzagging and held on upon his normal course at 17 knots, increasing to 18 knots twelve minutes later. Admiral Beatty's 2.25 flag signal to his destroyers was repeated by searchlight to the *Barham* at 2.30 ; it cannot, however, be definitely established whether or not the message was passed on to Admiral Evan-Thomas on the bridge. Even if it was, some minutes would elapse before it reached him. The 2.32 signal ("Alter course, leading ships together, the rest in succession, to S.S.E") was also made by flags, and repetition by searchlight would also have entailed a loss of some minutes. It was, therefore, not until 2.40 that the 5th Battle Squadron followed Admiral Beatty in his endeavour to get between the enemy and Horn Reefs.[2] Seeing that the battle cruisers were increasing speed, Admiral Evan-Thomas was left over ten miles astern and unable to see what they were doing. This distance, however, Admiral Beatty's alterations of course soon enabled him to reduce.

The *Galatea*, after seeing the big cloud of smoke, from which she inferred the presence of a fleet fifteen miles to the eastward, went off to the north-westward with her consort, the *Phaeton*, in order to draw the enemy on and enable Admiral Beatty to cut them off. The enemy cruisers gave chase, but at 2.45 they seemed to have altered to the northward.[3] Commodore Alexander-Sinclair, however, continued his efforts to entice them north-west, and about 3.20 he was able

[1] See Diagram 16. [2] See Diagram 18. [3] See Diagrams 19 and 20.

to report they were following him in that direction. As his signals came in Admiral Beatty gradually altered course, till by 3.0 p.m. he was steering east, a course which he judged would prevent the enemy getting back round Horn Reefs without an action. In fact he was actually steering direct for Admiral Hipper, who at this time was passing about twenty-nine miles right ahead of him in the wake of the chasing cruisers. A quarter of an hour later, however, as the *Galatea* continued to report she was leading the enemy N.W., Admiral Beatty altered still more to the northward till he was steering north-east. This continued for about ten minutes, when five columns of heavy smoke came into sight on his starboard bow.[1] At the same time the *Galatea* reported she could see more smoke E.S.E. of her, indicating another squadron astern of the ships that were chasing her, and at 3.29 Admiral Beatty, seeing he was heading too far north, turned back to east. The result of these movements was that all the ships of our 1st and 3rd Light Cruiser Squadrons which had been closing the *Galatea* were well to the north-west of him, and Admiral Evan-Thomas, by increasing speed and cutting the corner, had got up to within six miles on his port quarter.

Admiral Beatty's new course was well judged for achieving his purpose of cutting the enemy off from the Bight. Up till 3.20 each Admiral was still unaware of the other's presence, but at that time, Admiral Hipper, though still some fourteen miles away upon the *Lion's* starboard bow, sighted two columns of British battle cruisers steering towards him. So much less was the visibility to the eastward that it was not until about twelve minutes later, when he had been on his easterly course about three minutes, that Admiral Beatty sighted the enemy's five battle cruisers on his port bow. Simultaneously the Germans were aware that the British force was heading to cross their wake. For Admiral Hipper it meant his chief's plan could be carried no further. For the moment there was nothing for it but to endeavour to fall back on Admiral Scheer before it was too late, and to try to draw the enemy within his reach. Accordingly he immediately recalled his light cruisers and himself swung round sixteen points to starboard (3.33).[2] For Admiral Beatty it was the long-desired chance of getting back what he had missed at the Dogger Bank. As Admiral Hipper's force turned back towards the Bight he called the *New Zealand* and *Indefatigable* into line astern (3.34) and signalled to Admiral Evan-Thomas to turn east, speed twenty-five knots,

[1] See Diagram 21. [2] See Diagram 22.

as the enemy was in sight, and to the 9th Flotilla to take station ahead of the *Lion*, while the 13th Flotilla was to get two points on her starboard bow.

When the German battle cruisers were sighted they were hull down eleven miles away on the dim horizon. It was impossible to see what they were doing, and Admiral Beatty held on as he was at twenty-five knots to close, while the 5th Battle Squadron, six miles on his port quarter, turned on the same course (E.). A few minutes later a seaplane which had gone up from the *Engadine* reported that the course of the enemy was south, and similar signals were sent about the same time by the *Galatea* and *Falmouth*, but these all referred to the enemy's light cruisers.[1] By this time the enemy must have been well within the effective range of the *Lion's* 13.5 inch guns, but Admiral Beatty was still holding his fire. It would seem that, owing to the atmospheric conditions, accurate range-finding to the eastward was difficult. The observations from the flagship made the enemy further away than they actually were. As our ships were the more lightly armoured and had guns of heavier calibre the advantage of fighting at long range was obvious, and for some minutes Admiral Hipper had been anxiously expecting his enemy to open fire.[2] At 3.45 Admiral Beatty, in order to bring all guns to bear and to clear the smoke, signalled to form a compass line of bearing N.W. on a course E.S.E. Admiral Hipper's idea of reducing the odds against him was to reserve his fire till the last moment, so as to close as near as possible before the action began. But now, as soon as he saw what Admiral Beatty was doing, he opened fire. Simultaneously Admiral Beatty did the same, believing he was still over 18,000 yards away. In truth the range can hardly have been so great. Many of the first German

[1] See Diagram 23.

[2] According to both Scheer and Hase, the Germans believed that our battle cruisers could outrange theirs. This was partly true; Hase states that their extreme range was 180 hectometres (19,674 yards). In Admiral Beatty's "Fighting Orders" he gives his maximum ranges as follows: 13·5-inch guns, 23,000 and 24,000 yards; 12-inch guns, 18,500 yards; but, as the result of his experience gained at the Battle of Jutland, he lays down 16,000 yards as the most advantageous range for engaging, his reasons being:

"(*a*) To utilise the advantages of our heavier projectiles.
(*b*) To minimise the disadvantages of our lighter protection.
(*c*) To outrange the enemy's torpedoes.
(*d*) The time of flight (twenty-six seconds) is suitable for controlling double salvoes and attaining a high rate of fire.
(*e*) The range is not too great for efficient observation of fire.
(*f*) 16,000 yards is well inside the maximum range of 12-inch guns."

salvoes were far over,[1] but looking westward the visibility was very good and the mistake was quickly corrected. In a minute or two our ships were firing through giant columns of water and spray as the enemy's shell fell and burst all round them. So far as can be calculated from various data, it would seem that the distance at which our ships opened may have been as low as 16,000 yards, but whatever it was this much is certain, that it was an intense relief to the Germans that we did not open fire from a longer distance, when the superiority which they believed our heavier guns gave us would have denied them the possibility of making effective reply.

His other advantage Admiral Beatty was bent on using to pay back what he had himself suffered at the Dogger Bank. Having one ship more than his opponent, he was able, while preserving the rule of keeping all the enemy under fire, to order the *Princess Royal*, his next astern, to concentrate with him on the *Lützow*, in which Admiral Hipper was leading. But the *Queen Mary*, which was third in the line, having apparently missed the signal for distribution of fire, took her opposite number, the *Seydlitz*, so that until she realised what was happening, the *Derfflinger*, which was second in the enemy's line, was left undisturbed for nearly ten minutes.[2] In the rear half of our line a similar error occurred. The *Tiger*, the *Queen Mary's* next astern, appeared also to have missed the signal, so that she and the *New Zealand*, who had correctly taken the fourth ship, were both on the *Moltke*, while the *Indefatigable* and *Von der Tann* enjoyed an undisturbed duel.[3]

Seeing that our ships were clearly defined against the bright western sky, the Germans were able to pick up the range very quickly, and hits came fast. Admiral Hipper was also distributing his fire along our line, and in the first few minutes the *Lion* and *Tiger* were both hulled twice. Though Admiral Beatty was gradually bringing the enemy nearer and nearer abeam by a succession of small turns to starboard, the range continued to diminish so fast that the enemy was able to open rapid fire with both main and

[1] Commander von Hase, gunnery officer of the *Derfflinger*, says that his first few salvoes were over, though he began at 3.48 with 15,000 metres (16,400 yards). With the sixth salvo at 3.52 he straddled, the range being then 11,900 metres (13,000 yards). *Kiel and Jutland*, pp. 145–7.

[2] Hase, *Kiel and Jutland*, pp. 149, 150.

[3] The signal for the distribution of fire is not recorded in the signal logs of either the *Tiger* or the *New Zealand*. It was made by flags from the *Lion* at 3.46. At 3.47 there was another flag signal to turn together E.S.E., and in half a minute came the signal, also made by flags, to open fire.

secondary armament. By 3.54 it was down to about 13,000 yards. The *Lion* was now steering about S.S.E., parallel to the enemy's course, and with a steady range both sides were in hot action. But it was too fierce to last, and in another minute Admiral Hipper turned his ships sharply away to S.E. into line ahead. Admiral Beatty, too, bore away about two points to south (3.57), and the action continued with the range now opening rapidly. To Admiral Evan-Thomas, who was now over seven miles astern, the new movement was hidden in clouds of gun smoke, and having as yet seen nothing of the German battle cruisers, he held on to the eastward.

During this part of the action the *Queen Mary* registered two hits on the *Seydlitz*, one of which pierced and disabled one of the midship turrets in which most of the crew were killed. To some extent our fire had been hampered by a division of the 9th Flotilla, which, in its strenuous endeavour to get ahead into a favourable position for attack, was trying to pass up the engaged side of the battle cruisers and almost blinding the *Princess Royal* and *Tiger* with its smoke.[1]

At 3.58, immediately after he turned to the southward, Admiral Beatty, like his opponent, signalled to increase the rate of fire, and about this time the *Derfflinger* received her first hit. Her gunnery officer described how the shells burst with a terrific roar as they struck the water, raising colossal pillars of livid green water, which rose higher than the masts, and hung in the air for five or ten seconds before they crashed down in clouds of spray. For our own people things were no less lively. With main and secondary armament in action the German salvoes were being delivered about every twenty seconds, and our ships too were in a forest of waterspouts. It was one of the hottest moments of the action, when every nerve had to be strained to the utmost, and Admiral Beatty, having the enemy well abaft his beam, signalled to the 13th Flotilla that it seemed a good opportunity to attack. Five minutes later, while the fight still raged at its hottest, the *Lion* received a nearly fatal blow. A heavy shell struck Q-turret, entered the gun-house, burst over the left gun, and killed nearly the whole of the guns' crews, and it was only the presence of mind and devotion of the officer of the turret, Major F. J. W. Harvey, R.M.L.I., when

[1] These destroyers ("L" class) were some of those which had lately come from the Harwich Force, and were slower than those attached to the Grand Fleet. The officer commanding them reported: "Owing to lack of speed my division was not able to get ahead, and I therefore had to remain on the engaged side of the battle cruiser squadron or drop astern. I chose to remain where I was, rather than lose all chance of making a torpedo attack."

almost incapacitated with a mortal wound, that saved the flagship from sudden destruction.[1] The shot must have come from the *Lützow*, for the *Derfflinger* had been all the time on the *Princess Royal*. At the other end of the line the duel between the *Indefatigable* and the *Von der Tann* had been growing in intensity till, at about 4.0, the British ship was suddenly hidden in a burst of flame and smoke. A salvo of three shots had fallen on her upper deck and must have penetrated to a magazine. She staggered out of the line, sinking by the stern when another salvo struck her; a second terrible explosion rent her, and at 4.5 she turned over and all trace of her was gone.[2]

There can be little doubt she suffered the fate from which Major Harvey had just saved the *Lion*, but in the roar and turmoil of the action no more was known than that she with her 57 officers and 960 men was gone. Two men were picked up later by the German torpedo-boat *S 68*. So intense indeed was now the storm of the fight, so thick about the ships the spouting columns of shell-tossed water, so blinding the smoke and flame, that only a few in the fleet knew so much. But now the opposing lines had got upon slightly diverging courses the strain began to slacken. A fire had broken out on board the *Lion* from the last hit. To the Germans she appeared to fall out of the line, but what she did was to incline away to starboard in order to confuse the enemy's fire control, and so continued to open the range till by 4.5 the German guns could no longer reach, and Admiral Hipper ceased fire.

Admiral Evan-Thomas, who till this time had been steering E. by S. direct for the enemy, was nearly eight miles away. Five minutes earlier he had had a blurred glimpse of the German light cruisers which our 1st and 3rd Light Cruiser Squadrons were chasing, and with a few salvoes at 18,000 yards had forced them to disappear to the eastward. It was now (4.5) he saw Admiral Hipper's force for the first time, and directly afterwards discovered that Admiral Beatty had turned south. He at once conformed, and as soon as he was settled on the new course the *Barham* opened fire on the rearmost enemy. The range was estimated at 19,000 yards, and the target very dim, but the *Von der Tann* was straddled almost

[1] In spite of both his legs being shot off he was able to pass the word down to close the magazine doors and flood the magazines. He thus prevented the fire which started from reaching the ammunition, and so saved the ship, an action for which he was awarded the Victoria Cross after death.

[2] See Diagram 24.

at once, and the Germans took to zigzagging to confuse the range. The shooting indeed seems to have been magnificent. The Germans saw the salvoes falling absolutely together and closely concentrated, and were full of admiration for the remarkable fire direction it revealed. It was nothing, they thought, but the poor quality of the British bursting charges that saved them from disaster.[1] After five minutes the *Barham* shifted to the second ship from the rear and the action became more general, but at the great range little could be done. The German line was so obscured by haze and smoke that seldom more than one or two ships could be seen, and often there was nothing to lay on but the flashes of the guns.

For Admiral Hipper was in action again. At 4.10, being then eleven miles away abaft the beam of the *Lion*, he inclined inwards a couple of points, and as Admiral Beatty simultaneously altered still more to port to press his van, he was able at 4.17 to re-open fire at extreme range. The *Lion* had not yet been able entirely to master the fire that was smothering her. To the Germans she must have been invisible, for the *Derfflinger*, mistaking the *Princess Royal* for the flagship, began firing on the next astern, which the *Seydlitz* was also engaging. Thus the *Queen Mary*, at from 15,800 to 14,500 yards, became the target of both these ships. For about five minutes she stood it gallantly. She was fighting splendidly. The Germans say full salvoes were coming from her with fabulous rapidity.[2] Twice already she had been straddled by the *Derfflinger*, when at 4.26 a plunging salvo crashed upon her deck forward. In a moment there was a dazzling flash of red flame where the salvo fell, and then a much heavier explosion rent her amidships.[3] Her bows plunged down, and as the *Tiger* and *New Zealand* raced by her to port and starboard, her propellers were still slowly revolving high in the air. In another moment, as her two consorts were smothered in a shower of black debris, there was nothing of her left but a dark pillar of smoke rising stemlike till it spread hundreds of feet high in the likeness of a vast palm tree.[4] Two such successes were beyond anything the Germans had reason to expect. Admiral Scheer's plan had broken down, and yet they were gaining even more than he

[1] The actual explanation was that our armour-piercing shells broke up on oblique impact without penetrating the armour.

[2] Hase, *Kiel and Jutland*, pp. 157–8. [3] See Diagram 25.

[4] The casualties were 57 officers and 1,209 men killed; 2 officers and 5 men wounded. Seventeen of her crew, one of whom died, were rescued by the *Laurel*, one by the *Petard* and two by the German destroyer *V28*.

could have hoped from it. But Admiral Hipper was far from out of the wood. The 5th Battle Squadron had well hold of the enemy's rear; under the increasing fire the shooting of the German ships was growing unsteady; and from ahead of them the 13th Flotilla was developing the attack for which the moment had come.

This flotilla comprised some of the best and latest of our destroyers—*Nestor* (Commander The Hon. E. B. S. Bingham), *Nomad* (Lieutenant-Commander P. Whitfield), *Nicator* (Lieutenant in command J. E. A. Mocatta), *Pelican* (Lieutenant-Commander K. A. Beattie), *Narborough* (Lieutenant-Commander G. Corlett) *Petard* (Lieutenant-Commander E. C. O. Thomson), *Obdurate* (Lieutenant-Commander C. H. H. Sams), and *Nerissa* (Lieutenant-Commander M. G. B. Legge), with the *Turbulent* (Lieutenant-Commander D. Stuart), and *Termagant* (Lieutenant-Commander C. P. Blake), of the 9th Flotilla and the *Moorsom* (Commander J. C. Hodgson) and *Morris* (Lieutenant-Commander E. S. Graham) of the 10th Flotilla. At 4.15 Captain J. U. Farie in the flotilla cruiser *Champion* gave the order to attack, and led by Commander Bingham in the *Nestor*, in five minutes the five foremost boats were far enough advanced to cross the *Lion's* bows about a mile ahead.[1] The last four, having been thrown out by a light cruiser having to cross the line, were a little later and acting independently. Once clear the *Nestor* led for a favourable attacking position. The enemy were some eight miles off to the north-east, and as our destroyers raced for them they could see the exhilarating sight of a German flotilla emerging from the smoke with the apparent intention of delivering a like attack on our battle cruisers. In fact, so Admiral Scheer tells us, Commodore Heinrich of the *Regensburg*, the leader of Admiral Hipper's attached flotillas, seeing the plight his chief was in when our 5th Battle Squadron got his range, determined to deliver an attack to relieve him.[2] Commander Bingham immediately turned north to intercept it, and soon a hot fight began. Combined with the fire of our ships it was more than the Germans could endure. Though more numerous than our own destroyers, they were smaller and had a weaker gun armament, so, without pressing their attack home to effective range, they fired ten torpedoes hastily and retired. To avoid the attack Admiral Evan-Thomas had turned away two points, but hardly any of the torpedoes reached him, and none took effect. Part of the foiled flotilla was to be seen seeking safety round the rear of their squadron and part round the van. These last Com-

[1] See Diagrams 24, 25 and 26. [2] Scheer, *High Seas Fleet*, p. 144.

mander Bingham turned to chase at his utmost speed, while our other divisions went after the rest.

The *Nicator* was now the only boat with him, for the *Nomad*, his next astern, had been disabled by a shell in her boilers. But, nothing daunted, he continued to chase till he had reached a good position for the *Lützow*, when, turning to attack, he fired two torpedoes at 5,000 yards. But Admiral Hipper was ready for him with the same foiling manœuvre as our own, and just as the *Nestor* fired the Germans suddenly turned away (4.30), and both torpedoes missed. The *Nicator* had no better luck. But Commander Bingham was not yet satisfied, and followed by the *Nicator* he turned eastward after his prey. Undeterred by a rain of shell from the secondary armament of the enemy, as well as from the *Regensburg*, now assisted by four destroyers of the 2nd Flotilla, they pressed on and fired again at 3,500 yards. Again there was no hit, and miraculously dodging the enemy's rapid salvoes they turned back to escape.

By this time Lieutenant-Commander Thomson in the *Petard*, having become separated from his division, was endeavouring to attack with the *Turbulent*, followed by the *Nerissa* and *Termagant*, as well as the *Morris* and *Moorsom* of the 9th Flotilla, who had attached themselves to the party. In the first onset he had fired a torpedo at the leading German destroyer, *V 27*, which seems to have taken deadly effect, for she was soon seen to be lying stopped with her decks awash, but all the boats were too much engaged in the mêlée with the enemy's destroyers to be able to get at the squadron. It was a wild scene of groups of long low forms vomiting heavy trails of smoke and dashing hither and thither at thirty knots or more through the smother and splashes, and all in a rain of shell from the secondary armament of the German battle cruisers, as well as from the *Regensburg* and the destroyers, with the heavy shell of the contending squadrons screaming overhead. Gradually a pall of gun and funnel smoke almost hid the shell-tormented sea, and beyond the fact that the German torpedo attack had failed, little could be told of what was happening, when, at 4.43, the *Lion* ran up the destroyers' recall.[1] As they all turned to obey, it was seen that midway between the lines the *Nestor's* first antagonist, *V 27*, and another destroyer, *V 29*, were sinking. Near to them was the *Nomad* in a like condition, and as the *Petard* ran back she came across the *Nestor* scarcely able to crawl. Commander Bingham in dodging back from his second gallant attack had had two

[1] See Diagram 26.

boilers put out of action by the *Regensburg*. The *Petard* offered him a tow, but he refused to expose another destroyer to what now looked like certain destruction.

The meaning of the destroyer recall was that in the midst of the turmoil the tables had been once more turned and the fight had assumed an entirely new aspect. Ten minutes earlier (4.33) Commodore Goodenough, commanding the 2nd Light Cruiser Squadron in the *Southampton*, which was then nearly two miles ahead of the *Lion* on her port bow, suddenly sent the surprising signal that battleships were in sight south-east of him.[1] Closing them at full speed he was able in five minutes to make them out to be the German battle fleet. So startling a development was scarcely credible. Admiral Beatty had still no reason to think Admiral Scheer had left the Jade, but there was the signal, and it was immediately confirmed by the *Champion*, who was also ahead and supporting her destroyers. What was to be done? Admiral Beatty, who since 4.30 had been inclining away from the enemy to open the range, turned at once to port direct for the position where the apparition had been reported, while Admiral Evan-Thomas held on, firing heavily on the German battle cruisers as they turned away before the destroyer attack. Wholly unexpected as Admiral Scheer's arrival was, all doubt was quickly at an end. Two minutes after the *Lion* altered course she could see the leading German battleship less than twelve miles away to the south-eastward, and then an apparently interminable line of battleships came into view, attended by light cruisers and a swarm of destroyers. There could be no question as to what it meant, and at 4.40 Admiral Beatty swung back sixteen points in succession to north-west, and then northward to join the Commander-in-Chief by the shortest possible course.[2]

The signal was " general," but it was made by flags, and Admiral Evan-Thomas, who was eight miles astern, could not see it. He was busy at the time with the enemy, and was just making a signal to " concentrate in pairs from the rear." He saw the turn, but being in hot chase, he rightly judged his duty was to hold on as he was. This he did till eight minutes later, when, as the *Lion* and *Barham* had approached each other on opposite courses within two miles, Admiral Beatty signalled direct to the battle squadron to turn back sixteen points to starboard. But as they were closing each other at the rate of nearly a mile a minute, Admiral Evan-Thomas had passed before he could carry out the order, and so he turned up in succession astern of the

[1] See Diagram 25. [2] See Diagram 26.

battle cruisers, as the enemy began to fire on the turning point. Commodore Goodenough elected to disregard the general signal, and held on at twenty-five knots direct for the new enemy, bent on reporting in detail their composition and if possible making a torpedo attack. So, inspired by the old tradition of the service, he raced on at full speed into the jaws of death till he had seen all that was needful. His boldness perhaps saved him.. As he was heading direct for the enemy, possibly they could not be certain what his squadron was, for he held on to within 13,000 yards of them before he turned back north-west, and it was not till then, when it could be seen his ships had four funnels, that they were fired on. Though they were immediately drenched with the splashes from the enemy's closely falling salvoes, yet by clever zigzagging all escaped injury.

What he had seen—and it was a sight no British ship had enjoyed since the war began—was the German High Seas Fleet deployed in battle order, line ahead. In the van, led by Rear-Admiral Behncke in the *König*, came the 3rd Squadron, seven of the "König" and "Kaiser" classes, the latest German Dreadnoughts. Following them were nine more Dreadnoughts—five "Helgolands," with twelve 12-inch guns and four "Nassaus" with twelve of 11-inch. In the rear was the 2nd Squadron of six pre-Dreadnoughts. He himself, in the fleet flagship *Friedrich der Grosse*, was eighth ship in his selected post of command between the van and centre, and in company were five cruisers of the 4th Scouting Group and three and a half flotillas of destroyers, led by the light cruiser *Rostock*. At 3.54 he had heard that Admiral Hipper was engaged with the enemy and was leading them towards him. Apparently it was some time before he learnt the exact position, for it was not till 4.5 that he altered to a north-westerly course to support his battle cruisers and to prevent the premature retreat of the enemy. With this object, a quarter of an hour later, believing the chance he had worked for had come, he turned to the westward so as to bring Admiral Beatty between two fires. But he had scarcely begun the movement when he heard of our 5th Battle Squadron having appeared on the scene, and immediately turned north to save Admiral Hipper from the trap in which till that moment he thought he had caught his opponent.

He held on this course until 4.42 when he turned two points to port; at 4.58 he made a further turn of two points to port which brought him on to a north-westerly course and led him towards our destroyers as they were retiring in response to

Admiral Beatty's recall. Helpless, right in his track lay the *Nomad* and the *Nestor*. As the battleships came on, both boats were quickly smothered with their fire, yet before they had to be abandoned both had fired their last torpedoes at their new assailants and what was left of the crews had taken to the riddled boats, from which they were soon rescued by a German destroyer. The *Nicator* and *Petard* as they retired also got in four shots between them at the battle cruisers. Three came from the *Petard*, the last of which, fired just before 5.0, hit the *Seydlitz*. It took her on the starboard side forward under the armoured belt, tearing a hole 13 feet by 39, and put her No. 1 15-centimetre gun permanently out of action, but so well was she constructed that she was able to carry on. Though twenty torpedoes had been fired, this was the only damage done to the German fleet; yet, small as was the result, the whole affair must ever stand as an exemplary piece of flotilla work in battle. Not only had our destroyers foiled the attempt of the German flotillas, but had broken through them, and with the opposing ship-fire unsubdued, had pushed home their attack with unsurpassed dash and daring. Though the positive effects were small, yet the courage and determination our men had displayed were not without effect on the action. They had certainly forced the German battle cruisers to continue their turn away during the highly critical minutes when our battle cruisers were making the sixteen-point turn and would otherwise have been exposed to severe punishment. As between the opposed flotillas it had been a fair trial of strength, and though in losses honours were easy, for on each side two boats had been sunk, the faith of the Germans in the superiority of their destroyer service must have been shaken.

By the time our two destroyers went down our two squadrons were out of sight from the rest of the flotilla, but could be heard still firing. Admiral Hipper after his turn away had resumed his southerly course, just as Admiral Beatty was making his sixteen-point turn to N.W. After he had hauled round another four points to North, firing broke out again almost immediately, the *Lion* engaging the *Von der Tann*, the left-hand ship of the enemy. A few salvoes only had been fired at extreme range, when Admiral Hipper, in his turn, altered round sixteen points to starboard in succession to take up his station ahead of the advancing German battle fleet. In the mist and the resulting confusion of smoke, Admiral Beatty once more lost sight of the enemy, and for about six minutes firing ceased. By five o'clock, however, the German battle cruisers could again be dimly seen steering to the northward. Once more Admiral Beatty engaged them, and almost immediately the *Lion* received another bad hit, giving rise to a fire which, but for the closed magazine door, must have put an end to her. It was little our battle cruisers could do, for while they showed up clearly against the glowing western sky, the increasing mist so obscured the eastern horizon, that Admiral Hipper's ships were soon barely visible. Only on the flashes of the guns was it possible to get a target, or when from time to time the sun broke through the clouds to light up the enemy's line and dazzle his eyes. As Admiral Beatty ran out of range firing became intermittent, and within eight minutes ceased altogether. At 5.10 he reduced to 24 knots, and made his way northward to join the main fleet.[1]

Away on his port quarter Admiral Evan-Thomas was having the same trouble.[2] By the time his turn northward was completed he was some three miles astern of the battle cruisers and nearly abreast of the *König*, so that he at once became engaged with Admiral Scheer's van squadron, as well as with Admiral Hipper. To reduce the range the whole German battle fleet had turned north-west by divisions, and in this formation was trying to close the range. The *Barham* had hardly turned before she was badly hit by a heavy shell which caused many casualties and wrecked her wireless gear. Those of the enemy ships that were within range seemed to be concentrating on the turning point, but the *Valiant*, her next astern, got round without being touched. The *Warspite* was no less fortunate, and as *Malaya*, the rear ship, turned it was evident that she was the target of a whole division or more. Salvoes were falling all round her at the rate of six a minute. By hauling out to port, however, she escaped, but for the next twenty minutes she was constantly straddled,and was twice so badly hit below the water line that she began to list. It was then decided to open fire short with the 6-inch starboard battery in order to set up a screen, but before the order was passed another heavy shell burst inside it, devastating guns and crew and starting a fire amidst the havoc it had wrought.[3]

For a time Admiral Evan-Thomas kept a northerly course, as Admiral Beatty had done, the *Barham* and the *Valiant* firing on the enemy's battle cruisers while his two rear ships engaged the battleships.[4] Thus, as Admiral Scheer was coming

[1] See Diagram 27. [2] See Diagram 26.

[3] The casualties in the 5th Battle Squadron were chiefly suffered in this period. *Barham* had 26 killed and 37 wounded, *Malaya* lost 63 killed and 33 wounded. For over half an hour she bore the brunt of the fighting.

[4] See Diagram 27.

on north-west the courses converged, and Admiral Evan-Thomas was unable, in spite of his superior speed, to increase the range, and all his squadron remained under a heavy fire, which they returned as well as the bad light permitted. Two destroyers of the 13th Flotilla, which had not yet been in action, made a bold attempt to close. These were the *Onslow* (Lieutenant-Commander J. C. Tovey) and the *Moresby* (Lieutenant-Commander R. V. Alison), who, having been detached to screen the seaplane carrier, had missed the big attack. But on rejoining Admiral Beatty when he turned north they saw their opportunity in the approaching German battle fleet. Then, about 5.0 p.m., as the Admiral altered to N.N.W., the *Onslow*, steering N.N.E., with the *Moresby* close astern, found herself diverging from our battle cruisers and closing those of the enemy. As they seemed to have no screen ahead of them, the opportunity was not to be resisted, and the *Onslow* led on to close nearer. Before, however, the range was low enough to please her, four light cruisers appeared. They were Admiral Hipper's light scouting group, which had just turned north again. Instantly they developed so accurate and heavy a fire on the two destroyers that they were forced to turn away and scatter. The *Onslow* swung to port and abandoned her bold attempt. The *Moresby*, however, was more fortunate. Having turned to starboard and started to run south she soon found herself in position to attack the van of the advancing German battle fleet, and closing to within 8,000 yards she gave a long-range torpedo to the third ship in the line. It missed, but both boats got back from their brilliant adventure with their fighting capacity unimpaired.

By this time (5.20) Admiral Evan-Thomas had inclined to port till he was steering approximately in the wake of the battle cruisers N.N.W., and as the range then opened, the fury of the running fight was abating. The Germans soon found themselves unable to reach our ships, while they themselves were still under fire. Hits were made on both their battle cruisers and battleships; the *Grosser Kürfürst*, *Markgraf*, *Lützow* and *Derfflinger* all being hit on the water line, while the *Seydlitz* also received considerable damage. By 5.30, however, the pursuit was dropped, though firing continued intermittently. So the first phase of the battle ended with all our squadrons hastening northward under the quiet evening sky to join the Commander-in-Chief, and the Germans following at their utmost speed in response to Admiral Scheer's signal to pursue the enemy.

CHAPTER XVIII

JUTLAND—THE SECOND PHASE

First Contact of the Battle Fleets

When at 5.30 the firing died away Admiral Jellicoe was twenty-three miles to the northward, with his three Dreadnought squadrons in divisions in line ahead disposed abeam.[1] Rear-Admiral Hood with the 3rd Battle Cruiser Squadron (*Invincible*, *Inflexible* and *Indomitable*), with the light cruisers *Chester* and *Canterbury* and four destroyers, was twenty-one miles ahead, but too far to the eastward to be seen by the *Lion*. Spread in advance were two cruiser squadrons, the 1st Cruiser Squadron (*Defence*, *Warrior*, *Duke of Edinburgh* and *Black Prince*), under Rear-Admiral Arbuthnot, forming the starboard half of the line, and the *Minotaur*, *Cochrane* and *Shannon* of the 2nd Cruiser Squadron the port half, under Rear-Admiral H. L. Heath, with his fourth ship, the *Hampshire*, as linking ship. Directly ahead of the battle squadrons as anti-submarine screen was Commodore Le Mesurier's 4th Light Cruiser Squadron (*Calliope*, *Constance*, *Comus*, *Royalist* and *Caroline*). The light cruisers attached to the battle squadrons, *Active*, *Boadicea*, *Blanche* and *Bellona*, had fallen astern into the stations assigned for the approach.[2] Thus disposed his advanced ships should have covered a front of forty miles. But owing to the continually decreasing visibility they had been forced to close in order to keep visual touch till their front was reduced to some twenty-five miles.

In the main fleet Vice-Admiral Burney, commanding the 1st Battle Squadron, formed the starboard wing with the 6th Division (*Marlborough*, *Revenge*, *Hercules* and *Agincourt*), and next to him was the 5th Division (*Colossus*, *Collingwood*,

[1] See Diagram 28.

[2] Cruising Disposition No. 1: *Cochrane*, *Shannon*, *Minotaur*, centre of screen, *Defence*, *Warrior*, *Duke of Edinburgh*, *Black Prince*, *Hampshire* (linking ship). Cruisers spread eight miles apart. (At 3.10 the centre of the screen had been ordered to be sixteen miles ahead of the battle fleet.) The 4th Light Cruiser Squadron was four miles ahead of the battle fleet and the attached light cruisers on the flanks.

Neptune and *St. Vincent*), led by Rear-Admiral Gaunt. On the port flank was the 2nd Battle Squadron, the strongest section of the fleet, under Vice-Admiral Jerram (*King George V*), who was leading the wing division (*Ajax, Centurion* and *Erin*), with his other division next (*Orion, Monarch, Conqueror* and *Thunderer*), led by Rear-Admiral Leveson. In the centre was the 4th Squadron, led by Vice-Admiral Sturdee at the head of his starboard division (*Benbow, Bellerophon, Temeraire* and *Vanguard*), and at the head of the other division (*Superb*, with the flag of Rear-Admiral Duff, *Royal Oak* and *Canada*) was Admiral Jellicoe in the fleet flagship *Iron Duke*. He thus had under his own hand, without counting the four ships of the 5th Squadron, a fairly homogeneous force of twenty-four Dreadnoughts, against Admiral Scheer's sixteen and the six ships of the older pre-Dreadnought squadron. As the Germans had no gun heavier than 12-inch, while our main armament ranged from 12-inch to 15-inch, Admiral Jellicoe had also a considerable superiority in gun power, but, on the other hand, the German ships were better protected and had more torpedo tubes.[1]

From this marked inequality in the main weapon of the two admirals arose a corresponding difference of tactics, and particularly in their views of how to use their minor forces in battle. Each was equally bent on a combination of all arms, but each had his own method, correctly based on his relative strength in primary units. Since Admiral Jellicoe was so much superior in battleships, his best chance of a decisive success was to get in a smashing blow with his main weapon, while Admiral Scheer would naturally seek to avoid such a blow, or at least to weaken it by energetic use of his minor forces. It was fully expected that for this purpose he would use mines, submarines and destroyers, but in fact he had nothing but destroyers. Accordingly his destroyers were given a highly offensive function, and to enable them to exercise it with facility they were more or less equally divided into two groups, the one in the van (3rd and 1st Half Flotillas) and the other in rear (5th and 7th Flotillas), both on the disengaged side of the battle squadrons. On the other hand, since it was fundamental with Admiral Jellicoe that the blow with his dominant weapon should be given with the utmost violence, it was essential that his Dreadnought force should not be interfered with or have its attention distracted by minor attack from the enemy. His destroyers were therefore given a function that was primarily defensive. Their instructions were to confine

[1] For the organisation of the Grand Fleet see Appendix B.

themselves at first to repelling torpedo attacks which the enemy might threaten, but subject to this restriction commanders of units were given full discretion for delivering their attack as and when they saw occasion. Cruisers and light cruisers were charged with like primary duties, either independently against similar types of ship or in support of destroyers; but here again commanders of squadrons were given the freest possible hand as to how they played their parts in the tactical combination. On this conception of co-ordination they, as well as the destroyers, had their battle stations at either end of the line in the positions from which they could best contribute to the free action of the battle fleet without masking its fire.

One other material factor had an equally strong effect on Admiral Jellicoe's tactics. Seeing that his battle fleet was superior to that of the enemy in numbers as well as in weight of gun power and effective range, his advantage was to open the action out of effective torpedo range—which was taken to be 15,000 yards—and not to come to close range till the enemy began to be dominated. Without keeping in mind these fundamental considerations it is impossible to follow the battle with a just appreciation of what was or was not done.

At 2.20, when Admiral Jellicoe began to take in the *Galatea's* signals, he was still nearly twelve miles from his two o'clock rendezvous, owing to the delay caused by examining vessels which the fleet encountered to see that they were not enemy scouts.[1] As at first the reports of the enemy indicated nothing more than light cruising forces, possibly even only destroyers, he kept on at the economical speed of his destroyers, zigzagging as before, but ordered the fleet to raise steam for full speed (2.35). As soon, however, as the reports made it evident that something more serious might be in question he ceased zigzagging and resumed his normal course S. 50 E., increasing speed to seventeen knots (2.43). Not content with this, twelve minutes later he increased by another knot, and almost at once called for steam to be raised for full speed with all dispatch and signalled to prepare for action (3.0). Then, in accordance with his pre-arranged plan, he altered course S.E. by S., in the direction of Horn Reefs, and ordered his cruisers to push on sixteen miles ahead of him. It was an order they must have some difficulty in

[1] According to the *Iron Duke's* reckoning she was at two o'clock nineteen and a half miles N. 40 W. of the rendezvous, but she seems actually to have been four miles further on, in Lat. 57° 54½′ N., Long. 3° 52′ E., that is, fifteen and a half miles from the rendezvous.

carrying out, for he was increasing to nineteen knots when he received Admiral Beatty's 3.15 position. Neither flagship's dead reckoning, as we have seen, was quite correct. The position which the *Iron Duke* gave at 3.26 made the two flagships seventy-one miles apart and bearing N. 16 W. Admiral Beatty had given his course and speed as N.E. twenty-three knots, while the *Galatea* said she was leading the enemy N.W. On this information Admiral Jellicoe concluded that some enemy cruisers and destroyers were being chased to the northward by the battle cruiser fleet, and he now ordered all flag officers to inform their divisions of the situation, and at 3.35 he himself warned Commodore Hawksley, who as Commodore "F" was commanding the Grand Fleet flotillas, that the enemy should be in touch with our cruisers by four o'clock.

So far all seemed going well. But the signal had hardly been made when the outlook was entirely changed. An urgent message came in from the *Lion* that the enemy's battle cruisers with a large number of destroyers had come into sight bearing N.E.; another followed quickly giving their course as south-easterly (S. 55 E.), and then a third (3.55) that Admiral Beatty was engaged with them. All hope of an early encounter was now shattered. It looked more than ever like a repetition of former raids, but without loss of time Admiral Jellicoe increased to twenty knots and ordered Admiral Hood to proceed ahead immediately to support the battle cruiser fleet.

The *Invincible*, in which Admiral Hood's flag was flying, was then about twenty-five miles on the port bow of the *Iron Duke*, and a little ahead of station, for when at 3.15 Admiral Hood heard from the *Galatea* of the enemy's light cruisers coming northward, he had inclined to the eastward at twenty-two knots to head them off. Half an hour later, when he knew they had turned to the southward, he altered back to S. 26 E., and when the welcome order came to push ahead he was about forty-three miles from the position the *Lion* had given S. by W. of him. But as he had no margin of speed there was little hope of overtaking Admiral Beatty on that course. He had therefore altered to S.S.E.—with what unforeseen good effect will be seen later—and sped away at twenty-five knots.

Then for an anxious half-hour all was silence; not a word reached the Commander-in-Chief of how his colleague was faring. Of the 5th Battle Squadron he had heard nothing. He telegraphed (4.17) to know if it was in company with the battle cruisers. The reassuring reply was "Yes, I am engaging enemy." Then as the battle fleet pressed southward he thought of the open Skagerrak and the unguarded waters behind him, and at 4.38 ordered Admiral Tupper with the 10th Cruiser Squadron to close the blockade against outgoing raiders by taking up the eastern patrol area.

The message had hardly been despatched when in the *Iron Duke's* wireless room was heard the call of the *Southampton*, followed by the message, "Have sighted enemy battle fleet bearing approximately S.E. . . . course North." It was the first that had been heard of Admiral Scheer that day, since he had been reported apparently in the Jade, yet it was confirmed in a few minutes by Admiral Beatty. The message came in mutilated and confusing, but for the Commander-in-Chief it was enough, and at 4.47 the whole fleet was reading the stirring general signal "Enemy's battle fleet coming north." If Admiral Jellicoe had any doubt as to what lay before him it was quickly set at rest by Commodore Goodenough's boldness in pressing his reconnaissance home. The detailed report he was able to make to Admiral Beatty he also sent to the Commander-in-Chief, and at 4.51 Admiral Jellicoe signalled to the Admiralty "Fleet action is imminent." [1]

Everywhere as the long-despaired-of news was whispered through the air and sped along the wires excitement grew. Dockyards all round the coast were astir and tugs were getting up steam to assist crippled ships, and nowhere was the tension higher than in the squadrons that were still chafing in port. At Harwich when the half-read battle signals told clearly enough what was happening in the North Sea Commodore Tyrwhitt was straining in the leash that held him. It had always been understood that if a fleet action became imminent he was to join the Commander-in-Chief with all speed, and he had just asked for instructions; but the minutes went by and none came. From the Thames at 5.0 Admiral Bradford signalled to the Admiralty that he was moving out from the Swin to the Black Deep light-vessel. Then Commodore Tyrwhitt could bear it no longer,

[1] Admiral Beatty's signal is a typical example of the difficulty of conveying accurate information in action. His own W/T having been shot away, he semaphored to the *Princess Royal*, his next astern, as he was turning north, "Report enemy's battle fleet to Commander-in-Chief bearing S.E." The message she sent was entered in her log thus: "S.O. Battle Cruiser Fleet to Commander-in-Chief via *Princess Royal*: Urgent-priority. Have sighted enemy's battle fleet bearing S.E. My position Lat. 56° 36′ N., Long. 6° 04′ E." By some of the ships the message was taken in correctly. In the *Iron Duke* it read: "26–30 battleships probably bearing S.S.E. steering S.E.," but in the light of the *Southampton's* signal the enemy's course was rightly interpreted.

and at 5.15 he too informed the Admiralty he was proceeding to sea. He still had time to deal with a half-beaten enemy trying to escape through the waters with which he was so familiar, and so reap the reward of all the strenuous work on which he had been incessantly engaged since the war began. But the Admiralty were not yet in a position to give him the necessary orders. Crossing his message came the reply to his request for instructions: "Complete with fuel. You may have to relieve light cruisers and destroyers in battle cruiser fleet later." So dismal a part could not be tamely accepted until at least the effect of his last telegram was known, and he held on hopefully.

The Admiralty's responsibilities in the southern area were too heavy for them to fall in with his obvious wish.[1] It was in any case of the last importance that his force should be complete with fuel and ready to carry out whatever duty was ultimately assigned to it. Twenty minutes later Commodore Tyrwhitt read with sinking heart his next instruction, "Return at once and await orders."

At 5.30 Admiral Beatty, from whom the enemy was temporarily obscured, was continuing his course N.N.W. to close the Commander-in-Chief. Admiral Evan-Thomas, who was four miles astern on a northerly course, was still in action. Ever since Admiral Beatty had lost sight of the enemy, the 5th Battle Squadron had been almost continuously engaged, the flagship and the *Valiant* with the German battle cruisers at 19,000 to 20,000 yards, and the two rear ships with the battle fleet, but it could hardly be seen except for the flashes of its guns. It was only now and then that a ship showed up long enough to be taken as a target. Our ships, on the other hand, were well defined against a bright yellow horizon, and since, in spite of the squadron's speed, it had not yet got beyond the enemy's range, the rear ships, *Warspite* and *Malaya*, were suffering from the leading German battleships. The cause of the inability to drop the enemy was that Admiral Scheer was still heading in quarter line to close the range. Only by an inclination to the westward could Admiral Evan-Thomas counter the move, and that would have thrown his squadron off the line to meet Admiral Jellicoe. Up to this time neither admiral was at all sure where the Commander-in-Chief was, but as his estimated bearing was N. 16 W., Admiral Beatty at 5.33 hauled round to N.N.E. Seven minutes before, Admiral Hipper, on receiving Admiral Scheer's order for a "general chase," had conformed to his Chief's inclination to the westward, so that the courses of

[1] See *ante*, p. 302.

all squadrons were now converging, with the result that by 5.40 Admiral Beatty could again make out his adversary in the mist only 14,000 yards away, and the action broke out again in renewed fury.[1] Simultaneously Admiral Evan-Thomas also saw the enemy's battle cruisers, and both the *Barham* and the *Valiant* added their fire to that of Admiral Beatty, while the *Warspite* and *Malaya* continued to engage the now dim forms of Admiral Scheer's leading battleships. Under the concentrated fire, with the light now in our favour, Admiral Hipper's squadrons began to suffer severely, but hauling away slightly to open the range they stood up to their barely visible opponents, as yet in complete ignorance of the perilous situation which was just developing.

At 5.33 Admiral Napier, leading the 3rd Light Cruiser Squadron in the *Falmouth* four miles ahead of the *Lion*, sighted the *Black Prince*, starboard wing ship of Admiral Arbuthnot's 1st Cruiser Squadron, and so finally visual touch was established between the two sections of the Grand Fleet. As this squadron formed the starboard section of Admiral Jellicoe's advanced screen, her station was on the extreme westward flank. With the decreasing visibility Admiral Arbuthnot was inclining inwards to close Admiral Heath on his left and steering south-east diagonally across the battle cruiser course. The *Black Prince* was therefore nearest to the enemy, and just as Admiral Beatty re-opened fire was able to report battle cruisers five miles south of her. They were our own that she saw, but whether or not she mistook them for Germans, the signal was received by the Commander-in-Chief as reporting enemy battle cruisers, and only deepened the perplexity of the sparse and confusing information he had been getting from the southward. Assuming that the enemy's battle fleet would be only a few miles astern of the battle cruisers, the *Black Prince's* message made its position some twenty miles north-westward of where the last message from Commodore Goodenough placed it, and Admiral Jellicoe rightly concluded that the battle cruisers seen must be our own.[2] It was thus with everything in extreme uncertainty that contact with the enemy began to be felt, and it was felt very close. As early as 3.10, when it was known that Admiral Beatty was in touch with something more than destroyers, Admiral Jellicoe had ordered the screen to get sixteen miles ahead, but he himself was increasing speed so rapidly that they had not been able to gain half the distance.

[1] See Diagram 29.

[2] The *Black Prince's* signal was by wireless timed 5.42, but was not read by the Commander-in-Chief till considerably later.

Deployment could not be postponed much longer, and little time was left for signals to get through to the Commander-in-Chief which would determine the all-important factor of the exact position of the enemy's battle fleet.

At the moment, however, that his starboard wing had contact with Admiral Beatty something even more important was happening on the opposite flank. Here Admiral Hood, in response to the order to support Admiral Beatty, had reached about twenty-five miles ahead of the battle fleet with the 3rd Battle Cruiser Squadron. One of his attached light cruisers, the *Canterbury*, was about five miles further forward; the other, the *Chester*, was the same distance to the westward on his starboard beam, while his four destroyers, *Shark*, *Acasta*, *Ophelia* and *Christopher*, formed his anti-submarine screen ahead. The *Chester* was thus nearest to the enemy; at 5.27 her commander, Captain R. N. Lawson, hearing the sound of guns to the south-westward, had turned in that direction to investigate.[1] Soon he could see far-away flashes breaking the mist where the 5th Battle Squadron was still fighting, and in another minute or two the form of a three-funnelled cruiser with some destroyers took shape crossing ahead of him. Realising at once that she was an enemy, he turned to starboard to bring his guns to bear, but as this movement brought one of the destroyers in admirable position for attack on his port bow he swung north and was opening fire on his phantom enemy when he saw she was not alone. Two other ghost-like forms were astern of her, and in a minute or two the *Chester* was smothered in bursting shell. Within five minutes she had three of her guns disabled: the majority of the guns' crews were lying dead or wounded, and with only her after gun in action she turned away north-eastward at utmost speed, dodging the salvoes like a snipe.[2]

It was Admiral Boedicker's light cruiser squadron (2nd Scouting Group) she had run into, as on Admiral Hipper's disengaged side it was continuing to the northward some four miles on his starboard beam, and the ships chasing the *Chester*

[1] See Diagram 28.

[2] Two light cruisers which had been ordered and were building at Messrs. Cammell Laird's for the Greek Government were purchased and taken over in 1915. They were renamed *Birkenhead* and *Chester*. The former was completed in September 1915, but the *Chester* was less far advanced, and was only commissioned on 2nd May, 1916. The *Birkenhead* and *Chester*, which were considerably heavier (5,250 tons) than the "C" class cruisers, resembled very closely the "Chatham" class. They carried a main armament of ten 5·5-inch guns. The speed of the *Birkenhead* was twenty-five knots, and that of the *Chester* twenty-six knots.

were the *Frankfurt* (flag), *Wiesbaden*, *Pillau* and *Elbing*. The *Chester* seemed doomed, but rescue was at hand. Directly Admiral Hood heard the firing abaft his starboard beam he swung round north-west (5.37). As the German cruisers were closing to the eastward the courses quickly converged. In a few minutes our battle cruisers could see emerging from the mist the *Chester* zigzagging in the storm of shell splashes that were drenching her, and almost at once her eager pursuers came into view.[1] Immediately they saw their danger they swung round to starboard on the opposite course to Admiral Hood, but it was too late. As they passed, his guns crashed into them, while the *Chester* escaped across the *Invincible's* bows, firing her last shots as she ran northward into safety.[2] As for Admiral Boedicker, he only escaped the 12-inch salvoes that were smothering him by recourse to his torpedoes. To avoid them Admiral Hood had to turn away, and the enemy was soon lost in the mist, but not before the *Wiesbaden* was a wreck and both the *Pillau* and *Frankfurt* badly hit.

But the episode did not end here. When Admiral Hood turned to the rescue of the *Chester* his four destroyers were left on his port quarter, and they soon caught sight of the German cruisers running towards them south-east, half hidden by shell splashes. The division was led by Commander Loftus Jones in the *Shark*, the same intrepid officer who by his resolute dogging of Admiral von Ingenohl's cruiser screen at dawn on the day of the Scarborough raid had caused the whole High Seas Fleet to turn back to its base. Seeing the excellent chance that had fallen to him, he led off to make the most of it, followed by the *Acasta* (Lieutenant-Commander J. O. Barron), *Ophelia* (Commander L. G. E. Crabbe)—both officers had been with him in his previous exploit—and the *Christopher* (Lieutenant-Commander F. M. Kerr).[3] As they approached they could see that ahead of the flying cruisers a number of enemy destroyers were evidently developing an attack on Admiral Hood, but as soon as the Germans were aware of the *Shark's* direction they turned to

[1] See Diagram 29.

[2] Beside the loss of three of her ten 5·5-inch guns the *Chester* had several holes in and above her armour. Her after control was destroyed, but her engines were practically uninjured. Her casualties were seventy-seven (thirty-five killed or died of wounds and forty-two wounded). Amongst the killed was the boy Jack Cornwell, who for his exemplary conduct in the action was awarded a posthumous Victoria Cross. Indeed the behaviour of all concerned marked the affair as highly creditable to a new ship that had not been quite a month in commission. At daylight on June 1 she was ordered to proceed to the Humber, where she arrived at 5.0 p.m.

[3] See Diagram 30.

protect Admiral Boedicker. A very hot engagement was the result. The *Shark* got off a torpedo at one of the cruisers, but was quickly smothered with the fire of the squadron and its destroyers, and by the time Commander Jones knew he had frustrated the attack on Admiral Hood and had turned back, his boat was brought to a standstill. His old comrade, Lieutenant-Commander Barron, rushed up to take him in tow, but he would not hear of the *Acasta*, which was also badly damaged, being sunk for him, and ordered her to leave him. At this moment Captain P. M. R. Royds in the *Canterbury* appeared coming up to the rescue from the south-east. By turning to the southward he enticed the cruisers to chase, and for a while the *Shark* was left in peace. Presently, however, more destroyers, which Admiral Hipper had ordered to attack Admiral Hood in order to cover his retirement, came up and poured in a merciless fire.[1] In a moment her after gun was hit, and its crew killed, and Commander Jones, who was himself controlling its fire, had a leg shot away at the knee. Yet he continued to encourage his men to fight the only gun he had left, until the *Shark* went down with her flag still flying.[2]

So, maintaining to the last the finest traditions of the Service, she came to her end. Upon her, as she lay helpless yet unbeaten, the vast forces of which she formed so small a part were converging to the crisis of the long-foreseen day. Fourteen miles north-west Admiral Jellicoe was coming at high speed towards her, still in cruising order, for as yet no word, other than half-a-dozen differing reports,[3] had come in to tell him where the German battle fleet was, and he was trying vainly to ascertain its exact position that he might judge how best to deploy. Six miles south-west of him was Admiral Beatty. Heavily engaged again, and supported by the fire of the 5th Battle Squadron, he had forced the German battle cruisers to turn east, and he was altering to starboard in conformity when at 5.56, he had sight of the leading

[1] The 12th Half Flotilla and the 9th Flotilla.

[2] An able seaman, C. C. Hope, thus describes the scene after the captain was disabled: "The gaff on which the ensign was flying was shot away, and Captain Jones asked what was wrong with the flag, and appeared greatly upset. Then I climbed and unbent the ensign from the gaff. I passed it down to Midshipman Smith, R.N.R., who hoisted it on the yardarm. Commander Jones seemed then to be less worried." A petty-officer got the wounded captain to a life-saving raft, but a few hours later he died of exhaustion, to be awarded subsequently a posthumous Victoria Cross. The six survivors were eventually picked up by the Danish steamer *Vidar*.

[3] There was a difference of over eight miles in the enemy's position as reported by various vessels, and, although the messages sent from the Admiralty at 5.0 and 5.45 gave, as we now know, the position and course fairly accurately, little reliance was placed upon them.

battleships of the Grand Fleet, four miles to the northward. "Thereupon," he says in his report, "I altered course east and proceeded at utmost speed."[1] Though his reasons for doing so are not recorded, it was clearly of importance that he should keep firm hold of the enemy's battle cruisers, so as to prevent them from sighting our battle fleet and reporting it to Admiral Scheer. If, as he apparently thought most likely, Admiral Jellicoe was going to deploy to starboard, that being the flank nearest to the enemy, his easterly course would do no harm, and the reasons which eventually convinced his chief that a deployment to starboard was tactically inadmissible can scarcely have been in his mind.

But for Admiral Jellicoe the movement was difficult to understand. On the conflicting information he had he was still expecting to meet the enemy right ahead, and as soon as he made out our battle cruisers heading across his bows and engaged with an unseen enemy he flashed to Admiral Beatty the query, "Where is the enemy's battle fleet?" (6.1). Something was evidently wrong, for Admiral Beatty had appeared much further to the westward than his position signals had indicated. Both flagships, in fact, were out of their reckoning. The *Lion's* error was nearly seven miles west, and that of the *Iron Duke* over four miles east, so that the cumulative error was about eleven miles. To Admiral Jellicoe it now seemed probable that instead of the enemy being found ahead they would appear a little on his starboard bow, and in order to gain ground in that direction he at once altered to south (6.2).[2] A few minutes later, a rapid calculation, however, convinced him that his new course would not do. It brought the "guides"—that is, the leading ships of divisions—into echelon, or, in technical phrase, they were "disposed quarterly" with the starboard wing forward, a disposition very unfavourable for a deployment to the eastward since it could not bring the line at right angles to the bearing of the enemy. This was tactically essential for a good deployment, and before it could be done the port guides must be brought up on the flagship's beam. But it was now evident from various indications that the enemy was too near for this disposition to be completed in time. A further effect of the errors in reckoning was that he was likely

[1] The signal "alter course in succession to east" was made at 6.0. At 5.56 he had signalled "Alter course in succession to N.E. by E. Speed 25 knots," and at this speed he continued for the next twenty-five minutes, when he increased a knot.

[2] See Diagram 30.

to get contact twenty minutes sooner than he expected.[1] It was therefore vital to get the fleet into the best position immediately attainable for instant deployment in either direction, and at 6.6, as the best he could do, he signalled course S.E., to bring the guides approximately abreast again.

Just then Admiral Beatty, who was beginning to pass across the starboard division of the battle fleet only two miles ahead of the *Marlborough*, flashed back his reply to the Commander-in-Chief's query, but it only said "Enemy's battle cruisers bearing S.E." This did no more than deepen the obscurity. About ten minutes earlier Admiral Jellicoe had heard from Commodore Goodenough that the enemy's battle fleet had altered course to north and that their battle cruisers bore S.W. from it. On this information it was incomprehensible that the battle cruisers should have been sighted first, and at his wits' end to fathom the situation the Commander-in-Chief repeated to Admiral Beatty, "Where is the enemy's battle fleet?" At the moment the *Lion* had no enemy in sight. There was no immediate answer, and precious minutes went by with no further light to determine the right direction for deployment.

The Commander-in-Chief's perplexity was not lightened by the fact that Admiral Beatty in giving the bearing of the enemy battle cruisers had omitted their course. In fact he had lost sight of them, and did not know what it was. The reason was that Admiral Hipper, finding himself in a corner too hot for him, had turned away, and with his flagship in flames was retiring with all speed on Admiral Scheer. But danger still lay in his path. For now came the *Ophelia's* chance. Driven off when the *Shark* attacked, Commander Crabbe had returned for another attempt, and was rewarded by a fair shot at the German battle cruisers. The torpedo missed, but these bold attacks were not without effect upon Admiral Hipper. With Admiral Beatty engaging him to port and British destroyers continually attacking him, he was confirmed in the impression which the appearance of Admiral Hood's battle cruisers had made upon his mind, and he says it was because he felt sure that he had run into our main fleet that he swung back to retire on Admiral Scheer. This information he had passed to his chief before he turned north-eastwards again upon the same course as the battle fleet (6.14). But even now he did not find rest from the worry of the insistent British destroyers. Indeed, he was soon in a worse predicament than ever, for he found himself attacked upon both bows at once. To port was one of Admiral

[1] See Diagram 31.

Beatty's destroyers, the *Onslow*, to starboard was the *Acasta*. After Lieutenant-Commander Tovey in the *Onslow* had been foiled in his attempt to attack with the *Moresby* during the run north, he had taken station on the engaged bow of the *Lion*, and as Admiral Beatty turned east he could see the *Wiesbaden*, in an excellent position for using his torpedoes, only 6,000 yards away. He immediately dashed at her, firing as he went to within 2,000 yards, when suddenly he found himself upon the port bow of the enemy's battle cruisers. The *Onslow* at once came under the fire of the advancing ships, but the chance against the battle cruisers was too tempting to resist, and at 8,000 yards from the van ship Lieutenant-Commander Tovey ordered all torpedoes to be fired. But, as luck would have it, at that very moment a heavy shell struck the *Onslow* amidships and she was enveloped in clouds of escaping steam. Only one torpedo was got off, but Lieutenant-Commander Tovey, thinking all had been fired and finding his speed greatly reduced, began to creep away to retire.

He too had missed, but the *Acasta* had not yet done. As Admiral Hipper returned north-eastwards she was just leaving the crippled *Shark*, and Lieutenant-Commander Barron, seeing the *Lützow* coming up on his port quarter, an admirably placed target, turned to attack. With a storm of shell the enemy strove to baffle her attack. Yet undeterred, Lieutenant-Commander Barron fired. The shot seemed to go fairly home with a great explosion, and he sped away with his boat so torn with shell that she could neither stop nor steer.[1]

Meanwhile the *Onslow* had also been busy. Lieutenant-Commander Tovey, having discovered as he retired that all his torpedoes had not been spent, as he thought, had fired one of them as he passed close to the *Wiesbaden*, which hit her fairly under the conning tower. The explosion could be clearly seen and heard, but she did not sink. Scarcely had he noted his success when another and a far more important target presented itself. Some five miles away a whole line of German battleships loomed up in the mist advancing upon him at high speed. What was he to do? He had two torpedoes still in his tubes, but his engines were failing, his speed was down to ten knots, and to turn to attack meant almost certain destruction, and yet he turned. One destroyer

[1] The *Acasta* has been given the credit for having made a successful shot on the *Seydlitz* during this attack, but it is now known from German sources that the *Seydlitz* was only torpedoed once—by the *Petard*, earlier in the action. See *ante*, p. 342.

more or less, so he reasoned, mattered little, while two torpedoes fired from an ideal position might materially affect the action, and in this admirable spirit of devotion he decided to attack again. Making for the advancing battleships he waited till his sights were on, and at 8,000 yards fired his remaining torpedoes. Fair to cross the enemy's line they ran as he struggled away, but the Germans manœuvred to avoid them, and there was no hit. So bold an attack with a crippled ship deserved a better result, but the sacrifice that he faced was not required of him, and two days later he got safely back to port.[1]

Having avoided the *Onslow's* attack Admiral Scheer held on again, and so did Admiral Hipper, for ahead of him could be seen one of his ships in sore distress. Burning fiercely lay the helpless *Wiesbaden*, still afloat, and some British cruisers were pouring into her a concentrated fire. It was Admiral Arbuthnot with the 1st Cruiser Squadron that had appeared in the thick of the fighting. We have last seen him closing in towards the 2nd Cruiser Squadron as the visibility decreased, till by 5.50 he was right ahead of the *Iron Duke*.[2] The *Warrior* was with him, the *Duke of Edinburgh* two miles to starboard, and the *Black Prince* out of sight to the westward. At that time the glitter of the *Chester's* action with Admiral Hipper's light cruisers became visible on his starboard bow, and he turned to port to bring his guns to bear just as Admiral Hipper was turning away from the concentrated fire of our battle cruisers and the 5th Battle Squadron. As the enemy became faintly visible Admiral Arbuthnot opened fire, but seeing his salvoes fall short he turned to the southward, and as he ran down to close saw the *Wiesbaden* lying disabled and in flames. At the moment when he himself made his turn southward Admiral Beatty had led round to the eastward to keep his teeth in Admiral Hipper, and now the *Defence* saw the battle cruisers coming up fast from the westward across her course.[3] But Admiral Arbuthnot was not to be baulked. The Battle Orders laid it down clearly that the first duty of cruisers in a fleet action was to engage the enemy's cruisers,[4] and with the *Warrior* close astern, firing with all guns that would bear he held on so close athwart the *Lion's* bows that she was forced

[1] After struggling away from the action the *Onslow* was taken in tow by the *Defender*, another crippled destroyer, and both succeeded in getting in to Aberdeen on June 2.

[2] See Diagram 29.

[3] See Diagram 30.

[4] Prior to deployment their duty was that of reconnaissance in conjunction with, and in support of, the light cruisers.

to deviate from her course to clear, while the *Duke of Edinburgh*, which was coming down more to the westward, turned east on Admiral Beatty's disengaged side. Both the *Defence* and *Warrior* had already hit the doomed *Wiesbaden*. Still Admiral Arbuthnot, in spite of straddling salvoes, held on till within 5,500 yards of his prey he turned to starboard. Both ships were now in a hurricane of fire, which the Germans were concentrating with terrible effect to save their burning ship, and there quickly followed yet another of the series of those appalling catastrophes which make this battle so tragically memorable. Four minutes after crossing the *Lion's* bows, the *Defence* was hit by two heavy salvoes in quick succession, and the Admiral and his flagship disappeared in a roar of flame (6.20). The *Warrior* barely escaped a similar fate. Labouring away with damaged engines she was only saved by the *Warspite* of the 5th Battle Squadron. At the critical moment, for reasons that will appear directly, this ship was seen to leave the line, and flying the " Not under control " signal she made a complete circle round the damaged cruiser. For a while both were in a rain of shell, till the storm of the battle passed to the eastward and they were left in peace. So ended the first bold, if ill-judged, attempt at individual action by a spirited squadron commander.

Against the loss of one ship Admiral Scheer had now to his credit the destruction of two battle cruisers and one cruiser, but of this he was unaware at the time.[1] Suddenly the whole scene changed. As the cloud of smoke and flame in which the *Defence* had perished died away, the leading ships of the two German lines could see, out of the grey beyond, an interminable line of huge ships stretching across their course with both ends of it lost in the mist.[2] For Admiral Scheer, who believed that our fleet was operating in dispersed detachments, the sight came with a shock of surprise. Within range ahead of him a mass of British Dreadnoughts were deploying, and, confident as he might have been in the success of his bold and well-laid plan, he had met his match. Instead of cutting off a detached squadron of his enemy, as he hoped, he suddenly found himself in present danger of being entrapped by at least the bulk of the Grand Fleet.

Until Admiral Jellicoe was almost in sight of the German battle fleet he still could not tell where it was by several miles. Owing to unavoidable errors in reckoning, the reports he

[1] Admiral Jellicoe did not know the extent of his own losses until the forenoon of the following day.

[2] Hase, *Kiel and Jutland*, pp. 177–8.

had been receiving were too conflicting for more than wide approximation. It was a situation which his long experience of manœuvres had led him to anticipate, and one against which he had done his best to provide. Seeing that correct deploying depended absolutely on knowing the enemy's exact position, course and speed, he had insisted in his Battle Orders on the importance of securing visual touch at the earliest moment, and had issued a special warning that the necessary precision was not to be expected from wireless. He himself had arranged for visual touch with the *Hampshire* as connecting ship between his light cruiser screen and his advanced scout line, but, as we have seen, the high speed at which he had been coming down ever since he knew the enemy was at sea made it impossible for that line to get far enough ahead. In the battle cruiser force things were still worse. Though Commodore Goodenough had kept admirable station astern all through, Admiral Beatty in the rapid changes of course in the early part of the action had for a while lost touch with his other two squadrons, and they were not able to get into visual contact again with the *Lion* until 5.0, when it was too late to extend either of them to link up with the Commander-in-Chief's advanced screen. Thus it was that Admiral Jellicoe had nothing to guide him but the confusing wireless messages which led him to believe that the German battle fleet must be farther advanced and more to the eastward than it actually was. It was indeed only due to the effect of the preliminary fighting that he was not more seriously misled. During the chase northward Admiral Scheer's fleet had straggled out, and at 5.45, when he began to scent the presence of our battle fleet, he was forced to slacken speed and allow his slower squadrons to close up into battle order.[1] Five minutes later he could hear the *Wiesbaden* saying she was out of control, and he ordered the fleet to incline two points to starboard towards her. But for this the head of his line must have been some miles more to the westward than it was when it came into view.

In spite of all doubt, however, Admiral Jellicoe, after hearing where the enemy battle cruisers were, was becoming convinced he would have to deploy to the eastward, and (6.8) ordered his three flotillas of destroyers to take up the necessary disposition.[2] But at 6.14, four minutes after he

[1] See Diagram 29.

[2] This was Disposition No. 1, under which two flotillas would be to port of the line of approach and one to starboard. Preparatory to deployment one flotilla would take station three miles on the starboard bow of the starboard wing, and one three miles on the port bow of the port wing, the third

had repeated his urgent inquiry as to where the enemy's battle fleet was, all doubt was set at rest. Just before the *Lion* had cleared the *Defence*, the head of Admiral Scheer's line suddenly appeared out of the gloom on her starboard beam, and Admiral Beatty signalled " Have sighted the enemy's battle fleet bearing S.S.W." In the course of the next few minutes his leading vessels were heavily engaged with the van of the enemy's battle fleet. The *Barham* had also seen them to S.S.E. and was trying to get a message through, but her flags could not be seen, and her wireless was not received till it was too late to be of use.

Many had been the critical situations which British admirals in the past had been called upon suddenly to solve, but never had there been one which demanded higher qualities of leadership, ripe judgment and quick decision, than that which confronted Admiral Jellicoe in this supreme moment of the naval war. There was not an instant to lose if deployment were to be made in time. The enemy, instead of being met ahead, were on his starboard side. He could only guess their course. Beyond a few miles everything was shrouded in mist; the little that could be seen was no more than a blurred picture, and with every tick of the clock the situation was developing with a rapidity of which his predecessors had never dreamt. At a speed higher than anything in their experience the two hostile fleets were rushing upon each other; battle cruisers, cruisers and destroyers were hurrying to their battle stations, and the vessels steaming across his front were shutting out all beyond in an impenetrable pall of funnel smoke.[1] Above all was the roar of battle both ahead and to starboard, and in this blind distraction Admiral Jellicoe had to make the decision on which the fortunes of his country hung.

His first and natural impulse was, he says, to deploy on the starboard flank, which was nearest to the enemy.[2] But for this the decisive intelligence had come too late and he was too near. Heavy shells were already falling between the lines of his divisions, and if he deployed, as his natural impulse was, it would mean that Admiral Burney, whose

---

being two miles abeam of the port flotilla. On deployment to the eastward he would thus have two flotillas in the van and one in the rear. The three-mile distance was selected as being the best for enabling flotillas to deliver attacks on the enemy battle fleet and to repel similar attacks on our own.

[1] In addition to the battle cruisers, several light cruisers and destroyers, the *Duke of Edinburgh*, in particular, was pouring forth a dense volume of smoke, while the burning *Wiesbaden* contributed to the general smother.

[2] Jellicoe, *The Grand Fleet, 1914–16*, p. 348.

squadron was the oldest and least powerful in the fleet, would receive the concentrated fire of the enemy's best ships and almost certainly a heavy destroyer attack while in the act of deployment. To increase the disadvantage he would be compelled as he deployed to turn to port in order to avoid having his "T" crossed, and this would mean that the fleet would be turning at least twelve points in the thick of the enemy's fire, and, what is still more important, the action would be opened well within torpedo range of the enemy's battleships—a hazard which in Admiral Jellicoe's system it was vital to avoid.

It is scarcely to be doubted that his reasoning was correct. We now know that such an opening with the visibility as low as it was would have given his adversary exactly the opportunity he prayed for. The tactics on which Admiral Scheer's whole conception of offensive action with an inferior fleet was undoubtedly based were a rapid and overwhelming concentration with gun and torpedo on part of his opponent's line, followed by a withdrawal under cover of a smoke screen before a counter-concentration could be brought to bear—a bold manœuvre which the High Seas Fleet had persistently practised. A possible alternative for Admiral Jellicoe was deployment on the flagship in the centre, but this was too complicated at such a juncture. Nothing, then, remained but to form his line to port on Admiral Jerram, and at 6.15 he signalled for him to lead the deployment S.E. by E.[1]

The wisdom of the decision was quickly apparent. Scarcely had Admiral Burney turned his division when it came under fire from the van of the German fleet at about 14,000 yards—a range which was within the effective capacity of the long-range torpedoes of the enemy's capital ships.[2]

[1] To continue the course S.E. would have led nearer to the enemy, but for this there was no clear signal. Equal speed deployment could be signalled with a numeral flag indicating the number of points away from the course the fleet was on, but the signal had never been made with a zero flag. After a rapid consultation with his staff, Admiral Jellicoe decided that an unfamiliar signal made at such a juncture was too hazardous, and might well lead to confusion. He therefore did the next best thing, by ordering a course S.E. by E.—that is, one point away from his S.E. course. Deployment south-westward on his starboard wing would have involved the fleets passing each other on opposite courses and leave open to the enemy a clear line of retreat to the northward. See Diagram 31.

[2] The German ships had a much stronger torpedo armament than our own. All of them had from four to six submerged tubes. The best armed of ours had four, and half of them only two. On the other hand, our gun armament was greatly superior, and for this reason Admiral Jellicoe judged that to get the utmost advantage he must engage at not less than 15,000 yards, which was deemed to be the effective range of the enemy's torpedo.

It was only as the smoke of the vessels steaming across his front slowly drifted clear that the divisions turning ahead of Admiral Burney could successively come to his assistance, but fortunately he had other and more powerful support. When Admiral Evan-Thomas first sighted the *Marlborough* he believed that the fleet had already deployed: it was too thick for any other division to be seen, and he concluded that she was leading the line. By that time he had turned to the eastward after Admiral Beatty, and like him was steering to cross ahead of the enemy. He was again hotly engaged, and as he was on a course that converged with that of Admiral Burney at a greatly superior speed he was gradually drawing into his battle station ahead of the *Marlborough*. But the real state of the case quickly became plain. As he drew ahead he could see that the fleet was only just forming line, and that the deployment was consequently to the eastward. In these circumstances his proper battle station was at the head of the line with the battle cruisers. But to reach that position was now out of the question. To follow Admiral Beatty across the front of the battle fleet would make the interference worse than it already was, and he decided his only course was to make a wide turn and lead on as best he could into his alternative battle station astern.[1]

In waters alive as they now were with rapidly moving ships it was no easy task. With Admiral Beatty's light cruisers and destroyers as well as the flotillas of the battle fleet making for their own battle stations in all directions, the manœuvre called for nerve and dexterity of a high order. To add to the hazard the *Warspite's* steering gear began to give way under the wounds she had received. As she put her helm over it jammed, and this was why she swerved out of the line just in time to save the *Warrior*, and how as she circled round the crippled cruiser the two ships became the focus of the enemy's fire. The *Onslow*, limping away, saw the *Warspite* apparently stopped in a forest of water spouts, doomed as it seemed to destruction, but replying to the enemy's fire with all her guns—an inspiring sight for the lonely destroyer.[2] With his other three ships Admiral Evan-Thomas led on, and dropping neatly into his station, re-opened a fire, the accuracy and the effect of which were the admiration of friend and foe.[3]

At the other end of the line there was an equally fine

[1] By the Battle Orders, if the fleet deployed towards Heligoland, as it was now doing, both he and Admiral Beatty were to take station ahead. Otherwise he would be astern, with the battle cruisers ahead.

[2] *The Fighting at Jutland*, p. 258. [3] See Diagram 32.

stroke of seamanship. Shortly after 6.0 p.m., while Admiral Hood was still engaging the enemy's light cruisers, he heard firing to the westward and turned towards it. Not a ship was to be seen, but the distant thud of guns soon increased to a continuous roll of thunder, and the horizon was lit by whirling sheets of flame. Then out of the lurid obscurity appeared the *Lion* and her sisters in hot fight, and he held on to meet them with the fine intention of turning up ahead of their van. It was no easy feat. For at this juncture the torpedo attack which Admiral Hipper had launched to cover his retirement developed. As our battle cruisers turned to avoid it the line was thrown into confusion. But no harm was done. The torpedoes passed harmlessly, the line quickly re-formed and in the most brilliant manner Admiral Hood swung his squadron into station ahead of the *Lion*.[1] It was all high testimony to what training and seamanship could achieve. Such a maze of crossing ships were the waters at both ends of the line in which the deployment took place that officers held their breath, collisions seemed inevitable, but all went well, and in that fateful hour was reaped the harvest which in the long years of preparation had been laboriously sown by Admiral Jellicoe and his predecessors, Sir Arthur Wilson, Sir Francis Bridgeman, Sir William May and Sir George Callaghan.

Thus did Admiral Jellicoe attain the tactical position which, on his unrivalled experience of manœuvres and exercises under those masters, he had regarded as the most desirable. "Action on approximately similar courses," he wrote in his Battle Orders, "will be one of the underlying objects of my tactics, because it is the form of action likely to give the most decisive results." He was in single line with a fast division ahead and astern and every prospect of engaging the enemy on similar courses. For as soon as the Germans realised that large forces were in front of them the *König* had led to the eastward on a course which they probably took to be parallel to that of the enemy (6.27). It was in fact parallel to the course Admiral Beatty was steering to get ahead of the battle fleet, and the haze and smoke must have effectually prevented Admiral Scheer from seeing that our deployment was being made on a course that sharply converged with his own. Possibly also the movement was made to cover Admiral Hipper, who, five minutes earlier, under the fire of our battle cruisers, had turned to the southward on a nearly parallel course with

[1] The *Invincible* and *Indomitable* turned away to starboard, the *Inflexible*, which was rear ship, to port.

Admiral Hood, and was again suffering severely, the *Lützow* herself being hardly under control.

While Admiral Scheer was thus apparently trying to meet a situation which he had not yet fathomed, to Admiral Jellicoe it gradually became plain. He had just settled down on the deployment course, but as Admiral Beatty was heading to cross he had to reduce speed to 14 knots to allow the battle cruisers to clear. Now, however, their smoke so far drifted away that he could get occasional glimpses of the German ships as the sun declined in the north-west and now and then lit one or more of them up. He could see they were turning to the eastward, with our battle cruisers hotly engaging their van. Obviously it was the moment to deliver the crushing blow for which his whole tactical scheme was devised, and eager to seize the occasion he signalled for the fleet to turn to south-south-east by sub-divisions in order to close. But a moment's reflection convinced him he must forgo the move. The necessity for reducing speed to let Admiral Beatty get clear had checked an otherwise perfect deployment; ships astern of him became bunched, and his two rear squadrons had not yet reached the turning point. There was thus an awkward angle in the line, and in such a position the movement would have rendered it practically impossible to complete the deployment. There was, moreover, a further difficulty. Though Admiral Beatty, by increasing to twenty-six knots, had cleared the rear of the line, he was still masking the van and rapidly converging on the battleships, while Admiral Jerram was inclining to port away from the enemy in order to obtain more sea room. There was nothing, therefore, for Admiral Jellicoe to do but cancel the signal and hold on as he was, nor was it till 6.33 that the battle cruisers were well enough ahead to allow him to increase again to his battle speed of seventeen knots. Thus the enforced passage of Admiral Beatty across the battle front, due to the sudden appearance at the moment of contact of the enemy battle fleet on an unexpected bearing, which necessitated deployment on the port wing, spoiled a promising opening to the action. The first duty of our battle cruisers, as laid down in the Grand Fleet Battle Orders, was to destroy the enemy battle cruisers. It was incumbent upon them also at the commencement of an action to take up their battle station at the head of our line in order to frustrate any attempt on the part of the enemy battle cruisers to attack the van of our battle fleet with torpedoes at long range. In the circumstances Admiral Beatty's movement was inevitable.

It was not indeed till this time (about 6.30) that the

flagship in the centre got into action with the enemy's battle fleet. As the *König* led round to the eastward the *Iron Duke* and the ships astern fired at her and any enemy vessels they could see, but now it was only here and there between the slowly drifting patches of smoke-laden haze that they could occasionally get a target.

At 6.32 Admiral Beatty reached his station ahead of the battle fleet. Ahead of him again was Admiral Hood with his three battle cruisers, leading the fleet, and leading it in a manner worthy of the honoured name he bore. Upon him was concentrated the fire of three or four of Admiral Hipper's five ships.[1] Under pressure of the oncoming British Dreadnoughts they had turned again to the southward. For the past ten minutes the action between them and the "Invincibles" had been growing hot upon similar courses, and Admiral Hood with Captain A. L. Cay, his flag-captain, at his side was directing it from the bridge. Having the advantage of the light he was giving more than he received. The range was down below 9,000 yards, but it was the greatest that visibility would permit, and he was doing too well to alter. "Several shells," says Commander von Hase of the *Derfflinger*, "pierced our ship with a terrific force and exploded with a tremendous roar which shook every seam and rivet. The captain had again frequently to steer the ship out of the line to get clear of the hail of fire." So heavy was the punishment he was inflicting that Admiral Hood hailed Commander Dannreuther, his gunnery officer, in the control top, and called to him, "Your firing is very good. Keep at it as quickly as you can. Every shot is telling." They were the last words he is known to have spoken. Just then the mist was riven and from the *Derfflinger* her tormentor was suddenly silhouetted against a light patch of sky. Then as another salvo from the *Invincible* straddled her she began rapid salvoes in reply, in which probably the *König* joined with as many. One after another they went home on the *Invincible*. Flames shot up from the gallant flagship, and there came again the awful spectacle of a fiery burst, followed by a huge column of dark smoke which, mottled with blackened debris, swelled up hundreds of feet in the air, and the mother of all battle cruisers had gone to join the other two that were no more. As her two consorts

[1] The *Lützow* had apparently fallen out of the line, and possibly another was keeping her company. Admiral Napier, who was close by with part of the 3rd Light Cruiser Squadron, reports coming across two detached battle cruisers steering east. They engaged him with their secondary armament, and both his ships fired torpedoes at the leading enemy.

swerved round her seething death-bed they could see she was rent in two; her stem and stern rose apart high out of the troubled waters as though she had touched the bottom, and near by a group of half a dozen men were clinging to a life raft, cheering the ships as they raced by to continue the fight.[1] So in the highest exultation of battle—doing all a man could do for victory—the intrepid Admiral met his end, gilding in his death with new lustre the immortal name of Hood.

[1] The survivors were Commander H. E: Dannreuther, Lieutenant C. S. Sandford, C.P.O. Thompson and three other ratings, most of whom had been in the control top. They were picked up by the *Badger*, of the 1st Flotilla.

CHAPTER XIX

JUTLAND—THE THIRD PHASE

6.30 to Nightfall

THE explosion in which the *Invincible* perished heralded a new phase of the action. A period of manœuvring ensued comparable with that when from May 28 to June 1 Lord Howe strove to bring Villaret-Joyeuse to action a hundred and twenty-two years before. But now a tactical contest of days was condensed into hours. Admiral Scheer had come suddenly upon his enemy in the act of deployment, but instead of being able to throw him into confusion by a concentrated attack on part of his line, he found his own van being enveloped by a superior force ready for action. Persuaded as he was by the reports of his submarines that the Grand Fleet had been split up, he did not as yet realise that he was face to face with the whole of it. But he could divine enough. Out of the mist which shrouded his enemy, fire was coming from about eight points of the compass. Fortunately for him, the smoke-laden air was saving him from the full weight of it. The British battle fleet had almost completed its deployment, and although it also was baffled by patches of mist and hanging smoke that appeared and dissolved at intervals so that only a few of the enemy could be seen at a time, nearly all ships were firing and getting hits, while they themselves suffered not at all. The head of the German line was already being smashed in. The *Lützow* was completely disabled, and Admiral Hipper was about to board a destroyer in order to shift his flag. The *Derfflinger*, with her masts and rigging cut to shreds and water pouring through a large hole in her bows as she rose and fell to the swell, was little better off. The head of the German battle line was being forced to the eastward, and one of the "Königs" was seen to be blazing fore and aft.[1] So boldly had Captain E. H. F. Heaton-Ellis in the *Inflexible* led on past the wreck

[1] Several of our vessels reported this ship as having sunk shortly afterwards (*Jutland Despatches* (Cmd. 1068), p. 18). What they mistook for a sinking ship was probably the disabled *Lützow*.

of the lost flagship, that the rest of the German battle cruisers, thinking it must be the van of our battle fleet, swerved away to the westward (6.35).[1]

Admiral Scheer thus found himself in an awkward predicament. Completely out-manœuvred, he had no choice but to get his neck out of the noose. But this was no easy matter. To retire in succession was not to be thought of, for the turning point would be a deathtrap as the long line of the enemy's fleet encircled it, while, on the other hand, his own fleet was in nearly the worst possible position for a turn away together. His rear had not yet reached the eastward turning point, and was still steering north-east; his van battle division was going south-east, so that as the battle cruisers had turned to the westward he had three kinks in his line. Yet a turn together was his only chance. Even though the extended order in which his ships were steaming allowed them ample room to manœuvre, to attempt such a thing with the fleet as it was and under fire was attended with no small risk, but the exigency had been foreseen and a special measure provided to meet it.[2]

In the German tactical manuals it was termed the *Gefechtskehrtwendung* (battle turn away), a simultaneous withdrawal analogous to that attributed to the French at the end of the sailing period which had baffled our greatest tacticians to counter. So vital was it for an inferior fleet to be able to disengage at any moment that it had been sedulously practised by the Germans in all conditions of the line. This was well known to us, and in the exercises we had practised since the war began, an effective reply to the manœuvre had constantly been sought, but none had been found. The only possible means of preventing the enemy's escape was a resolute and immediate chase, but to baffle pursuit the *Kehrtwendung* was to be made under cover of a destroyer attack and a smoke screen which would at once conceal the direction of the retreat and check the pursuit. A century earlier, in the days of close action, slow speed, and towering masts, such devices for concealing tactical movements would have been of little avail, but under modern conditions in the misty North Sea, with fleets engaging at high speed on the limits of visibility, they had every chance of success.

Yet it was not without misgiving that Admiral Scheer

[1] See Diagram 32.

[2] Admiral Scheer's plans show his ships to have been at this time between four and five cables apart. In the Grand Fleet ships in column were two and a half cables apart.

decided to perform the manœuvre. It had never been attempted under fire, several of his ships were crippled, the fleets were very close, and should the enemy, with his superior speed, penetrate his intention and turn to follow, his situation would be perilous in the extreme. But, like the resolute commander he proved himself to be, he did not hesitate, and at 6.33, just after the *Invincible* blew up, he made the manœuvring signal, at the same time launching his destroyers to deliver their covering attack and to set up the protecting smoke screen.[1] The effect was all he could desire. In two or three minutes his fleet, already only visible from the British ships by glimpses, had disappeared, and all firing ceased.[2]

It soon appeared to Admiral Jellicoe that the enemy must have turned away, though whether they had turned right back to the south-westward, directly away from him, or to a course for Heligoland, he was unable to discover. What was he to do? An immediate turn by divisions, in order to follow, was out of the question. It would have placed his fleet in a position directly open to a possibly overwhelming attack from the long-range torpedoes in the enemy's capital ships; and this, it must be remembered, was a danger, at that time new and unmeasured, to which no capable tactician could venture to expose his fleet, above all in the opening stages of an action. Nor did the viciousness of the expedient end here. For it would have brought the German destroyers directly ahead of the advancing British fleet, in the best possible position for launching every available torpedo.

A turn in succession was equally undesirable, for though fewer ships would have been laid open to torpedo attack, the fleet must have been led straight into the waters now occupied by the enemy. Such a hazard could not be accepted. The German capital ships were all believed to carry mines, and might reasonably be expected to lay them as they retired. Nor would such a turn have enabled the British fleet to re-engage immediately, for some minutes had elapsed since the enemy had turned and the range was opening rapidly.

Another alternative was to turn right round to the westward and so maintain his position to the northward, but this would only have brought the enemy upon a bow bearing instead of ahead, and the torpedo menace would not have been appreciably reduced. The only way in which this difficulty could have been even partially met was to divide the

[1] The signal read: Turn together sixteen points to starboard and form single line ahead in the opposite direction. [2] See Diagram 33.

fleet and undoubtedly in clear weather and with plenty of daylight something might possibly have been done in this way to foil the enemy's evasive tactics. But in the prevailing atmospheric conditions, and so late in the day, co-ordination between independent squadrons would have been impossible, and the well-known risk which for two centuries had forced all navies to cling to the single line of battle in spite of all its drawbacks—the risk of independent squadrons being overwhelmed individually by a concentrated enemy—would have been very great in the prevailing conditions and in the face of so able a tactician as Admiral Scheer.

The alternative to forcing the enemy to engage by the independent action of squadrons was to follow him up closely with the whole fleet. With a sufficient superiority of speed it has always been regarded as the most effective method, but the introduction of minelayers and submarines had restricted its merit, and as early as October, 1914, Admiral Jellicoe, in a memorandum he submitted to the Admiralty, had explained the modification of the time-honoured tactics which the new developments involved. In certain conditions, which were those in which he considered it most likely the German fleet would be met, he did not intend "to comply with enemy tactics by moving in the invited direction." "If, for instance," he wrote, "the enemy were to turn away from an advancing fleet, I should assume the intention was to lead us over mines and submarines, and should decline to be so drawn." In reply he received from the new Board, which Lord Fisher had just joined as First Sea Lord, an assurance "of their full confidence in your contemplated conduct of the fleet in action."[1] After six months' experience of the war his views were unshaken, and on April 5, 1915, he had again submitted his intentions to the Board for approval, and again no exception was taken to them.

But, as it happened, the principles laid down in these memoranda did little or nothing to affect his tactics. The situation on his first contact with the High Seas Fleet differed from that which the memoranda contemplated. True he had every reason to believe that submarines were present. He knew many were in the North Sea, and ship after ship reported sighting one. The situation he had visualised in the memoranda was one in which the enemy would be seeking an action in the open sea deliberately. Now he knew he had surprised them and that there was little risk of their having time to prepare a minefield or even a submarine trap. The dominating consideration of the movement he made was therefore quite different from that which his memoranda emphasised,

[1] *Jutland Despatches*, p. 601.

and his " contemplated conduct of the fleet in action " in no way affected what followed.

In the constant search before the battle for an effective counter to the manœuvre which he had so surely foreseen, and with which he was now faced, he had come to the conclusion that " nothing but ample time and superior speed can be an answer, and this means that unless the meeting of the fleets takes place fairly early in the day, it is most difficult, if not impossible, to fight the action to a finish." But the day was already far advanced, and in the face of Admiral Scheer's evasive tactics and of the low visibility it is difficult to see, even now, how the action, so well begun, could have been pushed to a decision.

Nothing then remained for Admiral Jellicoe, since he could not tell in what direction the enemy had retired, but to place himself as soon as possible athwart their line of retreat to the Bight, for along that line, sooner or later, they were almost certain to be discovered. His ships were so disposed as to be able instantly to form line of battle on a course parallel to that line, and in order to maintain them in this disposition, Admiral Jellicoe now turned by divisions to south-east (6.44) as the best means of attaining the required position, so far as he could divine the situation.[1]

It was still obscure, and from the battle cruisers, who, being three miles on the starboard bow of the battle fleet, had been in a better position to gauge what had happened than himself, he obtained little help to penetrate it. They also had ceased firing, a sure indication that the enemy were not yet heading for their base—the more so since he could see that Admiral Beatty was hauling round gradually to starboard. Accordingly, having no news of the enemy from the van, as soon as his turn was complete (6.50) he signalled to Admiral Burney, who was furthest to the westward, " Can you see any enemy battleships ? " The reply was, " No ! " For Admiral Jellicoe this was enough. Convinced that he had now made enough to the eastward to bring him between the enemy and their base, he ordered the guides of his divisions to lead four more points to starboard, and signalled to the battle cruiser squadrons that the course of the fleet was now south (6.54).

This course had already been anticipated by Captain Kennedy, who was now senior officer of what was left of Admiral Hood's squadron, and for the past five minutes the *Inflexible*, which was still leading, had been steering south. Some minutes elapsed before Admiral Beatty received this

[1] See Diagram 34.

course from the Commander-in-Chief,[1] but, having followed the *Inflexible's* lead, he too was steering south.

Nothing was in sight, and to maintain his station on the battle fleet he now (6.55) reduced speed to eighteen knots. At the same time, ordering the *Inflexible* and *Indomitable* to take station astern of him, he began to circle to starboard, but owing to a failure of the gyro compass the turn was carried much farther than he intended before the defect was noticed. The consequence was that a complete circle had to be made, so that by 7.1 he was once again where he had been when the turn started.[2] The effect of the mishap was to delay his progress to the southward by about seven minutes, and when he received the Commander-in-Chief's signal to steer south, he was already heading to the south-westward to regain touch with the enemy with the *Inflexible* and *Indomitable* in station in rear of his line.

The German smoke screen had, in fact, been entirely successful, but the half-hearted destroyer attack had failed. A few torpedoes crossed our lines, and to avoid them some divisions had to turn away, but they had little or no effect on Admiral Jellicoe's closing movement. Just as it was complete, however, Admiral Burney signalled that his flagship, the *Marlborough*, had been hit by a torpedo. Where it came from is difficult to say, but so far as can be seen it was most probably fired by the *Wiesbaden*, which was still afloat. The blow was severe, but not fatal; the *Marlborough* was not even put out of action. As for the ill-fated *Wiesbaden*, her gallant struggle was near its inevitable end. Being the only enemy ship now visible, she came under a heavier fire than ever, and some ten minutes later the flames with which she had been struggling were quenched beneath the sea.

Meanwhile, Admiral Scheer, with his line disordered by the *Kehrtwendung* manœuvre, had turned to the westward. His four Dreadnought divisions in reverse order were disposed quarterly, that is, in echelon, with the rear division leading; south of them the two pre-Dreadnought divisions, similarly disposed, were trying to get into station ahead, while Admiral Hipper's battered battle cruisers were coming up on his port quarter. The leading ships had been badly damaged, but at this cost Admiral Scheer cleverly extricated his fleet from the trap in which his adversary had so nearly caught him, and could hope to steal away in night cruising order with considerable success to

[1] Admiral Beatty in his despatch of June 12 states that he did not receive the signal till 7.6.

[2] See Diagram 35.

his credit. But for escape in this way it was still too early. There was more than an hour to sunset, and in the long twilight of those latitudes it was too dangerous to attempt.[1] Crippled as many of his ships were, they might well be overtaken, and long before dark the enemy would be able, if he came south—which Admiral Jellicoe was actually doing—to force him to action again with every advantage. The result could only be a severe reverse, and since his enemy would be in a position to cut him off from the Bight, it might well mean annihilation. "There was," he says, "only one way of avoiding this."[2] It was to advance again regardless of consequences and launch all his destroyers against our line. The manœuvre, he calculated, could not fail after his last move to come as a surprise that would upset his enemy's plans for the rest of the day, and if the attack was only pushed home with enough violence on some part of their line he could hope to escape for the night. It was a desperate expedient, but emboldened by the skill with which his captains had carried out the last *Kehrtwendung* under fire, he determined to stake his fate upon it. His idea, so he says, was to strike at the enemy's centre under cover of a destroyer attack while the battle cruisers held our van, and shortly before 7.0 he signalled the fleet to turn back together 16 points to starboard—i.e., back to the eastward.[3]

Such is the explanation of his intentions which Admiral Scheer chose to give to the world. It may well be that he

[1] Sunset was at 8.7.

[2] *Jutland Despatches*, p. 594.

[3] The analogy between the explanation which Admiral Scheer gives of his conduct at this time and the Trafalgar Memorandum is so close that the inspiration is evident. We have a fast advance squadron, a main body of Dreadnoughts with a reserve of pre-Dreadnoughts, as well as the two attacks on centre and van. Compare also Admiral Scheer's comment (*High Seas Fleet*, p. 155): "The manœuvre would be bound to surprise the enemy and upset his plans for the rest of the day," with Nelson's remark to Keats (Despatches vii, 241 *note*): "I think it will surprise and confound the enemy. They won't know what I am about." But Nelson added: "It will bring forward a pell-mell battle, and that is what I want," while Admiral Scheer concludes: "If the blow fell heavily it would facilitate breaking loose at night." Further falsity in the analogy is that Nelson, fighting close with short-range guns, had no fear of mutual interference of squadrons. Moreover, under modern conditions of high freedom of movement and long-range guns, any part of the attacked fleet could at once succour another. Under sail it could not do so, and it was on this that Nelson mainly relied for success against a superior enemy. It would almost seem, indeed, that Admiral Scheer fell into the not uncommon error of endeavouring to apply a historical precedent without sufficiently considering the extent to which development of material reduced its applicability to the conditions of his own time. It may at least be taken as a reminder that the value of history in the art of war is not only to elucidate the resemblance of past and present, but also their essential differences.

justly gauged the appetite and the ignorance of the German public in naval matters, but it cannot be reconciled with his high reputation as a tactician, or even with sanity. In the relative dispositions of the two fleets as he judged them to be, to thrust at the enemy's centre in line ahead was deliberately to expose himself to having his "T" crossed by a superior fleet, and we may well believe, as is told, that subsequently his Chief-of-Staff remarked that had he attempted such a stroke in manœuvres he would have been promptly ordered to haul down his flag. Fortunately the ascertained facts of this phase of the action indicate clearly enough that his intentions were very different and much wiser.

From his own diagrams we know that when he turned away sixteen points at 6.35 he believed the British fleet was disposed on an arc extending from east by south of him to north-east by north about seven miles distant, and that it was steering south-eastward. Assuming a normal battle speed of 18 knots, this would mean that at 7.0, when he had turned back eastward for his alleged attempt at the centre, his enemy would be some fifteen miles away on an arc bearing from him between south-east and east. The diagrams further show that at this time he thought he could see "individual heavy enemy ships" (which he took to be "Queen Elizabeths") bearing north-east seven miles, and just turning to the eastward, and on these his van opened fire as it came on the easterly course.[1] Possibly the sight of them may have suggested that the enemy's fleet had been divided in order to force him to action. If so the counter movement was obvious. A course to the east would cut off the detached ships and at the same time give a fair chance of crossing astern of the main body. Further, the course would carry him past the *Wiesbaden*, whose crew he was bent on rescuing, and once clear to the eastward he would have his enemy at gunnery advantage against the western horizon. From such a position, moreover, each time he launched his destroyers to attack he would be driving the enemy further off the line of retreat to Horn Reefs. Such a device then for extricating his fleet from the trap in which he found himself was much more to be expected from his ability than the incredible folly of which it was his humour to accuse himself. It is scarcely to be doubted therefore that he was already seeking "to break loose," as he says. That he hoped to surprise his enemy is equally credible, but Admiral Jellicoe

[1] What he saw was probably the isolated *Warspite*, and Commodore Goodenough's squadron, which had seen the turn to the eastward. See *post*, p. 376.

had penetrated the situation acutely enough to be ready for him, and again it was Admiral Scheer who was surprised.

At 6.55 Admiral Jellicoe had turned south, and when he had been on this course for five minutes a message came in from the *Lion* saying " Enemy are to westward." [1] The information only went to confirm him that he was in the position he desired, and at 7.5 he turned three points to starboard in order to close. He knew almost immediately that Admiral Scheer's movement had been accurately detected. As usual, Commodore Goodenough with the 2nd Light Cruiser Squadron was where he was most wanted. Having clung to the enemy as long as possible during the running fight north, he had not followed Admiral Beatty across the front of the battle fleet, but when in the deployment the 5th Battle Squadron formed up in rear of the line, he had taken his proper battle station on its starboard quarter. There he remained during the first of the fighting, but when the enemy disappeared he ran down to the southward to try to regain touch. Thus when the *König* led back to the eastward he was only 12,000 yards away, and immediately came under fire. But, as before, he stoutly held his ground till at 7.4 he was able to report that the enemy had turned back.[2] Then he withdrew again to his station with another bold and well-judged piece of cruiser work added to his already fine record.

The information made clear to the Commander-in-Chief beyond all doubt that what he had already prepared for was coming. A few minutes after he had made the turn together to close the enemy, the ships immediately ahead of him reported a submarine a little on the port bow. Unaware that it was but one of the many false alarms that day, he immediately turned upon it. The turn, which was to the south again, had the additional advantage of bringing back his columns into line ahead, ready for any required manœuvre, and it was high time; for now he could see a number of destroyers, apparently supported by a light cruiser, approaching on his starboard bow. Astern of him Admiral Sturdee saw them too, and at 7.8 signalled to the Commander-in-Chief " Enemy destroyers south-west." A minute or two later, when the southerly turn was complete, Admiral Burney was seen to be re-opening fire. Out of the mist to the westward the van of the enemy's fleet was just coming into sight,

[1] See Diagram 35.

[2] *Southampton*, to S.O., B.C.F. Urgent. Priority. Enemy battle fleet steering E.S.E. Enemy bears from me S.S.W. Number unknown. My position Lat. 57° 02′ N., 6° 07′ E.

and it was on them he was firing. Six minutes earlier he had fired his last salvo at the *Wiesbaden*, and now he could see what he took to be the *König* and some of her sisters on his starboard bow, and at 7.12 his division had everything in action—primary armament on the ships and secondary on the 3rd Flotilla which was now attacking.

The *Marlborough* opened a devastating fire on the leading ship. Fourteen salvoes were fired in six minutes, and of these at least four gave distinct hits. In the sixth salvo a large cloud of grey and white smoke sprang up near the enemy's foremast, while in the twelfth two hits could be clearly seen under the bridge and rather low.[1]

The *Revenge*, Admiral Burney's second ship, took the enemy for " Kaiser " class battleships. She too opened fire on the leading ship, but seeing that her target was already under a heavy fire, she shifted on to the fourth ship and fired rapid salvoes. Sixteen in all were fired, and several hits were observed.

The third ship of the division, the *Hercules*, seeing three battle cruisers to the left of these battleships, opened fire upon the second of them, and scored hits with her fifth and sixth salvoes, while the *Revenge*, her next ahead, reports firing a torpedo, which was seen to run true, at the rear battle cruiser, the *Von der Tann*. Following the *Hercules* was the *Agincourt*, the rear ship, and she too saw four enemy battleships, which she rightly judged to be their 5th Division, appearing out of the mist. She opened fire at 11,000 yards, obtained four straddles and observed effective hits.

Meanwhile our 5th Division, led by Admiral Gaunt in the *Colossus*, had also come into action. The division was well ahead of the *Marlborough*, so it was the enemy battle cruisers that became the target as they appeared out of the mist upon the starboard beam. They were very close, and at ranges between 9,000 and 8,000 yards all four ships poured in an overwhelming fire, to which the German ships were unable to make any effective reply. The *Colossus* alone was hit by two shells, which only inflicted minor damage.

Admiral Jellicoe could see his rear divisions in hot action, though in the smother of the fight the ships could not be made out with certainty. But whatever the enemy was that was coming into action, it was evident to the Commander-in-Chief that his rear was dangerously threatened, and he signalled (7.12) to Admiral Burney to form into line astern of the 4th Division. At the same time Admiral Sturdee, who, according to the established rule, had inclined two

[1] See Diagram 36.

points away from the destroyers, conformed to his intention by turning up astern of him. As the enemy came on and the position became clear, Admiral Jellicoe saw that by completing his line of battle he could cross his adversary's "T," and at 7.16 he ordered Admiral Jerram to take station ahead. So, at last, the battle fleet had its turn, and in a few minutes nearly the whole of it was engaged at ranges between 9,000 and 12,000 yards in an overwhelming attack on the enemy's battle cruisers and the van of their battle fleet. At 7.13 the *Iron Duke* opened fire on the *König*, followed by the rest of the centre squadron at ranges varying from 11,000 to over 14,000 yards, according as battle cruisers or battleships gave them a target through the smoke of the enemy's guns and burning ships. Admiral Jerram's squadron also came into action with the enemy battleships a minute or two later, but at longer ranges.

Thus it was that when Admiral Scheer on his easterly course came in sight of the Grand Fleet he found his opponent had surprised him in the worst possible position. Instead of gaining a clear path to eastward, he was rushing to destruction into the arms of a much superior force disposed on a quadrant athwart his course. So much he could see, but little more. For the Grand Fleet was to him nothing but a long vista of formidable shapes half seen in the increasing gloom of the eastern horizon, while groups of his own ships from time to time were defined between the shifting veils of mist against the glow of the western horizon. For the second time he found himself enveloped in a flaming arc of gun-flashes, and now they were so near that his predicament was more critical than ever. The surprise had been complete, and realising at once that his plan for extricating his fleet had been baffled, he saw his only chance of escape was to risk another *Kehrtwendung*, and he immediately (about 7.12) launched his destroyers to attack and raise a smoke screen in order to cover the precarious manœuvre. This time the conditions rendered it even more dangerous than before.[1] The enemy was closer and his line was as badly bent. The van had already turned on a similar course to the enemy to bring their guns to bear, and they were under a heavy and accurate fire, which threatened every moment to grow more violent and destructive as the range decreased. The British fire was rapidly extending from rear to van, and for the German battle cruisers the situation was specially desperate, but, unequal as was the contest, they had to stand the punishment. For no sooner had Admiral Scheer sent out his destroyers than he saw the

[1] See Diagram 37.

cover they could afford was not enough, and that something more must be done and done quickly if the *Kehrtwendung* was not to end in disaster. There was nothing for it but the battle cruisers. If need was they must be sacrificed to save the battle fleet, and in desperation he had ordered them to press home a forlorn attack on the enemy's van.[1]

For such an exigency the Germans had a signal corresponding to our old ones for attacking the van, centre or rear, and for close action. But their love of heroic gesture was not content with such simplicity. They called it "*Ran an den feind*," literally "charge the enemy"—a headlong rush on the objective indicated regardless of consequences—and the signification of the signal was "Press for a decision with every means at your disposal. Charge. Ram."[2] The battle cruisers were still under the command of Captain Hartog of the *Derfflinger*, for Admiral Hipper had not yet been able to transfer his flag; the *Lützow* was out of action and still burning, and Captain Hartog had only just succeeded in forming the four that were left into line. All were badly damaged, but Captain Hartog, without flinching, led off on his "death ride" against the British van.

To call it a "death ride," as they did, was no exaggeration, even had they been less crippled than they were. Admiral Gaunt's division was still upon them, and most of the divisions of the battle fleet to port of him, though all were now engaged in repelling the destroyer attacks, were also firing at the devoted German battle cruisers as they came from time to time into view against the western glow, while away before their port beam Admiral Beatty had found them again.

At 7.10, when the battle fleet came into action, he was about eight miles to the south-eastward of Admiral Burney and three miles sharp on the port bow of Admiral Jerram. Ten minutes earlier, having turned to the same course as the battle fleet and steaming at eighteen knots to keep his station on the port wing, he began to haul to starboard to try to regain touch with the enemy, till he was going south-west by south. On this course at 7.15, being then from two to three miles further to the eastward than the battleship division

[1] Admiral Scheer's confused narrative (*High Seas Fleet*, pp. 156–7) leaves the order of events uncertain at this point, but Commander von Hase (*Kiel and Jutland*, p. 196) clearly states that the signal for the battle cruisers to push home their attack was made at the same time as that for the *Kehrtwendung*—that is, about 7.12. According to Admiral Scheer's diagrams (*Jutland Despatches*) the latter signal was hauled down five minutes later.

[2] Cf. Hase (*Kiel and Jutland*, p. 125), who says that the signal entered in the log was "Charge the enemy. Ram. Ships denoted are to attack without regard to consequences."

which was nearest to the enemy, he suddenly made out some of the German ships west-north-west of him. They were over 18,000 yards away, but as the sun had now sunk behind the clouds the visibility in that direction had improved so much that in a couple of minutes he could open fire, and at the same time he increased speed to head off what he took to be the van of the enemy's line.[1]

The peril of the Germans was thus sensibly increased, nor could they make any effective reply. A rippling ring of gun-flashes was all they could see as salvo after salvo from the battle fleet crashed into them out of the thundering void. In a couple of minutes the *Derfflinger* had two turrets blown to pieces, her decks were a shambles, she was ablaze fore and aft and all her fire control gear out of action. She was blinded by the smoke from the burning *Lützow* and the agony of the rest can scarcely have been less. It seemed only a question of minutes for the end to come when a signal from their Commander-in-Chief gave them relief.

The German turn away was to starboard, but the Admiral himself turned to port. Possibly there was some confusion. "My intention," Admiral Scheer explains, "was to get through and to save the ships ahead of the *Friedrich der Grosse* from a difficult situation in carrying out the manœuvre" (meaning presumably to give them more room to turn). He admits that his evolution might have led the ship astern to think there had been a mistake in signalling, but Admiral Schmidt, he says, who was leading the 1st Squadron in the *Ostfriesland*, understood, and without waiting for the ships astern of him to turn first, as was the rule for minimising the risk of collision, immediately turned his ship to starboard and thus forced his ships round. "This action," comments Admiral Scheer, "gave satisfactory evidence of the capable handling of ships and the leaders' intelligent grasp of the situation," but it certainly also indicates that the *Kehrtwendung* was carried out with some precipitancy.[2] Thanks to the risk taken, the battleships were all fairly round by 7.20. Then Admiral Scheer signalled to his forlorn hope to break off their rush and simply "manœuvre off the enemy's van," and at the same time he sent out the destroyers' recall. Fitfully the firing died away; like a Homeric mist the smother of haze and smoke thickened impenetrably between the combatants, and Admiral Scheer, for the time at least, had saved his fleet; but

[1] The *Lion's* first salvo was at 17,500 yards and the range was corrected "up" to 18,300. The *Princess Royal* gives the range as 18,000 and the *Tiger* as 19,800 at 7.16.

[2] Scheer, *High Seas Fleet*, pp. 157–8.

no more. His surprise tactics had not had the effect he expected, they had not upset his enemy's plans for the rest of the day, nor had his attack "fallen heavily enough," as he says he hoped, to facilitate his "breaking loose at night."[1]

So effective, however, was the smoke screen which the destroyers set up that, combined with the mist and the failing light, it sufficed for some time to prevent Admiral Jellicoe from having any idea of what the enemy was about. All he knew was that as Admiral Scheer disappeared he had made a series of attacks with his numerous destroyers.[2] They opened with the 11th half flotilla, but so hot was their reception that they fired their torpedoes as soon as they were within extreme range. Eleven were fired, but none took effect. For Admiral Jellicoe performed the manœuvre which long and well-ascertained experiment had proved to be the only way of avoiding such an attack. Admiral Jerram, who had not yet been able to get into station ahead, was ordered to turn his ships away four points together, and to the rest of the fleet he made the "Preparative," which meant they were to turn away two points by sub-divisions (7.21). Then after an interval judged by the time it would take for the torpedoes to reach the line the turn was made, but almost immediately Commander R. M. Bellairs, who had charge of the special instrument designed for the purpose, informed the Admiral that the turn already made was not enough and he signalled for another two points to port. At the moment he was practically without protection from his light craft. Owing to his recent strenuous efforts to close the enemy's battle fleet, all his own flotillas had not yet been able to get up into their battle stations, and all he had for counter attack was Commodore Le Mesurier's 4th Light Cruiser Squadron.[3] This squadron was in station on the port wing, and on receiving a signal from the Commander-in-Chief to attack, went round across the course of the fleet at utmost speed. They were quickly engaged, and under their fire, combined with that of the battleships, it would seem that in the second attack also the enemy destroyers were unable to press near enough to be

[1] Scheer, *High Seas Fleet*, p. 155.

[2] He had in all six and a half flotillas. Attached to the battle fleet were the 3rd, 5th, 7th and the 1st half flotilla; with the battle cruisers were the 2nd, 6th and 9th. A third of them were not available for the covering attack. The 7th Flotilla was astern of the battle fleet; the 1st half flotilla and most of the 12th and 18th half flotillas were away guarding the disabled *Lützow*. Each flotilla consisted of eleven boats and was organised in two half flotillas numbered consecutively, the first and second forming the 1st Flotilla, the third and fourth forming the 2nd Flotilla, etc.

[3] *Calliope, Constance, Comus, Royalist, Caroline.*

effective. A number of torpedoes were fired, but thanks to the turn away they were nearing the end of their run when they crossed our line and were easily avoided.

Ten minutes later followed a third attack from the 3rd and 5th Flotillas attached to the German battle fleet, but with no better success.[1] They, it seems, at once encountered Commodore Le Mesurier, who launched his squadron against them with so much energy that Admiral Jellicoe, being still unaware of the extent of the German withdrawal, had to warn him not to get too near the enemy's battleships. So hot, indeed, was his counter attack that the German destroyers never even had sight of our fleet. In all three attacks not one of our ships had been touched, while in the first attempt one of the enemy destroyers, *S 35*, had been sunk and apparently several others damaged. The failure of the German flotillas to obtain any positive result under conditions so favourable, was due to the ease with which their torpedoes were avoided. At this time the Germans had not succeeded to the extent our own people had done in concealing the tracks of torpedoes, and consequently their approach could be seen in plenty of time for the necessary action to be taken.[2]

The one effective feature of the attack was the smoke screen, which the destroyers developed so thickly as they returned that nothing could be seen of the German fleet. No report of how complete the turn away was had reached the Commander-in-Chief, and as the rear ships were still firing he could only conclude that his inability to see the enemy was due to the fouling of the western horizon. The guns he heard in his rear were really the last that were being fired at the retreating destroyers. This he could not tell, and he ordered the fleet to alter course five points towards the enemy—that is, to south by west (7.35)—expecting at any moment to have sight of them again as the smother cleared. It was the course in any case which, until he knew where they were, would ensure maintaining his dominant position between them and their base—the only way he could see of eventually forcing the enemy to decisive action. But further information came almost immediately. Admiral Beatty on his south-westerly course could still see a few of the enemy, but not distinctly enough to engage them, and at 7.40 a signal (timed ten minutes earlier) was received from him saying that the enemy bore N.W. by W. from him about ten miles. He was

[1] See Diagrams 38 and 39.

[2] This was one of the surprises of the battle, and had it been known previously it might have modified the instructions for avoiding torpedo attack.

out of sight, and the *Lion's* position as given by the signal was obviously wrong, but Admiral Jellicoe, calculating correctly that she was five or six miles ahead of his van, immediately signalled for line ahead and turned to S.W., the course Admiral Beatty had given.[1]

The situation, however, was still far from clear. At 7.45 Commodore Goodenough, who had apparently seen the German turn away at 7.15, sent an urgent message to say that at that time the enemy had detached a number of ships of unknown type which were steering N.W. Shortly after this the Commander-in-Chief received two important messages from Admiral Beatty. At 7.45 he had sent a message to say that the leading enemy battleship bore from him N.W. by W. on a course about S.W. The message was passed *en clair* by searchlight, so that it reached the Commander-in-Chief at 7.59. He at once turned the fleet by divisions to the westward in order to close and informed Admiral Beatty to that effect. For twenty minutes he held that course, and during that time, the second message sent at 7.50 reached him.[2] It was in these words: "Submit van of battleships follow battle cruisers. We can then cut off whole of enemy's battle fleet." This was received in the *Iron Duke* at 7.54, but being made by wireless had to be deciphered, and did not come to the Admiral's hands until shortly after eight. By 8.7 Admiral Jerram, who, on his own initiative had been steaming at a greater speed than the rest of the fleet, was now well ahead, and had the Commander-in-Chief's order to follow the battle cruisers.[3]

It was quick work. Admiral Jellicoe cannot have hesitated a moment in adopting his colleague's proposal. It is true that Admiral Beatty's ships were in no condition to meet battleships, but it was the last chance of bringing the enemy to action before dark.

The situation was still obscure, nor is it clear on what

[1] The position the *Lion* gave was Lat. 56° 56′, Long. 6° 16′, which would have made her two miles on the *Iron Duke's* port beam at 7.30. She was actually five or six miles farther to S.W., so that at 7.40 she was about five and a half miles ahead of Admiral Jerram.

[2] See Diagram 40.

[3] Owing to the continual alteration of course to starboard "in divisions," in order to close the enemy, it had become necessary for Admiral Jerram, having the van squadron, to steam at higher speed than the rest of the fleet in order to get into his station as line ahead was reformed and to obtain a clear range. At 7.20 the fleet speed had been reduced by signal to fifteen knots and increased again to seventeen at 8.0. During most of this period Admiral Jerram on his own initiative was steaming nineteen knots, with the ships of his squadron keeping station upon him.

evidence Admiral Beatty made his confident suggestion. By that time he had completely lost sight of the enemy in the smoke screen, and altering course himself to west-south-west he was sending away the 1st and 3rd Light Cruiser Squadrons to sweep to the westward and try to locate the head of the German line. As for the Commander-in-Chief, he was still deeper in the dark. He had received no accurate information, either from his own ships or from the Admiralty, as to the strength or composition of the German fleet, still less of its order and disposition. Nor could he ascertain the all-important facts with his own eyes. All that he had sighted was the dim shapes of a few ships, but whether they were van, centre or rear it was impossible to tell. Now even these had faded away, and whether their vanishing from view was caused by a thickening of the mist or a tactical movement he could only guess. The situation was indeed so completely wrapped in mystery as to baffle even his remarkable powers of penetration, and it was some considerable time before the obscurity was in any way relieved.

As soon as Admiral Scheer had withdrawn his fleet well out of range beyond the smoke screen he had turned to the southward, hoping apparently that if the British fleet started to chase him to the westward he would be able to slip away to the Horn Reefs south of them. At all events, having now no doubt, as he says, that he was in contact with the whole British fleet, he had decided that his only chance was to make for Horn Reefs by the shortest route and in close formation, and that to foil any attempts to intercept him he must devote all his destroyers to night attacks even at the risk of having to fight an action at daylight without them.

To bring about such a meeting he was sure would be our object, and that we should consequently endeavour by strong attacks in the twilight and using flotillas at night to force him to the westward. The result could scarcely be doubtful with his fleet in the condition it was. His van battle divisions had suffered further severe damage in the last encounter, and his battle cruisers were in still worse plight. Admiral Hipper had not yet succeeded in finding one fit to carry his flag. When he had got up alongside the *Seydlitz* he found her down by the bows and all her wireless gone, and was told she had shipped several thousand tons of water. Then he tried the *Moltke*, but she was under too heavy a fire to stop for him, and as for the *Derfflinger*, she proved to be in even worse condition than the *Seydlitz*. It was not until 9.50 that he hoisted his flag in the *Moltke*, having been on board the *G39* for about three hours.[1]

It was at 7.53 that Admiral Scheer, determined not to be forced to the westward further than could be helped, ventured to turn to the south, with his disordered fleet gradually closing up in reverse order. His pre-Dreadnought squadron was now on the starboard bow of the battle fleet, and the battle cruisers with their attached light cruisers were to the east of them, doing the best their reduced speed would allow to get into station ahead, while Admiral Scheer's own light cruiser squadron (4th Scouting Group) had taken the place of Admiral Hipper's light cruisers as advanced screen. So they steamed anxiously on upon the southerly course. It was not the direct route for Horn Reefs, but it was as near to it as presumably he thought it wise to attempt, and even so it was enough to bring about what he apprehended.

Meanwhile, Admiral Jerram was at a loss how to obey the order he had received to follow our battle cruisers. In asking for the van squadron Admiral Beatty had not given his position, and the Commander-in-Chief had therefore assumed that the *Lion* and *King George V* were in visual touch. But in fact they were not, and Admiral Jerram had no means of knowing where the battle cruisers were. But now firing was suddenly heard somewhere on his port beam. It was no sure guide—gun-fire at sea is always difficult to locate—but it was at least an indication, and on it Admiral Jerram took action. Signalling to his squadron " Follow me," he turned two points to port, which brought him west-south-west, and called up Admiral Beatty to know his position, course and speed (8.21). There was no reply, so he held on as he was.[3]

The meaning of the firing he heard was that Admiral Napier, in the *Falmouth*, in sweeping westward with the 3rd Light Cruiser Squadron on Admiral Beatty's orders to locate the head of the enemy's line, had run into contact with their advanced cruiser squadron. At 8.10 he had been able to report to Admiral Beatty that ships were in sight north by west, and five minutes later he sighted five enemy light cruisers west by north steering across his bows. It was the 4th Scouting Group, then steering south ahead of the German

[1] According to the original German text (p. 360) Admiral Hipper boarded the *Moltke* at 10.05 (9.05 G.M.T.). In the appendix at p. 534, however, the following signals are recorded :—" *G 39* to *Moltke*, visual, received 10.50 p.m.—A. C. Scouting Forces will board *Moltke* " ; " *Moltke* to *G 39*, visual, received 10.55 p.m.—*Moltke* has stopped." It would appear, therefore, that 10.05 in the text is a missprint for 10.50.

[2] Up to the time the order was given the *Minotaur*, of the 2nd Cruiser Squadron, had been in sight of both ships, but she had just passed out of sight from the *King George V*. She signals 8.10 and 8.55. (*Jutland Despatches.*)

[3] See Diagram 41.

battle fleet. He immediately turned parallel and opened fire. His ships, being spread a mile apart to the southward of him, could at first afford him no support, but as he closed them they came successively into action. A sharp fight ensued until about 8.32, when the Germans, having had enough, turned eight points away, and though the British turned after them, they were soon lost to sight in the growing darkness. At 8.15 Admiral Beatty had turned to the same course as the battle fleet, but four minutes later he caught sight of the German battle cruisers and pre-Dreadnought squadron coming south, and turning away a point to port he opened fire. At the same time Admiral Jellicoe had further light. Some ten minutes earlier Commodore Hawksley, who, in the light cruiser *Castor*, was on his port bow with part of the 11th Flotilla, saw smoke in the W.N.W. and pushed out to investigate.[1] Commodore Le Mesurier followed in support with the first division of the 4th Light Cruiser Squadron,[2] and before Admiral Jerram had started in search of the battle cruisers, he was able to inform him that twelve enemy destroyers were in sight to the N.W. From the course they were steering they seemed to be making for our battle cruisers, but with the help of the *Castor* and her destroyers Commodore Le Mesurier quickly drove them off, and as he pressed on in chase came in sight of the German battle fleet steering south. Turning to a similar course the *Calliope* fired a torpedo at 6,500 yards, and then, coming under fire from three battleships, was forced to retire. For ten minutes she was in a boil of splashes, but by zigzagging managed to escape. Admiral Jellicoe now knew what to do. The enemy were fairly well located, and at 8.28 he turned the fleet by divisions S.W. towards the sound of Admiral Beatty's guns—a movement which brought it into line ahead again.

The position, therefore, could scarcely be better. While Admiral Beatty had firm hold of the enemy's van squadrons well ahead of them, Admiral Jellicoe was coming into line of battle abreast of their main body on a converging course. By no possibility, even if Admiral Jerram had known how to make for the battle cruisers directly he got the order, could he have been up in time to reinforce them. Nor was his assistance needed. Already the German ships under Admiral Beatty's fire were suffering, with no means of making effective reply; for again in the deepening dusk they could see nothing

[1] Commodore Hawksley was Captain "D" of the 11th Flotilla and also Commodore "F," commanding all the Grand Fleet flotillas.

[2] *Calliope* (broad pendant), *Constance* and *Comus*.

but the gun-flashes of their assailants. Upon Admiral Hipper's squadron the punishment fell most severely. The *Derfflinger* had another turret temporarily put out of action. The *Seydlitz* also suffered serious damage; it was more than in their crippled condition they could endure, and only the action of Admiral Mauve's pre-Dreadnought squadron saved them. These old ships, being now ahead, had come into action for the first time, and at last had their chance, so Admiral Scheer says, of justifying Admiral Mauve's importunity to be allowed to accompany the fleet. It was little they could do, but they stoutly held their ground till their battle cruisers and light forces had passed to their disengaged side. For Admiral Scheer the position was impossible. Threatened with what he most apprehended—an attack in force in the twilight to press him to the westward—he turned away for the third time before our battle fleet had sight of him, and by 8.35, as he was once more lost in the thickening mists, the firing ahead was dying away.

Again Admiral Jellicoe was puzzled to know the reason. On his starboard bow the *Comus* of the 4th Light Cruiser Squadron was still in action, and when he asked what she was firing at she replied, "Enemy's battle fleet west." Unable to penetrate the situation, Admiral Jellicoe then signalled to Admiral Beatty to indicate the bearing of the enemy (8.46).[1] Hardly had the message gone when a signal came in from the *Falmouth*, flagship of the 3rd Light Cruiser Squadron, giving the bearing of the enemy as north and their course W.S.W.[2] Admiral Jerram was also sending an urgent message that our battle cruisers were not in sight (8.44), and ten minutes later Admiral Beatty was asking the *Minotaur* where Admiral Jerram was, but as she had lost sight of him since 8.10 she could not tell. The *Lion's* main wireless had been shot away and she received the Commander-in-Chief's message indirectly, and before Admiral Beatty got his last query he sent to Admiral Jellicoe the information for which he had been asking, "Enemy battle cruisers and pre-Dreadnought battleships," it said, "bear from me N.34W. distant ten to eleven miles steering S.W." He then gave his position and S.W. as his course.[3]

With sufficient accuracy he could now determine where

[1] See Diagram 42.

[2] Her own position she gave as Lat. 56° 42′ N., Long. 5° 37′ E., which was about five miles north of her actual position.

[3] The "time of origin" of this message is entered in the *Lion's* log as 8.40; "time of despatch" 8.59. Its receipt by the *Iron Duke* is noted as 9.5.

the enemy were and what they were doing, and further light came from Commodore Goodenough, who had his squadron in station astern. He could be heard in action, and reported that he was engaging destroyers which from the westward were trying to attack the 5th Battle Squadron. The 2nd Light Cruiser Squadron sighted a " V " class torpedo boat, upon which the *Southampton* and *Dublin* opened fire, hitting her amidships. This can only have been the *V48*, which was sunk later by the destroyers of the 12th Flotilla. Firing could also be heard ahead. The *Caroline* and *Royalist*, of the 4th Light Cruiser Squadron, had just seen what they took to be the German pre-Dreadnought squadron, and the senior officer, Captain H. R. Crooke, made the signal to attack with torpedo (8.50). Admiral Jerram who still could not make out where Admiral Beatty was, and was expecting to sight him at any moment, at once signalled " Negative the attack. Those are our battle-cruisers." Captain Crooke, however, could see more clearly, and having no doubt as to what he had sighted, took upon himself the responsibility of ignoring the order and proceeded with the attack. In spite of the storm of fire that met them the *Caroline* fired two torpedoes and the *Royalist* one at 8,000 yards. Then, smothered with shell, they made off, and though both were straddled again and again they escaped under a screen of funnel smoke little the worse for their adventure. As for our destroyers, though they were in their battle stations astern of the *Caroline*, they could make no attempt to attack, for owing to the uncertainty of Admiral Beatty's whereabouts, Admiral Jerram was in too much doubt about the enemy's identity to open fire, and without battleship support a destroyer attack before dark is not tactically sound.

Though no harm was done to the enemy, the affair was of value to the Commander-in-Chief. He now knew for certain that he was still in a good position between the Germans and their base, and that it was at least possible to force them further to the west. But the sun had set nearly an hour before; the gloom all round was deepening into darkness, and any further attempt to engage must involve a night action. This, like Lord Howe on the same day in 1794, he was determined not to hazard.[1] Modern developments had only hardened the long-established objections which condemned fleet actions by night as inadmissible, and

[1] See the despatch in Barrow's *Life of Howe*, p. 232. With a misty night coming on and an adversary so skilful at turning away it was equally impossible for Admiral Jellicoe to bring the enemy " properly to action," that is, in a manner likely to secure decisive results.

for Admiral Jellicoe all that remained was to determine what course to take so as to intercept the enemy in the morning.

"I was loth to forgo," he wrote in his despatch, "the advantage of position which would have resulted from an easterly or westerly course, and I therefore decided to steer to the southward, where I should be in a position to renew the engagement at daylight." This was at nine o'clock, while the firing was still going on. About ten minutes later he heard from Admiral Jerram that our battle cruisers were in sight west-north-west on a south-westerly course, but in fact it was the enemy's battle cruisers, not our own, that he had seen. There was nothing to suggest the error, and the message as received did nothing to modify Admiral Jellicoe's intentions. All it indicated was that he now had his whole force well together, and at 9.17 he made a general signal for the fleet to assume night cruising order in close formation so as to ensure keeping visual touch through the dark hours and to avoid the risk of ships mistaking each other for the enemy.[1]

The organisation which the signal specified brought the fleet into columns of squadrons instead of columns of divisions —that is, it was now in three columns instead of six, with the 5th Battle Squadron on the port flank. Admiral Beatty remained detached in advance of the main body. At 9.16 he had taken in the Commander-in-Chief's signal to all squadron commanders and flotilla captains that the course of the fleet was south, and in view of the gathering darkness he seems to have come to the same conclusion as his Chief, that it was unwise for him to attempt to engage again before daylight. The reasons he gave in his report were his own distance from the battle fleet and the damaged condition of the battle cruisers, while the enemy were concentrated and accompanied by numerous destroyers; and finally our strategical position was "such as to make it appear certain that we should locate the enemy at daylight under most favourable circumstances." On this appreciation, he says, "I did not consider it desirable or proper to close the enemy battle fleet during the dark hours. I therefore concluded that I should be carrying out the Commander-in-Chief's wishes by turning to the course of the fleet, reporting to the Commander-in-Chief that I had done so. My duty in this situation was to ensure that the enemy fleet could not regain its base by passing round the southern flank of our forces. I therefore turned to south at 9.24 p.m. at

[1] The actual signal was, "Assume second organisation. Form divisions in line ahead, columns disposed abeam to port. Columns to be one mile apart." See Diagram 43.

seventeen knots . . . with the 1st and 3rd Light Cruiser Squadrons spread to the southward and westward."

Nothing probably could have more nicely interpreted what was in Admiral Jellicoe's mind. The crux of the strategical situation was the possibility of the enemy slipping away to the eastward either ahead or astern during the night. There were three ways by which Admiral Scheer could seek the safety of his base. One was by Horn Reefs and the Amrum bank; the second was by a passage to the westward of Heligoland, and the third by making the Frisian coast and so along the German swept channel from the Ems to the Jade. On the course Admiral Jellicoe had chosen with the battle cruiser fleet ahead of him he calculated he was "favourably placed to intercept the enemy should he make for his base by steering for Heligoland or towards the Ems."[1] But his disposition did not so well provide for the Horn Reefs route should the enemy attempt to reach it by passing across the northward of our fleet. True, he had the three Harwich submarines lying in wait on a line from the Vyl light-vessel, but that was not enough to deny the enemy the Horn Reefs passage. As an additional precaution he therefore ordered the *Abdiel* to proceed in accordance with her original instructions and extend the minefield south of the submarine patrol line. But, what was far more important, he took the fine decision (at 9.27) of massing the whole of his flotillas five miles astern of the fleet. The risk involved was not great. True it would leave him without an anti-submarine screen during the night, but he could count with fair certainty on having his destroyers about him again at dawn. Meanwhile their presence five miles astern would ensure him against attempts of the enemy's flotillas on his rear, and had the great advantage of exposing the Germans to a massed torpedo attack should they endeavour to pass north of him.

So with the battle fleet well closed up in night cruising order, the destroyers astern and the battle cruiser fleet some twelve miles a little before his starboard beam, he held on south, as, big with fate, the night closed down.

[1] *Jutland Despatches*, p. 21.

CHAPTER XX

JUTLAND—THE FOURTH PHASE

The Night

As Admiral Jellicoe was doing all that time-honoured tradition and his own experience taught him, to ensure that the enemy should not get away without a decision, his adversary appears to have made up his mind as to what was his best chance of avoiding one. Foiled once if not twice in his attempt to get by to the eastward, he could no longer delay another determined effort to cross.[1] At all hazards he must take the most direct way home, though it involved another attempt to push across the enemy's wake and the possibility of receiving another shock such as had baffled his first effort. Accordingly at 9.10—that is, seven minutes before Admiral Jellicoe had given directions to take up night cruising order—he made the necessary signals. The first was for the main body of the fleet to maintain a course S.S.E.¾ E. at 16 knots. This was the rallying course in case of accidents, and it led in the direction of Horn Reefs. The organisation the fleet was to assume followed: 1st Battle Squadron, 3rd Battle Squadron, 2nd Battle Squadron; Battle Cruisers in the rear; 2nd Scouting Group ahead and the 4th Scouting Group to starboard.[2] He did not, however, turn at once on the specified course. It would look as though he was unwilling to approach the Grand Fleet till it had had time to draw well ahead, and beyond the two scouting groups nearly all his destroyers were thrown out to feel for it. Shortly after 9.30 the van began to lead round to port on the course for Horn Reefs.

That he expected to find the way clear is hardly credible. Presumably he was feeling for his enemy, and as the courses of the two fleets were now fast converging his advanced guard cruisers came into action almost immediately. What they struck was the destroyer rear guard where the *Castor* with the 11th Flotilla had taken station on the wing nearest the enemy,

[1] See Diagram 43.

[2] The *Westfalen* (Captain Redlich) of the 1st Battle Squadron was leading the line.

with Commodore Hawksley at the head of two divisions and Commander H. E. Sulivan in the *Kempenfelt* leading the remainder. About half an hour after Admiral Scheer's change of course, the Commodore, peering through the darkness, could make out ships on his starboard bow. What they were it was impossible to tell, and he was making towards them when they showed challenging lights. To add to the doubt as to their identity the first two signals they made were correct for the British challenge of the day, but the other two were wrong. For Commodore Hawksley, however, the uncertainty was soon set at rest. Suddenly the two leading strangers switched on searchlights and at 2,000 yards opened fire. Hitting began at once on both sides. Four times shells got home on the *Castor*, causing heavy casualties. One set her motor barge on fire, and so fiercely did it blaze that the whole ship became a brilliantly lighted target, and she turned away, but not before she had fired a torpedo. The enemy seemed also to turn away to avoid it, and they now disappeared. Each of the leading destroyers of the *Castor's* half-flotilla *Marne* and *Magic*, had also fired one torpedo, but they were so blinded by the rapid flashes of the *Castor's* guns that neither could see to fire more, while as for the rest of the destroyers, they were so certain that a mistake was being made, and that the strangers were some of our own ships, that they refrained from firing at all. So in the first hour of darkness the incalculable hazards of a night action were exemplified.[1]

Abortive as the affair was it can only have appeared to Admiral Scheer as the kind of attack he was expecting to be made in order to force him to the westward. To all appearance it had been frustrated by his van cruisers, but he nevertheless seems to have found it advisable to give way a little, for at the time he would have got his cruisers' report he altered a point to starboard (10.6).[2] But this proved insufficient to clear him. Commodore Hawksley had hardly resumed his southerly course after the fleet when Admiral Scheer could see that another engagement had started to eastward of him. Here Commodore Goodenough with the 2nd Light Cruiser Squadron was trying to keep his station in rear of the battle fleet. He had fallen a good deal astern of the Commander-

[1] The German vessels engaged at this time with the 11th Flotilla were the *Hamburg* and *Elbing* of the 4th Scouting Group, both of which ineffectively fired a torpedo, and almost immediately afterwards the *Frankfurt* and *Pillau* of the 2nd Scouting Group opened fire. The *Hamburg* received considerable damage in this encounter, and three of her stokers and all the crew of her No. 3 gun were seriously wounded.

[2] See Diagram 44.

in-Chief, for he had been keeping in touch with the *Marlborough*, which, owing to her torpedo damage, was unable to do more than 16 knots. Admiral Burney's division was consequently about four miles astern of station, and at 10.0 Admiral Evan-Thomas found it necessary to turn the 5th Battle Squadron back to look for him. In spite of Admiral Scheer's last inclination to starboard the two fleets were still on converging courses, and the result was that the 4th Scouting Group, which had apparently taken station on his port beam, soon found themselves abreast of Commodore Goodenough.[1]

For him the meeting was no surprise. For some time the play of searchlights and gun-flashes to the westward, where the *Castor* had been in action, had warned him that the enemy was not far away. With starboard gun crews closed up ready for instant action an intense look-out was being kept, when, against the faint glow that still tinged the western horizon, the silhouettes of five cruisers took shape.[2] They were very close, and clearly on a converging course. There could be little doubt what they were. For a moment or two recognition lights began to twinkle from both lines, when, at a range of eight hundred yards, Captain A. C. Scott of the *Dublin* was sure enough to fire. The shell could be seen to tear a hole in the side of one of the strangers; instantaneously a dozen searchlights were switched on to him and the *Southampton*, and they were smothered with rapid fire by the whole enemy squadron. In a moment all was a roar of passing and exploding shell and a wild confusion of gun-flashes, dazzling searchlight beams and rapid changes of course. It was work in the old style at point-blank range, with missing hardly possible on either side. But the enemy were far from having it their own way. Captains C. B. Miller and A. A. M. Duff of the *Nottingham* and *Birmingham* had judiciously kept their searchlights quiet, and the enemy, unable to see them, left them alone to develop a rapid and destructive fire. At the first glimpse of the Germans, moreover, the *Southampton* had got a torpedo tube ready, and while her deck, bridges and superstructure were being swept in the storm of shell, it was fired. A bright explosion was seen in the enemy's line, and then suddenly they switched off their searchlights and vanished into the gloom. In a quarter of an hour it was all over. The *Southampton* had had all her midship guns' crews and most of her searchlight parties wiped out, she was

[1] *Stettin* (Commodore von Reuter), *München, Frauenlob, Stuttgart, Hamburg.*

[2] See Diagram 45 (A).

blazing like a beacon with cordite fires, expecting every moment to blow up, and her casualties were thirty-five killed and forty-one wounded. The *Dublin* fared better, having only two ships on her, but she too lost heavily. She was on fire between decks, her navigator was killed and her charts all destroyed, so that, as she soon after lost touch with the *Southampton*, she could not tell where she was and was not able to rejoin her squadron until 10.15 a.m. the following day. As for the Germans, seeing that for those deadly minutes the *Nottingham* and *Birmingham* had been pouring in rapid fire at point-blank practically undisturbed, they can scarcely have suffered less.[1] One ship was lost with all hands, for the *Southampton's* torpedo found its billet in the *Frauenlob*, and in a quarter of an hour she went down with her 12 officers and 308 men. Her end was not seen; for the *Southampton* and *Dublin*, under the crushing concentration, had been forced to turn away to master their fires. This was soon done, and the Commodore held on to the eastward till he came across the 5th Battle Squadron, when he gathered his scattered squadron (less the *Dublin*) to form a rear guard against destroyer attack.

With his wireless put out of action and his squadron temporarily out of touch it was impossible for Commodore Goodenough to communicate his news to the Commander-in-Chief. The glitter of the action could be seen in the *Iron Duke*, but its significance was not grasped. Admiral Jellicoe had fully expected a torpedo attack would be made on his rear, and the need of guarding against it was one of the reasons that decided him to mass his flotillas astern. He had little doubt that what he anticipated was happening, and shortly before 11.0—that is, about the time the *Frauenlob* went down —Commodore Hawksley received from him the query: "Are you engaging enemy destroyers?" The reply was already on its way, crossing the Commander-in-Chief's message, and it said "Have been engaged with enemy cruisers," and the inference in the *Iron Duke* was that these were ships acting in support of destroyers.

Destroyers indeed had been sighted in the vicinity of the flotilla which was next to the Commodore to the eastward. This was the 4th Flotilla, under Captain C. J. Wintour.[2]

[1] The German returns for 4th Scouting Group in this and the previous action with the *Falmouth* give the losses for the *Stettin*, *München* and *Hamburg* killed 31, wounded 71. Those of the *Stuttgart* are not recorded. The *Frauenlob* (sunk) 320.

[2] Captain Wintour had only twelve boats with him. He was leading the 1st half flotilla in the flotilla leader *Tipperary*, with Commander W. L. Allen leading the 2nd half in the *Broke*. The two boats that were left of the *Shark* division,

At about 10.0 he was turning sixteen points into his assigned station on a southerly course when three of his rear boats were aware of three or four enemy destroyers to the northward, who fired four torpedoes at them, but before our people could get off more than a round or two in reply they disappeared into the darkness. Shortly afterwards the *Garland*, which was one of the destroyers that had fired, sighted a light cruiser of the " Graudenz " class to westward going south, and Captain Wintour held on upon the same course in accordance with his orders (10.35). Five minutes later the *Boadicea*, Admiral Jerram's attached light cruiser, was reporting enemy ships on her starboard beam. None of these reports reached the flagship, the observations not being deemed of sufficient importance to justify betraying the position of the battle fleet by signalling them to the Commander-in-Chief. So far, then, he had no information to modify his belief that he was still between the enemy and their base. There was nothing, therefore, to suggest a change of plan, and he continued his southerly course.

Admiral Scheer, however, may have had something more definite to go upon, for the 9.27 general signal to the British flotillas had been intercepted by the German wireless station at Neumünster and passed to him, but whether the message actually came to his hand cannot be definitely established. What he did know was that his advanced cruisers had been in contact with some of our destroyers, and in all probability he was also informed that his searching destroyers had located others of ours to the south of them, but had found no trace of the battleships. On these indications it must have seemed that our fleet had drawn far enough ahead for him to risk an attempt to escape by passing across his enemy's wake. At all events, shortly after half-past ten he altered course to port upon a course S.E. by S., direct for the Horn Reefs light-vessel.

By this time the sky had become overcast, the night was very dark, and he was feeling his way with the 2nd Scouting Group in line ahead, and his available destroyers spread before him in a wide " V " formation E.N.E. and S.S.W. from

---

Ophelia and *Christopher*, were screening Admiral Beatty's squadron. Another division, *Owl*, *Hardy* and *Midge*, were with the armoured cruisers. The remaining three of the twenty were refitting. The 1st half flotilla consisted of the *Spitfire*, *Sparrowhawk*, *Garland*, *Contest*; the 2nd half of *Achates*, *Ambuscade*, *Ardent*, *Fortune*, with the *Porpoise* and *Unity*, of the last division, following. At this time they were in two columns, but half an hour later Captain Wintour ordered the *Broke* to form her divisions astern of him.

the van ship.[1] It was with the port wing of these ships that Captain Wintour must have come into contact, but for nearly an hour nothing more broke the calm and blackness of the night. The reason may have been that some time after the *Castor's* action the German fleet had inclined away a little to starboard, and was not converging so much as it had been up to ten o'clock. Whatever the cause, the long spell of quiet could only confirm the Commander-in-Chief in his belief that the enemy were to the westward of him, and he was holding on to the southward, while Admiral Burney's division, unbeknown to him, was falling farther and farther astern. Some fifteen miles away before the *Iron Duke's* starboard beam was Admiral Beatty, with all the battle cruisers screened by two divisions of the 1st Flotilla and the *Christopher* and *Ophelia* of the 4th Flotilla.[2] On his starboard quarter was the 3rd Light Cruiser Squadron with the 1st in company. The latter he had ordered to take station four miles on his starboard beam and to keep a sharp look-out for the enemy north by west; but the *Lion* was out of sight and the light cruisers were only able to take station on her assumed position. Admiral Beatty, too, must have been fairly sure the fleet was holding the Germans away from their base and expecting to find them to the westward in the morning. But in fact they had crossed astern of him more than an hour before, and Admiral Scheer, heading for the Horn Reefs, was some fifteen miles to the north-eastward of the *Lion*, when at 11.30 the fight broke out again and the power of Admiral Jellicoe's massed flotillas to bar the escape of the High Seas Fleet was put to a fiery test.

When the hour came—the hour that was to decide the question which had been the food of so much thought and experiment during the years of preparation—Captain Wintour was leading his flotilla south in line ahead. To the eastward, but nearly seven miles away, was Captain Farie in the light cruiser *Champion*, leading the seven remaining boats of the 13th Flotilla,[3] with the *Termagant* and *Turbulent* of the 10th. Close abeam of him were the four Harwich boats of the 9th Flotilla,[4] with the *Morris* of the 10th.[5] And

[1] Scheer, *High Seas Fleet*, p. 160. The screen consisted of the 2nd, 5th and 7th Flotillas and part of the 6th and 9th, possibly about forty destroyers. A great many of the boats, he says, had fired all their torpedoes in the day fighting; some were astern protecting the *Lützow*, and others were held back by the flotilla leaders in case of emergency.

[2] See Diagram 45 (B).

[3] *Obdurate, Moresby, Nerissa, Narborough, Nicator, Pelican, Petard.*

[4] *Lydiard, Liberty, Landrail, Laurel.*

[5] The *Moorsom* had been sent back owing to damaged oil tanks, due to a hit in the afternoon action.

then, also well in station, came Captain A. J. B. Stirling leading fourteen boats of the 12th Flotilla in the *Faulknor*. Between the two groups there was thus a wide space owing to the fact that the eastern flotillas were keeping station on Admiral Burney's division, which was still dropping more and more astern owing to the *Marlborough's* injuries.

This was the position when, towards 11.20, Captain Wintour and the leading boats of his solitary flotilla were aware of a shadowy line of ships to starboard on a converging course. Whether they were friend or foe it was impossible to tell, and he held on for some minutes with all torpedo tubes trained to starboard. Still they made no sign, and at last, as they were evidently drawing ahead of him and had closed to less than 1,000 yards, he ventured to give the challenge.[1] Salvoes, accurate and rapid, at point blank followed instantaneously, and in a minute the *Tipperary* burst into flames, almost lost to sight in brilliantly illuminated splashes. Yet she fired both her torpedoes. The four boats of her division did the same, and so did the *Broke*. Some of the rear boats, still uncertain that a mistake was not being made, held their fire till accidentally one of the enemy's beams lit up the rear ship. Then it was plain to see what they had to deal with, and they also attacked. Several of the boats claim to have hit. Explosions were plainly seen; there were gaps in the line of staring searchlights. How many hits were made is uncertain, but one at least of the cruisers received her death blow. It was the *Elbing* of the 2nd Scouting Group, part of the advanced screen of the High Seas Fleet. In face of the destroyer attack they had turned away and tried to escape by passing through the line of the leading battle squadron. The *Frankfurt* and the *Pillau* succeeded, but the *Elbing*, less fortunate, was badly rammed by the *Posen*. She did not sink at once, but had soon to be abandoned.[2]

All that man could do Captain Wintour had done, but he was now no more. The first salvo had swept away the *Tipperary's* bridge, on which he stood, and she was left a mass of burning wreckage.[3] Lieutenant-Commander C. W. E. Trelawny in the *Spitfire* was next astern. Unable to reload his tubes for another attack—his torpedo davit had been disabled

[1] It would appear that on hearing of this first contact the van of the High Seas Fleet hauled away a little to starboard, and then led in again to E.S.E. to resume its station. Consequently by 11.20 there was a substantial kink in the line.

[2] Damage was also sustained by the *Westfalen*, *Nassau* and *Rheinland*, all of which were hit in their foremost funnels and searchlights. Their casualties were ten killed and thirty-eight wounded.

[3] Nine of the *Tipperary's* crew were rescued by the German *S.53*.

—he had to be content with smashing an enemy's searchlight with gunfire, and then came back to his leader's assistance. In the fierce glare of the flames he could see nothing. All around was impenetrable blackness, till out of it he suddenly saw what he took to be two German cruisers coming down upon him. Then followed one of the most remarkable incidents of the battle. "The nearer one," he wrote, "altered course to ram me apparently. I therefore put my helm hard-a-port and the two ships rammed each other port bow to port bow. . . . I consider I must have considerably damaged this cruiser, as twenty feet of her side plating was left on my forecastle." As the two ships met at full speed the enemy fired her forward guns, over the *Spitfire.* She was too close for their utmost depression to secure a hit, but the blast blew away her bridge, searchlight platform and foremost funnel, and left officers and men half stunned and entangled in a mass of wreckage. Her forecastle was torn open, sixty feet of her bow plating was shorn away, and she took fire. As soon as Lieutenant-Commander Trelawny had extricated himself from the ruin of the bridge he threw overboard the steel chest containing the secret books. Only by a miracle could a destroyer survive such an adventure, but, wonderful to relate, she did survive. And the wonder increases now that we know it was no mere cruiser she had met in full career, but the German Dreadnought *Nassau.* Thanks to those who designed and constructed her the *Spitfire* was able to limp away with three boilers still going, and in due course came home carrying the plating and part of the anchor gear of her mighty antagonist as trophies of the conflict.[1]

As for the remainder of the fleet, this uproar and confusion so close at hand was too much for it, and with the firing at its height the van led away to starboard until it was steering S.S.W., nearly eight points off its course for home. Eight minutes later Admiral Scheer, who had just reached the turning point, made a peremptory signal, ordering the fleet to steer S.E. by S., and by 11.34 the *Westfalen* had again turned on the direct course for Horn Reefs.

Meanwhile the *Broke* had taken the *Tipperary's* place. Commander Allen found that half a dozen boats had got into line astern of him, and in the order *Sparrowhawk, Garland, Contest, Ardent, Fortune, Porpoise,* he was leading them southward, where he judged he should find the enemy again.[2] He was not far wrong. In a few minutes—it was about 11.40—he could see a large ship on his starboard bow heading to cross his course. He challenged. The answer was again

[1] See Diagram 45 (B).

[2] See Diagram 45 (C).

a blaze of searchlights and a burst of rapid fire. Commander Allen swung to port to bring his tubes to bear. Lieutenant-Commander S. Hopkins in the *Sparrowhawk* did the same, and then to his horror he saw that the *Broke*, instead of steadying her helm, was continuing to swing and coming straight for him. As the *Broke* turned she had been hit by a salvo which put her out of control. There was no time to avoid a collision, and she crashed into the *Sparrowhawk* just before the bridge. Only by a hair's breadth the *Garland* avoided the *Sparrowhawk* and turned away, but the *Contest*, coming next, did not see the trouble in time and cut five feet of her stern clean off as she lay locked with the *Broke*.[1]

What it was they had come upon was not clear. Searchlights and gun-flashes seemed to be all round them. Some were sure the first ship encountered was of the "Westfalen" type, and it seems they had hit the head of the German battle fleet as it was passing across Admiral Jellicoe's wake. The attack was not without effect, for one torpedo got home on the *Rostock*, flagship of Commodore Michelsen, commanding the destroyers, and she was severely damaged. She, like the *Elbing* (abandoned and sunk about 3.40 a.m.), managed to keep afloat for a time, and crawling away to the southward was eventually also (4.25 a.m.) abandoned and sunk by her crew. After the collision, which put the *Broke* and *Sparrowhawk* out of action, Commander R. B. C. Hutchinson in the *Achates* took command of the 2nd half flotilla, and continued south after the battle fleet. The *Contest*, not much injured by the collision, was with them, and the *Garland* had rejoined and had taken station in the line when more battleships were seen ahead. Then followed another wild scene of din and glare like the last. Commander Hutchinson, believing some of our own cruisers were between him and the enemy, held his fire till it was too late to attack. The *Ambuscade* discharged her two remaining torpedoes before she and the *Achates* were chased off by cruisers to the eastward, and, unable to cross ahead of the enemy's line after our battle fleet, had to make for the northward to circle back that way. Meanwhile the next astern, the *Ardent*, was attacking a ship which had picked up her next astern the *Fortune* (Lieutenant-Commander F. G. Terry), and was smothering her with salvoes. The *Ardent* fired a torpedo

[1] The *Broke* again came into action with two enemy destroyers early the next morning, but escaped to the northward, with the intention of making Scapa or Cromarty. Owing, however, to a strong breeze springing up from the north-west she had to keep away to the south and arrived in the Tyne at 5.0 p.m. on June 3.

which was believed to have hit, but the *Fortune* had been badly hit, and though already in flames and sinking, she was gallantly firing her guns to the last at her big adversary. She was being fired at by the battleship *Rheinland* which the *Porpoise* sighted abaft her starboard beam, but before the latter could attack she was struck by a heavy shell, which put her out of action. Yet she was able to crawl away, while the *Ardent* was now the only one of the flotilla fit for further service.

This destroyer now found herself alone, and having escaped with little injury, made away southwards in the hope of finding the rest of her division, which in fact had ceased to exist. What she fell in with was something quite different. The German battle fleet, in spite of our flotilla attacks, was still holding on for Horn Reefs, and had just achieved a wholly unexpected success. Ever since Admiral Arbuthnot's cruiser squadron had been practically wiped out at the moment of deployment, the *Black Prince* (Captain T. P. Bonham) had not been seen. She had completely lost touch, and had fallen far astern, and it would seem that she was making the best of her way south after the fleet, when she now suddenly found herself close abreast of the German centre. In a moment she was in a glare of searchlights, a tornado of shell at point-blank rent her from stem to stern, and in two minutes she was a mass of flames. For a while she was seen as a floating furnace, and then, with an appalling explosion, sank with all hands (12.10).

Undisturbed by the incident, the Germans held on their course, so that in a minute or two Lieutenant-Commander A. Marsden in the *Ardent* saw smoke ahead of him, and thinking it came from his consorts he made towards it. Then the form of a large German ship loomed up, and without hesitation he attacked. Another torpedo was fired at very close range, but before he could see the result he was blinded by the searchlights of four battleships in line ahead.[1] Out of the glare came the inevitable hurricane of shell. In a minute or so the *Ardent* was a mass of scrap-iron, and switching off their lights the enemy disappeared and left her to sink in total darkness. She was lost with all hands (12.19) except Lieutenant-Commander Marsden and one man.

So ended the work of the gallant 4th Flotilla. Alone they had borne the brunt of the whole German battle fleet, and not a man had flinched. Again and again as a group of the enemy tore them with shell at point-blank and disappeared they sought another, and attacked till nearly every

[1] They were in fact the four leading German battleships.

boat had spent all her torpedoes or was a wreck. Such high spirit and skill had they shown that one thing was certain—the failure of the flotilla to achieve all that was generally expected from it was due to no shortcoming in the human factor. It was the power of the weapon itself that had been overrated.

During all this time of intermittent fighting in the rear-guard our battle fleet, never suspecting what it really meant, was holding on steadily to the southward. From the main body, with the Commander-in-Chief, the enemy star shells and the glare of the successive actions could be seen on the low clouds, first on their starboard quarter, gradually shifting to right astern and even further to the eastward, but captain after captain records the impression that it was our light cruisers and destroyers repelling an attack on the rear of the fleet. The *Vanguard*, of Admiral Sturdee's squadron, actually reports an attack on Admiral Jerram, whose squadron was on her starboard beam.[1] Admiral Burney, though he was several miles astern, and more to the eastward, could see no more. All he could tell was that there were short bursts of firing first on his starboard beam and then astern. The 5th Battle Squadron was at certain critical times nearest to the enemy and would seem to have been in a still better position to detect what was going on,[2] but Admiral Evan-Thomas only records that at 10.15 heavy firing was observed a little abaft the starboard beam, "which," he says, "I surmised to be attacks by enemy destroyers and light craft on our light cruisers and destroyers." At 10.39 there was similar firing on his starboard quarter, and again at 11.35 right astern, but it still seemed to be no more than a destroyer attack on cruisers. The *Valiant*, which was second in the squadron, saw the *Castor's* action much as it occurred, and at 11.30 another action two miles on her starboard quarter. The *Malaya*, her next astern, seems to have been the only ship that had any reason to believe that German battleships were being engaged by our flotillas. At 11.40 she could see some of our destroyers three

[1] The *Thunderer*, Admiral Jerram's rear ship, and the *Boadicea*, report having sighted an enemy cruiser at 10.30. This was either the *Moltke* or the *Seydlitz*, but fire was not opened upon her as it was considered inadvisable to show up the battle fleet unless there was an obvious intention to attack, and she stated she saw our destroyers afterwards attacking this cruiser.

[2] Admiral Evan-Thomas had now only three ships, *Barham*, *Valiant* and *Malaya*. The *Warspite*, owing to the damage she had received when the Grand Fleet was deploying, found she could do no more than 16 knots. She became isolated, and on asking for the position of the battle fleet received orders to make her way back to Rosyth.

points abaft her starboard beam attacking some big ships, but they seemed to be steering the same course as our own fleet. Then suddenly, amidst the din and glitter of the fight, it could be seen that one of the enemy had been hit by a torpedo. In the flash of the explosion the *Malaya* thought she could identify the leader of the ships that were being attacked as a Dreadnought of the " Westfalen " class. For some reason this important piece of information was not passed on to the Commander-in-Chief to warn him that he was drawing ahead of the enemy.

By that time, however, he had in his hands a highly important message from the Admiralty. This was timed 10.41, and was received in the *Iron Duke* at 11.5. It read as follows :—" German Battle Fleet ordered home at 9.14 p.m. Battle Cruisers in rear. Course S.S.E. ¾ E. Speed 16 knots." This message was a summary of three signals intercepted in the Admiralty, two at 9.55 and one at 10.10. The first was one which Admiral Scheer made at 9.14 ordering the retirement and giving the course the fleet was to steer during the night. The second, made at 9.29, gave the fleet's formation, while the third, timed 9.46, gave a slightly different course. A far more vitally important signal, however, taken in at the Admiralty also at 10.10, was an urgent request by Admiral Scheer for air reconnaissance at Horn Reefs. This information, which would have told Admiral Jellicoe beyond any doubt exactly what was his opponent's intention, was not forwarded to him. It is possible, however, that an earlier message sent by the Admiralty to the Commander-in-Chief at 9.58, which gave the position of Admiral Scheer's rear ship at 9.0, was considered sufficient indication of the route homewards that the enemy intended to take. But the inference was not so obvious to Admiral Jellicoe. This earlier Admiralty message stated the position to be Lat. 56.33 N., Long. 5.30 E., but this he could not accept as it made the German fleet some ten miles to the south-westward of his own van when he turned south, at which time he knew that it must have been well to the north-westward of the *Iron Duke*. Moreover, had the Admiralty position been correct, and had Admiral Scheer acted on his 9.14 order to make for the base, it was scarcely possible that some intimation of the movement would not have reached the flagship at least an hour earlier, and the last intimation Admiral Jellicoe had had was Commodore Hawksley's signal (sent by wireless at 10.50) that it was only cruisers that were engaging him. He could thus be sure that at least a portion of the enemy's fleet was in touch with his rear. He considered it highly improbable that Admiral Scheer, seeing night fighting ahead of him, would steer straight into it. It would more probably force him to the northward or westward. Should he take the risk, however, Admiral Jellicoe could hope that his massed destroyers would get a chance to attack. In default therefore of more trustworthy intelligence about the battleships he held on as he was, nor did the next information he received afford any ground for changing his appreciation. Within the next half-hour two more messages came in, and both of them went to show that Admiral Scheer was not yet making for home. One was from Commodore Goodenough. At last he had been able, through the *Nottingham*, whose wireless was intact, to report his action with the 4th Scouting Group. The message read : " Have engaged enemy cruisers at 10.15 bearing west-south-west," a clear indication that at that time the enemy was still to the westward of our battle fleet. The other message was from Captain Duff of the *Birmingham*, who, in retiring eastward after the action, had had to turn to port to avoid the 5th Battle Squadron, and so had lost company with the Commodore. What he had to say was : " Battle cruisers, unknown number probably hostile, in sight north-east, course south. My position Lat. 56.26 N., Long. 5.42 E."[1] The message could only confirm the Commander-in-Chief's belief that the German fleet was not making for Horn Reefs, and that the fighting that was going on could be nothing more than his rearguard repelling an attempt of the enemy light craft to attack from astern. We have seen how admirable the information from Commodore Goodenough's squadron had been all through, and in the circumstances it must have seemed more trustworthy, and was certainly more definite than the Admiralty intercept. With such conflicting evidence before him Admiral Jellicoe could do no other than accept that from his own vessels on the spot. To him, therefore, there was still nothing to warrant a change in his considered plan for the night, and he continued his course south.

Erroneous as was the impression which Captain Duff's message conveyed, the course given was correct. When the van of the German fleet came for the second time into contact with the 4th Flotilla it had turned sharply away to south-west. At 11.30, as we have seen, it turned back to south, and was actually on that course when Captain Duff

[1] There would appear to have been no enemy to the N.E. at this time.

made his report. In four minutes, however, the enemy resumed the course for Horn Reefs, but even when this brought their battle fleet in contact with the 4th Flotilla for the third time, no report of what it was attacking reached the Commander-in-Chief, so that the firing was only further evidence that it was the enemy's light forces making another attempt on his rear.

Although Admiral Scheer was thus left at the critical hour to pass astern of his enemy, with no interference from our battle fleet, he was not yet clear of our flotillas, and it was still not too late for Admiral Jellicoe to stop him. But the good fortune which the Germans had earned by their bold movement stood by them. As they were steering, and as our flotillas were disposed they should have run right into the western group. But it so happened that the southerly course which the group was steering had been interrupted. Overs from the fight with the 4th Flotilla had been falling among them, particularly on the 13th Flotilla, which was the westernmost.[1] In the bewilderment of searchlights, gun-flashes and explosions Captain Farie, who was leading it in the *Champion*, believed that he himself was being fired on, and judging that our own people were between him and the enemy, he considered it was impossible to deliver an attack. He therefore swerved away to the eastward. As, however, he made the turn without signal, only the two destroyers immediately astern followed him, and as he led them away to the eastward he forced the Harwich destroyers, which were next, as well as the 12th Flotilla, which was beyond them also, to turn away to port in order to clear. The effect was to open a road for the Germans to pass, and nothing was seen of them except two cruisers, now known to have been the *Frankfurt* and *Pillau*, all that remained of the leading scouting group. These two came upon the *Menace* and *Nonsuch*, the rear boats of the 12th Flotilla as it swung to the south-eastwards, and attacked them very close. So near a thing was it that the *Menace* barely avoided being rammed, while the *Nonsuch*, after an attempt to attack, only escaped by making off to the eastward at full speed, and was never able to rejoin her flotilla.

Thus the eastern group was broken up without having found opportunity to attack. The 12th Flotilla was forced right round to the north-east by the *Champion's* movement, and it was not till 12.20 that it was able to turn south again. The bulk of the *Champion's* flotilla, being unable to find her, had come up astern of Commander M. L. Goldsmith, who

[1] See Diagram 45 (C).

was leading the Harwich divisions in the *Lydiard*. The *Unity* had also found him, so that he now had a force of twelve destroyers and was leading them south-west at high speed, hoping to get on the far side of the enemy's battle fleet.[1] Though he did not know so many boats were following his lead, he was thus in a position to deal a serious blow, for he was actually steering to pass close ahead of the German van. After forcing their way past the last of the 4th Flotilla at midnight they had resumed the fixed course for home, so that they were steering nearly at right angles to the course of Commander Goldsmith's flotilla as it ran south-west. But, as luck would have it, by 12.25 he had passed across their course without seeing them. But so near a thing was it that the last four boats of the 13th Flotilla, as they followed him, had sight of them. The first two had passed, and were too late to attack, but the last two were right in the enemy's path. The *Petard* (Lieutenant-Commander Thomson), which was the rear boat but one, as she came on was suddenly aware of a dark mass six hundred yards away bearing close down upon her. That it was a German battleship was quickly clear, and the *Petard* was in admirable position for attack, but again the enemy's luck stood by them. Of all our destroyers the *Petard* was the only one that had fired all her torpedoes, and impotent for mischief she turned away to port, but only just in time to clear the enemy's stem. Then a blaze of searchlights revealed four battleships in line ahead—the same that had been attacked by the *Ardent*, which had just gone down a couple of miles to the northward. In a hail of shell from their secondary armament the *Petard* made off out of the beams, and was fortunate enough to get away with little injury, but not before she had seen the leading enemy ship crash into the *Turbulent*, the last boat in the line, and sink her with all hands. So for the night the flotilla attacks ended and the impossible had happened. In spite of the massed flotilla rear guard Admiral Scheer had succeeded in passing across his adversary's wake during the hours of darkness, and without injury to a single capital ship.[2]

As a strategical expedient for barring the passage of a battle fleet the flotillas had failed. With all conditions of light and weather as favourable as could be expected, they had been simply overpowered by the enemy's searchlights, star-shells and secondary armament. The spirit of attack had

[1] *Lydiard, Liberty, Landrail, Laurel* of the 9th Flotilla; *Morris, Termagant* and *Turbulent* of the 10th, *Unity* of the 4th, and *Nerissa, Nicator, Narborough, Pelican,* and *Petard* of the 13th.

[2] See Diagram 45 (D, E and F).

not been wanting, though some have thought that the organisation did not lend itself well to individual enterprise. Possibly with an organisation in smaller units they might have done more, but, on the other hand, the risk of mutual interference and the fear of mistaking friend for foe would have been greater. All we know is that the German organisation for repelling destroyer attack proved unexpectedly effective. During the various night attacks four of our destroyers were sunk and three disabled, and all they could justly claim to have sunk were two light cruisers. The enemy's battle fleet was intact.

The German destroyers, too, failed to realise expectations; for in spite of Admiral Scheer's special dispositions and his direct order to his flotillas to make night attacks,[1] not one was delivered. "It is remarkable," says Commander von Hase, "and much to be regretted, that throughout the whole night our destroyers searching for the English Grand Fleet failed to find them, although they knew exactly where they were last seen."[2]

The orders to the German destroyer flotillas for the night did not disclose the skill that is expected from a highly trained naval staff. Thus, the 2nd Flotilla, consisting of the fastest and most powerful boats, and, moreover, still having a full complement of torpedoes, was detailed for the area where it was least likely to have any chance of action. This flotilla returned via the Skagerrak, and reached Kiel the next day practically undamaged. The slowest boats, some with only one torpedo each, were detailed for the two most promising areas. Errors in reckoning and in signalling also contributed to the failure of the enemy to demonstrate his claimed superiority in night fighting.

[1] Scheer, *High Seas Fleet*, p. 159.
[2] Hase, *Kiel and Jutland*, p. 219.

CHAPTER XXI

JUTLAND—THE LAST PHASE

The First of June

High up in the North Sea summer nights are short. In little more than an hour after the midnight firing had died away dawn would begin to lift the veil which still denied to Admiral Jellicoe certainty that his judgment was correct. In an hour or so all eyes would be straining into the great horizon to know if there was to be another first of June—to take perhaps an even greater place in naval history than that which had immortalised the name of Howe. With no less intense expectation he and his captains had watched the coming of the morning sixscore years before. The grounds for confidence were as firm for the one Admiral as for the other. As Lord Howe made sure he had the enemy fairly to leeward, so Admiral Jellicoe had little doubt he was in a position between them and their bases and was equally in a position to force an action. It was to the northward that he expected them to reappear. With leaden feet the minutes went by as all watched for what the dawn would bring. Few doubted it would be what they desired and none what the result would be.

If there was any misgiving it was mistrust of the weather. As the night advanced the mists, which had cleared a little, began to thicken again, and a wind was getting up that promised anything but a fine summer day. Scattered over a wide battlefield injured ships were beginning to struggle with a rising sea. The *Sparrowhawk*, with her stern cut off, was still afloat, and so was the *Tipperary*, though she was sinking fast. The *Porpoise* and *Spitfire* could still steam, but the *Ardent* and *Fortune* were gone, while all the flotillas that had hitherto attacked were more or less dispersed, and most of them had fired all their torpedoes. Away to the northward, too, Admiral Hipper's shattered flagship, the *Lützow*, in hopeless plight, was being abandoned. So also were the light cruisers *Elbing* and *Rostock*, which had met their fate in the night action.

The only flotilla that could still bar the way to the German fleet was the 12th. The movements of the *Champion*, as we have seen, had forced it away to the eastward and northward, until it was nearly thirty miles to the north-north-eastward of the battle fleet. Thus it was that as it came south the German fleet had to pass across its course. Captain Stirling was leading the first half in the *Faulknor*, with the 1st Division (*Obedient*, *Mindful*, *Marvel* and *Onslaught*) on his starboard quarter and the 2nd Division (*Maenad*, *Narwhal*, *Nessus* and *Noble*) similarly disposed to port. Astern was Commander Sulivan, in the flotilla leader *Marksman*, with the second half (*Opal*, *Menace*, *Munster* and *Mary Rose*). Captain Stirling thus had at his disposal, besides the two flotilla leaders, twelve powerful 34-knot destroyers of the most recent type, each with four torpedo tubes.[1] To the eastward of him again was Captain Farie in the *Champion*, with the two destroyers *Obdurate* and *Moresby*, that had been able to follow his lead, so that both he and the 12th Flotilla were converging on the enemy's course.[2]

At 1.45, just as the first streaks of dawn were waking the black horizon, Captain Stirling could make out a line of large ships on his starboard bow, on a south-easterly course. It was still too dark and misty to tell what they were, but as he closed he recognised them as German battleships. Certain now they were not a squadron of our own fleet, he turned to a similar course and ordered Commander G. W. McO. Campbell in the *Obedient* to attack with the 1st Division. Then, increasing to 25 knots himself, he signalled to the Commander-in-Chief that enemy battleships were in sight, with what result will be seen later. But Commander Campbell was scarcely well on his way with the *Marvel* and *Onslaught* when he had to report that the enemy were no longer visible. They had, in fact, turned away six points or more together to avoid the attack. Captain Stirling now ordered the 1st Division to take station astern of him, and being sure the enemy would quickly resume their course, proceeded south-east at full speed to get into position to attack from ahead. Ten minutes later (2.6) judging himself to be far enough advanced, he led round sixteen points to starboard to deliver his attack. Almost immediately the enemy reappeared on his port bow, and so far as could be seen were made out to be five or six battleships with " Kaisers "

[1] Of the other four destroyers the *Nonsuch* had lost touch (see *ante*, p. 404). The *Mischief* had been detailed on leaving harbour to join the armoured cruisers destroyer screen and was still with them. The remaining two, *Napier* and *Mameluke*, were refitting.

[2] See Diagram 45 (G and H).

leading and old ships in the rear. The conditions were almost perfect for attack. The position of the leading destroyer was excellent. It was already too light for the searchlights of the ships to be of much use, and there was mist enough to make the darting destroyers a very difficult target. In high expectation the *Faulknor* led off with two torpedoes, one at the second in the line and one at the third. The *Obedient* followed with two torpedoes, and then the *Marvel* and *Onslaught* with four each. The *Mindful*, being unable to make the speed, owing to boiler defects, had steered straight for the enemy before the turn, but being masked by the other destroyers as they passed was unable to get in a shot. Gallant as was her attempt she was thus denied a part in this memorable attack. It had been carried through to the end in the most brilliant manner in the face of a heavy and well-controlled fire. This came not only from the battleships, but also from three cruisers in rear of them which, after starting to chase the *Faulknor*, turned back to meet the destroyers. So hot and accurate indeed was their greeting that the result of the attack could not be seen. All they knew was that in the middle of the enemy's line there had been a terrific explosion and one battleship had entirely disappeared (2.10). On our own side all got away by using a smoke screen with little or no damage, except the *Onslaught*, the last in the line. She was hit on the bridge as she turned away after her last shot, and her captain, Lieutenant-Commander A. G. Onslow, together with his first lieutenant, was killed.

The ship that had gone was the *Pommern*, and no trace of her or her unhappy crew was ever seen again. With her were lost 844 officers and men. What part of the fleet the flotilla had struck was difficult to tell, since the squadron attacked seemed to contain both Dreadnoughts and pre-Dreadnoughts. But there is no doubt that it was the rear of the battle fleet. The battle cruisers were astern and the bulk of the Dreadnoughts had already passed ahead of our flotilla. But owing to the previous efforts of our destroyers the German dispositions for the night had been thrown into some disorder. As attack followed attack, ships had been constantly forced to haul out of the line and circle till they could find a place in which to re-enter it, and thus stations had been lost and even squadrons intermingled.[1] The High

[1] Hase, *Kiel and Jutland*, p. 220. "We had frequently to stop because the whole line ahead of us was thrown into disorder by the numerous destroyer attacks. . . . Ships were frequently hauling out of the line and steering a circular course, and had to take station again wherever they could. In this way the *Nassau*, originally second ship in the line, gradually fell into the last place and became our next ahead."

Seas Fleet was thus in a worse condition than ever for the fully expected renewal of the battle. The Horn Reefs light-vessel was still some thirty miles ahead, daylight was making fast, and anxious eyes, aching for want of sleep, scanned the brightening horizon for what still lay between them and safety. Yet, precious as was every mile gained, they could not hold their course, and under Captain Stirling's fierce attack they were forced once more to turn away.

Though the movement lost them ground, it saved them from the rest of the flotilla. Commander Champion in the *Maenad* had led the 2nd Division (*Narwhal, Nessus, Noble*) round after the 1st, but, believing that Captain Stirling's intention was to close the enemy and attack to starboard, he had trained his tubes in that direction, and was not ready. However, not to be denied, he held on until he was able to fire one tube on the port side. Then, swinging both tubes to starboard, he turned back alone and closed to within 5,000 yards. The position was, of course, unfavourable, and in spite of the bold manner in which he pushed home his attack no ship was sunk, though at the time it appeared to the captain of the *Maenad* that a torpedo hit the fourth ship in the line, causing a terrific explosion. The *Narwhal*, his next astern, had also got in two shots from the port side with no better effect, but the rest of the division could not attack at all. As for the 3rd Division it had no better luck, being apparently headed off by the enemy's cruisers. Its leader the *Marksman* had disappeared, and the *Opal*, as soon as they were clear, led them round to the southward after the battle fleet with the rest of the *Maenad's* division following their lead.

Meanwhile, the *Champion*, with her two destroyers, *Obdurate* and *Moresby*, which were still with her, had heard the firing as she came down from the northward, and at 2.15 turned to the westward towards it. The movement brought her in touch with the missing *Marksman*, who followed her lead, and Captain Farie then led round to the southward (2.25). As he did so, ships were clearly seen to the southward, and the *Marksman* asked the *Champion* what they were. Her reply was: "Germans, I think," and for a while she held on towards them, but at 2.34 for some reason she started to make another cast to the eastward. Unhappily the turn was made a moment too soon, for by this time the Germans had resumed their course, and as the *Moresby*, the rearmost of the division, was following round, she had a glimpse through the mist of four pre-Dreadnoughts 4,000 yards to the westward, steering at full speed south-eastwards. "I considered action imperative," wrote her captain,

Lieutenant-Commander Alison, "hoisted 'Compass west,' hauled out to port and fired a high-speed torpedo." He had only one tube available, but an underwater concussion shook the destroyer as she sped away to rejoin her division. Sure enough a hit had been made, but not on the battleships. It was an attendant destroyer, *V 4*, that the torpedo found and sank, and the two forlorn rear squadrons of the enemy passed on unscathed after the Dreadnoughts with no unit of the Grand Fleet left between them and home.

The *Moresby's* spirited effort was the last stroke of the long-drawn battle. But Admiral Jellicoe had not yet given up hope of being able to deliver the blow which he had been prevented from striking when he first deployed. Unfortunately the wireless signal which Captain Stirling had sent at 1.52, immediately before his attack, never got through. Twenty minutes later, when the enemy had turned away for the second time, Captain Stirling sent another saying, "Enemy steering south-south-west," a course which was approximately direct for the *Iron Duke*. Both signals were repeated, but neither reached the flagship. Since 11.30 Admiral Jellicoe had had no information either from his cruisers or from Whitehall as to where the enemy was. Up to that time all the information showed that Admiral Scheer was well to the northward of him and steering south. If so, either he or Admiral Beatty ought soon to have sight of the enemy in the brightening dawn. But all was uncertain. By two o'clock Admiral Jellicoe had decided that if nothing was seen in another half-hour, by which time it would be full daylight, his best chance of regaining contact with the enemy was to hark back, and accordingly at 2.15 he made the general signal that at 2.30 the battle fleet would turn north and form single line ahead in the "5th Organisation."[1] Admiral Beatty, on the other hand, believed the enemy to be to the westward of him, and he regarded it as his function "to ensure that the enemy fleet did not regain its base by passing round the southern flank of our forces." "My intention," he wrote on June 12, "was to ask permission to sweep S.W. at daylight, but on receiving a signal that the Commander-in-Chief was turning to the north and ordering me to conform and close, I proceeded accordingly."[2]

At this time the German fleet was actually about thirty miles north-eastward of the *Iron Duke*, and only about an hour's steaming from Horn Reefs. Admiral Burney's division,

[1] That is, the 2nd Battle Squadron leading, followed by the 4th, with the 1st Battle Squadron astern. The 5th Battle Squadron on rejoining took station ahead.

[2] *Jutland Despatches*, p. 139.

which had fallen fully twelve miles astern of station, was little more than fifteen miles from the van of the enemy, but the bulkheads of the *Marlborough* were now showing signs of giving way, and Admiral Burney informed the Commander-in-Chief she could not be trusted to steam more than twelve knots. Now for the first time he heard that the *Marlborough's* division was dropping astern, and as day broke Admiral Gaunt, in the *Colossus*, leading the remainder of the 1st Battle Squadron, reported that Admiral Burney was not in touch, and the Commander-in-Chief found himself bereft of a whole division of battleships. The *Marlborough* had fallen out of the line, but fortunately the first flush of the dawn revealed the light cruiser *Fearless*, which had been unable to keep up with the 1st Flotilla, following the division. Signalling her to close (2.21), Admiral Burney was therefore able to shift his flag to the *Revenge*. Then, by direction of the Commander-in-Chief, he sent the *Fearless* back to escort the *Marlborough* into port, and with the *Hercules* and *Agincourt* held on to meet the fleet as it came north, and resume his station. The course the Commander-in-Chief was steering was not the course for Horn Reefs, yet we know it had been his fixed intention when he decided to proceed south through the night to close the Horn Reefs at dawn if nothing at that time had been seen of the enemy, and by stationing his flotillas five miles astern he had hoped it would not be difficult to gain early touch with some of them at daylight. But Admiral Scheer's bold push through them had upset all his plans. In the series of desperate conflicts that had taken place the destroyers were scattered far and wide, and to take the fleet right into the enemy's waters without cruiser and destroyer cover was contrary to all principle. The best he could do was to steer north till he could get his light forces about him. Even to proceed in single line without them was to run no small risk, but he was still in hopes he was between the enemy and their base. At any moment they might appear, and as the morning was very misty, with a visibility of only three or four miles, he must be ready for them on the instant. "Accordingly," he says, "I deemed it advisable to disregard the danger from submarines due to a long line of ships, and to form line of battle at once in case of meeting the enemy battle fleet before I had been able to get in touch with my cruisers and destroyers."[1]

So at 2.39 the *King George V* led round to starboard and, with the fleet in order of battle, less Admiral Burney's three ships, which were still out of sight on his starboard beam, and

[1] *Jutland Despatches*, p. 26.

with Admiral Evan-Thomas two miles ahead, the Commander-in-Chief proceeded northwards in search of his cruisers and flotillas, but without finding any trace of them. Nor was there any indication of the approach of Commodore Tyrwhitt with the Harwich Force to fill their place. He was still being held at his moorings, for, at the Admiralty, the intelligence they had was not considered full or clear enough to make certain that the whole of the High Seas Fleet was with Admiral Scheer. If part of it had been kept back there was thought to be still a possibility of a raid in the southern area. Whether or not their hesitation has to be set down as an excess of caution, matters little. For had Commodore Tyrwhitt been permitted to proceed at 5.0 p.m. the previous day, when the signal, "Fleet action imminent" was received, he could not have been in touch with the Grand Fleet till 4.0 a.m. without exhausting the destroyers' fuel, and then, as will be seen, it would have been too late for his arrival to affect the situation.

For about half an hour Admiral Jellicoe held on and no signal reached him to throw light on the movements of the enemy's battle fleet.[1] The prospect of coming upon it in the mists that shrouded the horizon was growing more and more remote as the eager minutes passed, but hope was still keen for a sight of ships that had been maimed. About 3.0 an important signal from the Admiralty reached him, telling him that enemy submarines were coming out from German ports, and that a damaged German ship, the *Lützow*, was at midnight in Lat. 56.26 N., Long. 5.41 E., steaming south at seven knots.[2] He shortly after signalled to Admiral Jerram, who was leading the fleet, to look out for a damaged battle cruiser ahead, when suddenly hope grew hot. Firing, which rapidly increased in intensity, was heard to the west-south-west. It might well mean that the battle cruisers had fallen in with the enemy, and he acted immediately. At 3.42 the fleet was turned sharply towards the sound of the guns, and he himself resumed "Guide of Fleet" in readiness to deal promptly with anything that might suddenly loom up out of the haze. But he was doomed to disappointment. It was but the *Indomitable* and some of the 3rd Light Cruiser Squadron driving off an airship which was observing the movements of Admiral Beatty's force, and in ten minutes the Commander-

[1] See Diagram 46.

[2] This message was timed 1.48, and received on board the *Iron Duke* at 2.40. It was received by the *Lion* through the *New Zealand* at 4.10, and from the Commander-in-Chief direct at 3.40.

in-Chief turned north again in line ahead and Admiral Jerram resumed the duty of "Guide."

There was now less hope than ever of bringing the enemy to action unless he could gather his destroyers, and he was still bent on finding them. By this time he knew there was no hope of the Harwich Force arriving in time to be of any use. Shortly after 3.0, when all fear of a raid on the southern area had passed away, the Admiralty had at last ordered Commodore Tyrwhitt to sea, and at 3.20 they sent a signal to the Commander-in-Chief to say that five light cruisers and thirteen destroyers had been ordered from Harwich to a rendezvous close to where he then was (Lat. 55.30 N., Long. 5.0 E.), to join him and replace vessels requiring fuel. But Commodore Tyrwhitt did better. By 3.50 he had slipped and was away with five light cruisers, two flotilla leaders and sixteen destroyers. This splendid force could now have no effect, not even had it arrived an hour before it actually started, and Admiral Jellicoe's only hope was quickly to find his own flotillas. So he held on to the northward, and as he did so an airship appeared. For three minutes it was engaged by the whole battle fleet, but it quickly disappeared.

It was now fairly clear that the enemy must know his position, but he was entirely ignorant of theirs, and was continuing northward to find his flotillas, of which he was still without news. Captain Stirling, it is true, with some of the 12th Flotilla had just got touch with Admiral Burney's division, and was able to report his successful action with the German battleships, far to the north on a south-east course. Of this the Commander-in-Chief was still unaware when, about 4.15, he read a startling message from the Admiralty. It was to say that at 2.30 the German main fleet was in a position only sixteen miles from Horn Reefs light-vessel, steering south-east by south at 16 knots.[1] For Admiral Jellicoe, therefore, there could be no illusions, but Admiral Beatty, who possibly may not yet have received the Admiralty message, still clung to his own appreciation. Convinced apparently that the northerly search must be wrong, at 4.4 he sent a message to the Commander-in-Chief pointing out that the enemy when last seen was to the westward, proceeding slowly S.W., and begged to be allowed to

[1] Received in the *Iron Duke* at 3.55 a.m. The time of origin of this message was 3.29 and the position given Lat. 55.33 N., Long. 6.50 E. Between 11.15 p.m. May 31 and 1.25 a.m. June 1 seven German signals had been deciphered in the Admiralty but were not passed on to Admiral Jellicoe. Each of these messages conveyed the information that the High Seas Fleet was proceeding home via the Horn Reefs Passage. See Appendix J.

sweep in that direction to locate them.[1] With the better information at his disposal the Commander-in-Chief could not agree to the proposal, and Admiral Beatty had to content himself with spreading his light cruisers well to the westward and ordering them to be careful to keep visual touch with him by linking ships. Then, a little later, refusing to admit that the enemy had slipped through our fingers, he made a signal to enhearten his men. " Damage yesterday," it ran, " was heavy on both sides. We hope to-day to cut off and annihilate the whole German fleet. Every man must do his utmost."

The Commander-in-Chief had no such hope. He saw too plainly the bitter truth that there was now no possibility of recovering the lost chance of the vital hour when he had first caught his skilful adversary unawares, and the latter, aided by misty conditions, had effected his escape. Admiral Jellicoe was already breaking up his line of battle, and by 4.30 the divisions of the fleet were turning into cruising order. It had scarcely settled down again on its northerly course when Admiral Beatty, who was just coming into sight of the port division, received from the *Iron Duke* the signal " Enemy fleet has returned to harbour."

Admiral Jellicoe was right. At 3.30 the High Seas Fleet had reached Horn Reefs. Since the first glimmer of dawn from every ship anxious eyes had been strained into the veil of mist, expecting every moment to find the Grand Fleet was upon them. The growing light revealed no trace of it. Since Admiral Scheer now knew that five airships which he had asked for were patrolling to seaward to protect him, he says he decided to wait where he was to cover the retreat of the two battle cruisers which had been unable to keep touch.[2] One of them, the *Seydlitz*, was not far away, coming slowly on, and in so precarious a condition from her wounds that no one could tell how much longer she could stand the strain of steaming. The other, Admiral Hipper's flagship, the *Lützow*, about which the Commander-in-Chief was specially concerned, was in a far worse case. When the Admiralty informed Admiral Jellicoe of her position she was nearly a hundred miles W.N.W. of Horn Reefs, and so heavily down by the bows that she could scarcely make any headway. The end indeed was very near. Deeper and deeper sank her bows till

[1] The Admiralty message was passed to the *Lion* by the *New Zealand* at 3.54. The time of origin of Admiral Beatty's request to the Commander-in-Chief is given as 3.50, the time of despatch being 4.4.

[2] Scheer, *High Seas Fleet*, pp. 163–4. In the report of the airship *L 11* she states that she was one of five airships which had gone up about midnight " to cover the flank of the High Seas Forces."

her propellers were out of water, and about 1.45 it was decided to abandon her. Four destroyers that were accompanying her took off the survivors of her crew, and then one of them sank her with a torpedo.

It was not till 3.30 that news of her fate reached Admiral Scheer, and then, he says, " I had no difficulty in drawing my own conclusions. As the enemy did not come down from the north, even with light forces, it was evident he was retiring." [1] This statement can only be accepted as a pardonable gloss on the truth to soften for the public benefit the undesirable admission that he withdrew the fleet in the face of the enemy. What actually happened he tells elsewhere with sufficient candour. At 2.0 the most northerly of the airship patrol reported that she had sighted a flotilla of enemy destroyers and half a dozen submarines fifty miles west of Bovbjerg, which is sixty miles north of Horn Reefs. They fired on her and she replied with bombs, but as our nearest destroyer was thirty miles to the southward it would look as though she had attacked the German flotilla which our destroyers had forced to make for their base by way of the Skagerrak. So thick was the low-lying mist over the sea that the mistake was pardonable, but she soon made another. Carrying on her reconnaissance to the northward as high as the Skagerrak she reported having sighted in the Jammersbucht a group of twelve large battleships and numerous cruisers proceeding south at high speed, but heavy cloud prevented her keeping touch with them.[2] Possibly this phantom fleet was a convoy: it was certainly no part of the British forces, but the news went forward and must have reached Admiral Scheer soon after he stopped off the Horn Reefs. About the same time he received more accurate information from another airship, *L 11*. At 3.0 she had seen clouds of smoke about half-way between Horn Reefs and Terschelling, and ten minutes later she reported what in the mist she took to be twelve large warships with numerous light craft steering N.N.E. at full speed, but as they fired on her she was forced to make away to the eastward. This was the battle cruiser fleet making to close the Commander-in-Chief,[3] but on receiving the report Admiral Scheer seems to have drawn an entirely wrong inference. He concluded that what the *L 11* had seen could only be a new force " which had just come up from the channel on

[1] Scheer, *High Seas Fleet*, p. 164.

[2] The Jammersbucht is a bay on the north-west coast of Denmark.

[3] Admiral Beatty was actually steering N.N.E. at this time. *L 11* reports fire was opened on her at 3.15, which accords with the reports of our battle cruisers.

hearing news of the battle to try to join up with the Grand Fleet and advance against us." In view of the fact that *L 24* had reported twelve large battleships as far north as the Jammersbucht, the appreciation was natural, but seeing that the northern force was said to be coming south at high speed, the advance of a new force from the southward is not to be reconciled with his alleged theory that his adversary was retiring. The action he took alone contradicts his assertion. While lying off Horn Reefs he seems to have called for the state of his ships. "The reports," he says, "received from the battle cruisers showed that the 1st Scouting Group could no longer fight a serious action. The ships in the van of the 3rd Squadron (i.e., the "König" class Dreadnoughts) must also have lost in fighting value. Of the fast light cruisers only the *Frankfurt*, *Pillau* and *Regensburg* were at my disposal. Owing to the bad visibility, further scouting by airships could not be counted on. It was, therefore, impossible to try to force a regular action on the enemy reported south. The consequences of such an encounter would have been a matter of chance. I therefore abandoned any further operations and gave the order to return to base." [1]

This can be taken as a reasonably frank statement of his reasons for leaving the field to the enemy, but further detail is available. At 3.24—that is, within a few minutes of receiving from *L 11* the report of the enemy to the south—he ordered his remaining battle cruisers to go in. A quarter of an hour later *L 11*, circling to the eastwards, reported "six large battleships with lighter forces on a northerly course." This was the rear of our battle fleet, and immediately after sighting them the airship saw them make the westward turn by divisions toward the sound of Admiral Beatty's guns that were still firing on her. It was at some little time before this report reached Admiral Scheer that he ordered the fleet to re-form preparatory to going in.[2] While the order was being executed *L 11* was keeping touch with the last seen squadron as being nearer to the High Seas Fleet than the first one, but she soon saw another nearer still. It was Admiral Burney's division making to the westward in conformity with the Commander-in-Chief's movement. The *Faulknor* was just joining it with the *Obedient* and *Marvel*, and the airship reported three battle cruisers and four smaller craft bearing N.E. between her and the German fleet. This was at 3.50,

[1] *Jutland Despatches*, p. 598.

[2] At 3.38 he made the signal for the fleet to re-form, 2nd Scouting Group astern; 4th Scouting Group ahead; destroyers to distribute for submarine screen; 2nd Battle Squadron to lead in. The airship signal was timed 3.40.

and at 3.54 Admiral Scheer made the general signal "Course S.E. Proceed into harbour eastward of Amrum bank."

Owing to the impossibility of knowing to a minute or two when the airship reports reached Admiral Scheer, we cannot follow with absolute certainty their relation to his final movements. But the general inference from the admitted facts is clear enough. Admiral Scheer on reaching Horn Reefs had decided that his fleet had suffered too severely in the previous day's fighting to be fit for a general action. Either when he decided to withdraw or just afterwards he must have known that at least three strong groups of British ships were near by to the westward and moving in a manner which could only suggest they were concentrating with a view, as he said, "of advancing upon him." There was no indication whatever that they were retiring, and his own position was impossible. He had no light cruisers with which to form a screen; in the mists that shrouded the sea he could not trust the airships, and he was consequently liable to be suddenly surprised by a greatly superior force. In such circumstances he could not afford to risk being brought to action, and the only safe course was to remove his fleet from the board. This he decided to do, taking his sheaves with him; they were enough for honour; and who shall blame his judgment, though it involved declining an action with a fleet obviously bent on fighting and leaving an undefeated enemy in possession of the field? That after being surprised by the concentrated Grand Fleet he had so cleverly drawn his head out of the noose, and with so much success to his credit, was enough to enrol his name high upon the list of fleet leaders.

But bold and skilful as he had been, he was still far from safe. Directly ahead of him as he made for the security of the Amrum channel were our three submarines, and beyond them the new minefield which had been laid an hour or two earlier by Commander Curtis in the *Abdiel*. The submarines *E 55*, *E 26* and *D 1* had just taken up the stations assigned to them under the plan of May 28, which had been cancelled when the sortie of the Germans rendered it unnecessary. Their position was equally good for the present situation. But unfortunately their instructions under the cancelled plan were to lie on the bottom till June 2. With these orders they had put to sea from Harwich on May 30, unaware of the sudden change in the situation. For all they knew their old orders stood, and the consequence was that they lay quietly on the bottom while the retiring German fleet passed over them, all unconscious of the peril they had so strangely escaped. Still they were not out of the wood. Between them and safety they had yet to pass the *Abdiel's* minefields, and to pass them without disaster could only be a miracle, seeing with what precision and ingenuity the new field had been laid. From a position fifteen miles S.W. of the Vyl lightship Commander Curtis had run a line of forty mines spaced at ten to the mile zigzagging on a mean course S. 9 E. Then turning S.34 W., he ran out another forty in the same way. By 2.4 the thing was done and he was speeding away north at thirty knots. So far as he could tell he had not been observed. True the lights of three fishing vessels had been seen, but it was so dark, with drizzling rain, and an overcast sky, that he felt sure they had not seen his ship and still less what she was doing. Besides this field there was the one he had also laid on May 4, or so much of it as had not been swept up in the interval, and between the two the fairway was only about ten miles wide.

Though there was no reason to believe that Admiral Scheer had any definite knowledge of the trap that had been laid for him he was naturally taking ordinary precautions. The 4th Scouting Group was disposed ahead, while all the destroyers present formed an anti-submarine screen. Care alone would scarcely have saved him from severe loss, but the good fortune which his bold push had earned him was not yet exhausted. As Admiral Scheer came down from the north-westward he passed between the lightship and the new minefield. But not unscathed. At 5.20 there was a loud explosion in the van of the 1st Battle Squadron and the *Ostfriesland* was seen to be in trouble. She had in fact fouled one of the mines which the *Abdiel* had laid on May 4, but the cause at first was not clear. No minefield was known to exist in the vicinity. An impression that it was a more dreaded form of underwater attack seems to have spread through the fleet and upset its equilibrium. " Several submarine attacks on our main fleet as it returned," says Admiral Scheer, " failed entirely," but we know that these attacks were but the outcome of overwrought imagination. As the explosion died away he signalled " Keep on," and in spite of the damage she had received the *Ostfriesland* was able to obey the order. No other casualty is recorded, though our submarines report having heard up to 5.30 eleven explosions of varying intensity. There is no reason, however, for believing they were caused by mines. The explanation is probably due to an alarm not far removed from panic which the mishap to the *Ostfriesland* appears to have spread through the overwrought fleet. Amongst the survivors from some of our lost ships, who had been rescued by German destroyers the previous afternoon, was an officer who reports that the ship in which he was a prisoner of war began firing wildly at phantom submarines, and we know that the *Stettin* about this time signalled that she was being fired on by one of her own battle squadrons. By 6.30, however, the whole of the surviving German capital ships were well out of reach, except possibly the *König*, which had taken in so much water that she had to wait three hours for the tide off Amrum bank before she could pass the channel, and the *Seydlitz*, which was approaching it in a precarious condition.[1]

During all this time Admiral Jellicoe was scouring the seas off Horn Reefs in search of crippled enemy ships making for the base. It was now his only hope, but some hope there was, since he knew the *Lützow* at least had been left far behind. At 4.30, as we have seen, he had formed cruising order for the double purpose of reducing risk from submarine attack and of searching on a wider front. The evolution was not yet complete when Captain Scott, of the *Dublin*, who had lost company with Commodore Goodenough's squadron during the night and was then steering north, reported an enemy cruiser in sight with two destroyers. The position she gave was about fifteen miles to the eastward of the *Iron Duke*, but it was only approximate, for her navigator had been killed and her charts damaged, and she must have been much nearer than she knew to Horn Reefs. For what she saw admits of only one explanation. Shortly after news reached the German fleet that the *Lützow* had been sunk and that the four attendant destroyers were coming on crowded with her crew, a signal was received to say that one of them had had her engines disabled and was in tow. Commodore Heinrich, second leader of flotillas, immediately turned back in the *Regensburg* to their assistance, " regardless," as Admiral Scheer says, " as to whether he might meet with superior English forces," a comment which scarcely harmonised with his expressed conviction that his adversary had retired. The destroyers, moreover, reported that they had twice encountered enemy cruisers and destroyers, but that on each occasion they attacked and successfully made their way into the Bight. It was in the second encounter the injured destroyer *G 40* is said to have been disabled, and it must have been the *Champion* and the destroyers that were with her that did the mischief. At 3.30, with the *Obdurate*, *Moresby*, *Marksman*, and *Maenad* she was heading

[1] Thirty-six hours later the *Seydlitz* crawled into the Jade and beached herself at the entrance.

N.N.W. when she caught sight of four enemy destroyers on the opposite course and engaged them. They certainly did not attack, but, hurrying on, were quickly lost in the haze, and the *Champion* held on her course. When the *Dublin* caught her glimpse of the *Regensburg* she had already joined the crowded destroyers and was steaming fast to the southward, but by this time the mist had grown so thick that, even as Captain Scott was turning to shadow her, she completely disappeared and nothing more was heard of her.

The *Dublin* report did not affect the Commander-in-Chief's movements. He held on north on the look-out for the crippled enemy ships, but Admiral Beatty, who had not parted with his destroyers, had also received her signal, and at 5.15, when he came into visual touch with the *Iron Duke*, he proposed making a sweep southward and eastward in search of the ship the *Dublin* had located, believing it must be the *Lützow*. This he did, turning at 5.43 to the south-east and keeping that course for half an hour, when, having sighted nothing, he altered to south. At 6.3 Admiral Jellicoe made a cast to the south eastward, and shortly afterwards received a message, timed 5.30, from the Admiralty informing him that the *Elbing* was still afloat at 3.47 without her crew in a position which was on his new course. But he sighted nothing.

About 7.0 a.m. Admiral Beatty sent a message to say that if he sighted nothing by 7.30 he proposed making a sweep north-east. The Commander-in-Chief's reply was to inform him of the *Abdiel's* minefield, and then that he would sweep to the northward, while Admiral Beatty was to keep to the eastward of him. Accordingly at 7.16 Admiral Jellicoe turned north, the 5th Battle Squadron, which formed the starboard column of the fleet, being then about thirty miles west-north-west of the Horn Reefs light-vessel. A quarter of an hour later Admiral Beatty swung round to N.N.E. Possibly owing to an error in his reckoning he did not hold this course long enough to carry out the Commander-in-Chief's instructions, but at 8.0 turned up north in the wake of the *Iron Duke*, some thirty miles astern.

Scattered far and wide over the waters which the British fleet was thus quartering were the debris of the action. The battle fleet on its northerly course was soon in the region in which the Germans had stolen away astern. It was the scene of the thickest of the destroyer fighting, and on all sides foul patches of oil, life-buoys and floating bodies, both friend and foe, told how deadly it had been. Further afield damaged ships that had survived were struggling for life in the solitude of the grey shroud that wrapped the rising sea. The *Sparrowhawk*, after the *Contest* had cut off her stern, was able to creep slowly to the westward. In this helpless condition about 3.30 her crew saw a large ship appearing slowly out of the mist, and she was soon made out to be a three-funnelled German cruiser. For ten minutes they watched her waiting in breathless suspense for their end, when as by a miracle she was seen to settle down and disappear.

What they saw was undoubtedly the light cruiser *Elbing*, of the 4th Scouting Group. Admiral Scheer reports that after her collision with the *Posen* she was abandoned and sunk about the time of the *Sparrowhawk's* alarm. The *Rostock*, the other light cruiser which sank during the morning, had been disabled by one of our destroyer's torpedoes in the night action with our 4th Flotilla. Though she was in a sinking condition her captain was still clinging to her, and according to the German Official History it was not till 4.25 that she eventually sank far to the southward of the *Sparrowhawk's* position. The helpless destroyer was now alone again for about an hour, when she saw what appeared to be a submarine. The only remaining gun was manned, but the object proved to be a life-saving raft carrying the survivors of the *Tipperary* which had sunk at about 2.0 a.m. After over an hour's effort they managed to get alongside and she took them off, and scarcely had she done so when she was gladdened by the sight of the *Dublin* and *Marksman* coming up out of the mist. The *Marksman* did all that was possible to take her in tow stern first, but hours of work proved all in vain, and at 8.45 Admiral Burney, with whose division they had come in touch, ordered her to be sunk by gunfire.

One of the other stricken destroyers, the *Acasta*, was still afloat and struggling on with the last of her oil when she was picked up and taken in tow by the *Nonsuch* of the 12th Flotilla.[1] Amidst the wreckage of the *Ardent* the *Marksman* rescued her captain, Lieutenant-Commander Marsden, while the *Obdurate* picked up two of his men, one of whom subsequently succumbed. They had all been five hours in the water. Near by, about 5.0, the *Maenad* saved from a raft ten of the *Fortune's* crew. The *Porpoise*, escorted by the *Garland*, made her way eventually into the Tyne, and so did the *Spitfire*—without assistance.

As for the capital ships, all were in station except the 6th

[1] The *Nonsuch* towed the *Acasta* till the evening of June 1, when a trawler unit and tugs were sent to their assistance. They were brought in to Aberdeen about 9.0 p.m. on the 2nd.

Division and the damaged *Marlborough* and *Warspite*.[1] The former, with the *Fearless* in company, was making her way at moderate speed for the Tyne, steering at first a south-westerly course to clear the intervening minefield laid by the Germans in 1915. Owing to her inability to maintain a sufficient speed there was considerable anxiety that she might fall to the enemy's submarines, and Admiral Jellicoe had called upon Commodore Tyrwhitt to send a division of destroyers to screen her. But the Harwich Force was still far to the southward, and long before touch with the *Marlborough* could be obtained the Germans had located her. About 10.0 she had sight of two enemy submarines, which dived; course was altered away from them, and it was not till three-quarters of an hour later that she was attacked by the *U46*. The torpedo came from astern, passed harmlessly to port, and she went on her way. For three hours longer her peril continued. The Harwich destroyers, which had been told off to her rescue, failed to find her, but by 2.0 p.m. she had sighted Commodore Tyrwhitt. He at once detached another division to escort her; the first one joined shortly afterwards, and she was thus able to proceed with little to fear from further submarine attack, and arrived in the Humber at 8.0 a.m. on June 2.

The *Warspite's* adventures were much the same, but her danger was greater. After reporting her speed reduced to sixteen knots at the opening of the battle fleet action she had been ordered to make her way to Rosyth, and straight in her path was part of the original submarine trap, for in consequence of the battle the "U" boats which had been stationed off our bases had been ordered to stay out another day. Fortunately by dint of strenuous exertions in shoring bulkheads and the like Captain E. M. Phillpotts in the morning had been able to get a speed of nineteen knots, and was zigzagging when at 9.35 two torpedoes (from the *U51*) passed him close on either side, but no submarine could be seen. He, therefore, at some risk increased to twenty-two knots and reported his danger to Rosyth. Escort was at once despatched to meet him, and in a couple of hours two destroyers appeared on the horizon, but at the same time a submarine (*U63*) was sighted very close. Captain Phillpotts put his helm over to ram her at full speed, and only missed by a few yards. The submarine was unable to attack, and by 8.15 p.m. he was safe in Rosyth.

As for the *Warrior*, which had been saved from the immediate fate of the rest of Admiral Arbuthnot's squadron, she had tried with engine rooms flooded to make her way to Cromarty.

[1] The 6th Division re-joined in the evening of June 1.

But her engines would hardly revolve, and having fallen in with the seaplane carrier *Engadine*, Captain V. B. Molteno ordered her to take him in tow. Together for about a hundred miles they struggled on till by 7.0 a.m. it was clear the *Warrior's* bulkheads were giving way, and that she could not float more than a few hours. While, therefore, it was still possible, Captain Molteno ordered her to be abandoned. Very skilfully Lieutenant-Commander C. G. Robinson brought the *Engadine* alongside and took on board the whole of the *Warrior's* company. Then in mid-sea some 160 miles to the eastward of Aberdeen, with the seas washing over her deck, she was left, and nothing more was ever seen of her.[1]

By about 8.50 the danger of the main fleet from attack by the submarines which the Germans were hurrying out had passed. Most of the battle fleet destroyers which were not disabled or obliged to make for port for lack of fuel had rejoined, and the Commander-in-Chief turned S.S.W., while Admiral Beatty kept on to the northward. As the battle fleet worked back more drifting wreckage was encountered, life-buoys of the *Black Prince* and much else the sea had claimed during the night. This course he held for an hour, till the battle cruisers were in touch, and then at 10.0 turned again north by west. In an hour's time he was once more amongst the wreckage which marked the trail on which Admiral Scheer had stolen away. It was now eight hours since the German fleet reached Horn Reefs, and during that time Admiral Jellicoe's ships had been sweeping in an area sixty miles long by fifty broad, which to the south was close up to the minefield danger area and to the east was twenty-five miles from the Horn Reefs light-vessel. In all that time, with the exception of the momentary glimpse of the *Regensburg*, no sign of the High Seas Fleet had been seen nor had any crippled ship been encountered. Admiral Jellicoe now therefore made up his mind that further search was useless, and at 10.44 he so informed the Admiralty. "The Harwich Force," he signalled, "not required except for destroyers to screen *Marlborough*. Am ascertaining no disabled ships are left and am returning to base. Whole area swept for disabled enemy cruisers without result." That was the end, and just after 11.0 he turned N.W. direct for Scapa, while Admiral Beatty, still apparently unwilling to admit the disheartening truth, diverged N.N.E.

[1] The *Engadine* with the survivors from the *Warrior* arrived at Rosyth at 1.35 a.m. on June 2.

APPENDIX A

DISTRIBUTION OF THE SHIPS OF THE GRAND FLEET BEFORE SAILING ON TUESDAY, MAY 30, 1916, WITH THE NAMES OF FLAG AND COMMANDING OFFICERS

The sea-going ships of the Grand Fleet were distributed between the three northern bases as follows:—

AT SCAPA FLOW

Iron Duke, Captain F. C. Dreyer, C.B. (Fleet Flagship). Flying the flag of Admiral Sir John R. Jellicoe, G.C.B., K.C.V.O., Commander-in-Chief; Vice-Admiral Sir Charles E. Madden, K.C.B., C.V.O., Chief-of-Staff.

Attached ships:
- Destroyer: *Oak*, Lieut.-Comm. D. Faviell, M.V.O.
- Flotilla Leader: *Abdiel*,[1] Commander B. Curtis.
- Light Cruiser: *Active*, Captain P. Withers.
- Seaplane Carrier: *Campania*,[2] Captain O. Schwann.
- Kite Balloon Ship: *Menelaus*,[3] Commander C. W. N. McCulloch.

First Battle Squadron

Marlborough, Captain G. P. Ross. Flying the flag of Vice-Admiral Sir Cecil Burney, K.C.B., K.C.M.G., Second-in-Command of the Grand Fleet; Captain E. P. F. G. Grant, Chief-of-Staff.
Revenge, Captain E. B. Kiddle.
Hercules, Captain L. Clinton-Baker.
Agincourt, Captain H. M. Doughty.
Colossus, Captain A. D. P. R. Pound. Flying the flag of Rear-Admiral E. F. A. Gaunt, C.M.G.
Collingwood, Captain J. C. Ley.
Neptune, Captain V. H. G. Bernard.
St. Vincent, Captain W. W. Fisher, M.V.O.
Royal Sovereign,[3] Captain A. T. Hunt, C.S.I.
Light Cruiser: *Bellona*, Captain A. B. S. Dutton.

---

[1] Fitted as a minelayer.
[2] Left Scapa at 11.45 a.m.; ordered back 4.37 a.m., May 31. See Note A, p. 326a.
[3] Remained in harbour.

FOURTH BATTLE SQUADRON

Benbow, Captain H. W. Parker. Flying the flag of Vice-Admiral Sir Doveton Sturdee, Bt., K.C.B., C.V.O., C.M.G.
Bellerophon, Captain E. F. Bruen.
Temeraire, Captain E. V. Underhill.
Vanguard, Captain J. D. Dick.
Royal Oak, Captain C. Maclachlan.
Superb, Captain E. Hyde-Parker. Flying the flag of Rear-Admiral A. L. Duff, C.B.
Canada, Captain W. C. M. Nicholson.
Emperor of India,[1] Captain C. W. R. Royds. (Second Flagship of the Squadron.)
Light Cruiser: *Blanche*, Captain J. M. Casement.

THIRD BATTLE CRUISER SQUADRON

Invincible, Captain A. L. Cay. Flying the flag of Rear-Admiral The Hon. H. L. A. Hood, C.B., M.V.O., D.S.O.
Indomitable, Captain F. W. Kennedy.
Inflexible, Captain E. H. F. Heaton-Ellis, M.V.O.

Temporarily attached ships:

Light Cruisers: *Chester*,[2] Captain R. N. Lawson.
Canterbury, Captain P. M. R. Royds.

SECOND CRUISER SQUADRON.[3]

Minotaur, Captain A. C. S. H. D'Aeth. Flying the flag of Rear-Admiral H. L. Heath, M.V.O.
Hampshire, Captain H. J. Savill.
Cochrane, Captain E. La T. Leatham.
Shannon, Captain J. S. Dumaresq, M.V.O.
Achilles,[1] Captain F. M. Leake.
Donegal,[4] Captain W. H. D'Oyly.

FOURTH LIGHT CRUISER SQUADRON

Calliope, Commodore C. E. Le Mesurier.
Constance, Captain C. S. Townsend.
Comus, Captain A. G. Hotham.
Caroline, Captain H. R. Crooke.
Royalist, Captain The Hon. H. Meade, D.S.O.

FOURTH FLOTILLA

Flotilla Leaders:
Tipperary, Captain C. J. Wintour (Captain D. IV).
Broke, Commander W. L. Allen.

Destroyers:
Achates, Commander R. B. C. Hutchinson, D.S.O.
Porpoise, Commander H. D. Colville.
Spitfire, Lieut.-Comm. C. W. E. Trelawny.
Unity, Lieut.-Comm. A. M. Lecky.

---

[1] In dockyard hands.
[2] Belonging to the Third Light Cruiser Squadron.
[3] Organised on May 30 out of the ships of the old Second and Seventh Cruiser Squadrons.
[4] On detached service.

Garland, Lieut.-Comm. R. S. Goff.
Ambuscade, Lieut.-Comm. G. A. Coles.
Ardent, Lieut.-Comm. A. Marsden.
Fortune, Lieut.-Comm. F. G. Terry.
Sparrowhawk, Lieut.-Comm. S. Hopkins.
Contest, Lieut.-Comm. E. G. H. Master.
Shark, Commander L. W. Jones.
Acasta, Lieut.-Comm. J. O. Barron.
Christopher, Lieut.-Comm. F. M. Kerr.
Owl, Commander R. G. Hamond.
Hardy, Commander R. A. A. Plowden.
Midge, Lieut.-Comm. J. R. C. Cavendish.
Ophelia,[1] Commander L. G. E. Crabbe.
Cockatrice.[2]
Paragon.[2]
Victor.[3]

Part of Eleventh Flotilla

Light Cruiser: *Castor*, Commodore J. R. P. Hawksley, M.V.O. (Commodore F., Captain D. XI).
Destroyers:
Marne, Lieut.-Comm. G. B. Hartford.
Manners, Lieut.-Comm. G. C. Harrison.
Michael, Lieut.-Comm. C. L. Bate.
Mons, Lieut.-Comm. R. Makin.

Twelfth Flotilla

Flotilla Leaders { *Faulknor*, Captain A. J. B. Stirling (Captain D. XII).
Marksman, Commander N. A. Sulivan.
Destroyers:
Obedient, Commander G. W. McO. Campbell.
Maenad, Commander J. P. Champion.
Opal, Commander C. G. C. Sumner.
Mary Rose, Lieut.-Comm. E. A. Homan.
Marvel, Lieut.-Comm. R. W. Grubb.
Menace, Lieut.-Comm. C. A. Poignand.
Nessus, Lieut.-Comm. E. Q. Carter.
Narwhal, Lieut.-Comm. H. V. Hudson.
Mindful, Lieut.-Comm. J. J. C. Ridley.
Onslaught, Lieut.-Comm. A. G. Onslow, D.S.C.
Munster, Lieut.-Comm. S. F. Russell.
Nonsuch, Lieut.-Comm. H. I. N. Lyon.
Noble, Lieut.-Comm. H. P. Boxer.
Mischief, Lieut.-Comm. The Hon. C. A. Ward, M.V.O.
Napier.[2]
Mameluke.[2]

---

[1] Temporarily attached. [2] In dockyard hands.
[3] Remained in harbour.

AT INVERGORDON

Second Battle Squadron

King George V, Captain F. L. Field. Flying the flag of Vice-Admiral Sir Martyn Jerram, K.C.B.
Ajax, Captain G. H. Baird.
Centurion, Captain M. Culme-Seymour, M.V.O.
Erin, Captain The Hon. V. A. Stanley, M.V.O., A.D.C.
Orion, Captain O. Backhouse, C.B. Flying the flag of Rear-Admiral A. C. Leveson, C.B.
Monarch, Captain G. H. Borrett.
Conqueror, Captain H. H. D. Tothill.
Thunderer, Captain J. A. Fergusson.
Light Cruiser: *Boadicea*, Captain L. C. S. Woollcombe, M.V.O.

First Cruiser Squadron

Defence, Captain S. V. Ellis. Flying the flag of Rear-Admiral Sir Robert Arbuthnot, Bt., M.V.O.
Warrior, Captain V. B. Molteno.
Duke of Edinburgh, Captain H. Blackett.
Black Prince, Captain T. P. Bonham.

Part of Eleventh Flotilla

Flotilla Leader: *Kempenfelt*, Commander H. E. Sulivan.
Destroyers:
Ossory, Commander H. V. Dundas.
Mystic, Commander C. F. Allsup.
Morning Star, Lieut.-Comm. H. U. Fletcher.
Magic, Lieut.-Comm. G. C. Wynter.
Mounsey, Lieut.-Comm. R. V. Eyre.
Mandate, Lieut.-Comm. E. McC. W. Lawrie.
Minion, Lieut.-Comm. H. C. Rawlings.
Martial, Lieut.-Comm. J. Harrison.
Milbrook, Lieut. C. G. Naylor.
Moon,[1] Commander (acting) W. D. Irvin.
Marmion.[2]
Musketeer.[2]

AT ROSYTH

Lion, Captain A. E. M. Chatfield, C.V.O. (Battle Cruiser Fleet Flagship). Flying the flag of Vice-Admiral Sir David Beatty, K.C.B., M.V.O., D.S.O. Captain R. W. Bentinck, Chief-of-Staff.

---

[1] On patrol; joined her flotilla about 2.0 p.m., May 31.
[2] In dockyard hands.

Fifth Battle Squadron

Barham, Captain A. W. Craig. Flying the flag of Rear-Admiral H. Evan-Thomas, M.V.O.
Valiant, Captain M. Woollcombe.
Warspite, Captain E. M. Phillpotts.
Malaya, Captain The Hon. A. D. E. H. Boyle, C.B., M.V.O.
Queen Elizabeth,[1] Captain G. P. W. Hope, C.B., A.D.C.

First Battle Cruiser Squadron

Princess Royal, Captain W. H. Cowan, M.V.O., D.S.O. Flying the flag of Rear-Admiral O. de B. Brock, C.B.
Queen Mary, Captain C. I. Prowse.
Tiger, Captain H. B. Pelly, M.V.O.

Second Battle Cruiser Squadron

New Zealand, Captain J. F. E. Green. Flying the flag of Rear-Admiral W. C. Pakenham, C.B., M.V.O.
Indefatigable, Captain C. F. Sowerby.
Australia,[1] Captain S. H. Radcliffe.

First Light Cruiser Squadron

Galatea, Commodore E. S. Alexander-Sinclair, M.V.O.
Phaeton, Captain J. E. Cameron, M.V.O.
Inconstant, Captain B. S. Thesiger, C.M.G.
Cordelia, Captain T. P. H. Beamish.

Second Light Cruiser Squadron

Southampton, Commodore W. E. Goodenough, M.V.O., A.D.C.
Birmingham, Captain A. A. M. Duff.
Nottingham, Captain C. B. Miller.
Dublin, Captain A. C. Scott.

Third Light Cruiser Squadron

Falmouth, Captain J. D. Edwards. Flying the flag of Rear-Admiral T. D. W. Napier, M.V.O.
Yarmouth, Captain T. D. Pratt.
Birkenhead, Captain E. Reeves.
Gloucester, Captain W. F. Blunt, D.S.O.

Part of First Flotilla

Light Cruiser: *Fearless*, Captain C. D. Roper (Captain D. I).
Destroyers:
Acheron, Commander C. G. Ramsey.
Ariel, Lieut.-Comm. A. G. Tippet.

---

[1] In dockyard hands.

Attack, Lieut.-Comm. C. H. N. James.
Hydra, Lieut. F. G. Glossop.
Badger, Commander C. A. Fremantle.
Goshawk, Commander D. F. Moir.
Defender, Lieut.-Comm. L. R. Palmer.
Lizard, Lieut.-Comm. E. Brooke.
Lapwing, Lieut.-Comm. A. H. Gye.
Botha.[1]
Jackal.[1]
Archer.[1]
Tigress.[1]
Phœnix.[2]

THIRTEENTH FLOTILLA

Light Cruiser: *Champion*, Captain J. U. Farie (Captain D. XIII).
Destroyers:
Nestor, Commander The Hon. E. B. S. Bingham.
Nomad, Lieut.-Comm. P. Whitfield.
Narborough, Lieut.-Comm. G. Corlett.
Obdurate, Lieut.-Comm. C. H. H. Sams.
Petard, Lieut.-Comm. E. C. O. Thomson.
Pelican, Lieut.-Comm. K. A. Beattie.
Nerissa, Lieut.-Comm. M. G. B. Legge.
Onslow, Lieut.-Comm. J. C. Tovey.
Moresby, Lieut.-Comm. R. V. Alison.
Nicator, Lieut. J. E. A. Mocatta
Negro.[1]
Nereus.[1]
Paladin.[1]
Penn.[1]
Pigeon.[1]
Nepean.[2]

PART OF NINTH FLOTILLA

Destroyers:
Lydiard, Commander M. L. Goldsmith.
Liberty, Lieut.-Comm. P. W. S. King.
Landrail, Lieut.-Comm. F. E. H. G. Hobart.
Laurel, Lieut. H. D. C. Stanistreet.

PART OF TENTH FLOTILLA

Destroyers:
Moorsom, Commander J. C. Hodgson.
Morris, Lieut.-Comm. E. S. Graham.
Turbulent, Lieut.-Comm. D. Stuart.
Termagant, Lieut.-Comm. C. P. Blake.

Seaplane Carrier

Engadine, Lieut.-Comm. C. G. Robinson.

---

[1] In dockyard hands. [2] Remained in harbour.

APPENDIX B

ORGANISATION OF THE GRAND FLEET AS IT SAILED ON MAY 30, 1916

BATTLE FLEET

Iron Duke (Fleet Flagship).

Organisation No. 2.	Second Battle Squadron.	Organisation No. 5.
1st Division.	*King George V.*	1st Division.
	Ajax.	
	Centurion.	
	Erin.	
	Orion.	2nd Division.
	Monarch.	
	Conqueror.	
	Thunderer.	

Organisation No. 2.	Fourth Battle Squadron.	Organisation No. 5.
2nd Division.	*Iron Duke.*	3rd Division.
	Royal Oak.	
	Superb.	
	Canada.	
	Benbow.	4th Division.
	Bellerophon.	
	Temeraire.	
	Vanguard.	

Organisation No. 2.	First Battle Squadron,	Organisation No. 5.
3rd Division.	*Marlborough.*	6th Division.
	Revenge.	
	Hercules.	
	Agincourt.	
	Colossus.	5th Division.
	Collingwood.	
	Neptune.	
	St. Vincent.	

Attached Light Cruisers	*Boadicea.*	Attached	*Oak* (Destroyer).
	Blanche.		*Abdiel* (Minelayer).
	Bellona.		
	Active.		

BATTLE CRUISERS

Third Battle Cruiser Squadron.

Invincible.
Inflexible.
Indomitable.

FF

Cruisers

First Cruiser Squadron.	Second Cruiser Squadron.
Defence.	*Minotaur.*
Warrior.	*Hampshire.*
Duke of Edinburgh.	*Cochrane.*
Black Prince.	*Shannon.*

Light Cruisers

Fourth Light Cruiser Squadron.

Calliope. *Caroline.*
Constance. *Royalist.*
Comus.

Light Cruiser: *Canterbury.*

Destroyer Flotillas

Twelfth Flotilla.	Eleventh Flotilla.	Fourth Flotilla.
Faulknor.	*Castor.*	*Tipperary.*
Marksman.	*Kempenfelt.*	*Broke.*
Obedient.	*Ossory.*	*Achates.*
Maenad.	*Mystic.*	*Porpoise.*
Opal.	*Moon.*	*Spitfire.*
Mary Rose.	*Morning Star.*	*Unity.*
Marvel.	*Magic.*	*Garland.*
Menace.	*Mounsey.*	*Ambuscade.*
Nessus.	*Mandate.*	*Ardent.*
Narwhal.	*Marne.*	*Fortune.*
Mindful.	*Minion.*	*Sparrowhawk.*
Onslaught.	*Manners.*	*Contest.*
Munster.	*Michael.*	*Shark.*
Nonsuch.	*Mons.*	*Acasta.*
Noble.	*Martial.*	*Ophelia.*
Mischief.	*Milbrook.*	*Christopher.*
		Owl.
		Hardy.
		Midge.

BATTLE CRUISER FLEET

Battle Cruisers

Lion (Fleet Flagship).

First Battle Cruiser Squadron.	Second Battle Cruiser Squadron.
Princess Royal.	*New Zealand.*
Queen Mary.	*Indefatigable.*
Tiger.	

Fifth Battle Squadron.

Barham. *Warspite.*
Valiant. *Malaya.*

Light Cruisers

First Light Cruiser Squadron.	Second Light Cruiser Squadron.	Third Light Cruiser Squadron.
Galatea.	*Southampton.*	*Falmouth.*
Phaeton.	*Birmingham.*	*Yarmouth.*
Inconstant.	*Nottingham.*	*Birkenhead.*
Cordelia.	*Dublin.*	*Gloucester.*
		Chester.

Destroyer Flotillas

First Flotilla.	Thirteenth Flotilla.	Ninth and Tenth Flotillas.
Fearless.	*Champion.*	*Lydiard.*
Acheron.	*Nestor.*	*Liberty.*
Ariel.	*Nomad.*	*Landrail.*
Attack.	*Narborough.*	*Laurel.*
Hydra.	*Obdurate.*	*Moorsom.*
Badger.	*Petard.*	*Morris.*
Goshawk.	*Pelican.*	*Turbulent.*
Defender.	*Nerissa.*	*Termagant.*
Lizard.	*Onslow.*	
Lapwing.	*Moresby.*	
	Nicator.	

Seaplane Carrier : *Engadine.*

APPENDIX C

SHIPS OF THE HIGH SEAS FLEET WITH THE NAMES OF FLAG AND COMMANDING OFFICERS, MAY 31, 1916

Friedrich der Grosse, Captain T. Fuchs (Fleet Flagship). Flying the flag of Vice-Admiral Scheer, Commander-in-Chief. Captain A. von Trotha, Chief-of-Staff.

First Battle Squadron

Ostfriesland, Captain von Natzmer. Flying the flag of Vice-Admiral E. Schmidt. Commander W. Wegener, Staff Officer.
Posen, Captain Lange. Flying the flag of Rear-Admiral Engelhardt.
Thüringen, Captain H. Küsel.
Helgoland, Captain von Kameke.
Oldenburg, Captain Höpfner.
Rheinland, Captain Rohardt.
Nassau, Captain H. Klappenbach.
Westfalen, Captain Redlich.

Second Battle Squadron

Deutschland, Captain H. Meurer. Flying the flag of Rear-Admiral Mauve, Squadron Commander. Commander Kahlert, Staff Officer.
Hannover, Captain W. Heine. Flying the flag of Rear-Admiral Freiherr von Dalwigk zu Lichtenfels.
Pommern, Captain Bölken.
Schlesien, Captain F. Behncke.
Schleswig Holstein, Captain Barrentrapp.
Hessen, Captain R. Bartels.

Third Battle Squadron

König, Captain Brüninghaus. Flying the flag of Rear-Admiral Behncke, Squadron Commander. Commander Freiherr von Gagern, Staff Officer.
Kaiser, Captain Freiherr von Kayserling. Flying the flag of Rear-Admiral Nordmann.
Grosser Kurfürst, Captain E. Goette.
Markgraf, Captain Seiferling.
Kronprinz, Captain C. Feldt.
Prinzregent Luitpold, Captain K. Heuser.
Kaiserin, Captain Sievers.

SCOUTING FORCES

First Scouting Group (Battle Cruisers)

Lützow, Captain Harder. Flying the flag of Vice-Admiral Hipper, Commanding the Scouting Forces. Commander E. Raeder, Staff Officer.
Seydlitz, Captain von Egidy.
Moltke, Captain von Karpf.
Derfflinger, Captain Hartog.
Von der Tann, Captain Zenker.

Second Scouting Group (Light Cruisers)

Frankfurt, Captain T. von Trotha. Flying the flag of Rear-Admiral Boedicker. Lieut.-Comm. Stapenhorst, Staff Officer.
Pillau, Captain Mommsen.
Elbing, Captain Madlung.
Wiesbaden, Captain Reiss.
Rostock, Captain O. Feldmann.
Regensburg, Captain Heuberer.

Fourth Scouting Group (Light Cruisers)

Stettin, Captain F. Rebensburg. Wearing the broad pendant of Commodore von Reuter. Commander H. Weber, Staff Officer.
München, Commander O. Böcker.
Frauenlob, Captain G. Hoffmann.
Stuttgart, Captain Hagedorn.
Hamburg, Commander von Gaudecker.

DESTROYER FLOTILLAS [1]

Rostock, Captain O. Feldmann. Wearing the broad pendant of Commodore Michelsen, Commanding the Destroyer Flotillas. Commander Junkermann, Staff Officer.
Regensburg, Captain Heuberer. Wearing the broad pendant of Commodore Heinrich, Second-in-Command.

FLOTILLA COMMANDERS

First Flotilla / 1st Half-Flotilla } Lieut.-Comm. C. Albrecht, *G 39*.[2]
Second Flotilla, Captain Schuur, *B 98*.
3rd Half-Flotilla, Commander Boest, *G 101*.
4th Half-Flotilla, Commander A. Dithmar, *B 109*.
Third Flotilla, Commander Hollmann, *S 53*.
5th Half-Flotilla, Lieut.-Comm. Gautier, *V 71*.
6th Half-Flotilla, Lieut.-Comm. Karlowa, *S 54*.
Fifth Flotilla, Commander Heinecke, *G 11*.
9th Half-Flotilla, Lieut.-Comm. Hoefer, *V 2*.
10th Half-Flotilla, Lieut.-Comm. F. Klein, *G 8*.
Sixth Flotilla, Commander M. Schultz, *G 41*.
11th Half-Flotilla, Lieut.-Comm. W. Rümann, *V 44*.
12th Half-Flotilla, Lieut.-Comm. Lahs, *V 69*.
Seventh Flotilla, Commander von Koch, *S 24*.
13th Half-Flotilla, Lieut.-Comm. G. von Zitzewitz, *S 15*.
14th Half-Flotilla, Commander H. Cordes, *S 19*.
Ninth Flotilla, Commander Goehle, *V 28*.
17th Half-Flotilla, Lieut.-Comm. Ehrhardt, *V 27*.
18th Half-Flotilla, Commander W. Tillessen, *V 30*.

SUBMARINES

In Command of Submarines, Captain Bauer.[3] Commander F. Lützow, Staff Officer.

U 24, Lieut.-Comm. R. Schneider.
U 32, Lieut.-Comm. Freiherr Spiegel von und zu Peckelsheim.
U 63, Lieut.-Comm. O. Schultze.
U 66, Lieut.-Comm. von Bothmer.
U 70, Lieut.-Comm. Wünsche.
U 43, Lieut.-Comm. Jürst.
U 44, Lieut.-Comm. Wagenführ.
U 52, Lieut.-Comm. H. Walther.
U 47, Lieut.-Comm. Metzger.
U 46, Lieut.-Comm. L. Hillebrand.
U 22, Lieut.-Comm. Hoppe.

---

[1] Each flotilla consisted of eleven destroyers, and was divided into two half-flotillas, the First Flotilla consisting of the 1st and 2nd Half-Flotillas, the Second Flotilla consisting of the 3rd and 4th Half-Flotillas, and so on.
[2] Denotes name of destroyer.
[3] On board the *Hamburg*.

U 19, Lieut.-Comm. R. Weissbach.
UB 22, Lieutenant Putzier.
UB 21, Lieut.-Comm. E. Hashagen.
U 53, Lieut.-Comm. Rose.
U 64, Lieut.-Comm. R. Morath.

AIRSHIPS

L 11, Commander V. Schütze.
L 17, Lieut.-Comm. H. Ehrlich.
L 14, Lieut.-Comm. d. R. Böcker.
L 21, Lieut.-Comm. M. d. R. Dietrich.
L 23, Lieut.-Comm. von Schubert.
L 16, Lieut.-Comm. Sommerfeldt.
L 13, Lieut.-Comm. d. R. Prölss.
L 9, Captain (Army) Stelling.
L 22, Lieut.-Comm. M. Dietrich.
L 24, Lieut.-Comm. R. Koch.

APPENDIX D

ORGANISATION OF THE HIGH SEAS FLEET AS IT SAILED ON MAY 31, 1916

BATTLESHIPS

Third Squadron.	*König.*	5th Division.
	Grosser Kurfürst.	
	Kronprinz.	
	Markgraf.	
	Kaiser.	6th Division.
	Kaiserin.	
	Prinzregent Luitpold.	
First Squadron.	*Friedrich der Grosse.* (Fleet Flagship.)	1st Division.
	Ostfriesland.	
	Thuringen.	
	Helgoland.	
	Oldenburg.	
	Posen.	2nd Division.
	Rheinland.	
	Nassau.	
	Westfalen.	
Second Squadron.	*Deutschland.*	3rd Division.
	Hessen.	
	Pommern.	
	Hannover.	4th Division.
	Schlesien.	
	Schleswig Holstein.	

CRUISERS

First Scouting Group (Battle Cruisers)	Second Scouting Group (Light Cruisers)	Fourth Scouting Group (Light Cruisers)
Lützow.	*Frankfurt.*	*Stettin.*
Derfflinger.	*Wiesbaden.*	*München.*
Seydlitz.	*Pillau.*	*Hamburg.*
Moltke.	*Elbing.*	*Frauenlob.*
Von der Tann.		*Stuttgart.*

DESTROYER FLOTILLAS

Rostock, Light Cruiser.
First Leader of Torpedo Boats.
First Flotilla (1st Half).
Third Flotilla.
Fifth Flotilla.
Seventh Flotilla.

Regensburg, Light Cruiser.
Second Leader of Torpedo Boats.
Second Flotilla.
Sixth Flotilla.
Ninth Flotilla.

APPENDIX E

LIST OF SHIPS SUNK

	BRITISH.	GERMAN.
Battleships	—	*Pommern*
Battle Cruisers	*Indefatigable* *Invincible* *Queen Mary*	*Lützow*
Cruisers	*Black Prince* *Defence* *Warrior*	—
Light Cruisers	—	*Elbing* *Frauenlob* *Rostock* *Wiesbaden*
Destroyers	*Ardent* *Fortune* *Nestor* *Nomad* *Shark* *Sparrowhawk* *Tipperary* *Turbulent*	*S 35* *V 4* *V 27* *V 29* *V 48*

APPENDIX F

BRITISH CASUALTIES

Ship.	Officers.			Men.		
	Killed.	Wounded.	Prisoners of War.	Killed.[1]	Wounded.	Prisoners of War.
Battleships :						
Barham	4	1	—	22	36	—
Colossus	—	—	—	—	5	—
Malaya	2	—	—	61 (4)	33	—
Marlborough . . .	—	—	—	2	—	—
Valiant	—	—	—	—	1	—
Warspite	1	3	—	13 (2)	13 (1)	—
Battle Cruisers :						
Indefatigable (sunk) .	57	—	—	960 (5)	—	2
Invincible (sunk) . .	61	—	—	965 (5)	—	—
Lion	6	1	—	93 (2)	43	—
Princess Royal . .	—	1	—	22 (2)	77	—
Queen Mary (sunk) .	57	2	1	1,209	5	1
Tiger	2	—	—	22	37	—
Cruisers :						
Black Prince (sunk) .	37	—	—	820 (5)	—	—
Defence (sunk) . .	54	—	—	849 (4)	—	—
Warrior [2] (sunk) . .	1	2	—	70	25	—
Light Cruisers :						
Calliope	—	2	—	10	7	—
Castor	—	1	—	13	22	—
Chester	2	3	—	33	39	—
Dublin	1	—	—	2	24	—
Southampton . . .	—	1	—	35 (1)	40	—
Flotilla Leaders :						
Broke	1	3	—	46	33	—
Tipperary (sunk) .	11	—	—	174	2	8
Destroyers :						
Acasta	1	—	—	5	1	—
Ardent (sunk) .	4	1	—	74	1	—
Defender	—	—	—	1	2	—
Fortune (sunk) . .	4	—	—	63	1	—
Moorsom	—	—	—	—	1	—
Nessus	2	—	—	5	7	—
Nestor (sunk) . . .	2	—	5	4	—	75
Nomad (sunk) . .	1	—	4	7	—	68
Onslaught	3	—	—	2	2	—
Onslow	—	—	—	2	3	—
Petard	2	1	—	7	5	—
Porpoise	—	—	—	2	2	—
Shark (sunk) . . .	7	—	—	79	2	—
Sparrowhawk (sunk) .	—	—	—	6	—	—
Spitfire	—	3	—	6	16	—
Turbulent (sunk) . .	5	—	—	85	—	13
Total	328	25	10	5,769	485	167

[1] The numbers in brackets indicate civilians and are included in totals.
[2] Casualties sustained prior to loss of ship.

APPENDIX G

GERMAN CASUALTIES[1]

Ship	Killed	Wounded
Battleships :		
Ostfriesland	1	10
Oldenburg	8	14
Rheinland	10	20
Nassau	11	16
Westfalen	2	8
Pommern	844	—
Schlesien	1	—
Schleswig-Holstein	3	9
König	45	27
Grosser Kurfürst	15	10
Markgraf	11	13
Kaiser	—	1
Prinzregent-Luitpold	—	11
Battle Cruisers :		
Lützow	115	50
Derfflinger	157	26
Seydlitz	98	55
Moltke	17	23
Von der Tann	11	35
Light Cruisers :		
Pillau	4	19
Elbing	4	12
Frankfurt	3	18
Wiesbaden	589	—
Rostock	14	6
Stettin	8	28
München	8	20
Frauenlob	320	1
Hamburg	14	25
Torpedo Boats	238	50
Totals	2,551	507

[1] Figures taken from the German Official History, *Der Krieg zur See: Nordsee*, Vol. 5, pp. 481-2.

APPENDIX H

HITS RECEIVED BY BRITISH SHIPS

Ship.	Number of hits by		Date of completion of repairs.	Remarks.
	Large Projectiles.	Small Projectiles.		
Battleships :				
Colossus . . .	2	—	—	
Barham . . .	6	—	4 July	
Malaya . . .	7	—	24 June	
Marlborough .	—	—	2 August	Hit by a torpedo.
Warspite . .	13	—	20 July	
Battle Cruisers :				
Lion	12	—	19 July	
Princess Royal .	6	—	15 July	
Tiger	10	—	2 July	
New Zealand .	1	—	—	
Light Cruisers :				
Chester . . .	—	17	25 July	
Dublin . . .	—	8	17 June	
Southampton .	—	18	20 June	
Castor . .	10	—	—	
Flotilla Leader :				
Broke . . .	—	9	31 August	Also damaged by collision.
Destroyers :				
Acasta . . .	—	2	2 August	
Contest . . .	—	—	19 June	In collision.
Defender . . .	1	—	23 June	
Moorsom . .	—	1	17 June	
Onslaught . .	—	1	23 June	
Onslow . . .	—	5	8 August	
Petard . . .	—	3	27 June	
Porpoise . . .	—	2	23 June	
Spitfire . . .	—	2	31 July	Also damaged by collision.

Vessels sunk are not included as the number of hits cannot be estimated. In many instances the above figures must be taken as approximate only.

HITS RECEIVED BY GERMAN SHIPS

Ship	Number of hits by		Date of completion of repairs	Remarks
	Large Projectiles	Small Projectiles		
Battleships :				
König . . .	10	—	21 July	
Grosser Kurfürst .	8	—	16 July	
Markgraf . .	5	—	20 July	
Kaiser . . .	2	—	—	
Ostfriesland . .	—	—	26 July	Struck a mine whilst returning to harbour.
Helgoland . .	1	—	16 June	
Oldenburg . .	—	1	—	
Nassau . . .	—	2	10 July	
Rheinland . .	—	1	10 June	
Westfalen . .	—	1	17 June	
Schleswig-Holstein	1	—	24 June	
Pommern . .	1	—	Sunk	Hit also by a torpedo.
Battle Cruisers :				
Lützow . . .	24	—	Sunk	
Derfflinger . .	17	9	15 October	
Seydlitz . . .	21	2	16 Sept.	Hit also by a torpedo.
Moltke . . .	4	—	30 July	
von der Tann .	4	—	2 August	
Light Cruisers :				
Frankfurt . . .	—	3	8 July	
Elbing . . .	—	1	Sunk	
Pillau . . .	1	—	17 July	
Wiesbaden . .	—	—	Sunk	
Rostock . . .	—	—	Sunk	Hit also by a torpedo.
Stettin . . .	—	2	20 July	
München . .	—	5	29 June	
Frauenlob . .	—	—	Sunk	Hit also by a torpedo.
Hamburg . .	—	4	15 June	
Torpedo Boats:				
S 50	—	1	—	
B 98 . . .	—	1	20 June	
G 40 . . .	—	1	15 June	
S 32	—	3	31 July	
S 51 . . .	—	1	19 June	
V 27 . . .	—	2	Sunk	
V 29 . . .	1	—	Sunk	Hit also by a torpedo.
S 35 . . .	—	—	Sunk	
G 41	—	1	—	
V 28 . . .	—	1	13 June	
V 48	—	—	Sunk	

Though there is reason to doubt their accuracy, these figures, as being more authoritative than our own estimates, are reproduced from the German Official History, *Der Krieg zur See : Nordsee*, Vol. 5, p. 477. It is obvious from such items as *Wiesbaden*, and *Derfflinger* that totals could bear no relation to actual fact. No totals, therefore, are shown.

The *Wiesbaden*, against whose name no hits are entered, had shell poured into her from time to time over a period of six hours by several of our capital ships. For the *Derfflinger* 17 heavy hits are entered, whereas a study of the German Official History and other high German authorities reveals a total of 23 specified and an additional 9 estimated hits.

APPENDIX J.

German Signals received in the Admiralty between 11.15 p.m. (31 May) and 1.25 a.m. (1 June).

(All times of origin (middle European Summer Time) are two hours fast on G.M.T. Decipher times G.M.T.)

0032 : C.-in-C. : Main fleet steering SE by S.
Deciphered : 11.15 p.m. (31st).

0032 :[1] O.C. 1st T.D. to all T.B.D. Flots : Be assembled by 4 a.m. at Horns Riff or course round Skaw.
Deciphered : 11.15 p.m. (31st).

0106 : C.-in-C. to H.S. Fleet : Our own main body at 1 a.m. 12 epsilon (56° 15′—5° 42′ E.) Course SE ¾ E.
Deciphered : 11.50 p.m. (31st).

0130 : C.-in-C. to H.S. Fleet : Our main forces are to resume course SE by S.
Deciphered : 12.0 midnight.

0136 : C.-in-C. to H.S. Fleet : The course ordered is SE ¾ S.
Deciphered : 12.5 a.m. June 1.

0243 : C.-in-C. to Lutzow ; Own main body's position at 2.30 a.m. 073 alpha (55°57′—6°15′ E.).
Deciphered : 1.20 a.m.

0303 : C.-in-C. to A.C. 2nd S.G.: Head of our own main fleet at 3 a.m. bottom of 87 alpha (55°50′—6°25′ E.).
Deciphered : 1.25 a.m.

[1] The signal received in the Admiralty was : " Be assembled by 4 a.m. with own main body at Horns Riff, or course round Skaw," but unfortunately by some mischance the words " with own main body " were omitted from the decipher. See p. 414 *n*.

INDEX

Abbreviations :

A.B.S. = Armed Boarding Steamer.
A.M.C. = Armed Merchant Cruiser.
A.P. = Auxiliary Patrol.
B. = Battleship.
B.Cr. = Battle Cruiser.
B.E.F. = British Expeditionary Force.
Cr. = Cruiser.
G.B. = Gunboat.
L.Cr. = Light Cruiser.
L.V. = Light Vessel.
M.E.F.=Mediterranean Expeditionary Force.
M/L = Minelayer.
Mon. = Monitor.
M/S = Minesweeper.
N.T.O. = Naval Transport Officer.
R.G.B. = River Gunboat.
S/M = Submarine.
S.N.O. = Senior Naval Officer.
Sq. = Squadron.
S.S. = Steamship.
S.V. = Sailing Vessel.
T.B. = Torpedo Boat.
T.B.D. = Destroyer.
T.G.B. = Torpedo Gunboat.

D

E

G

M

N

O

X

Y

Z